Rick Steves'

SPAIN & PORTUGAL
2003

Rick Steves'

SPAIN & PORTUGAL

2003

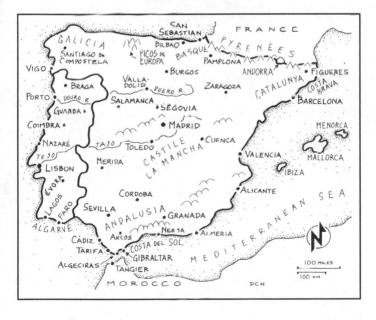

AVALON
TRAVEL

Other ATP travel guidebooks by Rick Steves
Rick Steves' Best of Europe
Rick Steves' Europe 101: History and Art for the Traveler (with Gene Openshaw)
Rick Steves' Europe Through the Back Door
Rick Steves' Mona Winks: Self-Guided Tours of Europe's Top Museums
  (with Gene Openshaw)
Rick Steves' Postcards from Europe
Rick Steves' France (with Steve Smith)
Rick Steves' Germany, Austria & Switzerland
Rick Steves' Great Britain
Rick Steves' Ireland (with Pat O'Connor)
Rick Steves' Italy
Rick Steves' Scandinavia
Rick Steves' Amsterdam, Bruges & Brussels (with Gene Openshaw)
Rick Steves' Florence (with Gene Openshaw)
Rick Steves' London (with Gene Openshaw)
Rick Steves' Paris (with Steve Smith and Gene Openshaw)
Rick Steves' Rome (with Gene Openshaw)
Rick Steves' Venice (with Gene Openshaw)
Rick Steves' Phrase Books: French, German, Italian, Portuguese, Spanish, and
  French/Italian/German

Text © 2002, 2001, 2000, 1999, 1998, 1997, 1996 by Rick Steves
Maps © 2002 Europe Through the Back Door. All rights reserved.

Printed in the USA by R.R. Donnelley. First printing January 2003
Distributed by Publishers Group West

For the latest on Rick Steves' lectures, guidebooks, tours, and public
television series, contact Europe Through the Back Door, Box 2009, Edmonds,
WA 98020, tel. 425/771-8303, fax 425/771-0833, www.ricksteves.com,
or e-mail: rick@ricksteves.com.

ISBN 1-56691-460-4
ISSN 1084-4414

Europe Through the Back Door Managing Editor: Risa Laib
Europe Through the Back Door Editors: Jill Hodges, Cameron Hewitt
Avalon Travel Publishing Series Manager & Editor: Kate Willis
Copy Editor: Kate McKinley
Research Assistance: Carlos Galvin
Production & Typesetting: Kathleen Sparkes, White Hart Design
Design: Linda Braun
Cover Design: Janine Lehmann
Maps and Graphics: David C. Hoerlein, Rhonda Pelikan, Zoey Platt
Front matter color photos: p. i, Boats in Porto's Harbor, Portugal ©
  Trip/S.Reddy; p. iv, St. Catarina Chapel, Azulejos, Portugal © Trip/S. Reddy
Cover Photo: Giralda Tower and Cathedral, Sevilla, Spain;
  © Blaine Harrington III

Distributed to the book trade by Publishers Group West, Berkeley, California

CONTENTS

Top Destinations in Spain and Portugal

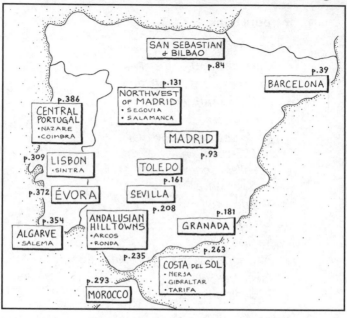

INTRODUCTION

Like a grandpa bouncing a baby on his knee, Iberia is a mix of old and new, modern and traditional. Spain and Portugal can fill your travel days with world-class art treasures, folk life, exotic foods, sunshine, friendly people, and castles where the winds of the past still howl. And, in spite of its recent economic boom, Iberia (particularly Portugal) remains Europe's bargain basement. Tourism is huge here. Spain, with 40 million inhabitants, entertains 50 million visitors annually. Iberia is very popular—and on your trip, you'll learn why.

This book breaks Spain and Portugal into their top big-city, small-town, and rural destinations. It then gives you all the information and opinions necessary to wring the maximum value out of your limited time and money. If you plan a month or less in Iberia, this lean and mean little book is all you need.

Experiencing Spain and Portugal's culture, people, and natural wonders economically and hassle-free has been my goal for 25 years of traveling, tour guiding, and writing. With this book, I pass on to you the lessons I've learned, updated for 2003.

Rick Steves' Spain & Portugal is a tour guide in your pocket, with a balanced, comfortable mix of exciting cities and cozy towns topped off with an exotic dollop of Morocco. It covers the predictable biggies and stirs in a healthy dose of Back Door intimacy. Along with seeing a bullfight, the Prado, and flamenco, you'll buy cookies from cloistered nuns in a sun-parched Andalusian town and recharge your solar cells in an Algarve fishing village. You'll eat barnacles with green wine in a Portuguese village and scramble the ramparts of an ancient Moorish castle. I've been selective, including only the most exciting sights and experiences. For example, there are countless whitewashed Andalusian hill towns; I recommend the best two—Arcos and Ronda.

The best is, of course, only my opinion. But after two busy decades of travel writing, lecturing, and tour guiding, I've developed a sixth sense for what travelers enjoy.

This Information Is Accurate and Up-to-Date

This book is updated every year. Most publishers of guidebooks that cover a region from top to bottom can afford an update only every two or three years, and then the research is often by letter. Since this book is selective, covering only the places I think make the best month or so in Iberia, it can be personally updated each summer. Even with annual updates, things change. But if you're traveling with the current edition of this book, I guarantee you're using the most up-to-date information in print (for the latest, see

www.ricksteves.com/update). Trust me, you'll regret trying to save
a few bucks by traveling with old information. If you're packing
an old book, you'll quickly learn the seriousness of your mistake ...
in Europe. Your trip costs about $10 per waking hour. Your time
is valuable. This guidebook saves lots of time.

Planning Your Trip

This book is organized by destinations. Each destination is covered
as a mini-vacation on its own, filled with exciting sights and homey,
affordable places to stay. In each chapter, you'll find the following:

Planning Your Time, a suggested schedule with thoughts
on how best to use your limited time.

Orientation, including tourist information, city transportation, and an easy-to-read map designed to make the text clear and
your arrival smooth.

Sights with ratings: ▲▲▲—Don't miss; **▲▲**—Try hard
to see; **▲**—Worthwhile if you can make it; no rating—Worth
knowing about.

Sleeping and **Eating,** with addresses and phone numbers
of my favorite budget hotels and restaurants.

Transportation Connections to nearby destinations by train,
bus, or car, with recommended roadside attractions for drivers.

The **appendix** is a traveler's tool kit, with telephone tips, a
climate chart, a list of festivals, and cultural background.

Browse through this book, choose your favorite destinations,
and link them up. Then have a great trip! You'll travel as a temporary local, getting the absolute most out of every mile, minute,
and dollar. You won't waste time on mediocre sights because,
unlike other guidebooks, this one covers only the best. Since
your major financial pitfall is lousy, expensive hotels, I've worked
hard to assemble the best accommodations values for each stop.
And, as you travel the route I know and love, I'm happy you'll be
meeting some of my favorite Spanish and Portuguese people.

Trip Costs

Five components make up your trip cost: airfare, surface transportation, room and board, sightseeing/entertainment, and
shopping/miscellany.

Airfare: Don't try to sort through the mess yourself. Get and
use a good travel agent. A basic round-trip flight from the United
States to Madrid or Lisboa should cost $700 to $1,000 (less in winter), depending on where you fly from and when. Always consider
saving time and money by flying "open-jaw" (into one city and out
of another, e.g., into Barcelona and out of Lisbon).

Surface Transportation: For a three-week whirlwind trip

linking all of my recommended destinations, allow $350 per person for second-class trains and buses ($500 for first-class trains) or $600 per person (based on 2 people sharing) for a three-week car rental, tolls, gas, and insurance. Car rental is cheapest to arrange from home in the United States. While train passes (generally designed to be purchased in your home country—before arriving in Iberia) are a convenience, you may save money by simply buying tickets as you go (see "Transportation," below).

Room and Board: While most travelers will spend more (because they've got it and it's fun), you can thrive in Iberia on $50 a day per person for room and board. A $50-a-day budget allows $5 for lunch, $15 for dinner, and $30 for lodging (based on 2 people splitting the cost of a $60 double room that includes breakfast). That's doable. Students and tightwads will do it on $30 ($15 per bed, $15 for meals and snacks). But budget sleeping and eating require the skills and information covered below (or more extensively in *Rick Steves' Europe Through the Back Door*).

Sightseeing and Entertainment: In big cities, figure $3 to $5 per major sight (Prado, Picasso Museum), $2 for minor ones (climbing church towers), and about $30 for splurge experiences (flamenco, bullfights). An overall average of $10 a day works for most. Don't skimp here. After all, this category directly powers most of the experiences all the other expenses are designed to make possible.

Shopping and Miscellany: Figure $1 per coffee, beer, ice-cream cone, and postcard. Shopping can vary in cost from nearly nothing to a small fortune. Good budget travelers find that this category has little to do with assembling a trip full of lifelong and wonderful memories.

Exchange Rates
I list prices in euros throughout the book. Both Spain and Portugal use the euro currency.

> 1 euro (€) = about $1.

One euro is broken down into 100 cents. You'll find coins ranging from 1 cent to 2 euros, and bills from 5 euros to 500 euros.

Prices, Times, and Discounts
The telephone numbers and hours of sights listed in this book are accurate as of mid-2002. Iberia is always changing, and I know you'll understand that this, like any other guidebook, starts to yellow even before it's printed.

In Europe—and in this book—you'll be using the 24-hour

clock. After 12:00 noon, keep going—13:00, 14:00, and so on. For anything over 12, subtract 12 and add p.m. (14:00 is 2:00 p.m.).

In peak season, May through September, sightseeing attractions are wide open. Off-season, roughly October through April, expect shorter hours, more lunchtime breaks, and fewer activities. Confirm your sightseeing plans locally, especially when traveling off-season.

Though Portugal and Spain are in the same time zone, the time is one hour earlier in Portugal during daylight saving months. Moroccan is in an earlier time zone, so it can be up to two hours earlier than Spanish time.

While discounts for sightseeing and transportation are not listed in this book, seniors (60 and over), students (with International Student Identity Cards), and youths (under 18) sometimes get discounts—but only if they ask.

When to Go
Spring and fall offer the best combination of good weather, light crowds, long days, and plenty of tourist and cultural activities. Summer and winter travel both have their predictable pros and cons. July and August are most crowded and expensive in coastal areas, less crowded but uncomfortably hot and dusty in the interior. Air-conditioning is worth the splurge in summer. For weather specifics, see the climate chart in the appendix.

Whenever you anticipate crowds, particularly in summer, call hotels in advance (call from one hotel to the next, with the help of your fluent receptionist) and try to arrive early in the day.

Sightseeing Priorities
Depending on the length of your trip, here are my recommended priorities.

3 days:	Madrid, Toledo
5 days, add:	Barcelona
7 days, add:	Lisbon
10 days, add:	Andalucía, Sevilla
14 days, add:	Granada, Algarve
17 days, add:	Costa del Sol, Morocco
20 days, add:	Coimbra, Nazaré
22 days, add:	Salamanca, Segovia

Red Tape, Business Hours, and VAT Refunds
You currently need a passport but no visa and no shots to travel in Spain, Portugal, and Morocco.

For visitors, Iberia is a land of strange and frustrating schedules. Many businesses respect the afternoon siesta. When it's 100 degrees in the shade, you'll understand why.

In Spain and Portugal, the biggest museums stay open all day. Smaller ones often close for a siesta. Shops are generally open from 9:00 to 13:00 and from 15:00 (or 16:00 in Spain) to 19:00 (or 20:00 in Spain), longer in touristy places. Small shops are often open on Saturday only in the morning and are closed all day Sunday.

VAT Refunds for Shoppers: Wrapped into the purchase price of your Iberian souvenirs is a Value Added Tax (VAT) that's generally about 14 percent (specifically, 13.8 percent in Spain, 14.5 percent in Portugal). If you make a purchase of more than €90 in Spain (or more than €58 in Portugal) at a store that participates in the VAT refund scheme, you're entitled to get most of that tax back. Personally I've never felt that VAT refunds are worth the hassle, but if you do, here's the scoop.

If you're lucky, the merchant will subtract the tax when you make your purchase (this is more likely to occur if the store ships the goods to your home). Otherwise, here's what you'll need to do:

Get the paperwork. Have the merchant completely fill out the necessary refund document, called a "cheque." You'll have to present your passport at the store.

Have your cheque(s) stamped at the border at your last stop in the European Union by the customs agent who deals with VAT refunds. It's best to keep your purchases in your carry-on for viewing, but if they're too large or dangerous (such as knives) to carry on, then track down the proper customs agent to inspect them before you check your bag. You're not supposed to use your purchased goods before you leave. If you show up at customs wearing your new flamenco costume, officials might look the other way— or deny you a refund.

To collect your refund, you'll need to return your stamped documents to the retailer or its representative. Many merchants work with a service, such as Global Refund or Cashback, which have offices at major airports, ports, or border crossings. These services, which extract a 4 percent fee, can refund your money immediately in your currency of choice or credit your card (within two billing cycles). If you have to deal directly with the retailer, mail the store your stamped documents and then wait. It could take months.

Banking

Bring a Visa or MasterCard with a four-digit PIN so you can use the same card to withdraw cash from ATMs and to charge any expensive items. Both Spain and Portugal have readily available, easy-to-use, 24-hour ATMs with English instructions. They'll save you time and money (on commission fees). I traveled painlessly throughout Spain and Portugal in 2002 with my Visa debit card. Get details at your bank and bring an extra copy of your

Whirlwind Three-Week Trip

card (or another of your cards) just in case one gets demagnet-
ized or gobbled up by a machine. Pack along some cash or a few
traveler's checks as a backup. If you're planning on getting cash
advances from your regular credit card, be sure to ask the card
company about fees before you leave.

Banks are generally open Monday through Friday nonstop
from 9:00 to 14:00 in Spain, and in Portugal from 8:30 to 15:00,
often with a lunch break.

Spanish banks charge acceptable commissions for changing
traveler's checks. American Express offices (found only in big
cities) offer mediocre rates but change any type of traveler's
check without a commission. Portugal's banks charge outrageous,
unregulated commissions ($8–15). Shop around. Sometimes the
hole-in-the-wall exchange offices offer better deals than the bank.
Look for the rare American Express office. Better yet, use a cash
machine. I've changed my last traveler's check.

Language Barrier
Spain presents the English-speaking traveler with the most formi-
dable language barrier in Western Europe. Learn the key phrases.
Travel with a phrase book, particularly if you want to interact

Spain & Portugal's Best Three-Week Trip

Day	Plan	Sleep in
1	Arrive in Madrid	Madrid
2	Madrid	Madrid
3	El Escorial, Valley of Fallen, Segovia	Segovia
4	Segovia and Salamanca	Salamanca
5	Salamanca, Coimbra	Coimbra
6	Coimbra, Batalha, Fátima, Nazaré	Nazaré
7	Beach day in Nazaré, Alcobaça side trip	Nazaré
8	Nazaré, Lisbon	Lisbon
9	Lisbon	Lisbon
10	Lisbon side trip to Belém and Sintra	Lisbon
11	Lisbon to Evora to the Algarve	Salema
12	Free beach day, Sagres	Salema
13	Across Algarve, Sevilla	Sevilla
14	Sevilla	Sevilla
15	Andalucía's Route of White Villages	Arcos
16	Arcos, Jerez, Tarifa	Tarifa
17	A day in Morocco	Tarifa
18	Gibraltar, Costa del Sol	Nerja
19	Nerja to Granada	Granada
20	Granada	Granada
21	Through la Mancha to Toledo	Toledo
22	Toledo	Toledo/Madrid/fly

While this itinerary is designed to be done by car, it can be done by train and bus (7–8 bus days and 4–5 train days). For three weeks without a car, I'd modify it to start in Barcelona and finish in Lisbon. From Barcelona, fly or take the night train to Madrid (see Toledo, Segovia, and El Escorial as side trips); take the night train to Granada; bus along Costa del Sol to Tarifa (visit Morocco —likely from nearby Algeciras); bus to Arcos, Sevilla, and Algarve; and take the train to Lisbon. This skips Coimbra and Salamanca and assumes you'll fly open-jaw into Barcelona and fly out of Lisbon. If you're catching the train from Lisbon back to Madrid, you can sightsee your way in three days (via Coimbra and Salamanca) or simply catch the night train to Madrid.

with local people. You'll find that doors open quicker and with more smiles when you can speak a few words of the language.

Portuguese is more difficult then Spanish to learn and pronounce. However, the Portuguese speak more English—it's required in school and their movies are subtitled, while the Spanish get their Hollywood dubbed. Spanish and French are also widely understood in Portugal, but locals visibly brighten up when you know and use a few key Portuguese words.

My Spanish and Portuguese phrase books, which include a traveler's dictionary, will help you hurdle the language barrier. You'll find the Survival Phrases in the appendix of this book useful as well. Considering the fun of eating Spanish tapas, the tapas phrase list is particularly helpful. Use this and you'll eat much better than the average tourist.

Travel Smart

Your trip to Spain and Portugal is like a complex play—easier to follow and really appreciate on a second viewing. While no one does the same trip twice to gain that advantage, reading this book in its entirety before your trip accomplishes much the same thing. This book is filled with practical history and cultural tips, so read even the chapters on destinations you don't plan to visit or you may miss some fun and helpful factoids.

Reread entire chapters of this book as you arrive in a new destination, and visit local tourist information offices. Buy a phone card or cell phone and use it for reservations and confirmations. Use taxis in the big cities, bring along a water bottle, and linger in the shade. Connect with the cultures. Set up your own quest for the best cream cake, cloister, fish soup, or whatever.

Enjoy the friendliness of the local people. Ask questions. Most locals are eager to point you in their idea of the right direction. Wear your money belt, pack a pocket-size notepad to organize your thoughts, and practice the virtue of simplicity. Those who expect to travel smart, do.

Design an itinerary that enables you to hit the festivals, bullfights, and museums on the right days. As you read this book, note the problem days: Mondays, when many museums are closed, and Sundays, when public transportation is meager. Treat Saturday as a weekday (though transportation connections can be less frequent than on Mon–Fri).

Plan ahead for banking, laundry, post-office chores, and picnics. Maximize rootedness by minimizing one-night stands. Mix intense and relaxed periods. Every trip (and every traveler) needs at least a few slack days. Pace yourself. Assume you will return.

Reservations for Granada's Alhambra: The only Iberian

sight you might want to reserve tickets for in advance is this remarkable Moorish hilltop stronghold, consisting of palaces, gardens, a fortress, and a rich history. You can make reservations for the Alhambra upon arrival in Spain (ideally before you reach Granada), but I mention it here for those who like to have things nailed down before they leave home. For more information, check the Granada chapter (see "Sights—The Alhambra," page 186).

Theft Alert: Thieves target tourists throughout Spain and Portugal, especially in Barcelona, Madrid, Sevilla, and Lisbon. While hotel rooms are generally safe, cars are commonly broken into, purses are snatched, and pockets are picked. Thieves zipping by on motorbikes grab handbags from pedestrians. A fight or commotion is created to enable pickpockets to work unnoticed. Be on guard, use a money belt, and treat any disturbance around you as a smoke screen for theft. Don't believe any "police officers" looking for counterfeit bills. When traveling by train, keep your backpack in sight and get a *couchette* (bed in an attendant-monitored sleeping car) for safety on overnight trips. Drivers should park carefully and leave nothing of value in the car.

Tourist Information

Your best first stop in a new city is the Turismo (tourist information office—abbreviated as TI in this book). Get a city map and advice on public transportation (including bus and train schedules), special events, and recommendations for nightlife. Many Turismos have information on the entire country. When you visit a Turismo (TI), try to pick up maps for towns you'll be visiting later in your trip.

While the TI has listings of all lodgings and is eager to book you a room, use its room-finding service only as a last resort (bloated prices, fees, no opinions, and they take a cut from your host). You'll get a far better value by using the listings in this book and going direct.

The national tourist offices in the United States are a wealth of information. Before your trip, get their free general information packet and request any specific information you want, such as city maps and schedules of upcoming festivals.

Tourist Office of Spain: Check the Web sites www.okspain .org or www.tourspain.es, and contact the nearest office.

In New York: 666 5th Ave., 35th floor, New York, NY 10103, tel. 212/265-8822, fax 212/265-8864, e-mail: oetny@tourspain.es.

In Illinois: 845 N. Michigan Ave., Suite 915E, Chicago, IL 60611, tel. 312/642-1992, fax 312/642-9817, e-mail: chicago @tourspain.es.

In Florida: 1221 Brickell Ave., Suite 1850, Miami, FL 33131, tel. 305/358-1992, fax 305/358-8223, e-mail: oetmiami@tourspain.es.

In California: 8383 Wilshire Blvd., Suite 956, Beverly Hills, CA 90211, tel. 323/658-7188, fax 323/658-1061, e-mail: losangeles@tourspain.es.

Portuguese National Tourist Office: 590 5th Ave., 4th floor, New York, NY 10036, tel. 800/PORTUGAL or 212/354-4403, fax 212/764-6137, www.portugalinsite.com, e-mail: tourism@portugal.org. Videotapes, maps, and information on regions, castles, and beach resorts. Very helpful.

Moroccan National Tourist Office: 20 E. 46th St., Suite 1201, New York, NY 10017, tel. 212/557-2520, fax 212/949-8148, www.tourism-in-morocco.com. Good country map. Information on cities and regions.

Gibraltar Information Bureau: 1156 15th St. N.W., Suite 1100, Washington, D.C. 20005, tel. 202/452-1108, fax 202/452-1109.

Recommended Guidebooks

You may want some supplemental travel guidebooks, especially if you are traveling beyond my recommended destinations. When you consider the improvement it will make in your $3,000 vacation, $25 or $35 for extra maps and books is money well spent. For several people traveling by car, the extra weight and expense of a small trip library are negligible.

Lonely Planet's guides to Spain and Portugal are thorough, well-researched, and packed with good maps and hotel recommendations for low- to moderate-budget travelers (but they're not updated annually—check to see when it was published). Students and vagabonds will like the hip *Rough Guide: Spain* and *Rough Guide: Portugal* (written by insightful British researchers—also not updated annually) and the highly opinionated *Let's Go: Spain & Portugal* (by Harvard students, thorough hostel listings, updated annually, includes Morocco). *Let's Go* is best for backpackers with a train pass interested in the youth and night scene. Older travelers enjoy Frommer's Spain and Portugal guides even though they, like the Fodor guides, ignore alternatives that enable travelers to save money by dirtying their fingers in the local culture. The popular, skinny Michelin Green Guides to Spain and Portugal are excellent, especially if you're driving. They're known for their city and sightseeing maps, dry but concise and helpful information on all major sights, and good cultural and historical background. English editions are sold in Iberia. The well-written and thoughtful Cadogan guides to Spain and Portugal are excellent for A students on the road. The encyclopedic Blue Guides to Spain and Portugal are dry as the plains in Spain but just right for some.

The Eyewitness series has editions covering Spain, Barcelona,

Madrid, Sevilla/Andalucía, Portugal, and Lisbon (published by
Dorling Kindersley, sold in the United States or Iberia). They're
extremely popular for their fine graphics, 3-D cutaways of buildings, aerial-view maps of historic neighborhoods, and cultural
background. The downside: They're heavy, and if you pull out
the art, the print that's left is pretty skimpy.

Juan Lalaguna's *A Traveller's History of Spain* provides a
readable background on this country's tumultuous history. John
Hopper's *The New Spaniards* provides an interesting look at Spain
today. Portuguese history is mentioned (but not thoroughly
covered) in various guidebooks, such as Cadogan, Eyewitness,
and the Michelin Green Guide.

Rick Steves' Books and Videos

Rick Steves' Europe Through the Back Door 2003 gives you budget
travel tips on minimizing jet lag, packing light, planning your
itinerary, traveling by car or train, finding beds without reservations, changing money, outsmarting thieves, avoiding rip-offs,
hurdling the language barrier, staying healthy, taking great
photographs, using your bidet, keeping up with high-tech inno-
vations for smart travel such as virtually disposable cellphones,
and much more. The book also includes chapters on 35 of my
favorite "Back Doors," three of which are in Iberia.

Rick Steves' **Country Guides** are a series of eight guidebooks including this book—covering Great Britain, Ireland,
France, Italy, Scandinavia, Germany/Austria/Switzerland, and
the Best of Europe. All are updated annually; most are available
in bookstores in December, the rest in January.

My **City Guides** feature Rome, Venice, Florence, Paris,
London, and—new for 2003—*Rick Steves' Amsterdam, Bruges &
Brussels*. These practical guides offer in-depth coverage of the
sights, hotels, restaurants, and nightlife in these grand cities
along with illustrated tours of their great museums. They're
updated annually and come out in December and January.

Rick Steves' Europe 101: History and Art for the Traveler
(with Gene Openshaw, 2000) tells the story of Europe's peoples,
history, and art. Written for smart people who were sleeping
in their history and art classes before they knew they were going
to Europe, *101* really helps Europe's sights come alive.

Rick Steves' Mona Winks (with Gene Openshaw, 2001)
provides fun, easy-to-follow, self-guided tours of Europe's
top 25 museums and cultural sites in London, Paris, Rome,
Venice, Florence, and Madrid. Madrid's Prado is the thickest
tour in the book.

Rick Steves' Spanish Phrase Book and *Portuguese Phrase Book* give you the words and survival phrases necessary to communicate your way through a smooth and inexpensive trip.

My new public television series, *Rick Steves' Europe*, includes a show on Lisbon. My original series, *Travels in Europe with Rick Steves*, has six half-hour shows on Spain and Portugal. These earlier shows still air on public television throughout the United States. They are also available in information-packed home videos, along with my two-hour slide-show lecture on Spain and Portugal (order online at www.ricksteves.com or call us at 425/771-8303 for our free newsletter/catalog).

Rick Steves' Postcards from Europe, my autobiographical book, packs 25 years of travel anecdotes and insights into the ultimate 2,000-mile European adventure. Through my guidebooks I share my favorite European discoveries with you. *Postcards* introduces you to my favorite European friends.

All of my books are published by Avalon Travel Publishing (www.travelmatters.com).

Maps

The maps in this book, drawn by Dave Hoerlein, are concise and simple. Dave, who is well-traveled in Spain and Portugal, has designed the maps to help you locate recommended places and get to the TIs, where you'll find more in-depth, free maps of the cities or regions.

Don't skimp on maps. For an overall Europe trip, consider my *Rick Steves' Europe Planning Map*, which is geared for the traveler and shows sightseeing destinations prominently (order online at www.ricksteves.com or call 425/771-8303 for free newsletter/catalog). Excellent Michelin maps are available—and cheaper than in the United States—throughout Iberia in bookstores, newsstands, and gas stations. Train travelers can do fine with a simple rail map (such as the one that comes with a train pass) and city maps from the TIs. Drivers should invest in good 1:400,000 maps and learn the keys to maximize the sightseeing value.

Tours of Spain and Portugal

Travel agents can tell you about all the normal tours, but they won't tell you about ours.

At Europe Through the Back Door, we offer 17-day tours of Spain and Portugal featuring most of the highlights in this book (departures April–Oct). The tours come in two versions: fully guided (24–26 people on a big roomy bus with two great guides) and the cheaper BBB—bus, bed, and breakfast—version (28 people with an enthusiastic escort, ideal for families and independent travelers). We also offer one-week in-depth getaways

to Barcelona (departures Feb–Dec, 20 people maximum). For
details, call 425/771-8303, ext. 217, or see www.ricksteves.com.

Transportation
By Car or Train?
Cars are best for three or more traveling together (especially
families with small kids), those packing heavy, and those scouring
the countryside. Trains and buses are best for solo travelers, blitz
tourists, and city-to-city travelers.

Overview of Trains and Buses
Public transportation in Spain is becoming as slick, modern, and
efficient as in northern Europe. Portugal is straggling in train
service but offers excellent bus transportation. The best public
transportation option is to mix bus and train travel. Always verify
bus or train schedules before your departure. Never leave a station
without your next day's schedule options in hand. In either Spain
or Portugal, to ask for a schedule at an information window, say,
"*Horario para* _____–_____ [fill in names of cities], *por favor.*"
(The local TI will sometimes have schedules available for you to
take or copy.) To study train schedules in advance, see www
.renfe.es (Spain), www.cp.pt (Portugal), or http://bahn.hafas.de
/bin/query.exe/en (for international connections).

Trains
While you could save money by purchasing tickets as you go,
you may find the convenience of a railpass worth the extra cost.
You can buy a "flexi" railpass for Spain, Portugal, or all Iberia
that allows travel for a given number of days over a longer period
of time. If your trip also includes neighboring France, choose
the Eurail Selectpass (see chart on page 14). Spain also offers a
rail-and-drive pass, which gives you the ease of big-city train
hops and the flexibility of a car for rural areas such as the Andalusian hill towns. Remember, even if you have a train pass, take
advantage of bus connections when they are more convenient
than the train connections.

    Spain: The long second-class train rides from Madrid to
either Barcelona or Lisbon cost $50 each; from Madrid to
either Sevilla or Granada cost about $40 each. First class costs
50 percent more—often as much as a domestic flight. Using
a railpass to cover these trips can be a good value.

    If you're buying point-to-point tickets, note that round-
trip tickets are 20 percent cheaper than two one-way tickets.
You can get a round-trip discount even if you start with a

Cost of Public Transportation

Prices listed are for 2002. My free *Rick Steves' Guide to European Railpasses* has the latest on 2003 prices. To get the railpass guide or an order form, call us at 425/771-8303 or visit www.ricksteves.com/rail.
Saverpass prices are per person for 2 or more people traveling together. Kids 4-11 half adult or saver fare on all rail-only passes. Youth prices for under 26 only.

SPAIN FLEXIPASS

	1st class	2nd class
Any 3 days in 2 months	$200	$155
Extra rail days (max. 7)	35	30

IBERIC FLEXIPASS

	1st class Individual	1st class Saverpass
Any 3 days in 2 months	$205	$200
Any 4 days in 2 months	250	240
Any 5 days in 2 months	295	278
Any 6 days in 2 months	340	305
Extra rail days (next 4, per day)	45	25

Covers Spain and Portugal. Pass holders pay an $11-$25 reservation fee for the fast Talgo and AVE trains. For $85-$205, take a "Night Talgo" sleeper train from Madrid to Paris or Barcelona to Paris, Zurich, or Milan.

PORTUGUESE FLEXIPASS

1st class: Any 4 days out of 15 for $105.

Iberia:

Map shows approximate point-to-point one-way 2nd class rail fares in $US. 1st class costs 50% more. Add up fares for your itinerary to see whether a railpass will save you money.

SPAIN RAIL & DRIVE PASS

Any 3 rail days and 2 car days in 2 months.

	1st class	extra car day
Economy car	$239	$39
Compact car	249	49
Intermediate car	259	59
Compact automatic	265	59

Prices are per person for 2 traveling together. Solo travelers pay $50-$75 extra. 3rd and 4th persons sharing car buy only the railpass. Extra rail days (2 max.) cost $36. To order Rail & Drive passes, call Rail Europe at 800/438-7245.

EURAIL SELECTPASS

This pass covers travel in three adjacent countries.

	1st class Selectpass	1st class Saverpass	2nd class Youthpass
5 days in 2 months	$346	$294	$243
6 days in 2 months	380	322	266
8 days in 2 months	444	378	310
10 days in 2 months	502	428	352

one-way ticket—as long as you save the ticket and make a return trip. For example, if you buy a one-way ticket from Barcelona to Madrid, visit Madrid, then decide to return to Barcelona, you can bring your one-way Barcelona–Madrid ticket to the train station and get a 40 percent discount on your return trip (this equals a

Public Transportation Routes

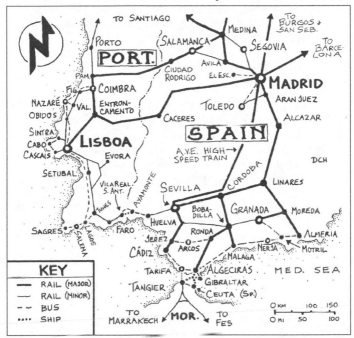

total 20 percent discount for the round-trip). Travelers under age 26 can buy cheap train tickets in Wasteels or C.T.S. offices in most major train stations.

RENFE (the acronym for the Spanish national train system) used to be "Relatively Exasperating, and Not For Everyone," but it is getting better. To save time in Spain, consider buying tickets or reservations at the RENFE offices located in over 100 city centers. These are more central and less crowded/confusing than the train station. Or, for information and reservations, dial RENFE's national number (tel. 902-240-202) from anywhere in Spain.

Spain categorizes trains this way:

The high-speed train called the **AVE** (pron. AH-vay, stands for Alta Velocidad Española) whisks travelers between Madrid and Sevilla in less than three hours. AVE is almost entirely covered by the Eurailpass (a seat reservation fee from Madrid to Sevilla costs Eurailers about €14 in second class; €29 for first class includes meal). A Madrid–Barcelona link is in the works, likely to be finished in 2004. Franco left Spain a train system that didn't fit Europe's gauge. AVE trains run on European-gauge tracks.

The **Talgo** is fast, air-conditioned, and expensive, and runs on AVE rails. **Intercity** and **Electro** trains fall just behind Talgo in speed, comfort, and expense. **Rapido, Tranvia, Semi-directo,** and **Expreso** trains are generally slower. **Cercania** are commuter trains for big-city workers and small-town tourists. **Regional** and **Correo** trains are slow, small-town milk runs. Trains get more expensive as they pick up speed, but all are cheaper per mile than their northern European counterparts.

AVE trains can be priced differently according to their time of departure. Peak hours (*punta*) are most expensive, followed by *llano* and *valle* (quietest and cheapest times).

In Spain, *salidas* means "departures" and *llegadas* is "arrivals." On train schedules, "LMXJVSD" are the days of the week, starting with Monday. A train that runs "LMXJV-D" doesn't run on Saturdays. *Laborables* can mean Monday through Friday or Monday through Saturday. Most train stations have handy luggage lockers.

Overnight Trains in Iberia: Overnight trains (and buses) are usually less expensive and slower than the daytime rides. Most overnight trains have berths and beds that you can rent (not included in the cost of your train ticket or railpass). Sleeping berths (*litera*) cost $15. A *coche-cama*, or bed in a classy quad compartment, costs $20; and a bed in a double costs $25. For long trips I go overnight on the train or fly (domestic shuttle flights are generally under $100). Travelers with first-class reservations are entitled to the use of comfortable "Intercity" lounges in train stations in Spain's major cities.

The overnight train between Lisbon and Madrid is a pricey Hotel Train called the "Lusitania" (fares listed in Lisbon chapter under Transportation Connections; discounts with railpass; for info on Hotel Trains, see below). No cheaper rail option exists between Iberia's capital cities. You can save money by taking a bus, or save time by taking a plane.

Overnight Trains to/from Europe: Expensive Hotel Trains connect France, Italy, and Switzerland with Spain. All of these fancy overnight trains (known collectively as Talgo Night) have fancy names: Francisco de Goya (Madrid–Paris), Joan Miró (Barcelona–Paris), Pau Casals (Barcelona–Zurich), and Salvador Dalí (Barcelona–Milan). These trains are not covered by railpasses, but railpass holders (of Eurail, Eurail Select, Spain, Iberic, France, Italy, and consecutive-day Swiss passes) can get discounted fares on routes within their pass boundaries; you'll give up a flexi-day and pay about half the full fare, which ranges from a $75 second-class quad *couchette* to a posh $205 Gran Class single compartment. (Full fares range from $145 in a quad to a $425 Gran Class single.) If you can easily afford to take a Hotel Train, consider flying instead to save time.

To avoid the expensive luxury of a Hotel Train, you can take a cheaper train trip that involves a transfer at the Spanish border (at Irun on Paris runs, at Cerbère on the eastern side). You'll connect to a normal night train with $20 *couchettes* on one leg of the trip. This plan is more time-consuming, and may take two days of a flexipass.

Portugal: Portugal has mostly slow milk-run trains and an occasional Expreso. Departures and arrivals are *partidas* and *chegadas*, respectively. On Portuguese train schedules, *diario* means "daily," *mudanca de comboio* means "change trains," *so* means "only," and *não* means "not." This is a typical qualifier: *"Não se efectua aos sabados, domingos, e feriados oficiais"* ("Not effective on Saturdays, Sundays, and official holidays"). Or *"So se efectua aos ... "* ("Only effective on ... ").

Buses

In either Spain or Portugal, ask at the tourist office about travel agencies that sell bus tickets to save you time if the bus station is not central. Don't leave a bus station to explore a city without checking your departure options and buying a ticket in advance if necessary (and possible). Bus service on holidays, Saturdays, and especially Sundays can be dismal.

You can (and most likely will be required to) stow your luggage under the bus. For longer rides, give some thought to which side of the bus will get the most sun, and sit on the opposite side. Even if a bus is air-conditioned and has curtains, direct sunlight can still get unpleasantly hot.

Iberian drivers and station personnel rarely speak English. Buses usually lack WCs but stop every two hours or so for a break (usually 15 min, but can be up to 30). In either Spain or Portugal, ask the driver "How many minutes here?" (*"¿Cuantos minutos aquí?"*) so you know if you have time to get out. Bus stations have WCs (rarely with toilet paper) and cafés offering quick and cheap food.

Both Spain and Portugal have a number of different bus companies, sometimes running buses to the same destinations and using the same transfer points. If you have to transfer, make sure to look for a bus with the same name/logo as the company you bought the ticket from.

A few buses are entirely nonsmoking; others are nonsmoking only in the front. When you buy your ticket for a long-distance bus (8 hours or more), ask for nonsmoking (*no fumadores* in Spanish, *não fumador* in Portuguese). It's usually pointless, since passengers ignore the signs, but it's a statement.

Your ride will likely come with a soundtrack: taped music (usually American pop in Portugal, Spanish pop in Spain), a radio, or sometimes videos. If you prefer silence, bring earplugs.

Portugal: Off the main Lisbon–Porto–Coimbra train lines, buses are usually a better bet. In cases where buses and trains serve the same destination, the bus is often more efficient, offering more frequent connections and sometimes a more central station.

Bus schedules in Portugal are clearly posted at each major station. Look for "*Partidas*" (departures), not "*Chegadas*" (arrivals). On schedules, exceptions are noted, such as "*Excepto sabados e domingos*" (Except Saturdays and Sundays). More key Portuguese "fine-print" words: Both *as* and *aos* mean "on." *De* means "from," as in "from this date to that date." *Feriado* means "holiday." *Directo* is "direct." *Ruta* buses are slower because they make many stops en route. Posted schedules list most, but not all, destinations. If your intended destination isn't listed, check at the ticket/info window for the most complete schedule information. For long trips your ticket might include an assigned seat.

Spain: Spain's bus system is more confusing than Portugal's because it has more bus companies (though they're usually clustered within one building). The larger stations have an information desk with all the schedules. In smaller stations, check the destinations and schedules posted on each office window.

Taxis

Most taxis are reliable and cheap. Drivers generally respond kindly to the request, "How much is it to ____, more or less?" (Spanish: "*¿Cuanto cuesta a ____, mas o menos?*" Portuguese: "*Quanto cuesta a ____, mais o menos?*"); if there's a long line-up of taxis, ask this question of one of the taxi drivers stuck farther back in line who has time (rather than ask at the head of the line where you might feel pressured to get in the cab and go). Spanish taxis have more extra add-ons (luggage, nighttime, Sundays, train-station or airport pickup, and so on). Rounding the fare up to the nearest large coin (maximum of 10 percent) is adequate for a tip. City rides cost $3 to $5. Keep a map in your hand so the cabby knows (or thinks) you know where you're going. Big cities have plenty of taxis. In many cases, couples travel by cab for little more than two bus or subway tickets.

Car Rental

It's cheapest to rent a car through your travel agent well before your departure. You'll want a weekly rate with unlimited mileage. Figure about $200 a week. For three weeks or longer, it's cheaper to lease; you'll save money on taxes and insurance. Easycar.com is a good car-rental option if you're looking for a cheap car to pick up and drop in Madrid or Barcelona (book through their Web site).

Comparison shop through your agent. Remember, you can turn in your car at any office on any day (normally with credit for

Standard European Road Signs

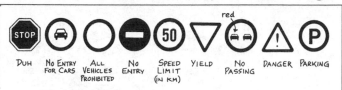

| STOP | No Entry For Cars | All Vehicles Prohibited | No Entry | Speed Limit (in km) | Yield | No Passing | Danger | Parking |

Duh   No Entry   All   No   Speed   Yield   No   Danger   Parking
For Cars   Vehicles   Entry   Limit   Passing
Prohibited   (in km)

early turn-in or extra charge for extension). Also remember that rental offices usually close from midday Saturday until Monday.

I normally rent a small economy model. For peace of mind, I splurge for the CDW insurance (Collision Damage Waiver, about $15 a day), which covers virtually the full value of the car in case of an accident. A few "gold" credit cards include CDW insurance if you rent the car using the card; quiz your credit-card company on the worst-case scenario. Travel Guard offers CDW for $6 a day (U.S. tel. 800/826-1300, www.travelguard.com). With the luxury of CDW, you'll enjoy Iberia's highways, knowing you can bring back the car in an unrecognizable shambles and just say, "S-s-s-sorry."

Driving

Driving in Iberia is great—sparse traffic and generally good roads. While the International Driver's License is officially required (cheap and easy to obtain from the nearest AAA office; bring 2 photos and $10), I drive in Iberia with only my U.S. driver's license. (The Spanish version of AAA is the Real Automobil Club; Portugal's is the Automobil Clube de Portugal.)

Good maps are available and inexpensive throughout Iberia. Freeways in Spain and Portugal come with tolls (about $4 per hour) but save huge amounts of time. Always pick up a ticket as you enter a toll freeway. In Portugal, don't use the no-stop-necessary speed lane (labeled *Reservada a Aderentes*, reserved for locals with a monthly pass) or you'll pay for a trip across the country in order to exit—a lesson I learned the expensive way. On freeways, navigate by direction (*norte, oeste, sur, este*). Also, since road numbers can be confusing and inconsistent, navigate by city names.

In Portugal, statistically one of Europe's most dangerous places to drive, you'll see lots of ambulances on the road. Drive defensively. If you're involved in an accident, you will be blamed and in for a monumental headache. Seat belts are required by law. Expect to be stopped for a routine check by the police (be sure your car-insurance form is up-to-date). Small towns come with speed traps and corruption. Tickets, especially for foreigners,

Driving in Spain & Portugal

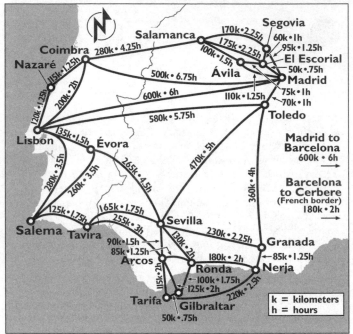

Segovia
170k • 2.25h
Salamanca
175k • 2.25h
60k • 1h
95k • 1.25h
Coimbra 280k • 4.25h
100k • 1.5h
El Escorial
Nazaré
Ávila
50k • .75h
Madrid
500k • 6.75h
415k • 1.25h
75k • 1h
200k • 2h
600k • 6
70k • 1h
120k • 1.25h
110k • 1.25h
580k • 5.75h
Toledo
Lisbon 135k • 1.5h Évora

Madrid to
Barcelona
600k • 6h

470k • 5h

280k • 3.5h
265k • 4.5h
360k • 4h

Barcelona
to Cerbere
(French border)
180k • 2h

260k • 3.5h
125k • 1.75h 165k • 1.75h
Salema Tavira
255k • 3h
Sevilla
230k • 2.25h Granada
90k • 1.5h
130k • 2h
85k • 1.25h
85k • 1.25h
Arcos
180k • 2h Nerja
Ronda
100k • 1.75h
115k • 2h
125k • 2h
220k • 2.5h
Tarifa Gilbraltar
50k • .75h

k = kilometers
h = hours

are issued and paid for on the spot. Insist on a receipt so the money is less likely to end up in the cop's pocket.

Gas and diesel prices are controlled and the same everywhere—around $4 a gallon for gas, less for diesel. *Gasolina* is either normal or super; unleaded is now widely available. Note that diesel is called *gasoleo*.

Get used to metric. A liter is about a quart, four to a gallon; a kilometer is six-tenths of a mile. To convert kilometers to miles, drop the last digit, then multiply by six (90 km: 9 x 6 = 54 mph; 120 km/hr: 12 x 6 = 72 mph).

Choose parking places carefully. Leave valuables in the trunk during the day and leave nothing worth stealing in the car overnight. While you should avoid parking lots with twinkly asphalt, thieves break car windows anywhere, even at stoplights. If your car's a hatchback, take the trunk cover off at night so thieves can look in without breaking in. Parking attendants all over Spain holler, "*Nada en el coche*" ("Nothing in the car"). And they mean it. Ask at your hotel for advice on parking. In cities you can park safely but expensively in guarded lots.

Telephones, Cell Phones, Mail, and E-mail

You cannot travel smartly in Iberia without using the telephone—to reserve and confirm hotel rooms, check sightseeing plans, and call home. A few tips will minimize frustration.

At a phone booth, make calls by using a phone card (*tarjeta telefónica* in Spanish, *cartão telefónico* in Portuguese) rather than feeding in a bunch of coins.

There are two types of phone cards you can buy: The kind you insert in a phone (sold at post offices and many newsstand kiosks) and a PIN card that's not inserted into a phone. You can use a PIN card from almost any phone, even from your hotel room (unless it has an older touch-tone model—try switching it from "pulse" to "tone"). You dial the access number listed on the card, then follow the prompts, dialing your scratch-to-reveal personal identification number (PIN) and finally the number you want to call.

PIN cards are made by numerous different (sometimes fly-by-night) companies. While you can buy them at most kiosks and newsstands, the best selection is usually at hole-in-the-wall shops catering to immigrants (who are the leading experts on calling home cheaply). Ask for an international calling card specifically for the United States if that's where you'll be calling. (Different PIN cards work better for different destinations.) PIN cards offer cheaper per-minute rates for international calls, but they don't consistently work as well as the insertable cards. In Portugal, I bought one that advertised in English, "Call Home!" but it worked only for calls within Portugal. Try to confirm that the card will work for calls to America (the salesclerk may not know), and buy a lower-denomination card in case the card is defective. Either type of phone card works only in the country where it's purchased.

To use an insertable card, simply stick it into the slot on the phone, wait for a dial tone and digital readout to show how much value remains on your card, and dial your local, long-distance, or international call; the cost of the call is automatically deducted from your card.

Portuguese phones are even-tempered, but Spanish phones refuse to be rushed. After you "*inserta*" your "*tarjeta*" (phone card) into the Spanish phone, wait until the digital display says "*Marque numero*" and then dial. Dial slowly and deliberately. Push the square R button to get a dial tone for a new call.

Dialing Direct: All phone numbers in Spain and Portugal are nine-digit numbers (without area codes) that can be dialed direct throughout each country; for example, in Madrid you dial a nine-digit number whether you're calling across the street or calling Barcelona.

To dial international calls direct, you'll need the international access codes and country codes (see the appendix). Spanish time is generally six/nine hours ahead of the east/west coast of the United States. Portuguese time is five/eight hours ahead.

USA Direct Services: Since direct-dialing rates have dropped, calling cards (offered by AT&T, MCI, and Sprint) are no longer the good value they used to be. In fact, they are a rip-off. You'll likely pay $3 for the first minute with a $4 connection fee; if you get an answering machine, it'll cost you $7 to say "Sorry I missed you." Simply dialing direct (even from your hotel room) is generally a much better deal.

Cell Phones: Many travelers in Iberia buy cheapie cell phones—about $70 on up—to make local and international calls. The cheapest phones work only in the country where they're sold; the pricier phones work throughout Europe (but it'll cost you about $40 per country to outfit the phone with the necessary chip and prepaid phone time). Because of their expense, cell phones are most economical for travelers staying in one country for two weeks or more. If you're interested, stop by one of the ubiquitous phone shops or at a cell-phone counter in a department store. Find an English-speaking clerk to help you. Confirm with the clerk whether the phone works only in Spain or Portugal or throughout Europe. To understand all the extras, get a brand that has instructions in English. Make sure the clerk shows you how to use the phone—practice making a call to the store or, for fun, to the clerk's personal cell phone. You'll need to pick out a policy; different policies offer, say, better rates for making calls at night or for calling cell phones rather than fixed phones. I get the basic fixed rate: a straight 30 cents per minute to the United States and 15 cents per minute to any fixed or cell phone in the home country at any hour. Receiving calls is generally free. When you run out of calling time, buy more time at a newsstand. Upon arrival in a different country, purchase a new chip (which comes with a new phone number). Remember, if you're on a tight budget, skip cell phones and buy PIN phone cards instead.

Mail: To arrange for mail delivery, reserve a few hotels along your route in advance and give their addresses to friends or use the mail services of American Express, free for AmEx cardholders (and a minimal fee to others). Allow 10 days for a letter to arrive. Phoning and e-mail are so easy that I've dispensed with mail stops altogether.

E-mail: E-mail use among Iberian hoteliers is increasing. I've listed e-mail addresses when possible. Some family-run pensions can become overwhelmed by the volume of e-mail they receive, so be patient if you don't get an immediate response. Internet service providers can change with alarming frequency, so if your e-mail message to a hotel bounces back, search for the hotel name in a

search engine such as Google (www.google.com) to see if it has
a new Web site. If that doesn't work, fax or call the hotel.

Cybercafés and little hole-in-the-wall Internet access shops
(offering a few computers, no food, and cheap prices) are popular
in most cities. If the extension .com doesn't work, try .es for Spain
or .pt for Portugal.

If you're planning to log on with your laptop from your hotel
room, you'll need an Internet service provider that has local phone
numbers for each country you'll visit. While an American modem
cable plugs into European phone jacks, you may have to tweak
your settings to make your computer recognize a pulse instead of
the U.S. dial tone. Bring a phone jack tester that reverses line
polarity as needed.

Sleeping

In the interest of smart use of your time, I favor hotels (and restaurants) handy to your sightseeing activities. Rather than list
hotels scattered throughout a city, I describe my favorite couple
of neighborhoods and recommend the best accommodations
values in each, from $10 bunks to $180 doubles.

Spain and Portugal (along with France) offer the best accommodation values in Western Europe. Most places are government-
regulated, with posted prices. While prices are low, street noise is
high (Spaniards are notorious night owls). Always ask to see your
room first. Check the price posted on the door, consider potential
night-noise problems, ask for another room, or bargain down the
price. You can request *con vista* (with a view) or *tranquilo* or *calado*
(quiet). In most cases, the view comes with street noise. Breakfast
may or may not be included in your room cost. It is often used as
a bargaining chip. Ask before accepting a room. Most of the year,
prices are soft.

All rooms have sinks with hot and cold water. Rooms with
private bathrooms are often bigger and renovated, while the
cheaper rooms without bathrooms often will be dingier and/or
on the top floor. Any room without a bathroom has access to a
bathroom on the corridor. Towels aren't routinely replaced
every day, so you should drip-dry and conserve.

Types of Accommodations

Hotels: Don't judge hotels by their bleak and dirty entryways.
Landlords, stuck with rent control, often stand firmly in the way of
hardworking hoteliers who'd like to brighten up their buildings.

Any regulated place will have a complaint book (*libro de recla-
maciones* in Spanish and *livro de reclamações* in Portuguese). A request
for this book will generally solve any problem you have in a jiffy.

Sleep Code

To give maximum information in a minimum of space, I use this code to describe accommodations listed in this book. Prices listed are per room, not per person. When there is a range of prices in one category, the price will fluctuate with the season; these seasons are posted at the hotel desk. Especially in resort areas, prices go way up in July and August. In Spain, some hotels include the 7 percent I.V.A. tax in the room price, others tack it onto your bill. Hotel breakfasts, while rarely included in Spain, are often included in Portugal.

- **S** = Single room (or price for one person in a double).
- **D** = Double or twin. Double beds are usually big enough for nonromantic couples.
- **T** = Triple (often a double bed with a single bed moved in).
- **Q** = Quad (an extra child's bed is usually cheaper).
- **b** = Private bathroom with toilet and shower or tub.
- **s** = Private shower or tub only (the toilet is down the hall).
- **CC** = Accepts credit cards (Visa and MasterCard, rarely American Express).
- **no CC** = Does not accept credit cards; pay in local cash.
- **SE** = Speaks English. This code is used only when it seems predictable that you'll encounter English-speaking staff.
- **NSE** = Does not speak English. Used only when it's unlikely you'll encounter English-speaking staff.

According to this code, a couple staying at a "Db-€90, CC, SE" hotel would pay a total of €90 (about $90) for a double room with a private bathroom. The hotel accepts credit cards or cash in payment, and the staff speaks English.

Hotels are officially prohibited from using central heat before November 1 and after April 1 (unless it's unusually cold); prepare for cool evenings if you travel in spring and fall. Summer can be extremely hot. Consider air-conditioning, fans, and noise (since you'll want your window open), and don't be shy about asking for ice at the fancier hotels. Many rooms come with mini-refrigerators (if it's noisy at night, unplug it). Conveniently, expensive business-class hotels often drop their prices in July and August, just when the air-con comfort they offer is most important.

Most hotel rooms with air-conditioners come with control

sticks (like a TV remote) that generally have the same symbols and features: fan icon (click to toggle through wind-power from light to gale); louver icon (choose steady air flow or waves); snow flake and sunshine icons (heat or cold, depending on season); clock ("O" setting: run x hours before turning off; "I" setting: wait x hours to start); and the temperature control (20° or 21° Celsius is the normal sleeping temperature).

You can usually save time by paying your bill the evening before you leave instead of paying in the busy morning, when the reception desk is crowded with tourists wanting to pay up, ask questions, or check in.

Historic Inns: Spain and Portugal also have luxurious, government-sponsored, historic inns. These *paradores* (Spain) and *pousadas* (Portugal) are often renovated castles, palaces, or monasteries, many with great views and stately atmospheres. These can be a very good value (doubles $80–200), especially for younger people (30 and under) and seniors (60 and over), who often get discounted rates; for details and family deals, see www.parador.es (Spain) and www.pousadas.pt (Portugal). If you're not eligible for any deals, you'll get a better value by sleeping in what I call "poor-man's paradors"—elegant normal places that offer double the warmth and Old World intimacy for half the price.

Rooms in Private Homes: In both Spain and Portugal you'll find rooms in private homes, usually in touristy areas where locals decide to open up a spare room and make a little money on the side. These rooms are usually as private as hotel rooms, often with separate entries. Especially in resort towns, the rooms might be in small apartment-type buildings. Ask for a *cama*, *habitacion*, or *casa particulare* in Spain and a *quarto* in Portugal. They're cheap ($10–25 per bed without breakfast) and usually a good experience.

Hostels and Campgrounds: Spain and Portugal have plenty of youth hostels and campgrounds, but considering the great bargains on other accommodations, I don't think they're worth the trouble and don't cover them in this book. Hotels and *pensiones* are easy to find, inexpensive, and, when chosen properly, a fun part of the Spanish and Portuguese cultural experience. If you're on a starvation budget or just prefer camping or hosteling, plenty of information is available in the backpacker guidebooks, through the national tourist offices, and at local tourist information offices.

Making Reservations
Even though Easter, July, and August are often crowded, you can travel at any time of year without reservations. But given the high stakes, erratic accommodation values, and the quality of the gems I've found for this book, I'd recommend calling ahead for rooms.

In peak times or for big cities, you can reserve long in advance. Otherwise, simply call several days in advance as you travel. For maximum flexibility—especially off-season—you might make a habit of calling between 9:00 and 10:00 on the day you plan to arrive, when the hotel knows who'll be checking out and just which rooms will be available. Use the telephone and the convenient phone cards. Most hotels listed are accustomed to English-only speakers. A hotel receptionist will trust you and hold a room until 16:00 without a deposit, though some will ask for a credit-card number. Honor (or cancel by phone) your reservations. Long distance is cheap and easy from public phone booths. Don't let these people down—I promised you'd call and cancel if for some reason you won't show up. Don't needlessly confirm rooms through the tourist office; they'll take a commission.

Those on a tight budget save pocketfuls of euros by traveling with no reservations and taking advantage of the discounted prices that hotels offer when it's clear they'll have empty rooms that day. Some of the hotels I recommend offer discounted prices if you have this book; mention this book—and claim the discount— when you call to reserve.

If you know exactly which dates you need and want a particular place, reserve a room well in advance before you leave home. To reserve from home, call, e-mail, or fax the hotel. Simple English usually works. To fax, use the handy form in the appendix (online at www.ricksteves.com/reservation). Confirm the need and method for a deposit. A two-night stay in August would be "2 nights, 16/8/03 to 18/8/03" (Europeans write the date day/month/year, and hotel jargon uses your day of departure). You'll often receive a response back requesting one night's deposit. If they accept your credit card number as the deposit, you can pay with your card or cash when you arrive; if you don't show up, you'll be billed for one night. Reconfirm your reservations a day or two in advance for safety. If you have hotel confirmations in writing, bring them along.

Eating in Spain

Spaniards eat to live, not vice versa. Their cuisine is hearty and served in big, inexpensive portions. You can eat well in restaurants for $10.

The Spanish eating schedule frustrates many visitors. First off, many restaurants close during August. Secondly, when restaurants are open, they serve meals "late." Because most Spaniards work until 19:30, supper (*cena*) is usually served around 21:00 or 22:00. And, since few people want a heavy meal that late, lunch (*almuerzo*)—also served late (13:00–16:00)—is the largest meal of the day. Don't buck this system. Generally, no self-respecting *casa*

Tips on Tipping

Tipping in Spain and Portugal isn't as automatic and generous as it is in the United States, but for special service, tips are appreciated, if not expected. As in the United States, the proper amount depends on your resources, tipping philosophy, and the circumstance, but some general guidelines apply.

Restaurants: In most restaurants, service is included—your menu typically will indicate this by noting *servicio incluido*. Still, if you like to tip and you're pleased with the service, it's customary to leave up to 5 percent. If service is not included (*servicio no incluido*), tip up to 10 percent. Leave the tip on the table. It's best to tip in cash even if you pay with your credit card. Otherwise the tip may never reach your server.

Taxis: To tip the cabbie, round up. For a typical ride, round up to the next euro on the fare (to pay a €13 fare, give €14); for a long ride, to the nearest 10 (for a €75 fare, give €80). If the cabbie hauls your bags and zips you to the airport to help you catch your flight, you might want to toss in a little more. But if you feel like you're being driven in circles or otherwise ripped off, skip the tip.

Services: Tour guides at public sites sometimes hold out their hands for tips after they give their spiel; if I've already paid for the tour, I don't tip extra, though some tourists do give a euro or two, particularly for a job well done. I don't tip at hotels, but if you do, give the porter a euro for carrying bags and leave a couple of euros in your room at the end of your stay for the maid if the room was kept clean. In general, if someone in the service industry does a super job for you, a tip of a couple of euros is appropriate . . . but not required.

When in doubt, ask. If you're not sure whether (or how much) to tip for a service, ask your hotelier or the TI; they'll fill you in on how it's done on their turf.

de comidas (house of eating—when you see this label, you can bet it's a good traditional eatery) serves meals at American hours.

You might consider having a small *pincho* (bar snack) with a coffee in the late morning, relaxing over your main meal at 15:00, and a light tapas snack for dinner later.

Don't expect "my name is Alan and I'll be your waiter tonight" cheery service. Service is often *serioso*—it's not friendly or unfriendly . . . just proficient.

Although not fancy, Spanish cuisine comes with an endless variety of regional specialties. Two famous Spanish dishes are paella and gazpacho. Paella features saffron-flavored rice as a background for whatever the chef wants to mix in—seafood, sausage, chicken, peppers, and so on. While paella is pretty heavy for your evening meal, jump (like everyone else in the bar) at the opportunity to snare a small plate of paella when it appears hot out of the kitchen in a tapas bar. Gazpacho, an Andalusian specialty, is a chilled soup of tomatoes, bread chunks, and spices—refreshing on a hot day and commonly available in the summer. Spanish cooks love garlic and olive oil. The cheapest meal is simply a *bocadillo de jamon* (ham on French bread sandwich), sold virtually anywhere.

For a budget meal in a restaurant, try a *plato combinado* (combination plate), which usually includes portions of one or two main dishes, a vegetable, and bread for a reasonable price; or the *menu del día* (menu of the day), a substantial three- to four-course meal that usually comes with a carafe of house wine.

Spain is one of the world's leading producers of grapes and that means lots of excellent wine: both red *(tinto)* and white *(blanco)*. Major wine regions include Valdepeñas, Penedès, Rioja, and Ribera del Duero. Sherry, a fortified wine from the Jerez region, ranges from dry *(fino)* to sweet *(dulce)*—Spaniards drink the *fino* and export the *dulce*. *Cava* is Spain's answer to champagne. Sangría (red wine mixed with fruit juice) is popular and refreshing. To get a small draft beer, ask for a *caña* (pron. can-yah). Spain's bars often serve orange juice *(zumo de naranja)*. For something completely different, try *horchata de chufa*, a sweet, milky beverage made from earth almonds. If ordering mineral water in a restaurant, request a *botella de agua grande* (big bottle). They push the more profitable small bottles.

Breakfast
Hotel breakfasts are generally €5 and optional. While they are handy and not expensive, it's very easy to start your day with a Spanish flair at the corner bar or at a colorful café near the town market hall.

Key Words for Breakfast *(Desayuno)*

café solo	black espresso
café con leche	coffee with milk
zumo de fruta	fruit juice
zumo de naranja	orange juice
...natural	...fresh-squeezed
pan	bread

tortilla española	potato omelet (standard dish cooked each morning, served in cheap slices)
churros	long, greasy, cigar-shaped donuts
porras	fat *churros*
chocolate	hot, pudding-like chocolate usually served with *churros* for dunking
sandwich (*toast*)	Wonder bread (toasted)
...*con jamon/queso/* ...*mixto*	...with ham/cheese/ both
...*mixto con huevo*	...with ham and cheese topped with an over-easy egg

Tapas Tips

You can eat well any time of day in tapas bars. Tapas are small portions, like appetizers, of seafood, salads, meat-filled pastries, deep-fried tasties, and on and on—normally displayed under glass at the bar (costing about €1 up to €10 for seafood). But don't limit yourself to what you see on the bar. A huge variety of more appetizing, interesting plates are being thrown together in a little back room kitchen. Get a menu and explore.

Chasing down a particular bar for tapas nearly defeats the purpose and spirit of tapas. Tapas are impromptu. Just drop in to any lively place. Be assertive or you'll never be served. *Por favore* is a key word—it grabs a guy's attention. Don't worry about paying until you're ready to leave (he's keeping track of your tab). To get the bill ask: *La cuenta?* (or *la dolorosa*—meaning literally "the sadness"—always draws a confused laugh). Bars come with a formidable language barrier. A small working vocabulary is essential for tapas proficiency (see below).

Eating and drinking at a bar is usually cheapest if you eat or drink at the counter (*barra*). You may pay a little more to eat sitting at a table (*mesa*) and still more for an outdoor table (*terraza*). Locate the price list (often posted in fine type on a wall somewhere) to know the menu options and price tiers. In the right place, a quiet snack and drink on a terrace on the town square is well worth the extra charge. But the cheapest seats sometimes get the best show. Sit at the bar and study your bartender—he's an artist.

When searching for a good bar, I look for the noisy places with piles of napkins and food debris on the floor (go local and toss your trash, too), lots of locals, and the TV blaring. Popular television shows include bullfights and soccer games, American sitcoms, and Spanish interpretations of soaps and silly game shows (you'll see Vanna Blanco).

The small tapas are most common in the south. In the north you'll likely be stuck with larger *ración* portions. While tapas are served all day, the real action begins late—21:00 at the earliest. But for beginners, an earlier start is easier and comes with less commotion.

Get a fun, inexpensive sampler plate. Ask for *un ración canapes variados* to get a plate of various little open-face sandwiches. Or ask for a *surtido de* (an assortment of...) *charcuteria* (a mixed plate of sausage), *queso* (cheese), or *mixto* (meat and cheese). *Un surtido de jamon y queso* means a plate of different hams and cheeses. That, bread, and two glasses of red wine on the right square—and you've got a romantic (and $10) dinner for two.

Terms

pincho	bite-size portion (not always available)
pinchito	tiny *pincho*
tapas	snack-size portions (not always available)
ración	larger portions—half a meal, occasionally available as "$^1/_2$ *ración*"
frito	fried
...*la plancha*	...sautéed
¿Quanto cuesta una tapa?	How much per tapa?

Sandwich Words

canape	tiny open-face sandwich
pulguitas	small closed baguette sandwich
montadito	tiny *bocadillo* (*montadito de* ... means "little sandwiches of...")
bocadillos	baguette sandwiches, cheap and basic, a tapa on bread
flautas	sandwich made with flute-thin baguette
pepito	yet one more word for a little sandwich
sandwich (toast)	Wonder bread (toasted) with meat and/or cheese
con jamon, *con queso*, or *mixto*	with ham, with cheese, or both

Typical Tapas

aceitunas	olives
almendras	fried almonds
atun	tuna
bacalao	cod

banderilla	a mini skewer of spicy, pickled veggies—eat all at once for the real punch (it's named after the spear matadors use to spike the bull)
bombas	fried meat and potatoes ball
boquerones	fresh anchovies
cabrillas	snails, cheap and not as good as French escargot
calamares fritos	fried squid rings
caracoles	snails (May–Sept)
cazon en adabo	marinated white fish
champiñones	mushrooms
croquetas de . . .	greasy, breaded balls of milky flour paste with . . .
empanadillas	pastries stuffed with meat or seafood
ensaladas (rusa)	salads (Russian)
espinacas (con garbanzos)	spinach (with garbanzo beans)
gambas (a la plancha, al ajillo)	shrimp (sautéed, with garlic)
gazpacho	cold garlic soup
guiso	stew
mejillones	mussels
pan	bread
paella	saffron rice dish with fish (when it appears fresh out of the kitchen, grab a little plate)
patatas bravas	fried chunks of potato with creamy tomato sauce
pescaditos fritos	assortment of fried little fish
picos	little breadsticks (free)
pimiento (relleno)	peppers (stuffed)
pisto	mixed sautéed vegetables
pulpo	octopus
queso	cheese (or a beautiful woman)
queso manchego	sheep cheese
rabas	squid tentacles
rabo de toro	bull-tail stew
revuelto de . . . . . . setas	scrambled eggs with . . . . . . wild mushrooms
tabla serrana	hearty plate of mountain meat and cheese
tortilla de jamón/queso	potato omelet with ham/cheese
variado fritos	typical Andalusian mix of various fried fish

Cured Meats *(Charcuteria)*

salchichón	sausage
jamón iberico	best ham, from acorn-fed baby pigs
jamón serrano	cured ham
chorizo	spicy sausage
lomo	pork

Typical Desserts

flan de huevo	crème caramel
arroz con leche	rice pudding
helados (variados)	ice cream (various flavors)
fruta del tiempo	fruit in season
un queso	cheese

Drinks

caña	small glass of draft beer
coble	tall glass of beer
tinto de la casa	house red wine
un tinto	a small glass of house red wine
chato	small glass of house wine
Rioja	a region known for quality red wine
tinto de verano	a lighter sangria
mucho cuerpo	full-bodied
afrutado	fruity
seco	dry
dulce	sweet
vermu	vermouth
refresco	soft drink
aqua con/sin gas	water with/without bubbles
un vaso de aqua del grifo	glass of tap water
una jarra de agua	pitcher of tap water
¡Salud!	Cheers!

For quality wine, ask for *crianza* (old), *reserva* (older), or *gran reserva* (oldest).

Eating in Portugal

The Portuguese meal schedule, while still late, is less cruel than Spain's. Lunch (*almoço*) is the big meal, served between noon and 14:00, while supper (*jantar*) is from 20:00 to 22:00. Tapas, therefore, are not such a big deal. You'll eat well in restaurants for $8.

Eat seafood in Portugal. Fish soup (*sopa de peixe*) and shellfish soup (*sopa de mariscos*) are worth seeking out. *Caldo verde* is a popular vegetable soup. *Frango no churrasco* is roast chicken; ask for *piri-piri* sauce if you like it hot and spicy. *Porco a alentejana* is an interesting combination of pork and clams. As in Spain, garlic and olive oil are big. *Meia dose* means half portion, while *prato do dia* is the daily special. If appetizers (olives and bread, a veritable mini-buffet of temptations) are brought to your table before you order, they are not free. If you don't want the unordered food, ask to have it removed—or you'll end up nibbling...and paying for it.

For a quick snack, remember that cafés are usually cheaper than bars. *Sandes* (sandwiches) are everywhere. The Portuguese breakfast *(pequeno almoço)* is just *café com leite* and a sweet roll, but due to the large ex-pat English community, a full British "fry" is available in most touristy areas. A standard, wonderful local pastry is the cream tart, *pastel de Nata* (called *pastel de Belém* in Lisbon).

Portuguese wines are cheap and decent. *Vinho da casa* is the house wine. *Vinho verde* is a young, light wine from the north that goes well with seafood. The Alentejo region (look for bottles labeled "Borba") is known for its quality red. The Dão region also produces fine red wines. And if you like port wine, what better place to sample it than its birthplace—Porto? Beer *(cerveja)* is also popular—for a small draft beer, ask for *uma imperial*. Freshly squeezed orange juice *(sumo de laranja)*, mineral water *(agua mineral)*, and soft drinks are widely available.

Stranger in a Strange Land
We travel all the way to Europe to enjoy differences—to become temporary locals. You'll experience frustrations. Certain truths that we find "God-given" or "self-evident," such as cold beer, ice in drinks, bottomless cups of coffee, hot showers, and bigger being better, are suddenly not so true. One of the benefits of travel is the eye-opening realization that there are logical, civil, and even better alternatives. A willingness to go local ensures that you'll enjoy a full dose of European hospitality.

While Europeans look bemusedly at some of our Yankee excesses—and worriedly at others—they nearly always afford us individual travelers all the warmth we deserve.

Back Door Manners
While updating this book, I heard over and over again that my readers are considerate and fun to have as guests. Thank you for traveling as temporary locals who are sensitive to the culture. It's fun to follow you in my travels.

Send Me a Postcard, Drop Me a Line
If you enjoy a successful trip with the help of this book and would like to share your discoveries, please fill out the survey at the end of this book (online atwww.ricksteves.com/feedback) and send it

to me at Europe Through the Back Door, Box 2009, Edmonds, WA 98020. I personally read and value all feedback.

For our latest travel information, visit www.ricksteves.com. For any updates to this book, check www.ricksteves.com/update. My e-mail address is rick@ricksteves.com. Anyone is welcome to request a free issue of our *Back Door* quarterly newsletter.

Judging from the happy postcards I receive from travelers, it's safe to assume you're on your way to a great, affordable vacation—with the finesse of an independent, experienced traveler. Thanks, and *buen viaje!*

BACK DOOR TRAVEL PHILOSOPHY
from *Rick Steves' Europe Through the Back Door*

Travel is intensified living—maximum thrills per minute and one of the last great sources of legal adventure. Travel is freedom. It's recess, and we need it.

Experiencing the real Europe requires catching it by surprise, going casual ... "through the Back Door."

Affording travel is a matter of priorities. (Make do with the old car.) You can travel—simply, safely, and comfortably—anywhere in Europe for $80 a day plus transportation costs. In many ways, spending more money only builds a thicker wall between you and what you came to see. Europe is a cultural carnival, and, time after time, you'll find that its best acts are free and the best seats are the cheap ones.

A tight budget forces you to travel close to the ground, meeting and communicating with the people, not relying on service with a purchased smile. Never sacrifice sleep, nutrition, safety, or cleanliness in the name of budget. Simply enjoy the local-style alternatives to expensive hotels and restaurants.

Extroverts have more fun. If your trip is low on magic moments, kick yourself and make things happen. If you don't enjoy a place, maybe you don't know enough about it. Seek the truth. Recognize tourist traps. Give a culture the benefit of your open mind. See things as different but not better or worse. Any culture has much to share.

Of course, travel, like the world, is a series of hills and valleys. Be fanatically positive and militantly optimistic. If something's not to your liking, change your liking. Travel is addictive. It can make you a happier American as well as a citizen of the world. Our Earth is home to six billion equally important people. It's humbling to travel and find that people don't envy Americans. They like us, but, with all due respect, they wouldn't trade passports.

Globe-trotting destroys ethnocentricity. It helps you understand and appreciate different cultures. Travel changes people. It broadens perspectives and teaches new ways to measure quality of life. Many travelers toss aside their hometown blinders. Their prized souvenirs are the strands of different cultures they decide to knit into their own character. The world is a cultural yarn shop. And Back Door Travelers are weaving the ultimate tapestry. Come on, join in!

SPAIN
(ESPAÑA)

- 506,000 square kilometers, or 195,000 square miles (three-fourths the size of Texas), 85 percent of the Iberian Peninsula
- 40 million people (80 people per square kilometer, 80 percent in towns and cities)
- 1 euro (€1) = about $1

Spain may seem poor compared to northern Europe, but it has a richness—of history, of depth, of a people who have made a good life out of little. From the stirring *sardana* dance in Barcelona to the sizzling rat-a-tat-tat of flamenco in Sevilla, this country creates its own beat despite the heat. Spaniards are proud and stoic, and can be hard to get to know—but once you've made a connection, you've got a friend for life.

If you fly over Spain, you'll see that parts of the country are parched as red-orange as a desert. But the country manages to thrive, especially in the cool of the evening. Spaniards are notorious night owls. Many clubs and restaurants don't even open until after midnight. The antidote for late nights is a midday nap. The siesta is taken by locals—and by most businesses (about 13:00–16:00).

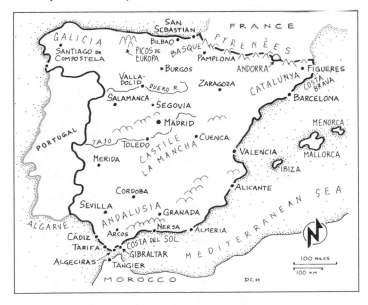

Spain is in Europe, but not *of* Europe—it has a unique identity and history. After a stint with the Romans, Spain was conquered by the North African Moors, who took over the Iberian Peninsula in just seven years. From 711 to 1492, Spain's Moorish occupiers left their mark on the country's history, architecture, and culture. Many of the top tourist sights in southern Spain, such as Granada's Alhambra, are actually Moorish.

As the last Moors were chased out of Spain, Isabel and Ferdinand united several separate Iberian kingdoms into a single nation, marking the beginning of Spain's Golden Age (1500–1700). Columbus and other explorers sailed the ocean blue, turning Spain into a naval and colonial superpower.

Devoutly Catholic Spain spearheaded the notorious Inquisition during the Counter-Reformation. Little remains of this period except the stern El Escorial palace near Madrid.

As other countries exploited science and technology to their benefit, Spain exploited only the rapidly depleting wealth of its quarrelsome colonies. Hence, while much of Europe forged ahead, Spain fell into a centuries-long decline.

Spain and Portugal were the only European countries to keep their fascist dictators after World War II. Generalissimo Francisco Franco came to power during the bloody Spanish Civil War in the 1930s and ruled for 40 years. When Franco finally died in 1975, his handpicked and carefully schooled successor, Prince Juan Carlos of Bourbon, surprised everyone by voluntarily turning his power over to a democratic parliament. Spain is still waking up to freedoms that were impossible only a generation ago.

You've heard of Basque nationalists, but every other region of Spain also has its own dialect, customs, and (often half-hearted) separatist movement. Basques, Catalonians, Andalusians, Galicians—even Castilians and Leonese—they're all Spanish second.

Whether Spanish or Basque or Leonese, everyone has an opinion about bullfighting. Consider watching a bullfight, live or on TV (good bullfighters are the Michael Jordans of Spain). To many foreigners—as well as some Spaniards—*la corrida de toros* is a cruel, barbaric custom. To fans, it's equal parts sport and art.

BARCELONA

Barcelona is Spain's second city and the capital of the proud and distinct region of Catalunya. With Franco's fascism now history, Catalan flags wave once again. Language and culture are on a roll in Spain's most cosmopolitan and European corner.

Barcelona bubbles with life in its narrow Gothic Quarter alleys, along the grand boulevards, and throughout the chic, grid-planned new town. While Barcelona had an illustrious past as a Roman colony, Visigothic capital, 14th-century maritime power, and in more modern times—a top Mediterranean trading and manufacturing center, it's most enjoyable to throw out the history books and just drift through the city. If you're in the mood to surrender to a city's charms, let it be in Barcelona.

Planning Your Time

Sandwich Barcelona between flights or overnight train rides. There's little of earth-shaking importance within eight hours by train. It's as easy to fly into Barcelona as into Madrid, Lisbon, or Paris for most travelers from the United States. Those renting a car can cleverly start here, fly to Madrid, see Madrid and Toledo, and pick up the car as they leave Madrid.

On the shortest visit, Barcelona is worth one night, one day, and an overnight train or evening flight out. The Ramblas is two different streets by day and by night. Stroll it from top to bottom at night and again the next morning, grabbing breakfast on a stool in a market café. Wander the Gothic Quarter, see the cathedral, and have lunch in Eixample (pron. eye-SHAM-plah). The top two sights in town, Gaudí's Sacred Family Church and the Picasso Museum, are usually open until 20:00. The illuminated fountains (on Montjuïc) are a good finale for your day.

Barcelona

Of course, Barcelona in a day is insane. To better appreciate the city's ample charm, spread your visit over two or three days.

Orientation

Orient yourself by locating these essentials on the map: Barri Gòtic/Ramblas (old town), Eixample (fashionable modern town), Montjuïc (hill covered with sights and parks), and Sants Station (train to Madrid). The soul of Barcelona is in its compact core—the Barri Gòtic (Gothic Quarter) and the Ramblas (main boulevard). This is your strolling, shopping, and people-watching nucleus. The city's sights are widely scattered, but with a map and a willingness to figure out the sleek subway system (or a few euros for taxis), all is manageable.

Tourist Information

There are four useful **TIs** in Barcelona: at the **airport** (an office in both terminal A and terminal B, daily 9:00–21:00, tel. 934-784-704);

at the **Sants train station** (daily 8:00–20:00, near track 6); and **Plaça de Catalunya** (daily 9:00–21:00, on main square near recommended hotels, look for red sign; has room-finding service). The TI at Plaça de Catalunya offers walking tours in English of the Gothic Quarter (€7, 2 hrs, Sat–Sun at 10:00, meet at TI, call to reserve, toll call tel. 906-301-282—€0.40/minute, www.barcelonaturisme.com) and also has a half-price ticket booth—"Tiquet 3"—where you can drop by in the early evening (3 hours before showtime) to see what tickets are available. The all-Catalunya TI office is at **Passeig de Gràcia** 107 (Mon–Sat 10:00–19:00, Sun 10:00–13:00, tel. 932-384-000).

At any TI, pick up the free small map or the large city map (€1.20), the brochure on public transport, and the free quarterly *See Barcelona* guide with practical information on museum hours, restaurants, transportation, history, festivals, and so on.

Throughout the summer, you'll see young red-jacketed tourist info helpers on the streets in the touristed areas of town.

Arrival in Barcelona

By Train: Although many international trains use the França Station, all domestic (and some international) trains use Sants Station. Both França and Sants have baggage lockers and subway stations: França's station is Barceloneta (2 blocks away), and Sants' is Sants Estacio (under the station). Sants Station has a good TI, a world of handy shops and eateries, and a classy, quiet Sala Euromed lounge for travelers with first-class reservations (TV, free drinks, study tables, and coffee bar). Subway or taxi to your hotel. Most trains to/from France stop at the subway station Passeig de Gràcia, just a short walk from the center (Plaça de Catalunya, TI, hotels).

By Plane: Barcelona's **El Prat de Llobregat Airport,** 12 kilometers southwest of town, is connected cheaply and quickly by **Aerobus** (immediately in front of arrivals lobby, 4/hr until 24:00, 20 min to Plaça de Catalunya, buy €3.30 ticket from driver) or by RENFE **train** (walk through the overpass from airport to station, 2/hr at :13 and :43 after the hour, 20 min to Sants Station and Plaça de Catalunya, €2.20). A **taxi** to or from the airport costs under €18. The airport has a post office, pharmacy, left luggage, and ATMs (avoid the gimmicky machines before the baggage carrousels, use the bank-affiliated ATMs at the far-left end of arrival hall as you face the street). Airport info: tel. 932-983-467 or 932-983-465.

Getting around Barcelona

By Subway: Barcelona's Metro, among Europe's best, connects just about every place you'll visit. It has five color-coded lines. Rides cost €1. The T-10 Card for €5.60 gives you 10 tickets good for all local bus and Metro lines as well as the separate FGC line and RENFE train lines. Pick up the TI's guide to public transport. One-, two-, and three-day passes are available (for €4.20, €7.60, and €10.80).

By Hop-on Hop-off Bus: The handy Tourist Bus (*Bus Turistic*) offers two multistop circuits in colorful double-decker buses (red route covers north Barcelona—most Gaudí sights; blue route covers south—Gothic Quarter, Montjuïc) with multilingual guides (27 stops, 2 hours per route, April–Dec 9:00–21:30, buses run every 8–20 min, most frequent in summer, buy tickets on bus). Ask for a brochure (which has a good city map) at the TI or at a pick-up point. One-day (€14) and two-day (€18) tickets include about 20 percent discounts on the city's major sights—which will likely reimburse you for half the tour cost over the course of your visit.

By Taxi: Barcelona is one of Europe's best taxi towns. Taxis are plentiful and honest (€1.20 drop charge, €0.80/km, extras posted in window). Save time by hopping a cab (Ramblas to Sants Station—€4, luggage—€0.80/piece).

Helpful Hints

Theft Alert: You're more likely to be pickpocketed here—especially on the Ramblas—than about anywhere else in Europe. Most of the crime is nonviolent, but muggings do occur. Be on guard. Leave valuables in your hotel, and wear a money belt.

Here are a few common street scams, easy to avoid if you recognize them. Most common is the too-friendly local who tries to engage you in conversation by asking for the time, whether you speak English, and so on. If you suspect the person is more interested in your money than your time, ignore him and move on. A common street gambling scam is the pea-and-carrot game, a variation on the shell game. The people winning are all ringers and you can be sure that you'll lose if you play. Also beware of groups of women aggressively selling carnations, people offering to clean off a stain from your shirt, and people picking things up in front of you on escalators. If you stop for any commotion or show on the Ramblas, put your hands in your pockets before someone else does. Assume any scuffle is simply a distraction by a team of thieves.

U.S. Consulate: Passeig Reina Elisenda 23 (tel. 932-802-227).

Emergency Phone Numbers: Police—092, Emergency—061, directory assistance—010.

24-hour Pharmacy: Near the Boqueria Market at #98 on the Ramblas.

American Express: AmEx offices are at Passeig de Gràcia 101 (with all the travel agency services, Mon–Fri 9:30–18:00, Sat 10:00–12:00, Metro: Diagonal, tel. 934-152-371) and at La

Ramblas 74, opposite the Liceu Metro station (banking services only, daily 9:00–24:00, tel. 933-011-166).

Local Guides: The Barcelona Guide Bureau is a co-op with plenty of excellent local guides who give personalized four-hour tours for €150 (Via Laietana 54, tel. 932-682-422 or 933-107-778, www.bgb.es; Joanna Wilhelm is good). Barcelona Guided Tours leads daily walking tours (departing from Plaça Catalunya, Mon–Fri, 10:30 for the Gothic Quarter, 13:00 for Modernism, €13, tel. 653-622-763 for details).

Internet Access: When **easyEverything** arrived, prices for Internet access fell all over town. Europe's favorite Internet access—with piles of computers, drinks, and munchies—is open 24/7 and offers zippy access (€1/30 min) at two central locations: one is half a block west of Plaça de Catalunya on Ronda Universitat and another near the seedy bottom of the Ramblas at #31. The rival **BBiGG** is at Calle Comtal 9, near Plaça de Catalunya (daily 9:00–02:00, 300 terminals, tel. 933-014-020).

Cheap Rental Cars: Consider Easycar.com for its great rates (tel. 902-182-028,www.easycar.com).

Introductory Walk:
From Plaça de Catalunya down the Ramblas

A ▲▲▲ sight, Barcelona's central square and main drag exert a powerful pull as many visitors spend a major part of their time here doing laps on the Ramblas. Here's a top-to-bottom orientation walk:

Plaça de Catalunya—This vast central square, littered with statues of Catalan heroes, divides old and new Barcelona and is the hub for the Metro, bus, airport shuttle, and both hop-on and hop-off buses (red northern route leaves from El Corte Inglés, blue southern route from west side of Plaça). The grass around its fountain is the best public place in town for serious necking. Overlooking the square, the huge **El Corte Inglés** department store offers everything from bonsai trees to a travel agency, plus one-hour photo developing, haircuts, and cheap souvenirs (Mon–Sat 10:00–22:00, closed Sun, pick up an English directory flier, supermarket in basement, 9th-floor terrace cafeteria/restaurant with great city view—take elevator from entrance nearest the TI, tel. 933-063-800).

Four great boulevards start from Plaça de Catalunya: the Ramblas, the fashionable Passeig de Gràcia, the cozier but still fashionable Rambla Catalunya, and the stubby, shop-filled, pedestrian-only Portal de L'Angel. Homesick Americans can even find a Hard Rock Café. Locals traditionally start or end a downtown rendezvous at the venerable Café Zurich.

"You're not in Spain, You're in Catalunya!"

This is a popular pro-nationalist refrain you might see on T-shirts or stickers around town. Catalunya is *not* the land of bullfighting and flamenco that many visitors envision when they think of Spain (best to wait until you're in Madrid or Sevilla for those).

The region of Catalunya—with Barcelona as its capital—has its own language, history, and culture, and the people have a proud independent spirit. Historically, Catalunya has often been at odds with the central Spanish government in Madrid. The Catalan language and culture have been repressed or outlawed at various times in Spanish history, most recently during the Franco era. Three of Barcelona's monuments are reminders of that suppression: The Parc de la Ciutadella was originally a much-despised military citadel, constructed in the 18th century to keep locals in line. The Castle of Montjuïc, built for similar reasons, has been the site of numerous political executions, including hundreds during the Franco era. The Sacred Heart Church atop Tibidabo, completed under Franco, was meant to atone for the sins of Barcelonans during the Spanish Civil War—the main sin being opposition to Franco. Although rivalry between Barcelona and Madrid has calmed down in recent times, it rages any time the two cities' football clubs meet.

To see real Catalan culture, look for the *sardana* dance (described in "Sights") or an exhibition of castellers. These teams of human-castle builders come together for festivals throughout the year to build towers that can reach over 15 meters (50 feet)

Cross the street from the café to reach...

Ramblas Walk Stop #1: The top of the Ramblas—Begin your ramble 20 meters down at the ornate fountain (near #129).

More than a Champs-Élysées, this grand boulevard takes you from rich at the top to rough at the port in a 1.5-kilometer, 20-minute walk. You'll raft the river of Barcelonan life past a grand opera house, elegant cafés, retread prostitutes, pickpockets, power-dressing con men, artists, street mimes, an outdoor bird market, great shopping, and people looking to charge more for a shoeshine than you paid for the shoes.

Grab a bench and watch the scene. Open up your map and read some history into it: You're about to walk right across medieval Barcelona from Plaça de Catalunya to the harbor. Notice how the higgledy-piggledy street plan of the medieval town was high, topped off by the bravest member of the team—a child! The Gràcia festival in August and the Mercè fesitival in September are good times to catch the castellers.

The Catalan language is irrevocably tied to the history and spirit of the people here. Since the end of the Franco era in the mid-1970s, the language has made a huge resurgence. Now most school-age children learn Catalan first and Spanish second. Although Spanish is understood here (and the basic survival words are the same), Barcelona speaks Catalan. Here are the essential Catalan phrases:

Hello	*Hola*	(OH-lah)
Please	*Si us plau*	(see oos plow)
Thank you	*Gracies*	(GRAH-see-es)
Goodbye	*Adeu*	(ah-DAY-oo)
Exit	*Sortida*	(sor-TEE-dah)
Long live Catalunya!	*Visca Catalunya!*	(BEE-skah . . .)

Most place-names in this chapter are listed in Catalan. Here is a pronunciation guide:

Barcelona	bar-sah-LOH-nah
Plaça de Catalunya	PLAS-sah duh cat-ah-LOON-yah
Eixample	eye-SHAM-plah
Passeig de Gràcia	PAH-sage duh grass-EE-ah
Catedral	CAH-tah-dral
Barri Gòtic	BAH-rrree GAH-teek
Montjuïc	MOHN-jew-eek

contained within the old town walls—now gone but traced by a series of roads named Ronda (meaning "to go around"). Find the Roman town, occupying about 10 percent of what became the medieval town—with tighter roads yet around the cathedral. The sprawling modern grid plan beyond the Ronda roads is from the 19th century. Breaks in this urban waffle show where a little town was consumed by the growing city. The popular Passeig de Gràcia boulevard was literally the road to Gràcia (once a town, now a characteristic Barcelona neighborhood).

Rambla means "stream" in Arabic. The Ramblas used to be a drainage ditch along the medieval wall that once defined what's now called the Gothic Quarter. "Las Ramblas" is plural, a succession of five separately named segments, but address numbers treat it as a single long street.

From Plaça de Catalunya down the Ramblas

You're at Rambla Canaletes, named for the fountain. The black-and-gold Fountain of Canaletes is the beginning point for celebrations and demonstrations. Legend says that one drink from the fountain ensures that you'll return to Barcelona one day. All along the Ramblas you'll see newspaper stands (open 24 hours, selling phone cards) and ONCE booths (selling lottery tickets that support Spain's organization of the blind, a powerful advocate for the needs of disabled people).

Got some change? As you wander downhill, drop coins into the cans of the human statues (the money often kicks them into entertaining gear). Warning: Wherever people stop to gawk, pickpockets are at work.

Walk 100 meters downhill to #115 and...

Ramblas Walk Stop #2: Rambla of the Little Birds— Traditionally, kids bring their parents here to buy pets, especially on Sundays. Apartment-dwellers find birds, turtles, and fish easier to handle than dogs and cats. Balconies with flowers are generally living spaces, those with air-conditioning are generally offices. The Academy of Science's clock (at #115) marks official Barcelona time—synchronize. The Champion supermarket (at #113) has cheap groceries and a handy deli with cooked food to go. A newly-discovered Roman necropolis is in a park across the street, 50 meters behind the big modern Citadines Hotel (go through the passageway at #122). Local apartment-dwellers blew the whistle on contractors who hoped they could finish their building before anyone noticed the antiquities they had unearthed. Imagine the tomb-lined road leading into the Roman city of Barcino 2,000 years ago.

Another 100 meters takes you to Carrer del Carme (at #2), and...

Ramblas Walk Stop #3: Baroque Church—The big plain church lining the boulevard is Baroque, unusual in Barcelona. While Barcelona's Gothic age was rich (with buildings to prove it), the Baroque age hardly left a mark (the city's importance dropped when New World discoveries shifted lucrative trade to ports on the Atlantic). The Bagues jewelry shop across Carrer del Carme from the church is known for its Art Nouveau jewelry (exactingly duplicated from the c. 1898 molds of Masriera, displayed in the window; buzz to get inside). At the shop's side entrance, step on the old-fashioned scales (free, in kilos) and head down the lane opposite (behind the church, 30 meters) to a place expert in making you heavier. Café Granja Viader (follow the narrow lane behind the church; see "Eating," below) has specialized in baked and dairy delights since 1870.

Stroll through the Ramblas of Flowers to the subway stop marked by the red M (near #100), and...

Ramblas Walk Stop #4: La Boqueria—This lively produce

market is an explosion of chicken legs, bags of live snails, stiff fish, delicious oranges, and sleeping dogs (#91, Mon–Sat 8:00–20:00, best mornings after 9:00, closed Sun). The Conserves shop sells 25 kinds of olives (straight in, near back on right, 100-gram minimum, €0.20–0.40). Full legs of ham (*jamón serrano*) abound; *Paleta Iberica de Bellota* are best and cost about €120 each. Beware: *Huevos de toro* are bull testicles—surprisingly inexpensive... and oh so good. Drop by a cafe for an *espresso con leche* or breakfast (*tortilla española*—potato omelet). For lunch and dinner options, consider La Gardunya, located at the back of the market (see "Eating," below).

The Museum of Erotica is your standard European sex museum—neat if you like nudes and a chance to hear phone sex in four languages (€7.20, daily June–Sept 10:00–24:00, shorter hours Oct–May, across from market at #96).

At #100, Gimeno sells cigars (appreciate the dying art of cigar boxes). Go ahead... buy a Cuban cigar (singles from €1). Tobacco shops sell stamps.

Farther down the Ramblas at #83, the Art Nouveau Escriba Café—an ornate world of pastries, little sandwiches, and fine coffee—still looks like it did on opening day in 1906 (daily 8:30–21:00, indoor/outdoor seating, tel. 933-016-027).

Fifty meters farther, find the much-trod-upon anchor mosaic (a reminder of the city's attachment to the sea) created by noted abstract artist Joan Miró that marks the midpoint of the Ramblas. (The towering statue of Columbus in the distance marks the end of this hike.) From here, walk down to the Liceu Opera House (reopened after a 1994 fire, tickets on sale Mon–Fri 14:00–20:30, tel. 902-332-211; 30-minute €5 tours in English daily at 10:00, reserve in advance, tel. 934-859-914). From the Opera House, cross the Ramblas to Café de l'Opera for a beverage (#74, tel. 933-177-585). This bustling café, with modernist decor and a historic atmosphere, boasts it's been open since 1929, even during the Spanish Civil War. Continue to #46; turn left down an arcaded lane to a square filled with palm trees...

Ramblas Walk Stop #5: Plaça Reial—This elegant neoclassical square comes complete with old-fashioned taverns, modern bars with patio seating, a Sunday coin and stamp market (10:00–14:00), Gaudí's first public works (the two colorful helmeted lampposts), and characters who don't need the palm trees to be shady. Herbolari Ferran is a fine and aromatic shop of herbs, with fun souvenirs such as top-quality saffron, or *safra* (Mon–Sat 9:30–14:00 & 16:30–20:00, closed Sun, downstairs at Plaça Reial 18). The small streets stretching toward the water from the square are intriguing but less safe.

Back across the Ramblas, **Palau Güell** offers an enjoyable look at a Gaudí interior (€3 for 75-min English/Spanish tour,

usually open Mon–Sat 10:00–19:00, Carrer Nou de la Rambla
3–5, tel. 933-173-974). If you'll see Casa Milà, skip the climb
to this rooftop.

Farther downhill, on the right-hand side, is...
Ramblas Walk Stop #6: Chinatown—This is the world's only
Chinatown with nothing even remotely Chinese in or near it. Named
for the prejudiced notion that Chinese immigrants go hand in hand
with poverty, prostitution, and drug dealing, the actual inhabitants
are poor Spanish, Arab, and Gypsy people. At night the Barri Xines
features prostitutes, many of them transvestites, who cater to sailors
wandering up from the port. A nighttime visit gets you a street-
corner massage—look out. Better yet—stay out.
The Rambla of the Sea—The bottom of the Ramblas is marked
by the Columbus Monument. And just beyond that, **La Rambla de
Mar** ("Rambla of the Sea") is a modern extension of the boulevard
into the harbor. A popular wooden pedestrian bridge—with waves
like the sea—leads to Maremagnum, a soulless Spanish mall with
a cinema, huge aquarium, restaurants (see recommended Tapas
Maremagnum), and piles of people. Late at night it's a rollicking
youth hangout. It's a worthwhile stroll.

Ramblas Sights at the Harbor

Columbus Monument (Monument a Colóm)—Marking the
point where the Ramblas hits the harbor, this 60-meter-tall (197-
foot) monument built for an 1888 exposition offers an elevator-
assisted view from its top (€2, June–Sept daily 9:00–20:30, Oct–
March Mon–Fri 10:00–13:30 & 15:30–18:30, Sat–Sun 10:00–18:30,
April–May until 19:30, the harbor cable car offers a better—if less
handy—view). It's interesting that Barcelona would so honor the
man whose discoveries ultimately led to its downfall as a great
trading power. It was here in Barcelona that Ferdinand and Isabel
welcomed Columbus home after his first trip to America.
Maritime Museum (Museo Maritim)—Housed in the old royal
shipyards, this museum covers the salty history of ships and navigation from the 13th to the 20th century, showing off the Catalan
role in the development of maritime technology (for example, the
first submarine is claimed to be Catalan). With fleets of seemingly
unimportant replicas of old boats explained in Catalan and Spanish,
landlubbers may find it dull—but the free audioguide livens it up
for sailors (€5.40, daily 10:00–19:00, closed Mon off-season). For
just €0.60 more, visit the old-fashioned sailing ship *Santa Eulàlia*,
docked in the harbor across the street.
Golondrinas—Little tourist boats at the foot of the Columbus
Monument offer 30-minute harbor tours (€3.20, daily 11:00–20:00).
A glass-bottom catamaran makes longer tours up the coast (€8 for

75 min, 4/day, daily 11:30–18:30.) For a picnic place, consider one
of these rides or the harbor steps.

Sights—Gothic Quarter (Barri Gòtic)

The Barri Gòtic is a bustling world of shops, bars, and nightlife
packed between hard-to-be-thrilled-about 14th- and 15th-century
buildings. The area around the port is seedy. But the area around
the cathedral is a tangled yet inviting grab bag of undiscovered
courtyards, grand squares, schoolyards, Art Nouveau storefronts,
baby flea markets (Thursdays), musty junk shops, classy antique
shops (Carrer de la Palla), street musicians strumming Catalan folk
songs, and balconies with domestic jungles behind wrought-iron
bars. Go on a cultural scavenger hunt. Write a poem.

▲**Cathedral**—As you stand in the square facing the cathedral,
you're facing what was Roman Barcelona. To your right, letters
spell out BARCINO—the city's Roman name. The three towers
on the building to the right are mostly Roman.

The colossal **cathedral,** started in about 1300, took 600 years
to complete. Rather than stretching toward heaven, it makes a
point of being simply massive (similar to the Gothic churches of
Italy). The west front, though built according to the original plan,
is only 100 years old (note the fancy, undulating rose window).
The cathedral welcomes visitors daily (8:00–13:30 & 16:30–19:30;
cloisters: daily 9:00–13:00 & 17:00–19:00; tel. 933-151-554).

The spacious interior—characteristic of Catalan Gothic—was
supported by buttresses. These provided walls for 28 richly ornamented chapels. While the main part of the church is fairly plain,
the chapels, sponsored by local guilds, show great wealth. Located
in the community's most high-profile space, they provided a kind
of advertising to illiterate worshipers. Find the logos and symbols
of the various trades represented. The Indians Columbus brought
to town were supposedly baptized in the first chapel on the left.

The **chapels** ring a finely carved 15th-century choir (*coro*).
Pay €1 for a close-up look (with the lights on) at the ornately
carved stalls and the emblems representing the various knights of
the Golden Fleece who once sat here. The chairs were folded up,
giving VIPs stools to lean on during the standing parts of the Mass.
Each was creatively carved and—since you couldn't sit on sacred
things—the artists were free to enjoy some secular fun here. Study
the upper tier of carvings.

The **high altar** sits upon the tomb of Barcelona's patron saint,
Eulàlia. She was a 13-year-old local girl tortured 13 times by
Romans for her faith and finally crucified on an X-shaped cross.
Her X symbol is carved on the pews. Climb down the stairs for a
close look at her exquisite marble sarcophagus.

Barcelona's Gothic Quarter Sights

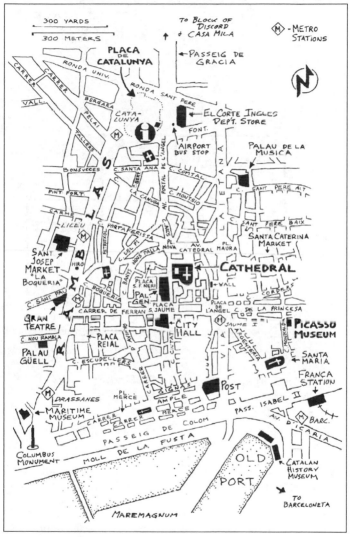

Ride the **elevator** to the roof and climb a tight spiral staircase up the spire for a commanding view (€1.40, Mon–Fri 10:30–12:30 & 16:30–18:00, closed Sat–Sun, start from chapel left of high altar).

Enter the **cloister** (through arch, right of high altar). From there, look back at the arch, an impressive mix of Romanesque and

Barcelona's Cathedral

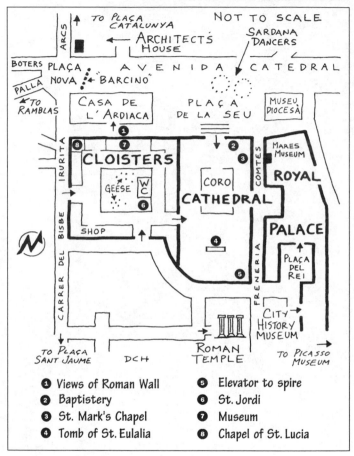

NOT TO SCALE

- ❶ Views of Roman Wall
- ❷ Baptistery
- ❸ St. Mark's Chapel
- ❹ Tomb of St. Eulalia
- ❺ Elevator to spire
- ❻ St. Jordi
- ❼ Museum
- ❽ Chapel of St. Lucia

Gothic. A tiny statue of St. George slaying the dragon stands in the garden. Jordi (George) is one of the patron saints of Catalunya and by far the most popular boy's name here. Though cloisters are generally found in monasteries, this church added one to accommodate more chapels—good for business. Again, notice the symbols of the trades or guilds. Even the pavement is filled with symbols—similar to Americans getting their name on a brick for helping to pay for something.

Long ago the resident geese—there are always 13 in memory of Eulàlia—functioned as an alarm system. Any commotion would get them honking, alerting the monk in charge.

From St. Jordi, circle to the right (past a WC hidden on the left). The skippable little €0.60 **museum** (far corner) is one plush room with a dozen old religious paintings. In the corner the dark, barrel-vaulted Romanesque Chapel of Santa Lucia was a small church predating the cathedral and built into the cloister. The candles outside were left by people hoping for good eyesight (Santa Lucia's specialty). Farther along, the Chapel of Santa Rita (her forte: impossible causes) usually has the most candles. Complete the circle and exit at the door just before the place you entered.

Walk uphill, following the church. From the end of the apse turn right 50 meters up Carrer del Paradis to the **Roman Temple** (Temple Roma d' August). In the corner a sign above a millstone in the pavement marks "Mont Tabor, 16.9 meters." Step into the courtyard for a peek at a surviving corner of the imposing temple which once stood here on the city's highest hill, keeping a protective watch over Barcino (free, daily 10:00–14:00 & 16:00–20:00).

Plaça del Rei—The Royal Palace sat on King's Square (a block from the cathedral) until Catalunya became part of Spain in the 15th century. Then it was the headquarters of the local Inquisition. Columbus came here to show King Ferdinand souvenirs from what he thought was India.

▲City History Museum—For a walk through the history of the city, take an elevator down 20 meters (and 2,000 years) to stroll the streets of Roman Barcelona. You'll see sewers, models of domestic life, and bits of an early Christian church. Then a new exhibit in the 11th-century count's palace shows you Barcelona through the Middle Ages (€3.50 includes museum, presentation, and visits to Pedralbes Monastery and Verdaguer House Museum, see museum pamphlet for details; June–Sept Tue–Sat 10:00–20:00, Sun 10:00–14:00, closed Mon; Oct–May Tue–Sat 10:00–14:00 & 16:00–20:00, Sun 10:00–14:00, closed Mon, Plaça del Rei, tel. 933-151-111).

Frederic Mares Museum—This classy collection combines medieval religious art with a quirky bundle of more modern artifacts—old pipes, pinups, toys, and so on (Tue–Sat 10:00–15:00, Sun 10:00–14:00, closed Mon, Carrer del Comtes, off Plaça de la Seu, next to cathedral, tel. 933-105-800).

▲*Sardana* Dances—The patriotic *sardana* dances are held at the cathedral (most Sun at 12:00) and at Plaça de Sant Jaume (often on Sun at 18:00 in spring and summer, 18:30 in fall and winter). Locals of all ages seem to spontaneously appear. They gather in circles after putting their things in the center—symbolic of community and sharing (and the ever-present risk of theft). Holding hands, they raise their arms as they hop and sway gracefully to the band. The band (*cobla*) consists of a long flute, tenor and soprano oboes,

strange-looking brass instruments, and a tiny bongolike drum
(tambori). The rest of Spain mocks this lazy circle dance, but, considering what it takes for a culture to survive within another culture's
country, it is a stirring display of local pride and patriotism.

Shoe Museum (Museu del Calçat)—Shoe-lovers enjoy this
two-room shoe museum (with a we-try-harder attendant) on the
delightful Plaça Sant Felip Neri (€1.20, Tue–Sun 11:00–14:00,
closed Mon, 1 block beyond outside door of cathedral cloister,
behind Plaça de G. Bachs, tel. 933-014-533). The huge shoe
at the entry is designed to fit the foot of the Columbus Monument at the bottom of the Ramblas.

Plaça de Sant Jaume—On this stately central square (pron.
jau-mah) of the Gothic Quarter, two of the top governmental
buildings in Catalunya face each other: The Barcelona city hall
(Ajuntament, free Sun 10:00–13:30) and the seat of the auto-
nomous government of Catalunya (Palau de la Generalitat).
Sardana dances take place here many Sundays (see "*Sardana*
Dances," above).

▲▲▲**Picasso Museum**—This is the best collection of Picasso's
(1881–1973) work in Spain, and—since he spent his formative
years (age 14–21) in Barcelona—the best collection of his early
works anywhere. It's scattered through two Gothic palaces, six
blocks from the cathedral.

Picasso's personal secretary amassed a huge collection of his
work and bequeathed it to the city. Picasso, happy to have a fine
museum showing off his work in the city of his youth, added to
the collection throughout his life. (Sadly, since Picasso vowed
never to set foot in a fascist, Franco-ruled Spain and he died
2 years before Franco, the artist never saw the museum.)

This is a great chance to see Picasso's earliest, more realistic
art; to appreciate his genius; and to better understand his later,
more challenging art (€5, free on first Sun of month, Tue–Sat
10:00–20:00, Sun 10:00–15:00, closed Mon, free and required bag
check, Montcada 15–19, Metro: Jaume, tel. 933-196-310). If there's
a line at the ticket window, use the second ticket booth (down the
street at #21). The ground floor offers a handy array of services
(bookshop, WC, bag check, and cafeteria). For a good lunch, see
"Eating near the Picasso Museum" under "Eating," below.

While the rooms are constantly rearranged, the collection is
always presented chronologically. With the help of thoughtful
English descriptions for each stage, it's easy to follow the evolution
of Picasso's work. You'll see his art evolve in these twelve stages:

Stage 1—Boy wonder, age 12–14, 1895–1897: Pablo's
earliest art is realistic and serious. A budding genius emerges at
age 12 as Pablo moves to Barcelona and gets serious about art.

Even this young, his portraits of grizzled peasants show great psychological insight and flawless technique. You'll see portraits of Pablo's first teacher, his father *(Padre del Artista)*. Displays show his art-school work. Every time Pablo starts breaking rules, he's sent back to the standard classic style. The assignment: Sketch nude models to capture human anatomy accurately. Three self-portraits (1896) show the self-awareness of a thoughtful genius blossoming. When Pablo was 13, his father quit painting to nurture his young prodigy. Look closely at the portrait of his mother *(Retrato de la Madre del Artista)*. Pablo, then age 15, is working on the fine details and gradients of white in her blouse and the expression in her cameo-like face. Notice the signature. Spaniards keep both parents' surnames: Pablo Ruiz Picasso. Pablo was closer to his mom than his dad. Eventually he kept just his mom's name.

Stage 2—Málaga, exploration of nature: During a short trip to Málaga, Picasso dabbles in Impressionism (unknown in Spain at the time).

Stage 3—Sponge, influenced by local painters: As a 15-year-old, Pablo dutifully enters art-school competitions. His first big painting—while forced to show a religious subject *(First Communion)*—is more an excuse to paint his family. Notice his sister Lola's exquisitely painted veil. This painting was heavily influenced by local painters.

Science and Charity—which won second prize at a fine-arts exhibition—got Picasso the chance to study in Madrid. Now Picasso conveys real feeling. The doctor (Pablo's father) represents science. The nun represents charity and religion. But nothing can help as the woman is clearly dead (notice her face and lifeless hand). Pablo painted a little perspective trick: Walk back and forth across the room to see the bed stretch and shrink. Four small studies for this painting, hanging in the back of the room, show how this was an exploratory work. The frontier: light.

Picasso travels to Madrid for further study. Finding the stuffy fine-arts school in Madrid stifling, Pablo hangs out in the Prado Gallery and learns by copying the masters. Notice his nearly perfect copy of Felipe IV by Valázquez.

Stage 4—Independence: Having absorbed the wisdom of the ages, in 1898, Pablo visits Horta, a rural Catalan village, and finds his artistic independence.

Stage 5—Sadness, 1899–1900: Pablo's good friend dies, he's poor, and without love. He returns to Barcelona. It's 1900 and Art Nouveau is the rage. Upsetting his dad, Pablo quits art school and falls in with the avant-garde crowd. These bohemians congregate daily at the Four Cats (slang for "a few crazy people"— see "Eating," below). Further establishing his artistic freedom, he paints portraits—no longer of his family . . . but of his new friends. Still a teenager, Pablo puts on his first one-man show.

Stage 6—Paris, 1900–1901: Nineteen-year-old Picasso arrives in Paris, a city bursting with life, light, and love. Dropping the surname Ruiz, Pablo establishes his commercial brand name: "Picasso." Here the explorer Picasso goes Bohemian, befriending poets, prostitutes, and artists. He paints Impressionist landscapes like Monet, posters like Toulouse-Lautrec, still-lifes like Cezanne, and bright-colored Fauvist works like Matisse. (La Espera—with her bold outline and strong gaze—pops out from the Impressionistic background.) It was Cezanne's technique of "building" a figure with "cubes" of paint that inspired Picasso to soon invent Cubism.

Stage 7—Blue Period, 1901–1904: The bleak weather and poverty Picasso experiences in Paris leads to his "Blue Period." He cranks out piles of blue art just to stay housed and fed. With blue—the coldest color—backgrounds and depressing subjects, this period was revolutionary in art history. Now the artist is painting not what he sees but what he feels. The touching portrait of a mother and child, *Desamparados* (*Despair*, 1903), captures the period well. Painting misfits and street people, Picasso, like Velázquez and Toulouse-Lautrec, sees "the beauty in ugliness." Back home in Barcelona, Picasso paints his hometown at night from rooftops *(Terrats de Barcelona)*. Still blue, here we see proto-Cubism . . . five years before the first real Cubist painting.

Stage 8—Rose: The woman in pink *(Retrato de la Sra. Canals)*, painted with classic "Spanish melancholy," finally lifts Picasso out of his funk, moves him out of the blue and into a happier "Rose Period" (of which this museum has only one painting).

Stage 9—Cubism, 1907–1920: Pablo's invention in Paris of the shocking Cubist style is well known—at least I hope so, since this museum has no true Cubist paintings. In the age of the camera, the Cubist gives just the basics (a man with a bowl of fruit) and lets you finish it.

Stage 10—Eclectic, 1920–1950: Picasso is a painter of many styles. We see a little post-Impressionistic Pointillism in a portrait that looks like a classical statue. After a trip to Rome, he paints beefy women, inspired by the three-dimensional sturdiness of ancient statues. The expressionist horse symbolizes to Spaniards the innocent victim. In bullfights, the horse—clad with blinders and pummeled by the bull—has nothing to do with the fight. To take the symbolism in a deeper, more human direction, to Picasso the horse was feminine and the bull masculine. Picasso would mix all these styles and symbols—including this image of the horse—in his masterpiece *Guernica* (in Madrid) to show the horror and chaos of modern war.

Stage 11—Picasso and Velázquez, 1957: Notice the print

of Velázquez's *Las Meninas* (in Madrid's Prado) that introduces this section. Picasso, who had great respect for Velázquez, painted over 50 interpretations of the painting many consider the greatest painting by anyone ever. These two Spanish geniuses were artistic equals. Picasso seems to enjoy a relationship with Velázquez. Like artistic soul mates, they spar and tease. He dissects Velázquez, and then injects playful uses of light, color, and perspective to horse around with the earlier masterpiece. In the big black-and-white canvas, the king and queen (reflected in the mirror in the back of the room) are hardly seen while the self-portrait of the painter towers above everyone. The two women of the court on the right look like they're in a tomb—but they're wearing party shoes. In these rooms, see the fun Picasso had playing paddleball with Velázquez's masterpiece—filtering Velázquez's realism through the kaleidoscope of Cubism.

  Stage 12—Windows, 1957: All his life Picasso said, "Paintings are like windows open to the world." Here we see the French Riviera—with simple black outlines and Crayola colors, he paints sun-splashed nature and the joys of the beach. He died with brush in hand, still growing. To the end—through his art—he continued exploring and loving life. As a child, Picasso was forced to paint as an adult. Now, as an old man (with little kids of his own and an also-childish artist Chagall for a friend), he paints like a child.

Textile and Garment Museum (Museu Textil i de la Indumentaria)—If fabrics from the 12th to 20th centuries leave you cold, have a *café con leche* on the museum's beautiful patio (€3.50, Tue–Sat 10:00–18:00, Sun 10:00–15:00, closed Mon, free entrance to patio—an inviting courtyard with a WC and coffeeshop, which is outside museum but within the walls, 30 meters from Picasso Museum at Montcada 12–14).

▲▲**Catalan Concert Hall (Palau de la Música Catalana)**—This concert hall, finished in 1908, features *the* best modernist interior in town. Inviting arches lead you into the 2,000-seat hall. A kaleidoscopic skylight features a choir singing around the sun while playful carvings and mosaics celebrate music and Catalan culture. Admission is by tour only and starts with a relaxing 20-minute video (€5, 1 hr, in English, daily on the hour 10:00–15:00, maybe later, tel. 932-967-200). Ask about concerts (300 per year, inexpensive tickets, www.palaumusica.org).

Sights—Eixample

Uptown Barcelona is a unique variation on the common grid-plan city. Barcelona snipped off the building corners to create light and spacious eight-sided squares at every intersection. Wide sidewalks, hardy shade trees, chic shops, and plenty of Art Nouveau fun make the Eixample a refreshing break from the old town. For the best Eixample example, ramble Rambla Catalunya (unrelated to the more famous Ramblas) and pass through Passeig de Gràcia (described below, Metro: Passeig de Gràcia for Block of Discord or Diagonal for Casa Milà).

The 19th century was a boom time for Barcelona. By 1850 the city was busting out of its medieval walls. A new town was planned to follow a gridlike layout. The intersection of three major thoroughfares—Gran Vía, Diagonal, and Meridiana—would shift the city's focus uptown.

The Eixample, or "Expansion," was a progressive plan in which everything was made accessible to everyone. Each 20-block-square district would have its own hospital and large park, each 10-block-square area would have its own market and general services, and each five-block-square grid would house its own schools and day-care centers. The hollow space found inside each "block" of apartments would form a neighborhood park.

While much of that vision never quite panned out, the Eixample was an urban success. Rich and artsy big shots bought plots along the grid. The richest landowners built as close to the center as possible. For this reason, the best buildings are near the Passeig de Gràcia. While adhering to the height, width, and depth limitations, they built as they pleased—often in the trendy new modernist style.

Sights—Gaudí's Art and Architecture

Barcelona is an architectural scrapbook of the galloping gables and organic curves of hometown boy Antonio Gaudí. A devoted Catalan and Catholic, he immersed himself in each project, often living on-site. He called Parc Güell, La Pedrera, and the Sagrada Familia all home.

▲▲▲**Sagrada Familia (Holy Family) Church**—Gaudí's most famous and persistent work is this unfinished landmark. He worked on the church from 1883 to 1926. Since then, construction has moved forward in fits and starts. Even today, the half-finished church is not expected to be completed for another 50 years. One reason it's taking so long is that the temple is funded exclusively by private donations and entry fees. Your admission helps pay for the ongoing construction (€6, daily April–Oct 9:00–20:00, Nov–March 9:00–18:00; €3 extra for tours in English: 4/day April–Oct, usually 2/day Nov–March; Metro: Sagrada Familia, tel. 932-073-031, www.sagradafamilia.org).

When the church is finished, a dozen 100-meter spires (representing the apostles) will stand in groups of four and mark the three entry facades of the building. The center tower (honoring Jesus), will reach 170 meters up (560 feet) and be flanked by 125-meter-tall towers (400 feet) of Mary and the four evangelists. A unique exterior ambulatory will circle the building like a cloister turned inside out.

1. Passion Facade (on the side where you enter): This shows Gaudí's spiritual drive. Inspired by Gaudí's vision, it's full of symbolism from the Bible (find the stylized alpha and omega over the door; Jesus, hanging on the cross, has an open book for hair; the grid of numbers all add up to 33—Jesus' age at the time of his death). The distinct face of the man on the lower left is a memorial to Gaudí.

Judge for yourself how the recently completed and controversial Passion facade by Josep Maria Subirachs fits with Gaudí's original formulation. Now look high above: The colorful ceramic caps of the columns symbolize the mitres (formal hats) of bishops. This is only a side entrance. The nine-story apartment flat to the right will be torn down to accommodate the grand front entry of this church.

Now walk down to your right to the . . .

2. Museum (in church basement): The museum displays physical models used for the church's construction. As you wander, you'll see how the church's design is a fusion of nature, architecture, and religion. The columns seem light, with branches springing forth and capitals that look like palm trees. The U-shaped choir hovers above the nave, tethered halfway up the columns. Find the hanging model showing how Gaudí used gravity to calculate the perfect parabolas incorporated into the church design (the mirror above this model shows how the right-side-up church is derived from this).

Gaudí lived on the site for more than a decade and is buried in the crypt. When he died in 1926, only the stubs of four spires stood above the building site. A window allows you to look down into the neo-Gothic 19th-century crypt (which is how the church began) to see the tomb of Gaudí. There's a move afoot to make Gaudí a saint. Perhaps some day, this tomb will be a place of pilgrimage. Gaudí was certainly driven to greatness by his passion for God. When undertaking a lengthy project, he said, "My client [meaning God] is not in a hurry." You'll peek into a busy workshop where the slow and steady building pace is maintained.

Outside, just after leaving the building, you'll encounter the . . .

3. Nativity Facade: This really shows Gaudí's vision. It was the only real decorative part of the church finished in his lifetime, and shows scenes from the birth and childhood of Jesus along with angels playing musical instruments.

Finally you walk through the actual . . .

4. Construction Zone: With the cranking cranes, rusty forests of rebar, and scaffolding requiring a powerful faith, the Sagrada Familia Church offers a fun look at a living, growing,

Gaudí & Moderniste Sights

bigger-than-life building. Take the lift on the Passion side
(€1.20) or the stairs on the Nativity side (free but often miserably
congested) up to the dizzy lookout bridging two spires. You'll
get a great view of the city and a gargoyle's-eye perspective of
the loopy church. If there's any building on earth I'd like to see,
it's the Sagrada Familia . . . finished.

▲**Palau Güell**—This is a good chance to enjoy a Gaudí interior
(see "Introductory Walk—Ramblas," above). Curvy.

▲▲**Casa Milà (La Pedrera)**—This Gaudí exterior laughs down
on the crowds filling Passeig de Gràcia. Casa Milà, also called
La Pedrera (the Quarry), has a much-photographed roller coaster
of melting-ice-cream eaves. This is Barcelona's quintessential
modernist building.

Visits come in three parts: apartment, attic, and rooftop.
Buy the €6 ticket to see all three. Starting with the apartment,
an elevator whisks you to the *Life in Barcelona 1905–1929* exhibit

Modernisme

The Renaixensa (Catalan cultural revival) gave birth to Modernisme (Catalan Art Nouveau) at the end of the 19th century. Barcelona is its capital. Its Eixample neighborhood shimmers with the colorful, leafy, flowing, blooming shapes of Modernisme in doorways, entrances, facades, and ceilings.

Meaning "a taste for what is modern," this free-flowing organic style lasted from 1888 to 1906. Breaking with tradition, artists experimented with glass, tile, iron, and brick. Decoration became structural. It comes with three influences: nature, exotic (such as Chinese), and a fanciful Gothic twist to celebrate Catalan's medieval glory days. Modernisme was a way of life as Barcelona burst into the 20th century.

Antoni Gaudí is Barcelona's most famous modernist artist. From four generations of metalworkers, a lineage of which he was quite proud, he incorporated ironwork into his architecture and came up with novel approaches to architectural structure and space.

Two more modernist architects famous for their unique style are Lluís Domènech i Muntaner and Josep Puig i Cadafalch. You'll see their work on the Block of Discord.

(well-described in English). Then you walk through a sumptuously furnished Art Nouveau apartment. Upstairs in the attic, wander under brick arches—enjoying a multimedia exhibit of models, photos, and videos of Gaudí's works. From there a stairway leads to the fanciful rooftop where chimneys play volleyball with the clouds. From here, you can see Gaudí's other principal works, the Sagrada Familia, Casa Batllo, and Parc Güell (daily 10:00–20:00; free tours in English Mon–Fri at 17:30, Sat–Sun and holidays at 11:00; Passeig de Gràcia 92, Metro: Diagonal, tel. 934-845-995). At ground level of Casa Milà, poke into the dreamily painted original entrance courtyard (free). The first floor hosts free art exhibits. During the summer, a concert series called "Pedrera by Night" features live music—jazz, flamenco, tango—a glass of champagne, and the chance to see the rooftop illuminated (€9, July–Sept Fri–Sat at 22:00, tel. 934-845-900).

▲The Block of Discord—Four blocks from Casa Milà you can survey a noisy block of competing late-19th-century facades. Several of Barcelona's top modernist mansions line Passeig de Gràcia (Metro: Passeig de Gràcia). Because the structures look as though they are trying to outdo each other in creative twists, locals nicknamed the block between Consell de Cent and Arago, the "Block of Discord." First (at #43) and most famous is Gaudí's Casa Batlló, with skull-like balconies and a tile roof that suggests a cresting dragon's back (Gaudí based the work on the popular St. Jordi-slays-the-dragon legend). By the way, if you're tempted to snap your photos from the middle of the street, be careful—Gaudí died under a streetcar.

Next door, at Casa Amatller (#41), check out architect Puig i Cadafalch's creative mix of Moorish, Gothic, and iron grillwork. This is the only place in town to purchase Modernist Route combo-tickets. For €3.60, you get a 50 percent discount to 10 of the most important modernist sights in Barcelona (valid for 1 month). Even if you only see Sagrada Familia and Casa Milà, you'll save money with this ticket.

On the corner (at #35) is Casa Lleo Morera, by Lluís Domènech i Muntaner, who did the Catalana Concert Hall (you'll see similarities). The perfume shop halfway down the street has a free and interesting little perfume museum in the back. The Hostal de Rita restaurant, just around the corner on Carrer Arago, serves a fine three-course lunch for a great price at 13:00 (see "Eating," below).

▲Park Güell—Gaudí fans enjoy the artist's magic in this colorful park (free, daily 9:00–20:00) and small Gaudí Museum (€2.50, daily 10:00–20:00, closes off-season at 18:00, red Tourist Bus or bus #24 from Plaça de Catalunya; €6 by taxi). Gaudí intended this garden to be a 60-residence housing project—a kind of gated community—rather than a park. As a high-income housing development, it flopped. As a park, it's a delight offering another peek into the eccentric genius of Gaudí. From the bus stop, you'll hike uphill three blocks to the main (lower) entry to the park. (Taxis take you right there.) Notice the mosaic medallions that say "park" in English, reminding folks that this is modeled on an English garden.

Imagine living here 100 years ago, when this gated community was filled with Barcelona's wealthy. Stepping past fancy gate houses (which now house a good bookshop and an audiovisual intro), you walk by Gaudí's wrought-iron gas lamps (1900–1914)—his dad was a blacksmith and he always enjoyed this medium. Climb the grand stairway past the ceramic dragon fountain. At the top drop by the Hall of 100 Columns, a produce market for the neighborhood's 60 mansions. The fun columns—each different, made from concrete and rebar, topped with colorful ceramic and studded with broken bottles and bric-a-brac—add to the market's vitality. After shopping, continue up. Look left down the playful "pathway of columns" that support a long arcade. Gaudí drew his inspiration from nature, and this arcade is like a surfer's perfect "tube." From here, continue up to the terrace. Sit on a colorful bench—designed to fit your body ergonomically—and enjoy one of Barcelona's best views. Look for the Sagrada Familia church in the distance.

When considering the failure of Park Güell, consider also that it was an idea just a hundred years ahead of its time. Back then high-society ladies didn't want to live so far from the cultural action. Today, the surrounding neighborhoods are some of the wealthiest in town and a gated community here would be a big hit.

Sights—Barcelona's Montjuïc

The Montjuïc (Mount of the Jews), overlooking Barcelona's hazy port, has always been a show-off. Ages ago it had the impressive fortress. In 1929 it hosted an international fair, from which most of today's sights originated. And in 1992 the Summer Olympics directed the world's attention to this pincushion of attractions.

There are many ways to reach Montjuïc: on the blue Tourist Bus route (see "Getting around Barcelona," above);by bus #50 from the corner of Gran Vía and Passeig de Gràcia (€1, every 10 min); take the Metro to Parallel and catch the funicular (€1.70 one-way, €2.50 round-trip, Mon–Sat 10:45–20:00, closed Sun); or by taxi (about €7). The first three options leave you at the *teleférico* (cable car), which you can take to the Castle of Montjuïc (€3.20 one-way, €4.50 round-trip, daily 11:00–21:00, less off-season, tel. 934-430-859). Alternatively, from the same spot, you can walk uphill 20 minutes through the pleasant park. Only a taxi gets you doorstep delivery. From the port, the fastest and most scenic way to Montjuïc is via the 1929 Transbordador Aereo (at tower in port, ride elevator up to catch dangling gondola, €7.20 round-trip, 4/hr, daily 10:30–19:00, tel. 934-430-859).

Castle of Montjuïc—The castle offers great city views and a military museum (€1.20, Tue–Sun 9:30–20:00, closed Mon). The seemingly endless museum houses a dull collection of guns, swords, and toy soldiers. An interesting section on the Spanish-American War covers Spain's valiant fight against American aggression (from its perspective). Unfortunately, there are no English descriptions. Those interested in Jewish history will find a fascinating collection of ninth-century Jewish tombstones. The castle itself has a fascist past. It was built in the 18th century by the central Spanish government to keep an eye on Barcelona and stifle citizen revolt. When Franco was in power, the castle was the site of hundreds of political assassinations.

▲**Fountains (Font Magica)**—Music, colored lights, and huge amounts of water make an artistic and coordinated splash on summer nights (Fri–Sun, 20-min shows start on the half-hour,

21:30–24:00, in summer Thu eve, too, from Metro: Plaça Espanya, walk toward towering National Palace).

Spanish Village (Poble Espanyol)—This tacky five-acre model village uses fake traditional architecture from all over Spain as a shell to contain gift shops. Craftspeople do their clichéd thing only in the morning (not worth your time or €6). After hours it's a popular local nightspot.

▲▲**Catalan Art Museum (Museo Nacional d'Art de Catalunya)**—Often called "the Prado of Romanesque art," this is a rare, world-class collection of Romanesque art taken mostly from remote Catalan village churches in the Pyrenees (saved from unscrupulous art dealers—many American).

The Romanesque wing features frescoes, painted wooden altar fronts, and ornate statuary. This classic Romanesque art—with flat 2-D scenes, each saint holding his symbol, and Jesus (easy to identify by the cross in his halo)—is impressively displayed on replicas of the original church ceilings.

In the Gothic wing, fresco murals give way to vivid 14th-century paintings of Bible stories on wood. A roomful of paintings by the Catalan master Jaume Huguet (1412–1492) deserves a close look.

Before you leave, ice-skate under the huge dome over to the air-conditioned cafeteria. This was the prime ceremony room and dance hall for the 1929 International Exposition (museum €5, Tue–Sat 10:00–19:00, Thu until 21:00, Sun 10:00–14:30, closed Mon, tel. 936-220-375). The museum is in the massive National Palace building above the fountains, near Plaça Espanya (Metro: Plaça Espanya, then hike up or ride the bus; the blue Tourist Bus and bus #50 stop close by).

▲**Fundació Joan Miró**—For something more up-to-date, this museum—showcasing the modern-art talents of yet another Catalan artist—has the best collection of Joan Miró art anywhere. You'll also see works by other modern Spanish artists (such as Alexander Calder's *Mercury Fountain*). If you don't like abstract art, you'll leave scratching your head, but those who love this place are not faking it . . . they understand the genius of Miró and the fun of abstract art.

As you wander, consider this: Miró believed that everything in the cosmos is linked—colors, sky, stars, love, time, music, dogs, men, women, dirt, and the void. He mixed these things creatively, as a poet uses words. It's as liberating for the visual artist to be abstract as it is for the poet: Both can use metaphors rather than being confined to concrete explanations. Miró would listen to music and paint. It's interactive, free interpretation. He said, "For me simplicity is freedom."

To enjoy Miró's art: 1) meditate on it, 2) read the title (for example, *The Smile of a Tear*), 3) meditate on it again. There's no correct answer, it's pure poetry. Devotees of Miró say they fly with him and don't even need drugs. Take advantage of the wonderful audioguide, included with admission (€7.20, July–Sept Tue–Sat 10:00–20:00, Thu until 21:30, Sun 10:00–14:30, closed Mon, Oct–June closes at 19:00 Tue–Sat).

More Sights—Barcelona

▲**Monastery of Pedralbes**—Long a museum showing off the monastery's six centuries of history (with a peaceful cloister and cells set up for worship, giving a peek into the everyday life of the cloistered nuns), the monastery now also houses an exquisite Thyssen-Bornemisza collection of paintings. The small, two-room collection features medieval art (with a pristine Fra Angelico altarpiece), along with German (Cranach), Italian Renaissance (Titian), Baroque (Valázquez, Rubens), and Late Venetian Baroque (Canaletto, Guardi) works. Unfortunately, it's far from the center (€3, Tue–Sun 10:00–14:00, closed Mon, buses: #22, #63, #64, #75, tel. 932-801-434).

Tibidabo—Tibidabo comes from the Latin for "to thee I shall give," the words the devil used when he was tempting Christ. It's still an enticing offer: At the top of Barcelona's highest peak, you're offered the city's oldest fun-fair, the neo-Gothic Sacred Heart Church, and—if the weather and air quality are good—a near-limitless view of the city and the Mediterranean.

Getting there is part of the fun: Start by taking the FGC line—similar to but separate from the Metro, also covered by the T-10 ticket—from the Plaça de Catalunya station (under Café Zurich) to the Tibidabo stop. The red Tourist Bus stops here, too. Then take Barcelona's only remaining tram—the Tramvia Blau—from Plaça John F. Kennedy to Plaça Dr. Andreu (€2.40, 2–4/hr). From there, take the cable car to the top (€2.40, tel. 906-427-017).

Citadel Park (Parc de la Ciutadella)—Barcelona's biggest, greenest park, originally the site of a much-hated military citadel, was transformed in 1888 for a World's Fair (Universal Exhibition). The stately Triumphal Arch at the top of the park was built as the main entrance. Inside you'll find wide pathways, plenty of trees and grass, the zoo, the Geology and Zoology Museums, and the Modern Art Museum (see below). In Barcelona, which suffers from a lack of real green space, this park is a haven. Enjoy the ornamental fountain that the young Antonio Gaudí helped design, and consider a jaunt in a rowboat on the lake in the center of the park (€1.20/person for 30 min). Check out the tropical Umbracle greenhouse and the Hivernacle winter garden, which has a pleasant café-bar (daily 8:00–20:00, Metro: Arc de Triomf, east of França train station).

Modern Art Museum (Museu d'Art Modern)—This manageable museum in Citadel Park exhibits Catalan sculpture, painting, glass, and furniture by Gaudí, Casas, Llimona, and more (€3, Tue–Sat 10:00–19:00, Thu until 21:00, Sun 10:00–14:30, closed Mon).

Barcelona's Beach—Take the trek through the charming Barceloneta neighborhood to the tip of this man-made peninsula. The beaches begin here and stretch for four kilometers up the coast to the Olympic Port and beyond. Everything you see here—palm trees, cement walkways, and tons of sand—was installed in the mid-1980s in an effort to shape up the city for the 1992 Olympic Games. The beaches are fine for sunbathing (beach chair rental €3/day), but the water quality is questionable for swimming. Take a lazy stroll down the seafront promenade to the Olympic Port, where you'll find bars, restaurants, and, at night, dance clubs.

Nightlife in Barcelona

Refer to the *See Barcelona* guide (free from TI) and find out the latest at a TI. Sights open daily until 20:00 include the Picasso Musuem, Casa Milà, and Gaudí's Sagrada Famila and Parc Güell. On Thursday, the Modern Art Museum and Catalan Art Museum stay open until 21:00 and the Joan Miró museum until 21:30. On Montjuïc, the fountains on Plaça Espanya make a splash on weekend evenings (Fri–Sun, plus Thu in summer).

For music, consider a performance at Casa Milà ("Pedrera by Night" summer concert series), the Liceu Opera House, or the Catalan Concert Hall (all listed above). Two decent music clubs are La Boite (477 Diagonal, near El Corte Inglés) and Jamboree (on Plaça Reial).

Sleeping in Barcelona
(€1 = about $1, country code: 34)
Sleep Code: S = Single, **D** = Double/Twin, **T** = Triple, **Q** = Quad, **b** = bathroom, **s** = shower only, **CC** = Credit Cards accepted, **no CC** = Credit Cards not accepted, **SE** = Speaks English, **NSE** = No English.

To help you easily sort through these listings, I've divided the rooms into three categories, based on the price for a standard double room with bath (during high season):

    Higher Priced—Most rooms more than €150.
    Moderately Priced—Most rooms €150 or less.
    Lower Priced—Most rooms €100 or less.

Book ahead. If necessary, the TI at Plaça de Catalunya has

a room-finding service. Barcelona is Spain's most expensive city. Still, it has reasonable rooms. Cheap places are more crowded in summer; fancier business-class places fill up in winter and offer discounts on weekends and in summer. Prices listed do not include the 7 percent tax or breakfast (ranging from simple €3 spreads to €13.25 buffets) unless otherwise noted. While many recommended places are on pedestrian streets, night noise is a problem almost everywhere (especially in cheap places, which have single-pane windows). For a quiet night, ask for "*tranquilo*" rather than "*con vista.*"

Sleeping in Eixample
For an uptown, boulevardian neighborhood, sleep in Eixample, a 10-minute walk from the Ramblas action.

MODERATELY PRICED
Hotel Gran Vía, filling a palatial mansion built in the 1870s, offers Botticelli and chandeliers in the public rooms; a sprawling, peaceful sun garden; and 54 spacious, comfy, air-conditioned rooms. While borderline ramshackle, it's charming and an excellent value (Sb-€70, Db-€105, Tb-€130, prices valid through 2003 but only by reserving direct with this book, CC, Internet access, elevator, quiet, Gran Vía de les Corts Catalanes 642, 08007 Barcelona, tel. 933-181-900, fax 933-189-997, e-mail: hgranvia@nnhotels.es, Juan Gomez SE).

Hotel Continental Palacete is a new place filling a 100-year-old chandeliered mansion. With flowery wallpaper and cheap but fancy furniture under ornately gilded stucco, it's gaudy in the city of Gaudí. But it's friendly, clean, quiet, and well located and the beds are good. Owner Señora Vallet (whose son, José, runs the recommended Hotel Continental—see "Hotels with Personality on or near the Ramblas," below) has a creative vision for this 19-room hotel (Sb-€95-150, Db-€120-150, Tb-€150-180, includes breakfast, CC, air-con, 2 blocks north of Plaça de Catalunya at corner of Carrer Diputacio, Rambla de Catalunya 30, tel. 934-457-657, fax 934-450-050, www.hotelcontinental.com, e-mail: palacete@hotelcontinental.com).

LOWER PRICED
Hotel Residencia Neutral, with a classic Eixample address and 28 very basic rooms, is a family-run time warp (tiny Sb-€27, Ds-€41, Db-€47, extra bed-€9, €4 breakfast in pleasant breakfast room, CC, elevator, no air-con, thin walls and some street noise, elegantly located 2 blocks north of Gran Vía at Rambla Catalunya 42, 08007 Barcelona, tel. 934-876-390, fax 934-876-848, owner Ramon SE). Its sister hotel, **Hotel Universal,** lacks the friendly

feel and is stark but well located (Db-€55, Sb-€42, no breakfast, Arago 281, tel. 934-879-762).

Sleeping in Business-Class Comfort near Plaça de Catalunya and the Top of the Ramblas

These nine places have sliding glass doors leading to plush reception areas, air-conditioning, and newly renovated modern rooms. Most are on big streets within two blocks of Barcelona's exuberant central square (zip code: 08002 unless otherwise noted). Being business hotels, they have hard-to-pin-down prices fluctuating wildly with the demand.

HIGHER PRICED

Hotel Catalonia Albinoni, the best located of all these places, elegantly fills a renovated old palace with wide halls, hardwood floors, and 74 modern rooms with all the comforts. It overlooks a thriving pedestrian boulevard. Front rooms have views; balcony rooms on the back are quiet and come with sun terraces (Db-€166, extra bed-€18, CC, family rooms, air-con, elevator, a block down from Plaça de Catalunya at Portal de l'Angel 17, tel. 933-184-141, fax 933-012-631, e-mail: albinoni@hoteles-catalonia.es).

Hotel Duques de Bergara boasts four stars. It has splashy public spaces, slick marble and hardwood floors, 150 comfortable rooms, and a garden courtyard with a pool a world away from the big-city noise (Sb-€144, Db-€180, Tb-€204, CC, air-con, elevator, a half-block off Plaça de Catalunya at Bergara 11, tel. 933-015-151, fax 933-173-442, www.hoteles-catalonia.es, e-mail: duques@hoteles-catalonia.es).

Hotel Occidental Reding, on a quiet street a five-minute walk west of the Ramblas and Plaça de Catalunya action, rents 44 modern business-class rooms (Db-€110 in low season, €160 in high, extra bed-€42, CC, air-con, elevator, near Metro: University at Gravina 5, 08001 Barcelona, tel. 934-121-097, fax 932-683-482, e-mail: reding@occidental-hoteles.com).

Hotel Barcelona is another big, American-style hotel with 72 bright, prefab, comfy rooms (Sb-€143, Db-€170, Db with terrace-€215, CC, air-con, elevator, a block from Plaça de Catalunya at Caspe 1–13, tel. 933-025-858, fax 933-018-674, e-mail: hotelbarcelona@husa.es).

Hotel Duc de la Victoria, with 150 rooms, is a new, professional-yet-friendly business-class hotel, buried in the Gothic Quarter but only three blocks off the Ramblas (Sb/Db-€160 Mon–Thu and €125 Fri–Sun, summer rate Db-€100, superior rooms—bigger and on a corner with windows on 2 sides—are worth €15 extra, air-con, elevator, CC, groups get weekend rate,

Barcelona's Gothic Quarter Hotels

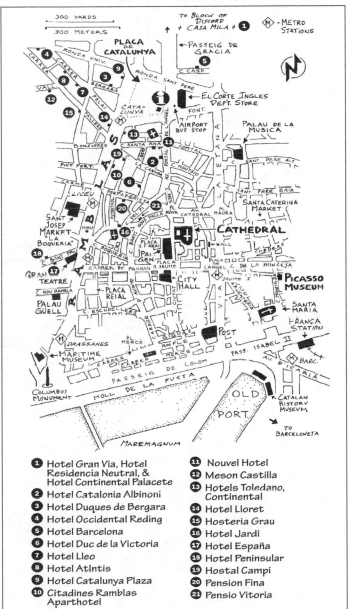

1. Hotel Gran Via, Hotel Residencia Neutral, & Hotel Continental Palacete
2. Hotel Catalonia Albinoni
3. Hotel Duques de Bergara
4. Hotel Occidental Reding
5. Hotel Barcelona
6. Hotel Duc de la Victoria
7. Hotel Lleo
8. Hotel Atlntis
9. Hotel Catalunya Plaza
10. Citadines Ramblas Aparthotel
11. Nouvel Hotel
12. Meson Castilla
13. Hotels Toledano, Continental
14. Hotel Lloret
15. Hosteria Grau
16. Hotel Jardi
17. Hotel España
18. Hotel Peninsular
19. Hostal Campi
20. Pension Fina
21. Pensio Vitoria

Duc de la Victoria 15, tel. 932-703-410, fax 934-127-747,
www.nh-hoteles.com).

MODERATELY PRICED
Hotel Lleo is a well-run business hotel with 90 big, bright,
and comfortable rooms and a great lounge (Db-€120–130,
on weekends-€144, summer Db special-€100, add about
€10 for extra person, CC, air-con, elevator, 2 blocks west
of Plaça de Catalunya at Pelai 22, tel. 933-181-312, fax 934-
122-657, www.hotel-lleo.es, e-mail: reservas@hotel-lleo.es).

   Hotel Atlantis is a solid business-class hotel with 50
rooms and great prices for the area (Sb-€85, Db-€105,
Tb-€125, CC, air-con, elevator, Pelayo 20, tel. 933-189-012,
fax 934-120-914, www.hotelatlantis-bcn.com, e-mail:
hotelatlantis@retemail.es).

   Catalunya Plaza, an impersonal business hotel right
on the square, has tight mod rooms with all the air-conditioning
and minibar comforts (Sb-€120, Db-€144–210 in busy times,
CC, elevator, Plaça de Catalunya 7, tel. 933-177-171, fax
933-177-855, e-mail: catalunya@city-hotels.es).

   Citadines Ramblas Aparthotel is a clever concept offering 130 apartments by the day in a bright, modern building
right on the Ramblas. Prices range with the seasonal demand
and rooms come in two categories (studio apartment for 2
with sofa bed or twin and kitchenette-€127–145, apartment
with real bed and sofa bed for up to 4 people-€190–216,
includes tax, CC, laundry, Ramblas 122, tel. 932-701-111,
fax 934-127-421, e-mail: barcelona@citadines.com).

Hotels with "Personality" on or near the Ramblas

MODERATELY PRICED
Nouvel Hotel, an elegant, Victorian-style building on a handy
pedestrian street, has royal lounges and 71 comfy rooms (Sb-€88–
100, Db-€145–158, includes breakfast, manager Gabriel promises
10 percent discount when booking direct with this book, CC,
air-con, Carrer de Santa Ana 18, tel. 933-018-274, fax 933-018-370,
www.hotelnouvel.com, e-mail: info@hotelnouvel.com).

   Meson Castilla is well located, with 56 clean rooms, but
it's also pricey, a bit sterile (less quirky), and in all the American
guidebooks. It's three blocks off the Ramblas in an appealing
university neighborhood (Sb-€90, Db-€115, Tb-€150, Qb
apartment-€175, includes buffet breakfast, CC, air-con, elevator, Valldoncella 5, 08001 Barcelona, tel. 933-182-182, fax
934-124-020, e-mail: hmesoncastilla@teleline.es).

LOWER PRICED

Hotels Toledano, Residencia Capitol, Continental, and Lloret overlook the Ramblas (at the top, very near Plaça de Catalunya) and offer classic tiny view-balcony opportunities if you don't mind the noise. The last three (Jardi, España, and Peninsular) are a few blocks away from the boulevard at about its midpoint. These places are generally family-run with ad-lib furnishings, more character, and much lower prices.

Hotel Toledano, overlooking the Ramblas, is suitable for backpackers and popular with dust-bunnies. Small, folksy, and borderline dumpy, it's warmly run by Albert Sanz, his father Juan, Juanma, and trusty Daniel on the nightshift (Sb-€29, Db-€50, Tb-€63, Qb-€71, CC, front rooms have Ramblas-view terraces, back rooms have air-con and no noise—request your choice when you call; Rambla de Canaletas 138, tel. 933-010-872, fax 934-123-142, www.hoteltoledano.com, e-mail: reservas@hoteltoledano.com). The Sanz family also runs **Hostal Residencia Capitol** one floor above—quiet, plain, cheaper, and also appropriate for backpackers (S-€22, D-€34, Ds-€39, Q-€51, 5-bed room-€58).

Hotel Continental has comfortable rooms, double-thick mattresses, and wildly clashing carpets and wallpaper. To celebrate 100 years in the family, José includes a free breakfast and an all-day complimentary coffee bar. Choose a Ramblas-view balcony or quiet back room (Db with double bed-€70, with twin-€80, with balcony-€94, extra bed-€12, includes tax, special family room, CC, fans in rooms, elevator, Internet access, Ramblas 138, tel. 933-012-570, fax 933-027-360, www .hotelcontinental.com, e-mail: ramblas@hotelcontinental.com).

Hotel Lloret is a big, dark, Old World place on the Ramblas with plain, neon-lit rooms. A dark, dusty elevator cage fills the stairwell like Darth Vader—but on a hot day, you're glad it's there (Sb-€46, Db-€70, Tb-€84, extra bed-€6, choose a noisy Ramblas balcony or *tranquilo* in the back, CC, air-con in summer, Rambla de Canaletas 125, tel. 933-173-366, fax 933-019-283).

Hosteria Grau is a homey, almost alpine place, family-run with 27 clean and woody rooms just far enough off the Ramblas (S-€27, D-€45, Ds-€47, Db-€53, family suites with 2 bedrooms-€112, €6 extra charged July–Sept, CC, fans, 200 meters up Calle Tallers from Ramblas at Ramelleres 27, 08001 Barcelona, tel. 933-018-135, fax 933-176-825, www.intercom.es/grau, e-mail: hgrau@lix.intercom.es, Monica SE).

Hotel Jardi is a clean and newly remodeled place on a breezy little square in the Gothic Quarter. Tight little balcony rooms overlooking the peaceful leafy square are most expensive

(Db-€75 with square view, €70 on interior, extra bed-€10, CC, air-con, elevator, halfway between Ramblas and cathedral on Plaça Sant Josep Oriol #1, tel. 933-015-900, fax 933-425-733, e-mail: hoteljardi@retemail.es). Rooms with balconies enjoy an almost Parisian ambience and minimal noise.

Hotel España is a big, creaky circa 1900 place with lavish public spaces still sweet with Art Nouveau decor. While it's 100 meters off the Ramblas on a borderline seedy street, it feels safe (75 rooms, Sb-€46, Db-€88, Tb-€120, includes tax and breakfast, air-con, elevator, near Metro: Liceu at Sant Pau 9, tel. 933-181-758, fax 933-171-134, www.hotelespanya.com, e-mail: hotelespanya@hotelespanya.com).

Hotel Peninsular, farther down that same street, is thoughtfully run and a unique value in the old center. A former monastery, the 80 still basic and thinly furnished rooms—once monks' cells— gather prayerfully around a peaceful courtyard (S-€22, Sb-€45, D-€45, Db-€65, Tb-€80, prices include tax and breakfast and are the same year-round, CC, air-con, elevator, Carrer Sant Pau, tel. 933-023-138, fax 934-123-699, Alex and Augustin SE).

Humble Cheaper Places Buried in Gothic Quarter
Hostal Campi—big, quiet, and ramshackle—is a few doors off the top of the Ramblas. The streets can be noisy, so request a quiet room in the back (24 rooms, D-€38, Db-€46, T-€50, no CC, Canuda 4, tel. & fax 93-301-3-545, e-mail: hcampi@terra.es, friendly Sonia and Margarita SE). **Pension Fina** offers more cheap sleeps (25 rooms, S-€30, D-€45, Db-€50, no CC, Portaferrissa 11, tel. & fax 933-179-787). **Pensio Vitoria** has loose tile floors and 12 basic rooms, each with a tiny balcony. It's more dumpy than homey, but consider the price (D-€26, Db-€34, T-€30, Tb-€36, cheaper off-season, CC, a block off daydreamy Plaça dei Pi at Carrer la Palla 8, tel. & fax 933-020-834, Andres SE).

Eating in Barcelona
Barcelona, the capital of Catalan cuisine, offers a tremendous variety of colorful places to eat. Many restaurants close in August (or July), when the owners vacation.

Eating Simply yet Memorably near the Ramblas and in the Gothic Quarter
Taverna Basca Irati serves 40 kinds of hot and cold Basque *pintxos* for €1 each. These are open-faced sandwiches—like Basque sushi but on bread. Muscle in through the hungry local crowd. Get an empty plate from the waiter, then help yourself.

It's a Basque honor system: You'll be charged by the number of toothpicks left on your plate when you're done. Wash it down with a €1 glass of Rioja (full-bodied red wine), Txakoli (spritely Basque white wine), or *sidra* (apple wine) poured from on high to add oxygen and bring out the flavor (daily 12:00–24:00, a block off the Ramblas, behind arcade at Carrer Cardenal Casanyes 17, near Metro: Liceu, tel. 933-023-084).

Juicy Jones, next door, is a tutti-frutti vegetarian place with garish colors, a hip veggie menu (served downstairs), and a stunning array of fresh-squeezed juices served at the bar (lunch and dinner menu-€7, daily 10:00–24:30, Carrer Cardenal Casanyes 7). Pop in for a quick "juice of the day."

Restaurant Elisabets is a happy little neighborhood eatery popular with locals for its "home-cooked" three-course €7 lunch special. Stop by for lunch, survey what those around you are enjoying, and order what looks best (Mon–Sat 13:00–16:00, closed Sun, tapas only in the evening, 2 blocks west of Ramblas on far corner of Plaça Bonsucces at Carrer Elisabets 2, tel. 933-175-826).

Café Granja Viader is a quaint time warp, family-run since 1870. This feminine place—specializing in baked and dairy delights, toasted sandwiches, and light meals—is ideal for a traditional breakfast (note the "Esmorzars" specials posted). Try a glass of *orxata* (horchata—almond milk, summer only), *llet mallorquina* (Majorca-style milk with cinnamon, lemon, and sugar), or *suis* (literally, "Switzerland"—hot chocolate with a snowcap of whipped cream). Described on the Ramblas walk above, it's a block off the boulevard behind El Carme church (Mon 17:00–20:45, Tue–Sat 9:00–13:45 & 17:00–20:45, closed Sun, Xucla 4, tel. 933-183-486).

La Gardunya, located at the back of La Boqueria market, offers tasty meat and seafood meals made with fresh ingredients bought directly from the market (€9 lunch menus include wine and bread, €11.50 dinner menus don't include wine, Mon–Sat 13:00–16:00 & 20:00–24:00, closed Sun, Carrer Jerusalem 18, tel. 933-024-323).

Tired tourists consider **La Poma** for a good pizza, pasta, salads in a bright modern setting at the top of the Ramblas with comfortable views of all the street action (daily 9:00–24:00, Ramblas 117).

Homesick tourists flock to **The Bagel Shop,** which offers fresh bagels and brownies (Mon–Sat 9:30–21:30, Sun 11:00–16:00, Carrer Canuda 25, tel. 933-024-161).

Shoestring tourists buy **groceries** at El Corte Inglés (Mon–Sat 10:00–22:00, closed Sun, supermarket in basement, Plaça de Catalunya) and Champion Supermarket (Mon–Sat 9:00–22:00, closed Sun, Ramblas 113).

Dining in the Gothic Quarter

A chain of five bright, modern restaurants with high-quality traditional cuisine in classy bistro settings with great prices has stormed Barcelona. Because of their three-course (with wine) €7 lunches and €13 dinners, all are crowded with locals and tourists in the know. They take no reservations and are marked by long lines at the door. Arrive 15 minutes before opening or be prepared to wait. The first three are within a block of the Plaça Reial, the fourth is near the Catalan Concert Hall, and the fifth (Hostal de Rita) is described in the Eixample section below: **La Fonda** (daily 13:00–15:30 & 20:30–23:30, a block from Plaça Reial at Escudellers 10, tel. 933-017-515); **Les Quinze Nits** (on La Plaça Reial at #6—you'll see the line, tel. 933-173-075); **La Crema Canela** (feels cozier than the others in this chain, daily 13:30–15:45 & 20:00–24:00, Ptge. Madoz 6, 30 meters north of Plaça Reial, tel. 933-182-744); and **La Dolca Herminia** (2 blocks toward Ramblas from Catalan Concert Hall at Magdalenes 27, tel. 933-170-676).

Els Quatre Gats, Picasso's hangout (and the place he first showed off his paintings), still has a bohemian feel in spite of its tourist crowds. Before the place was founded in 1897, the idea of a café for artists was mocked as a place where only *quatre gats*—"four cats," meaning crazies—would go (€27 meals, Mon–Sat 8:30–24:00, Sun 17:00–24:00, live piano Mon–Sat from 21:00, Sun from 20:00, CC, Montsio 3, tel. 933-024-140).

El Pintor Restaurante serves perhaps the best €30 dinner in town. Under medieval arches and rough brick with candles and friendly service you'll enjoy Catalan and Mediterranean cuisine (daily 13:30–16:30 & 20:0024:00, from Plaça de Sant Jaume walk north on Carrer Sant Honorat to #7, reserve for eve, tel. 933-014-065).

Restaurante Agut, buried deep in the Gothic Quarter four blocks off the harbor, is a fine place with an enticing menu (in English) for local-style food in a local-style setting. It's almost dressy with white table cloths and candles (Tue–Sat 13:30–16:00 & 21:00–24:00, closed Sun, Mon, and Aug, Carrer Gignas 16, reservations smart for dinner, tel. 933-151-709).

Eating Out at Sea—Maremagnum

Tapasbar Maremagnum is a big, rollicking sports-bar kind of tapas restaurant, great for large groups. It's a fun way to end your Ramblas walk, a 10-minute stroll past the Columbus Monument straight out the dock, with breezy harbor views and good local food with emphasis on the sea (daily 11:00–24:00, Moll d'Espanya, tel. 932-258-180, www.tapasbar.es).

Barcelona's Gothic Quarter Restaurants

1. Taverna Basca Irati
2. Rest. Elisabets
3. Café Granja Viader
4. La Gardunya
5. La Poma
6. The Bagel Shop
7. La Fonda
8. Les Quinze Nits
9. La Crema Canela
10. La Dolca Herminia
11. Els Quatre Gats
12. El Pintor Rest.
13. Rest. Agut
14. Tapasbar Maramagnum
15. El Xampanyet
16. Self Naturista
17. Bio Center
18. Fresc Co
19. La Bodegueta, L' Hostal de Rita & Quasi Queviures
20. To Cova Fumada & Bar Electricidad
21. Tapas places on Carrer Merce

Eating Near the Picasso Museum

El Xampanyet, a fun and characteristic bar, specializes in tapas and anchovies. A *sortido* (assorted plate) of meat (*carne*) or fish (*pescado*) costs about €6 with tomato bread (12:00–15:30 & 19:00–24:00, half a block beyond Picasso Museum at Montcada 22, tel. 933-197-003).

Vegetarian near Plaça de Catalunya and off the Ramblas

Self Naturista is a quick, no-stress buffet that makes vegetarians and health-food lovers feel right at home. Others may find a few unidentifiable plates and drinks. The food seems tired—pick what you like and microwave it—but the place is very handy (Mon–Sat 11:30–22:00, closed Sun, near several recommended hotels, just off the top of Ramblas at Carrer de Santa Ana 11–17).

Bio Center, a Catalan soup-and-salad place popular with local vegetarians, is better but not as handy (Mon–Sat 13:00–17:00, closed Sun, Pintor Fortuny 25, Metro: Catalunya, tel. 933-180-343). This street has several other good vegetarian places.

Fresc Co is a healthy and hearty buffet in a sleek and efficient cafeteria. A clever scheme: For one cheap price (€7 for lunch, €9 for dinner and on weekends), you get a drink and all the salad, pasta, soup, pizza, and dessert you want. Choose from two locations: west of Plaça de Catalunya at Ronda Universitat 29 or a block off the Ramblas (near La Boqueria market) at Carme 16 (daily 12:45–24:00, tel. 914-474-388).

Juicy Jones is a juice bar with a modern, fun veggie restaurant in back (just off the Ramblas at midpoint, described above).

Eating in the Eixample

The people-packed boulevards of the Eixample (Passeig de Gràcia and Rambla Catalunya) are lined with appetizing places with breezy outdoor seating. Many trendy and touristic tapas bars offer a cheery welcome and slam out the appetizers.

La Bodegueta is an unbelievably atmospheric below-street-level bodega serving hearty wines, tapas, and *flautas*—sandwiches made with flute-thin baguettes. Its daily €8 lunch special (3 courses with wine) is served from 13:00 to 16:00 (Mon–Sat 7:00–24:00, Sun 19:00–24:00, Rambla Catalunya 100, at intersection with Provenza, Metro: Diagonal, tel. 932-154-894). A long block from Gaudí's Casa Milà, this makes a fine sightseeing break.

Hostal de Rita is a fresh and dressy little place serving Catalan cuisine near the Block of Discord. Their three-course-with-wine lunch (€6.60, Mon–Fri at 13:00) and dinner (€12, daily from 20:30) specials are a great value (a block from the Passeig de

Gracia Metro stop, near corner of Carrer de Pau Claris and Carrer Arago at Arago 279, tel. 934-872-376). Like its four sister restaurants described above, its prices attract long lines, so arrive just before the doors open or wait.

Quasi Queviures serves upscale tapas, sandwiches, or the whole nine yards—classic food served fast from a fun menu with modern decor and a sports-bar ambience. For €10 you can try three tiny dishes and a glass of wine (daily 7:00–24:00, between Gran Via and Via Diputacio at Passeig de Gràcia 24, tel. 933-174-512).

Sandwich Shops

Bright, clean, and inexpensive sandwich shops are proudly holding the cultural line against the fast-food invasion hamburgerizing the rest of Europe. You'll find great sandwiches at **Pans & Company** and **Bocatta**, two chains with outlets all over town. Catalan sandwiches are made to order with crunchy French bread. Rather than butter, locals prefer *pa amb tomaquet* (pron. pah ahm too-MAH-kaht), a mix of crushed tomato and olive oil. Study the instructive multilingual menu fliers to understand your options.

Eating near the Harbor in Barceloneta

Barceloneta is a charming beach suburb of the big city. A grid plan of long, narrow, laundry-strewn streets surrounds the central Plaça Poeta Boscan. For an entertaining evening, wander around the perimeter of this slice-of-life square. Plenty of bakeries, pastry shops, and tapas bars ring a colorful covered produce market. Drop by the two places listed here or find your own restaurant (an unpleasant 15-min walk, Metro: Barceloneta, or taxi). During the day a lively produce market fills one end of the square. At night kids play soccer and ping-pong.

Cova Fumada is the neighborhood eatery. Josep Maria and his family serve famously fresh fish (Mon–Fri 17:30–20:30, closed Sat–Sun and Aug, Carrer del Baluarte 56, on corner at Carrer Sant Carles, tel. 932-214-061). Their *sardinas a la plancha* (grilled sardines, €3) are fresh and tasty. *Bombas* (potato croquets with pork, €1) are the house specialty. It's macho to have it *picante* (spicy with chili sauce); gentler taste buds prefer it *alioli*, with garlic cream. Catalan *bruschetta* is *pan tostado* (toast with oil and garlic, €1). Wash it down with *vino tinto* (house red wine, €0.60).

At **Bar Electricidad,** Lozano is the neighborhood source for cheap wine. Drop in. It's €1.10 per liter; the empty plastic water bottles are for takeaway. Try a €0.70 glass of Torroja Tinto, the best local red; Priorato Dulce, a wonderfully sweet red; or the homemade candy-in-heaven Vermouth (Mon–Sat 8:00–13:00

& 15:00–19:00, closed Sun, across square from Cova Fumada, Plaça del Poeta Bosca 61, tel. 932-215-017, NSE).

The Olympic Port, a swank marina district, is lined with harborside restaurants and people enjoying what locals claim is the freshest fish in town (a short taxi ride past Barceloneta from the center).

Tapas on Carrer Merce in the Gothic Quarter

While tapas aren't as popular in Catalunya as they are in the rest of Spain, Barcelona boasts great *tascas*—colorful local tapas bars. Get small plates (for maximum sampling) by asking for "*tapas*," not "*raciónes.*" Glasses of *vino tinto* go for about €0.50.

While trendy uptown places are safer, better lit, and come with English menus and less grease, these places will stain your journal.

From the bottom of the Ramblas (near the Columbus Monument), hike east along Carrer Clave. Then follow the small street that runs along the right side of the church (Carrer Merce), stopping at the *tascas* that look fun. For restaurant dining in the area, Restaurante Agut (described above) comes with table-cloths and polite service. But for a montage of edible memories, wander Carrer Merce west to east considering these places and stopping wherever looks most inviting:

La Jarra is known for its tender *jamón canario con patatas* (baked ham with salty potatoes). Across the street, **La Pulperia** serves up fried fish. A block down the street, at **Tasca del Molinero** you can sauté your chorizo *al diablo* (sausage from hell). It's great with the regional specialty, *pan con tomate*. Across the street, **La Plata** keeps things wonderfully simple, serving extremely cheap plates of sardines, little salads, and small glasses of keg wine. **Tasca el Corral** serves mountain favorites from northern Spain such as *queso de cabrales* (very moldy cheese) and chorizo (spicy sausage) with *sidra* (apple wine sold by the €4 bottle). **Sidreria Tasca La Socarrena** (at #21), being a *sidreria*, is the only place that serves hard cider by the glass. At the end of Carrer Merce, **Bar Vendimia** serves up tasty clams and mussels (hearty *raciónes* for €3 a plate—they don't do smaller portions so order sparingly). Their *pulpo* (octopus) is more expensive and the house specialty. Carrer Ample and Carrer Gignas, the streets paralleling Carrer Merce inland, have more refined barhopping possibilities.

Transportation Connections—Barcelona

By train to: Lisboa (1/day, 17 hrs with change in Madrid, €107), **Madrid** (7/day, 7–9 hrs, €31–41), **Paris** (3/day, 11–15 hrs, €72–102, night train, reservation required), **Sevilla** (3/day, 11 hrs,

€38), **Granada** (2/day, 12 hrs, €46), **Málaga** (2/day, 14 hrs, €39), **Nice** (1/day, 12 hrs, €58, change in Cerbère), **Avignon** (5/day, 6–9 hrs, €38). Train info: tel. 902-240-202.

By bus to: Madrid (12/day, 8 hrs, half the price of a train ticket, departs from station Barcelona Nord at Metro: Marina).

By plane: To avoid 10-hour train trips, check the reasonable flights from Barcelona to Sevilla or Madrid. Iberia Air (tel. 902-400-500) and Air Europa (tel. 902-401-501 or 932-983-907) offer $80 flights to Madrid. Airport info: tel. 932-983-467.

NEAR BARCELONA: FIGUERES, CADAQUES, SITGES, AND MONTSERRAT

Four fine sights are day-trip temptations from Barcelona. For the ultimate in Surrealism and a classy but sleepy port-town getaway, consider a day or two in Cadaques with a stop at the Dalí Museum in Figueres. Figueres is an hour from Cadaques and two hours from Barcelona. For the consummate day at the beach, head 45 minutes south to the charming and gay-friendly resort town, Sitges. Pilgrims with hiking boots head an hour into the mountains for the most sacred spot in Catalunya—Montserrat.

FIGUERES

▲▲▲**Dalí Museum**—This is the essential Dalí sight. Inaugurated in 1974, the museum is a work of art in itself. Dalí personally conceptualized, designed, decorated, and painted it, intending to showcase his life's work. Highlights include the epic Palace of the Wind ceiling, the larger-than-life Mae West room (complete with fireplaces for nostrils), fun mechanical interactive art (Dalí was into action; bring lots of coins), and the famous squint-to-see Abraham Lincoln. Other major and fantastic works include the tiny *Spectre du Sex-Appeal, Soft Self Portrait,* and the red-shoe riddle of *Zapato y Vaso de Leche.* The only real historical context provided is on the easy-to-miss and unlabeled earphone info boxes in the Mae West room. While not in English, it's plenty entertaining (€9, daily July–Sept 9:00–19:45, Oct–June 10:30–17:45, last entry 45 min before closing, free bag check has your bag waiting for you at the exit, tel. 972-677-500). Dalí, who was born in Figueres in 1905, is buried in the museum. From the train station, follow Museu Dalí signs to the museum.

Connections: Figueres is an easy day trip from Barcelona or a stopover (trains from France stop in Figueres; lockers at station). Trains from Barcelona depart Sants Station or the RENFE station at Metro: Passeig de Gràcia (hrly, 2 hrs, €15 round-trip).

CADAQUES

Since the late 1800s, Cadaques has served as a haven for intellectuals and artists alike. Salvador Dalí, raised in nearby Figueres, brought international fame to this sleepy Catalan port in the 1920s. He and his wife, Gala, set up home and studio at the adjacent Port Lligat. Cadaques inspired Surrealists such as Eluard, Magritte, Duchamp, Man Ray, Buñuel, and García Lorca. Even Picasso was drawn to this enchanting coastal *cala* (cove), and he painted some of his Cubist works here.

In spite of its fame, Cadaques is laid-back and feels off the beaten path. If you want a peaceful beach-town escape near Barcelona, there's no better place. From the moment you descend into the town, taking in whitewashed buildings and deep blue waters, you'll be struck by the port's tranquility and beauty. Have a glass of *vino tinto* or *cremat* (a traditional brandy-and-coffee drink served flambé-style) at one of the seaside cafés and savor the lapping waves, brilliant sun, and gentle breeze.

The **Casa Museu Salvador Dalí,** once Dalí's home, gives fans a chance to explore his labyrinthine compound (€8, Tue–Sun 10:30–21:00, closes spring and fall at 18:00, closed Mon and winter, 30-min walk over hill from Cadaques to Port Lligat, limited visits, call to reserve a time, tel. 972-251-015).

The **TI** is at Carrer Cotxe 2 (Mon–Sat 9:00–14:00 & 16:00–21:00, Sun 10:00–13:00, shorter hours and closed Sun off-season, tel. 972-258-315).

Sleeping and Eating: These affordable options are conveniently located in the main square, around the corner from the TI and across from the beach—**Hostal Marina** (D-€27, Ds-€33, Db-€48, breakfast-€3, CC, Riera 3, tel. & fax 972-258-199) and **Hostal Cristina** (24 rooms, D-€36, Ds-€42, Db-€48, CC, La Riera, tel. & fax 972-258-138, David and Rebecca SE). **Hotel Llane Petit,** many of whose 37 spacious rooms have view balconies, is on the harbor, a 10-minute walk south of the city center (Db-€65–100, CC, air-con, elevator, Dr. Bartomeus 37, tel. 972-251-020, fax 972-258-778, http://interhotel.com/spain/es/hoteles/2645.html,SE).

For a fine dinner, try **Casa Anita,** down a narrow street from La Residencia. Sitting with others around a big table, you'll enjoy house specialties such as *calamars a la plancha* (grilled squid) and homemade *helado* (ice cream). Muscatel from a glass *porron* finishes off the tasty meal (Juan and family, tel. 972-258-471).

Connections: Cadaques is reached by Sarfa buses from Figueres (3/day, 50 min, €3) or from Barcelona (5/day, 2.5 hrs, €10.50, 2/day off-season, tel. 932-656-508).

Sights near Barcelona

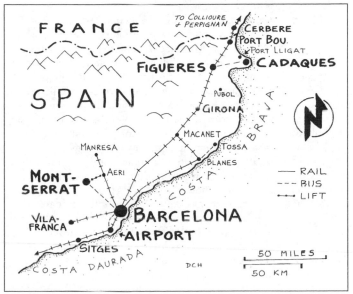

SITGES

Sitges is one of Catalunya's most popular resort towns and a world-renowned vacation destination among the gay community. Despite its jet-set status, the old town has managed to retain its charm. Nine beaches extend about 1.5 kilometers southward from town. Stroll down the seaside promenade, which stretches from the town to the end of the beaches. About halfway down, the crowds thin out, and the beaches become more intimate and cove-like. Along the way, restaurants and *chiringuitos* (beach-front bars) serve tapas, paella, and drinks. Take time to explore the old town's streets and shops. On the waterfront, you'll see the 17th-century Sant Bartomeu i Santa Tecla Church. It's a quick hike up for a view of town, sea, and beaches.

Connections: Southbound trains depart Barcelona from Sants Station and from the RENFE station at Plaça de Catalunya (hrly, €4.20 round-trip).

MONTSERRAT

Montserrat, with its unique rock formations and mountain monastery, is a popular day trip from Barcelona (50 km away). This has been Catalunya's most important pilgrimage site for a thousand years. Hymns ascribe this "serrated mountain" to little angels who carved the rocks with golden saws. Geologists blame 10 million years of nature at work.

Montserrat's top attraction is **La Moreneta,** the statue of the Black Virgin, which you'll find within the basilica (daily 8:00–10:30 & 12:00–18:30). The Moreneta, one of the patron saints of Catalunya, is the most revered religious symbol in the province.

Inside the basilica, be sure to see the Virgin close-up (behind the altar). Pilgrims touch her orb; the rest is protected behind glass. Then descend into the prayer room for a view of the Moreneta from behind. Pilgrims dip a memento of their journey into the holy water or even leave a personal belonging (such as a motorcycle helmet for safety) here to soak up more blessings.

Stop by the audiovisual center for some cultural and historical perspective. The interactive exhibition, which includes computer touch-screens and a short video, covers the mountain's history and gives a glimpse into the daily lives of the monastery's resident monks (€2, daily 9:00–18:00, tel. 938-777-701).

The first hermit monks built huts at Montserrat around A.D. 900. By 1025 a monastery was founded. The **Montserrat Escolania,** or choir school, soon followed and is considered to be the oldest music school in Europe. Fifty young boys, who live and study in the monastery itself, make up the choir, which offers performances (Mon–Sat at 13:00 & 18:45, Sun at 12:00, choir on vacation in July). Note: Catch the early show. If you attend the evening performance, you'll miss the last funicular down the mountain.

The **Museu de Montserrat** offers prehistoric tools, religious art, ancient artifacts, and a few paintings by masters such as El Greco, Caravaggio, Monet, Picasso, and Dalí (€4.50, July–Sept daily 9:30–19:00, Oct–June Mon–Fri 10:00–18:00, Sat–Sun 9:30–18:30).

The Moreneta was originally located in the **Santa Cova** (holy cave), a 40-minute hike down from the monastery. The path is lined with statues depicting scenes from the life of Christ. While the original Black Virgin statue is now in the basilica, a replica sits in the cave. A three-minute funicular ride cuts 20 minutes off the hike (€1.60 one-way, €2.50 round-trip).

The **Sant Joan funicular** (see below) continues another 250 meters above the monastery (€3.80 one-way, €6.10 round-trip). At the top of the funicular, a 20-minute walk takes you to the Sant Joan chapel and the starting point of numerous hikes, described in the TI's "Six Itineraries from the Monastery" brochure.

Sleeping: You can sleep in the old **monks' cloister**—now equipped with hotel and apartment facilities—far more comfortably than did its original inhabitants (D-€77, fine restaurant attached, tel. 938-777-701).

Connections: Ferrocarriles Catalanes trains leave hourly for Montserrat from Barcelona's Plaça Espanya (€12 round-trip, cash only, Eurailpass not valid, tel. 932-051-515). The Trans-Montserrat ticket includes the train trip, cable-car ride, and unlimited funicular rides (€20). The TotMontserrat ticket includes all of this, plus the museum and a self-serve lunch (€34). If you plan to do it all, you'll save a little money (roughly €1.80) with either ticket (buy at Plaça Espanya or TI). If you don't plan on taking either funicular, it's cheaper to buy just the train ticket (includes cable car).

To get from Barcelona to Montserrat, enter the Plaça Espanya Metro station next to the Plaza Hotel. Follow signs to the "FF de la Generalitat" underground station, then look for train line R5 (direction Manresa, departures at :36 past each hour, 45 min). Get off at the Aeri de Montserrat stop at the base of the mountain, where the cable car awaits (the round-trip from Barcelona includes cable-car ride, 4/hr). To be efficient, note that departures at :15 past the hour make the trains leaving at : 36 past the hour. The last efficient departure is at 18:15. The last cable-car departs the monastery at 18:45 (17:45 off-season), entailing a 45-minute wait for the train.

SAN SEBASTIÁN, BILBAO, AND THE BASQUE REGION

If you're traveling between Spain and France, the coastal resort of San Sebastián and the Guggenheim Bilbao modern art museum merit a quick visit, if only to see what all the fuss is about.

This is Basque country, or in Spanish, Pais Vasco. In some ways, Pais Vasco has more in common with the neighboring Basque region in France than it does with Spain. The Spanish and French Basque regions share a flag (white, red, and green), cuisine, and common language (Euskara). Insulated from mainstream Europe for centuries, the plucky Basques have for over 7,000 years just wanted to be left alone.

For 40 years, Generalissimo Franco did his best to tame the separatist-minded Basques. The bombed city of Guernica, halfway between San Sebastián and Bilbao, survives as a tragic example of his efforts to suppress Basque independence.

Today the Basque terrorist organization, ETA (which stands for Basque, country, and freedom), is supported by a tiny minority of the population. They focus their anger on political targets and go largely unnoticed by tourists.

The area is officially bilingual and you'll see signs in Euskara and Spanish, even though few residents speak Euskara. Because Franco so effectively blunted Basque expression, the language is Spanish by default.

Today's Basque lands are undergoing a 21st-century renaissance as the dazzling new architecture of the Guggenheim Bilbao modern art museum and the glittering resort of San Sebastián are drawing enthusiastic crowds. And for a fun border stop, drop by little Hondarribia, for a good first (or last) dose of Spain.

SAN SEBASTIÁN (DONOSTIA)

Shimmering above the breathtaking bay of La Concha, elegant and prosperous San Sebastián (Donostia in Basque) has a favored location with golden beaches lining its perfectly round bay, capped with twin peaks at either end and a cute little island in the center. A pedestrian-friendly beachfront promenade runs the length of the bay, with an intriguing old town at one end and a smart shopping district in the center. It's a big city with about 180,000 residents and almost that many tourists in high season (July–Sept). With a romantic setting, the soaring statue of Christ gazing over the city, and the late-night lively old town, San Sebastián has a distinct Rio de Janiero aura. While there's no compelling museum to visit, the city and its setting are reason enough to come.

Planning Your Time

San Sebastián is worth a day. Start your morning at the hill of Monte Igueldo (described below; consider a taxi to the funicular). Then stroll the waterfront walkway to and through the old town and port (taking time to explore). Then head up to the hill of Monte Urgull. Everything is within walking distance; skip the double-decker hop-on-hop-off bus tours.

Orientation

The San Sebastián we're interested in surrounds the Bay of Concha (Bahia de la Concha), and can be divided into three areas: Playa de la Concha (best beaches), the shopping district (called *centro romantico*, just east of Playa de la Concha), and the skinny, straight streets of the old town (called *parte vieja*, to the north of the shopping district). It's all bookended by mini-mountains: Monte Urgull to the north and east, Monte Igueldo to the south and west. The River (Rio) Urumea divides central San Sebastián from the beachfront extension called Gros (of no interest unless you want to see Spanish surfers).

Tourist Information: The main TI, which lies between the shopping area and old city a block from the river, has complete information on city and regional sights. Pick up the excellent booklet in English (called Donostia/San Sebastián); of its three well-described walking tours, the Old Quarter/Monte Urgull walk is the best. The TI also has bus and train schedules (June–Sept Mon–Sat 8:00–20:00, Sun 10:00–14:00; Oct–May Mon–Sat 9:00–14:00, 15:30–19:00, Sun 10:00–14:00, Calle Reina Regente 3, tel. 943-481-166).

Useful Phone Numbers: For a taxi, call 943-464-646. For the police, dial 943-467-766. For flight information, call San Sebastián's airport (in Hondarribia, 19 km away) at 943-668-500.

San Sebastián

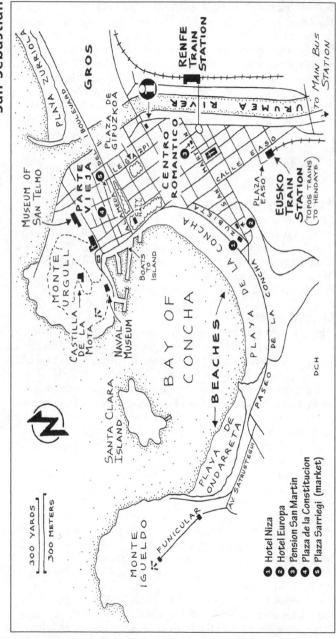

1 Hotel Niza
2 Hotel Europa
3 Pension San Martin
4 Plaza de la Constitucion
5 Plaza Sarriegi (market)

Arrival in San Sebastián

By Train: If you're coming on a Topo train from Hendaye on the French border, get off at the Eusko Tren station. It's a level 15-minute walk to the center. Exit the station and walk across the long plaza, then walk eight blocks down Calle Easo to reach the beach. The old town will be to your right, Playa de la Concha to your left.

If you're arriving by train from elsewhere in Spain, you'll get off at the RENFE station. It's just across the bridge (Puente Maria Christina) from the shopping district. To reach the beach, cross the bridge, take your first right along the river, then first left on Calle San Martin, then right on Calle Easo.

By Bus: If you're arriving by bus from Hondarribia, hop off at pretty Plaza de Gipuzkoa (first stop after crossing the river, in shopping area, near TI). To reach the TI, walk down Legazpi and turn right on the parkway boulevard, Alameda del Boulevard.

By Car: Follow *Centro Ciudad* signs into San Sebastián's center and park in a pay lot (many are well signed).

Sights—San Sebastián

Old City (Parte Veija)—Huddling securely in the shadow of its once protective Monte Urgull, the old town is where San Sebastián was born about a thousand years ago. Lively tapas (*pintxos*, pron. PEEN-chohs) bars, heavy Baroque churches, and surprise plazas entertain locals and tourists 24 hours a day. Note that the raucous nightlife and street noise in this part of town means that many hotels in this area are not for light sleepers.

Plaza de la Constitución—This striking square, where bullfights used to be held (notice the seat numbering on the balconies), is a fine place to sample a plate of pintxos with a glass of *txacoli* (pron. tax-OH-lee), the local light, sparkling white wine that is often theatrically poured form high above the glass.

Museum of San Telmo—Formerly a Dominican monastery, this museum proudly displays paintings of Basque artists (free, Tue–Sat 10:30–13:00 & 16:00–20:00, Sun 10:30–14:00, Plaza Zuloaga 1, tel. 943-424-970).

Cruise—Small boats cruise from the old town's port to the island in the bay (Isla Santa Clara) where you can hike the trails and have lunch at the lone café (€2.5 round-trip, every 30 min, 10:00–19:00, until 20:00 June–Sept).

Naval Museum—Located at the port, the museum shows this seafaring city's history and provides a link between the Basque culture and the sea (€2, Tue–Sat 19:00–13:30 & 16:00–19:30, Sun 11:00–14:00, closed Mon).

Monte Urgull—The once-mighty castle (Castilla de la Mota)

atop the hill deterred most attackers, allowing the city to prosper
in the Middle Ages. The museum of San Sebastián history, located
within the castle, is mildly interesting. The best views from the hill
are not from the statue of Christ, but from the ramparts on the left
side as you face the hill, just above the port's aquarium.

Monte Igueldo—For the best views, ride the funicular up the
hill of Monte Igueldo, a mirror image of Monte Urgull. The views
into the distant green mountains, along the coast, and over San
Sebastián are sensational day or night. The entrance to the funicular is behind the tennis club on the far western end of Playa de
Ondarreta, which extends from Playa de la Concha to the west
(€1.50, daily 8:00–18:00, until 20:00 June–Aug).

Sleeping in San Sebastián
**(€1 = about $1, country code: 34, zip code: 20007,
unless otherwise noted)**
Sleep Code: **S** = Single, **D** = Double/Twin, **T** = Triple, **Q** = Quad,
b = bathroom, **s** = shower only, **CC** = Credit Cards accepted,
no CC = Credit Cards not accepted, **SE** = Speaks English,
NSE = No English.

　　Best Western's **Hotel Europa,** a block from the beach,
is pricey but central and has all of the comforts (Db-€116–140,
CC, San Martin 52, tel. 943-470-880, fax 943-471-730,
www.hotel-europa.com).

　　Hotel Niza, with its waterfront setting on the western edge
of Playa de la Concha, offers the best overall value. Half of its
rooms (some with balconies) overlook the bay. All of its rooms
are comfortable and pleasantly decorated, and share the same
million-euro view breakfast room/café (Db-€90–115, CC, Zubieta
56, tel. 943-426-663, fax 943-441-251, www.hotelniza.com, SE).

　　Pension San Martin, in the shopping area a few blocks
from beaches and the old town, has a forgettable entry with
comfortable and well-cared-for rooms (Db-€35–55, CC, San
Martin 10, San Sebastián 20005, tel. 943-428-714).

　　If you want to stay in the lively old town above a tapas bar and
can stand non-stop noise, **Pension Amaiur** is the place (S-€30,
D-€50, T-€75, family room-€85, kitchen facilities, Internet access-
€1/18 min, excursions available, next to Santa Maria church, Calle
31 de Agosto 44, San Sebastián 20003, tel. 943-429-654, www
.pensionamaiur.com, e-mail: reservas@pensionamaiur.com).

Eating in San Sebastián
Basque cuisine—mixing influences from the mountains, sea,
Spain, and France—stands far apart from traditional Spanish
cuisine, and is considered by many to be Spain's best. It's

dominated by seafood, tomatoes, garlic, and red peppers. You'll
see lots of *bacalao* (salted cod), best when cooked *a la bizkaina*
(with tomatoes, onions, and roasted peppers); *merluza* (hake), a
light white fish prepared in a variety of ways; and *chipirones en su
tinta* (squid served in their own black ink). Carnivores will find
plenty of lamb (try *chuletas de buey* for massive lamb chops). Local
brews include *sidra* (hard apple cider), *txacoli* (light white wine),
and *Izarra* (an herbal-flavored brandy).

San Sebastián's old town provides the ideal backdrop for
tapas hopping. The selection of tapas is amazing. Every other
shop seems to be a tapas bar, especially on these streets: Calles
Fermin Calebeton, San Jeronimo, and 31 de Agosto.

For reasonably-priced meals served in an appealing setting,
try **Bodégon Alejandro** (closed Wed, in the thick of the old city
on Calle Fermin Calebeton 4, tel. 943-477-737). **Casa Urola**, a
few steps away, is also good and a bit more traditional (Calle
Fermin Calebeton 22, tel. 943-421-175).

For picnics, try the public market at Plaza Sarriegi not far
from the TI.

Transportation Connections—San Sebastián
All Barcelona, Madrid, and Paris trains require reservations.

By train to: Barcelona (2/day, 8.5–9.5 hrs, plus 10-hr night
train except on Sat), **Madrid** (Sun–Fri: 4/day, Sat: 2/day, 6–8.5 hrs,
plus daily 10.5-hr night train), **Hendaye/French border** (2/hr,
30 min, departs Eusko Tren station at :15 and :45 after the hour
7:00–22:00), **Paris** (get to Hendaye—see above, then 4/day,
5.5 hrs, or 8.5-hr night train).

By bus to: Bilbao (2/hr from 6:00–22:30, 70 min, departs
San Sebastián's main bus station on Plaza Pio XII, on the river
2 blocks below Euska Tren station, bus tel. 902-101-210; once
in Bilbao, buses leave you a 30-minute walk to the museum),
Hondarribia (5/hr, 45 min, many bus stops, most central is on
Plaza de Gipuzkoa in shopping area).

BILBAO AND THE GUGGENHEIM MUSEUM
In the last five years, the cultural and economic capital of the
Pais Vasco, Bilbao (pop. 1 million), has seen a transformation
like no other Spanish city. Entire sectors of the industrial city's
long-depressed port have been cleared away to allow construction
of a new Opera House, convention center, and the stunning
Guggenheim museum of modern art.

Tourist Information: Bilbao's main TI is across the river
from the train station (on Paseo del Arenal 1), though the office

Basque Region

across from the Guggenheim is more convenient for most
(Mon–Fri 9:00–14:00 & 16:00–19:30, Sat–Sun 10:00–14:00,
tel. 944-795-760).

Arrival in Bilbao

Finding the museum is easy: Pink signs guide drivers and walkers
to this city's most famous sight. Still it's handy to be able to ask:
¿Donde está el museo Guggenheim?

By Train: Bilbao's RENFE station is on the river in central
Bilbao, a pleasant 20-minute walk through the downtown to the
museum; ask for a map of Bilbao at the train information office
(or pay €4 for a taxi).

By Bus: Buses stop at the Termibus station on the eastern
edge of downtown, about 1.5 kilometers southwest of the museum,
leaving you with a less appealing 30-minute walk. Your best bet
is a taxi (€4.50).

By Car: The museum is signed from the freeway; look for
the pink signs to the Guggenheim and follow them to the
museum parking.

Sights—Bilbao

▲▲▲**Guggenheim Bilbao**—Frank Gehry's remarkable building
opened in 1998, reinvigorating the modern art and architectural
world. The consensus of most travelers is that this titanium tile-
clad building, looking like a huge silvery Cubist fish, overwhelms

the art within it. Take some time to admire the outside of the museum before you plunge in.

Guarding the main entrance is artist Jeff Koons' dog, (13 meters/ 42 feet tall), who is made of flowers and is called "Puppy." Inside you'll find an impressive atrium from which the other galleries branch off. Pick up a map and plan your attack. Thanks to the fact that this museum is part of the Guggenheim "family" of museums, the permanent collection of modern paintings is strong—but it is perpetually rotating and not as impressive as collections you can see in Madrid, London, and Paris. You'll probably see at least a Miró, a Modgliani, and a Picasso or two. Although many Basques would love it to be here, one painting you won't see is Picasso's famous *Guernica*, named after the nearby Basque town bombed to smithereens by Hitler's Luftwaffe at Franco's request in 1936.

The best approach to your visit is simply to immerse yourself in a modern art happening, rather than count on seeing a particular work or an artist's works.

The building's walls can be moved to best display the ever-changing special exhibits and installments *del día*, often consisting of huge post-WWII minimalist works that you may struggle to "get."

The museum offers free audioguides and guided tours in English; call 944-359-090 for the schedule (entry: €8.50, July–Aug daily 9:00–21:00; Sept–June Tue–Sun 10:00–20:00, closed Mon; café, no photos, Metro: Moyua, Abandoibarra Et. 2, tel. 944-359-080, www.guggenheim-bilbao.es).

Transportation Connections—Bilbao

By bus to: **San Sebastián** (2/hr from 6:00–22:30, 70 min, departs Bilbao's Termibus station, arrives in San Sebastián at Plaza Pio XII).

HONDARRIBIA

For a taste of small-town Pais Vasco, dip into this enchanting, seldom-visited town. Much smaller and easier to manage than San Sebastián, Hondarribia allows travelers a stressless opportunity to enjoy Basque culture.

The town comes in two parts: the lower port town, and the historic, balcony-lined streets of the hilly upper town. The **TI** is located between the two, two blocks up from the port on Jabier Ugarte Kalea 6 (Mon–Fri 9:30–14:00 & 16:00–18:30, Sat 10:00–14:00, closed Sun, tel. 943-645-458). You can follow their self-guided tour of the old town (English brochure available) or just lose yourself within the walls. Explore the wrought-iron railings and plazas of the upper city. Today Charles V's odd, squat castle is a parador (Db-€140, CC, Plaza de Armas 14, tel. 943-645-500,

e-mail: hondarribia@parador.es). Tourists are allowed to have a
sangria in the *muy* cool bar, though the terraces are for guests only.
In the modern, lower town, straight shopping streets serve a local
clientele and a pleasant walkway takes strollers along the beach.

Transportation Connections—Hondarribia
By bus to: **San Sebastián** (3/hr, 45 min to go 19 km), **Hendaye/
French border** (3/hr, 20 min). The bus stop in Hondarribia is
across from the post office, one block below the TI.

By boat to: **Hendaye** (2/hr, 10 min, runs about 11:00–19:00).

MADRID

Today's Madrid is upbeat and vibrant, still enjoying a post-Franco renaissance. You'll feel it. Even the living-statue beggars have a twinkle in their eyes.

Madrid is the hub of Spain. This modern capital—Europe's highest, at more than 615 meters (2,000 feet)—has a population of more than four million and is young by European standards. Only 400 years ago, King Philip II decided to move the capital of his empire from Toledo to Madrid. One hundred years ago Madrid had only 400,000 people, so 90 percent of the city is modern sprawl surrounding an intact, easy-to-navigate historic core.

Dive headlong into the grandeur and intimate charm of Madrid. The lavish Royal Palace, with its gilded rooms and frescoed ceilings, rivals Versailles. The Prado has Europe's top collection of paintings. The city's huge Retiro Park invites you for a shady siesta and a hopscotch through a mosaic of lovers, families, skateboarders, pets walking their masters, and expert bench-sitters. Save time for Madrid's elegant shops and people-friendly pedestrian zones.

The city is working hard—installing posts to keep cars off sidewalks, restoring old buildings, and making the streets safer after dark—to make Madrid more livable . . . and fun to visit.

On Sundays, cheer for the bull at a bullfight or bargain like mad at a mega–flea market. Lively Madrid has enough street-singing, barhopping, and people-watching vitality to give any visitor a boost of youth.

Planning Your Time
Madrid's top two sights, the Prado and the palace, are each worth a half day. On a Sunday (Easter–Oct), consider allotting extra

time for a bullfight. Ideally, give Madrid two days and spend
them this way:

Day 1: Breakfast of *churros* (see "Eating," below) before a
brisk, good-morning-Madrid walk for 20 minutes from Puerta
del Sol to the Prado; spend the rest of the morning at the Prado;
afternoon siesta in Retiro Park or modern art at Centro Reina
Sofia *(Guernica)* and/or Thyssen-Bornemisza Museum; dinner
at 20:00, with tapas around Plaza Santa Ana.

Day 2: Follow this book's "Puerta del Sol to Royal Palace
Walk"; tour the Royal Palace, lunch near Plaza Mayor; afternoon
free for other sights, shopping, or side trip to El Escorial (open
until 19:00). Be out at the magic hour—before sunset—when
beautifully lit people fill Madrid.

Note that the Prado, Thyssen-Bornemisza Museum, and
El Escorial all close on Monday. For good day-trip possibilities
from Madrid, see the next two chapters ("Northwest of Madrid"
and "Toledo").

Orientation

The historic center is enjoyably covered on foot. No major sight
is more than a 20-minute walk or a €3.50 taxi ride from Puerta
del Sol, Madrid's central square. Divide your time between the
city's top three attractions: the Royal Palace, the Prado, and its
barhopping, contemporary scene.

The Puerta del Sol marks the center of Madrid. The Royal
Palace to the west and the Prado Museum and Retiro Park to the
east frame Madrid's historic center. Southwest of Puerta del Sol is
a 17th-century district with the slow-down-and-smell-the-cobbles
Plaza Mayor and memories of pre-industrial Spain. North of
Puerta del Sol runs Gran Vía, and between the two are lively
pedestrian shopping streets. Gran Vía, bubbling with expensive
shops and cinemas, leads to the modern Plaza de España. North
of Gran Vía is the gritty Malasaña quarter, with its colorful small
houses, shoemakers' shops, sleazy-looking hombres, milk vendors,
bars, and hip night scene.

Tourist Information

Madrid has five TIs: **Plaza Mayor** at #3 (Mon–Sat 10:00–20:00,
Sun 10:00–15:00, tel. 915-881-636); **near the Prado Museum**
(Mon–Sat 9:00–19:00, Sun 9:00–15:00, Duque de Medinaceli 2,
behind Palace Hotel, tel. 914-294-951); **Chamartin** train station
(Mon–Sat 8:00–20:00, Sun 9:00–15:00, tel. 913-159-976); **Atocha**
train station (daily 9:00–21:00); and at the **airport** (daily 8:00–
20:00, tel. 913-058-656). The general tourist information number
is 915-881-636 (www.munimadrid.es). During the summer, small

Madrid

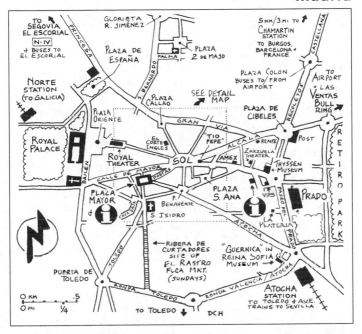

temporary stands with yellow umbrellas pop up at touristed places such as Puerta del Sol, and their yellow-shirted student guides are happy to help out lost tourists. Confirm your sightseeing plans and pick up a city map and the *Enjoy Madrid* publication. The free bus map has the most detailed map of the center. The TI has the latest on bullfights and zarzuela (the local light opera).

For entertainment listings, the TI's free *En Madrid/What's On* is not as good as the easy-to-decipher Spanish-language weekly entertainment guide *Guía del Ocio* (€1, sold at newsstands), which lists events, restaurants, and movies ("v.o." means a movie is in its original language rather than dubbed).

If you're heading to other destinations in this book, ask any Madrid TI for free maps and brochures (ideally in English). Since many small-town TIs keep erratic hours and run out of these pamphlets, get what you can here. You can get schedules for buses and some trains, avoiding unnecessary trips to the various stations. The TI's free and amazingly informative *Mapa de Comunicaciones España* lists all the Turismos and highway SOS numbers with a road map of Spain. (If they're out, ask for the route map sponsored by the Paradores Hotel chain.)

Arrival in Madrid

By Train: Madrid's two train stations, Atocha and Chamartín, are both on subway lines with easy access to downtown Madrid. Each station has all the services. Chamartín handles most international trains. Atocha generally covers southern Spain including the AVE trains to Sevilla. Both stations offer long-distance trains (*largo recorrido*) as well as smaller, local trains (*regionales* and *cercanías*) to nearby destinations. To travel between Chamartín and Atocha, don't bother with the subway (which involves a transfer)—the *cercanías* trains are faster (6/hr, 12 min, €1.20, free with railpass—show it at ticket window in the middle of the turnstiles, departing from Atocha's track 2 and generally Chamartín's track 2 or 3—but check the Salidas Immediatas board for the next departure).

Chamartín: The TI is opposite track 19. The impressively large *Centro de Viajes/Travel Center* customer-service office is in the middle of the building. You can use the Club Intercity lounge if you have a first-class railpass and first-class seat or sleeper reservations. The *cercanías* platforms cluster around track 5. The station's Metro stop is Chamartín. (If you arrive by Metro at Chamartín, follow signs to *Información* to get to the lobby rather than signs to *Vías*, which send you directly to the platforms.)

Atocha: Atocha is split into two halves, connected by a corridor of shops. On one side are the slick AVE trains, some Talgo trains, and a botanical garden (in the towering old-station building, complete with birds, places to sit, and a cafeteria). On the other side of the station you'll find the local *cercanías, regionales,* some Talgos, and the Metro stop named Atocha RENFE. (Note that the stop named simply "Atocha" is a different Metro in Madrid—not at the train station.) Each side of the station has separate schedules; this can be confusing if you're in the wrong side of the building. The tiny TI handles tourist info only—not train info (Mon–Sat 9:00–21:00, Sun 9:00–13:00, 50 meters straight ahead of the Metro's turnstiles, ground floor). For train info, try the customer-service office called *Atención al Cliente* (daily 7:00–23:00); although there's one office for each half of the building, the office on the AVE side (just off the botanical garden) is more likely to speak English.

Atocha's Club AVE is a lounge reserved solely for AVE business or first-class ticket-holders or Eurailers with a reservation (likely closed in 2003 for renovation, daily 6:30–22:30, upstairs on AVE side of station, free drinks, newspapers, showers, and info service).

To buy tickets at Atocha for the local *cercanías* trains (for example, to Toledo), go to the middle of the *cercanías* side and get your ticket from ticket windows in the small rectangular offices (marked *Venta de Billetes sin reserva*). You can buy AVE and other long-distance train tickets in the bigger ticket offices in either half of the building; the airier *Taquillas* office on the AVE side (next to *Atención al Cliente* off the botanical garden) is more pleasant. Since station ticket offices can get really crowded, it's often quicker to buy your ticket at an English-speaking travel agency (such as in El Corte Inglés) or at the downtown RENFE office, which offers train information, reservations, tickets, and minimal English (Mon–Fri 9:30–20:00, closed Sat–Sun, CC, go in person, 2 blocks north of the Prado at Calle Alcala 44, tel. 902-240-202, www.renfe.es). For more transportation details, see "Connections" at the end of the chapter.

By Bus: Madrid's three key bus stations, all connected by Metro, are Larrea (for Segovia, Metro: Príncipe Pío), Estación Sur Autobuses (for Toledo, Àvila, and Granada, on top Metro: Méndez Alvaro, tel. 914-684-200), and Estación Intercambiador (for El Escorial, in Metro: Moncloa). For details, see "Transportation Connections" at the end of this chapter.

By Plane: For information on Madrid's Barajas Airport, see "Transportation Connections" at the end of this chapter.

Getting around Madrid

By Subway: Madrid's subway is simple, speedy, and cheap (€1/ride, runs 6:00–1:30). The €5, 10-ride Metrobus ticket can be shared by several travelers and works on both the Metro and buses (sold at kiosko, tobacco shops, and in Metro). The city's broad streets can be hot and exhausting. A subway trip of even a stop or two saves time and energy. Most stations offer free maps (*navegamadrid*; www.metromadrid.es). Navigate by subway stops (shown on city maps). To transfer, follow signs to the next subway line (numbered and color-coded). End stops are used to indicate directions. Insert your ticket in the turnstile, then retrieve it as you pass through. Green *Salida* signs point to the exit. Using neighborhood maps and street signs to exit smartly can save lots of walking.

By Bus: City buses, while not as easy as the Metro, can be useful (bus maps at TI or info booth on Puerta del Sol, €0.90 tickets sold on bus, or €5 for a 10-ride Metrobus—see "By Subway," above; buses run 6:00–24:00).

By Taxi: Madrid's 15,000 taxis are easy to hail and reasonable (€1.40 drop, €0.70 per km; €4 supplement for airport, train/bus stations, bags, Sunday, and night service). Threesomes travel as cheaply by taxi as by subway. A ride from the Royal Palace to the Prado costs about €3.50.

Helpful Hints

Theft Alert: Be wary of pickpockets, anywhere, anytime, but particularly on Puerta del Sol (main square), the subway, and crowded streets. Assume a fight or any commotion is a scam to distract people about to become victims of a pickpocket. Wear your money belt. The small streets north of Gran Vía are particularly dangerous, even before nightfall. Muggings occur, but are rare. Victims of a theft can call 902-102-112 for help (English spoken).

Embassies: The U.S. Embassy is at Serrano 75 (tel. 915-872-200); the Canadian Embassy is at Nuñez de Balboa 35 (tel. 914-233-250).

Travel Agencies and Free Maps: The grand department store, El Corte Inglés, has two travel agencies (on first and seventh floors, Mon–Sat 10:00–22:00, just off Puerta del Sol) and gives out free Madrid maps (at the information desk, immediately inside the door, just off Puerta del Sol at intersection of Preciados and Tetuan; has post office and supermarket in basement). El Corte Inglés is taking over the entire intersection; the main store is the tallest building, with the biggest sign.

American Express: The AmEx office at Plaza Cortes 2 sells train and plane tickets, and even accepts Visa and MasterCard (Mon–Fri 9:00–19:30, Sat 10:00–14:00, closed Sun, 2 blocks from Metro: Banco de España, opposite Palace Hotel, tel. 913-225-445).

Books: For books in English, try **Fnac Callao** (Calle Preciados 8, tel. 915-956-190), **Casa del Libro** (English on ground floor in back, Gran Vía 29, tel. 915-212-219), and **El Cortes Inglés** (guidebooks and some fiction, in its Libreria branch kitty-corner from main store, see listing within "Travel Agencies," above).

Laundromat: The self-service Lavamatique is the most central, just west of the Prado (Mon–Sat 9:00–20:00, closed Sun, Cervantes 1).

Internet Access: The popular **easyEverything** offers 250 fast, cheap terminals 24/7 at Calle de la Montera (a block above Puerta del Sol and a block below piles of tattoo shops and prostitutes). **NavegaWeb**, centrally located at Gran Vía 30, is also good (daily 9:00–24:00). **BBiGG** is at Calle Alcalá 21 (daily 9:00–02:00, 300 terminals, near Puerta del Sol, tel. 916-647-700). **Zahara's** Internet café is at the corner of Gran Vía and Mesoneros (Mon–Fri 9:00–24:00, Sat–Sun 9:00–24:00).

Tours of Madrid

Madrid Vision Hop-On Hop-Off Bus Tours—Madrid Vision offers three different hop-on hop-off circuits of the city (historic, modern, and monuments). Buy a ticket (€10/1 day, €13/2 days) and you can hop from sight to sight as you like, listening to a recorded commentary along the way. Each route has about 15 stops and takes about 75 minutes, with buses departing every 10 or 15 minutes. The three routes intersect at the south side of Puerta del Sol (at #5, daily 10:00–19:00, until 21:00 in summer, tel. 917-791-888).

Walking Tours—British expatriate Stephen Drake-Jones gives entertaining, informative walks of historic old Madrid almost nightly (along with more specialized walks, such as Hemingway, Civil War, and Bloody Madrid). A historian with a passion for the memory of Wellington (the man who stopped Napoleon), Stephen is the founder and chairman of the Wellington Society. For €25 you become a member of the society for one year and get a free two-hour tour that includes stops at two bars for local drinks and tapas. Eccentric Stephen takes you back in time to sort out Madrid's Hapsburg and Bourbon history. Chairman Stephen likes his wine. If that's a problem, skip the tour. Tours start at the statue on Puerta del Sol (maximum 10 people, tel. 609-143-203 to confirm tour and reserve a spot, www.wellsoc.org, e-mail: chairman@wellsoc.org). Members of the Wellington Society can take advantage of Stephen's help line (if you're in a Spanish jam, call him to translate and intervene) and assistance by e-mail (for questions on Spain, your itinerary, and so on). Stephen also does private tours and day trips to great spots in the countryside for small groups (about €350 per group per day, explained on his Web site).

Typical Big Bus City Sightseeing Tours—Juliatours offers standard, inexpensive guided bus tours departing from Gran Vía 68 (tel. 915-599-605). Consider these tours: a three-hour city tour (€19, daily at 9:45 and 15:00); Madrid by Night (€12, a 2-hour floodlit overview, nightly at 20:30); Valley of the Fallen and El Escorial (€42, makes the day trip easy, covering both sights adequately with commentary en route, Tue–Sun at 8:45 and 15:00); and a marathon tour of El Escorial, Valley of the Fallen, and Toledo (€85, Tue–Sun at 8:30). If you want to pick up a rental car in Toledo, you could take this tour, stowing your luggage under the bus, then leave the tour at Toledo.

Introductory Walk: From Madrid's Puerta del Sol to the Royal Palace

Connect the sights with the following walking tour. Allow an hour for this one-kilometer (half-mile) walk, not including your palace visit.

▲▲**Puerta del Sol**—Named for a long-gone medieval gate with the sun carved onto it, Puerta del Sol is ground zero for Madrid. It's a hub for the Metro, buses, and pickpockets.

Stand by the statue of King Charles III and survey the square. Because of his enlightened urban policies, Charles III (who ruled until 1788) is affectionately called the "best mayor of Madrid." He decorated the city squares with fine fountains, got those meddlesome Jesuits out of city government, established the public school system, made the Retiro a public park rather than a royal retreat, and generally cleaned up Madrid.

Look behind the king. The statue of the bear pawing the strawberry bush and the madrono trees in the big planter boxes are symbols of the city. Bears used to live in the royal hunting grounds outside Madrid. And the madrono trees produce a berry that makes the traditional *madroño* liqueur.

The king faces a red-and-white building with a bell tower. This was Madrid's first post office, established by Charles III in the 1760s. Today it's the governor's office, though it's notorious for having been Franco's police headquarters. An amazing number of those detained and interrogated by the Franco police "tried to escape" by flying out the windows to their deaths. Notice the hats of the civil guardsmen at the entry. It's said the hats have square backsides so the men can lean against the wall while enjoying a cigarette.

Crowds fill the square on New Year's Eve as the rest of Madrid watches the action on TV. As Spain's "Big Ben" atop the governor's office chimes 12 times, Madrileños eat one grape for each ring to bring good luck through the coming year.

Cross Calle Mayor. Look at the curb directly in front of the entrance of the governor's office. The scuffed-up marker is "kilometer zero," marking the center of Spain. To the right of the entrance, the plaque on the wall marks the spot where the war against Napoleon started. Napoleon wanted his brother to be king of Spain. Trying to finagle this, Napoleon brought nearly the entire Spanish royal family to France for negotiations. An anxious crowd gathered outside this building awaiting word of the fate of their royal family. This was just after the French Revolution, and there was a general nervousness between France and Spain. When locals heard that Napoleon had appointed his brother as the new king of Spain, they gathered angrily in the streets. The French guard simply massacred the mob. Goya, who worked just up the street, observed the event and captured the tragedy in his paintings *2nd of May, 1808* and *3rd of May, 1808*, now in the Prado.

Walking from Puerta del Sol to Plaza Mayor: On the corner of Calle Mayor and Puerta del Sol, across from McDonald's, is the busy *confiteria* Salon la Mallorquina (daily 9:00–21:00). Cross Calle Mayor to go inside. The shop is famous for its sweet Napolitana cream-filled pastry (€1) and savory, beef-filled *agujas* pastries (€1.50)—if you can't finish yours, the beggar at the front door would love to. See the racks with goodies hot out of the oven. Look back toward the entrance and notice the tile above the door

Heart of Madrid

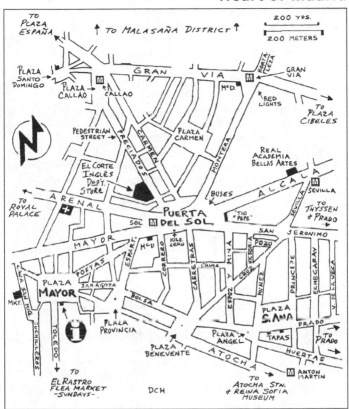

with the 18th-century view of the Puerta del Sol. Compare this with today's view out the door. This was before the square was widened, when a church stood where the Tío Pepe sign stands today. The French used this church to detain local patriots awaiting execution. (The venerable Tío Pepe sign, advertising a famous sherry for over 100 years, was Madrid's first billboard.)

Cross busy Calle Mayor (again), round McDonald's, and veer left up the pedestrian alley called Calle de Postas. The street sign shows the post coach heading for that famous first post office. Medieval street signs included pictures so the illiterate could "read" them. Fifty meters up the street, at Calle San Cristobal, drop into Pans & Company, a popular sandwich chain. Pick up their translated flier illustrating that Spain is a country of four languages: Catalan (spoken in and around Barcelona), Euskara

(Basque), Galego (a Gaelic language spoken in northwest Spain—Galicia), and Castilian (what we call Spanish). From here, hike up Calle San Cristobal. Within two blocks, you'll pass the local feminist bookshop (Libreria Mujeres) and reach a small square. At the square notice the big, brick 17th-century Ministry of Foreign Affairs building (with the pointed spire)—originally a jail for rich prisoners who could afford the cushy cells. Turn right and walk down Calle de Zaragoza under the arcade into...

Plaza Mayor—This square, built in 1619, is a vast, cobbled, traffic-free chunk of 17th-century Spain. Each side of the square is uniform, as if a grand palace were turned inside out. The statue is of Philip III, who ordered the square's construction. Upon this stage, much Spanish history was played out: bullfights, fires, royal pageantry, and events of the gruesome Inquisition. Reliefs serving as seatbacks under the lampposts tell the story. During the Inquisition, many were tried here. The guilty were paraded around the square (bleachers were built for bigger audiences, the wealthy rented balconies) with billboards listing their many sins. They were then burned. The fortunate were slowly strangled as they held a crucifix, hearing the reassuring words of a priest as this life was squeezed out of them.

The square is painted a democratic shade of burgundy—the result of a citywide vote. Since Franco's death in 1975, there's been a passion for voting here. Three different colors were painted as samples on the walls of this square, and the city voted for its favorite.

A stamp-and-coin market bustles here on Sundays from 10:00 to 14:00, and on any day it's a colorful and affordable place to enjoy a cup of coffee. Throughout Spain, lesser *plazas mayores* provide peaceful pools in the river of Spanish life. The TI is at #3, on the south side of the square. The building decorated with painted figures, on the north side of the square, is the Casa de la Panaderia, which used to house the Bakers' Guild (interior closed to public).

The Torre del Oro Bar Andalu is a good place for a drink to finish off your Plaza Mayor visit (northwest corner of square, to the left of the Bakers' Guild, daily 8:00–15:00 & 18:00–24:00). This bar is a temple to bullfighting. Warning: They push expensive tapas on tourists. A *caña* (small beer) shouldn't cost more than €1.50. The bar's ambience is "Andalu" (Andalusian). Look under the stuffed head of Barbero the bull. At eye level you'll see a *puntilla*, the knife used to put a bull out of its misery at the arena. This was the knife used to kill Barbero.

Notice the breath-taking action caught in the bar's many photographs. At the end of the bar in a glass case is the "suit of lights" the great El Cordobes wore in his ill-fated 1967 fight.

From Plaza Mayor to the Royal Palace

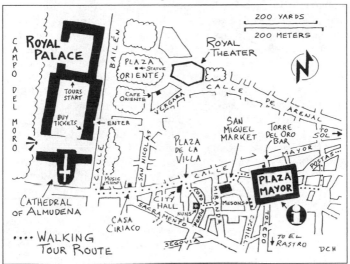

With Franco in attendance, El Cordobes went on and on, long after he could have ended the fight, until finally the bull gored him. El Cordobes survived; the bull didn't. Find Franco with El Cordobes at the far end, to the left of Segador the bull. Under the bull is a photo of El Cordobes' illegitimate son, El Cordobes, kissing a bull. Disowned by El Cordobes and using his dad's famous name after a court battle, El Cordobes is one of this generation's top fighters.

Walking from Plaza Mayor to the Royal Palace: Leave Plaza Mayor on Calle Cuidad Rodrigo (far right corner from where you entered the square, and to your right as you exit Torre del Oro). You'll pass a series of fine turn-of-the-20th-century storefronts and shops such as the recommended Casa Rua, famous for its cheap *bocadillos de calamares*—fried squid-ring sandwiches.

From the archway you'll see the covered Mercado de San Miguel (green iron posts, on left). Before you enter the market, look left down the street Cava de San Miguel. If you like sangria and singing, come back around 22:00 and visit one of the *mesones* (such as Guitarra, Tortilla, or Boqueron) that line the street. These cavelike bars stretch way back and get packed with locals who—emboldened by sangria, the setting, and Spain—might suddenly just start singing. It's a lowbrow, electric keyboard, karaoke-type ambience, best on Friday and Saturday nights.

Wander through the newly renovated produce market and

consider buying some fruit (Mon–Fri 9:00–14:30 & 17:15–20:15, Sat 9:00–14:30, closed Sun). Leave the market on the opposite (downhill) side and follow the pedestrian lane left. At the first corner, turn right, and cross the small plaza to the modern brick convent. The door on the right says *venta de dulces;* to buy inexpensive sweets from the cloistered nuns, buzz the *monjas* button, then wait patiently for the sister to respond over the intercom. Say *"dulces"* (pron. DOOL-thays) and she'll let you in (Mon–Sat 9:30–13:00 & 16:00–18:30, closed Sun). When the lock buzzes, push open the door and follow the sign to *torno,* the lazy Susan that lets the sisters sell their baked goods without being seen (smallest quantities: half, or *medio,* kilo). Of the many choices (all good), consider *pastas de almendra* (crumbly) or *mantecados de yema* (moist and eggy).

Follow Calle del Codo (where those in need of bits of armor shopped—see the street sign) uphill around the convent to Plaza de la Villa, the city-hall square. Ahead, four flags—of city, state, nation, and Europe—grace the city hall. The statue in the garden is of Don Bazan—mastermind of the Christian victory over the Muslims at the naval battle of Lepanto in 1571. This pivotal battle, fought off the coast of Greece, ended the Muslim threat to Christian Europe. The mayor's office is behind the don.

From here, busy Calle Mayor leads downhill a couple more blocks to the Royal Palace. Halfway down (on the left) there's a tiny square opposite the recommended Casa Ciriaco restaurant (#84). The statue memorializes the 1906 anarchist bombing that killed 23 people as the royal couple paraded by on their wedding day. While the crowd was throwing flowers, an anarchist threw a bouquet lashed to a bomb from a balcony of #84 (the building was a hotel at the time). Photos of the event hang just inside the door of the restaurant.

Continue down Calle Mayor. Within a couple of blocks you'll come to a busy street, Calle de Bailen. (The Garrido-Bailen music store is *the* place to stock up on castanets, unusual flutes, and Galician bagpipes.) Across the busy street is the **Cathedral of Almudena,** Madrid's new cathedral. Built between 1883 and 1993, its exterior is a contemporary mix and its interior is neo-Gothic with a colorful ceiling, glittering 5,000-pipe organ, and the 13th-century coffin (empty, painted leather on wood, in a chapel behind the altar) of Madrid's patron saint, Isidoro. Next to the cathedral is the . . .

▲▲**Royal Palace (Palacio Real)**—Europe's third-greatest palace (after Versailles and Vienna's Schönbrunn) with arguably the most lavish interior, is packed with tourists and royal antiques. After a fortress burned down on this site, King Phillip V commissioned this huge 18th-century palace as a replacement. Phillip V was very

French (born in Versailles). He ruled Spain for 40 years and never learned to speak Spanish. He ordered this palace built to be his own Versailles. It's big—over 2,000 rooms with tons of lavish tapestries, a king's ransom of chandeliers, priceless porcelain, and bronze decor covered in gold leaf. While the royal family lives in a mansion a few kilometers away, the place still functions as a royal palace and is used for formal state receptions and tourist daydreams.

A simple one-floor, 24-room, one-way circuit is open to the public. You can wander on your own or join an English tour (get time of next tour and decide as you buy your ticket; tours depart about every 20 min). The tour guides, like the museum guidebook, show a passion for meaningless data. Your ticket includes the armory and the pharmacy, both on the courtyard and worth a quick look (€6 without a tour, €7 with a tour, April–Sept Mon–Sat 9:00–19:00, Sun 9:00–16:00; Oct–March Mon–Sat 9:30–18:00, Sun 9:00–15:00, last tickets sold an hour before closing, palace can close without warning if needed for a royal function; note the beer-stein urinals—the rage in Madrid—in the WC just past the ticket booth; Metro: Opera, tel. 915-597-404 or 914-548-800). The €2 audioguides cover only marginally more of interest than what I describe below (and would never mention beer-stein urinals). The palace is most crowded on Wednesdays, when it's free for locals.

If you tour on your own, here are a few details beyond what you'll find on the little English descriptions posted in each room:

The Palace Lobby: In the old days, horse-drawn carriages would drop you off here. Today, a sign divides the visitors waiting for a tour and those going in alone.

The Grand Stairs: Fancy carpets are rolled down (notice the little metal bar-holding hooks) for formal occasions. At the top of the first landing, the blue and red coat of arms is of the current—and popular—constitutional monarch, Juan Carlos. While Franco chose him to be the next dictator, J.C. knew Spain was ripe for democracy. Rather than become "Juan the Brief" (as some were nicknaming him), he turned real power over to the parliament. You'll see his (figure) head on the back of the Spanish euro coin. At the top of the stairs (before entering first room, right of door) is a white marble bust of J.C.'s great-great-g-g-g-great-grandfather Phillip V. The grandson of France's King Louis XIV, he began the Bourbon dynasty in Spain in 1700. That dynasty survives today with Juan Carlos.

Guard Room: The guards hung out here. Notice the clocks. Charles IV, a great collector, amassed over 700—all in working order and displayed throughout the palace.

Hall of Columns: Originally a ballroom, today this room is used for formal ceremonies. (For example, this is the place where Spain formally joined the European Union in 1985—see plaque on far wall.) The tapestries (like most you'll see in the palace) are 17th-century Belgian.

Throne Room: Red velvet walls, lions, and frescoes of Spanish scenes symbolize the monarchy in this rococo riot. The chandeliers are the best in the house. The thrones are only from 1977. This is where ambassadors give their credentials to the king, who receives them relatively informally . . . standing rather than seated in the throne. Two rooms later you'll find . . .

Charles IV Antechamber: The four paintings are of King Charles IV (looking a bit like a dim-witted George Washington) and his wife (who wore the pants in the palace)—all originals by Goya. Velázquez's masterpiece *Las Meninas* originally hung here. The ceiling fresco, the last great work by Tiepolo, celebrates the vast Spanish empire—upon which the sun also never set. Find the American Indian (hint: follow the rainbow to the macho, red-caped conquistador). The clock, showing Cronus, god of time, in marble, bronze, and wood, sits on a music box. The gilded decor you see throughout the palace is bronze with gold leaf.

Gasparini Room: This room, its painted stucco ceiling and inlaid Spanish marble floor restored in 1992, was the royal dressing room. The Asian influence was trendy at the time. Dressing, for a divine monarch, was a public affair. The court bigwigs would assemble here as the king, standing on a platform—notice the height of the mirrors—would pull on his leotards. In the next room, the silk wallpaper is new; notice the J.C.S. initials of King Juan Carlos and Queen Sofia. Passing through the silk room, you reach the . . .

Charles III Salon: This salon, decorated in 19th-century neoclassical style, is dominated by a chandelier in the shape of the fleur-de-lis (symbol of the Bourbon family). The thick walls separating each room hide service corridors for servants who scurried about generally unseen.

Porcelain Room: The 300 separate plates that line this room were disassembled for safety during the Civil War. (Find the little screws in the greenery that hide the seams.) The Yellow Room leads to the . . .

Gala Dining Room: Five or six times a year the king entertains up to 150 guests at this bowling lane–size table—which can be extended to the length of the room. Find the two royal chairs. (Hint: With the modesty necessary for 21st-century monarchs, they are just a tad higher than the rest.) The parquet floor was the preferred dancing surface when balls were held in this fabulous room. The table in the next room would be lined with an exorbitantly caloric dessert buffet.

Cinema Room: In the early 20th century the royal family enjoyed "Sunday afternoons at the movies" here. Today it stores glass cases filled with the silver tableware used for fancy dining functions.

Stradivarius Room: The queen likes classical music. When you perform for her, do it with these precious 300-year-old violins. About 300 Antonius Stradivarius-made instruments survive. This is the only matching quartet: two violins, a viola, and a cello. The next room was the children's room—with kid-sized musical instruments.

Royal Chapel: The Royal Chapel is used only for funerals. The royal coffin sits here before making the sad trip to El Escorial to join the rest of Spain's past royalty.

Billiards and Smoking Rooms: The billiards room and the smoking room were for men only. The porcelain and silk of the smoking room imitates a Chinese opium den which, in its day, was furnished only with pillows.

Queen's Boudoir: The next room was for the ladies, decorated just after Pompeii was excavated and therefore in fanciful ancient-Roman style. You'll exit down the same grand stairway you climbed 24 rooms ago.

Across the courtyard is a fine park view and the **armory** displaying the armor and swords of El Cid, Ferdinand, Charles V, and Phillip II. Near the exit is a cafeteria and a bookstore, which has a variety of books on Spanish history.

As you leave the palace, walk around the corner to the left along the palace exterior to the grand yet people-friendly Plaza de Oriente. Throughout Europe, energetic governments are turning formerly car-congested wastelands into public spaces like this. Madrid's latest mayor is nicknamed "the mole" for all the digging he's doing. Where's all the traffic? Under your feet.

To return to Puerta del Sol: With your back to the palace, face the equestrian statue of Philip IV and (behind the statue) the Royal Theater (*Teatro Real*, neoclassical, rebuilt in 1997, open for visits Tue–Fri at 13:00, Sat–Sun at 11:30, closed Mon, tel. 915-160-660). Walk behind the Royal Theater (on the right, passing Café de Oriente—a favorite with theater-goers) to another square where you'll find the Opera Metro stop and Calle Arenal which leads back to Puerta del Sol.

Sights—Madrid's Museum Neighborhood

Three great museums are in east Madrid. From the Prado to the Thyssen-Bornemisza Museum is a five-minute walk; Prado to Centro Reina Sofia is a 10-minute walk.

Museum Pass: If you plan to visit all three museums, you'll save 25 percent by buying the Paseo del Arte combo-ticket (€7.75, sold at each museum). Note that the Prado and Centro Reina Sofia museums are free on Saturday afternoon and Sunday (and anytime for those under 18 and over 65); the Prado and Thyssen-Bornemisza are closed Monday; and the Reina Sofia is closed Tuesday.

▲▲▲**Prado Museum**—The Prado holds my favorite collection of paintings anywhere. With more than 3,000 canvases, including entire rooms of masterpieces by Velázquez, Goya, El Greco, and Bosch, it's overwhelming. Pick up the English floor plan as you enter. Take a tour or buy a guidebook (or bring along the Prado chapter from *Rick Steves' Mona Winks*—available without maps and photos for free at www.ricksteves.com/prado). Focus on the Flemish and northern (Bosch, Dürer, Rubens), the Italian (Fra Angelico, Raphael, Titian), and the Spanish art (El Greco, Velázquez, Goya).

Follow Goya through his stages, from cheery *(The Parasol)* to political *(2nd of May, 1808* and *3rd of May, 1808)* to dark ("Negras de Goya": e.g., *Saturn Devouring His Children).* In each stage, Goya asserted his independence from artistic conventions. Even the standard court portraits from his "first" stage reflect his politically liberal viewpoint, subtly showing the vanity and stupidity of his royal patrons by the looks in their goony eyes. His political stage, with paintings such as the *3rd of May, 1808,* depicting a massacre of Spaniards by Napoleon's troops, makes him one of the first artists with a social conscience. Finally, in his gloomy "dark stage," Goya probed the inner world of fears and nightmares, anticipating our modern-day preoccupation with dreams. Also, seek out Bosch's *The Garden of Earthly Delights*—a three-paneled altarpiece showing creation, the "transparency of earthly pleasures," and the resulting hell. Bosch's self-portrait looks out from hell (with the birds leading naked people around the brim of his hat), surrounded by people suffering eternal punishments appropriate to their primary earthly excesses.

The art is constantly rearranged by the Prado's management, so even the Prado's own maps and guidebooks are out of date. Regardless of the latest location, most art is grouped by painter, and better guards can point you in the right direction if you say, "*¿Dónde está . . . ?*" and the painter's name as Españoled as you can (e.g., Titian is "Ticiano" and Bosch is "El Bosco"). The Murillo entrance—at the end closest to the Atocha train station—often has shorter lines. Lunchtime, from 14:00 to 16:00, is least crowded (€3; free on Sat afternoon after 14:30, all day Sun, and to anyone under 18 and over 65; covered by €7.75 Paseo del Arte combo-ticket; Tue–Sat 9:00–19:00, Sun 9:00–14:00, closed Mon, last

Madrid's Museum Neighborhood

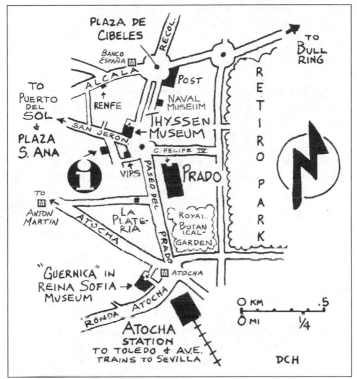

PLAZA DE CIBELES

RECOL.

TO BULL RING

BANCO ESPAÑA Ⓜ

ALCALA

POST

TO PUERTO DEL SOL & PLAZA S. ANA

RENFE

NAVAL MUSEUM

SAN JERON.

THYSSEN MUSEUM

C. FELIPE IV

R E T I R O   P A R K

VIPS

PASEO DEL PRADO

PRADO

TO Ⓜ ← ANTON MARTIN

ATOCHA

LA PLATE- RIA

ROYAL BOTAN ICAL- GARDEN

"GUERNICA" IN REINA SOFIA → MUSEUM

Ⓜ ATOCHA

ATOCHA

RONDA

ATOCHA STATION TO TOLEDO & A.V.E. TRAINS TO SEVILLA

0 KM .5
0 MI ¼

DCH

entry 30 min before closing; free, mandatory baggage check after your things are scanned just like at the airport; no water bottles inside; photos allowed but no flash; cafeteria at Murillo end; Paseo de Prado, Metro: Banco de España or Atocha—each a 15-min walk from the museum, tel. 913-302-800, http ://museoprado.mcu.es). Cabs picking you up at the Prado are likely to overcharge. Insist on the fare meter.

While you're in the neighborhood, consider a visit to the Charles III Botanical Garden (listed under "Sights Near the Prado," below).

▲▲**Thyssen-Bornemisza Museum**—Locals call this stunning museum simply the Thyssen (pron. tee-sun). It displays the impressive collection that Baron Thyssen (a wealthy German married to a former Miss Spain) sold to Spain for $350 million. It's basically minor works by major artists and major works by minor artists (major works by major artists are in the Prado).

But art lovers appreciate how the good baron's art complements the Prado's collection by filling in where the Prado is weak (Impressionism). For a delightful walk through art history, ride the elevator to the top floor and do the rooms in numerical order from Primitive Italian (room 1) to Surrealism and Pop Art (room 48). It's kitty-corner from the Prado at Paseo del Prado 8 in Palacio de Villahermosa (€5, or €7 to add current exhibition; covered by €7.75 Paseo del Arte combo-ticket, children under 12 enter free, Tue–Sun 10:00–19:00, closed Mon, ticket office closes at 18:30, audioguide-€3, free baggage check, café, shop, no photos, Metro: Banco de España or Atocha, tel. 914-203-944, www.museothyssen.org). If you're tired, hail a cab at the gate and zip straight to the Centro Reina Sofia.

▲▲**Centro Reina Sofia**—In this exceptional modern-art museum, ride the fancy glass elevator to the second floor and follow the room numbers for art from 1900 to 1950. The fourth floor continues the collection from 1950 to 1980. The museum is most famous for Picasso's *Guernica* (room 6), an epic painting showing the horror of modern war. Guernica, a village in northern Spain, was the target of the world's first saturation-bombing raid, approved by Franco and carried out by Hitler. Notice the two rooms of studies for *Guernica*, filled with iron-nail tears and screaming mouths. *Guernica* was exiled to America until Franco's death, and now it reigns as Spain's national piece of art.

The museum also houses an easy-to-enjoy collection by other modern artists, including more of Picasso (3 rooms divide his art into pre–civil war, *Guernica*, and post–civil war) and a mind-bending room of Dalís (room 10). Enjoy a break in the shady courtyard before leaving (€3, free Sat afternoon after 14:30 and all day Sun, always free to those under 18 and over 65; covered by €7.75 Paseo del Arte combo-ticket; hardworking audioguide-€2.50, Mon and Wed–Sat 10:00–21:00, Sun 10:00–14:30, closed Tue, good brochure, no photos, no tours in English, free baggage check, Santa Isabel 52, Metro: Atocha, across from Atocha train station, look for exterior glass elevators, tel. 914-675-062, http://museoreinasofia.mcu.es).

Sights Near the Prado

▲**Retiro Park**—Siesta in this 350-acre green and breezy escape from the city. At midday on Saturday and Sunday, the area around the lake becomes a street carnival, with jugglers, puppeteers, and lots of local color. These peaceful gardens offer great picnicking and people-watching. From the Retiro Metro stop, walk to the big lake (El Estanque), where you can cheaply rent a rowboat. Past the lake, a grand boulevard of statues leads to the Prado.

Charles III's Botanical Garden (Real Jardín Botánico)—After your Prado visit, you can take a lush and fragrant break in this sculpted park, wandering among trees from around the world. The flier in English explains that this is actually more than a park—it's a museum of plants (€1.50, daily 10:00–20:00, until 18:00 in winter, entry opposite Prado's Murillo entry, Plaza de Murillo 2).

Naval Museum—This tells the story of Spain's navy from the Armada to today (free, Tue–Sun 10:00–14:00, closed Mon, a block north of the Prado across boulevard from Thyssen-Bornemisza Museum).

More Sights—Madrid

Chapel San Antonio de la Florida—Goya's tomb stares up at a splendid cupola filled with his own frescoes. On June 13, local ladies line up here to ask St. Anthony for a boyfriend, while outside a festival rages, with street musicians, food, and fun (€2, Tue–Fri 10:00–14:00 & 16:00–20:00, Sat–Sun 10:00–14:00, closed Mon, July and Aug only 10:00–14:00, Glorieta de San Antonio de la Florida, Metro: Príncipe Pío, tel. 915-420-722). This chapel is near the bus station with service to Segovia. If you're day tripping to Segovia, it's easy to stop by before or after your trip.

Next door to the chapel is Restaurante Casa Mingo, popular for its cheap chicken, chorizo, and *cabrales* cheese served with cider. Ask the waiter to pour the cider for you. For dessert, try the *tarta de Santiago* almond cake (daily 11:00–24:00, Paseo de la Florida 34, tel. 915-477-918).

Royal Tapestry Factory (Real Fabrica de Tapices)—Have a look at the traditional making of tapestries (€2, some English tours, Mon–Fri 10:00–14:00, closed Sat–Sun and Aug, Calle Fuenterrabia 2, Metro: Menendez Pelayo, take Gutenberg exit, tel. 914-340-550, call before visiting as it has been closed for restoration). You can actually order a tailor-made tapestry (starting at $10,000).

Moncloa Tower (Faro de Moncloa)—This tower's elevator zips you up 92 meters (300 feet) to the best skyscraper view in town (€1.20, Tue–Fri 10:00–14:00 & 17:00–19:00, Sat–Sun 10:30–17:30, closed Mon, Metro: Moncloa, tel. 915-448-104). If you're going to El Escorial by bus, this is a convenient sight near the bus station.

Teleferico—For city views, ride this cable car from downtown over Madrid's sprawling city park to Casa de Campo (€2.60 one-way, €3.60 round-trip, daily from 11:00, fall and winter from 12:00, departs from Paseo del Pintor Rosales, Metro: Arguelles, tel. 915-417-450, www.teleferico.com). Do an immediate round-trip to skip Casa de Campo's strange mix of rental rowboats, prostitutes, a zoo, addicts, and an amusement park.

Shopping

Shoppers focus on the colorful pedestrian area between Gran Vía and Puerta del Sol. The giant Spanish department store El Corte Inglés is a block off Puerta del Sol and a handy place to pick up just about anything you need (Mon–Sat 10:00–21:30, closed Sun, free maps at info desk, supermarket in basement).
▲El Rastro—Europe's biggest flea market, held on Sundays and holidays, is a field day for shoppers, people-watchers, and thieves (9:00–15:00, best before 12:00). Thousands of stalls titillate more than a million browsers with mostly new junk. If you brake for garage sales, you'll pull a U-turn for El Rastro. Start at the Plaza Mayor and head south or take the subway to Tirso de Molina. Hang on to your wallet. Munch on a *pepito* (meat-filled pastry). Europe's biggest stamp market thrives simultaneously on Plaza Mayor.

Nightlife

▲▲▲Bullfight—Madrid's Plaza de Toros hosts Spain's top bull-fights on Sundays and holidays from March through mid-October and nearly every day during the San Isidro festival (May through mid-June—generally sold out long in advance). Fights start between 17:00 and 19:00 (early in spring and fall, late in summer). Tickets range from €3.50 to €100. There are no bad seats at the Plaza de Toros; paying more gets you in the shade and/or closer to the gore. (The action often intentionally occurs in the shade to reward the expensive-ticket holders.) To be close to the bullring, choose areas 8, 9, and 10; for shade 1, 2, 9, 10; for shade/sun: 3, 8; for the sun and cheapest seats: 4, 5, 6, 7. (Note that fights advertised as "Gran Novillada con Picadores" feature younger bulls and rookie matadors.)

Hotels and booking offices are convenient but they add 20 percent and don't sell the cheap seats. Telephone both offices before you buy (Plaza Carmen 3—daily 9:30–13:30 & 16:00–19:00, tel. 915-312-732 and Calle Victoria 3—daily 10:00–14:00 & 17:00–19:00, tel. 915-211-213). To save money, stand in the bullring ticket line. About a thousand tickets are held back to be sold on the five days leading up to a fight, including the day of the fight. The bullring is at Calle Alcala 237 (Metro: Ventas, tel. 913-562-200, www.las-ventas.com).

Madrid's **bullfighting museum** is not as good as Sevilla's or Ronda's (Museo Taurino, at the back of bullring, free, Tue–Fri & Sun 9:30–14:30, closed Sat–Mon and early on fight days, tel. 917-251-857).

See the appendix for more on the "art" of bullfighting.

▲▲**Zarzuela**—For a delightful look at Spanish light opera that even English speakers can enjoy, try zarzuela. Guitar-strumming Napoleons in red capes; buxom women with masks, fans, and castanets; Spanish-speaking pharaohs; melodramatic spotlights; and aficionados clapping and singing along from the cheap seats where the acoustics are best—this is zarzuela ...the people's opera. Originating in Madrid, zarzuela is known for its satiric humor and surprisingly good music. The season, which runs from January through June, features a mix of zarzuela and traditional opera. The rest of the year is devoted to ballet. You can buy tickets at Theater Zarzuela (€8–28, box office open 12:00–18:00 for advance tickets or until showtime for that day, Jove-llanos 4, near the Prado, Metro: Banco de España, tel. 915-245-400, http://teatrodelazarzuela.mcu.es). The TI's monthly guide has a special zarzuela listing.

▲**Flamenco**—While Sevilla is the capital of flamenco, Madrid has two easy and affordable options.

Taberna Casa Patas attracts big-name flamenco artists. At this intimate (30-table) and smoky venue you'll pay €25 (for cover and first drink) and 90 minutes later you'll know why this place is called, literally, "the house of legs." Since this is for locals as well as tour groups, the flamenco is contemporary and may be jazzier than your notion—it depends on who's performing (Mon–Thu at 22:00, Fri–Sat at 21:00 and 24:00, closed Sun, reservations are smart, Canizares 10, tel. 914-298-471 or 913-690-496, www.casapatas.com). Its restaurant is a logical place for dinner (Mon–Sat from 20:00) before the show or, since this place is three blocks south of the recommended Plaza Santa Ana tapas bars, this could be your post-tapas-crawl entertainment.

Las Carboneras is more downscale—an easygoing, folksy little place a few steps from Plaza Mayor with a nightly 60-minute flamenco show (€15 includes a stool in the back and a drink, €32 gets you a table up front with dinner and unlimited cheap drinks, Mon–Thu at 22:30, Fri–Sat at 23:00, closed Sun, earlier shows possible if a group books, reservations possible but generally not necessary, Plaza del Conde de Miranda 1, tel. 915-428-677).

Regardless of what your hotel receptionist may want to sell you, other flamenco places like Arco de Cuchilleros (Calle de los Cuchilleros 7), Café de Chinitas (Calle Torija 7, just off Plaza Mayor), and Torres Bermejas (off Gran Vía) are filled with tourists and pushy waiters.

Mesones—Just west of Plaza Mayor, the lane called Cava de San Miguel is lined with *mesones*, long, skinny cave-like bars famous for drinking and singing late into the night. Toss lowbrow locals, Spanish karaoke, electric keyboards, crass tourists, cheap sangria, and greasy calamari in a late-night blender and turn it on. Probably lively only on Friday and Saturday, but you're welcome to pop in to several and see what you can find.

Sleeping in Madrid
(€1 = about $1, country code: 34)
Sleep Code: **S** = Single, **D** = Double/Twin, **T** = Triple, **Q** = Quad, **b** = bathroom, **s** = shower only, **CC** = Credit Cards accepted, **no CC** = Credit Cards not accepted, **SE** = Speaks English, **NSE** = No English. Breakfast is not included unless noted. In Madrid, the 7 percent IVA tax is sometimes included in the price.

To help you easily sort through these listings, I've divided the rooms into three categories, based on the price for a standard double room with bath during high season:

Higher Priced—Most rooms €100 or more.
Moderately Priced—Most less than €100.
Lower Priced—Most rooms less than €60.

Madrid has plenty of centrally located budget hotels and *pensiónes.* You'll have no trouble finding a sleepable double for $30, a good double for $60, and a modern air-conditioned double with all the comforts for $100. Prices are the same throughout the year, and it's almost always easy to find a place. Anticipate full hotels May 15 to May 25 (the festival of Madrid's patron Saint Isidro) and the last week in September (conventions). All of the accommodations I've listed are within a few minutes' walk of Puerta del Sol.

Sleeping in the Pedestrian Zone between Puerta del Sol and Gran Vía
(zip code: 28013)
Predictable and away from the seediness, these are good values for those wanting to spend a little more. Their formal prices may be inflated, and some offer weekend and summer discounts whenever it's slow. Use Metro: Sol for all but Hotel Opera (Metro: Opera). See map on page 116 for location.

HIGHER PRICED
Hotel Arosa charges the same for all of its 134 rooms, whether they're sleekly remodeled Art Deco or just aging gracefully. Ask for a remodeled room with a terrace (Sb-€108, Db-€168, Tb-€224, 20 percent cheaper July–Aug, tax not included, breakfast-€12, CC, air-con, memorably tiny triangular elevator, Calle Salud 21, a block off Plaza del Carmen, tel. 915-321-600, fax 915-313-127, e-mail: arosa@hotelarosa.com).

The huge **Hotel Liabeny** is a business-class hotel with

222 plush, spacious rooms and all the comforts (Sb-€105, Db-€140, Tb-€162, 25 percent cheaper July–Aug, tax not included, breakfast-€12, CC, air-con, if one room is smoky ask for another, off Plaza Carmen at Salud 3, tel. 915-319-000, fax 915-327-421, www.liabeny.com, e-mail: liabeny@apunte.es).

Hotel Opera, a serious, modern hotel with 79 classy rooms, is located just off Plaza Isabel II, a four-block walk from Puerta del Sol toward the Royal Palace (Sb-€75, Db-€105, Db with big view terrace-€114, Tb-€137, tax not included, buffet breakfast-€8, CC, air-con, elevator, ask for a higher floor—there are 8—to avoid street noise; consider their "singing dinners" offered nightly at 22:00—average price €42—reservations wise, Cuesta de Santo Domingo 2, Metro: Opera, tel. 915-412-800, fax 915-416-923, www.hotelopera.com, e-mail: reservas@hotelopera.com). Hotel Opera's cafeteria is understandably popular.

Hotel Santo Domingo has artsy paintings, an inviting lounge, and 120 rooms, each decorated differently (Sb-€120, Db-€178, tax not included, pricier superior rooms are not necessary, CC, air-con, elevator, smoke-free floor, facing Metro: Santo Domingo, Plaza de Santo Domingo 13, tel. 915-479-800, fax 915-475-995, www.hotelsantodomingo.com). Prices drop €30—and breakfast is included—on weekends (Fri–Sun) and July–Aug.

MODERATELY PRICED

Hotel Europa has red-carpet charm: a royal salon, plush halls with happy muzak, polished wood floors, an attentive staff, and 80 squeaky-clean rooms with balconies overlooking the pedestrian zone or an inner courtyard (Sb-€52, Db-€65, Tb-€93, Qb-€110, Quint/b-€125, tax not included, breakfast-€5, easy phone reservations with credit card, CC, fans, elevator, fine lounge on 2nd floor, Calle del Carmen 4, tel. 915-212-900, fax 915-214-696, www.hoteleuropa.net, e-mail: info@hoteleuropa.net, Antonio and Fernando Garaban and their helpful and jovial staff, Javi and Jim, SE). The convenient Europa cafeteria/restaurant next door is a great scene, fun for breakfast, and a fine value any time of day.

Hotel Regente is a big and traditional place with 145 tastefully decorated but comfortable air-conditioned rooms, a great location, and a great value (Sb-€52, Db-€78, Tb-€90, tax not included, breakfast-€4.50, CC, midway between Puerta del Sol and Plaza del Callao at Mesonero Romanos 9, tel. 915-212-941, fax 915-323-014, e-mail: info@hotelregente.com).

Euromadrid Hotel—like a cross between a Motel 6 and an old hospital—rents 43 white rooms in a modern but well-worn shell (big Sb-€56, Db-€78, tight Tb-€88, includes buffet breakfast but not tax, CC, air-con, discounted rate for

Madrid's Center Hotels & Restaurants

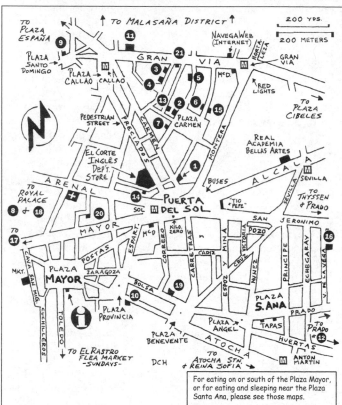

1. Hotel Europa & Cafeteria
2. Hostal Acapulco & Hostal Triana
3. Hotel Regente
4. Hotel Santo Domingo
5. Hotel Arosa
6. Hotel Anaco
7. Hotel Liabeny
8. To Hotel Opera
9. Euromadrid Hotel
10. Hotel Plaza Mayor
11. Hotels at Gran Via #44
12. Hotel Green Lope de Vega, La Platería Bar Museo, & VIPS/Starbucks
13. Rest. Puerto Rico
14. Casa Labra Taberna Rest.
15. Artemisia II
16. Artemisia I
17. To Casa Ciriaco
18. To La Bola Taberna & Café Ricordi
19. Bar Majaderitos
20. Chocolatería San Ginés
21. Zahara Internet Café

parking-€12/day, Mesonero Romanos 7, tel. 915-217-200, fax 915-214-582, e-mail: clasit@infonegocio.com).

The basic **Hotel Anaco** has a drab color scheme and a dreary lobby, but offers 39 quiet, comfortable rooms in a central location (Sb-€72, Db-€89, Tb-€120, tax not included, breakfast-€4.20, CC, air-con, elevator, smoke-free floor, Tres Cruces 3, a few steps off Plaza del Carmen and its underground parking lot, tel. 915-224-604, fax 915-316-484, e-mail: info@anacohotel.com).

Hotel Plaza Mayor, with 30 newly renovated and solidly outfitted rooms, is beautifully situated a block off Plaza Mayor (Sb-€48, Db-€70, corner "suite" Db-€75, Tb-€85, CC, air-con, elevator, Calle Atocha 2, tel. 913-600-606, fax 913-600-610, e-mail:info@h-plazamayor.com, Fedla SE).

LOWER PRICED
Hostal Acapulco, overlooking the fine little Plaza del Carmen, rents 16 bright rooms with air-conditioning and all the big hotel gear. The neighborhood is quiet enough that it's smart to request a room with a balcony (Sb-€35, tiny Db-€42, Db €47, Tb-€60, CC, elevator, Salud 13, 4th floor, tel. 915-311-945, fax 915-322-329, e-mail: hostal_acapulco@yahoo.es, Anna SE).

Hostal Triana, at the same address as Acapulco and also a fine deal, is bigger—with 40 rooms—and offers a little less charm for a little less money (Sb €32, Db-€40, Tb-€54, €2 extra for air-con, half the rooms have only fans, elevator, CC, laundry service, Calle de la Salud 13, tel. 915-326-812, fax 915-229-729, www.hostaltriana .com, e-mail: hostaltriana@nauta.es, Victor Gonzalez SE).

The next three are in the same building at Gran Vía 44, overlooking the busy street. All are cheap and work in a jam. **Hostal Helena,** on the top floor, is a homey burgundy-under-heavy-drapes kind of place renting eight fine rooms. Enjoy the great little roof garden (S-€30, Ds-€42, Db-€54, Tb-€54, CC, elevator, Gran Vía 44, tel. 915-411-529, NSE). The next two are well-worn with stark rooms and traffic noise: **Hostal Residencia Valencia** (Sb-€32, Ds-€44, Db-€47, Tb-€62, includes tax, CC, 5th floor, tel. 915-221-115, fax 915-221-113, e-mail: hostalvalencia@wanadoo.es, Antonio SE) and **Hostal Residencia Continental** (Sb-€29, Db-€42, includes tax, CC, 3rd floor, tel. 915-214-640, fax 915-214-649, www.hostalcontinental.com, e-mail: continental@mundivia.es, Andres SE).

Sleeping on or near Plaza Santa Ana
(zip code: 28012 unless otherwise noted)
The Plaza Santa Ana area has small, cheap places mixed in with fancy hotels. While the neighborhood is noisy at night, it has a

rough but charming ambience, with colorful bars and a central
location (3 min from Puerta del Sol's Tío Pepe sign; walk down
Calle San Jerónimo and turn right on Príncipe; Metro: Sol). To
locate hotels, see map on the next page.

HIGHER PRICED
Suite Prado, two blocks toward the Prado from Plaza Santa Ana,
is a good value, offering 18 sprawling, elegant, air-conditioned
suites with a modern yet homey feel (suites are all the same size
charging €120 for single, €150 double, and €172 triple occu-
pancy, sitting rooms, refrigerators, kitchens, extra kid free, breakfast at café next door-€3.60, CC, elevator, Manuel Fernandez y
Gonzalez 10, at intersection with Venture de la Vega, 28014
Madrid, tel. 914-202-318, fax 914-200-559, www.suiteprado.com,
e-mail: hotel@suiteprado.com, Anna SE).

LOWER PRICED
Residencia Hostal Lisboa, across the street from Suite Prado
(above), is also a good value (25 rooms, Sb-€45, Db-€53,
Tb-€70, CC, air-con, elevator, Ventura de la Vega 17, tel.
914-294-676, fax 914-299-894, www.hostallisboa.com, e-mail:
hostallisboa@inves.es, SE).
    Hostal R. Veracruz II, between Plaza Santa Ana and Puerta
del Sol, rents 22 decent, quiet rooms (Sb-€36, Db-€49, Tb-€63,
no breakfast, CC, elevator, air-con, Victoria 1, 3rd floor, tel.
915-227-635, fax 915-226-749, NSE).
    Because of the following two places, I list no Madrid youth
hostels. At these cheap hotels, fluent Spanish is spoken, bathrooms are down the hall, and there's no heat during winter. For
supercheap beds in a dingy time warp, consider **Hostal Lucense**
(13 rooms, S-€15–18, D-€18–21, Db-€30–36, T-€27, €1.20 per
shower, no CC, Nuñez de Arce 15, tel. 915-224-888, run by Sr.
and Sra. Muñoz, both interesting characters, Sr. SE) and **Casa
Huéspedes Poza** (14 rooms, same prices, street noise, and owners—
but Sr. does the cleaning, at Nuñez de Arce 9, tel. 915-224-871).

Sleeping Near the Prado
(zip code: 28014)

HIGHER PRICED
Hotel Green Lope de Vega is your best business-class hotel
value near the Prado. A four-star place opened in 2000, it's a
"cultural themed" hotel inspired by the 18th-century writer
Lope de Vega. It feels cozy and friendly for a formal business-
class hotel (60 rooms, Sb-€125, Db-€155, Tb-€198, 1 child

Plaza Santa Ana Area

1. Taurina Cerveceria
2. Museo del Jamón
3. Casa del Abuelo
4. Casa Toni
5. La Ria
6. Cerveceria de Santa Ana & La Moderna
7. Bar Viva Madrid
8. Bar El Oso & El Madroño
9. Artemisia I

10. Taberna Casa Patas
11. Hostal Lucense & Poza
12. Hostal Veracruz II
13. Suite Prado
14. Residencia Hostal Lisboa
15. To Hostals Gonzalo & Cervantes
16. To Taberna de Dolores

sleeps free, prices about 20 percent lower on weekends and during most of the summer, CC, air-con, elevator, easy parking, Calle Lope de Vega 49, tel. 913-600-011, fax 914-292-391, www .green-hoteles.com, e-mail: lopedevega@green-hoteles.com, SE).

LOWER PRICED
Two fine budget places are at Cervantes 34 (Metro: Anton Martin). **Hostal Gonzalo**—with 15 spotless, comfortable rooms, well run by friendly and helpful Javier—is deservedly in all the guidebooks.

Reserve in advance (Sb-€36, Db-€44, Tb-€56, CC, elevator, 3rd floor, tel. 914-292-714, fax 914-202-007). Downstairs, the nearly as polished **Hostal Cervantes,** also with 15 rooms, is also good (Sb-€36, Db-€45, Tb-€57, CC, 2nd floor, tel. 914-298-365, fax 914-292-745, www.hostal-cervantes.com, SE).

Eating in Madrid

In Spain, only Barcelona rivals Madrid for taste-bud thrills. You have three dining choices: an atmospheric sit-down meal in a well-chosen restaurant, an unmemorable basic sit-down meal, or a stand-up meal of tapas in a bar or (more likely) in several bars. Many restaurants are closed in August (especially through the last half).

Eating Cheaply North of Puerta del Sol

Restaurante Puerto Rico has good meals, great prices, and few tourists (Mon–Sat 13:00–16:30 & 20:30–24:00, closed Sun, Chinchilla 2, between Puerta del Sol and Gran Vía, tel. 915-322-040).

Hotel Europa Cafeteria is a fun, high-energy scene with a mile-long bar, traditionally clad waiters, great people-watching, local cuisine, and super prices (daily 7:30–24:00, next to Hotel Europa, 50 meters off Puerta del Sol at Calle del Carmen 4, tel. 915-212-900).

Corte Inglés' seventh-floor cafeteria is popular with locals (Mon–Sat 10:00–11:30 & 13:00–16:15 & 17:30–20:00, closed Sun, has nonsmoking section, just off Puerta del Sol at inter-section of Preciados and Tetuan).

Casa Labra Taberna Restaurante is famous among locals as the place where the Spanish Socialist party was founded in 1879...and where you can get great cod. Packed with locals, it's a wonderful scene with three distinct sections: the stand-up bar (cheapest, 2 different lines for munchies and drinks), a peaceful little sit-down area in back (a little more expensive but still cheap; good €4 salads), and a fancy little restaurant (€15 lunches). Their tasty little €1 *bacalao* (cod) dishes put it on the map (daily 11:00–15:30 & 18:00–23:00, a block off Puerta del Sol at Calle Tetuan 12, tel. 915-310-081).

Vegetarian: **Artemisia II** is a hit with vegetarians who like good, healthy food in a smoke-free room (great €9 three-course lunch menu, daily 13:30–16:00 & 21:00–24:00, CC, 2 blocks north of Puerta del Sol at Tres Cruces 4, a few steps off Plaza Carmen, tel. 915-218-721). **Artemisia I** is like its sister (same hours, 4 blocks east of Puerta del Sol at Ventura de la Vega 4 off San Jerónimo, tel. 914-295-092).

Eating on or near Plaza Mayor

Many Americans are drawn to Hemingway's favorite, **Sobrino del Botín** (daily 13:00–16:00 & 20:00–24:00, CC, Cuchilleros 17, a block downhill from Plaza Mayor, tel. 913-664-217). It's touristy, pricey (€24–30 average), and the last place he'd go now, but still, people love it and the food is excellent. If phoning to make a reservation, choose between the downstairs (for dark, medieval-cellar ambience) or upstairs (for a still-traditional but airier and lighter elegance). While this restaurant boasts it's the oldest in the world (dating from 1725), a nearby restaurant brags, "Hemingway never ate here."

Restaurante los Galayos is less touristy and plenty *típico* with good local cuisine (daily 8:00–24:00, lunch specials, lunch from 13:00, dinner anytime, arrive early or make a reservation, 30 meters off Plaza Mayor at Botoneras 5, tel. 913-663-028). For many, dinner right on the square at a sidewalk café is worth the premium (consider Cerveceria Pulpito, southwest corner of the square at #10).

La Torre del Oro Bar Andalu on Plaza Mayor has soul. Die-hard bullfight aficionados hate the gimmicky Bull Bar listed under "Tapas," below. Here the walls are lined with grisly bullfight photos from annual photo competitions. Read the gory description above in the Introductory Walk. Have a drink but be careful not to let the aggressive staff bully you into high-priced tapas you don't want (daily 8:00–15:00 & 18:00–24:00, closed Jan, Plaza Mayor 26, tel. 913-665-016).

Plaza Mayor is famous for its *bocadillos de calamares*. For a cheap and tasty squid-ring sandwich, line up at **Casa Rua** at Plaza Mayor's northwest corner, a few steps up Calle Ciudad Rodrigo (daily 9:00–23:00). Hanging up behind the bar is a photo/ad of Plaza Mayor from the 1950s, when the square contained a park.

Eating on Calle Cava Baja, South of Plaza Mayor

Few tourists frequent this traditional neighborhood—Barrio de los Austrias, named for the Hapsburgs. It's three minutes south of Plaza Mayor, or a 10-minute walk from Puerta del Sol. The street, Cava Baja, is lined with a diverse array of restaurants and tapas bars and clogged with locals out in search of a special meal. For a good authentic Madrileño dinner experience, take time to survey the many places along this street between the first and last listings described below and choose your favorite. A key wine-drinking phrase is *mucho cuerpo* (full-bodied).

Posada de la Villa serves Castilian cuisine in a 17th-century posada. Peek into the big oven to see what's cooking (€30 meals, Mon–Sat 13:00–16:00 & 20:00–24:00, closed Sun and Aug, Calle Cava Baja 9, tel. 913-661-860).

El Schotis is less expensive and specializes in bull stew and fish dishes. Named after a popular local dance, the restaurant retains the traditional character of old Madrid (daily 12:00–17:00 & 20:00–24:00, Calle Cava Baja 11, tel. 913-653-230).

Julian de Tolosa, a classy, elegantly simple place popular with locals who know good food, offers a small, quality menu of Basque cuisine from T-bone steak to red *tolosa* (Toulouse) beans (Mon–Sat 13:30–16:00 & 21:00–24:00, Sun 13:30–16:00, Calle Cava Baja 18, tel. 913-658-210).

Taberna los Lucio has good tapas, salads, egg dishes, and wine (Wed–Mon 13:00–16:00 & 20:30–24:00, closed Tue, Calle Cava Baja 30, tel. 913-662-984).

For a splurge, dine with power-dressing locals at **Casa Lucio.** While the king and queen of Spain eat here, it's more stuffy than expensive (daily 13:00–17:00 & 21:00–24:00, Calle Cava Baja 35, unless you're the king or queen, reserve several days in advance, tel. 913-653-252).

Taberna Tempranillo, ideal for hungry wine-lovers, offers tapas and 250 kinds of wine. Use their fascinating English menu to assemble your dream meal. Arrive by 20:00 or wait (daily 13:00–15:30 & 20:00–24:00, closed Aug, Cava Baja 38, tel. 913-641-532).

Eating near Calle Cava Baja
El Madroño is a fun tapas bar that preserves chunks of old Madrid. A tile copy of Velázquez' famous *Drinkers* grins from its facade. Inside, look above the stairs for photos of 1902 Madrid. Study the coats of arms of Madrid through the centuries as you try a *vermut* on tap and a €2 sandwich (Tue–Sun 10:00–24:00, closed Mon, Plaza Puerta Cerrada 7, tel. 913-645-629).

Taberna los Austrias, two blocks away, serves tapas, salads, and light meals on wood-barrel tables (daily 12:00–16:00 & 20:00–24:00, Calle Nuncio 17).

Next door is **Taberna de los 100 Vinos** (Tavern of 100 Wines), a classy wine bar serving top-end tapas and fine wine by the glass—see the chalk board (Tue–Sat 13:00–16:00 & 20:00–24:00, closed Sun–Mon, Calle Nuncio 17).

Eating near the Royal Palace
Casa Ciriaco is popular with locals who appreciate good traditional cooking (€25 meals, Thu–Tue 13:30–16:00 & 20:30–24:00, closed Wed and Aug, halfway between Puerta del Sol and the Royal Palace at Calle Mayor 84, tel. 915-480-620). It was from this building in 1906 that an anarchist bombed the royal couple on their wedding day (for details, see "Introductory Walk," above). A photo of the carnage is inside the front door.

Eating South of Plaza Mayor

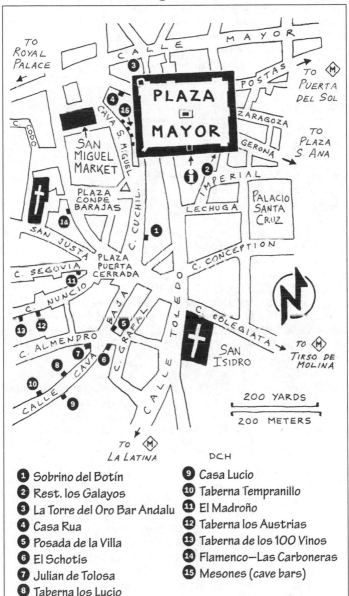

1 Sobrino del Botín
2 Rest. los Galayos
3 La Torre del Oro Bar Andalu
4 Casa Rua
5 Posada de la Villa
6 El Schotis
7 Julian de Tolosa
8 Taberna los Lucio

9 Casa Lucio
10 Taberna Tempranillo
11 El Madroño
12 Taberna los Austrias
13 Taberna de los 100 Vinos
14 Flamenco—Las Carboneras
15 Mesones (cave bars)

La Bola Taberna specializes in *cocido Madrileño*—Madrid stew. This is a touristy but tastefully elegant and friendly place stewing various meats, carrots, and garbanzo beans in earthen jugs. The €15 stew, which consists of two courses (first you enjoy the broth as a soup) is big enough to split (weekdays 13:00–16:00 & 20:30–23:00, often closed Sat–Sun, no CC, midway between the Royal Palace and Gran Vía at Calle Bola 5, tel. 915-476-930).

Café Ricordi, just a block from the Royal Theater, is a delightfully romantic little spot, perfect for theater-goers. You can enjoy tiny sandwiches with a glass of wine, coffee, and an elegant sweet, or a full meal in this café/bar/restaurant (daily 11:00–24:00, Calle Arrieta 5, tel. 915-479-200).

Eating near the Prado

Each of the big-three art museums has a decent cafeteria. Or choose from these three places, all within a block of the Prado:

La Plateria Bar Museo is a hardworking little café/wine bar with a good menu for tapas, light meals, and hearty salads (listed as *raciones* and $^1/_2$ *raciones* on the chalk board). Its tables spill onto the leafy little Plaza de Platarias de Matinez (daily 8:00–24:00, directly across busy boulevard Paseo del Prado from Atocha end of Prado, tel. 914-291-722).

Taberna de Dolores, a winning formula since 1908, is a commotion of locals enjoying €2 *canapes* (open-face sandwiches), tasty *almejas* (clams) and *cañas* (small beers) at the bar or at a few tables in the back (daily 13:00–24:00, Plaza de Jesus 4, tel. 914-292-243).

VIPS is where good-looking, young tour guides eat cheap and filling salads. This bright, popular chain restaurant is engulfed in a big bookstore (daily 9:00–24:00, across Paseo del Prado boulevard from northern end of Prado in Galeria del Prado under Palace Hotel facing Plaza Canovas). Spain's first Starbucks opened in April 2001, just next door.

Fast Food and Picnics

Fast Food: For an easy, light, cheap meal, try **Rodilla**—a popular sandwich chain with a shop on the northeast corner of Puerta del Sol at #13 (Mon–Fri 9:30–23:00, opens on Sat at 10:00, Sun at 11:00). **Pans & Company,** with shops throughout Madrid and Spain, offers healthy, tasty sandwiches and chef's salads (daily 9:00–24:00, on Puerta del Sol, Plaza Callão, Gran Vía 30, and many more).

Picnics: The department store **El Corte Inglés** has a well-stocked **deli** downstairs (Mon–Sat 10:00–22:00, closed Sun). A perfect place to assemble a cheap picnic is downtown Madrid's neighborhood market, **Mercado de San Miguel.** How about breakfast surrounded by early-morning shoppers in the market's café? (Mon–Fri 9:00–14:30 & 17:15–20:15, Sat 9:00–14:30, closed Sun; to reach the market from Plaza Mayor, face the colorfully painted building and exit from the upper left-hand corner.) The **Museo del Jamón** (Museum of Ham) sells cheap picnics to go (see tapas pub-crawl dinner below).

Churros con Chocolate

If you like danish and coffee in American greasy-spoon joints, you must try the Spanish equivalent: Greasy *churros* (or the thicker *porras*) dipped in pudding-like hot chocolate. **Bar Majaderitos** is a good bet (daily 7:00–22:30, Sun from 9:00, best in morning, 2 blocks off Tío Pepe end of Puerta del Sol, south on Espoz y Mina, turn right on Calle de Cadiz). Their tasty grilled cheese (with ham and/or egg) sandwich rounds out your breakfast. With luck, the *churros* machine in the back will be cooking. Notice the expressive WC signs.

The classy **Chocolatería San Ginés** is much loved by locals for its *churros* and chocolate (Tue–Sun 19:00–7:00, closed Mon). While empty before midnight, it's packed with the disco crowd in the wee hours; the popular Joy disco is next door. Dunk your *churros* into the pudding-like hot chocolate, as locals have done here for over 100 years (from Puerta del Sol, take Calle Arenal 2 blocks west, turn left on book-lined Pasadizo de San Ginés, you'll see the café—it's at #5, tel. 933-656-546).

Tapas: The Madrid Pub-Crawl Dinner

For maximum fun, people, and atmosphere, go mobile and do the "tapa tango," a local tradition of going from one bar to the next, munching, drinking, and socializing. Tapas are the tooth-pick appetizers, salads, and deep-fried foods served in most bars. Madrid is Spain's tapa capital—tapas just don't get any better. Grab a toothpick and stab something strange, but establish the prices first, especially if you're on a tight budget or at a possible tourist trap. Some items are very pricey, and most bars push larger *raciones* rather than smaller *tapas*. The real action begins late (around 20:00). But for beginners, an earlier start, with less commotion, can be easier. The litter on the floor is normal; that's where people traditionally toss their trash and shells. Don't worry about paying until you're ready to go. Then ask for *la cuenta* (the bill).

Very important: Before embarking upon this culinary adven-ture (which could, if done properly, be a highlight of your trip), study and use the "Tapas Tips" section in this book's introduction (page 29).

Prowl the area between Puerta del Sol and Plaza Santa Ana. There's no ideal route, but the little streets (in this book's map) between Puerta del Sol, San Jerónimo, and Plaza Santa Ana hold tasty surprises. Nearby, the street Jesus de Medinaceli is also lined with popular tapas bars. Below is a five-stop tapa crawl. These places are good, but don't be blind to making discoveries on your own.

1. From Puerta del Sol, walk east a block down Carrera de San Jerónimo to the corner of Victoria Street. Across from the Museo del Jamón, you'll find **La Taurina Cervecería,** a bull-fighters' Planet Hollywood (daily 8:00–24:00). Wander among trophies and historic photographs. Each stuffed bull's head is named, along with its farm, awards, and who killed him. Among the many gory photos study the first post: It's Che Guevara, Orson Welles, and Salvador Dalí all enjoying a good fight. Around the corner, the Babe Ruth of bullfighters, El Cordobes, lies wounded in bed. The photo below shows him in action. Kick off your pub crawl with a drink here. Inspired, I went for the *rabo de toro* (bull-tail stew, €10.50)—and regretted it. If a fight's on, the place will be packed with aficionados gathered around the TV. Across the street at San Jerónimo 5 is the...

2. Museo del Jamón (Museum of Ham), tastefully decorated—unless you're a pig (or vegetarian). This frenetic, cheap, stand-up bar is an assembly line of fast and simple *bocadillos* and *raciones*. Options are shown in photographs with prices. For a small sandwich, ask for a *chiquito* (€0.60, unadvertised). The best ham is the pricey *jamón Iberico*—from pigs who led stress-free lives in acorn-strewn valleys. Just point and eat (daily 9:00–24:00, sit-down restaurant upstairs). Next, forage halfway up Calle Victoria to the tiny...

3. La Casa del Abuelo, for seafood-lovers who savor sizzling plates of tasty little *gambas* (shrimp) and *langostinos* (prawns). Try *gambas a la plancha* (grilled shrimp, €4), *gambas al ajillo* (pron. ahh-hheee-yoh, shrimp version of escargot, cooked in oil and garlic and ideal for bread dipping—€5.50), and a €1.20 glass of red wine (daily 11:30–15:30 & 18:30–23:30, Calle Victoria 12). Continue uphill and around the corner to...

4. Casa Toni, for refreshing bowls of gazpacho—the cold tomato-and-garlic soup (€1.50, available all year but only popular when temperatures soar). Their specialty is *berenjena*, deep-fried slices of eggplant (€3.60) and *champiñones*—sauteed mushrooms (daily 11:30–16:00 & 18:00–23:30, closed July, Calle Cruz 14). Now it's...

5. Your choice. Madrid is the New York City of Spain for cuisine—you can find anything. This is your chance to try colorful specialties from regions you won't be visiting. For instance, across from the shrimp place (stop #3), **Oreja de Oro** (Golden Ear) is named for what it sells—sautéed pig's ears (*oreja*—€2.50). While the pig's ears are a Madrid specialty, the place is Galician and people come here for *pulpo* (octopus), *pimientos de padron* (green peppers . . . some sweet and a few hot surprises), and the distinctive *ribeiro* (pron. ree-BAY-roh) wine, served Galician-style, in characteristic little ceramic bowls (to disguise its lack of clarity). On the next street over, **Sidreria La Creacion** is Asturian (the mountainous north of Spain), serving Asturian munchies and cider, traditionally poured high through the air to be oxygenated; notice the goofy wall pumps over buckets for that purpose (Nunez de Arce 14). The neighborhood is thriving with people and taste treats. Explore. **La Ria,** at Pasaje Matheu 5, is famous for its mussels (€3, *con limon* or *picante*, slurp the meat, scoop the juice with the shell, and toss the shells on the floor as you smack your lips).

If you're hungry for more, and want a more trendy, up-to-date tapas scene, head for Plaza Santa Ana. The south side of the square is lined with lively bars offering good tapas, drinks, and a classic setting right on the square. Consider **Cerveceria de Santa Ana** (tasty tapas with two zones: rowdy beer-hall and classier sit-down) and **La Moderna** (wine, paté, and cheese plates).

If you're picking up speed and looking for a place filled with old tiles and young people, power into **Bar Viva Madrid** (Calle Manuel Fernandez y Gonzalez, tel. 914-293-640). The same street has other late-night bars filled with music.

For a more gentle late-night slice of Madrid, hike over to **Bar el Oso y el Madroño,** where the proprietor serves patrons and happily cranks his 19th-century mechanical organ (commotion and new friends at the bar, tables in back, closed Mon and Aug, Calle la Bolsa 4, 2 blocks south of Puerta del Sol, tel. 915-227-796).

Transportation Connections—Madrid

By train to: Toledo (9/day, 1 hr, from Madrid's Atocha station—the *cercanias* [pron. theyr-kah-NEE-ahz] section, not the AVE section; if day-tripping there's a direct Madrid–Toledo express at 8:34 and a Toledo–Madrid express at 18:56), **Segovia** (9/day, 2 hrs, both Chamartin and Atocha stations), **Ávila** (8/day, 90 min, from Chamartin and Atocha), **Salamanca** (5/day, 2.5 hrs, from Chamartin), **Barcelona** (7/day, 8 hrs, mostly from Chamartin, 2 overnight), **Granada** (2/day, 6–9 hrs), **Sevilla** (18/day, 2.5 hrs by AVE, 3.5 hrs by Talgo, from Atocha), **Córdoba** (17 AVE trains/day, 2 hrs, from Atocha), **Málaga** (6/day, 4 hrs, from Atocha), **Lisbon** (1/day departing at 20:45, 10 hrs, pricey over-night Hotel Train from Chamartin), **Paris** (4/day,

12–16 hrs, 1 direct overnight—an expensive Hotel Train, from Chamartin).

Spain's AVE (pron. AH-vay) bullet train opens up some good itinerary options. Pick up the brochure at the station. Prices vary with times and class. The basic Madrid–Sevilla second-class fare is €63 (€12 less on the almost-as-fast Talgo). AVE is heavily discounted for Eurail passholders (the Madrid–Sevilla second-class trip costs Eurailers about €9). So far AVE only covers Madrid–Córdoba–Sevilla, but in 2004 it will extend to Barcelona. Consider this exciting day trip to Sevilla from Madrid: 7:00 depart Madrid, 8:45–12:40 in Córdoba, 13:30–21:00 in Sevilla, 23:30 back in Madrid. Reserve each AVE segment (tel. 902-240-202 for Atocha AVE info). General train info: tel. 902-240-202.

By bus to: Segovia (2/hr, 1.25 hrs, first departure 6:30, last return at 21:30, La Sepulvedana buses, Paseo de la Florida 11, from Metro: Príncipe Pío go past Hotel Florida Norte and look for yellow mailbox—near it is the Sepulvedana bus station, tel. 915-304-800). For **Ávila** (8/day, 2 hrs), **Toledo** (2/hr, 60–75 min), and **Granada** (9/day, 5 hrs) catch a bus from Estación sur Auto-buses (which sits squarely atop Metro: Méndez Alvaro, with eateries and a small TI—open daily 9:00–20:45, Avenida de Méndez Alvaro, tel. 914-684-200). Buses for **Salamanca** (hrly. 2.5 hrs) leave from the Conde de Casal station (Calle Fernández Shaw 1, Metro: Conde de Casal, Auto-Res, tel. 902-020-999, www.auto-res.net).

By bus, train, and car to El Escorial: Buses leave from the basement of Madrid's Moncloa Metro stop and drop you in the El Escorial center (4/hr, 45 min, in Madrid take bus #664 or #661 from Intercambiador's bay #3, tel. 918-969-028). One bus a day (except for Mon, when sights are closed) is designed to let travelers do the Valley of the Fallen as a side trip from El Escorial; the bus leaves El Escorial at 15:15 (15-min trip) and leaves the Valley of the Fallen at 17:30. Trains run to El Escorial but let you off a 20-minute walk (or a shuttle-bus ride, 2/hr) from the monastery and city center. By car, it's easy to visit El Escorial and the Valley of the Fallen on the way to Segovia (note sights closed Mon).

Drivers Note: Avoid driving in Madrid. Rent your car when you depart. To leave Madrid from Gran Vía, simply follow signs for A6 (direction Villalba or Coruña) for Segovia, El Escorial, or Valley of the Fallen (see that chapter for details). It's cheapest to make car-rental arrangements before you leave home. In Madrid, consider Easycar.com (great rates, tel. 902-182-028, www.easycar.com), **Europcar** (central reservations tel. 902-105-030, San Leonardo 8 office tel. 915-418-892, Chamartin station tel. 913-231-721, airport tel. 913-937-235), **Hertz** (central reservations tel. 902-402-405,

Gran Vía 88 tel. 915-425-803, Chamartin station tel. 917-330-400, airport tel. 913-937-228), **Avis** (Gran Vía 60 tel. 915-472-048, airport tel. 913-937-222), **Alamo** (central reservations tel. 902-100-515), and **Budget** (central reservations tel. 901-201-212, www.budget.es). Ask about free delivery to your hotel. At the airport, most rental cars are returned at Terminal 1.

Madrid's Barajas Airport

Sixteen kilometers east of downtown, Madrid's modern airport has three terminals. You'll likely land at Terminal 1, which has a helpful English-speaking TI (marked "Oficina de Información Turistica," Mon–Fri 8:00–20:00, Sat 9:00–13:00, closed Sun, tel. 913-058-656); an ATM (part of the BBVA bank) far busier than the lonely American Express window; a 24-hour exchange office (plus shorter-hour exchange offices); a flight info office (marked simply "Information" in airport lobby, open 24 hrs/day, tel. 902-353-570); a post-office window; a pharmacy; lots of phones (buy a phone card from the machine near the phones); a few scattered Internet terminals (small fee); eateries; a RENFE office (where you can get train info and buy train tickets; daily 8:00–21:00, tel. 913-058-544); and on-the-spot car-rental agencies (see above). The three terminals are connected by long indoor walkways; it's about an eight-minute walk between terminals (the Metro is in Terminal 2).

Iberia is Spain's airline, connecting many cities in Spain as well as international destinations (Velázquez 130, phone answered 24 hrs/day, tel. 902-400-500, www.iberia.com).

Getting between the Airport and Downtown: By public transport, consider an affordable, efficient **airport bus/taxi combination.** Take the airport bus (#89, usually blue) from the airport to Madrid's Plaza Colón (€2.40, 4/hr, 20–30 min, leaves Madrid 4:30–24:00, leaves airport 5:15–2:00; stops at both Terminals 1 and 2; at the airport the bus stop is outside Terminal 1's arrivals door—cross the street filled with taxis to reach stop marked Bus on median strip; at Plaza Colón the stop is usually underground, though may be above ground at Calle Serrano). Then, to reach your hotel from Plaza Colón, catch a taxi (insist on meter, ride to hotel should be far less than €6, to avoid supplement charge for rides from a bus station, it's a little cheaper to go upstairs and flag down a taxi). Or from Plaza Colón, take the subway (from the underground bus stop, walk up the stairs and face the blue "URBIS" sign high on a building—the subway stop, M. Serrano, is 50 meters to your right; it takes two transfers to reach Puerta del Sol). At the airport, remember it's bus #89 you want; ignore bus #101, a holdover from the time when the airport didn't have a Metro stop (it runs to the Canillejas Metro stop on Madrid's outskirts).

You can take the **Metro** all the way between the airport and downtown. The airport's futuristic Aeropuerto Metro stop in Terminal 2 provides a cheap but time-consuming way into town (€1, or get a shareable 10-pack for €4.50; takes 45 min with 2 transfers; at airport, access Metro at check-in level; from Terminal 1 arrivals level, stand with your back to baggage claim, then go to your far right, up the stairs, and follow red-and-blue Metro diamond signs to Metro station, 8-minute walk; to get to Puerta del Sol from the airport, transfer at Mar de Cristal to brown line #4 direction Arguelles, then transfer at Goya to red line #3 direction Cuatro Caminos).

For a **taxi** to or from the airport, allow €20 (€4 airport supplement is legal). Cabbies routinely try to get €30—a rip-off. Insist on the meter.

NORTHWEST OF MADRID:
EL ESCORIAL, VALLEY OF THE FALLEN, SEGOVIA, ÁVILA, AND SALAMANCA

Before slipping out of Madrid, consider several fine side trips northwest of Spain's capital city, all conveniently reached by car, bus, or train.

Spain's lavish, brutal, and complicated history is revealed throughout Old Castile. This region, where the Spanish language Castilian originated, is named for its many castles—battle scars from the long-fought Reconquista.

An hour from Madrid, tour the imposing and fascinating palace of the Monasterio de San Lorenzo de El Escorial, headquarters of the Spanish Inquisition. Nearby at the awesome Valley of the Fallen, pay tribute to the countless victims of Spain's bloody civil war.

Segovia, with its remarkable Roman aqueduct and romantic castle, is another worthwhile side trip. At Ávila, you can walk the perfectly preserved medieval walls. And at Salamanca, enjoy Spain's best town square, caffeinated with a frisky college-town ambience.

Planning Your Time

See El Escorial and the Valley of the Fallen together in less than a day (but not on Monday, when sights are closed). By car, do them en route to Segovia; by bus, make it a day trip from Madrid.

Segovia is worth a half-day of sightseeing and is a joy at night. Ávila, while not without charm, merits only a quick stop (if you're driving and in the area) to marvel at its medieval walls and, perhaps, check out St. Teresa's finger.

Salamanca, with its art, university, and Spain's greatest Plaza Mayor, is worth a day and a night but is stuck out in the boonies. On a three-week Barcelona–Lisbon "open-jaw" itinerary, I'd hook south from Madrid and skip Salamanca. If you're doing

Sights near Madrid

a circular trip, Salamanca is a natural stop halfway between Portugal and Madrid.

In total, these sights are worth a maximum of three days if you're in Iberia for less than a month. If you're in Spain for just a week, I'd still squeeze in a quick side-trip from Madrid to El Escorial and the Valley of the Fallen.

EL ESCORIAL

The Monasterio de San Lorenzo de El Escorial is a symbol of power rather than elegance. This 16th-century palace, 50 kilometers northwest of Madrid, gives us a better feel for the Counter-Reformation and the Inquisition than any other building. Built at a time when Catholic Spain felt threatened by Protestant "heretics," its construction dominated the Spanish economy for a generation (1563–1584). Because of this bully in the national budget, Spain has almost nothing else to show from this most powerful period of her history.

The giant, gloomy building looks more like a prison than a palace (gray-black stone, 200 meters long, 150 meters wide, over

160 kilometers of passages, 2,600 windows, 1,200 doors, 1,600 overwhelmed tourists). Four hundred years ago, the enigmatic, introverted, and extremely Catholic King Philip II ruled his bulky empire and directed the Inquisition from here. To 16th-century followers of Luther, this place epitomized the evil of Catholicism. Today it's a time capsule of Spain's "Golden Age," packed with history, art, and Inquisition ghosts.

It was conceived by Phillip II to serve several purposes: a grand mausoleum for Spain's royal family starting with his father, Charles V; a monastery to pray (a lot) for the royal souls; a small palace to use as a Camp David of sorts for Spain's royalty; and a school to embrace humanism in a way that promoted the Catholic faith.

The Monasterio looks confusing at first, but you simply follow the arrows and signs in one continuous walk-through. This is the general order you'll follow (though some rooms may be closed for renovation):

The **Chamber of the Honor Guards** is hung with 16th-century tapestries including fascinating copies of Bosch's most famous and preachy paintings (which Phillip II fancied). Don't miss El Greco's towering painting of the *Martyrdom of St. Maurice*. This was the artist's first commission after arriving in Spain from Venice. It was too subtle and complex for the king, so El Greco moved on to Toledo to find work.

Downstairs (Sala 1) is the fascinating **Museum of Architecture** (Museo de Arquitectura) with long parallel corridors of easy-to-appreciate models of the palace and some of the actual machinery and tools used to construct it. Huge stone-pinching winches, fat ropes, and rusty old mortar spades help convey the immensity of this project. At the big model, notice how the complex is shaped like a grill, and recall how San Lorenzo was martyred by burning (throughout the palace the symbol associated with the saint is a square grill). The "grill handle" is the actual living quarters of the royal family or palace. The rest—the monastery and school—gathered around the huge basilica.

Detouring upstairs you'll find the **Hall of Battles** (Sala de Batallas), lined with frescos celebrating Spain's great military victories and providing an interesting peek at 16th-century warfare.

From here a corridor lined with various family trees (some scrawny, others lush and fecund) leads into the royal living quarters (the building's grill handle). Immediately inside the first door find the small portrait of Phillip II flanked by two large portraits of his daughters. The palace was like Phillip—austere. Notice the simple floors, plain white walls, and bare-bones chandelier. This was the bedroom of one of his daughters. Notice the sheet warmer beside

El Escorial

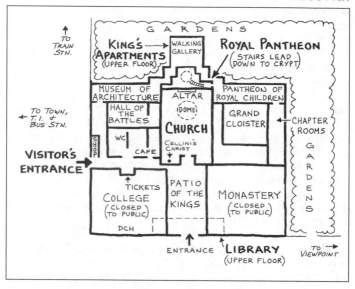

her bed—often necessary here at over 1,000 meters (3,400 feet) above sea level. Bend down to notice the view from her bed... of the high altar in the basilica next door.

In the next room notice the reclinable sedan chair that the king, thick with gout, was carried in (for 7 days) on his last trip from Madrid to El Escorial. He wanted to be here when he died.

The **Audience Chamber** is now a portrait gallery filled with Hapsburg royals. The paintings of unattractive people that line the walls provide an instructive peek at the consequences of inbreeding among royals—a common problem throughout Europe in those days. The Spanish emperor Charles V was the most powerful man in Europe. The guy next to Charles with the good-looking legs was his illegitimate son—famous for his handsome looks, thanks to a little fresh blood. Many other portraits show the unhappy effects of mixing blue blood with more of the same blue blood. When one king married his niece, the result was the Charles II. His severe underbite (an inbred royal family trait) was the least of his problems. An epileptic before that disease was understood, poor "Charles the Mad" would be the last of the Spanish Hapsburgs. He died without an heir in 1700, ushering in the continent-wide War of Spanish Succession, and the dismantling of Spain's empire.

In the **Walking Gallery,** the royals got their exercise

privately, with no risk of darkening their high-class skin with a tan. Study the 16th-century maps lining the walls. The slate strip on the floor is a sundial. It lined up with a (now plugged) hole in the wall so that at noon a tiny beam hit the middle of the three lines. Palace clocks were set by this. Where the ray crossed the strip indicated the date and sign of the zodiac.

As you enter the King's Antechamber, look back to study the fine inlaid wooden door (a gift from the German emperor celebrating the exciting humanism of the age).

Phillip II's bedroom is austere like his daughter's. Look at the king's humble bed...barely queen size. He too could view Mass at the basilica's high altar without leaving his bed. Notice the red box next to his pillow—holding the royal bed pan. But don't laugh—the king's looking down from the wall behind you. Phillip died in this room in 1598. Follow the route his body took from here down to the **Royal Pantheon** (Panteón Real), the gilded resting place of 26 kings and queens...four centuries' worth of Spanish monarchy. All the kings are included—but only those queens who became mothers of kings.

There is a post mortem filing system at work here. The first and greatest, Charles V and his Queen Isabella, flank the altar on the top shelf. Her son, Philip II, rests below Charles and opposite (only) one of Phillip's four wives, and so on. There is a waiting process, too. Before a royal corpse can rest in this room, it needs to decompose for several decades. The three empty niches are already booked. The bones of Juan Carlos' grandparents, Alfonso XIII and Victoria Eugenia (who died in 1941 and 1964, respectively) are just about ready to be moved in. Juan Carlos' father, Don Juan (who died in the 1993), is also on the wait list. But where does that leave Juan Carlos? Or his mom? This hotel is *todo completo*.

The next rooms are filled with the tombs of lesser royals: Each bears that person's name (in Latin), relation to the king, and slogan or epitaph. They lead to the lazy Susan–like **Pantheon of Royal Children** (Panteón de los Infantes) that holds the remains of various royal children who died before the age of seven (and their first Communion).

The **Chapter Rooms** (Salas Capitulares), where the monks met to do church business, are lined with big-name paintings: Ribera, El Greco, Titian, and Velázquez. (More great paintings are in the monastery's Museum of Painting, or Pinacoteca.) The **cloister** glows with bright, newly restored paintings by Tibaldi.

Follow the signs to the **basilica.** The altar is spectacular when illuminated (put a €1 coin in the small box near the church entrance, just before the gated doors). In the center of the altar wall, find the flame-engulfed grill featuring San Lorenzo (St. Laurence) meeting his famous death—and taking "turn the other cheek" to new extremes. With your back to the altar go to the right corner for the artistic highlight of the basilica: Cellini's marble sculpture *The Crucifixion*. Jesus' features are supposedly modeled after the Shroud of Turin. Cellini carved this from Carrara marble for his own tomb in 1502 (according to the letters under Christ's feet).

Last comes the immense **library** *(biblioteca)*—where it's clear that education was a priority for the Spanish royalty. Savor this room. The ceiling (by Tibaldi, depicting various disciplines labeled in Latin, the lingua franca of the multinational Hapsburg empire) is a burst of color. At the far end of the room, the elaborate model of the solar system looks like a giant gyroscope, revolving unmistakably around the Earth. As you leave, look back above the door. The plaque warns "Excomunion . . . "—you'll be excommunicated if you take a book without checking it out properly. Who needs late fees when you hold the keys to hell?

Admission to the palace is €6 (April–Sept Tue–Sun 10:00–19:00, enter before ticket office closes at 18:00, closed Mon; Oct–March palace closes at 18:00; tel. 918-905-904).

You'll find scanty captions in English within the palace. For more information, get the *Visitor's Guide: Monastery of San Lorenzo El Real de El Escorial*, which follows the general route you'll take (€6, available at any of several shops in the palace). While you can pay €7 for admission with a guided tour, English-speakers generally have a long wait for a group to form. I'd rent the €2 audioguide instead.

Arrival in El Escorial: Those arriving by bus enjoy a pleasant 10-minute stroll from the station through the town of San Lorenzo de El Escorial. Exit the bus station from the back ramp which leads over the parked buses, turn left and follow the newly cobbled pedestrian lane (Calle Juan de Leyra) a few blocks until it dead-ends at Duque de Medinaceli, where you'll turn left and see the palace. Stairs lead past several decent eateries, through a delightful park, past the TI (Mon–Thu 11:00–18:00, Fri–Sun 10:00–19:00, tel. 918-905-313), and directly to the tourist entry of the immense palace/monastery.

Eating: To shop for a picnic, stop by the Mercado Publico on Calle del Rey 9, a four-minute walk from the palace (Mon–Fri 9:00–14:00 & 17:00–20:00, Sat 10:00–14:00, closed Thu afternoon and Sun). For a change from Spanish fare, consider pizza at Tavolata Reale (Plaza de Las Animas, a block from Monasterio entrance, tel. 918-094-591) or Restaurante China Hong Kong (Calle San Anton 6, tel. 918-961-894).

Transportation Connections—El Escorial

From Madrid: Buses leave from the basement level of Madrid's Moncloa Metro stop and drop you in the town center of San Lorenzo de El Escorial, a 10-minute walk from the Monasterio (4/hr, 45 min, in Madrid take bus #664 or #661 from Intercambiador's bay #3, tel. 918-904-100).

The **train** is less convenient. Although trains leave twice hourly from Madrid's Atocha and Chamartin stations, you're dropped a 20-minute walk (through Casita del Principe park) or shuttle-bus ride (2/hr) from the San Lorenzo de El Escorial town center and Monasterio.

To Valley of the Fallen: Without a car, the easiest way there is to negotiate a deal with a taxi (to take you there, wait 30 minutes and bring you back to El Escorial). Otherwise one bus a day connects the Valley of the Fallen with El Escorial (15 min, leaves El Escorial at 15:15, leaves Valley of the Fallen at 17:30, €7 round-trip includes admission to the site, no bus on Mon when sites are closed).

By car it's quite simple. Taxi to your car rental office (or ask if they'll deliver the car to your hotel). Pick up the car by 8:30 and ask directions to highway A6. From Gran Vía in central Madrid it's easy: follow signs to A6 (direction Villalba or Coruña). The freeway leads directly out of town. Stay on the A6 past the first El Escorial exit. At kilometer 37 you'll see the cross marking the Valley of the Fallen ahead on the left. Exit 47 takes you to both the Valley of the Fallen (after 1 km, a granite gate on right marks Valle de los Caídos turn-off) and El Escorial (follow signs).

The nearby **Silla de Felipe** (Philip's Seat) is a rocky viewpoint where the king would come to admire his palace being built. Leaving El Escorial, follow signs to A6 Guadarrama. After about 10 km you pass the Valley of the Fallen and hit the freeway for Madrid, Segovia, and Toledo.

VALLEY OF THE FALLEN (EL VALLE DE LOS CAÍDOS)

Ten kilometers (6 miles) from El Escorial, high in the Guadarrama Mountains, a 150-meter-tall granite cross marks an immense and powerful underground monument to the victims of Spain's 20th-century nightmare—its civil war (1936–1939).

Approaching by car or bus, you enter the sprawling park through a granite gate(€4.80, or €7 to include round-trip bus from El Escorial, April–Sept Tue–Sun 10:00–19:00, closed Mon, last entry 60 min before closing, Oct-March closes at 18:00, tel. 918-907-756). The best views of the cross are from the bridge. Above you, the tiny chapels along the ridge mark the Stations of the Cross, where pilgrims stop on their hike to this memorial.

The immense cross (built like a chimney, from the inside) weighs over 200,000 tons. Since it's built directly over the dome of the subterranean basilica, a team of seismologists keeps a careful eye on things.

The stairs that lead to the imposing monument are grouped in sets of tens, meant to symbolize the Ten Commandments (including "Thou shalt not kill"—hmm). The emotional *pietà* draped over the entrance was sculpted by Juan de Avalos, the same artist who created the dramatic figures of the four evangelists at the base of the cross. It must have had a powerful impact on mothers who came here to remember their fallen sons.

A solemn silence and a stony chill fill the basilica—at 265 meters (870 feet) long, larger than St. Peter's. Many Spaniards pass under the huge, foreboding angels of fascism to visit the grave of General Franco—an unusual place of pilgrimage, to say the least.

After walking through the two long vestibules, stop at the iron gates of the actual basilica. The line of torch-like lamps adds to the ambience of a shrine. Notice the bare rock still showing on the ceiling. Franco's prisoners, the enemies of the right, dug this memorial out of solid rock from 1940 to 1959. The sides of the monument are lined with copies of 16th-century Brussels tapestries of the Apocalypse, and side chapels contain alabaster copies of Spain's most famous statues of the Virgin Mary.

Interred behind the high altar and side chapels (marked "RIP, 1936–1939, died for God and country") are the remains of the approximately 50,000 people, both Republicanos and Franco's Nacionalistas, who lost their lives in the war. Regrettably the urns are not visible, so it is Franco who takes center stage. His grave, strewn with flowers, lies behind the high altar. In front of the altar is the grave of José Antonio, the founder of Spanish fascism. Between these fascists' graves the statue of a crucified Christ is lashed to a timber Franco himself is said to have felled. The seeping stones seem to weep.

As you leave, stare into the eyes of those angels with swords and two right wings and think about all the "heroes" who keep dying "for God and country," at the request of the latter. A Mass closes off the entire front of the basilica (altar and tombs) to the public daily from 11:00 to 12:15. The resident boys' choir (the "White Voices"—Spain's answer to the Vienna Boys' Choir) generally sings during the Mass (you can sit through the service, but not sightsee during this time). The €2 audioguide is heavy on the theological message of the statues and tapestries and ignores Franco.

The expansive view from the monument's terrace includes the peaceful, forested valley and sometimes snow-streaked mountains. A small snack bar and picnic tables are near the parking lot and bus stop. Basic overnight lodging is available at the monastery behind the cross (100 rooms, D-€40, includes meals and a pass to enter and leave the park after hours, tel. 918-905-494, fax 918-961-542, NSE). A meditative night here is good mostly for monks.

For information on how to reach the Valley of the Fallen from El Escorial by bus, see "Transportation Connections—El Escorial," above.

SEGOVIA

Eighty kilometers (50 miles) from Madrid, this town of 55,000 boasts a great Roman aqueduct, a cathedral, and a castle. Segovia is a medieval "ship" ready for your inspection. Start at the stern—the aqueduct—and stroll up Calle de Cervantes to the prickly Gothic masts of the cathedral. Explore the tangle of narrow streets around the playful Plaza Mayor and then descend to the Alcázar at the bow. Since the city is over 900 meters (3,000 feet) above sea level and just northwest of a mountain range exposing it to the north, people from Madrid come here for a break from the summer heat.

Orientation

Tourist Information. Segovia has two tourist offices: one at Plaza del Azoguejo (at the base of the aqueduct, daily 10:00–20:00, tel. 921-462906 or 921-462-914, e-mail: segoviaturism @interbook.net) and one on Plaza Mayor that covers both Segovia and the region (at #10, Mon–Fri 9:00–15:00 & 17:00–19:00, Sat–Sun 10:00–14:00 & 17:00–20:00, tel. 921-460-334).

Arrival in Segovia: The train station is a 30-minute walk from the center. Take a city bus from the station to get to Calle de Colón, about 100 meters from Plaza Mayor (catch bus on the same side of the street as the station—confirm by asking, *"¿Para Plaza Mayor?"*; 2/hr, €0.70, pay driver). Taxis are a reasonable option (€4 to Plaza Mayor). If you arrive by bus, it's a 15-minute walk to the center (turn left out of the bus station and continue straight across the street, jog right and you're on Avenida de Fernandez Ladreda, which leads to the aqueduct). Day-trippers can store luggage at the train station (buy €3 tokens at ticket window), but not at the bus station. If arriving by car, see "Transportation Connections," below.

Helpful Hint: If you buy handicrafts such as tablecloths from street vendors, make sure the item you're buying is the one you actually get; some unscrupulous vendors substitute inferior goods at the last minute.

Sights—Segovia

▲**Roman Aqueduct**—Segovia was a Roman military base and needed water. So Emperor Trajan's engineers built a 15-kilometer-long (9-mile) aqueduct. The famous and exposed section of the 2,000-year-old *acueducto Romano* is 770 meters (2,500 feet) long and 30 meters (100 feet) high, has 118 arches, was made without any mortar, and can still carry a stream of water. On Plaza Azoguejo, a grand stairway leads from the base of the aqueduct to the top—offering close-up looks at the imposing work.

Cathedral—Segovia's cathedral (built 1525–1768, the third on this site) was Spain's last major Gothic building. Embellished to the hilt with pinnacles and flying buttresses, the exterior is a great example of the final, overripe stage of Gothic, called Flamboyant. The dark, spacious, and elegantly simple interior provides a delightful contrast (€2, free only on Sun 9:00–14:00; daily March–Oct 9:00–18:30, Nov–Feb 9:30–17:30). In the chapel to the immediate left of the entry, notice the dramatic gilded, wheeled "Carroza de la Custodia." The Holy Communion wafer is placed in the top of this temple-like cart and paraded through town each year during the Corpus Christi festival. The painting *Tree of Life*, by Ignacio Ries (as you enter, go right, to the last chapel—the painting is on the wall to the left of the altar), shows hedonistic mortals dancing atop the tree of life. As a skeletal Grim Reaper prepares to receive them into hell, Jesus rings a bell imploring them to wake up before it's too late. The peaceful cloister, opposite the cathedral entrance, contains a small museum (closed Sun 9:00–14:00).

▲**Alcázar**—Once a favorite summer residence and hunting palace of the monarchs of Castile, this castle burned in 1862. What you see today is rebuilt—a Disneyesque exaggeration of the original. It's still fun to explore the fine Moorish decor, historic furnishings, and grand Segovia view from its tower. After its stint as a palace, Alcázar was a prison for 200 years and then a Royal Artillery School. Since the fire, it's basically been a museum. As you wander, you'll see a big mural of Queen Isabella the Catholic being proclaimed Queen of Castile and Leon in Segovia's main square in 1474. The Hall of the Monarchs is lined with statues of all the rulers of Castile and Leon until Spain was unified. In the chapel, note the painting of St. James the Moorslayer—with Moorish heads literally rolling at his feet. He's the patron saint of Spain, and his name was the rallying cry in the centuries-long Christian crusade to push the Moors back into Africa. The well on the terrace marks the end of the 15-kilometer-long Roman aqueduct. From here you can enjoy such fine views as the mountain nicknamed "Mujer Muerta" (the dead woman—can you see why?).

Segovia

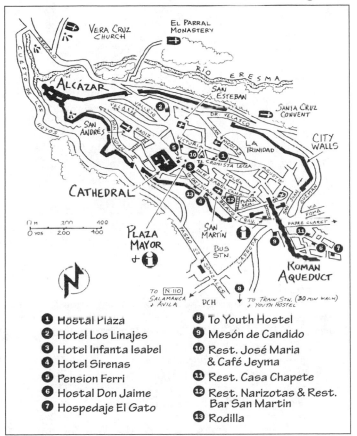

1 Hostal Plaza
2 Hotel Los Linajes
3 Hotel Infanta Isabel
4 Hotel Sirenas
5 Pension Ferri
6 Hostal Don Jaime
7 Hospedaje El Gato

8 To Youth Hostel
9 Mesón de Candido
10 Rest. José Maria & Café Jeyma
11 Rest. Casa Chapete
12 Rest. Narizotas & Rest. Bar San Martin
13 Rodilla

Tour guides like to say that Isabel first met Ferdinand at this castle and that Columbus came here to get his fantasy financed (€3.20, April–Sept daily 10:00–19:00, Oct–March until 18:00, audioguide-€3, get the free English leaflet, tel. 921-460-759).

Church of San Justo—This church, near the base of the aqueduct in the newer part of town, has well-preserved 12th- and 13th-century frescoes and a storks' nest atop its tower (free, Mon–Sat 11:00–13:30 & 17:00–19:00; in winter 11:00–13:45 & 16:00–19:00; closed Sun and when the caretaker, Rafael, needs to run an errand; near base of aqueduct, a couple of blocks from Plaza Azoguejo, in the newer side of town). Kind old Rafael may let you risk climbing the (dangerous) bell tower for "the best view of Segovia."

Historic Segovia Walk from the Main Square to the Aqueduct

This 15-minute walk is all downhill from the city's main square along the pedestrian-only street to the Roman aqueduct. It's most enjoyable just before dinner, when it's cool and filled with locals strolling.

Start on Segovia's inviting **Plaza Mayor**, once the scene of bullfights, with spectators jamming the balconies. In the 19th century the bullfights were stopped. When locals complained, they were given a more gentle form of entertainment—bands in the music kiosk. The Romanesque church opposite the city hall is where Isabel was proclaimed Queen of Castile in 1474. The symbol of Segovia is the aqueduct. Find it in the seals on the Theater Juan Bravo and atop the city hall. Head down Calle de Isabella Católica (downhill, to right of Hotel Infanta Isabel), tempting yourself with the local pastry in the window display of the corner bakery.

After 100 meters, at the first intersection, on the right you'll see the Corpus Christi Convent. You're welcome to pop in, knock on the window, ask the nun for the key (*La llave, por favor*; pron. lah YAH-vay, por fah-vor), and see the church, which was a synagogue, which was a mosque.

After another 100 meters, you come to the complicated Plaza de San Martin, a commotion of history centered around a striking statue of Juan Bravo. When Charles V, a Hapsburg who didn't even speak Spanish, took power, he moved to assert his rule over Castile. This threatened the local nobles, who—inspired and led by Juan Bravo—revolted in 1521. While Juan Bravo lost the battle and lost his head, he's still a symbol of Castilian pride. This statue was erected on the 400th anniversary of his death.

On the same square, the 12th-century Church of St. Martin is Segovian Romanesque in style (a mix of Christian Romanesque and Moorish styles). The 14th-century Tower of Lozoya, behind the statue, is one of many fortified towers that marked the homes of feuding local noble families. Clashing loyalties led to mini–civil wars (as in Italy with the families of Romeo and Juliet during the same age). In the 15th century, as Ferdinand and Isabel centralized authority in Spain, nobles were required to lop their towers. All over Segovia you'll see the stubby towers (once tall) of 15th-century noble mansions.

At the bottom of the square stands the bold and bulky House of Siglo XV. Its fortified style was typical of 15th-century Segovian houses. Later, in a more peaceful age, the boldness of these houses was softened with the decorative stucco work—Arabic-style floral and geometrical patterns—that you see today. At Plaza del Platero

Oquendo, 50 meters farther downhill, you'll see a similar house with a cropped tower.

At the next corner find the "house of a thousand pyramids" with another truncated tower. This building, maintaining its original Moorish design, has a wall just past the door, blocking your view from the street. This wall, the architectural equivalent of a veil, hid this home's fine courtyard—Moors didn't flaunt their wealth. Step inside to see art students at work and perhaps an exhibit on display.

From here, stroll 100 meters and you'll see the Roman aqueduct, which marks the end of this walk.

Sights—Near Segovia

Vera Cruz Church—This 12-sided 13th-century Romanesque church, built by the Knights Templar, once housed a piece of the "true cross" (€1.50, Tue–Sun 10:30–13:30 & 15:30–19:00, closed Mon and Nov, closes at 18:00 in winter, outside of town beyond the castle, a 20-min walk from main square, tel. 921-431-475). There's a postcard view of the city from here, and more views follow as you continue around Segovia on the small road below the castle, labeled *ruta turistica panoramica*.

▲**La Granja Palace**—This "Little Versailles," 10 kilometers south of Segovia, is much smaller and happier than El Escorial. The palace and gardens were built by the homesick French-born King Philip V, grandson of Louis XIV. It's a must for tapestry-lovers. Entry to the palace includes a required 45-minute guided tour, usually in Spanish (€4.80, June–Sept Tue–Sun 10:00–18:00, closed Mon; Oct–May Tue–Sat 10:00–13:30 & 15:00–17:00, Sun 10:00–14:00; tel. 921-470-019). Twelve buses a day (fewer on Sun) make the 20-minute trip from Segovia (catch at the bus station) to San Idlefonso la Granja. The park is free (daily 10:00–19:00).

Sleeping in Segovia
(€1 = about $1, country code: 34, zip code 40001)

Sleep Code: **S** = Single, **D** = Double/Twin, **T** = Triple, **Q** = Quad, **b** = bathroom, **s** = shower only, **CC** = Credit Cards accepted, **no CC** = Credit Cards not accepted, **SE** = Speaks English, **NSE** = No English.

To help you easily sort through these listings, I've divided the rooms into three categories, based on the price for a standard double room with bath during high season:

Higher Priced—Most rooms €85 or more.
Moderately Priced—Most less than €85.
Lower Priced—Most rooms less than €30.

The best places are on or near the central Plaza Mayor. This is where the city action is: the best bars, most touristic and *típico* eateries, and the TI. During busy times—on weekends and in July and August—arrive early or call ahead. The 7 percent IVA tax and breakfast aren't included. Buses from the station go to Plaza Mayor (near most of these recommended hotels).

In the Old Center near Plaza Mayor

HIGHER PRICED

Hotel Los Linajes is ultraclassy, with rusticity mixed into its newly-poured concrete. This poor man's parador is a few blocks beyond the Plaza Mayor, with territorial views and modern, air-conditioned niceties (Sb-€60, Db-€85, big Db-€110, Tb-€102, cheaper off-season, breakfast-€7, CC, elevator, parking-€10, Dr. Velasco 9, tel. 921-460-475, fax 921-460-479, e-mail: hotelloslinajes@terra.es). From Plaza Mayor, take Escuderos downhill; at the five-way intersection, angle right on Dr. Velasco. Drivers, follow brown hotel signs from the aqueduct to its tight but handy garage.

Hotel Infanta Isabel, right on Plaza Mayor, is the ritziest hotel in the old town, with 37 elegant rooms (big Sb-€62, Db-€84–98 depending on room size, some rooms with plaza views, 20 percent off in winter, CC, elevator, valet parking-€9, tel. 921-461-300, fax 921-462-217, www.hotelinfantaisabel.com, e-mail: hinfanta@teleline.es, SE).

MODERATELY PRICED

Hostal Plaza, just off Plaza Mayor, has a *serioso* management, snaky corridors, and faded bedspreads. But its 26 rooms are clean and cozy (S-€22, 1 Sb-€33, D-€30, Db-€37, Tb-€51, CC, parking, Cronista Lecea 11, tel. 92-146-0-303, fax 921-460-305).

The big, stuffy, hotelesque, but centrally located **Hotel Sirenas** rents comfortable rooms with a well-worn elegance (Sb-€47, Db-€50-60, CC, air con, elevator, 3 blocks down from Plaza Mayor at Calle Juan Bravo 30, tel. 921-462-663, fax 921-462-657, e-mail: hotelsirenas@terre.es, NSE).

LOWER PRICED

Pensión Ferri, half a block off Plaza Mayor, is a quiet, dumpy, five-room place cheaper than the youth hostel (S-€12, D-€19, shower-€2, no CC, Escuderos 10, half block off Plaza Mayor, tel. 921-460-957, NSE).

Outside of the Old Town, near the Aqueduct

MODERATELY PRICED

Hostal Don Jaime, near the base of the aqueduct, opposite the Church of San Justo, is shiny-new, clean, well maintained, and family-run (S-€22, D-€30, Db-€38, Tb-€48, Qb-€55, CC, Ochoa Ondategui 8; from TI at aqueduct, cross under the aqueduct, go right, angle left, then snake uphill for 2 blocks, tel. & fax 921-444-787, SE).

Hospedaje El Gato is another new, very clean, family-run place on the same quiet nondescript street just outside the old town; its 10 rooms are modern and comfortable (Sb-€20, Db-€32, Tb-€46, CC, air-con, bar serves breakfast and good tapas, uphill from Hostal Don Jaime and aqueduct at Plaza Salvador 10, tel. 921-423-244, fax 921-438-047, www.infosegovia .com/alojamiento/elgato, e-mail: elgato@tottel.com).

LOWER PRICED

The **Segovia Youth Hostel** is a great hostel—easygoing, comfortable, clean, friendly, very cheap—and open to members only (€13 beds, open July–Aug only, Paseo Conde de Sepulveda 4, between the train and bus stations, tel. 921-441-111).

Eating in Segovia

Eating Roast Suckling Pig

Look for Segovia's culinary claim to fame, roast suckling pig (*cochinillo asado:* 21 days of mother's milk, into the oven, and onto your plate—oh, Babe). It's worth a splurge here or in Toledo or Salamanca. While you're at it, try *sopa Castellana*— soup mixed with eggs, ham, garlic, and bread.

Mesón de Candido, one of the top restaurants in Castile, is famous as *the* place to spend €25 on a memorable dinner. Even filled with tourists, it's a grand experience. Take time to wander around and survey the photos of dignitaries who've suckled here (daily 13:00–16:30 & 20:00–23:00, Plaza Azoguejo 5, air-con, CC, under aqueduct, tel. 921-428-103 for reservations, gracious Alberto and family SE).

José Maria is the place to pig out in the old town (a block off Plaza Mayor). While it doesn't have the history or fanfare of Candido's, locals claim it serves the best roast suckling pig in town. Still, it's filled mostly with tourists (daily 13:00–16:00 & 20:00–23:30, CC, air-con, Cronista Lecea 11, tel. 921-466-017).

Restaurante Casa Chapete, a homey little place filled with smoke and happy locals and not a tourist in sight, serves the traditional lamb and pig dishes—but only for lunch (€15 3-course meals including wine, daily 12:00–16:00, 2 blocks beyond aqueduct, across from recommended Hostal Don Jaime at Calle Ochoa Ondategui 7, tel. 921-421-096).

Eating (No Pig) in the Old Center

Segovia's playful Plaza Mayor provides a great backdrop for a light lunch, dinner, or drink. Grab a table at the place of your choice and savor the scene. For me, **Café Jeyma** has the best setting and cathedral view. Survey their tapas selection at the bar. They'll happily make you an assorted plate of (*surtido de ...*) mini-pastries (*empanadillas*) and little sandwiches (*canapes*) for €6.

Narizotas serves more imaginative and non-Castilian alternatives to the gamey traditions. You'll dine outside on a delightful square or inside with modern art under medieval timbers. Their "Right Hand Left Hand" sampler menu (€27) provides a time-consuming but wonderful eating experience (daily 13:00–16:00 & 21:00–24:00, CC, midway down Calle Juan Bravo at Plaza de Medina del Campo 1, tel. 921-462-679).

Restaurante Bar San Martin is a no-frills place popular with locals, with a lively tapas bar, great outdoor seating on the same square by the fountain, and a smoky restaurant in the back. They can assemble a *surtido de canapes*—assorted plate of small sandwiches (€22 traditional menu ... with pig, daily 13:00–16:00 & 20:30–23:00, Plaza de San Martin 3, tel. 921-462-466).

Rodilla, the popular chain, offers a great assortment of cheap and tasty sandwiches and salads (long hours daily, on Calle Juan Bravo, at intersection with Calle de la Herreria).

Inexpensive bars and eateries line Calle de Infanta Isabel, just off Plaza Mayor. For nightlife, the bars on Plaza Mayor, Calle de Infanta Isabel, and Calle Isabel la Católica are packed. And there are a number of discos along the aqueduct.

An **outdoor produce market** thrives on Plaza de los Huertos (Thu 8:00–14:00). Nearby, a few stalls are open Monday through Saturday on Calle del Croista Ildefonso Rodriguez.

Transportation Connections—Segovia

By train to: Madrid (9/day, 2 hrs, both Chamartin and Atocha stations). If day-tripping from Madrid, look for the *cercanias* (commuter train) ticket window and departure board in either of Madrid's train stations. Pick up a return schedule here or from the Segovia TI. Train info: tel. 902-240-202.

By bus to: La Granja Palace (12/day, 20 min), **Ávila** (5/day but only 1 on weekends, 60 min), **Salamanca** (3/day, 3–4 hrs, transfer in Labajos; consider busing from Segovia to Ávila for a visit, then continuing to Salamanca by bus or train; tel. 921-427-705), **Madrid** (2/hour, 1.25 hrs, quicker than train, La Sepulvedana buses from Madrid's Larrea bus station, Metro: Príncipe Pío, just past Hotel Florida Norte at Paseo de la Florida 11, tel. 921-427-707).

By car: Leave Madrid on A6. Exit 39 gets you to Segovia ia a slow, winding route over the scenic mountain. Exit 60 (after a long €2 toll tunnel) gets you there quicker. At the Segovia aqueduct, turn into the old town (the side where the aqueduct adjoins the crenellated fortress walls).

Parking: You can park for free on the south side of Via Roma (runs east of aqueduct) and in the neighborhood directly south of Via Roma. Free parking is also available in the Alcázar's lot, but you must move your car out by 19:00, when the gates close. Outside of the old city, there's an Acueducto Parking underground garage kitty-corner from the bus station.

If you want to park near Plaza Mayor, be legal or risk an expensive ticket. Buy a ticket from the nearby machine to park in areas marked by blue stripes, and place the ticket on your dashboard (€0.25 for 30 min, 90-min maximum 9:00–20:00; free parking 20:00–9:00, Sat afternoon, and all day Sun).

Segovia to Salamanca (160 km): Leave Segovia by driving around the town's circular road, which offers good views from below the Alcázar. Then follow signs for Ávila (road N110). Notice the fine Segovia view from the three crosses at the crest of the first hill. The Salamanca road leads around the famous Ávila walls to the right. The best wall view is from the signposted Cuatro Postes, 1.5 kilometers northwest of town. Salamanca (N501) is clearly marked, about an hour's drive away.

About 30 kilometers before Salamanca, you might want to stop at the huge bull on the left of the road. There's a little dirt lane leading right up to it. As you get closer, it becomes more and more obvious it isn't real. Bad boys climb it for a goofy photo. For a great photo op of Salamanca, complete with river reflection, stop at the edge of the city (at the light before the first bridge).

In Salamanca, the only safe parking is in a garage; try the underground lot at Plaza Santa Eulalia.

ÁVILA

A popular side trip from Madrid, Ávila is famous for its perfectly preserved medieval walls, as the birthplace of St. Teresa, and for its yummy *yemas*. For over 300 years, Ávila was on the battlefront between the Muslims and Christians, changing hands several times. Today, perfectly peaceful Ávila's old town is charming. With several fine churches and monasteries, it makes for an enjoyable quick stop between Segovia and Salamanca (each about an hour away by car).

Tourist Information: The TI has fine free maps and organizes walking tours (facing the cathedral, tel. 920-211-387).

Arrival in Ávila: Approaching by bus, train, or car, you'll need to make your way through the nondescript modern part of town to find the walled old town. The bus and train stations are within a 15-minute walk of the cathedral and wall. By car, park as close as you can to the cathedral (road signs direct you to the nearby gate, Puerta de San Vicente).

On a quick stop, everything that matters is within a few blocks of the cathedral (actually part of east end of wall).

Sights—Ávila

▲**The Wall**—Built from around 1100, Ávila's fortified wall is the oldest, most complete, and best preserved in Spain. The only access is from gates on either side of the cathedral (€3.50, Tue–Sun 11:00–20:00, closed Mon). While it's fun to walk the walls, the open bits are about 300 meters on either side of the cathedral with no information or attempt to make them interesting and no exit possible other than returning to where you entered.

The best views are actually from street level (especially along the north side, which drivers will see as they circle to the right from Puerta de San Vicente to catch the highway to Salamanca). The best overall view of the walled town is about 1.5 kilometers away on the Salamanca road (N501) at a clearly marked turn-out for the Cuatro Postes (four posts).

Cathedral—While it started as Romanesque, Ávila's cathedral, finished in the 16th century, is considered the first Gothic cathedral in Spain. Its position—with its granite apse actually part of the fortified wall—underlines the "medieval alliance between cross and sword." You can view the nave from near the entry for free or pay a small fee to tour its sacristy, cloister, and museum (which includes an El Greco painting).

Convent of Saint Teresa—Built in the 17th century on the spot where the saint was born, this convent is a big hit with pilgrims (5-min walk from cathedral). A lavishly gilded side chapel marks the actual place of her birth and a room of relics connected to the shop (30 meters to the right of the church entrance) shows off Teresa's finger, complete with a fancy ring.

Yemas—These pastries, made by local nuns, are like a soft-boiled egg yolk cooled and sugared. They're sold all over town. The Las Delicias del Convento shop is actually a retail outlet for the cooks of the convent (10:00–14:00 & 16:30–20:30, a block from TI, at Calle Reyes Católicos 12, tel. 920-220-293).

Ávila

TO
SALAMANCA & **6**
VIA N-501

BASILICA OF
SAN VICENTE

TO
SEGOVIA
VIA N-501

AVENIDA DE MADRID

P

PLAZA
FUENTE
EL SOL

WALLS

BRIEVA

MÚSEN
RUBI
CHAPEL

LOPEZ NUNEZ

PLAZA
MERCADO
CHICO

EST. DOM.

DEL TOSTADO

CONDE VAL.

MARKET

1

TOMÁS

VICT.

2

i

REYES CATOLICOS

PUERTA
SAN VICENTE

PUERTA
PESO DE
LA HARINA

TO
TRAIN & BUS
STATIONS

SAN

LEAL.

PLAZA
ITALIA

LES QUINAS

FERR.

3

SE

GUNDO

CATHEDRAL

PUERTA
DEL
ALCAZAR

CONVENT
OF
SAINT TERESA

CVB.

PEPRO

PLA Y DEN.

DON GER.

PUERTA
DEL RASTRO

WALLS

4

7

5

N

PARQUE
DEL RASTRO

FRAN. GALLEGO

P

BCH

200 YARDS

200 METERS

1 Hotel Placio de los Velada

2 Hotel Continental

3 La Bodeguita de San Segundo

4 Yemas

5 Access point to wall

6 To Quatro Postes Viewpoint

7 St. Teresa's Finger

Sleeping and Eating in Ávila
(€1 = about $1, country code: 34)

Two hotels—one antique classy, the other antique cheap—face the cathedral. **Hotel Palacio de los Velada** is a centuries-old palace with 145 elegant rooms surrounding a huge and inviting arcaded courtyard (Db-€120, CC, air-con, elevator, Plaza de la Catedral 10, tel. 920-255-100, fax 920-254-900, e-mail: palaciov@ctv.es). **Hotel Continental** reeks of long-gone elegance with grand, musty public rooms and 57 basic bedrooms (S-€16, D-€26, Db-€35, CC, Plaza de la Catedral 4, tel. 920-211-502, fax 92-0211-563).

Eating: For a classy light lunch, **La Bodeguita de San Segundo** serves fine wine by the glass with sandwiches and tapas (along the outside of wall near cathedral at San Segundo 19, tel. 920-214-247).

Transportation Connections—Ávila

While there are no lockers at Ávila's bus station, you can leave
bags at the train station—a 10-minute walk away.

To: **Segovia** (3 buses/day, 45 min), **Madrid** (1 train/hr, 2 hrs,
more frequent connections with Chamartin station than Atocha; plus
8 buses/day, Larrea bus station in Madrid, Paseo de la Florida 11,
Metro: Príncipe Pío, tel. 921-427-707), **Salamanca** (4 trains/day,
2 hrs; 4 buses/day, 2 hrs). Train info: tel. 922-240-202.

SALAMANCA

This sunny sandstone city boasts Spain's grandest plaza, its
oldest university, and a fascinating history, all swaddled in a
strolling, college-town ambience. Salamanca—a youthful and
untouristy Toledo—is a series of monuments and clusters of
cloisters. The many students help keep prices down. Take a *paseo*
with the local crowd down Rua Mayor and through Plaza Mayor.
The young people congregate until late in the night, chanting
and cheering, talking and singing. When I asked a local woman
why young men all alone on the Plaza Mayor suddenly break
into song, she said, "Doesn't it happen where you live?"

Orientation

Tourist Information: The Turismo will relocate in 2003 but
will likely be on the Plaza Mayor (and open daily 9:30–17:30,
tel. 923-218-342). Pick up their free map, city brochure, and current list of museum hours. Summertime-only TIs also spring
up at the train and bus stations. There's little in the way of organized tourism for the English-speaking visitor. The small tourist
tram you'll see about town does 20-minute loops through the
city with a Spanish narration (€3, daily 10:00–14:00 &16:00–
20:00, leaves from new/old cathedrals).

Arrival in Salamanca: From Salamanca's train and bus
stations to Plaza Mayor, it's a 20-minute walk, an easy bus ride
(€0.65—pay driver), or a €4 trip by taxi. Day-trippers can store
bags in either station (€2).

From the train station: To walk to the center, exit left and
walk down to the ring road, cross it at Plaza España, then angle
slightly left up Calle Azafranal. Or you can take bus #1 from the
train station, which lets you off at Plaza Mercado (the market),
next to Plaza Mayor.

From the bus station: To walk to the center, exit right and
walk down Avenue Filiberto Villalobos; take a left on the ring
road and the first right on Ramon y Cajal. Or take bus #4 (exit
station right, catch bus on same side of the street as the station)
to the city center; the closest stop is on Gran Vía, about four

blocks from Plaza Mayor (ask the driver or a fellow passenger, "*¿Para Plaza Mayor?*").

Drivers will find a handy underground parking lot at Plaza Santa Eulalia (€0.75/hr, €9/day, open 24/7); some hotels give you a discount stamp on your parking receipt.

Helpful Hints

Internet Access: BBiGG is at Plaza de España 1 (daily 9:00–02:00, 150 terminals, tel. 923-250-063). **Cyberplace Internet** is on Plaza Mayor (daily 10:30–24:00, near TI at Plaza Mayor 10, 1st floor, tel. 923-264-281). The **Internet Bar,** down the alley under Plaza Mayor's clock tower, is also good (same hours). Perhaps your most appealing Internet access is at the laundry (see below).

Self-Service Laundry: It's a five-minute walk from Plaza Mayor (Mon–Fri 9:30–14:00 & 16:00–20:00, Sat 10:00–14:00, closed Sun, €6.50 for wash and dry, helpful attendant, Paseje Azafranal 18, located in passageway a half-block north of Plaza Santa Eulalia). Cleverly, it has about a dozen online computers (€1/30 min).

Travel Agency: Viajes Salamanca, which books flights, trains, and some buses, has two branches on Plaza Mayor at #11 and #24 (tel. 923-211-414 or 923-215-215, www.viajessalamanca.com).

Local Guide: Ines Criado Velasco, a good English-speaking guide, is happy to tailor a town walk to your interests (€60/2 hrs—a special rate for readers of this book, €75/3–5 hrs, €100/all day, for groups of 1–50, tel. 923-212-273, cellular 609-557-528, e-mail: icriado@interbook.net).

Sights—Salamanca

▲▲**Plaza Mayor**—Built in 1729, this ultimate Spanish plaza is a fine place to nurse a cup of coffee and watch the world go by. The town hall, with the clock, grandly overlooks the square. The Arch of the Toro (built into the eastern wall) leads to the covered market. While most European squares honor a king or saint, this square—ringed by famous Castilians—is for all the people. Look at the square niches above the colonnade surrounding the square for depictions of writers such as Cervantes, heroes and conquistadors such as Columbus and Cortez, and kings and dictators such as Franco. Plaza Mayor has long been Salamanca's community living room. Each day old-timers gather, remembering an earlier time when the girls would promenade clockwise around the colonnade while the boys would cruise counter-clockwise . . . looking for the perfect *queso* (cheese), as they'd call a cute dish. Perhaps the best time of all for people-watching is Sunday after Mass (13:00–15:00) when the grandmothers gather here in their Sunday best. (Notice that nearly any woman in her 70s is very short—a product of

Salamanca

trying to grow up during Spain's hungry and very difficult Civil War years.) Imagine the excitement of the days (until 1893), when bullfights were held in the square. How about coffee at the venerable Art Nouveau Café Novelty?

▲▲**Cathedrals, Old and New**—These cool-on-a-hot-day cathedrals share buttresses and are both richly ornamented. You get to the old through the new. Before entering the new church, check out its ornate front door (west portal). The facade is decorated Plateresque—Spain's version of Flamboyant Gothic. At the side door (on the next facade, around the corner to the left as you face the main entrance), look for the astronaut added by a capricious restorer in 1993. This caused an outrage in town, but now locals shrug their shoulders and say, "He's the person closest to God." I'll give you a chance to find him on your own. Otherwise, look at the end of this listing for him.

The "new" cathedral, built from 1513 to 1733, is a mix of Gothic, Renaissance, and Baroque (free and lackluster). The music (sometimes live) helps. The *coro*, or choir, blocks up half of the church, but its wood carving is sumptuous; look up to see the elaborate organ.

The entrance to the old cathedral (12th-century Romanesque) is near the rear of the new one (€3, free English leaflet, daily 10:00–13:30 & 16:00–19:30, closes at 12:30 and 17:30 in off-season; during Mass the old cathedral is free, but the cloister isn't). Sit in a front pew to study the altarpiece's 53 scenes from the lives of Mary and Jesus (by the Italian Florentino, 1445) surrounding a precious 12th-century statue of the Virgin of the Valley—Salamanca's patron virgin. High above, notice the dramatic Last Judgment fresco with Jesus sending condemned souls into the literal jaws of hell.

Then head into the cloister (off the right transept) and explore the chapels, notable for their unusual tombs, ornate altarpieces, and ceilings with leering faces. In the Capilla de Santa Barbara (second on the left as you enter) you can sit like students did when they were quizzed by a stern circle of professors for their final exam—feet nervously pressed against the well-worn feet of the tomb of the Salamanca bishop who founded the University around 1230. (The Salamanca University originated with a group of teacher/priests who met in this room.) Capilla San Bartolome de Los Anajas, the farthest from the cloister entrance, has a gorgeously carved 16th-century alabaster tomb (with the dog and lion making peace—or negotiating who gets to eat the worried-looking rabbit—at its foot) and a wooden 16th-century Mudejar organ (Mudejar is the Gothic-Islamic style of the Moors in Spain after the Christian conquest.) The museum, made up of three rooms on the main floor, is a gallery of 15th-century Castilian paintings.

Find that astronaut: He's just a little guy, about the size of a Ken-does-Mars doll, entwined in the stone trim to the left of the door, roughly three meters (10 feet) up. If you like that, check out the dragon (an arm's length below). Historians debate whether he's eating an ice cream cone or singing karaoke.

▲▲University—Salamanca University, the oldest in Spain (est. 1230), was one of Europe's leading centers of learning for 400 years. Columbus came here for travel tips. Today, while no longer so prestigious, it's laden with history and popular with Americans enjoying its excellent summer program. The old lecture halls around the cloister, where many of Spain's Golden Age heroes studied, are open to the public (€2.40, Mon–Sat 9:30–13:30 & 16:00–19:30, Sun 10:00–13:30, enter from Calle Libreros, tel. 923-294-400, ext. 1150). The ornately decorated grand entrance of the university is a great example of Spain's Plateresque style—masonry so intricate it looks like silverwork. The people studying the facade aren't art fans. They're trying to find a tiny frog on a skull that students looked to for good luck.

But forget the frog. Follow the facade's symbolic meaning. It was made in three sections by Charles V. The bottom celebrates the Catholic Monarchs. Ferdinand and Isabel saw that the university had no buildings befitting its prestige, and granted the money for this building. The Greek script says something like "From the monarchs, this university. From the university, this tribute as a thanks."

The immodest middle section celebrates the grandson of Ferdinand and Isabel, Charles V, appearing with his queen; the Hapsburg double-headed eagle; and the complex coat of arms of the mighty Hapsburg empire. Since this is a Renaissance structure, Greek and Roman figures are in the shells. And, as a statement of educational independence from medieval Church control, the top shows the pope flanked by Hercules and Venus.

After paying admission, you get a free English leaflet full of details; to follow it, go left (clockwise around the courtyard) upon entering.

In the Hall of Fray Luis de León, the narrow wooden beam tables and benches—whittled down by centuries of studious doodling—are originals. Professors spoke from the Church-threatening *catedra*, or pulpit. It was to here that free-thinking brother Luis de León returned, after the Inquisition jailed and tortured him for five years for challenging the Church's control of the word of God by translating part of the Bible into Castilian. He started his first post-imprisonment lecture with, "As we were saying...." Such courageous men of truth believed the forces of the Inquisition were not even worth acknowledging.

The altarpiece in the nearby chapel depicts professors swearing to Mary's virginity. (How did they know?) Climb upstairs for a peek into the oldest library in Spain. Outside the library, look into the courtyard at the American sequoia, brought here 150 years ago and standing all alone. Notice also the big nests in the bell tower. Storks stop here from February through August on their annual journey from northern Europe to Morocco. There are hundreds of such stork nests in Salamanca.

As you leave the university, you'll see the statue of Fray Luis de León. Behind him, to your left, is the entrance to a peaceful courtyard containing the Museum of the University, notable for Gallego's fanciful 16th-century *Sky of Salamanca* (included in university admission, no photos allowed in museum).

Still looking for the frog? It's on the right pillar of the facade, nearly half-way up, on the left-most of three skulls.

▲**Museo Art Nouveau y Art Deco**—Located in the Casa Lis, this museum—with its beautifully displayed collection of stained glass, jewelry, cancan statuettes, and toy dolls—is a refreshing change of pace. Nowhere else in Spain will you enjoy a modernist (or Art Nouveau) building filled with art and furnishings from that same age. The €0.30 English leaflet thoughtfully describes each part of the collection (€2, April–mid-Oct Tue–Fri 11:00–14:00 & 17:00–21:00, Sat–Sun 11:00–21:00; mid-Oct–March Tue–Fri 11:00–14:00 & 16:00–19:00, Sat–Sun 11:00–20:00, closed Mon, no photos, Calle Gibraltar 14, between the new/old cathedrals and the river, tel. 923-121-425, www.museocasalis.org).

Church of San Esteban—Dedicated to St. Stephen (Esteban) the martyr, this complex contains a cloister, tombs, museum, sacristy, and church. Tour it in this order: fancy facade outside, altarpiece in main nave, upstairs to sit in the choir, and finally a browse through the museum.

Before you enter, notice the Plateresque facade and its bas-relief of the stoning of St. Stephen. The crucifixion above is by Cellini. Once inside, follow the free English pamphlet. The nave is overwhelmed by a Churriguera altarpiece that replaced the original Gothic one in 1693. You'll see St. Francis on the left, Saint Dominic on the right, and a grand monstrance holding the Communion wafers in the middle, all below a painting of St. Stephen being stoned. This is a textbook example of the Churrigueresco style named after Jose Churriguera. Quietly ponder the dusty, gold-plated cottage cheese, as tourists retch and say "too much" in their mother tongue.

Upstairs step into the balcony choir loft for a fine overview of the nave and a rare opportunity to actually sit in the old wooden choir stalls. Go ahead, flip up the misericord, which allows old and tired Mass-goers to almost sit while they "stand." The big spinable book holder in the middle of the room held big music books—large enough for all to chant from in an age when there weren't enough books for everyone.

The museum next door has chilled glass cases preserving illustrated 16th-century Bibles and choir books. Notice also how the curved ivory Filipino saints all look like they're carved out of an elephant's tusk. And don't miss the fascinating "chocolate box reliquaries" on the wall from 1580. Survey whose bones are collected between all the inlaid ivory and precious woods (€1.20, daily 9:00–13:30 & 16:00–20:00, closed at 19:00 in winter).

Convento de las Dueñas—Next door, the much simpler *convento* is a joy. It consists of a double-decker cloister with a small museum of religious art. Check out the stone meanies exuberantly decorating the capitals on the cloister's upper deck (€1.50, daily 10:30–13:00 & 16:30–19:00, no English info). The nuns sell sweets daily except Sunday (€2.40/box, €0.60/small bag of cookies, no assortments possible even though their display box raises hopes).

Honorable Mention—Historians enjoy the low-slung Roman bridge, much of it original, spanning the Rio Tormes. The ancient pre-Roman headless bull (or boar) blindly guarding the entrance to the bridge is a symbol of the city. Nearby, at Parque Fluvial, you can rent rowboats.

▲**Tuna Music**—Traditionally, Salamanca's poorer students earned money to fund their education by singing in the streets. This 15th- to 18th-century tradition survives today as musical groups of students (representing the various faculties), dressed in the traditional black capes and leggings, play mandolins, guitars, and sing, serenading the public in the bars on and around the Plaza Mayor. They're out on weeknights (singing for tips from 22:00 until after midnight) because they make more serious money performing for weddings on weekends.

Sleeping in Salamanca
(€1 = about $1, country code: 34)
Sleep Code: **S** = Single, **D** = Double/Twin, **T** = Triple, **Q** = Quad, **b** = bathroom, **s** = shower only, **CC** = Credit Cards accepted, **no CC** = Credit Cards not accepted, **SE** = Speaks English, **NSE** = No English.

To help you easily sort through these listings, I've divided the rooms into three categories, based on the price for a standard double room with bath during high season:

Higher Priced—Most rooms €70 or more.
Moderately Priced—-Most less than €70.
Lower Priced—Most rooms less than €40.

Salamanca, being a student town, has plenty of good eating and sleeping values, and now, even a self-service laundry (see "Helpful Hints," above). All but one of my listings are on or within a three-minute walk of the Plaza Mayor. Directions are given from the Plaza Mayor, assuming you are facing the building with the clock (e.g., 3 o'clock is 90 degrees to your right as you face the clock). The 7 percent IVA tax generally is not included.

HIGHER PRICED
Hotel Las Torres, on Plaza Mayor, is a business-class place with 44 modern, spacious rooms and all the amenities. Its rooms with Plaza Mayor views cost the same as viewless rooms (Sb-€60, Db-€80, 30 percent more in Sept–Oct, tax extra, CC, air-con, elevator, skip their breakfast but enjoy their cafeteria, entry just off square at Consejo 4, Plaza Mayor 26, exit the plaza at 11 o'clock, 37002 Salamanca, tel. 923-212-100, fax 923-212-101, www .mmteam.com/lastorres, e-mail: lastorres@mmteam.com, SE).

Hotel Don Juan, a block off Plaza Mayor, has 16 classy,

Central Salamanca

⊤ = TAXI STAND

CLOCK TOWER

TO TRAIN STN.

TO ⑭

TORO

⑧

⑩
⑪

POZO AMARILLO

CORRE.

TO ⑤

①

⑨

⑪

PLAZA MAYOR

⑥

⑫

T.I.

⊤

PLAZA MERCADO

BERME.

TO BUS STN.

④

⊤

PLAZA POETA

BUS TO STN.

②

PLAZA ANGEL

③

N

TO ⑦

PLAZA PESO

NOT TO SCALE

SANCHEZ BARBERO

MAYOR

TO UNIVERSITY

DCH

❶ Hotel Las Torres
❷ Hotel Don Juan
❸ Hotel Salamanca Plaza
❹ Hotel Plaza Major
❺ To La Petit Hotel and
   La Fonda Casa de Comidas
❻ Hostal Los Angeles
❼ To Las Vegas Pension

❽ Rest. Chez Victor
❾ Café Novelty
❿ Rest. Isidoro
⓫ Rest. Dulcinea
⓬ Cervantes Bar
⓭ Café Real
⓮ To Coin Laundry
   Internet

comfy rooms and an attached restaurant (Sb-€55, Db-€74, Tb-€98, cheaper in Jan–Feb, CC, air-con, elevator, valet parking-€9/day, exit Plaza Mayor at about 5 o'clock and turn right to Quintana 6, 37001 Salamanca; tel. 923-261-473, fax 923-262-475, e-mail: hoteldonjuan@wanadoo.es, David SE).

Hotel Salamanca Plaza, which just opened in 2002, is a business-class hotel renting 38 bright, shiny modern rooms across the street from the covered market (Sb-€49, Db-€88, Tb/Qb-€125, CC, air-con, elevator, parking-€9, Plaza del Mercado 16, tel. 923-272-250, fax 923-270-932, www.salamancaplaza.com, e-mail: reservas@salamancaplaza.com, SE).

MODERATELY PRICED

Hostal Plaza Mayor has 19 small but welcoming rooms and a good location a block southwest of Plaza Mayor (Sb-€36, Db-€60, Tb-€90, CC, air-con, elevator, exit Plaza Mayor at 7 o'clock, Plaza del Corrillo 20, attached restaurant, tel. 923-262-020, fax 923-217-548).

Le Petit Hotel, while away from the characteristic core, is well located, facing a peaceful, well-tended park and a grand church just down the street from the police station (2 blocks east of Gran Vía). It rents 21 homey yet modern rooms. The rooms with views of the church are particularly bright; ask for a *vista de iglesias* (Sb-€34, Db-€41, Tb/Qb-€55, breakfast-€3, no CC, air-con, elevator, Ronda Sancti-Spiritus 39, about 6 blocks east of Plaza Mayor; exit Plaza Mayor at 3 o'clock and continue east, turn left on Gran Vía, right on Sancti Spiritus, and left after the church; tel. 923-600-773 or 923-600-774, no fax or e-mail, reserve by simply calling and leaving your name and time of arrival—no more than a month in advance, Hortensia NSE).

LOWER PRICED

Hostal Los Angeles, at about three o'clock, rents 11 simple but cared-for rooms, four of which overlook the square. Stand on the balcony and inhale the essence of Spain (S-€13, D-€25, Db-€36, T-€13, Tb-€42, Qb-€51, view rooms have full bathrooms, includes tax, Plaza Mayor 10, 37002 Salamanca, tel. & fax 923-218-166). To try for a view, request, *"Con vista, por favor."*

Las Vegas Pension—clean, bright, quiet, and cheap—is a cozy 12-room place run by a friendly mother-daughter team, Marisol and Immaculada (small S-€12, big S-€18, old Db-€24, new Db-€36, Tb-€42, CC, 2 blocks off Plaza Mayor, toward the cathedral at Melendez 13, first floor, tel. 923-218-749, e-mail: lasvegas@iponet.es, SE).

Eating in Salamanca

Dining Well

Restaurante Chez Victor is the result of the marriage of a French chef (Victor) and a Castilian food lover (Margarite). This family-run place, elegantly decorated with a feminine French touch and bouquets on the tables, serves modern and creative Franco/Castilian fare—perhaps your best €30 meal in town (Tue–Sat 14:00–16:00 & 21:00–23:30, Sun 14:00–16:00, closed Mon and Sun eve, CC, air-con, Espoz y Mina 26, tel. 923-213-123).

La Fonda Casa de Comidas is a dark, woody place with solid traditional cuisine, catering to locals, where you'll happily spend €20 for three courses (daily 13:45–16:30 & 21:00–23:30, a bit smoky, reserve on weekends, 30 meters down the arcade from corner of Gran Vía and Cuesta de Sancti Spiritus at La Reja 2, tel. 923-215-712.

Eating on Plaza Mayor

At **Café Real** or **Cervantes Bar,** enjoy a meal sitting on the finest square in Spain, savoring some of Europe's best people-watching. These bars, with little tables spilling onto the square, serve *raciones* and €2 glasses of wine. A *ración de la casa* (house specialty of hams, sausages, and cheese), a *ración* of *patatas bravas* (chunks of potatoes with tomato sauce), and two glasses of wine makes a nice dinner for two for about €23—one of the best eating values in all of Europe. (For dessert: Stroll with an ice cream cone from Café Novelty.) The interior of the Cervantes Bar, overlooking Plaza Mayor from one floor up, is a popular and characteristic student hangout serving tapas, salads, and meals (tapas served 10:00–13:30 & 19:00–21:00, meals only after 13:30 and 21:00, go up the stairs).

Café Novelty is Plaza Mayor's Art Nouveau cafe—dating from 1905, filled with character and literary memories (daily 8:00–24:00). Their ice cream sweetens a stroll around the plaza.

Eating Simple or Tapas

There are plenty of good, inexpensive restaurants between Plaza Mayor and Gran Vía, and as you leave the Plaza Mayor toward Rua Mayor. *Tostón* is the local term for the roast suckling pig. *Sopa de aja* is the local garlic soup. The tapas places along and around Rua Mayor are abundant and often overrun with students.

Restaurante Isidro is a thriving local favorite—a straightforward, hard-working local eatery with a good assortment of seafood and meat dishes (menu of the day-€8.50, Mon–Sat 13:00–16:00 & 20:00–24:00, Sun 13:00–16:00, CC, has seating in its *comedor*, Pozo Amarillo 19, about a block north of covered market, near Plaza Mayor, tel. 923-262-848).

Restaurante Dulcinea, on the same street, is a classier version of the Isidro with basic home-cooking in a bright dining room (no-stress menus of the day-€9 and €17, daily 13:00–16:00 & 20:00–24:00, Pozo Amarillo 5, tel. 923-217-843).

The **Rodilla** and **Pan & Company** sandwich chains are always fast and affordable. Pan & Company has a branch on Calle Prior across from Burger King and another on Rua Mayor (daily 10:00–24:00).

Picnics: The covered *mercado* (market) on Plaza Mercado has fresh fruits and veggies (Mon–Sat 8:00–14:30, closed Sun, on east side of Plaza Mayor). A small Consum grocery, three blocks east of Plaza Mayor, has just the basics (Mon–Sat 9:00–14:00 and

17:00–20:00, closed Sun). For variety, the big Champion Super-mercado is your best bet, but it's a six-block walk north of Plaza Mayor on Toro (Mon–Sat 9:15–21:15, closed Sun, across from Plaza San Juan de Sahagun and its church).

If you always wanted seconds at Communion, buy a bag of giant Communion wafers, a local specialty called *obleas*.

Transportation Connections—Salamanca

By train to: Madrid (3/day, 2.5 hrs, Chamartin station), **Ávila** (3/day, 1 hr), **Barcelona** (1/day, 8:00 departure, 10 hrs), **Coimbra** (1/day, 5 hrs, departs Salamanca station at about 4:38 in the morn-ing, no kidding; you can catch a taxi to the train station at any hour from Plaza Mercado—a few steps east of Plaza Mayor—and from Plaza Poeta Iglesias, which is across from the Gran Hotel, immedi-ately south of Plaza Mayor, €4 during day, €5 at night; for a bus option to Coimbra, see below.) Train info: tel. 902-240-202.

By bus to: Madrid (hrly, 2.5 hrs), **Segovia** (2/day, 4 hrs, transfer in Labajos or Ávila; consider a brief visit to Ávila en route), **Ávila** (4/day, 1.5 hrs), **Ciudad Rodrigo** (nearly hrly, 1 hr), **Barcelona** (2/day, 11 hrs), **Coimbra** (4/week, on Mon, Fri, Sat, and Sun, departs at 15:00, 4 hrs, €20, Alsa company, tel. 902-422-242,www.alsa.es). Bus info: tel. 923-236-717.

CIUDAD RODRIGO

Ciudad Rodrigo is worth a visit only if you're traveling from Salamanca to Coimbra (although buses connect Salamanca and Ciudad Rodrigo with surprising efficiency in about an hour).

This rough-and-tumble old town of 16,000 people caps a hill overlooking the Río Agueda. Spend an hour wandering among the Renaissance mansions that line its streets and exploring its cathedral and Plaza Mayor. Have lunch or a snack at El Sanatorio (Plaza Mayor 14). The tapas are cheap, the crowd is local, and the walls are a Ciudad Rodrigo scrapbook, including some bullfighting that makes the Three Stooges look demure.

Ciudad Rodrigo's cathedral—pockmarked with scars from Napoleonic cannon balls—has some entertaining carvings in the choir and some pretty racy work in its cloisters. Who says, "When you've seen one Gothic church, you've seen 'em all"?

The TI (2 blocks from Plaza Mayor, tel. 923-460-561) is just inside the old wall near the cathedral and can recommend a good hotel, such as Hotel Conde Rodrigo (34 rooms, Sb-€41, Db-€47, Tb-€63, CC, air-con, Plaza de Amayuelar 5, tel. 923-461-404, e-mail: h_c_rodrigo@ntserver.codeinf.com, SE).

TOLEDO

An hour south of Madrid, Toledo teems with tourists, souvenirs, and great art by day, delicious roast suckling pig, echoes of El Greco, and medieval magic by night. Incredibly well preserved and full of cultural wonder, the entire city has been declared a national monument.

Spain's historic capital is 2,000 years of tangled history—Roman, Visigothic, Moorish, and Christian—crowded onto a high, rocky perch protected on three sides by the Tajo (Tagus) River. It's so well preserved that the Spanish government has forbidden any modern exteriors. The rich mix of Jewish, Moorish, and Christian heritages makes it one of Europe's art capitals.

Perched strategically in the center of Iberia, Toledo was for centuries a Roman transportation hub with a thriving Jewish population. The city was a Visigothic capital back in 554 and—after a period of Moorish rule—Spain's political capital until 1561, when it reached its natural limits of growth as defined by the Tajo River Gorge. During its Golden Age, Toledo was famous for intellectual tolerance—a city for the humanities, where God was known by many names. When the king moved to more spacious Madrid, Toledo was mothballed, only to be rediscovered by 19th-century Romantic travelers who wrote of it as a mystical place.

Today Toledo thrives as a provincial capital and a busy tourist attraction. It remains the historic, artistic, and spiritual center of Spain. In spite of tremendous tourist crowds, Toledo sits enthroned on its history, much as it was when Europe's most powerful king and El Greco called it home.

Planning Your Time

To properly see Toledo's museums (great El Greco), cathedral (best in Spain), and medieval atmosphere (best after dark), you'll

Toledo

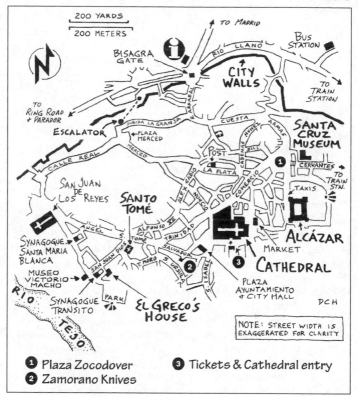

❶ Plaza Zocodover   ❸ Tickets & Cathedral entry
❷ Zamorano Knives

need two nights and a day. Plan carefully for lunch closings and note that a few sights are closed Monday.

Toledo is just 60 minutes away from Madrid by bus (2/hr), train (10/day), or taxi (about €65 one-way from Puerta del Sol— negotiate ride without a meter). A car is useless in Toledo. Ideally, see the town outside of car-rental time (pick up or drop your car here—Hertz is at train station, tel. 925-253-890, Avis is on Calle Armac below main square, tel. 925-214-535).

Orientation

Lassoed into a tight tangle of streets by the sharp bend of the Tajo River (called the Tejo where it hits the Atlantic, in Lisbon), Toledo has Spain's most confusing medieval street plan. But it's a small town of 65,000, the major sights are well signposted, and most locals will politely point you in the right direction.

El Greco's Art

Born on Crete and trained in Venice, Domenikos Theoto-copoulos (tongue-tied friends just called him "The Greek") came to Spain to get a job decorating El Escorial. He failed there but succeeded in Toledo, where he spent the last 37 years of his life. He mixed all three regional influences into his palette. From his Greek homeland, he absorbed the solemn, abstract style of icons. In Venice he learned the bold use of color and dramatic style of the later Renaissance. These styles were then fused in the fires of fanatic Spanish-Catholic devotion.

Not bound by the realism so important to his 16th-century contemporaries, El Greco painted dramatic visions of striking colors and figures—bodies unnatural and elongated as though stretched between heaven and earth. He painted souls, not faces. His work is on display at nearly every sight in Toledo. Thoroughly modern in his disregard of realism, he didn't impress the austere Spanish king. But his art seems as fresh as contemporary art today.

If driving into town, enjoy a scenic big-picture orientation by following the Ronda de Toledo signs on a big circular drive around the city. The best time for this is the magic hour before sunset when the top viewpoints are busy with tired old folks and frisky young lovers.

Look at the map and take a mental orientation-walk past Toledo's main sights. Starting in the central Plaza Zocódover, go southwest along the Calle Comercio. After passing the cathedral on your left, follow the signs to Santo Tomé and the cluster of other sights. The visitor's city lies basically along one small but central street—and most tourists never stray from this axis. Make a point to get lost. It's a small town, bounded on three sides by the river. When it's time to get somewhere, I pull out the map or ask, "*¿Dónde está Plaza Zocódover?*"

Tourist Information

Toledo has two TIs. The one that covers Toledo as well as the region is in a small, free-standing brick building just outside the Bisagra Gate (the last surviving gate of the 10th-century fortifications), where those arriving by train or bus enter the old town (Mon–Fri 9:00–18:00, Sat 9:00–19:00, Sun 9:00–15:00, longer hours in summer, tel. 925-220-843). The second TI is in front of the cathedral on Plaza Ayuntamiento (Mon 10:30–14:30, Tue–Sun 10:30–14:30 & 16:30–19:00, tel. 925-254-030). Consider the readable local guidebook, *Toledo, Its Art and Its History* (small version for €6, sold all over town). It explains all of the sights (which generally provide no on-site information) and gives you a photo to point at and say, *"¿Dónde está . . . ?"*

Arrival in Toledo

"Arriving" in Toledo means getting uphill to Plaza Zocódover. From the **train station,** that's a 20-minute hike, €3 taxi ride, or easy bus ride (#5 or #6, €0.80, pay on bus, confirm by asking, *"¿Para Plaza Zocódover?"*). You can stow extra baggage in the station's lockers (buy tokens at ticket booth). Consider buying a city map at the kiosk; it's better than the free one at the TI. If you're walking, turn right as you leave the station, cross the bridge, pass the bus station, go straight through the roundabout, and continue uphill to the TI and Bisagra Gate.

If you arrive by **bus,** go upstairs to the station lobby. You'll find lockers and a small bus-information office near the lockers and opposite the cafeteria. Confirm your departure time (probably every half hour on the hour to Madrid). When you buy your return ticket to Madrid—which you can put off until just minutes before you leave—specify you'd like a *directo* bus; the *ruta* trip takes longer (60 min vs. 75). From the bus station, Plaza Zocódover is a 15-minute walk (see directions from train station, above), €2.50 taxi ride, or short bus ride (catch #5 downstairs, underneath the lobby, €0.80, pay driver).

A new series of escalators runs near the Bisagra Gate, giving you a free ride up, up, up into town (daily 8:00–22:00). You'll end up near the synagogues and far from Plaza Zocódover (but this doesn't matter). It's great for drivers, who can park free in the streets near the base of the escalator or for a fee (€12/day) in the parking lot across from it. Toledo is no fun to drive in. If you don't park near the escalator, drive into town and park in the Garage Alcázar (opposite the Alcázar in the old town— €1.20/hr, €12/day).

Sights—Toledo

▲▲▲**Cathedral**—Holy Toledo! Spain's leading Catholic city has a magnificent cathedral. Shoehorned into the old center, its exterior is hard to appreciate. But the interior is so lofty, rich, and vast that it'll have you wandering around like a Pez dispenser stuck open, whispering "Wow."

Cost and Hours: While the basic cathedral is free, seeing the great art—located in four separate places within the cathedral

Toledo Cathedral

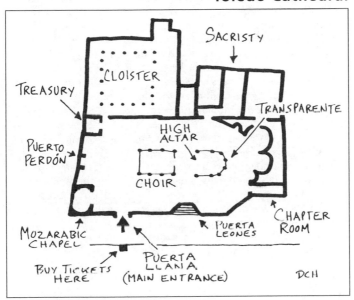

SACRISTY

CLOISTER

TREASURY

TRANSPARENTE

HIGH ALTAR

PUERTO PERDÓN

CHOIR

CHAPTER ROOM

MOZARABIC CHAPEL

PUERTA LEONES

BUY TICKETS HERE

PUERTA LLANA (MAIN ENTRANCE)

DCH

(the choir, chapter house, sacristy, and treasury)—requires a €4.80 ticket sold in the Tienda la Catedral shop opposite the church entrance (shop open Mon–Sat 10:30–18:30, Sun 14:00–18:00; also rents audioguides for €3). The strict dress-code sign covers even your attitude: no shorts, no tank tops...and no slouching.

The cathedral itself is free and open to the public daily (10:30–12:00 & 16:00–18:00, no WC in cathedral or cathedral shop). The four sights inside are open 10:30–18:00. Even though the cathedral closes from 12:00 to 16:00, if you have a ticket you can get in and tour the cathedral as well, with fewer crowds. (Note that the cloister is closed to everyone 13:00–15:30.)

Self-Guided Tour: Holy redwood forest, Batman! Wander among the pillars. Sit under one and imagine a time when the light bulbs were candles and the tourists were pilgrims—before the No Photo signs, when every window provided spiritual as well as physical light. The cathedral is primarily Gothic, but since it took over 200 years to build (1226–1495), you'll see a mix of styles—Gothic, Renaissance, and Baroque. Enjoy the elaborate wrought-iron work, lavish wood carvings, window after colorful window of 500-year-old stained glass, and a sacristy with a collection of paintings that would put any museum on the map.

This confusing collage of great Spanish art deserves a close look. Hire a private guide, freeload on a tour (they come by every few minutes during peak season), or follow this quick tour. Here's a framework for your visit:

High Altar: First, walk to the high altar to marvel through the iron grille at one of the most stunning altars in Spain. Real gold on pine wood, by Flemish, French, and local artists, it's one of the country's best pieces of Gothic art. About-face to...

Choir: Facing the high altar, the choir is famous for its fine carving and requires a piece of your four-part ticket. The lower wooden stalls are decorated with scenes celebrating the slow one-city-at-a-time Christian victory as the Muslims were pushed back into Africa. Each idealized castle has the reconquered town's name on it, culminating with the final victory at Granada in 1492. The upper stalls (which flank the grand throne of the archbishop) feature Old Testament figures carved out of alabaster. And, as is typical of choir decoration, the carvings on the misericords (the tiny seats allowing tired worshippers to lean while they "stand") feature the frisky, folksy, sexy, profane art of the day. Apparently, since you sat on it, it could never be sacred anyway. There are two fine pipe organs: one 18th-century Baroque and the other 19th-century neoclassical. Note the serene beauty of the 13th-century Madonna and Child at the front, thought to be a gift from the French king to Spain.

The iron grille of the choir is notable for the dedication of the man who built it. Domingo de Cespedes, a Toledo ironworker, accepted the commission to build the grille for 6,000 ducats. The project, which took from 1541 to 1548, was far more costly than he anticipated. The medieval Church didn't accept cost overruns, so to finish it, he sold everything he owned and went into debt. He died a poor—but honorable—man.

Chapter House: Face the altar and go around it to your right to the chapter house (*sala capitular*). Its lavish ceiling celebrates Italian Renaissance humanism with a ground-breaking fresco. You're surrounded by interesting Bible-storytelling frescoes and a pictorial review of 1,900 years of Toledo archbishops. Though the upper row of portraits were not painted from life, the lower portraits were, and therefore are of more historic and artistic interest. Imagine sitting down to church business surrounded by all this tradition and theology. As you leave, notice the iron-pumping cupids carved into the pear tree panels lining the walls.

The *transparente*, behind the high altar, is a unique feature of the cathedral. In the 1700s a hole was cut into the ceiling to let a sunbeam brighten the Mass. Melding this big hole into the Gothic church presented a challenge that resulted in a Baroque masterpiece. Gape up at this riot of angels doing flip-flops, babies breathing thin air, bottoms of feet, and gilded sunbursts. Study the altar, which looks chaotic but is actually thoughtfully structured: the good news of salvation springs from baby Jesus, up past the angel (who knows how to hold a big fish correctly), to the Last Supper high above, and beyond into the light-filled dome. I like it, as did, I guess, the long-dead cardinal whose faded red hat hangs from the edge of the hole. (A perk that only cardinals enjoy is choosing the place in the cathedral where their hat will hang until it rots.)

Sacristy: The cathedral's sacristy has 20 El Grecos as well as masterpieces by Goya, Titian, Rubens, Velázquez, Caravaggio, and Bellini. First, notice the fine perspective work on the 18th-century ceiling (frescoed by Lucca Giordano from Naples). Then walk to the end of the room for the most important painting in the collection. El Greco's first masterpiece, from 1579, *The Spoliation* (a.k.a. *The Denuding of Christ*) hangs above the marble altar. This was one of El Greco's first Toledo commissions after arriving from Venice. Notice the parallel contrasts: Jesus' delicate hand before a flaming red tunic and Jesus' noble face among the sinister mob. On the right is a rare religious painting by Goya, the *Betrayal of Christ*, which shows Judas preparing to kiss Jesus, identifying him to the Roman soldiers. Enjoy the many other El Grecos. Find the small but lifelike 17th-century carving of St. Francis by Pedro de Mena (to your right as you entered the door).

Treasury: The *tesoro* has plenty to see. The highlight is the three-meter-high, 430-pound monstrance—the tower designed to hold the Holy Communion bread (the Host) during the festival of Corpus Christi (body of Christ) as it parades through the city. Built in 1517 by a man named Arfe, it's made of 5,000 individual pieces held together by 12,500 screws. There are diamonds, emeralds, rubies, and 400 pounds of gold-plated silver. The inner part is 35 pounds of solid gold. Yeow. The base is a later addition from the Baroque period. Traditionally, it's thought that much of this gold and silver arrived in Columbus' first load home. To the right of the monstrance find the fancy sword of Franco. To the right of that is a gift from St. Louis, the king of France—a 700-year-old Bible printed and beautifully illustrated by French monks. (It's actually a copy, and the precious original is stored elsewhere.) Imagine the exquisite experience for medieval eyes of reading this, with its lavish illustrations. The finely painted small crucifix on the opposite side—by the great Gothic Florentine painter Fra Angelico—depicts Jesus alive on the back and dead on the front. This was a gift from Mussolini to Franco. Hmmm. There's even a gift in this room from Toledo's sister city, Toledo, Ohio.

If you're at the cathedral between 9:00 and 9:15, you can peek into the otherwise-locked **Mozarabic Chapel** *(Capilla Mozarabe).*

The Visigothic Mass, the oldest surviving Christian ritual in Western Europe, starts at 9:15 (9:45 on Sun). You're welcome to partake in this stirring example of peaceful coexistence of faiths—but once the door closes, you're a Visigoth for 30 minutes.

▲▲Santa Cruz Museum—For years, this museum has been in a confused state of renovation—not really open, not really closed. During renovation, the museum's cloister and a room full of its best art will be open and free. If the core of the building is filled with a temporary exhibit, you can generally wander in for a free look. The building's Plateresque facade is worth seeing anytime.

This great Renaissance building was an orphanage and hospital, built from money left by the humanist and diplomat Cardinal Mendoza when he died in 1495. The cardinal, confirmed as Chancellor of Castile by Queen Isabel, was so influential he was called "the third king." The building is in the form of a Greek cross under a Moorish dome. After renovation, the arms of the building—formerly wards—will be filled with 16th-century art, tapestries, furniture, armor, and documents. It'll be a stately, classical, music-filled setting with a cruel lack of English information (Mon–Sat 10:00–18:30, Sun 10:00–14:00, just off Plaza Zocódover, go through arch, Cervantes 3).

The collection includes 15 El Grecos. The highlight: the impressive *Assumption of Mary*—a spiritual poem on canvas (notice old Toledo on the bottom). Painted one year before El Greco's death in 1614, this is considered the culmination of his artistic development.

Find the lavish but faded Astrolabe Tapestry (c. 1480, Belgian) which shows a new world view at the dawn of the Renaissance and the age of discovery: God oversees all, as Atlas spins the Cosmos containing the circular Earth, and the wisdom gang (far right) heralds the new age.

An enormous blue banner hangs like a long, skinny tooth opposite the entry. This flew from the flagship of Don Juan of Austria and recalls the pivotal naval victory over the Muslims at the Battle of Lepanto in 1571 off the coast of Greece. Lepanto was a key victory in the centuries-long struggle of Christian Europe against the Muslim threat.

▲Alcázar—This huge former imperial residence—built on the site of Roman, Visigothic, and Moorish fortresses—dominates the Toledo skyline. The Alcázar became a kind of right-wing Alamo during Spain's civil war when a force of Franco's Nationalists (and hundreds of hostages) were besieged for two months. Finally, after many fierce but futile Republican attacks, Franco sent in an army that took Toledo and freed the Alcázar. The place was rebuilt and glorified under Franco. Today it's an army museum with civil war exhibits giving you an interesting—and right-wing—look at the horrors of Spain's recent past (€1.20, Tue–Sun 9:30–14:30, closed Mon).

▲**Tourist Train**—For great city views, hop on the cheesy Tren Imperial Tourist Tram. Crass as it feels, you get a 50-minute putt-putt through Toledo and around the Tajo River Gorge. It's a great way to get a general city overview and for non-drivers to enjoy views of the city from across the Tajo Gorge (€3.60, buy ticket from driver, daily from 11:00, leaves Plaza Zocódover on the hour, tape-recorded English/Spanish commentary, no photo stops but it goes slow; for the best views of Toledo across the gorge, sit on right side, not behind driver; tel. 925-142-274).

Sights—Southwest Toledo

▲**Santo Tomé**—A simple chapel holds El Greco's most-loved painting. *The Burial of the Count of Orgaz* couples heaven and earth in a way only The Greek could. It feels so right to see a painting left in situ where the artist put it 400 years ago. Take this slow. Stay a while—let it perform. The year is 1323. You're at the burial of the good count. After a pious and generous life, he left his estate to the Church. Saints Augustine and Steven have even come down for the burial—to usher the good count directly to heaven. "Such is the reward for those who serve God and his saints."

More than 250 years later, in 1586, a priest hired El Greco to make a painting of the burial to hang over the count's tomb. The painting has two halves divided by a serene line of noble faces. The physical world ends with the line of nobles. Above them a spiritual wind blows, as colors change and shapes stretch. Notice the angel, robe caught up in that wind, "birthing" the soul of the count through the neck of a celestial womb into Heaven—the soul abandoning the physical body to join Christ the Judge. Mary and John the Baptist both intervene on behalf of the arriving soul. This is Counter-Reformation propaganda—notice Jesus pointing to St. Peter who controls the keys to the pearly gates. Each face is a detailed portrait. El Greco himself (eyeballing you, 7th figure in from the left) is the only one not involved in the burial. The boy in the foreground—pointing to the two saints as if to say, "One's from the first century, the other's from the fourth… it's a miracle!"—is El Greco's son (€1.20, daily 10:00–18:45, until 17:45 off-season, free audioguide, tel. 925-256-098).

Museo El Greco and "El Greco's House"—Along with a replica of a house like El Greco's, you'll see about 20 El Greco paintings, including his masterful *View of Toledo* and portraits of the Apostles (€2, free Sat afternoon from 14:30 and all day Sun; Tue–Sat 10:00–14:00 & 16:00–17:45, Sun 10:00–13:45, closed Mon,

Samuel Levi 3). While many call this El Greco's House, it's actually a traditionally furnished Renaissance "monument house" built near where he likely lived.

Sinagoga del Transito (Museo Sefardi)—Built in 1366, this is the best surviving slice of Toledo's Jewish past (but it's likely closed through 2003 for renovation). The museum displays Jewish artifacts, including costumes, menorahs, and books, regrettably without a word of English description (€2.50, free Sat afternoon from 14:30 and all day Sun; Tue–Sat 10:00–14:00 & 16:00–17:45, Sun 10:00–13:45, closed Mon, near Museo El Greco, with same price and hours, on Calle de los Reyes Católicos).

Sinagoga de Santa Maria Blanca—This synagogue-turned-church with Moorish arches is an eclectic but harmonious gem and a vivid reminder of the three cultures that shared this city (€1.20, daily 10:00–14:00 & 15:30–19:00, closes off-season at 18:00, no photos allowed, Calle de los Reyes Católicos 2–4).

Museo Victorio Macho—After *mucho* El Greco, try Macho. Overlooking the gorge, this small, attractive museum—once the home and workshop of the early-20th-century sculptor Victorio Macho—offers several rooms of his bold work interspersed with view terraces. The highlight is *La Madre*, Macho's life-size sculpture of an older woman sitting in a chair. But the big draw for many is the air-conditioned theater featuring a fast-moving nine-minute video sweep through Toledo's history (for more information, you can request the 29-minute long version, €3, half price for young and old, Mon–Sat 10:00–19:00, Sun 10:00–15:00, request video showing in English, Plaza de Victorio Macho 2, between the two *sinagogas* listed above, tel. 925-284-225.)

The **river gorge view** from the Museo Vitorio Macho terrace (or free terraces nearby) shows well how the River Tajo served as a formidable moat protecting the city. Imagine trying to attack from this side. The 14th-century bridge on the right and the remains of a bridge on the left connected the town with the region's *cigarrales*—mansions of wealthy families with orchards of figs and apricots that dot the hillside even today.

San Juan de los Reyes Monasterio—St. John of the Monarchs is a grand, generally Flemish-style monastery, church, and cloisters—thought-provoking because the Catholic Monarchs (Isabel and Ferdinand) planned to be buried here. But after the Moors were expelled in 1492 from Granada, their royal bodies were planted there to show Spain's commitment to maintaining a Moor-free peninsula. Today the courtyard is a delightful spot where happy critters carved into the columns seem to chirp with the birds in the trees (€1.20, daily 10:00–13:45 & 15:30–18:45, San Juan de los Reyes 2, tel. 925-223-802).

And for Dessert: *Mazapan*

Toledo's famous almond-fruity-sweet *mazapan* is sold all over town. Locals say the best is made by **Santo Tomé** (several outlets, including a handy one on Plaza Zocódover, daily 9:00–22:22). Browse their tempting window displays. They sell *mazapan* goodies individually (2 for about €1, *sin relleno* is for purists, *de piñon* has pine nuts, *imperiales* is with almonds, others have fruit fillings) or in small mixed boxes. Their *Toledanas* is a crumbly cookie favorite with a subtle thread of pumpkin filling.

For a sweet and romantic evening moment, pick up a few pastries and head down to the cathedral. Sit on the Plaza del Ayuntamiento's benches (or stretch out on the stone wall to the right of the TI). The fountain is on your right, Spain's best-looking city hall is behind you, and her top cathedral, built back when Toledo was Spain's capital, shines brightly against the black night sky before you.

Shopping

Toledo probably sells as many souvenirs as any city in Spain. This is the place to buy medieval-looking swords, armor, maces, three-legged stools, and other nouveau antiques. It's also Spain's damascene center, where, for centuries, craftspeople have inlaid black steel with gold, silver, and copper wire.

At the workshop of English-speaking **Mariano Zamorano**, you can see swords and knives being made. Judging by what's left of Mariano's hand, his knives are among the sharpest (Mon–Sat 9:00–14:00 & 16:00–19:00, closed Sat afternoon and Sun, Calle Ciudad 19, near cathedral and Plaza Ayuntamiento, tel. 925-222-634, www.marianozamorano.com).

El Martes, Toledo's colorful outdoor flea market, bustles on Paseo de Marchen (near TI at Bisagra Gate) on Tuesdays from 9:00 to 14:00.

Sleeping in Toledo
(€1 = about $1, country code: 34)

Sleep Code: **S** = Single, **D** = Double/Twin, **T** = Triple, **Q** = Quad, **b** = bathroom, **s** = shower only, **CC** = Credit Cards accepted, **no CC** = Credit Cards not accepted, **SE** = Speaks English, **NSE** = No English. Breakfast and the 7 percent IVA tax are not included unless noted. Toledo's zip code is 45001, unless otherwise noted.

To help you easily sort through these listings, I've divided the rooms into three categories, based on the price for a standard double room with bath during high season:

Higher Priced—Most rooms €90 or more.
Moderately Priced—Most less than €90.
Lower Priced—Most rooms less than €60.

Madrid day-trippers darken the sunlit cobbles, but few stay to see Toledo's medieval moonrise. Spend the night. Spring and fall are high season; November through March and July and August are low. There are no private rooms for rent.

Sleeping near Plaza Zocódover

MODERATELY PRICED

Hotel Las Conchas, a new three-star hotel, gleams with marble and sheer pride. It's so sleek and slick it almost feels more like a hospital than a hotel. Its 35 rooms are plenty comfortable (Sb-€49, Db-€65, Db with terrace-€75, breakfast-€4.50, includes tax, 5 percent discount with this book, CC, air-con, near the Alcazar at Juan Labrador 8, tel. 925-210-760, fax 925-224-271, www. lasconchas.com, e-mail: lasconchas@ctv.es, Sole SE).

LOWER PRICED

Hotel Imperio is well run, offering 21 basic air-con rooms with marginal beds in a handy old-town location (Sb-€28, Db-€40, Tb-€54, includes tax, 5 percent discount with this book, CC, elevator, cheery café, from Calle Comercio at #38 go a block uphill to Calle Cadenas 5, tel. 925-227-650, fax 925-253-183, www.terra.es /personal/himperio, e-mail: himperio@teleline.es, friendly Pablo SE).

Hostal Centro rents 23 modern, clean, and comfy rooms just around the corner (Sb-€30, Db-€42, Tb-€60, no CC, roof garden, 50 meters off Plaza Zocódover, first right off Calle Comercio at Calle Nueva 13, tel. 925-257-091, fax 925-257-848, e-mail: hcentro4@aolavant.com, SE).

The quiet, modern **Hostal Nuevo Labrador,** with 12 clean, shiny, and spacious rooms, is another good value (Sb-€27, Db-€40, Tb-€52, Qb-€60, includes tax, no breakfast, CC, elevator, Juan Labrador 10, 45001 Toledo, tel. 925-222-620, fax 925-229-399, NSE).

Hotel Maravilla, wonderfully central and convenient, has gloomy, claustrophobic halls and 17 simple rooms (Sb-€25, Db-€40, Tb-€54, Qb-€65, includes tax, CC, back rooms are quieter, air-con, a block behind Plaza Zocódover at Plaza de Barrio Rey 7, tel. 925-228-317, fax 925-228-155, e-mail: hostalmaravilla@infonegocio.com, Felisa Maria SE).

Sleeping near the Bisagra Gate

HIGHER PRICED

Hostal del Cardenal, a 17th-century cardinal's palace built into Toledo's wall, is quiet and elegant with a cool garden and

Central Toledo

200 YARDS
200 METERS

N

BISAGRA GATE

TO MADRID & 7

BUS STATION

RIO LLANO

CITY WALLS

TO TRAIN STATION & 8

To 9

ESCALATOR

SUBIDA LA GRANJA

PLAZA MERCED

MERCED

CALLE REAL

CUESTA

SANTA CRUZ MUSEUM

CADENAS NUÑES

SILL

ARMAS

POST

LA PLATA

CERVANTES

TO TRAIN STN.

SAN JUAN DE LOS REYES

SANTO TOMÉ

ALEX GABIO

NUNCIO

COMERCIO

TAXIS

ANGEL

ALFONSO XII

S. TOME

TRINIDAD

SALVADOR

ALCÁZAR

SYNAGOGUE SANTA MARIA BLANCA

SAN JUAN DIOS

T. MORO

S. URSULA

ISABEL

CATHEDRAL

MUSEO VICTORIO MACHO

RIO TEJO

SYNAGOGUE TRANSITO

PARK

EL GRECO'S HOUSE

PLAZA AYUNTAMIENTO & CITY HALL

DCH

(see "Toledo's Plaza Zocódover" map)

NOTE: STREET WIDTH IS EXAGGERATED FOR CLARITY

① Plaza Zocódover
② Hotel Sol
③ Hostal & Rest. del Cardenal
④ Hotel Santa Isabel
⑤ La Posada de Manolo
⑥ Hotel Pintor El Greco
⑦ To Hostal Gavilánes II, Hostal Madrid & Hotel Maria Cristina
⑧ To Youth Hostel San Servando
⑨ To Parador Conde de Orgaz & Hotel La Almazara

⑩ Los Cuarto Tiempos Rest.
⑪ Casa Aurelio I
⑫ Casa Aurelio II & III on Sinagoga Street & Pizzeria Pastucci
⑬ Rest. Lopez de Toledo
⑭ Rest. La Perdiz
⑮ Rest. Meson Palacios
⑯ Bar Cerveceria Gambrinus
⑰ Taverna de Amboades
⑱ Mercado Municipal

a stuffy restaurant. This poor man's parador, at the dusty old gate of Toledo, is closest to the station but below all the old-town action—however, the new escalator takes the sweat out of getting into town (Sb-€56, Db-€90, Tb-€117, 20 percent cheaper mid-Dec through mid-March, breakfast-€6.50, CC, air-con, nearby parking-€12/day, *serioso* staff, enter through town wall 100 meters below Puerta Bisagra, Paseo de Reca-redo 24, 45004 Toledo, tel. 925-224-900, fax 925-222-991, www.cardenal.asernet.es, e-mail: cardenal@asernet.es).

LOWER PRICED
Hotel Sol, with 25 plain, modern, and clean rooms, is a great value on a quiet street halfway between the Bisagra Gate and Plaza Zocódover (Sb-€33, Db-€46, Tb-€58, includes tax, breakfast-€3.50, 10 percent discount with this book, CC, air-con, parking-€7/day 50 meters down lane off busy main drag at Hotel Real, Azacanes 8, 45003 Toledo, tel. 925-213-650, fax 925-216-159, www.fedeto.es/hotel-sol, José Carlos SE). Their "Hostal Sol" annex across the street is just as comfortable and a bit cheaper. A handy Laundro-mat is next door.

Sleeping beyond the Cathedral, Deep in Toledo

HIGHER PRICED
Hotel Pintor El Greco, at the far end of the old town, has 33 plush and modern-feeling rooms with all the comforts, yet it's in a historic 17th-century building. A block from Santo Tomé in a Jewish Quarter garden, it's very quiet (Sb-€80, Db-€104, plus tax, includes breakfast, CC, air-con, elevator, Alamillos del Transito 13, tel. 925-285-191, fax 925-215-819, www .hotelpintorelgreco.com).

MODERATELY PRICED
La Posada de Manolo rents 14 thoughtfully furnished rooms across from the downhill corner of the cathedral. Manolo Junior recently opened "The House of Manolo" according to his father's vision of a comfortable place with each of its three floors themed a little differently—Moorish, Jewish, and Christian (Sb-€36, Db-€66, big Db-€72, includes breakfast, 10 percent discount when booked directly with this book, CC, air-con, no elevator, nice view terrace, Calle Sixto Ramon Parro 8, tel. 925-282-250, fax 925-282-251, www .laposadademanolo.com, e-mail: laposadademanolo@wanadoo.es).

Toledo Plaza Zocódover

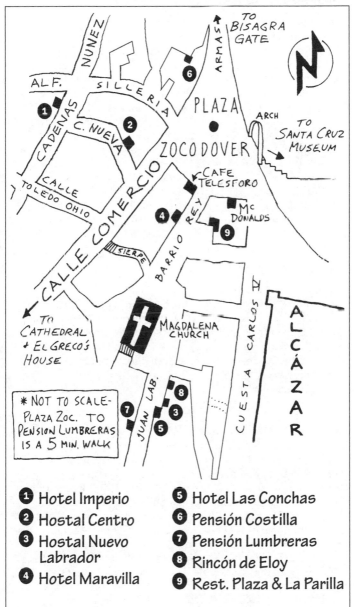

1 Hotel Imperio
2 Hostal Centro
3 Hostal Nuevo Labrador
4 Hotel Maravilla
5 Hotel Las Conchas
6 Pensión Costilla
7 Pensión Lumbreras
8 Rincón de Eloy
9 Rest. Plaza & La Parilla

Sleeping Cheap near Plaza Zocódover

LOWER PRICED
Hotel Santa Isabel, in a 15th-century building two blocks from
the cathedral, has 42 clean, modern, and comfortable rooms and
squeaky tile hallways (Sb-€29, Db-€43, Tb-€53, includes tax,
breakfast-€4, CC, air-con, elevator, great roof terrace, buried
deep in old town so take a taxi, not the bus; drivers enter from
Calle Pozo Amargo, parking-€6; Calle Santa Isabel 24, 45002
Toledo, tel. 925-253-120, fax 925-253-136, www.santa-isabel
.com, e-mail: santa-isabel@arrakis.es, SE).

Pensión Castilla, a family-run cheapie, has seven very basic
rooms (S-€15, Db-€25, extra bed possible, no CC, fans, Calle
Recoletos 6, tel. 925-256-318, Teresa NSE).

Pensión Lumbreras has a tranquil courtyard and 12 simple
rooms, some with views, including rooms 3, 6, and 7 (S-€19,
D-€33, reception is at Carlo V Hotel around the corner, Juan
Labrador 9, 45001 Toledo, tel. 925-221-571).

Sleeping outside of Town

MODERATELY PRICED
Hotel Maria Cristina, next to the bullring, is part 15th-century
and all modern. This sprawling 73-room hotel has all the comforts
under a thin layer of prefab tradition (Sb-€56, Db-€89, extra
bed-€30, suites available, breakfast-€5.50, plus tax, CC, air-
con, elevator, attached restaurant, parking-€7.20/day, Marques
de Mendigorria 1, tel. 925-213-202, fax 925-212-650, www
.hotelmariacristina.com, SE).

LOWER PRICED
On the road to Madrid (near bullring): There's a conspiracy
of clean, modern, and hard-working little hotels with comfy
rooms a five-minute walk beyond Puerta Bisagra near the bullring (Plaza de Toros, bullfights only on holidays) and bus station.
Drivers enjoy easy parking here. While it's a 15-minute uphill
hike to the old-town action, several buses go from just west of
Hostal Madrid directly to Plaza de Zocódover. Two good bets
are **Hostal Gavilánes II** (18 rooms, Sb-€33, Db-€42, Db
suite-€77, Tb-€56, Qb-€67, includes breakfast and taxes,
CC, air-con, parking-€5.50/day, Marqués de Mendigorría 14,
45003 Toledo, tel. & fax 925-211-628, NSE) and **Hostal
Madrid** (20 rooms, Sb-€29, Db-€37, Tb-€49, includes tax,
breakfast-€2.40, CC, air-con, parking-€6.50/day, Calle
Marqués de Mendigorría 7, 45003 Toledo, tel. 925-221-114,

fax 925-228-113, NSE). This *hostal* rents nine lesser rooms in an annex across the street.

Hostel: The **Albergue Juvenil San Servando** youth hostel is lavish but cheap, with small rooms for two, three, or four people; a swimming pool; views; and good management (106 beds, €8.50 per bed if under age 26, €11 if age 26 or older, hostel membership required, no CC, in San Servando castle 10-min walk from train station, 15-min hike from town center, over Puente Viejo outside town, tel. 925-224-554, reservations tel. 925-267-729, NSE).

Sleeping outside of Town with the Grand Toledo View

HIGHER PRICED

Toledo's **Parador Nacional Conde de Orgaz** is one of Spain's best-known inns, enjoying the same Toledo view El Greco made famous from across the Tajo Gorge (76 rooms, Sb-€60, Db-€114, Db with view-€129, Tb with view-€174, breakfast-€8.50, CC, 3 windy kilometers from town at Cerro del Emperador, 45002 Toledo, tel. 925-221-850, fax 925-225-166, www.parador.es, e-mail: toledo@parador.es, SE).

LOWER PRICED

Hotel Residencia La Almazara was the summer residence of a 16th-century archbishop of Toledo. Fond of its classic Toledo view, El Greco hung out here for inspiration. A lumbering old place with cushy public rooms, 28 simple bedrooms, and a sprawling garden, it's truly in the country but just three kilometers out of Toledo (Sb-€26, Db-€37, Db with view-€42, Tb-€48, 10 rooms have view, fans, CC, Ctra. de Piedrabuena 47, follow the signs from the circular Ronda de Toledo road, P.O. Box 6, Toledo 45080, tel. 925-223-866, fax 925-250-562, www.hotelalmazara.com, e-mail: hotelalmazara@ribernet.es).

Eating in Toledo

Dining in Traditional Elegance

A day full of El Greco and the romance of Toledo after dark puts me in the mood for partridge (*perdiz*), roast suckling pig (*cochinillo asado*), or baby lamb (*cordero*) similarly roasted after a few weeks of mother's milk. After dinner find a *mazapan* place (such as Santo Tomé) for dessert.

Los Cuatro Tiempos Restaurante offers gamey local specials in a tasteful and elegant setting with good service

(€25 dinners, daily 13:30–16:00 & 20:30–23:00, at downhill corner of cathedral at Sixto Ramon Parro 5, tel. 925-223-782).

Toledo's three **Casa Aurelio** restaurants all offer traditional cooking (game, roast suckling pig, traditional soup), a classy atmosphere, and good-value €30 meals (13:00–16:30 & 20:00–23:30, all closed Sun, each closed either Mon, Tue, or Wed, CC, air-con). All are within three blocks of the cathedral: Plaza Ayuntamiento 4 is festive (tel. 925-227-716), Sinagoga 6 is most *típico* (tel. 925-222-097), and Sinagoga 1 is new and dressiest (popular with Toledo's political class, tel. 925-221-392).

Restaurante Cason Lopez de Toledo, a fancy restaurant located in an old noble palace, specializes in Castilian food, particularly venison and partridge. Its character unfolds upstairs (€18 meals, Mon–Sat 13:30–16:00 & 20:30–23:30, closed Sun, Calle Silleria 3, near Plaza Zocódover, tel. 925-254-774).

Hostal del Cardenal Restaurante, a classic hotel restaurant near the Bisagra Gate at the bottom of town, is understandably popular with tourists for its decent traditional dishes (daily 13:00–16:00 & 20:30–23:30, Puerto de Recaredo 24, tel. 925-224-900).

For a splurge near the Santa Tomé sights, consider the classy **La Perdiz,** which offers partridge (as the restaurant's name suggests), venison, suckling pig, fish, and more (Tue–Sat 12:00–23:00, closes Sun about 16:00, closed Mon and first half of Aug, Calle de los Reyes Católicos 7, tel. 925-214-658).

Eating Simply but Well

Restaurante-Meson Palacios serves good food at cheap prices (Mon–Sat from 13:00 and from 19:30, closed Sun, on Alfonso X, near Plaza de San Vicente).

Rincón de Eloy is bright, modern, and a cool refuge for lunch on a hot day (€9 menu, Mon–Sat 13:00–16:00 & 20:00–22:30, closed Sun, air-con, Juan Labrador 16, near Alcázar, tel. 925-229-399).

Bar Cerveceria Gambrinus is a good tapas bar (*chapatas* are little sandwiches, *tablitas* are "little plates") with restaurant seating in its leafy courtyard or in back (daily 9:00–24:00, near Santa Tomé at Santa Tomé 10, tel. 925-214-440).

Restaurants Plaza and **La Parrilla** share a tiny square behind Plaza Zocódover (facing the Casa Telesforo on Plaza Zocódover, go left down alley 30 meters to Plaza de Barrio Rey). The bars and cafés on Plaza Zocódover are reasonable, seasoned with some fine people-watching.

At **Taverna de Amboades,** a humble but earnest wine-and-tapas bar near the Bisagra Gate, expert Miguel Angel enjoys explaining the differences among Spanish wines. To try some really good wines with quality local cheese and meat, drop by and let Miguel impress you (2 quality wines and a plate of cheese and meat for €7, Tue–Sat 19:30–24:00, also Thu–Sun 12:30–16:00, closed Mon, Alfonso VI 5, cellular 678-483-749).

Pizzeria Pastucci is the local favorite for pizza (Tue–Sun 12:00–16:00 & 19:00–24:00, closed Mon, near cathedral at Calle de la Sinagoga 10).

Picnics are best assembled at the **Mercado Municipal** on Plaza Mayor (on the Alcázar side of cathedral, open Mon–Sat until 14:00, closed Sun). This is a fun market to prowl, even if you don't need food. If you feel like munching a paper plate–size Communion wafer, one of the stalls sells crispy bags of *obleas*— a great gift for your favorite pastor.

Transportation Connections—Toledo
Far more buses than trains connect Toledo with Madrid.

To Madrid: by bus (2/hr, 60–75 min, *directo* is faster than *ruta*, Madrid's Estación sur Autobuses, Metro: Méndez Alvaro, Continental bus company, tel. 925-223-641), **by train** (9/day, 50–75 min, Madrid's Atocha station), **by car** (65 kilometers, 1 hr). Toledo bus info: tel. 925-215-850; train info: tel. 902-240-202.

To Granada: To get to Granada from Toledo, it's best to transfer in Madrid. Ideally, return to Madrid to spend the night, then catch the morning train to Granada (departs Chamartin station at 8:10, confirm time at station, 6 hrs).

LA MANCHA
(Visit only if you're driving between Toledo and Granada.) Nowhere else is Spain so vast, flat, and radically monotonous. La Mancha, Arabic for "parched earth," makes you feel small— lost in rough seas of olive-green polka dots. Random buildings look like houses and hotels hurled off some heavenly Monopoly board. It's a rough land where roadkill is left to rot, bugs ricochet off the windshield and keep on flying, and hitchhikers wear red dresses and aim to take you for the ride.

This is the setting of Cervantes' *Don Quixote*, published in the 17th century, after England sank the Armada and the Spanish Empire began its decline. Cervantes' star character fought doggedly for good, for justice, and against the fall of Spain and its traditional old-regime empire. Ignoring reality, Don Quixote was a hero fighting a hopeless battle. Stark La Mancha was the perfect stage.

The epitome of Don Quixote country, the town of **Consuegra** must be the La Mancha Cervantes had in mind. Drive up to the ruined 12th-century castle and joust with a windmill. It's hot and buggy here, but the powerful view overlooking the village, with its sun-bleached, light-red roofs; modern concrete reality; and harsh, windy silence makes for a profound picnic (a 1-hr drive south of Toledo). The castle belonged to the Knights of St. John (12th and 13th centuries) and is associated with their trip to Jerusalem during the Crusades. Originally built from the ruins of a nearby Roman circus, it has been newly restored (€1.50). Sorry, the windmills are post-Cervantes, only 200 to 300 years old.

If you've seen windmills, the next castle north (above Almonacid, 12 kilometers from Toledo) is free and more interesting than the Consuegra castle. Follow the ruined lane past the ruined church up to the ruined castle. The jovial locals hike up with kids and kites.

Route Tips for Drivers

Granada to Toledo (400 km, 5 hrs): The Granada–Toledo drive is long, hot, and boring (see "La Mancha," above). Start early to minimize the heat and make the best time you can. Follow signs for Madrid/Jaen/N323 into what some call the Spanish Nebraska—La Mancha. After Puerto Lapice, you'll see the Toledo exit.

Arriving in Toledo by car: View the city from many angles along the Circumvalación road across the Tajo Gorge. Stop at the street-side viewpoint or drive to Parador Conde de Orgaz just south of town for the view (from the balcony) that El Greco made famous in his portrait of Toledo.

As people have for centuries, you may enter Toledo via the Bisagra Gate. Or, to take advantage of the new escalator (opposite recommended Hostal del Cardenal, explained above), park across the street at the pay lot or free on the streets beyond. Those driving into town can park across the street from the Alcázar (€1.20/hr, €12/day).

Toledo to Madrid (65 km, 1 hr): It's a speedy *autovía* north, past one last bullboard to Madrid (on N-401). The highways converge into M30, which circles Madrid. Follow it to the left ("Nor" or "Oeste") and take the Plaza de España exit to get back to Gran Vía. If you're airport-bound, keep heading into Madrid until you see the airplane symbol (N-II). Turn in your rental car at terminal T-1.

GRANADA

For a time, Granada was the grandest city in Spain; but in the end, it was left in the historic dust. Today it's a provincial town with more than its share of history and bumper stickers reading, "Life is short. Don't run." We'll keep things fun and simple, settling down in the old center and exploring monuments of the Moorish civilization and monuments of its conquest. And we'll taste the treats of an African-flavored culture that survives today.

Granada's magnificent Alhambra fortress was the last stronghold of the Moorish kingdom in Spain. The city's exotically tangled Moorish quarter bustles under the grand Alhambra, which glows red in the evening while locals stroll, enjoying the city's cool late-night charms.

There is an old saying: "Give him a coin, woman, for there is nothing worse in this life than to be blind in Granada." This city has much to see, yet it reveals itself in unpredictable ways. It takes a poet to sort through the jigsaw-puzzle pieces of Granada. Peer through the intricate lattice of a Moorish window. Hear water burbling unseen among the labyrinthine hedges of the Generalife garden. Listen to a flute trilling deep in the swirl of alleys around the cathedral. Don't be blind in Granada—open your senses.

Planning Your Time

Granada is worth one day and two nights. Consider the night train connection with Madrid (or Barcelona), giving the city a night and a day. The Costa del Sol's best beach town, Nerja, is just two quick hours away (by bus), white hill towns such as Ronda are three hours away (bus or train), and Sevilla is an easy three-hour train ride. To use your time efficiently in Granada, reserve in advance for the Alhambra (see "Sights—The Alhambra," below).

In the morning, tour the cathedral and Royal Chapel (both closed roughly 13:00–16:00) and stroll the pedestrian-zone shopping scene. Do the Alhambra in the late afternoon. Be at the Albayzín viewpoint in the Moorish Quarter for sunset and then find the right place for a suitably late dinner.

Orientation

While modern Granada sprawls (300,000 people), its sights are all within a 20-minute walk of Plaza Nueva, where dogs wag their tails to the rhythm of the street musicians. Nearly all my recommended hotels are within a few blocks of Plaza Nueva. Make this the hub of your Granada visit.

Plaza Nueva was a main square back when kings called Granada home. This historic center is in the Darro River Valley, which separates two hills (the river now flows under the square). On one hill is the great Moorish palace, the Alhambra; and on the other is the best-preserved Moorish quarter in Spain, the Albayzín. To the southeast are the cathedral, Royal Chapel, and Alcaicería (Moorish market), where the city's two main drags, Gran Vía de Colón and Calle Reyes Católicos, lead away into the modern city.

Tourist Information

There are three TIs. The handiest—in the courtyard of what was a Moorish hotel 500 years ago—is at Corral del Carbon. It covers Granada as well as all Andalucía (Mon–Sat 9:00–19:00, Sun 10:00–14:00; from Plaza Isabel la Católica, take Calle Reyes Católicos in the opposite direction from Alhambra, take first left, walk through keyhole arch, tel. 958-225-990; festival office in the same courtyard—see "Helpful Hints," below). Another TI, focusing solely on Granada, is on Plaza de Mariana Pineda (Mon–Fri 9:30–19:00, Sat–Sun 10:00–14:00, 3 blocks south of Plaza Carmen and Puerta Real, tel. 958-247-128). The third TI is at the Alhambra entrance, across from the ticket windows (Mon–Sat 10:00–19:30, Sun 10:00–13:00). At any TI, get a free city map and verify your Alhambra plans. Bus and train schedules are posted in a small room next to the TI at Corral del Carbon. During peak season (April–Oct), TI kiosks sometimes pop up in Plaza Nueva and Bib-Rambla.

Arrival in Granada

By Train: Granada's train station is connected to the center by frequent buses, a €3.60 taxi ride, or a 20-minute walk down Avenida Constitución and Gran Vía de Colón. The train station has lockers. Reserve your train out upon arrival.

Exiting the train station, walk straight ahead down the

Granada

1 Hotel Residencia Macia
2 Hostal Residencia Britz
3 Hostal Gomerez
4 Hostal Navarro Ramos
5 Hostal Landazuri
6 Hostal Viena
7 Hotel Los Tilos

8 Royal Chapel entry
9 Cathedral entry
10 Naturi Albayzin Rest.
11 To Paseo de los Tristes
12 Alcaiceria
13 Hotel Anacapri
14 Hostal Residencia Lisboa

15 To Hotel Navas
16 Bodega Castaneda
17 Hotel Inglaterra
18 To Hotel Reina Cristina
19 Hotel Gran Via

tree-lined road. At the first major intersection (Avenida de la Constitución), you'll see the bus stop on your right. Take bus #9 or #11 and confirm by asking the driver, "*¿Catedral?*" (pron. kat-ay-dral; the nearest stop to Plaza Nueva, ticket-€0.85, pay driver). Get off when you see the fountain of Plaza Isabel la Católica in front of the bus at the stop near the cathedral; cross the busy Gran Vía and walk three short blocks to Plaza Nueva.

By Bus: Granada's bus station (with a café, ATMs, lockers, and a don't-bother-me-with-questions info office, tel. 958-185-480, or 902-422-242 for Barcelona or east coast destinations) is located on the outskirts of the city. To get to the center, either take a taxi (€4.20) or bus #3 (€0.85, pay driver). It's about a

20-minute ride by bus; nearing the center, the bus goes up
Gran Vía de Colón. For Plaza Nueva, get off at the stop for the
cathedral (cathedral not visible from bus), a half-block before
the grand square Plaza Isabel la Católica—from the bus you'll
see the big Banco Santander building across the square. From
this stop, you're a three-block walk from Plaza Nueva (facing
Banco Santander, go left up Calle Reyes Católicos).

By Car: Driving in Granada's historic center is restricted to
buses, taxis, and tourists with hotel reservations (tell the police
officer). The *autovía* (freeway) circles the city with a *circumvalación*
(Ronda Sur) road. To reach Plaza Nueva, take exit #129, direction
Centro, Recogidas. Calle Recogidas leads directly into the heart of
town. There will probably be a police block at Puerta Real (Victoria
Hotel). You can pull into Plaza Nueva if you have a hotel reservation:
There are posts with hotel buzzers on Calle Reyes Católicos and on
Calle Elvira on the approach to Plaza Nueva. You press a button
on the pillar for your hotel; the hotel buzzes back, releasing the road-
block to allow you through. Of Granada's many parking garages, one
is at Puerta Real and another is Parking San Agustin, near the cathedral, just off Gran Vía (€16/24 hrs, on Gran Vía as you approach
Plaza Isabel la Católica, turn right on Carcel Baja to reach garage).

By Plane: To get between the airport and downtown, you
can take a taxi (€17.50) or, much cheaper, the airport bus, timed
to leave when flights arrive and depart (6/day, 30 min, €3). Hop
on (or get off) at Gran Vía del Colón, nearly across from the
cathedral. Airport info: tel. 958-245-223.

Getting around Granada

With such cheap taxis, efficient minibuses, and nearly all points
of interest an easy walk from Plaza Nueva, you may not even need
the regular city buses. Three handy little red minibuses depart
frequently (roughly every 10 min until late in eve) from Plaza
Nueva: bus #30 goes up to the Alhambra and back; bus #31 does
the Albayzín loop (a few go through Sacromonte); and bus #32 connects the Alhambra and Albayzín (from Plaza Nueva, the bus goes
up to the Alhambra, returns to Plaza Nueva, then loops through
the Albayzín and ends at Plaza Nueva). The schedule is listed at the
bus stop and at the TI. You buy bus tickets (€0.85) from the driver.
Sharable Bonobus tickets for 10 trips (€5) or 21 trips (€109) save
you money if you'll be taking a lot of trips, or if you're part of a
group (buy from driver, valid on minibuses and city buses).

Helpful Hints

When you see women wanting to give you leaves or flowers, avoid
them like the plague. They may even grab at you. Firmly say no, and

walk away (for more information see Alcaicería under "Sights—Central Granada," below).

City Pass: The Bono Turístico city pass covers the Alhambra, cathedral, Royal Chapel, Caruja Monastery, and 10 free bus trips, plus other lesser sights and discounts on more (€18, valid for a week). When you buy your pass, the vendor schedules a time for your Alhambra visit. Passes are sold at the Royal Chapel, Alhambra, and Caja General de Ahorros bank on Plaza Isabel la Católica. You can save time by calling ahead to purchase your pass by credit card and it will be ready for you when you arrive at the vendor (12 percent commission, tel. 902-100-095). This pass works best for people who are staying two or more days, ideally off-season (because in peak-season there's a small risk you might not get into the Alhambra within 2 days). Note that some of the fancier hotels provide one free pass per room for stays of two nights or more during peak season.

Long-Distance Buses, Trains, and Flights: To save yourself a trip to the train or bus stations, get information from the TI (schedules posted next to TI at Corral del Carbon) or a travel agency. All travel agencies book flights, and many also sell long-distance bus and train tickets (generally open Mon–Fri 9:00–13:30 & 17:00–20:00, Sat 10:00–13:30, closed Sun; Viajes Bonanza is convenient at Calle Reyes Católicos 30, near main TI, tel. 958-223-578).

American Express: It's across from the main TI (Mon–Fri 9:00–20:00, Sat 10:00–14:00 & 15:00–19:00, closed Sun, Calle Reyes Católicos 31, tel. 958-224-512).

Internet Access: Navegaweb, a chain that sells tickets useable in other locations including Madrid and Barcelona, has 74 computers (daily 10:00–23:00, Calle Reyes Católicos 55, tel. 958-210-528). Madar Internet, one of many Internet points scattered throughout Granada, is in the midst of tea shops at Calderia Nueva 11 (20 computers, Mon–Fri 10:00–24:00, Sat–Sun 12:00–24:00, 2 long blocks off Plaza Nueva).

Post Office: It's on Puerta Real (Mon–Fri 8:30–20:30, Sat 9:30–14:00, closed Sun, tel. 958-221-138).

Festivals: From late June to early July the International Festival of Music and Dance offers some of the world's top classical music and art (ballet, flamenco, and zarzuela) nightly in the Alhambra at reasonable prices. The ticket office is open from mid-April through the festival (in Corral del Carbon, in same courtyard as TI, tel. 958-221-844). Tickets can also be booked online at www.granadafestival.org from February on. During the festival, flamenco is free every night at midnight; ask the ticket office or TI for the venue.

Local Guide: Margarita Landazuri, a local English-speaking guide, knows how to teach and has good rates (tel. 958-221-406); if she's busy, her partner, Miguel Angel, is also good.

Walking Tours: Run by locals, Granada Romántica's two-hour walking tour of the Albayzín ends with a drink and tapas (€17, 2/day year-round, tel. 958-210-127, cellular 630-262-840).

Sights—The Alhambra

A ▲▲▲ sight, this last and greatest Moorish palace is one of Europe's top sights. Attracting up to 8,000 visitors a day, it's the reason most tourists come to Granada. Nowhere else does the splendor of Moorish civilization shine so brightly.

The last Moorish stronghold in Europe is, with all due respect, really a symbol of retreat. Granada was only a regional capital for centuries. Gradually the Christian Reconquista moved south, taking Córdoba (1236) and Sevilla (1248). The Moors held Granada until 1492. As you tour their grand palace, remember that while Europe slumbered through the Dark Ages, Moorish magnificence blossomed—busy stucco, plaster "stalactites," colors galore, scalloped windows framing Granada views, exuberant gardens, and water, water everywhere. Water—so rare and precious in most of the Islamic world—was the purest symbol of life to the Moors. The Alhambra is decorated with water: standing still, cascading, masking secret conversations, and drip-dropping playfully.

The Alhambra—not nearly as confusing as it is—consists of four sights: Charles V's Palace (free, Christian Renaissance palace plopped on top of the Alhambra after the reconquest), Alcazaba (empty old fort with tower and views), Palacios Nazaries (exquisite Moorish palace), and Generalife Gardens (fancy gardens); for descriptions of these sites, see "The Alhambra in Four Parts," below. Note that some rooms or portions of the Alhambra may be closed for restoration.

Cost: The Alcazaba fort, Moorish palace (Palacios Nazaries), and Generalife Gardens require a €7 combo-ticket. (Only Charles V's Palace is free.) Audioguides are €3, available at the entrance and at Charles V's Palace. No map is included with your ticket, but a simple map comes with the audioguide. The bookshop adjacent to the ticket office sells guidebooks (see "Guidebooks," below; books are also sold at shops throughout the Alhambra) and the Official Map of the Alhambra, which looks great but doesn't mark sights clearly (€1.10, at least the backside has more detail).

Hours: The Alhambra is open daily from 8:30 to 20:00 (closes Nov–Feb at 18:00); ticket office closes an hour earlier (Alhambra closed on Dec 25 and Jan 1).

Alhambra by Moonlight: Late-night visits include only the Moorish palace and not the fort or gardens—but hey, the palace is 80 percent of the Alhambra thrills (March–Oct Tue–Sat 22:00–23:30, reserve ahead during peak season, ticket office

Alhambra

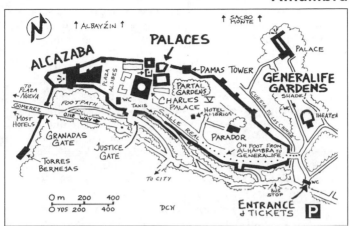

open 21:45–22:45; Nov–Feb only Fri–Sat 20:00–21:30, ticket
office open 19:45–20:15).

Getting a Reservation for the Alhambra: Some tourists
never get to see the Alhambra because the tickets can sell out fast.
It's smart to make a reservation in advance, especially if you know
the dates you'll be in Granada—and if you'll be visiting during
peak season (April–Oct) or on a bank holiday. Off-season, you
might be able to just walk right in. Still, it can be worth the peace
of mind and your valuable time to reserve ahead.

The Alhambra's top sight is the Moorish palace—Palacios
Nazaries. Only 400 visitors per half hour are allowed inside. Your
30-minute time span is printed on your ticket (you can request a
particular half hour). While you must enter Palacios Nazaries
within this time, once inside you may linger as long as you like.

The Alhambra is trying out some crowd-control techniques,
but only for visitors scheduled from 14:00 on. If your entry time
to Palacios Nazaries is before 14:00, you can enter the grounds
anytime in the morning, see the palace at your appointed time,
and then stay all day at the Alhambra if you choose. But if your
ticket is stamped for 14:00 or later, you can enter the site no earlier
than 14:00. For instance, if you have a reservation to visit Palacios
Nazaries between 16:30 and 17:00, you can enter the Alhambra
grounds as early as 14:00 and see the fort and Generalife Gardens
before the palace. (Because of the time restriction on afternoon
visits, morning times sell out the quickest, but for most travelers,
an afternoon allows ample time to see the site.) Here's the scoop
on how to make a reservation for the Alhambra.

Reserving in Advance: There are three possibilities, each costing a worthwhile €0.90 surcharge. With any of these options, you might be required to show your passport (as an identity card) when you pick up your ticket at the Alhambra, but in reality this rarely happens.

1. You can drop by any BBVA bank in Spain and make a reservation (Banco Bilbao Vizcaya Argentaria, Mon–Fri 8:30–14:15, closed Sat–Sun); you'll pay in advance and get a piece of paper that you take to the ticket window at the Alhambra (a minimum of 15 min before your allotted appointment time) to exchange for a ticket. The BBVA bank personnel usually speak just enough English to make this transaction (which takes about 10 min). If you know when you'll be in Granada, it's simplest to reserve a ticket soon after you arrive in Spain. BBVA banks are easy to find in virtually every Spanish town.

2. You can order by phone. If you're calling within Spain, dial 902-224-460. If calling internationally, dial the international access code first (00 for a European country, 011 for the U.S. or Canada), then 34-913-465936 (daily 8:00–18:00, can reserve between 1 day and a year in advance, use credit-card number to pay and you'll get a reference number to tell the ticket-window clerk at the Alhambra to get your ticket, you'll be advised to pick up your ticket an hour before your palace entry time).

3. Order online at www.alhambratickets.com (currently this Web site is in Spanish, but an English version will be added eventually).

If you're in Granada without a reservation: You have a number of alternatives, the first of which involves getting up unnaturally early.

1. Stand in line at the Alhambra. The Alhambra admits 8,000 visitors a day. Six thousand tickets are sold in advance (see above). Two thousand are sold each day at the Alhambra ticket window (near Generalife Gardens and parking lot). On busy days, tickets can sell out as early as 10:00.

The ticket office opens at 8:00. People start lining up about 7:30, but generally if you're in line by 8:15, you'll get an entry time. On a slow day you'll get in right away. During busy times you'll have an appointment for later that day. However, you're on vacation, and it's a pain to get up this early and miss breakfast to stand in line. It's more efficient to reserve in advance.

2. Consider getting Granada's Bono Turístico city pass if you'll be staying at least two days in the city. It costs €18, covers admission to the Alhambra and the city's other top sights, and includes a reservation for the Alhambra (scheduled when you buy the pass). The pass is valid for seven days. Usually you can

get into the Alhambra on the second day (possibly even the first). If you have only a day in Granada, this is risky. Even with two days, though it's probable you'll get in, there are no guarantees (especially during April–June and Sept–Oct). This pass is easiest to buy at the Royal Chapel (for details, see "Helpful Hints," above).

3. Make a reservation at a BBVA bank in Granada (possible for a following day, usually not the same day). People wait in line at the most visible BBVA bank in Granada—on Plaza Isabel la Católica—but any of the many BBVA branches in Granada (or anywhere in Spain) can make a reservation for you at a minimal €0.90 surcharge (bank hours Mon–Fri 8:30–14:00). You'll find a branch near Plaza Nueva at Plaza Carmen.

4. Your hotel (particularly if it's a 3- or 4-star) may be willing to book a reservation for you; ask when you reserve your room.

5. Take a tour of the Alhambra. The pricier hotels can book you on a €30 tour that includes Palacios Nazeries.

Getting to the Alhambra: There are three ways to get to the Alhambra.

1. From Plaza Nueva, hike 30 minutes up the street Cuesta de Gomerez. Keep going straight, with the Alhambra high on your left, and follow the street to the ticket pavilion at the far side of the Alhambra, near the Generalife Gardens.

2. From Plaza Nueva, catch a red minibus #30 or #32, marked "Alhambra" (€0.85, runs every 10 min).

3. Take a taxi (€3, taxi stand on Plaza Nueva).

Don't drive. If you do, you'll park on the far, far side of the Alhambra, and when you leave, one-way streets will send you into the traffic-clogged center of New Granada.

Planning Your Visit: It's a 10-minute walk to Palacios Nazaries from the entry. Be sure to arrive at the Alhambra with enough time to make it to the palace before your allotted half-hour appointment ends. The ticket-checkers at Palacios Nazaries are strict.

To minimize walking, see the Alcazaba fort and Charles V's Palace before your visit to Palacios Nazaries. Because the Alhambra is long (about a 10-min walk from end to end), you don't want to do a lot of backtracking, especially if it's hot. When you exit Palacios Nazaries, leave through the Partal Gardens (don't duck out early to visit the fort). This is your only chance to see these gardens and their great views of the Albayzín. You'll exit the gardens near the Alhambra entrance, and if you haven't seen the fort and Charles V's Palace yet, you'll need to backtrack to do so. (Note that, because of crowd-control restrictions, if you have an appointment for Palacios Nazaries after 14:00, you can't be admitted to the Alhambra any earlier than 14:00.)

Depending on your time, you can visit the Generalife Gardens before or after your visit to Palacios Nazaries. If you have any time to kill before your palace appointment, do it luxuriously at the parador bar (actually within the Alhambra walls). While you can find drinks, WCs, and guidebooks near the entrance of Palacios Nazaries, you'll find none inside the actual palace.

Cuisine: There are only three places to eat within the Alhambra walls: the restaurants at the parador and Hotel America, and a small bar/café kiosk in front of the Alcazaba fort (near entrance of Palacios Nazaries). You're welcome to bring in a picnic as long as you eat it in a public area.

Guidebooks: Consider getting a guidebook in town and reading it the night before to understand the layout and history of this remarkable sight before entering. The classic is *The Alhambra and the Generalife* (€6, includes great map, available in town and at shops throughout the Alhambra), but even better is the slick *Alhambra and Generalife in Focus*, which combines vibrant color photos and more readable text (€7.25, sold at Libreria next to TI in Corral del Carbon).

The Alhambra in Four Parts

1. Charles V's Palace—It's only natural for a conquering king to build his own palace over his foe's palace, and that's exactly what the Christian King Charles V did. The Alhambra palace wasn't good enough for Charles, so he built this one—destroying the dramatic Alhambra facade and financing his new palace with a salt-in-the-wound tax on Granada's defeated Moorish population. This palace, a unique circle within a square, is Spain's most impressive Renaissance building. It was designed by Pedro Machuca, a devotee of Michelangelo and Raphael. Stand in the circular courtyard, then climb the stairs. Imagine being here for one of Charles' bullfights. Charles' palace was never finished because his son Philip II moved the royal building focus to El Escorial. Inside the palace are two boring museums: Museo de Bellas Artes (€1.50, Tue 14:30–18:00, Wed–Sat 10:00–20:00, Sun 9:00–14:00, closed Mon, shorter hours off-season, located upstairs) and Museo de Alhambra, showing off some of the Alhambra's best Moorish art (free, Tue–Sat 9:00–14:30, closed Sun–Mon, on ground floor). The palace itself is free; to see only this, you can enter the Alhambra at either of the two gates located midway along the length of the grounds (between the fort and official entrance).

2. Alcazaba Fort—The fort, the oldest and most ruined part of the Alhambra, offers exercise and fine city views. What you see is mid–13th century, but there was probably a fort here in Roman times. Once upon a time this tower defended a town (or medina) of 2,000 Arabs living within the Alhambra walls. From the top find Plaza Nueva, the Albayzín viewpoint, and the mountains. Is anybody skiing today? Look to the south and think of that day in 1492 when the cross and flags of Aragon and Castile were raised on this tower and the fleeing Moorish King Boabdil looked back and wept. His mom chewed him out, saying, "Don't weep like a woman for what you couldn't defend like a man." Much later, Napoleon stationed his troops here, contributing substantially to its ruin when he left. Follow the signs down and around to the Palacios Nazaries (WCs to right of entry); if you're early, duck into the exhibit across from the palace entry. It's in Spanish, but the models of the Alhambra upstairs are easy to appreciate.

3. Palacios Nazaries—During the 30-minute window of time stamped on your ticket, enter the jewel of the Alhambra: The Moorish royal palace. You'll walk through three basic sections: royal offices, ceremonial rooms, and private quarters. Built mostly in the 14th century, this palace offers your best possible look at the refined, elegant Moorish civilization of Al-Andalus. If you can imagine a few tapestries, carpets, pillows, ivory-studded wooden furniture, and painted stucco, the place is much as it was for the Moorish kings. Rather then hire an interior decorator, the Moors just read the Koran: recommended color scheme—red (blood), blue (heaven), green (oasis), and gold (wealth). As you tour the palace, keep the palace themes in mind: water, no images, "stalactite" ceilings throughout—and few signs telling you where you are. Even today, the route constantly changes. Use the map to locate these essential stops.

Court of Myrtles: Walk through a few administrative rooms (the *mexuar*) and a small courtyard until you hit the big rectangular courtyard with a fish pond lined by a myrtle bush hedge—the Court of Myrtles (Patio de los Arrayanes). Moors loved their patios—with a garden, water, and under the sky. Women, who rarely went out, stayed in touch with nature here. The living quarters for the wives (the Koran allowed a man "all the women you can maintain with dignity") were upstairs. Notice the wooden "jalousies"—screens (erected by jealous husbands) allowing the cloistered women to look out without being clearly seen.

Boat Room: Head left (north) from the entry into the long, narrow antechamber to the throne room, called the "Boat Room." While it's understandable that many think this is named for the upside-down-hull shape of its fine cedar ceiling, the name is actually a corruption of the Arab word *baraka*, meaning "divine blessing and luck." This was the waiting room for meetings with the sultan, and blessings and luck are exactly what you'd need if you had business in the next room. Oh, it's your turn now . . .

Alhambra's Palacios Nazaries

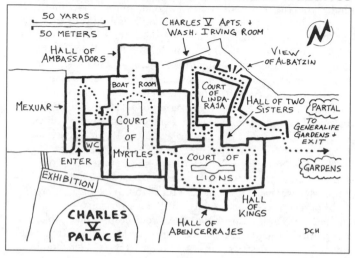

The Hall of the Ambassadors (Gran Salon de Embaja-dores): This functioned as a throne room. It was here that the sultan received foreign emissaries. The king's throne stood opposite the entrance. The ceiling, made of cedar of Lebanon—8,000 inlaid pieces—is original. The walls, even without their original paint and gilding, are still glorious. Note the finely carved Arabic script. Muslims couldn't make images of living things—that was God's work. But they could carve decorative religious messages. One phrase—"only Allah is victorious"—is repeated 9,000 times throughout the palace. Find the character for Allah—it looks like a cursive W with a nose on its left side. The swoopy toboggan blades underneath are a kind of artistic punctuation marking off one phrase.

In 1492 two historic events took place in this room. Culmin-ating a 700-year-long battle, the Reconquista was completed here as the last Moorish king, Boabdil, signed the terms of his surrender before packing light and fleeing to Africa. For four years Isabel had put off Columbus as she focused on the Recon-quista. That accomplished, Isabel and Ferdinand finally received Columbus in this room. Imagine the scene: The king, the queen, and the greatest minds from the University of Salamanca gathered here to hear Columbus make his case that the world was round— then a still-loony notion that got people burned a few years earlier. Ferdinand and the professors laughed, calling Columbus mad. But Isabel said *"Sí, señor."* Columbus fell to his knees (promising to wear a moneybelt and use the most current guidebooks available) and she gave him an ATM card and a wad of traveler's checks as a backup.

Continue deeper into the palace to a court where, 600 years ago, only the royal family and their servants could enter. It's the much-photographed...

Court of the Lions: The Patio de los Leones features a fountain with 12 lions. Why 12? Since the fountain was a gift from a Jewish leader celebrating good relations with the sultan (Granada had a big Jewish community), the lions probably represent the 12 tribes of Israel. During Moorish times, the fountain functioned as a clock, with a different lion spouting water each hour. (Conquering Christians disassembled the fountain to see how it worked and it's never worked since.) From the center, four streams went out—figuratively to the corners of the earth and literally to various apartments of the royal family. Notice how the court resembles, with its 124 columns, the cloister of a Catholic monastery. Six hundred years ago the Muslim Moors could read the Koranic poetry that ornaments this court, and they could understand the symbolism of this lush, enclosed garden (considered the embodiment of paradise or truth). Imagine—they appreciated this part of the palace even more than we do today.

On the right, off the courtyard, is a square room called the **Hall of the Abencerrajes (Sala de los Abencerrajes).** According to legend, the father of Boabdil took a new wife and wanted to disinherit the children of his first marriage—one of whom was Boabdil. In order to deny power to Boabdil and his siblings, he killed nearly the entire pro-Boabdil Abencerraje family. The sultan thought this would pave the way for the son of his new wife to be the next sultan. Happily, he stacked 36 Abencerrage heads in the pool under this sumptuous honeycombed stucco ceiling. But his scheme failed, and Boabdil ultimately assumed the throne. Bloody power struggles like this were the norm here in the Alhambra.

The Hall of the Kings (Sala de los Reyes) is at the end of the court opposite where you entered. Notice the ceilings of the three chambers branching off this gallery. Breaking from the tradition of imageless art, paintings on the goat-leather ceiling depict scenes of the sultan and his family. The center room shows a group portrait of the first 10 of the Alhambra's 22 sultans. The scene is a fantasy, since these people lived over a span of many generations. The two end rooms show scenes of princely pastimes, such as hunting and shooting skeet. In a palace otherwise devoid of figures, these offer a rare look at royal life in the palace.

The next room, the **Hall of the Two Sisters,** has another oh-wow stucco ceiling but no figures—only geometric patterns and stylized Arabic script quoting verses from the Koran.

Washington Irving Room: That's about it for the palace. From here you wander through a few more rooms including one (marked with a large plaque) where Washington Irving wrote *Tales of the Alhambra*. While serving as the U.S. ambassador to Spain in 1829, Irving lived in the Alhambra. It was a romantic time, when the place was home to Gypsies and donkeys. His "tales" kindled interest in the place, causing it to become recognized as a national treasure.

Hallway with a view: Stop at the open-air hallway for the best-in-the-palace view of the labyrinthine Albayzín—the old Moorish town on the opposite hillside. Find the famous viewpoint at the base of the white St. Nicolás church tower breaking the horizon. Creeping into the mountains on the right are the Gypsy neighborhoods of Sacromonte. Still circling old Granada is the Moorish wall (built in the 1200s to protect the city's population, swollen by Muslim refugees driven south by the Reconquista).

Leaving the Palacios Nazaries, follow signs to the Partal Gardens, go through the gardens, then follow signs directing you left to the Generalife Gardens or right to the exit.

4. Generalife Gardens—On the hillside to the east, the garden with carefully pruned hedges is Generalife (pron. henneraw-LEEF-ay). This most perfect Arabian garden in Andalucía was the summer home of the Moorish kings, the closest thing on earth to the Koran's description of heaven. If you have a long wait before your entry to the Palacios, tour these gardens first, then the Alcazaba fort and Charles V's Palace.

Sights—Central Granada

▲▲**Royal Chapel (Capilla Real)**—Without a doubt Granada's top Christian sight, this lavish chapel holds the dreams—and bodies—of Queen Isabel and King Ferdinand (€2.50, April–Sept Mon–Sat 10:30–13:00 & 16:00–19:00, Sun 11:00–13:00 & 16:00–19:00; Oct–March Mon–Sat 10:30–13:00 & 15:30–18:30, opens Sun at 11:00, no photos, entrance on Calle Oficios, just off Gran Vía de Colón; go through iron gate, tel. 958-227-848).

In the lobby, before you enter the chapel, notice the painting of Boabdil (on the black horse) giving the key of Granada to the conquering King Ferdinand. Boabdil wanted to fall to his knees, but the Spanish king, who had great respect for his Moorish foe, embraced him instead. They fought a long and noble war (for instance, respectfully returning the bodies of dead soldiers). Ferdinand is in red, and Isabel is behind him wearing a crown. Next to her (under a black hood) is their daughter Juana. And next to Juana is her husband, Philip the Fair, wearing a crown. Philip died young, and for two years Juana (known as "the Mad") kept his casket at her bedside, kissing his embalmed body good night. These four people are buried in this chapel. The painting is flanked by two large portraits of Ferdinand and Isabel.

Isabel decided to make Granada the capital of Spain (and burial place for Spanish royalty) for three reasons: 1) With the conquest of Granada, Christianity had overcome Islam in Europe; 2) her marriage with Ferdinand, followed by the conquest of Granada, had marked the beginning of a united Spain; and 3) in Granada, she agreed to sponsor Columbus' fateful voyage.

Step into the **chapel.** It's Plateresque Gothic—light and lacy, named for and inspired by the fine silverwork of the Moors. This was the most lavish interior money could buy 500 years ago. Because of its speedy completion, the chapel is an unusually harmonious piece of architecture.

The four **royal tombs** are Renaissance-style. Carved in Italy in 1521 out of Carrara marble, they were sent by ship to Spain. The faces based on death masks—are considered accurate. If you're facing the altar, Ferdinand and Isabel are on the right. (Isabel fans attribute the bigger dent she puts in the pillow to brains.) Philip the Fair and Juana are on the left. Philip was a Hapsburg. Their son, Charles V (known as Carlos I in Spain), was a key figure in European history, as his coronation merged the Holy Roman Empire (Hapsburg domain) with the Spanish empire. Europe's top king, he ruled a vast empire stretching from Bohemia to Bolivia (1519–1556).

When Phillip II, the son of Charles V, decided to build El Escorial and establish Madrid as the single capital of a single Spain, Granada lost power and importance.

More important, Spain declined. After the reign of Charles V, Spain squandered her awesome wealth trying to maintain this huge and impossible empire. She did it not for material riches, but to defend the romantic, quixotic dream of a Catholic empire ruled by one divinely ordained Catholic monarch against an irrepressible tide of nationalism and Protestantism that was sweeping across the country. Spain's relatively poor modern history can be blamed, in part, on her stubborn unwillingness to accept the end of this "old regime" notion.

Look at the fine carving on the tombs (unfortunately vandal-ized by Napoleon's troops). It's a humanistic statement with healthy, organic, realistic figures rising above the strict and heavy Gothic past.

From the feet of the marble tombs, step downstairs to see the actual coffins. They are plain. Isabel was originally buried as simply as a monk at the Franciscan monastery (in what is today the parador at the Alhambra). The fifth coffin (with PM on it) is that of a young Prince Michael, who would have been king of a united Spain and Portugal. A sad—but too long—story . . .

The **high altar** is one of the finest Renaissance works in Spain. It's dedicated to John the Baptist and John the Evangelist. In the center, you can see the Baptist and the Evangelist chatting as if over tapas (an appropriately humanist scene). Scenes from the Baptist's life are on the left: John beheaded after Salome's fine dancing and (below) John baptizing Jesus. Scenes from the Evangelist's life are on the right: John's martyrdom (a failed attempt to boil him alive in oil) and John on Patmos (where he wrote the last book of the Bible, Revelation). John is talking to the eagle that, according to legend, flew him to Heaven.

Anyone who paid for church art got his mug in it. Find Ferdinand and Isabel kneeling in prayer in opposite corners. The eagle banners around the room are not the aggressive, two-headed, claws-exposed Hapsburg eagles but eagles with halos (and crowns for bras). These are symbolic of the eagle that inspired John on Patmos.

The Plateresque (silver-filigree-style) arch leads to a small glass pyramid in the **treasury.** This holds Queen Isabel's silver crown ringed with pomegranates (symbolizing Granada), and King Ferdinand's sword. Beside the entry arch you'll see the devout Isabel's prayer book, in which she followed the Mass. The book and its sturdy box date from 1496. The fancy box on the other side of the door is the one that Isabel (cash-poor because of her military expenses) supposedly filled with jewels and gave to Columbus. Columbus sold these to finance his journey. Next, in the corner (and also behind glass), is the cross that Cardinal Mendoza, staunch supporter of Queen Isabel, carried into the Alhambra on that historic day in 1492. Next, the big silk, silver, and gold tapestry is the altar banner for the mobile campaign chapel of Ferdinand and Isabel, who always traveled with their army. In the next case you'll see the original Christian army flags raised over the Alhambra in 1492.

The room holds the first great art collection ever established by a woman. Queen Isabel amassed more than 200 great paintings. After Napoleon's visit, only 30 remained. Even so, this is a fine collection, all on wood, featuring works by Botticelli, Perugino, the Flemish master Memling, and less-famous Spanish masters.

Finally, at the end of the room, the two carved sculptures of Ferdinand and Isabel were the originals from the high altar. Charles V considered these primitive and replaced them with the ones you saw earlier.

Cathedral—One of only two Renaissance churches in Spain (the other is in Córdoba), Granada's cathedral is the second-largest in

Spain after Sevilla's. Its spacious and bright interior is a refreshing break from the dark Gothic and gilded-lily Baroque of so many Spanish churches. In a modern move back in the 18th century, the choir walls were taken out so that people could be involved in the worship. To make matters even better, an 18th-century bishop ordered the interior painted with lime (for hygienic reasons, during a time of disease). The people liked it, and it stayed white. Most of the side chapels are decorated in Baroque style. On the far wall (to the right of the high altar) is St. James the Moorslayer, with his sword raised high and an armored Moor under his horse's hooves. The Renaissance facade and paintings of the Virgin (1601–1661) in the rotunda are by Granada's own Alonso Cano (€2.50, April–Sept Mon–Sat 10:30–13:30 & 16:00–20:00, Sun 16:00–20:00; Oct–March Mon–Sat 10:30–13:30 & 16:00–19:00, Sun 16:00–19:00, audioguide-€3, entrance off Gran Vía de Colón through iron gateway, tel. 958-222-959).

Alcaicería—Originally an Arab silk market, this neighborhood (around the cathedral) still functions as a silk and jewelry market. Ignore the aggressive, obnoxious Gypsy women giving tourists sprigs of rosemary for good luck. (The flowers they used to give became too expensive. After somehow rerouting the magic power, they now use rosemary, which comes from the parks—for free.) By accepting the sprig you start a relationship. This, while free, leads to palm reading, which isn't.

Explore the mesh of tiny shopping lanes between the cathedral and Calle Reyes Católicos. Go on a photo and sound safari: popcorn machines popping, men selling balloons, leather goods spread out on streets, kids playing soccer, barking dogs, dogged shoeshine boys, and the whirring grind of bicycle-powered knife sharpeners.

The exuberant square behind the cathedral is **Bib-Rambla.** While today it's fine for coffee or a meal amidst the color and fragrance of flower stalls, in Moorish times this was a place of public execution. A block away, the square Pescaderia is a smaller, similarly lively version of Bib-Rambla.

Plaza Isabel la Católica—Granada's two grand boulevards, Gran Vía and Reyes Católicos, meet a block off Plaza Nueva at Plaza Isabel la Católica. Here you'll see a fine statue of Columbus unfurling a long contract with Isabel. It lists the terms of Columbus' MCDXCII voyage.

Isabel was driven by her desire to spread Catholicism. Columbus was driven by his desire for money. For adding territory to Spain's Catholic empire, Isabel promised Columbus the ranks of Admiral of the Oceans and Governor of the New World. To sweeten the pie, she tossed in 10 percent of all the riches he brought home. Isabel died thinking Columbus had found India or China. Columbus died poor and disillusioned.

From here, Calle Reyes Católicos leads to Puerta Real. There Acera de Darro takes you through modern Granada to the river via the huge El Corte Inglés department store and lots of modern commerce.

Paseo de los Tristes—In the cool of the evening—with dinner as a popular destination—consider strolling the Paseo de los Tristes (if you're tired, note that bus #31 and #32 stop here). This "walk of the sad ones" is the route of funeral processions to the cemetery at the edge of town.

Start at Plaza Nueva. The Church of Santa Anna, which stands at the far end of the square, was originally a mosque, its tower a minaret. Notice the ceramic brickwork. This is Mudejar art, the technique of the Moors used by Christians. Inside you'll see a fine Alhambra-style cedar ceiling. Follow Carrera del Darro along the River Darro under the Alhambra. (Nine kilometers upstream, part of the Darro is diverted to provide water for the Alhambra's many fountains.) Past the church, on your right is the turn-off for the Arab Baths (described below) and on the left Santa Catalina de Zafra, a convent of cloistered nuns (they worship behind a screen that divides the church's rich interior in half). Farther ahead, on the right, across from the Archaeological Museum, is the Church of San Pedro, the parish church of Sacromonte's Gypsy community. Within its rich interior is an ornate oxcart used to carry the Host on the annual pilgrimage to Rocio near Portugal. Finally, you reach the Paseo de los Tristes. Covered with happy diners, this is a great spot at night, under the floodlit Alhambra. From here the road arcs up (past a rank of "burro taxis" for those into adventure sports) into Sacromonte. And from here a lane (called Cuesta de los Chinos or Carretera del Rey Chico) leads up to the Alhambra "through the back door."

Arab Baths—Consider a visit to the Arab baths at Hammam Baños Arabes Al Andaluz. The 75-minute soak and a 15-minute massage cost €18; for a 90-minute bath only, it's €11 (daily 10:00–24:00, appointment times scheduled every hour, co-ed with mandatory swimsuits, quiet atmosphere encouraged, lockers available, just off Plaza Nueva at Santa Ana 16; from Plaza Nueva, it's the first right—over a bridge—past the church; reservation necessary, especially on weekends—some hoteliers are happy to call for you; tel. 958-229-978).

Sights—Albayzín

Explore Spain's best old Moorish quarter, with countless colorful corners, flowery patios, and shady lanes to soothe the 21st-century-mangled visitor. Climb high to the San Nicolás

Albayzín Neighborhood

NOTE: NOT TO SCALE. PLAZA NUEVA TO SAN NICOLAS IS A 20 MIN WALK UPHILL

❶ Bus stop for Albayzín loop
❷ Calderería Nueva (tapas bars, teterias)
❸ Plaza de Carvajales
❹ Restaurante Ladrillo I
❺ Restaurante Ladrillo II
❻ Casa Torcuato
❼ El Agua Casa de Vinos
❽ Mirador de Morayma
❾ Naturi Albayzín
❿ Bodega Castenada
⓫ Bus to Alhambra
⓬ Arab Baths

church for the best view of the Alhambra. Then wander through the mysterious backstreets.

Getting to the Albayzín: A handy city minibus threads its way around the Albayzín from Plaza Nueva (see Albayzín Circular Bus Tour, below), getting you scenically and sweatlessly to the St. Nicolás viewpoint. You can also taxi to the St. Nicolás church and explore from there. Consider having your cabbie take you on a Sacromonte detour en route.

If walking up, leave the west end of Plaza Nueva on Calle Elvira. After about 200 meters, turn right on Calderería Nueva. Follow this stepped street past tapas bars and *teterias* (see "Eating," below) as it goes left around the church, slants, winds, and zigzags up the hill, heading basically straight. Pass the peach-colored building on your left (resisting the temptation to turn left on Muladar Sancha). When you reach a T-intersection, go left on Calle del Almirante. Near the crest, turn right on Camino Nuevo de San Nicolás, then walk several blocks to the street that curves up left (look for brown sign Mirador de San Nicolás, where a street sign would normally be). Soon you'll see steps leading up to the church's viewpoint.

▲▲San Nicolás Viewpoint—For one of Europe's most romantic viewpoints, be here at sunset when the Alhambra turns red and the Albayzín widows share the benches with local lovers and tourists. In 1997 President Clinton made a point to bring his family here—a favorite spot from a trip he made as a student.

Exploring the Albayzín: From the San Nicolás viewpoint you're at the edge of a neighborhood even people of Granada recognize as a world apart. From the viewpoint turn your back to the Alhambra and walk north (passing the church on your right and the Biblioteca Municipal on your left). A lane leads past a white stone arch (on your right)—now a chapel built into the old Moorish wall. At the end of the lane, step down to the right through the 11th-century "New Gate" (Puerta Nueva—older than the Alhambra) and into **Plaza Larga.** In medieval times this tiny square (called "long," because back then it was) was the local marketplace. It still is a busy market each morning, with locals blaring their cheap, pirated cassettes as if to prove there is actually music on them. Casa Pasteles, at the near end of the square, serves good coffee and cakes.

Leave Plaza Larga on Calle Agua de Albayzín (as you face Casa Pasteles it's to your right). The street, named for the public baths that used to line it, shows evidence of the Moorish plumbing system—gutters. Back when Europe's streets were filled with muck, Granada actually had Roman Empire–style gutters with drains leading to clay and lead pipes.

This road leads to a T-intersection. You can turn left for the recommended restaurant Casa Torcuato (a block away, see "Eating," below) or right for the recommended El Ladrillo (2 blocks away). Or just explore. You're in the heart of the Albayzín. Poke into an old church. They're plain by design— to go easy on the Muslim converts who weren't used to being surrounded by images as they worshiped. You'll see lots of real Muslim culture living in the streets, including many recent Spanish converts. Those aren't the Spice Girls, just Gypsy teenagers—as influenced by TV as any teenagers these days.

Albayzín Circular Bus Tour—The handy Albayzín bus #31 makes the 15-minute loop, departing from Plaza Nueva about every 10 minutes (pay driver €0.85, better views on the right, bus #32 does the same loop but—depending on where you catch it—goes to Alhambra first). While good for a lift to the top of the Albayzín, I'd stay on for an entire circle (and return to the Albayzín later for dinner—either on foot or by bus). While a few #31 buses detour up Sacromonte (see schedule at bus stop), all pass its entrance. Two stops later the driver announces the San Nicolás mirador (viewpoint). The next stop is San Miguel el Bajo (a fun square with several fine little restaurants). Just after that you get a commanding view of modern Granada on the left. Hitting the city's main drag, Gran Vía, you make a U-turn at the Garden of the Triumph, celebrating the Immaculate Conception of the Virgin Mary (notice her statue atop a column). Behind Mary stands the old Royal Hospital—built in the 16th century for Granada's poor by the Catholic kings after the Reconquista in hopes of winning the favor of Granada's conquered residents. From here you zip past the cathedral and home to Plaza Nueva.

Sights—Sacromonte and Granada's Gypsies

Spain's Gypsies came from India via Egypt. The Spanish word for Gypsy, *Gitano*, means "Egyptian." They settled mostly in the south, where they found people less racist and more tolerant. Ages ago a Spanish king, exasperated by Gypsy problems, actually declared that these nomads must stay in one place and get a religion—any religion. In most of Spain, Gypsies are more assimilated into the general community, but Granada's Sacromonte district is a large and distinct Gypsy community. Granada's Gypsies arrived in the 16th century and have stuck together ever since. Today 50,000 Gypsies call Granada home.

Spaniards, who consider themselves accepting and not racist, claim that in maintaining such a tight community, the Gypsies segregate themselves. The Gypsies call Spaniards *Payo* ("Whites").

Sacromonte has one main street. Camino del Sacromonte is lined with caves primed for tourists and restaurants ready to fight over the bill. Intriguing lanes run above and below this main drag.

Formerly Europe's most disgusting tourist trap, famous for its cave-dwelling, foot-stomping, flamenco-dancing Gypsies, Sacromonte is not quite as bad as it used to be. Still, don't go here expecting to get a good value for anything. Flamenco is better in Sevilla.

Sights—Near Granada

Carthusian Monastery (La Cartuja)—A church with an interior that looks as if it squirted out of a can of whipped cream, La Cartuja is nicknamed the "Christian Alhambra" for its elaborate white Baroque stucco work. In the rooms just off the cloister, notice the gruesome paintings of martyrs placidly meeting their grisly fates. It's located 1.5 kilometers north of town on the way to Madrid. Drive north on Gran Vía de Colón and follow the signs or take bus #8 from Gran Vía de Colón (entry-€2.50, April–Sept Mon–Sat 10:00–13:00 & 16:00–20:00, Sun 10:00–12:00

& 16:00–20:00, Oct–March Mon–Sat 10:00–13:00 & 15:30–18:00, Sun 10:00–12:00 & 15:30–18:00, tel. 958-161-932).

Sleeping in Granada
(€1 = about $1, country code: 34)

Sleep Code: **S** = Single, **D** = Double/Twin, **T** = Triple, **Q** = Quad, **b** = bathroom, **s** = shower only, **CC** = Credit Cards accepted, **no CC** = Credit Cards not accepted, **SE** = Speaks English, **NSE** = No English. Breakfast and the 7 percent IVA tax are usually not included.

To help you easily sort through these listings, I've divided the rooms into three categories based on the price for a standard double room with bath during high season:

Higher Priced—Most rooms more than €100.
Moderately Priced—Most rooms €100 or less.
Lower Priced—Most rooms €50 or less.

In July and August, when the streets are littered with sun-stroke victims, rooms are plentiful. Crowded months are April, May, June, September, and October. Except for the Alhambra and near-train-station listings, all recommended hotels are within a five-minute walk of Plaza Nueva (see map on page 183). While few of the hotels have parking facilities, all can direct you to a garage (such as Parking San Agustin, just off Gran Vía de Colón, €16/24 hrs.)

Sleeping on or near Plaza Nueva
(zip code: 18009 unless otherwise noted)

Each of these is big, professional, plenty comfortable, and perfectly located. Prices vary with the demand.

HIGHER PRICED

Hotel Inglaterra, a chain hotel, is modern and peaceful, with 36 rooms offering all the comforts (Sb-€91–92, Db-€92–118, buffet breakfast-€9.50, tax extra, CC, elevator to 3rd floor only, air-con, Cettie Meriem 4, 18010 Granada, tel. 958-221-559, fax 958-227-100, www.nh-hoteles.com, e-mail: nhinglaterra@nh-hoteles.es).

MODERATELY PRICED

Hotel Residencia Macia, right on the colorful Plaza Nueva, is a hotelesque place with 44 clean, modern, and classy rooms. Choose between an on-the-square view or a quieter interior room (Sb-€43, Db-€64, Tb-€87, show this book upon arrival to get a 10 percent discount, good buffet breakfast-€5, tax extra, CC, air-con, elevator, Plaza Nueva 4, tel. 958-227-536, fax 958-227-533, e-mail: maciaplaza@maciahoteles.com, SE).

Hotel Anacapri is a bright, cool, marble oasis with 49 modern rooms and a quiet lounge (Sb-€54–60, Db-€72–84, extra bed-€18, CC, elevator, air-con, 2 blocks toward Gran Vía from Plaza Nueva at Calle Joaquin Costa 7, just a block from cathedral bus stop, tel. 958-227-477, fax 958-228-909, www.hotelanacapri.com, e-mail: reservas@hotelanacapri.com, helpful Kathy speaks Iowan).

Hotel Gran Vía, right on Granada's main drag, has a stately lobby with Euro-modern business-class rooms (Sb-€46–63, Db-€70–79, Tb-€93–106, show this book for a 10 percent discount on these prices, CC, air-con, elevator, 5-min walk from Plaza Nueva, Gran Vía de Colón 25, tel. 958-285-464, fax 958-285-591, e-mail: granvia@maciahoteles.com, SE).

Cheaper Places on Cuesta de Gomerez
(zip code: 18009)

LOWER PRICED

These are cheap and ramshackle lodgings on the street leading from Plaza Nueva up to the Alhambra.

Hostal Landazuri is run by friendly, English-speaking Matilda Landazuri and her son, Manolo. While most of its 18 rooms are well-worn, a few are newly renovated with new mattresses and windows. It has a great roof garden with an Alhambra view and a hardworking, helpful management. If your room gets too hot, ask for a fan (Sb-€28, D-€24, Db-€36, Tb-€40, simple €1.80 breakfast or their hearty €2.30 eggs-and-bacon breakfast, includes tax, no CC, Cuesta de Gomerez 24, tel. & fax 958-221-406). The Landazuris also run a good, cheap café.

Hostal Residencia Britz is a simple, no-nonsense place overlooking Plaza Nueva. All of its 24 basic rooms—with double-paned windows—are streetside. Bring earplugs (S-€19, D-€29, Db-€40, includes tax, no breakfast, CC, coin-op washing machine but no dryer, elevator, Plaza Nueva y Gomerez 1, tel. & fax 958-223-652).

Hostal Navarro Ramos has 15 rooms that are comfortable enough (S-€12, D-€19, Db-€29, Tb-€38, no breakfast, no CC, Cuesta de Gomerez 21, 1st floor, tel. 958-250-555, NSE).

Hostal Viena, run by English-speaking Austrian Irene (pron. ee-RAY-nay), is on a quieter side street with 29 basic backpacker-type rooms (S-€25, D-€35, Db-€42, Tb-€56, family rooms, includes tax, no breakfast, CC, air-con, Hospital de Santa Ana 2, 10 meters off Cuesta de Gomerez, tel. & fax 958-221-859, e-mail: hostalviena@hostelviena.com). Irene also manages the similar **Hotel Austria** nearby.

Hostal Gomerez is run by English-speaking Sigfrido Sanchez de León de Torres (who will explain to you how Spanish surnames work if you have the time). Clean and basic and listed in nearly

every country's student-travel guidebook, this is another fine
cheapie. Sigfrido is adding double-paned windows to the rooms.
Quieter rooms are in the back (S-€15, D-€23, T-€30, Q-€35,
includes tax, no breakfast, no CC, laundry service-€9, Cuesta de
Gomerez 10, 1 floor up, tel. & fax 958-224-437).

Sleeping near Plaza Carmen

Two blocks from the TI is the pleasant Plaza Carmen and the
beginning of Calle Navas, a pedestrian street offering a couple
of good values.

LOWER PRICED
Hotel Residencia Lisboa, which overlooks Plaza Carmen oppo-
site Granada's city hall, offers 28 simple but well-maintained rooms
with friendly owners (S-€18, Sb-€30, D-€27, Db-€40, T-€36,
Tb-€53, includes tax, no breakfast, CC, elevator, no public rooms,
Plaza de Carmen 27, tel. 958-221-413, fax 958-221-487, Mary and
Juan Jose).

   Hotel Navas, a block down Calle Navas, is a modern, well-
run, tour-friendly, business-class hotel with 49 spacious rooms
(Sb-€66, Db-€88, Tb-€105, breakfast buffet-€6, includes tax,
CC, air-con, elevator, attached restaurant, Calle Navas 24, tel.
958-225-959, fax 958-227-523, e-mail: navas@jet.es, SE).

Sleeping near the Cathedral

MODERATELY PRICED
Hotel Los Tilos offers 30 comfortable rooms, some with balconies, on the charming, traffic-free Bib-Rambla square behind
the cathedral. All clients are welcome to use the fourth-floor
view terrace overlooking the great café, shopping, and people-
watching neighborhood (Sb-€41, Db-€62, Tb-€73, includes
tax, 20 percent discount with this book and cash, breakfast
buffet-€5, CC, air-con, elevator, Plaza Bib-Rambla 4, tel.
958-266-712, fax 958-266-801, e-mail: clientes@hotellostilos
.com, friendly Jose-Maria SE).

   Reina Cristina has 43 quiet, elegant rooms a few steps
off Plaza Trinidad, a park-like square, near the lively Pescaderia
and Bib-Rambla squares. Check out the great Mudejar ceiling
and the painting at the entrance of this house, where the famous
Spanish poet Garcia Lorca hid before being executed by the
Guardia Civil (Sb-€56–59, Db-€83-88, Tb-€98-104, tax
extra, CC, air-con, elevator, Tablas 4, tel. 958-253-211, fax
958-255-728, www.hotelreinacristina.com, e-mail: clientes
@hotelreinacristina.com).

Sleeping near the Train Station

MODERATELY PRICED
Hotel Condor, with 104 modern rooms in a high-rise, has more four-star comfort than character. It's an eight-minute walk from the station, and 15 minutes—or a bus ride—to the center of town (Sb-€59–72, Db-€79–110, breakfast-€7.20, CC, laundry service, non-smoking floor, attached restaurant, Avenida de la Constitución 6, tel. 958-283-711, fax 958-283-850, e-mail: condor@maciahoteles.com).

Sleeping in or near the Alhambra
(zip code: 18009)
If you want to stay on the Alhambra grounds, there are two popular options—famous, overpriced, and often booked up. These are a kilometer up the hill from Plaza Nueva.

HIGHER PRICED
Parador Nacional San Francisco, offering 36 air-conditioned rooms in a converted 15th-century convent, is called Spain's premier parador (Db-€208, Tb-€275, breakfast-€11, free parking, CC, Real de la Alhambra, tel. 958-221-440, fax 958-222-264, e-mail: granada@parador.es, SE). You must book ahead six to eight months to spend the night in this lavishly located, stodgy, classy, and historic place. Any peasant, however, can drop in for a coffee, drink, snack, or meal (daily 8:00–11:00 & 13:00–16:00 & 20:30–23:00).

Next to the parador, the elegant and cozy **Hotel America** rents 17 rooms (Sb-€68, Db-€116, includes tax and breakfast, CC, closed Nov–Feb, tel. 958-227-471, fax 958-227-470, e-mail: hamerica@moebius.es, SE). Book three months in advance.

Eating in Granada
Traditionally, Granada bars serve a small tapas plate free with any beer or wine ordered. Two well-chosen beers can actually end up being a light meal. In search of an edible memory? A local specialty, *tortilla Sacromonte*, is a spicy omelet with pig's brain and other organs.

These places are peppered with lively eateries and tapas bars: Albayzín, Calle Elvira (near Plaza Nueva), Calle Navas (off Plaza Carmen), and Bib-Rambla and Pescaderia (a block apart from each other, just west of the cathedral).

Eating in the Albayzín
The most interesting meals hide out deep in the Albayzín quarter. Two good squares are near the San Nicolás viewpoint. Plaza San Miguel el Bajo has some charming restaurants and kids playing soccer (look for the view over the modern city a block away).

Plaza Larga, within two blocks of the first three listings below, also has good eateries (to find the square, ask any local, take bus #31 or #32 from Plaza Nueva, or follow directions and map above, in "Sights—Albayzín"). Warning: Thefts have increased after dark in the Albayzín; take the bus or a taxi back to your hotel after a late-night dinner.

For fish, consider **El Ladrillo,** with outdoor tables on a peaceful square (Plaza Fatima, just off Calle Pages), or **El Ladrillo II,** with indoor dining only and a more extensive menu (Calle Panaderos 35, off Plaza Larga, tel. 958-292-651). They both serve a popular *barco* (€7.25 "boatload" of mixed fried fish), a fishy feast that stuffs two to the gills. The smaller *medio-barco,* for €4.80, fills one adequately. (A *medio-barca* and a salad feed 2.) Yet another El Ladrillo, maybe featuring flamenco, recently opened (Agua 20); it's tricky to find—ask the folks at El Ladrillo II to show you the way. Each restaurant is open daily (12:00–24:00).

For fewer tourists, more locals and village atmosphere, and great inexpensive food, try **Casa Torcuato** (Mon–Sat 13:00–16:00 & 20:00–24:00, closed Sun, 2 blocks beyond Plaza Larga on Placeta de Carniceros, Calle Carniceros 4, tel. 958-202-039).

For a more romantic, candlelit setting with Alhambra views, reserve ahead for **El Agua Casa de Vinos** (€15 3-course meals—most with cheese fondue, Tue 20:00–23:00, Wed–Mon 13:30–16:00 & 20:00–23:00, CC, Placeta Aljibe de Trillo 7, halfway up Albayzín hill, below San Nicolás viewpoint, reservations necessary, tel. 958-224-356).

Mirador de Morayma, with a similarly intimate, garden-view-mansion ambience, also requires reservations (€24 meals, Mon–Sat 13:30–15:30 & 20:30–23:30, closed Sun, CC, Calle Pianista Garcia Carrillo 2, tel. 958-228-290).

Eating near Plaza Nueva

For people-watching ambience, consider the many restaurants on Plaza Nueva, Bib-Rambla, or Paseo de los Tristes.

The cheap and easy **Bodega Castaneda,** a half-block off Plaza Nueva, serves fine *ensaladas* and baked potatoes with a fun variety of toppings (on Calle Elvira, just 20 meters off Plaza Nueva, not the other bodega a block away with the same name—which doesn't serve baked potatoes).

Hippie Options on Calle Calderería Nueva: From Plaza Nueva walk two long blocks down Calle Elvira and turn right onto the wonderfully hip and Arabic-feeling Calderería Nueva, which leads uphill into the Albayzín. The street is lined with trendy *teterias*. These small tea shops, open all day, are good places to linger, chat, and imagine an America where marijuana was legal.

Some are conservative and unmemorable, and others are achingly romantic, filled with incense, beaded cushions, live African music, and effervescent young hippies. They sell light meals and a world-wide range of teas. The plush **Kasbah** has good (canned) music.

Naturi Albayzín is a vegetarian place with €7.75 three-course meals featuring classy couscous (Sat–Thu 13:00–16:00 & 19:00–23:00, Fri 19:00–23:00, Calle Calderería Nueva 10). Wafting up to the end of the teahouse street you'll find **Bar Restaurant Las Cuevas**—its rickety tables spilling onto the street—serving salads, pizzas, tapas, and wine to a fun family/bohemian crowd.

Dessert: **Los Italianos,** also known as **La Veneciana,** is popular among locals for its ice cream, *horchata* (almond drink), and shakes (daily 8:00–3:00, Gran Vía de Colon 4, across street from cathedral and Royal Chapel, tel. 958-224-034).

Markets: The Mercado San Augustin, while heavy on meat, also sells fruits and veggies. If nothing else, it's as refreshingly cool as a meat locker (Mon–Sat 8:00–15:00, closed Sun, has small café/bar, Calle Cristo San Augustin, a block north of cathedral, half-block off Gran Vía de Colón). Pescedaria, a block from Bib-Rambla, usually has some fruit stalls on its northern end, along with inviting restaurants on the square itself.

Transportation Connections—Granada

By train to: Barcelona (1/day, 12 hrs, handy night train), **Madrid** (1/day, 6 hrs, depart Granada at 7:55, confirm time at station), **Toledo** (only 1 train works well, with a transfer in Madrid, leave Granada at 7:55, confirm time at station, allow 10 hours including transfer in Madrid), **Algeciras** (3/day, 4 hrs; also 6 buses/day, 3.5–5 hrs), **Ronda** (3/day, 2.5 hrs), **Sevilla** (4/day, 3 hrs, transfer in Bobadilla; also 9 buses/day, 2.5–4 hrs), **Córdoba** (1/day, 4 hrs, transfer in Bobadilla; also 6 buses/day, 3 hrs), **Málaga** (3/day, 3 hrs, transfer in Bobadilla; also 16 buses/day, 2 hrs). Train info: tel. 902-240-202.

By bus to: Nerja (3/day, 2 hrs, more frequent with transfer in Motril), **Sevilla** (9/day, 2.5 hrs *directo*, 4 hrs *ruta;* plus trains, above), **Córdoba** (6 buses/day, 3 hrs; plus trains, above), **Málaga** (16/day, 2 hrs; plus trains, above), **Algeciras** (6/day, 3.5-5 hrs, some are *directo*, some are *ruta*), **Linea/Gibraltar** (2/day, 5 hrs). Bus info: tel. 958-185-480.

To better handle the winding roads, some tourists like to reserve a seat at the front of the bus (generally seats 1–30). You can call the station to reserve a seat—they'll hold it until 40 minutes before departure (tel. 958-185-480, or 902-422-242 for Barcelona or east coast destinations). Or, if you don't want to show up early to claim your seat, you can buy your ticket in advance with a credit card (tel. 902-330-400).

SEVILLA

This is the flamboyant city of Carmen and Don Juan, where bull-fighting is still politically correct and where little girls still dream of growing up to become flamenco dancers. While Granada has the great Alhambra, and Córdoba the remarkable Mezquita, Sevilla has a soul. It's a great-to-be-alive-in kind of place.

Sevilla, the gateway to the New World in the 16th century, boomed when Spain did. Explorers such as Amerigo Vespucci and Ferdinand Magellan sailed from its great river harbor. In the 17th century, local artists such as Velázquez, Murillo, and Zurbarán made it a cultural center. Sevilla's Golden Age, with its New World riches, ended when the harbor silted up and the Spanish empire crumbled.

In the 19th century, Sevilla was a big stop on the Romantic "Grand Tour of Europe." To build on this tourism, Sevilla planned the World Exposition of 1929. Bad year. The Expo crashed with the stock market. In 1992 Sevilla got a second chance at a World's Fair. This Expo was a success, leaving the city with an impressive infra-structure: new airport, train station, seven bridges, and the super AVE bullet train making Sevilla a 2.5-hour side-trip from Madrid.

Today Spain's fourth-largest city (pop. 700,000) is Andalucía's leading city, buzzing with festivals, life, color, and castanets. James Michener wrote, "Sevilla doesn't *have* ambience, it *is* ambience." Sevilla has its share of impressive sights, but the real magic is the city itself, with its tangled Jewish Quarter, riveting flamenco shows, thriving bars, and teeming evening *paseo*.

Planning Your Time

If ever there were a big Spanish city to linger in, it's Sevilla. On a three-week trip, spend two nights and a day here. On a shorter trip, zip here on the slick AVE train for a day trip from Madrid.

The sights—the cathedral and the Alcázar (about 3 hrs) and a wander through the Santa Cruz district (1 hr)—are few and simple for a city of this size. You could spend half a day touring its other sights (described below). Stroll along the bank of the Guadalquivir River and cross the Bridge of Triana for a view of the tower (Torre del Oro) and cathedral. An evening is essential for the *paseo* and a flamenco show. Bullfights are on most Sundays, April through October. Sevilla's Alcázar is closed on Monday.

Córdoba (described at the end of this chapter) is worth a stop-over if you're taking the AVE.

Orientation

For the tourist, this big city is small. Sevilla's major sights, including the lively Santa Cruz district and the Alcázar, surround the cathedral. The central boulevard, Avenida de la Constitución (with TI, banks, and a post office), zips right past the cathedral to Plaza Nueva (gateway to the shopping district). Nearly everything is within easy walking distance. With taxis so reasonable (€2.50 minimum), friendly, and easy, I rarely bother with the bus.

Tourist Information

Sevilla has several handy tourist offices: **Central** office is a block toward the river from the cathedral (Mon–Fri 9:00–19:00, Sat 10:00–14:00 & 15:00–19:00, Sun and festivals 10:00–14:00, Avenida de la Constitución 21, tel. 954-221-404). The less crowded **county/city TI** is at Plaza Triunfo (across from cathedral, Mon–Fri 10:30–14:00). There is also a **train station TI** (Mon–Fri 9:00–20:00, Sat–Sun 10:00–14:00, tel. 954-537-626) and a TI near the bus station (see "Arrival" below).

At any TI, ask for the city map (far better than the one in the promo city magazine); the English-language magazines *Welcome Olé* and *The Tourist*; a current listing of sights, hours, and prices; and a schedule of bullfights. The free monthly events guide, *El Giraldillo*, in nearly readable Spanish, covers cultural events in all of Andalucía with a focus on Sevilla. If heading south, ask for the "Route of the White Towns" brochure and a Jerez map (€0.60 each). Helpful Web sites are www.turismo.sevilla.org and www.andalucia.org.

Arrival in Sevilla

By Train: Trains arrive at the sublime Santa Justa station (banks, ATMs, TI, luggage storage). The town center, marked by the ornate Giralda Cathedral bell tower (visible from the front of the station), is a 30-minute walk, €4 taxi ride, or bus ride away (hike 2 blocks from station to catch bus #21 to cathedral; pay driver €1 as you board).

Sevilla

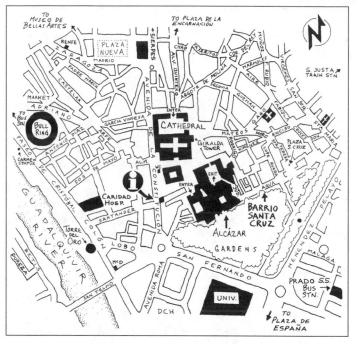

By Bus: Sevilla's two major bus stations have information offices, cafés, and luggage storage. The Prado de San Sebastian station covers Andalucía, Barcelona, and points east. To get downtown from the station, turn right on the major street Carlos V, then right again on Avenida de la Constitución (10-min walk).

The Plaza de Armas station (near the river, opposite Expo '92 site) serves southwest Spain, Madrid, Salamanca, and Portugal. To get downtown from this station, head toward the angled brick apartment building and cross the busy Boulevard Expiración. Go a half-block up Calle Arjona to the stop for bus #C4, which goes into town (€1, pay driver; get off at Puerta de Jerez, near main TI), or, even better, continue walking a couple more blocks to the helpful, uncrowded TI at Calle Arjona 28 (near Isabel II Bridge, Mon–Fri 8:00–20:45, Sat 8:00–14:00, closed Sun, tel. 954-505-600). From here you can catch bus #C4 or walk 15 minutes into the center (following map from TI).

By Car: Driving in Sevilla is difficult and many cars are broken into. I'd pay to park in a garage. To enter Sevilla, follow signs to *Centro Ciudad* (city center) and drive along the river. Ignore the bogus traffic wardens who direct you to an illegal spot, take a tip, and disappear later when your car gets towed. Consider hiring a taxi to lead you to your hotel, where you can get parking advice. The big garage under the bus station at Plaza de Armas is easy and cheap (€10/day). For short parking, the riverside Paseo de Cristobal Colón has two-hour meters and hardworking thieves.

Helpful Hints

Sevilla Festivals: Sevilla's peak season is April and May. And it has two one-week festival periods when the city is packed. While **Holy Week** (Semana Santa—the week between Palm Sunday and Easter Sunday—April 20 in 2003) is big all over Spain, it's biggest in Sevilla. Then (2 weeks after Easter), after taking enough time off to catch its communal breath, Sevilla holds its **April Fair.** This is a celebration of all that's Andalusian, with plenty of eating, drinking, singing, and merry-making. Book rooms well in advance for festival times. Warning: Prices can go sky-high and many hotels have four-night minimums.

    Train and Plane Tickets: The RENFE offices give out train schedules and sell train tickets. There's a RENFE Travel Center at the train station (daily 8:00–22:00, take a number and wait, call 902-240-202 for reservation and info) and one near Plaza Nueva in the center (Mon–Fri 9:30–14:00 & 17:30–20:00, Sat 10:00–13:30, closed Sun, CC, Calle Zaragoza 29, tel. 954-217-998, you can't work here if you speak English). Many travel agencies sell train tickets for the same price as the train station (look for train sticker in agency window).

    USIT Student Travel, with two offices near the cathedral, offers good budget flights for people of any age (Mateos Gago 2 and at Avenida de la Constitución 26, tel. 954-222-102).

    Telephone: A telephone office, Locutorio Público, has metered phone booths. Calls are slightly more expensive than calls made with Spanish phone cards, but you get a quiet setting with a seat (Mon–Fri 10:00–14:00 & 17:00–21:00, Sat 10:00–14:00, closed Sun, in passage at Sierpes 11, near intersection with Calle de Rafael Padura, tel. 954-226-800).

    Internet Access: Sevilla has lots of Internet cafes. Internet Workcenter is open 24/7 (on river side of Alcázar at San Fernando 1, tel. 954-212-074).

    Post Office: The post office is at Avenida de la Constitución 32, across from the cathedral (Mon–Fri 8:30–20:30, Sat 9:30–14:00, closed Sun).

    Laundry: Lavanderia Roma offers quick and economical drop-off service (€6 per load wash and dry, Mon–Sat 9:30–13:30 & 17:00–20:30, closed Sun, Castelar 2, tel. 954-210-535).

Tours of Sevilla

Guided City Walks—Concepción Delgado, an enthusiastic teacher and a joy to listen to, takes small groups on English-language-only walks. Using me as her guinea pig, Concepción has designed a fine two-hour introduction to the city, sharing important insights the average visitor misses. Her cultural show-and-tell is worthwhile, even on a one-day visit (€10, daily except Sun at 9:30 and 11:30, starting from statue in Plaza Nueva, always call to confirm departure and to reserve a place, tel. 902-158-226, cellular 616-501-100, www.sevi-ruta.com, e-mail: sevi-ruta@sevi-ruta.com).

Hop-on Hop-off Bus Tours—Two competing city bus tours leave from the curb near the riverside Golden Tower (Torre del Oro). You'll see the buses parked with salespeople handing out fliers. Each does about an hour-long swing through the city with a tape-recorded narration (green route slightly better because it includes María Luisa Park). The tours, which allow hopping on and off at four stops, are heavy on Expo '29 and Expo '92 neighborhoods of little interest in '03. While the narration does its best, Sevilla is most interesting where buses can't go (€11, departures daily 10:00–21:00).

Horse and Buggy Tours—A carriage ride is a classic and popular way to survey the city and a relaxing way to enjoy María Luisa Park (around €25 for a 45-min clip-clop, find English-speaking driver for better narration, if shared by 2 couples the ride is actually quite inexpensive).

More Tours—Visitours, a typical big bus-tour company, does all-day trips to Córdoba (€70, tel. 954-460-985).

American expat Daniel O'Beirne organizes and leads tours through Sevilla and Andalucía (starting at €45/half-day, discount for readers with this book). Dan's tours include the wine and horses of Jerez, Roman Sevilla, and Sephardic Sevilla. For more information, visit www.magicalspain.com.

For other guides, contact the Guides Association of Sevilla (tel. 954-210-037, e-mail: apitsevilla@alehop.com).

Sights—Cathedral and Giralda Tower

A ▲▲ sight, this is the third-largest church in Europe (after the Vatican's St. Peter's and London's St. Paul's) and the largest Gothic church anywhere. When they ripped down a mosque on the site in 1401, the Reconquista Christians bragged, "We'll build a cathedral so huge that anyone who sees it will take us for madmen." They built for 120 years. Even today, the descendants of those madmen proudly display an enlarged photocopy of their *Guinness Book of Records* letter certifying, "The cathedral with the largest area is: Santa Maria de la Sede in Sevilla, 126 meters long, 82 meters wide, and 30 meters high" (€6, Mon–Sat 11:00–18:00, free on Sun 14:30–19:00, last entry 1 hr before closing). There's only one way in for tourists, on the south end. Here's a tour:

Enter through the Alcázar side where you'll find a temporary exhibit, WC, and refreshing water fountain.

1. Restoration: Inside, the first thing you'll see is the restoration braces supporting huge pillars. A short video reviews the work being done here to keep this building up as they search for an answer to the problem of the pillars cracking. The likely solution is to empty them (they're hollow, filled with a rubble concrete) and fill them with a modern material that is more flexible.

2. High Altar: Sit down in front of the high altar in the center. The incredible main altarpiece *(retablo mayor)* clothed in gold leaf was constructed from 1482 to 1492. Twenty meters tall, with 36 scenes from the life of Jesus, it's composed of 1,500 figures. The artist used a perspective trick—notice how its statues get bigger as it gets higher. The design zigzags from the bottom (birth of Jesus) to the dizzying top (crucifixion).

3. The Choir: In front of the high altar, the choir features a 6,700-pipe organ played at the 10:00 Mass (free for worshippers). The big spinable book holder in the middle of the room held big music books—large enough for all to chant from in an age when there weren't enough books for everyone.

4. The Tomb of Columbus: In front of the cathedral's pilgrims' entrance are four kings carrying the tomb of Christopher Columbus. His pallbearers are the kings of Castile, Aragon, Leon, and Navarra (identify them by their team shirts). Columbus even traveled a lot posthumously. He was buried first in Spain, then in Santo Domingo, then Cuba, and—when Cuba gained independence from Spain, around 1900—he sailed home again to Sevilla. Are the remains actually his? Sevilla likes to think so. (There's a DNA study in the works . . . stay tuned.) The clock above dates from 1788. In the next chapel on the right is the fine painting of the Virgin Antiqua, the oldest art in the church. It was actually painted onto the prayer niche of the mosque which, when conquered in 1248, served as a church for 120 years—until it was torn down to be replaced by this huge church. All great explorers departing from Sevilla stopped to pray here before sailing. Follow signs to *tesoro*.

5. Treasury: The *tesoro* fills several rooms in the corner of the church. Start by marveling at the ornate 16th-century Plateresque dome of the main room, a grand souvenir from Sevilla's Golden Age. God is way up in the cupola. The three layers of figures below him show the heavenly host, relatives in Purgatory looking to Heaven and hoping you do them well, and the wretched in Hell, including a topless sinner engulfed in flames and teased cruelly by pitchfork-wielding monsters. The pure gold reliquaries hold hundreds of holy bones. One features "a piece of the true cross." Wandering deeper into the treasury, you'll find the first oval dome in Europe—the 16th-century chapter room where monthly meetings take place with the bishop (see his throne). Spain's most valuable crown is in the square, wood-paneled "room of ornaments." The Corona de la Virgen de los Reyes sparkles with 11,000 precious stones and the world's largest pearl—used as the torso of an angel.

To appreciate the ornate immensity of the church, hike to the rear. Can you see the angels trumpeting on their Cuban mahogany? A helpful information desk here has sheets with the current city museum hours. Near the high altar (opposite where you entered), a mirror on the floor gives a neck-friendly way to admire the fine Plateresque tracery on the ceiling. The exit sign leads to the Orange Patio and the exit, but first, some exercise . . .

6. Giralda Tower Climb: Your church admission includes entry to the bell tower. Notice the beautiful Moorish simplicity as you climb to its top, 100 meters up (330 feet), for a grand city view. The spiraling ramp was designed to accommodate riders on horseback—who galloped up five times a day to give the Muslim call to prayer.

7. Cloister: The cloister used to be the mosque's Court of the Naranjos (Oranges). Twelfth-century Muslims stopped at the fountain in the middle to wash their hands, face, and feet before praying. The ankle-breaking lanes between the bricks were once irrigation streams—a reminder that the Moors introduced irrigation to Iberia. The mosque was made of bricks; the church was made of stone.

8. As You Leave the Cloister: Notice also the fine Moorish-style arch (it's actually 16th-century Christian—the two coats of arms are a giveaway). As with much of the Moorish-looking art in town, it's the work of Moorish artists under Christian rule. The relief above the door shows the Bible story of Jesus ridding the temple of the merchants . . . a reminder to contemporary merchants that there will be no retail activity in the church. The plaque on the right is one of many scattered throughout town showing a place Cervantes—the great 16th-century Spanish writer—mentioned in his books. (In this case, the topic was pickpockets.) The huge green doors are a bit of the surviving pre-1248 mosque—wood covered with bronze.

9. Giralda Tower Exterior: Step across the street from the exit gate and look at the bell tower. Formerly a Moorish minaret from which Muslims were called to prayer, it became the cathedral's bell tower after the Reconquista. It's named for the 4,500-pound bronze statue symbolizing the Triumph of Faith (specifically the Christian defeat of the Muslims here) that caps it and serves as a weathervane. In fact, the name of the tower comes from the Spanish word for turning *(girando)*. In 1356 the original top of the tower fell. You're looking at a 16th-century Christian-built top with a ribbon of letters proclaiming, "The strongest tower is the name of God" (you can see *"Fortissima"*).

Needing more strength than their bricks could provide for the lowest section of the tower, the Moors used Roman-cut stones. Now circle around for a close look at the corner of the tower at ground level; you can actually read the Latin on one of the stones. The tower offers a brief recap of the city's history—sitting on a Roman foundation, a long Moorish period capped by our Christian age. Today, by law, no building can be higher then this statue.

More Sights—Central Sevilla

▲Alcázar—Originally a 10th-century palace built for the governors of the local Moorish state, this still functions as a royal palace... the oldest still in use in Europe. What you see today is an extensive 14th-century remodeling job, done by Moorish workmen (Mudejar) for the Christian King Pedro I. Pedro was nicknamed either "the Cruel" or "the Just," depending on which end of his sword you were on (€5, Tue–Sat 9:30–19:00, Sun 9:00 17:00, off-season Tue–Sat 9:30–17:00, Sun 10:30 13:00, closed Mon, tel. 954-502-323). The €3 audioguide is tempting and tries hard. But sorry, there's no way to make this palace worth a flowery hour of hard-to-follow commentary.

The Alcázar is a thought-provoking glimpse of a graceful Al-Andalus (Moorish) world that might have survived its Castilian conquerors—but didn't. But I have a tough time hanging any specific history on it. The floor plan is intentionally confusing, part of the style designed to make experiencing the place more exciting and surprising. While Granada's Alhambra was built by Moors for Moorish rulers, what you see here is essentially a Christian ruler's palace, built in the Moorish style.

Just past the turnstiles, walk through the Patio of the Lions and stop under the arch of the wall to orient yourself. Facing the Patio de la Monteria, you see the palace's three wings: Ahead is King Pedro the Cruel's Palace—giving a sense of his original 14th-century palace. The wing on the right is the 16th-century Admiral's Apartments. And on the left is the 13th-century Gothic Palace of Charles V.

Admiral's Apartments: When Queen Isabel debriefed Columbus here after his New World discoveries, she realized this could be big business. In 1503, she created this wing to administer Spain's New World ventures. Pop into the room just right of the grand and still-used reception room for a look at (mostly foreign) hand-held ornate fans and a long painting showing 17th-century Sevilla during Holy Week. Follow the procession—which is much like today's procession of traditional floats carried by teams of 24 to 48 men and a parade of KKK-looking penitents. Returning to the reception hall, on the right you'll find the Santa Maria de la Buenas Aires Chapel (St. Mary of the Fair Winds—or, as many Spanish boys would say, "of the good farts").

The Virgin of the Fair Winds was the patron saint of navigators and a favorite of Columbus. The fine Virgin of the Navigators altarpiece (painted by Alejo Fernandez in the 1530s) is said to have the only portrait of Columbus (blond guy on right) with Isabel and Ferdinand (on left with gold cape). Notice how the Virgin's cape seems to protect everyone under it—even the Indians in the dark background (the first time Indians were painted in Europe). On the left is a model of Columbus' *Santa Maria*, his flagship and the only one of his three ships not to survive the 1492 voyage. The family coat of arms of Columbus' descendants (who now live in Spain and Puerto Rico) is in the center of the back of the room. It reads: "To Castile and to Leon, Colón [that's Columbus in Spanish] gave a new world."

King Pedro the Cruel's Palace: This 14th-century nucleus of the complex, the real Alcázar, is centered around the elegantly proportioned Court of the Maidens (Patio de las Doncellas). A passageway leads to the second courtyard, the smaller and more delicate Dolls' Court (Patio de las Muñecas)—for the king's private and family life. The designers created a microclimate engineered for coolness: water, plants, pottery, thick walls, and darkness. Even with the inevitable hodge-podge of style that comes with 600 years of renovation, it's a fine example of Mudejar style—arguably the best in Spain. The decor is Moorish-style—you'll see peacocks, animals, and kings that you wouldn't find in Muslim decor, which doesn't allow images. The stylized Arabic script (creating a visual chant of Koranic verses in the Moorish buildings such as the Alahambra) survives, but now uses New Testament verses and propaganda phrases such as "dedicated to the magnificent Sultan Pedro—thanks to God!" Notice the sumptuous ceilings.

Gothic Charles V wing: Next climb a few steps and enter the Gothic wing of the palace. The tapestries—celebrating Emperor Charles V's 1535 victory in Tunis over the Turks—are from Brussels (1554). Study the great map with the unusual perspective—Africa being at the top. It's supposed to be from a Barcelona aerial perspective. Find the big fortified city in the middle (Barcelona), Lisboa, Gibraltar, Italy, Sicily, and the Mediterranean islands. The artist paints himself holding the legend—with a scale in both leagues and miles. This is an 18th-century copy of the original.

The garden: The best tended and safest in town, it's full of tropical flowers, wild cats, cool fountains, and hot tourists.

Archivo de Indias—The building (in Lonja Palace, across street from Alcázar) was designed by the same person who did El Escorial. Originally a market, it's the top building in Sevilla from its 16th-century glory days. Today it houses the archive of documents of the discovery and conquest of the New World. This could be fascinating, but little of importance is on display (old maps of Havana) and there's barely a word of English (closed in 2002 for renovation).

▲▲**Barrio de Santa Cruz**—Only the tangled street plan survives from the days when this was Sevilla's Jewish Quarter. The narrow streets—some with buildings so close they're called "kissing lanes"—were actually designed to maximize shade. Even today, locals claim the Barrio de Santa Cruz is three degrees cooler than the rest of the city. While its charm is trampled by tour groups in the mornings, this classy maze of lanes too narrow for cars, white-washed houses with wrought-iron latticework, and *azulejo* tile–covered patios is a great refuge from the summer heat and bustle of Sevilla. The TI map has a helpful Barrio de Santa Cruz inset, but it's best to just get lost. The Moors gave this region its characteristic glazed tiles… without any figures. In later centuries, Christians decorated their tiles with social scenes. Either way, the tiles made sense because they kept buildings cooler in the summer heat.

Forget about eating any of the oranges. They're bitter and used only to make vitamins, perfume, cat food, and that awful marmalade you can't avoid in England's B&Bs. Since the orange trees never lose their leaves, they're great for shade.

Hospital de la Caridad—Between the river and the cathedral is the Charity Hospital, founded by a nobleman in the 17th century. Peek into the fine courtyard. On the left, the chapel has some gruesome art (above both doors) illustrating that death is the great equalizer, and an altar so sweet only a Spaniard could enjoy it. The Dutch tiles depicting scenes of the Old and New Testament are a reminder of the time when the Netherlands were under Spanish rule in the mid-16th century (€3, Mon–Sat 9:00–13:30 & 15:30–19:30, Sun 9:00–13:00, tel. 954-223-232).

Torre del Oro/Naval Museum—Sevilla's historic riverside "golden tower" was the starting point and ending point for all shipping to the New World. It's named for the golden tiles that once covered it—not for all the New World booty that landed

here. Since the 13th century it has been part of the city's fortifications, with a heavy chain draped across the river to protect the
harbor. Today it houses a dreary little naval museum. Looking
past the dried fish and charts of knots, find the mural showing the
world-spanning journeys of Vasco da Gama and Juan Sebastian
Elcano; the model of the *Santa Maria* (the first ship to have landed
in the New World); and an interesting mural of Sevilla in 1740.
Enjoy the view from the balconies upstairs (€1, free Tue, Tue–Fri
10:00–14:00, Sat–Sun 11:00–14:00, closed Mon, tel. 954-222-419).

▲**Quickie Town Walk: Plaza Nueva to Calle Sierpes**—While
many tourists never get beyond the cathedral and the Santa Cruz
neighborhood, it's important to wander west into the lively shopping center of town, which also happens to be the oldest part of
Sevilla. Plaza Nueva—a 19th-century square facing the ornate city
hall—features a statue of Ferdinand III, a local favorite because
he freed Sevilla from the Moors in 1248. From here, wander down
Calle Tetuan into Sevilla's pedestrian-zone shopping center—
a delightful alternative to the suburban mall. This is a hit for
Spanish fashions (Zara, shoes, and so on).

Follow Calle Jovellanos (after checking out the frilly fancy
ladies' shoes at Pilar Burgos) to the right. At the first kink in the
lane is Capilla de San José—Saint Joseph's Chapel, located in the
historic carpenters' quarter (daily 8:00–12:30 & 18:30–20:30).
I have to say, it's excess like this that gives Baroque a bad name.
Check out the votive offerings—requests for help and thanks for
miracles—in the rear. Ten steps beyond the church is a glazed
tile scene showing the 1929 Sevilla fair.

Continue to Calle Sierpes, the best shopping street in town.
A commercial center for 500 years, it's the main street of the
Holy Week processions, when it's packed and the balconies bulge
with spectators.

Near Calle Sierpes and Calle Sagasta, a shop shows off traditional shawls and fans. Andalusian women have various fans to
match different dresses. The mantilla (ornate head scarf) comes
in black (worn only on Good Friday and by the mother of the
groom at weddings) and white (worn at bullfights during the
April fair). Cross Calle Sierpes to Calle Sagasta and notice it has
two names—the modern version and a medieval one: "Antiqua
Calle de Gallegos" ("Ancient Street of the Galicians"). With the
Christian victory in 1248, the Muslims were given one month to
evacuate. To consolidate Christian control here, settlers from
the north were planted. This street was home to the Galicians.

The street Calle Sagasta leads to Plaza del Salvador and
Sevilla's second-most-important church. Step in if it's open for
a good look at the figures carried through town during Holy

Week processions. Floats carrying scenes from the crucifixion are always followed by a float with a statue of a weeping Virgin. Sevilla's many adored Virgins are always portrayed weeping.

The church and surrounding streets are on the high ground where Phoenicians originally established the town. The Romans built their Forum here. The Arabs held their market here. Today it's fun to window shop in the colorful lanes that surround the church. Calle de Francos leads past a classy modern mall (Tiendas Peyre Centro at #40, nice air-conditioned café) back to the cathedral.

Sights—Near Plaza de España

University—Today's university was yesterday's *fabrica de tabacos* (tobacco factory), which employed 10,000 young female *cigareras*— including Bizet's Carmen. In the 18th century, it was the second-largest building in Spain, after El Escorial. Wander through its halls as you walk to Plaza de España. The university's bustling café is a good place for cheap tapas, beer, wine, and conversation (Mon–Fri 8:00–21:00, Sat 9:00–13:00, closed Sun).

▲**Plaza de España**—The square, the surrounding buildings, and the nearby María Luisa Park are the remains of the 1929 fair— where for a year the Spanish-speaking countries of the world enjoyed a mutual admiration fiesta. This delightful area, the epitome of World's Fair–style building, is great for people-watching (especially during the 14:00–15:00 and 19:00–20:00 peak *paseo* hours). Stroll through the park and along the canal. The highlight is what was the Spanish Pavilion. Its *azulejo* tiles (a trademark of Sevilla) show historic scenes and maps from every province of Spain (arranged in alphabetical order from Alava to Zaragoza). Climb to one of the balconies for a fine view. Beware, this is a classic haunt of thieves and con-artists. Believe no one here. Thieves, posing as lost tourists, will come at you with a map unfolded to hide their speedy, greedy fingers.

Sights—Away from the Center

▲**Museo de Bellas Artes**—Spain's second-best collection of paintings (after Madrid's Prado) features top Spanish artists such as Murillo and Zurbarán. While most Americans go for El Greco, Goya, and Velázquez (not a forte of this collection), this museum gives a fine look at the other, less-appreciated Spanish masters. Rather than exhausting, the museum—which occupies a former convent—is pleasantly enjoyable (€2, Tue 15:00–20:00, Wed–Sat 9:00–20:00, Sun 9:00–14:00, closed Mon, bus C1, C2, C3, or C4 to Pasarela de la Cartuja, Plaza Museo 9, tel. 954-220-790).

▲▲**Basilica Macarena**—Sevilla's Holy Week celebrations are Spain's grandest. During the week leading up to Easter, the city is packed with pilgrims witnessing 50 processions carrying about 100 religious floats. Get a feel for this event by visiting Basilica Macarena (built in 1947) to see the two most impressive floats and the darling of Semana Santa, the Weeping Virgin (Virgen de la Macarena or La Esperanza, church free, museum-€2.80, daily 9:30–13:00 & 17:00–20:00, taxi to Puerta Macarena or bus #C3 or C4 from Puerta Jerez).

Grab a pew and study Mary, complete with crystal teardrops. She's like a 17th-century doll with human hair and articulated arms, and even dressed with underclothes. Her beautiful expression—halfway between smiling and crying—is moving, in a Baroque way. Her weeping can be contagious; look around you. La Macarena is considered the protector of bullfighters (she's big in bullring chapels). In 1912 the bullfighter José Ortega, hoping for protection, gave her the five emerald brooches she wears. It worked for eight years . . . until he was gored to death in the ring. Filling a side chapel (on left) is the Christ of the Sentence (from 1654), showing Jesus the day he was condemned.

To see the floats that Mary and Jesus ride every Good Friday, head for the museum (through the door left of the altar).

The three-ton float, slathered in gold leaf, shows a commotion of figures acting out the sentencing of Christ (who's placed in the front of this crowd). Pontius Pilate is about to wash his hands. Pilate's mother cries as a man reads the death sentence. Relays of 50 men carry this—only their feet showing under the drapes—as they shuffle through the streets from midnight to 14:00 each Good Friday. Shuffle upstairs for another perspective.

La Esperanza follows the Sentencing of Christ in the procession. Her smaller (1.5-ton) float, in the next room, seems all silver and candles—"strong enough to support the roof but slender enough to quiver in the soft night breeze." Mary has a wardrobe of three huge mantels (each displayed here) worn in successive years. The big green one is from 1900. Her six-pound gold crown/halo is from 1913. This float has a mesmerizing effect on the local crowds. They line up for hours, clapping, weeping, and throwing roses as it slowly works its way through the city.

Before leaving, find the case of matador outfits (also upstairs) given to the church over the years by bullfighters in thanks for the protection they feel they received from La Macarena.

Outside, notice the best surviving bit of Sevilla's old walls. Originally Roman, what remains today is 12th-century Moorish, a reminder that for centuries Sevilla was the capital of the Moorish kingdom in Iberia. And yes, it's from this neighborhood that a local dance band changed the world by giving us "The Macarena."

Bullfighting

▲**Bullfights**—Spain's most artistic and traditional bullfighting is done in Sevilla's Plaza de Toros, with fights on most Sundays, Easter through October (at 18:30 or 19:30). Serious fights with adult matadors—called *corrida de toros*—are in April and October (and often sold out in advance). Summer fights are usually *novillada*, with teenage novices doing the killing. (*Corrida de toros* seats range from €20 for high seats looking into the sun to €100 for the first three rows in the shade under the royal box; *novillada* seats are half that—and easy to buy at arena a few minutes before showtime; get information at TI, your hotel, or call 954-210-315.) Sevilla's arena holds 14,000.

▲▲**Bullfight Museum**—Follow a two-language, 20-minute guided tour through the Plaza de Toros' strangely quiet and empty arena, its museum, the first-aid room where injured fighters are rushed, and the chapel where the matador prays before the fight. In the museum you'll see great classic scenes and the heads of a few bulls—awarded the bovine equivalent of an Oscar for a particularly good fight—and the mother of the bull that killed the famous matador Manolette in 1947; back then they killed the mother of any bull who killed a matador (€4, daily 9:30–14:00 & 15:00–19:00; or 9:30–15:00 on fight days though the chapel and horseroom are closed). See the appendix for more on the dubious "art" of bullfighting.

Nightlife

▲▲**Evening Paseo**—Sevilla is meant for strolling. The areas along either side of the river between the San Telmo and Isabel II bridges (Paseo de Cristobal Colón and Triana district; see "Eating," below), around Plaza Nueva, at Plaza de España, and throughout the Barrio de Santa Cruz thrive every non-winter evening. Spend some time rafting through this sea of humanity. Savor the view of floodlit Sevilla by night from the far side of the river—perhaps over dinner (but the seedy Alameda de Hercules district is best avoided).

▲▲▲**Flamenco**—This music-and-dance art form has its roots in the Gypsy and Moorish cultures. Even at a packaged "Flamenco Evening," sparks fly. The men do most of the flamboyant machine-gun footwork. The women concentrate on graceful turns and a smooth, shuffling step. Watch the musicians. Flamenco guitarists, with their lightning finger-roll strums, are among the best in the world. The intricate rhythms are set by castanets or the hand-clapping (called *palmas*) of those who aren't dancing at the moment. In the raspy-voiced wails of the singers you'll hear echoes of the Muslim call to prayer.

Like jazz, flamenco thrives on improvisation. Also like jazz, good flamenco is more than just technical proficiency. A singer or dancer with "soul" is said to have *duende*. Flamenco is a happening, with bystanders clapping along and egging on the dancers with whoops and shouts. Get into it. For a tourist-oriented flamenco show, your hotel can get you nightclub show tickets (happily, since they snare a hefty commission for each sale).

Los Gallos gives nightly two-hour shows at 21:00 and 23:30 (€27 ticket includes a drink, manager Nuria promises goosebumps and a €3 per person discount to those who book directly with Los Gallos and show this book—maximum 2 per book; arrive 30 min early for better seats without obstructed views, Plaza de Santa Cruz 11, tel. 954-216-981). **El Arenal** also does a good show (€29 including a drink, shows at 21:00 and 23:00, near bullring at Calle Rodo 7, tel. 954-216-492). **El Patio Sevillano** is more of a variety show (€26, shows at 19:30 and 22:00, next to bullring at Paseo de Cristobal Colón, tel. 954-214-120). These prepackaged shows can be a bit sterile, and an audience of tourists doesn't help. But I find both Los Gallos and El Arenal professional and riveting. El Arenal may have a slight edge on talent, but Los Gallos has a cozier setting, with cushy rather than hard chairs—and it's cheaper.

Casa para la Memoria de Alandalus (House for the Memory of Alandalus) offers more of an intimate concert with a smaller cast and more classic solos. In an alcohol-free atmosphere, tourists sit on folding chairs circling a small stage for shows featuring flamenco, Sephardic, or other Andalusian music. Summer concerts are nearly nightly at 20:30 and 22:30 (off-season at 21:00). Wednesday concerts are Sephardic rather than flamenco (€11, 60-min shows vary, Ximenez Enciso 28, in Barrio Santa Cruz, tel. 954-560-670).

Impromptu flamenco still erupts spontaneously in bars throughout the old town after midnight. Just follow your ears as you wander down Calle Betis, leading off Plaza de Cuba across the bridge. The **Lo Nuestro** and **Rejoneo** bars are local favorites (at Calle Betis 30 and 32).

For flamenco music without dancing, consider **La Carboneria Bar.** The sangria equivalent of a beer garden, it's a sprawling place with a variety of rooms leading to a big, open, tented area filled with young locals, casual guitar strummers, and nearly nightly flamenco music after midnight. Located just a few blocks from most of my recommended hotels, this is worth finding for anyone not quite ready to end the day (20:00–3:00, Levies 18, unsigned door).

Shopping

The popular pedestrian streets Sierpes, Tetuan, and Velázquez, as well as the surrounding lanes near Plaza Nueva, are packed with people and shops (see "Quickie Town Walk: Plaza Nueva to Calle Sierpes," above). Nearby is Sevilla's top department store, El Corte Inglés. While small shops close between 13:30 and 16:00 or 17:00, big ones like El Corte Inglés stay open (and air-conditioned) right through the siesta. It has a supermarket downstairs and a good but expensive restaurant (Mon–Sat 10:00–21:30, closed Sun).

Flea markets hop on Sunday: stamps and coins at Cabildo Square near the cathedral and animals at Alfalfa Square.

Sleeping in Sevilla
(€1 = about $1, country code: 34, zip code: 41004)
Sleep Code: **S** = Single, **D** = Double/Twin, **T** = Triple, **Q** = Quad, **b** = bathroom, **s** = shower only, **CC** = Credit Cards accepted, **no CC** = Credit Cards not accepted, **SE** = Speaks English, **NSE** = No English.

To help you easily sort through these listings, I've divided the rooms into three categories, based on the price for a standard double room with bath during high season:

Higher Priced—Most rooms €100 or more.
Moderately Priced—Most less than €100.
Lower Priced—Most rooms less than €55.

All of my listings are centrally located, within a five-minute walk of the cathedral. The first are near the charming but touristy Santa Cruz neighborhood. The last group is just as central but closer to the river, across the boulevard in a more workaday, less touristy zone. See the map on the next page.

Room rates as much as double during the two Sevilla fiestas (the week before Easter—April 20 in 2003—and two weeks or so after Easter). In general, the busiest and most expensive months are April, May, September, and October. Hotels put rooms on the discounted push list in July and August—when people with any sense avoid this furnace—and November through February. Prices rarely include the 7 percent IVA tax. A price range indicates low- to high-season prices (but I have not listed festival prices). Hoteliers speak enough English. Ground-floor rooms come with more noise. Ask for upper floors (*piso alto*). Many of these hotels are reportedly unreliable for reservations, particularly the small, family *pensiones* (as opposed to normal big hotels). Always telephone to reconfirm what you think is a reservation. If you do visit in July or August, the best values are central business-class places. They offer summer discounts and provide a necessary cool, air-conditioned refuge.

Sleeping in the Santa Cruz Neighborhood
These places are off Calle Santa Maria la Blanca and Plaza Santa Maria.

Sevilla Hotels

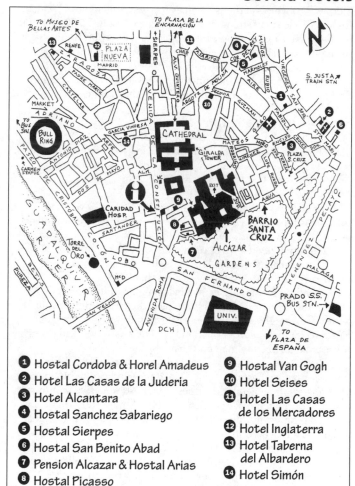

❶ Hostal Cordoba & Hotel Amadeus
❷ Hotel Las Casas de la Juderia
❸ Hotel Alcantara
❹ Hostal Sanchez Sabariego
❺ Hostal Sierpes
❻ Hostal San Benito Abad
❼ Pension Alcazar & Hostal Arias
❽ Hostal Picasso
❾ Hostal Van Gogh
❿ Hotel Seises
⓫ Hotel Las Casas de los Mercadores
⓬ Hotel Inglaterra
⓭ Hotel Taberna del Albardero
⓮ Hotel Simón

HIGHER PRICED

Hotel Las Casas de la Juderia has quiet, elegant rooms and
suites tastefully decorated with hardwood floors and a Spanish
flair. The rooms surround a series of peaceful courtyards. This
is a romantic splurge and a fine value (Sb-€72–86, Db-€107–129,
Db suite-€123–145, Qb suite-€180–200, extra bed-€30; low-
season prices—July, Aug, late-Nov–Feb—are discounted a further

10 percent to those with this book who ask; great buffet breakfast-€10, CC, air-con, elevator, valet parking-€12, on small traffic-free lane off Plaza Santa Maria, Callejon de Dos Hermanas 7, tel. 954-415-150, fax 954-422-170, www.casasypalacios.com, e-mail: juderia@zoom.es, SE).

MODERATELY PRICED
Hotel Amadeus is a little gem music-lovers will appreciate (it even has a couple of sound-proofed rooms with pianos—something I've never seen in Europe). It's lovingly decorated with a music motif around a little courtyard and a modern glass elevator that takes you to a roof terrace. While small, this 14-room place is classy and comfortable with welcoming public spaces (Db-€80, 2 suites, CC, air-con, Calle Farnesio 6, tel. 954-501-443, fax 954-500-019, www.hotelamadeussevilla.com, Maria Luisa SE).

Hotel Alcantara is a new place with more comfort than style or character. Well-located but strangely out of place in the midst of the Santa Cruz jumble, it rents 21 slick rooms at a good price (Sb-€64, Db-€80, fancy Db-€98, CC, air-con, elevator, Ximenez de Enciso 28, tel. 954-500-595, fax 954-500-604, www.hotelalcantara.net, e-mail: info@hotelalcantara.net).

Hostal Córdoba, a homier and cheaper option, has 12 tidy, quiet, air-conditioned rooms, solid modern furniture, and a showpiece plant-filled courtyard (S-€33, Sb-€45, D-€45-55, Db-€50-60, Nov–March 25 percent cheaper, includes tax, no CC, a tiny lane off Calle Santa Maria la Blanca, Farnesio 12, tel. 954-227-498).

LOWER PRICED
Hostal Sanchez Sabariego is a solid 10-room place with a folksy garden courtyard. The higher floors are most peaceful and air-conditioned (S-€28, Db-€42-50, no CC, sometimes hotel could be cleaner, laundry-€9/load, Corral del Rey 23, tel. 954-214-470, friendly Elena and Macu SE).

Hostal Sierpes, across the street, is a sprawling, 36-room place with fine lounges and a big, cool, airy courtyard. Rooms are small and basic with shiny new bathrooms (Sb-€34, Db-€50, Tb-€66, Qb-€82, breakfast-€5, CC, some air-con, noisy downstairs, quieter rooms upstairs, popular with backpackers, reconfirm reservations, parking-€10/day, Corral del Rey 22, tapas bar next door, tel. 954-224-948, fax 954-212-107, e-mail: reservas@hsierpes.com).

Hostal San Benito Abad, with eight humble rooms, faces a traditional Sevilla courtyard buried at the end of a deadend lane just off Plaza Santa Maria. The rooms are dark, with windows that open onto an inner courtyard. Communication here is very difficult, but the family is hard-working and offers some of the best cheap rooms in town (S-€16–18, D-€31, Db-€36, Tb-€48, no CC, a tiny lane next to Cano y Cueto at Calle Canarios 4, tel. 954-415-255, NSE).

Sleeping Cheap between the Alcázar and Avenida de la Constitucion

The places are small, quiet, and a bit funky.

LOWER PRICED

Pensión Alcázar rents eight pleasant rooms. The lower rooms have ceiling fans, the three top rooms are air-conditioned and have with terraces (Db-€35–45, extra bed-€12, Qb-€60–72, no CC, Dean Miranda 12, tel. 954-228-457, owners Micky and Liliane SE). Note: Taxi drivers often confuse this with *Hotel* Alcázar.

Hostal Arias is cool, clean, and no-nonsense. Its 14 basic rooms are air-conditioned and come equipped with medieval disco balls (big Sb-€34, Db-€44, Tb-€58, Qb-€65, Quint/b-€75, CC, nearby parking-€14/day, Calle Mariana de Pineda 9, tel. 954-226-840, fax 954-218-389, www.hostalarias.com, e-mail: reservas@hostalarias.com, manager Manuel Reina SE, but rest of staff doesn't).

Hostal Picasso has 17 smallish rooms with cans of bright paint spilled across all the walls (D-€40, Db-€53, extra bed-€22, 10 percent off with this book and cash, confirm your bill, CC, Calle San Gregorio 1, tel. & fax 954-210-864, e-mail: hpicasso@arrakis.es, Rocio SE).

Hostal Van Gogh, a 10-room place run by the Hostal Picasso, is less garishly decorated and a bit more comfortable (Db-€53, 10 percent off with this book and cash, air-con, Miguel de Manara 1, tel. & fax 954-563-727, www.ventalia .com/hvangogh, e-mail: hvangogh@arrakis.es).

Sleeping Classy near the Cathedral

HIGHER PRICED

Hotel Seises—a modern business-class place spliced tastefully into the tangled old town—offers a fresh and spacious reprieve for anyone ready for good old contemporary luxury. You'll eat breakfast amid Roman ruins. Its rooftop garden includes a pool and a great cathedral view (40 rooms, Sb-€96–132, Db-€126–180, extra bed-€30, lower prices in July, Aug, and winter, CC, air-con, elevator, 2 blocks northwest of cathedral at Segovias 6, tel. 954-229-495, fax 954-224-334, www.hotellosseises.com, e-mail: info@hotellosseises.com).

Hotel Las Casas de los Mercaderes feels like the Hotel Las Casas de la Juderia (listed above) because it's run by the same people. Traditional Andalusian in a modern way with all the comforts, it's beautifully located between the cathedral and the best shopping streets. It's in a late-night party zone, which could be a problem on weekends outside of summer, but most of its rooms are on the quiet back side (48 rooms, Sb-€68–84, Db-€99–122, 10 percent discount off low prices in July–Aug with this book, extra bed-€25, breakfast-€11, CC, air-con, elevator, parking-€13, Calle Alvarez Quintero 9, tel. 954-225-858, fax 954-229-884, www.casasypalacios.com, e-mail: mercaderes@zoom.es).

Hotel Inglaterra, a big blocky four-star place on the no-nonsense Plaza Nueva, has 109 rooms and all the professional amenities (high season April–May, low season rest of year, big Sb-€90–120, Db-€112–150, extra bed-€24–36, breakfast-€9, CC, air-con, nonsmoking floor, elevator, attached restaurant and Irish pub, American Express office, Plaza Nueva 7, tel. 954-224-970, fax 954-561-336, www.hotelinglaterra.es, e-mail: hotin@hotelinglaterra.es).

Sleeping West of Avenida de la Constitución

HIGHER PRICED
Hotel Taberna del Alabardero is a unique hotel with only seven rooms, taking the top floor of a famous poet's mansion (above the classiest restaurant in town—see below). It's well located and a great value but booked long in advance. The ambience is perfectly 1900 (Db-€135, Db suite-€165, includes breakfast, CC, air-con, elevator, closed in Aug, Zaragoza 20, tel. 954-502-721, fax 954-563-666, www.tabernadelalabardero.com).

MODERATELY PRICED
Hotel Simón is a classic 18th-century mansion with a faded-elegant courtyard. Although room quality varies, many of its 30 rooms are decorated with period furniture under high ceilings. On weekends, avoid rooms on the noisy street (Sb-€43–49, Db-€64–80, extra person-€18, high prices are only for April–May, continental breakfast-€4, CC, air-con, a block west of cathedral at Calle García de Vinuesa 19, tel. 954-226-660, fax 954-562-241, www.hotelsimonsevilla.com, e-mail: info@hotelsimonsevilla.com).

Eating in Sevilla

A popular Andalusian meal is fried fish, particularly marinated *adobo*. The soups, such as *salmorejo* (Córdoba-style super-thick gazpacho) and *ajo blanco* (almond-based), are light and refreshing.

If you're hungry for dinner before the Spaniards are, do the tapas tango, using the "Tapas Tips" from this book's introduction. Wash down your tapas with *fino* (dry sherry) or, more refreshing, *tinto de verano* (literally, "summer" red), an Andalusian red wine with soda, like a light sangria. A good light white wine is *barbadillo*.

Dining First Class

Corral del Agua Restaurante is a romantic pink-tablecloth place with classy indoor and charming courtyard seating (plan on €25 per meal, Mon–Sat 13:00–16:00 & 20:00–24:00, closed Sun, reservations smart, Callejon del Agua 6, tel. 954-220-714).

Taberna del Alabardero, one of Sevilla's finest restaurants, serves refined Spanish cuisine in chandeliered elegance just a couple of blocks from the cathedral. While the à la carte menu will add up to about €45 a meal, for €46 they offer a fun sampler menu with lots of little surprises from the chef. Or consider their €14 starter sampler followed by an entrée (daily 13:00–16:00 & 20:00–24:00, closed Aug, air-con, CC, reservations smart, Zaragoza 20, tel. 954-502-721). Their ground-floor dining rooms (elegant but nothing like upstairs) are popular with local office workers for their student-chef sampler menu (€10 for 3 delightful courses, Mon–Fri 13:00–16:30, €14 for same thing on Sat–Sun). To avoid a wait, arrive before 13:30.

Eating in Triana across the River

The colorful Triana District—south of the river, between the San Telmo and Isabel II bridges—is filled with fine and fun eateries.

Tapas: The riverside street, Calle Betis (the Roman name for the Guadalquivir River), is best for tapas bars. Before sitting down, walk to the Santa Ana church (midway between the bridges) where tables spill into the square in the shadow of the floodlit church spire. It feels like the whole neighborhood is out celebrating. On Plazuela Santa Ana each table has menus from two restaurants (and waiters do double duty): **Taberna la Plazuela** does simpler fare with enticing *tostones*—giant, fancy Andalusian *bruschetta*. **Restaurant Bistec** does grilled fish with enthusiasm. I liked *taquitos de merluza* (hake fish), but for a mix of fish, ask for *variado pescado* (daily 11:30–16:00 & 20:00–24:00, Plazuela de Santa Ana, tel. 954-274-759).

For tapas and a less gentle setting, head a block down the street where **Bar Santa Ana**—draped in bullfighting and Weeping

Restaurants and Flamenco in Sevilla

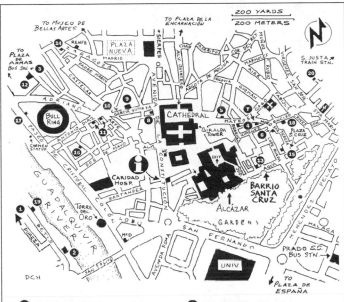

1 To Plazuela Santa Ana:
Bar Santa Ana, Taberna
Plazuela & Rest. Blstec

2 Rio Grande Rest. & Rest.
La Primera

3 To Rest. Maria Angeles

4 Bodega Santa Cruz

5 Cerveceria Giralda

6 Bar La Teresas

7 Rest. San Marco

8 Horno San Buenaventura

9 Bodega Morales

10 Fried-fish joint
& Bodegas Diaz Salazar

11 El Buzo Rest. & Cafeteria
Meson Serranito

12 Mercado del Arenal

13 Corral del Agua Rest.

14 Taberna del Alabardero

15 Los Gallos

16 El Arenal

17 El Patio Sevillano

18 Casa para la Memoria
del Alandalus

19 Lo Nuestro & Rejoneo

20 La Carboneria

Virgin memorabilia—is busy filling locals from a fun list of tapas
(long hours Mon–Sat, closed Sun, Pureza 82, tel. 954-272-102).
The **Pena Sevillista de Triana** (at Pureza 61) is Triana's soccer
fans' clubhouse (satellite TV—the biggest around—for all the
best matches and bullfights; wild on weekend soccer nights).

Riverside dinners: For a restaurant dinner (with properly
attired waiters and full menus as opposed to tapas), consider these

three (all are neighbors on Calle Betis, next to the San Telmo bridge). **Río Grande** is your candlelight-fancy option (€30 dinners, daily 13:00–16:00 & 20:00–24:00, tel. 954-273-956); its terrace is less expensive, more casual, and a better value. Next door, **Restaurante La Primera del Puente** serves about the same thing with nearly the same view for half the price (Thu–Tue 11:30–17:00 & 19:30–24:00, closed Wed and the last half of Aug, tel. 954-276-918).

At the Isabel II bridge, in the yellow bridge tower, **Restaurante María Angeles** offers romantic dining atop the tower (daily 3-course menus from around €15, tel. 954-337-498) but the real draw is the cheaper, more casual tables filling the sidewalk along the riverside here. **La Esquina del Puente** (along with a couple other places) serves *pescados fritos* (fried fish) *raciónes* of for €8 to locals out for maximum romance at a minimum price (Wed–Mon 12:00–17:00 & 20:00–23:00, closed Tue, Puente de Isabel II, tel. 954-330-069).

Tapas (or Italian) in the Santa Cruz Area

Plenty of atmospheric-but-touristy restaurants fill the old quarter near the cathedral and along Calle Santa María la Blanca.

For tapas, the Barrio de Santa Cruz is trendy, touristic, and *romántico*. From the cathedral, walk up Mateos Gago where several classic old bars—with the day's tapas scrawled on chalkboards—now keep tourists and locals well fed and watered. (Turn right at Meson del Moro for several more.)

Cerveceria Giralda (at Mateos Gago 1) is a standard meeting place for locals. It's famous for its fine tapas; posted on the wall you'll see the award it won at the Spanish tapas convention. A block farther you'll find . . .

Bodega Santa Cruz (a.k.a. Las Columnas) is another popular standby with good cheap tapas. At the next intersection, turn right off Mateos Gago onto Calle Meson del Moro, which leads past the recommended San Marco pizzeria to . . .

La Teresa is a fine and characteristic little bar draped in fun photos, including one of Ted Kennedy sandwiched between matadors and local intellectuals. It serves good tapas from a user-friendly menu (daily, Calle Santa Teresa 2, tel. 954-213-069). Just down Calle St. Teresa is the artist Murillo's house (free when open and a good example of a local courtyard). Calle St. Teresa continues past a convent of cloistered nuns to the most romantic little square in Santa Cruz (where you'll find the Las Gallos flamenco club, recommended above).

Restaurante San Marco offers pizza and basic fun Italian cuisine under the arches of what was an Arab bath in the Middle

Ages (and a disco in the 1990s). The food is cheap and basic, and the atmosphere is easygoing (daily 13:15–16:30 & 20:15–24:00, closed much of Aug, Calle Meson del Moro 6, tel. 954-564-390).

Eating Characteristically along Calle García de Vinuesa

I don't like the restaurants surrounding the cathedral. But many good places are just across Avenida de la Constitución. Calle Garcia de Vinuesa leads past several colorful and cheap tapas places to a busy corner surrounded with happy eateries.

Horno San Buenaventura, across from the cathedral, is slick, chrome, spacious, and handy for tapas, coffee, and desserts (tapas are posted on the pillar, good seating upstairs). Farther up Calle Garcia de Vinuesa you'll find **Bodega Morales** (#11, Mon–Sat, closed Sun, tel. 954-22-1242). Go in the back section to munch tiny sandwiches *(montaditos)* and tapas and sip wine among huge kegs. Nearby **Freiduria la Isla** (ask for it) is a fried-fish joint *(pescado frito)* that also sells wonderful homemade potato chips and fried almonds. Farther up Calle Garcia de Vinuesa, the lonely but potent **Bodegas Diaz Salazar** has more tapas than it seems (pick something adventurous from their menu and wash it down with sherry from the keg, it's cheap and the guys who run the place are well worn but fun). At the end of Calle Garcia de Vinuesa, angle right and you'll find several good places, including these two:

El Buzo Restaurant is a busy neighborhood place on a lively street corner with good outdoor seating and homey indoor seating, frisky service, and great fish (€15 meals, daily 12:00–24:00, Calle Antonio Diaz 5, tel. 954-210-231). Just down the street, **Cafeteria Meson Serranito** is full of bull lore and locals with €6 *platos combinados* (Antonio Diaz 4, tel. 954-211-243)

Picnickers forage at the covered fish-and-produce **Mercado del Arenal** (with a small café/bar for breakfast inside, Mon–Sat 9:00–13:00, closed Sun, not lively on Mon, on Calle Pastor y Landero at Calle Arenal, just beyond bullring). A livelier market recently opened, just across the Isabel II bridge in Triana.

Transportation Connections—Sevilla

To: Madrid (2.5 hrs by AVE express train, departures 7:00–23:00 on the hour—except 13:00, €10 reservation fee with railpass; 10 buses/day, €16.25), **Córdoba** (hrly, 1.5 hrs for €6; 50 min by speedy AVE for €18; 10 buses/day, 2 hrs), **Málaga** (5 trains/day, 2.5 hrs; 11 buses/day, 2.5 hrs), **Ronda** (11 trains/day, 3 hrs, change at Bobadilla; 5 buses/day, 3 hrs), **Tarifa** (4 buses/ day, 3.5 hrs), **La Línea/Gibraltar** (4 buses/day, 4 hrs), **Granada** (3 trains/day, 3 hrs; 8 buses/day, 3 hrs), **Arcos** (2 buses/day, 2 hrs), **Jerez** (almost hrly, 1.25 hrs), **Barcelona** (3 trains/day, 10–12 hrs), **Algeciras** (1 train/day, 5 hrs, change at Bobadilla; 10 buses/day, 4 hrs), **Lisboa** (fastest option by bus: 5–6 buses/week, departs Plaza de Armas station Tue–Sun at 15:00, off-season not on Wed, 7 hrs, €32 one-way, buy ticket at station, reservations not necessary, Eurolines, tel. 954-907-844, www.eurolines.es; slower option by bus: daily bus departs Plaza de Armas at 9:00, 9–10 hrs; or slowest, overnight option by train: you can take AVE to Madrid and then the pricey night train to Lisboa). Train info: tel. 902-240-202. Bus info: tel. 954-908-040 but rarely answered, go to TI for latest schedule info.

Driving south into Andalucía: See those chapters.

From Sevilla to Portugal's Algarve

Note that Portuguese time is one hour earlier than Spanish time during daylight saving months.

To Lagos/Salema: You have three possibilities: the direct bus (best, but only offered in peak season); a combination of buses (best choice for off-season weekdays); or a bus/ferry/train combination (best option for off-season weekends).

The direct bus between Lagos and Sevilla is a godsend (€15, 2/day, 5 hrs, schedule from Sevilla to Lagos: 7:30–11:00 & 16:30–20:00, runs daily May–Sept, sometimes starting in April and continuing into Oct, doesn't run in winter, tel. 954-908-040 or 954-901-160). The bus departs from Sevilla's Plaza de Armas bus station and arrives at the Lagos bus station. From Lagos take a 30-minute bus ride to Salema.

Off-season, it'll take you longer (8–10 hrs) to get from Sevilla to Lagos. The all-bus option is best on weekdays because bus frequency drops on weekends. On weekdays, you can catch a bus from Sevilla to Faro (2/day, allow 4 hrs with transfer in Huelva), then a bus from Faro to Lagos (7/day, 2 hrs) and from Lagos to Salema (nearly hrly, 30 min).

The bus/ferry/train combination takes the longest (about 10 hrs total). Get an early start: Sevilla–Ayamonte bus (4/day from Plaza de Armas station, fewer on weekends, 2.5 hrs; also see train option below) to Ayamonte at the border, ferry to Vila Real in Portugal (17/day, 26/day July–Sept, 15 min), train to Lagos (4/day, allow 4.5 hrs with transfer in Tunes or Faro). In Vila Real, you'll find ATMs near the dock (indoor ATM next to Hotel Guadiana, the big hotel kitty-corner from the dock; outdoor ATM to the left of hotel, up Rua do Dr. Teofilo Braga). Vila Real's bus station is at the dock (Vila Real by bus to: Lagos—7/day, 4 hrs, transfer in Faro; to Tavira—8/day, 40 min; to Évora—3/day, 4–6 hrs, transfer in Faro; to Lisboa—5/day, 5.25 hrs; frequency drops on weekends;

buy tickets at bus kiosk at dock). Vila Real's train station is a kilometer away from the ferry dock/bus station. To get to the train station from the dock, exit the dock straight on Rua Ayamonte, then take a right on Rua Eça de Queiroz.

Taking the train from Sevilla to the Algarve is slower and requires a transfer to a bus at Huelva (Sevilla–Huelva: 4 trains/day, 90 min; Huelva–Ayamonte: 10 buses/day, 1 hr, Huelva bus station tel. 959-256-900). The Sevilla–Ayamonte bus (4/day, fewer on weekends, 2.5 hrs) is preferable, cheap, direct, and less hassle.

By Car: Those driving from Sevilla to Portugal need to get to the Guadalquivir River (from most recommended hotels, follow signs to Torre del Oro). From there, signs for Huelva lead you right onto the excellent freeway and it's smooth sailing (toll-free, no rest stops, 1 hour to the border—set your watch back an hour; 2 hours to Tavira—great place for a break, 3 km off the road, and 2 more hours to Salema for your beach-town break). Unfortunately, the freeway runs out an hour before Salema. Still, continue west, following signs to Lagos and then Vila do Bispo. Fifteen minutes after Lagos you'll see a turn-off for Salema.

CÓRDOBA

Córdoba is one of Spain's three big Moorish cities. Even though it was the center of Moorish civilization in Spain for 300 years (and an important Roman city), Sevilla and Granada are far more interesting. Córdoba has a famous mosque surrounded by the colorful Jewish Quarter, and that's it.

The **Mezquita** (pron. meh-SKEET-ah) was the largest Islamic mosque in its day. Today you can wander past its ramshackle "patio of oranges" and into the cavernous 1,200-year-old building. Grab the English pamphlet at the door (which predictably describes the church's history much better than the mosque's). The interior is a moody world of 857 (formerly 1,013) rose- and blue-marble columns and as many Moorish arches. If a guide told me I was in the basement of something important, I'd believe him. The center was gutted to make room for an also-huge Renaissance cathedral (€6.50, Mon–Sat 10:00–19:00, Sun 14:00–19:00, until 18:30 July–Oct, tel. 957-470-512). The mosque is near the TI (Mon–Fri 9:30–20:00, Sat 10:00–20:00, Sun 10:00–14:00, closes early in winter, tel. 957-471-235). The TI also has a handy kiosk at the train station (with a room-finding service).

From the station to the mosque, it's a €2.40 taxi ride or a pleasant 30-minute walk (left on Avenida de America, right on Avenida del Gran Capitan, which becomes a pedestrian zone; when it ends ask someone "*¿Dónde está la mezquita?*" and you'll be directed downhill through the whitewashed old Jewish Quarter).

Sleeping and Eating in Córdoba: Two comfortable, air-conditioned, and expensive hotels are located within a five-minute walk of the station. **Hotel Gran Capitan** is closer (96 rooms, Db-€120, breakfast-€9, CC, parking-€10.50, Avenida de America 5, tel. 957-470-250, fax 957-474-643, www.occidental-hoteles.com, e-mail: pina@ch-es.com). **Hotel Sol los Gallos** is cheaper and has a pool (120 rooms, Sb-€78, Db-€99, extra bed-€23, 10 percent less July–Aug, breakfast-€8.50, CC, Avenida de Medina Azahara 7, tel. 957-235-500, fax 957-231-636, www.solmelia.com, e-mail: tryp.gallos@solmelia.com). For food, try **Taverna Salinas** (Tendidores 3, near mosque, tel. 957-480-135).

Transportation Connections—Córdoba

Now that Córdoba is on the slick AVE train line, it's an easy stopover between **Madrid** and **Sevilla** (15 trains/day, about 1.5 hours from each city, reservations required on all AVE trains).

By bus to: Granada (9/day, 3 hrs), **Málaga** (5/day, 3 hrs), **Algeciras** (4/day, 4.5–5 hrs; 2 direct, 2 with transfers in Bobadilla). The bus station is at Medina Azahara 29 (tel. 957-236-474).

ANDALUCÍA'S WHITE HILL TOWNS

Just as the American image of Germany is Bavaria, the Yankee dream of Spain is Andalucía. This is the home of bullfights, flamenco, gazpacho, pristine-if-dusty whitewashed hill towns, and glamorous Mediterranean resorts. The big cities of Andalucía (Granada, Sevilla, and Córdoba) and the Costa del Sol are covered in separate chapters. This chapter explores its hill-town highlights.

The Route of the White Towns, Andalucía's charm bracelet of cute towns, gives you wonderfully untouched Spanish culture. Spend a night in the romantic queen of the white towns, Arcos de la Frontera. Towns with "de la Frontera" in their names were established on the front line of the centuries-long fight to recapture Spain from the Muslims, who were slowly pushed back into Africa. The hill towns, no longer strategic, no longer on any frontier, are now just passing time peacefully. Join them. Nearby, the city of Jerez is worth a peek for its famous horses and a sherry.

Before you go, visit www.andalucia.com for information on hotels, festivals, museums, nightlife, and sports in the region.

Planning Your Time

While the towns can be (and often are) accessed from the Costa del Sol resorts via Ronda, Arcos makes the best home base. Arcos, near Jerez and close to interesting smaller towns, is conveniently situated halfway between Sevilla and Tarifa.

On a three-week Iberian vacation, the region is worth two nights and two days sandwiched between Sevilla and Tarifa. Spend both those nights in Arcos. See Jerez (horses and sherry) on your way in or out, spend a day hopping from town to town (Grazalema and Zahara, at a minimum) in the more remote interior, and enjoy Arcos early and late in the day.

Andalucía

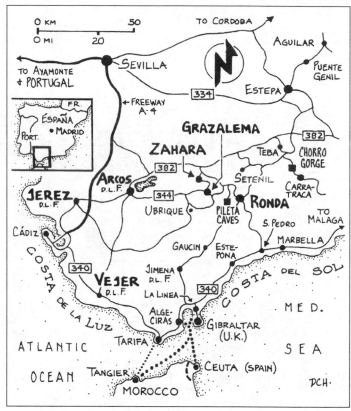

Without a car you might keep things simple and focus only on Arcos and Jerez (both well served by public buses). Spring and fall are high season throughout this area. In summer you'll find empty hotels and no crowds.

ARCOS DE LA FRONTERA

Arcos, smothering its hilltop and tumbling down all sides like an oversized blanket, is larger than the other Andalusian hill towns but equally atmospheric. The old center is a labyrinthine wonderland, a photographer's feast. Viewpoint-hop through town. Feel the wind funnel through the narrow streets as cars inch around tight corners. Join the kids' soccer game on the churchyard patio.

There are two towns: The fairy-tale old town and the fun-loving lower or new town. Check out the pleasant evening *paseo* and café scene, best at Plaza España and the adjacent Paseo Andalucía, the base of the hill where the new and old towns meet. Enjoy the moonlit view from the main square in the old town.

Though it tries, Arcos doesn't have much to offer other than its basic whitewashed self. The locally produced English guidebook on Arcos waxes poetic and at length about very little. You can arrive late and leave early and miss little.

Orientation

Tourist Information: The TI, on the main square across from the parador, is helpful and loaded with information, including bus schedules (March–Sept Mon–Sat 10:00–15:00 & 16:00–20:30, Sun 10:30–15:00, Oct–Feb Mon–Sat 10:00–19:30, Sun 10:30–15:00, Plaza del Cabildo, tel. 956-702-264).

Walking Tours: Year-round the TI organizes two different one-hour walking tours: Old Town and Patios of Arcos. They leave from the main square, are given in Spanish and/or English, and cost €3. Old-town walks include the church and general history (Mon–Fri at 10:30 and 17:00, Sat at 10:30 only, 1.5 hrs). Patio walks get you into private courtyards and cover lifestyles and Moorish influences (Mon–Fri at 12:00 and 18:30, Sat at 12:00, 2 hrs). Groups can hire a private guide through the TI for any walk any time (€36).

Arrival in Arcos: The bus station is on Calle Corregidores. To get to the old town from the bus station, catch a bus marked "Centro" (€1.20, 2/hr, runs 8:15–21:15, not on Sun), hop a taxi (€4), or take a 15-minute uphill walk: As you leave the station, turn left on Corregidores, angle left uphill, cross the four-way intersection, angle right uphill, and take Muñoz Vazquez up into town. Go up the stairs by the church to the main square and TI.

Parking is available in Arcos' main square (Plaza del Cabildo, ticket from machine €0.70/hr, only necessary Mon–Fri 9:30–14:00 & 18:00–21:00—confirm times on machine, can get €3 all-day ticket from old-town hotels, free Sat afternoon and all day Sun). If arriving to check in to a hotel, tell the uniformed parking man the name of your hotel. If there's no spot, you wait until one opens up (he'll help). Once you grab a spot, tell him you'll be back from your hotel with a ticket.

Helpful Hints: Café Ole offers Internet access in the new town on Plaza España. The little post office is in the old town at Paseo Boliches 26, a few doors away from Hotel Los Olivos (Mon–Fri 8:30–14:30, Sat 9:30–13:00, closed Sun). For laundry, Press To is full-service and reliable (Mon–Fri 9:00–13:30 & 17:00–20:30, Sat 9:00–14:00, closed Sun, in new town, across from recommended Hotel La Fonda on Calle Corredera).

Self-Guided Tour of the Old Town

Avoid this walk during the hot midday siesta.

1. Plaza del Cabildo: Stand at the viewpoint opposite the church on the town's main square. Survey the square, which in the old days doubled as a bullring: On your right is the parador, a former palace of the governor. On your left is the city hall (with the TI), below the 11th-century Moorish castle where Ferdinand and Isabel held Reconquista strategy meetings (closed to the public). Directly in front is the Church of Santa Maria. Notice the fine but unfinished church bell tower. The old one fell in the earthquake of 1755 (famous for destroying Lisboa). The new replacement was intended to be the tallest in Andalucía after Sevilla's—but money ran out. It looks like someone lives on an upper floor. They do. The church guardian lives there in a room strewn with bell-ringing ropes.

Enjoy the square's viewpoint. Belly up to the railing and look down. The people of Arcos boast that only they see the backs of the birds as they fly. Ponder the parador's erosion concerns (it lost part of its lounge in the 1990s—dropped right off), orderly orange groves, and fine views toward Morocco. An underground parking lot to clear up the square was considered but nixed because of the fragility of the land here. You're 100 meters (330 feet) above the river. This is the town's suicide departure point (for men—women jump from the other side).

2. Inside the Church of Santa Maria: After Arcos was re-taken from the Moors in the 13th century, this church was built—atop a mosque. Buy a ticket (€1, Mon–Fri 10:00–13:00 & 16:00–19:00, Sat 10:00–14:00, closed Sun) and step into the center, where you can see the finely carved choir. Notice the historic organ (built in 1789 with that many pipes). The fine Renaissance high altar—carved in wood—covers up a Muslim prayer niche surviving from the older mosque. The altar shows God with a globe in his hand on top, scenes from the life of Jesus on the right, and scenes from Mary's on the left. Circle the church counter-clockwise noticing the elaborate chapels. While most of the architecture is Gothic, the chapels are decorated in Baroque and Rococo. The ornate statues are used in the Holy Week processions. Sniff out the "incorruptible body" (meaning miraculously never rotting) of St. Felix—a third-century martyr. Felix may be nicknamed "the incorruptible," but take a close look at his knee. He's no longer skin and bones . . . just bones and the fine silver mesh that once covered his skin. Rome sent his body in 1764 after recognizing this church as the most important in Arcos. In the back of the church, under a huge fresco of St. Christopher (carrying his staff and baby Jesus), is a gnarly Easter candle from 1767.

Arcos de la Frontera

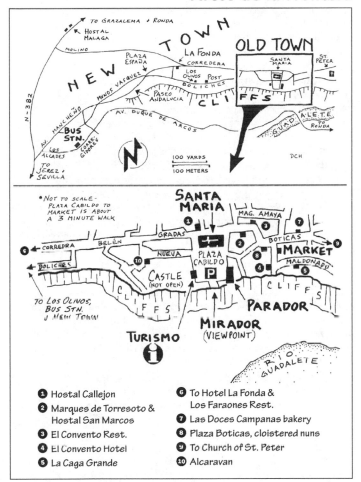

① Hostal Callejon
② Marques de Torresoto & Hostal San Marcos
③ El Convento Rest.
④ El Convento Hotel
⑤ La Caga Grande
⑥ To Hotel La Fonda & Los Faraones Rest.
⑦ Las Doces Campanas bakery
⑧ Plaza Boticas, cloistered nuns
⑨ To Church of St. Peter
⑩ Alcaravan

3. Church Exterior: Back outside, circle clockwise around the church. Down four steps, find the third-century Roman votive altar with a carving of the palm tree of life. While the Romans didn't build this high, they did have a town and temple at the foot of Arcos. This carved stone was found in the foundation of the old Moorish mosque that stood here before the first church was built.

Down a few more steps you come to the main entrance (west portal) of the church—open for worship on Sundays and every evening at 20:00 (19:00 in winter). This is a fine example of

Plateresque Gothic—Spain's last and most ornate kind of Gothic. In the pavement, notice the 15th-century magic circle: 12 red and 12 white stones—the white ones with various constellations marked. When a child came to the church to be baptized, the parents would stop here first for a good Christian exorcism. The exorcist would stand inside the protective circle and cleanse the baby of any evil spirits. While locals no longer use this (and a modern rain drain now marks the center), Sufis from a sect of Islam still come here in a kind of magical pilgrimage.

Continue around the church to the intersection below the flying buttresses. These buttresses were built to shore up the church when it was wounded by an earthquake in 1696. Thanks to these supports, the church survived the bigger earthquake of 1755. (Look at the arches propping up the houses downhill on the left; all over town, arches support earthquake-damaged structures.) The spiky security grille over the window above protected cloistered nuns when this building was a convent.

Sr. Gonzalez Oca's tiny barbershop at the corner has some exciting posters of bulls running Pamplona-style through the streets of Arcos during Holy Week—an American from the nearby Navy base at Rota was killed here by a bull in 1994. (Sr. Gonzalez Oca is happy to show off his posters; drop in and say, *"Hola."* Need a haircut? €5.50.) Downstairs in Sr. Oca's bar you can see a framed collection of all the euro coins of each of the 12 participating nations. Continuing along under the buttresses, notice the scratches of innumerable car mirrors on each wall (and be glad you're walking).

4. From the Church to the Market: Completing your circle around the church, turn left under more earthquake-damaged arches and walk down the bright, white Calle Escribanos. From now to the end of this walk you'll go basically straight until you come to the town's second big church (St. Peter's). After a block you hit Plaza Boticas. At the end of the street on your left is the finest restaurant in town (El Convento—see "Eating," below). On your right is the last remaining convent in Arcos. Notice the no-nunsense window grilles high above, with tiny peepholes in the latticework for the cloistered nuns to see through. Step into the lobby under the fine portico to find their one-way mirror and a blind spinning cupboard. Push the buzzer and one of the eight sisters inside will spin out some boxes of freshly baked cookies (€4.20) for you to consider buying. (Be careful, if you stand big and tall to block out the light, you can actually see the sister through the glass.) If you ask for *magdalenas*, bags of cupcakes will swing around (€1.50). These are traditional goodies made from completely natural ingredients (daily but not reliably 8:30–14:30 & 17:00–19:00). Buy some cupcakes to support their church work and give them to kids as you complete your walk.

The covered market *(mercado)* at the bottom of the plaza resides in an unfinished church. Notice the half-a-church-wall at the entry. The church was being built for the Jesuits, but construction stopped in 1767 when King Charles III, tired of the Jesuit appetite for politics, expelled the order from Spain. (Jesuits encountered no such tough treatment in South America.) The market is closed on Sunday and on Monday—when you rest on Sunday there's no produce, fish, or meat ready for Monday. Poke inside. It's tiny but has everything you need. Pop into the *servicio publico* (public WC)—no gender bias here.

5. From the Market to the Church of St. Peter: Continue straight (passing the market on your right) down Calle Boticas. Peek into private patios. These wonderful, cool-tiled courtyards filled with plants, pools, furniture, and happy family activities are typical of Arcos (and featured on the TI's Patios walks). Except in the mansions, these are generally shared by several families. Originally, each courtyard served as a catchment system, funneling rain water to a drain in the middle, which filled the well. You can still see tiny wells in wall niches with now-decorative pulleys for the bucket.

Look for Las Doce Campanas bakery, which sells traditional and delicious *sultana* cookies (€1 each). These big, dry macaroons (named for the sultans) go back to Moorish times. At the next corner, squint back above the bakery to the corner of the tiled rooftop. The tiny and very eroded mask was placed here to scare evil spirits from the house. This is Arcos' last surviving mask from a tradition that lasted until the mid-19th century.

At the next intersection notice the ancient columns on each corner. All over town these columns, many actually Roman (appropriated from their ancient settlement at the foot of the hill), were put up to protect buildings from reckless donkey carts.

As you walk down the next block, notice that the walls are scooped out on either side of the windows—a reminder of the days when women stayed inside but wanted the best possible view of any people-action in the streets. These also enabled boys in a more modest age to lean inconspicuously against the wall to chat up eligible young ladies.

At the old facade of San Miguel, duck right past a bar into the oldest courtyard in town—you can still see the graceful Gothic lines of this noble home. The bar is a club for retired men—always busy when a bullfight's on TV or during card-game times. The guys are friendly. Drinks are cheap (a stiff Cuba Libre costs €1.30). You're welcome to flip on the light and explore the old-town photos in the back room.

Just beyond (facing the elegant front door of that noble house), is Arcos' second church, St. Peter's. You know it's St. Peter's because St. Peter, mother of God, is the centerpiece of the facade. Let me explain. It really is the second church, having had an extended battle with Santa Maria for papal recognition as the leading church in Arcos. When the pope finally favored Santa Maria, St. Peter's parishioners even changed their prayers. Rather than honoring "Maria," they wouldn't even say her name. They prayed "Saint Peter, mother of God."

In the cool of the evening, the tiny square in front of the church—about the only flat piece of pavement around—serves as the old-town soccer field for neighborhood kids. Until a few years ago this church also had a resident bellman—notice the cozy balcony halfway up. He was a basket-maker and a colorful character—famous for bringing a donkey into his quarters that grew too big to get back out. Finally, he had no choice but to kill and eat the donkey.

Twenty meters beyond the church, step into the fine Galería de Arte San Pedro, featuring painting, pottery, and artisans in action. Walk inside. Find the water drain and the well.

From St. Peter's church, circle down and around back to the main square, wandering the tiny neighborhood lanes, peeking into patios, kicking a few soccer balls, and enjoying the views.

6. Circular Minibus Joyride: Arcos' little public bus circles through the town's one-way system and around the valley constantly, twice an hour, from 8:15 until 21:15 daily except Sunday (€1.30). For a fun and relaxing 30-minute tour, hop on. You can catch it just below the church near that mystical stone circle. Sit in the front seat for the best view of the tight squeezes and the schoolkids hanging out, as you wind through the old town. Passing under a Moorish gate, you enter a modern residential neighborhood, circle under the eroding cliff, and return to the old town via Plaza España. The bus generally stops for five minutes at Plaza España where you might get out to enjoy that slice-of-life scene.

Nightlife

New-Town Evening Action—The newer part of Arcos has a modern charm, as all the generations are out enjoying life in the cool of the evening around Plaza España (a 10-min walk from the old town). Several fine tapas bars border the square along with a good Egyptian restaurant (see "Eating," below).

The big park (Recinto Ferial) below the square is the late-night fun zone in the summer (June–Sept) when *carpas* (restaurant tents) fill with merrymakers, especially on weekends. The scene includes open-air tapas bars, disco music, and dancing. There are free live concerts here on Friday evenings throughout the summer.

Flamenco—On Plaza Cananeo in the old town, amateur flamenco sizzles on Thursday evening (free, from 22:00 July–Aug).

Sleeping in Arcos
(€1 = about $1, country code: 34, zip code: 11630)
Sleep Code: **S** = Single, **D** = Double/Twin, **T** = Triple, **Q** = Quad, **b** = bathroom, **s** = shower only, **CC** = Credit Cards accepted, **no CC** = Credit Cards not accepted, **SE** = Speaks English, **NSE** = No English. A price range reflects off-season to peak-season prices. Breakfast is not included, nor is the 7 percent IVA tax (unless noted below).

To help you easily sort through these listings, I've divided the rooms into three categories, based on the price for a standard double room with bath during high season:
> **Higher Priced**—Most rooms €100 or more.
> **Moderately Priced**—Most less than €100.
> **Lower Priced**—Most rooms less than €50.

Sleeping in the Old Town

HIGHER PRICED

Parador de Arcos de la Frontera is royally located, elegant, recently refurbished, and reasonably priced. If you're going to experience a parador, this might be the one (Sb-€80, Db-€110, breakfast-€9, CC, elevator, air-con, 24 rooms—8 with balconies, minibars, free parking, Plaza del Cabildo, tel. 956-700-500, fax 956-701-116, www.parador.cs, e-mail: arcos@parador.es, SE). Rooms with a terrace cost €6 extra. These can't be reserved in advance. Ask upon arrival.

MODERATELY PRICED

Hotel El Convento, deep in the old town just beyond the parador, is the best value in town. Run by a hardworking family, this cozy hotel offers 13 fine rooms—all with great views, half with view balconies. In 1998 I enjoyed a big party with most of Arcos' big shots present as they dedicated a fine room with a grand-view balcony to "Rick Steves Periodista Turistico"—so you know where I sleep when in Arcos (Sb-€49, Db-€61, third person or balcony-€12 extra, tax extra, CC, parking on Plaza del Cabildo-€3, Maldonado 2, tel. 956-702-333, fax 956-704-128, www.webdearcos.com/elconvento, e-mail: elconvento@viautil.com, Estefania SE). Bird-watch with breakfast on their view terrace with all of Andalucía spreading beyond your *café con leche*. The family also runs a good restaurant (see "Eating," below).

La Casa Grande is a lovingly appointed *Better Homes and Moroccan Tiles* kind of place renting six rooms with grand-view windows. Like in a lavish B&B, you're free to enjoy its fine view terrace, homey library, and classy courtyard, where you'll be served a traditional breakfast (Db-€67, Db suite-€79–85, Tb-€103–109, Qb suite with kitchen-€125, Maldonado 10, tel. 956-703-930, fax 956-717-095, www.lacasagrande.net, e-mail: lacasagrande @lacasagrande.net, friendly owners Elena and Ferran).

MODERATELY PRICED
Hotel Marques de Torresoto is a restored 17th-century palace run by a chain—which cuts into its personality. Still, it rents 15 decent rooms (few views) and comes with a peaceful courtyard. Once the home of a former Philippine governor, it has a grand Old World feeling (Sb-€43, Db-€58, Db with salon-€70, breakfast-€3.50, CC, air-con, across from Restaurante El Convento, Marques de Torresoto 4, tel. 956-700-717, fax 956-704-205, www.tugasa.com, e-mail: marques-torresoto@tugasa.com, SE).

LOWER PRICED
Hotel La Fonda is a great traditional Spanish inn with all 19 rooms off one grand hall above a tacky little lobby (Sb-€27, Db-€45, third person-€12, no breakfast, CC, request a quiet *tranquillo* room, Calle Corredera 83, tel. 956-700-057, fax 956-703-661, e-mail: lafonda@pobladores.com, SE).

Hostal San Marcos offers four air-conditioned rooms and a great sun terrace above a neat little bar in the heart of the old town (Sb-€18, Db-€30, Tb-€36, includes tax, less in winter, CC, Marques de Torresoto 6, tel. 956-700-721, e-mail: sanmarcosarcos@mixmail.com, Loli NSE).

Hostal Callejon de las Monjas, with a tangled floor plan and nine simple air-conditioned rooms, offers the best cheap beds in the old town—on a sometimes-noisy street behind the Church of Santa Maria (Sb-€18, D-€27, Db-€33, Db with terrace-€39, Tb-€44, includes tax, CC, air-con, Dean Espinosa 4, tel. & fax 956-702-302, NSE). Friendly Sr. Gonzalez Oca runs a tiny barbershop in the foyer and a restaurant in the cellar.

Sleeping in the New Town

MODERATELY PRICED
Hotel Los Olivos is a bright, cool, and airy place with a fine courtyard, roof garden, bar, view, friendly English-speaking folks, and easy parking. Unfortunately, this poor-man's parador is located on a motorbike-infested street. Since 12 of its 19 rooms

are on the quiet back side, it's smart to request a quiet room with no view (Sb-€38, Db-€62, Tb-€74, extra bed-€17, breakfast-€6, tax extra, 10 percent discount for readers of this book, CC, San Miguel 2, tel. 956-700-811, fax 956-702-018, http://terra.es /personal7/losolivosdelc, e-mail: losolivosdelc@terra.es, SE).

LOWER PRICED
If for some reason you want to sleep on the big, noisy road at the Jerez edge of town, a fine hotel nestles between truck stops on A-382: **Hostal Málaga** is surprisingly nice, with 19 clean, attractive rooms and a breezy two-level roof garden (Sb-€21, Db-€33, Qb apartment-€48, CC, air-con, easy parking, Ponce de Leon 5, tel. & fax 956-702-010, e-mail: hostalmalaga@teleline.es, Josefa speaks German). She also rents two apartments in the center of Arcos overlooking lively Plaza España (Db/Qb-€48). The highway on the Jerez side of Arcos is lined with cheap sleepable places.

Eating in Arcos
Restaurante El Convento, wonderfully atmospheric and graciously run by Señora María Moreno Moreno and her husband, Señor Roldan, serves what many readers report is the best meal of their trip (daily 13:00–16:00 & 19:00–22:30, near parador at Marques Torresoto 7, reservations necessary, tel. 956-703-222). The food is the best of traditional local cuisine and well worth the splurge. For a sampler of top-quality local cheese and ham, the *Sortido di Ricardo* promises four little explosions of taste. The hearty €24 menu of the day includes a fine house red wine and a glass of sherry with dessert. This is a good opportunity for game. And their Heaven's Bite dessert is well named.

The *típico* **Alcaravan** is two blocks off Plaza Cabildo under the castle. You can enjoy your tapas on its classy patio or inside what was actually the dungeon of the castle (closed Mon, Calle Nueva 1).

Los Faraones is a lively alternative serving spicy Egyptian cuisine in the new town near the *paseo* zone of Plaza España. Pay €9 for a Spanish menu or order à la carte for vegetarian and Egyptian (Tue–Sun from 12:30 and 19:30, closed Mon, Debajo del Corral 8, tel. 956-700-612). Helpful Hussein speaks English and can fire up a hubbly-bubbly with some apple tobacco—a memorable experience. Suck on it while watching the parade of people from your sidewalk perch.

Restaurante Marques de Torresoto offers good €18 à la carte meals (closed Mon–Tue, across from Restaurante El Convento, Marques de Torresoto 4).

The **Parador** is very expensive, though a costly drink on its million-dollar-view terrace can be a good value.

Transportation Connections—Arcos

By bus to: Jerez (hrly, 30 min), **Ronda** (4/day, 2 hrs), **Cádiz** (9/day, 1 hr), **Sevilla** (2/day, 2 hrs). From Jerez there are hourly connections to Sevilla. Two bus companies share the Arcos bus station. Their Jerez offices keep longer hours and know the Arcos schedules (Jerez tel. 956-342-174 or 956-341-063—make it clear you're in Arcos).

By car to: Sevilla (just over an hour if you pay €5 for the toll road).

RONDA

With 40,000 people, Ronda is one of the largest white towns; and with its gorge-straddling setting, it's also one of the most spectacular. While it can be crowded with day-trippers, nights are peaceful. And since it's served by train and bus, Ronda makes a relaxing break for nondrivers traveling between Granada, Sevilla, and Córdoba.

Ronda's main attractions are its gorge-spanning bridges, the oldest bullring in Spain, and an interesting old town. Spaniards know it as the cradle of modern bullfighting and the romantic home of old-time banditos. Its cliffside setting is as dramatic today as it was practical yesterday. For the Moors it provided a tough bastion, taken by the Spaniards only in 1485, seven years before Granada fell. To 19th-century bandits it was Bolivia without the boat ride.

Ronda's breathtaking ravine divides the town's labyrinthine old Moorish quarter and its new, noisier, and more sprawling Mercadillo quarter. A massive-yet-graceful 18th-century bridge connects these two neighborhoods. Most things of touristic importance (TI, post office, hotels, and bullring) are clustered within a few blocks of the bridge. While day-trippers from the touristy Costa del Sol clog the streets during the day, locals retake the town in the early evening. The *paseo* scene happens in the new town, on Ronda's major pedestrian street, Carrera Espinel.

Orientation

Tourist Information: The main TI is on the main square, Plaza España, opposite the bridge (Mon–Fri 9:00–19:00, Sat–Sun 10:00–14:00, tel. 952-871-272). Get the free Ronda map, excellent Andalusian road map, and a listing of the latest museum hours; consider buying maps of Granada, Sevilla, or the Route of the White Towns (€0.60 each). A second TI is located at Paseo Blas Infante, opposite the bullring (tel. 952-187-119).

Arrival in Ronda: The train station is a 15-minute walk from the center. To get to the center, turn right out of the station on

Avenida Andalucía, turn left at the roundabout (you will see the bus station is on your right), and then walk four blocks and you'll cross Calle Almendra (where several recommended hotels are located). At the pedestrian street (Carrera Espinel, a few blocks farther), turn right to reach the TI. From the bus station, cross the roundabout and follow directions above. A taxi to the center costs around €3.

Drivers coming up from the coast catch A376 at San Pedro de Alcantara and wind 50 kilometers into the mountains. A369 offers a somewhat longer, windy, but scenic alternative that takes you through a series of whitewashed villages. The handiest place to park is the underground lot at Plaza del Socorro (1 block from bullring, €0.90/hr, €10.75/24 hrs).

Tours of Ronda and Beyond

Rhonda Bus Tour—You may see a tiny Tajotur bus parked in front of the TI, gathering tourists for a drive outside of town to the most scenic places from which to view the gorge and bridge (€9, 45 min, English narration, runs erratically, up to 5 buses/day, tel. 616-909-483).

Local Guide—Energetic and knowledgeable Antonio Jesus Naranjo will take you on a two-hour walking tour of the city's sights (€60 on Mon–Sat, €90 on Sun, plus €1 per person, reserve early, tel. 952-879-215, cellular 639-073-763).

Guided Excursions—Helena Wirtanen, a personable guide from Finland, will take you to nearby Roman ruins and hill towns (starting at €30 per person, 4 hrs, tel. 952-875-556, cellular 656-932-820).

Sights—In Ronda's New Town

▲▲▲**The Gorge and New Bridge**—Ronda's main bridge, called Puente Nuevo (New Bridge), mightily spans the gorge. A bridge was built here in 1735 but fell after six years. This one was built from 1751 to 1793. The ravine, called El Tajo—110 meters (360 feet) down and 60 meters (200 feet) wide—divides Ronda into the whitewashed old Moorish town (La Ciudad) and the new town (El Mercadillo), which was built after the Christian reconquest in 1485. Look down ... carefully. Legend has it the architect fell to his death while inspecting it, and hundreds from both sides were thrown off this bridge during Spain's brutal civil war.

You can see the foundations of the original bridge (and a great view of the New Bridge) from the park named Jardines Ciudad de Cuenca. From Plaza España walk down Calle Villanueva and turn right on Calle Los Remedios at the sign for the park.

▲▲**Bullfighting Ring**—Ronda is the birthplace of modern

Ronda

200 YARDS
200 METERS

CITY WALL

TO COSTA DEL SOL, MALAGA

SANTA MARIA LA MAYOR

MONDRAGON PALACE

SOUTH

ARAB BRIDGE

MOORISH QUARTER

PUENTE NUEVO

GUADALEVIN RIVER

PARA-DOR

PLAZA ESPAÑA

INFO

PENAS   CANTOS   LOS REMEDIOS

PLAZA C. ABELA

VILLA

NUEVA

MERCA-DILLO QUARTER

CORTES

PLAZA DE TOROS

ALAMEDA

NARANJA   ESPINEL

POST

PLAZA MERCED

RAMON

ALMENDRA   SOUVIRON

MONTEREY

POZO

MADRID

SAN JOSE

DR. FLEMING

TO SEVILLA, ARCOS & PILETA CAVES

TO TRAIN STATION

ANDALUCIA

BUS STATION

❶ Royal	❼ Rest. Santa Pola	⓬ Casa del Marques de Salvatierra
❷ Ronda Sol	❽ Don Miguel	⓭ Puente Viejo
❸ Biarritz	❾ Reina Victoria	⓮ Hotel San Francisco
❹ Hostal Andalucía	❿ Museo del Bandolero	⓯ Hotel Rest. Alavera de los Baños
❺ El Tajo	⓫ Casa del Rey Moro	
❻ La Española		⓰ Hotel San Gabriel

bullfighting, and this ring was the first great Spanish bullring. In the early 1700s Francisco Romero established the rules of modern bullfighting and introduced the scarlet cape, held unfurled with a stick. His son Juan further developed the ritual or art, and his grandson Pedro was one of the first great matadors (killing nearly 6,000 bulls in his career).

To see the bullring, stables, and **museum,** buy tickets from the booth at the main entrance (which is at the back of the bull-ring, the farthest point from the main drag). The museum is located just before the entry into the arena.

This museum—which has translations in English—is a shrine to bullfighting and the historic Romero family. You'll see stuffed heads (of bulls), photos, artwork, posters, and costumes (€4, daily May–Sept 10:00–20:00, Oct–April 10:00–19:00, on main drag in new town, 2 blocks up and on left from the New Bridge and TI, tel. 952-874-132).

Take advantage of the opportunity to walk in the actual arena, with plenty of time to play *toro*, surrounded by 5,000 empty seats. The arena was built in 1784. Notice the 176 classy Tuscan columns. With your back to the entry, look left and you can see the ornamental columns and painted doorway where the dignitaries sit (over the gate where the bull enters). On the right is the place for the band—in the case of a small town like Ronda, a high school band.

Bullfights are scheduled for the first weekend of September and occur only rarely in the spring. For September bullfights, tickets go on sale the preceding July (tel. 952-876-967); *sol* means "sun" (cheap seats) and *sombra* means "shade" (pricier seats).

The Alameda del Tajo park, a block away, is a fine place for people-watching or a snooze in the shade.

Parador National de Ronda—Walk around and through this newest of Spain's fabled paradors. The views from the walkway just below the outdoor terrace are magnificent. Anyone is welcome at the cafés, but you have to be a guest to use the pool.

Sights—In Ronda's Old Town

Santa Maria la Mayor Collegiate Church—This 15th-century church shares a fine park-like square with orange trees and the city hall. Its Renaissance bell tower still has parts of the old minaret. It was built on and around the remains of Moorish Ronda's main mosque (which was itself built on the site of a temple to Julius Caesar). Partially destroyed by an earthquake, the reconstruction of the church resulted in the Moorish/Gothic/Renaissance/Baroque fusion (or confusion) you see today. Enjoy the bright frescoes, elaborately carved choir and altar, and the new bronze sculpture depicting the life of the Virgin Mary. The treasury displays vestments that look curiously like matadors' brocaded outfits (€2, daily May–Sept 10:00–20:00, Oct–April 10:00–19:00, in old town).

Mondragon Palace (Palacio de Mondragon)—This beautiful Moorish building was built in the 14th century, possibly as the residence of Moorish kings, and was carefully restored in the 16th century. It houses an enjoyable prehistory museum, with exhibits on Neolithic toolmaking and early metallurgy (many captions in English). Even if you have no interest in your ancestors, this is worth it for the architecture alone (€2, May–Sept Mon–Fri 10:00–19:00, Sat–Sun 10:00–15:00, Oct–April closes an hour earlier, on Plaza Mondragon in old town, tel. 952-878-450). Linger in the two small gardens, especially the shady one.

Wander out to the nearby Plaza de Maria Auxiliadora for more views and a look at the two rare *pinsato* trees (resembling firs) in the middle of the park; this is the only area of the country where these ancient trees are found.

Museo del Bandolero—This tiny museum, while not as intriguing as it sounds, is an interesting assembly of *bandito* photos, guns, clothing, and knickknacks. The Jesse Jameses of Andalucía called this remote area home, and brief but helpful English descriptions make this a fun detour. One brand of romantic bandits were those who fought Napoleon's army—often more effectively than the regular Spanish troops (€2.40, daily May–Sept 10:00–20:00, Oct–April 10:00–18:00, across main street below Church of Santa Maria la Mayor at Calle Armiñan 65, tel. 952-877-785).

Museo Joaquin Peinado—Housed in an old palace, this new museum features a Cubist collection by Joaquin Peinado, a pal of Picasso's (€3, Mon–Fri 10:00–14:00 & 15:30–18:30, Sat 10:00–14:00, closed Sun, Plaza del Gigante, tel. 952-871-585).

Walk through Old Town—From the New Bridge you can descend into a world of whitewashed houses, tiny grilled balconies, and winding lanes—the old town.

The **Casa del Rey Moro** garden may be in jeopardy if a five-star hotel opens on this site as planned. They may or may not offer access to "the Mine," an exhausting series of 365 stairs (like climbing down and then up a 20-story building) leading to the floor of the gorge. The Moors cut this zigzag staircase into the wall of the gorge in the 14th century. They used Spanish slaves to haul water to the thirsty town.

Fifty meters downhill from the garden is **Palace del Marques de Salvatierra** (closed to public). With the "distribution" following the Reconquista here in 1485, the Spanish king gave this fine house to the Salvatierra family. The facade is rich in colonial symbolism from Spanish America. Note the pre-Columbian-looking characters flanking the balcony above the door and below the family coat of arms.

Continuing downhill you come to **Puente Viejo** (Old Bridge), built in 1616 upon the ruins of an Arab bridge. From here look down to see the old Puente Romano, originally built by the Romans. Far to the right you can glimpse some of the surviving highly fortified Moorish city walls. Crossing the bridge you see stairs on the right leading scenically along the gorge back to the New Bridge via a fine viewpoint. Straight ahead bubbles the welcoming Eight Springs fountain.

Near Ronda: Pileta Caves

The Pileta Caves (Cuevas de la Pileta) are the best look a tourist can get at prehistoric cave painting in Spain. The caves, complete with stalagmites, bones, and 20,000-year-old paintings, are 22 kilometers from Ronda, past the town of Benaoján, at the end of the road.

Farmer Jose Pullon and his family live down the hill from the caves. He offers tours on the hour, leading up to 25 people through the caves, which were discovered by his grandfather. Call the night before to make sure no groups are scheduled for the time you want to visit—otherwise you'll have to wait (€6.50, daily 10:00–13:00 & 16:00–18:00, closes off-season at 17:00, closing times indicate last entrance, no reservations taken—just join the line, minimum of 12 people required for tour, bring flashlight, sweater, and good shoes, it's slippery inside, tel. 952-167-343). Sr. Pullon is a master at hurdling the language barrier. As you walk the cool kilometer, he'll spend over an hour pointing out lots of black, ochre, and red drawings (five times as old as the Egyptian pyramids), and some weirdly recognizable natural formations such as the Michelin man and a Christmas tree. The famous caves at Altamira are closed (though a new copycat has opened nearby); if you want to see real Neolithic paintings in Spain, this is it.

While possible without wheels (taking the Ronda–Benaoján bus—2/day, 8:30 & 13:00, 30 min—then a 2-hr, 5-km uphill hike), I wouldn't bother. You can get from Ronda to the caves by taxi (€25) and make your own way back or hire the taxi for a round-trip (€45). If you're driving, it's easy: Leave Ronda on the highway to Sevilla—C339, after a few kilometers exit left toward Benaoján, then follow the signs, bearing right just before Benaoján, up to the dramatic deadend. Leave nothing of value in your car. Nearby Montejaque has a great outdoor restaurant, La Casita.

Sleeping in Ronda
(€1 = about $1, country code: 34, zip code: 29400)

To help you easily sort through these listings, I've divided the rooms into three categories, based on the price for a standard double room with bath during high season:

Higher Priced—Most rooms €90 or more.
Moderately Priced—Most less than €90.
Lower Priced—Most rooms less than €50.

Ronda has plenty of reasonably priced, decent-value accommodations. It's crowded only during Holy Week (the week before Easter—April 20 in 2003) and throughout September. My recommendations are in the new town, a short walk from the New Bridge and a 10-minute walk from the train station. (The exceptions are Hostal Andalucía, across from the train station, and Reina Victoria, at the edge of town—and the gorge.) In the cheaper places, ask for a room with a *ventana* (window) to avoid the few interior rooms. Breakfast and the 7 percent IVA tax are usually not included.

HIGHER PRICED

You can't miss the striking **Parador de Ronda** on Plaza España. It's an impressive integration of stone, glass, and marble. All 78 rooms have hardwood floors and most have fantastic view balconies (ask about family-friendly duplexes). There's also a pool overlooking the bridge (Sb-€94, Db-€115–135, breakfast-€9, CC, garage-€8, Plaza España, tel. 952-877-500, fax 952-878-188, e-mail: ronda@parador.es, SE). Consider at least a drink on the terrace.

The royal **Reina Victoria,** hanging over the gorge at the edge of town, has a great view—Hemingway loved it—but you'll pay for it (89 rooms, Sb-€79, Db-€120, extra bed-€23, 10–15 percent less for smaller or non-view rooms and in June–Aug & Nov–Feb, breakfast-€9, CC, air-con, elevator, pool, free parking, 10-min walk from city center and easy to miss, look for intersection of Avenida Victoria and Calle Jerez, Jerez 25, tel. 952-871-240, fax 952-871-075, www.ronda.net/usuar/reinavictoria, e-mail: reinavictoriaronda@husa.es, SE).

Hotel La Casona, a beautiful splurge in the old town, is close to the Minarete de San Sebastian. The hotel features nine thoughtfully decorated rooms (some are suites), a swimming pool, and a garden (Db-€90, suites-€100–150, breakfast-€10, CC, air-con, Internet access, elevator, parking-€8, Marques de Salvatierra 5, tel. 952-879-595, fax 952-161-095, www.lacasonadelaciudad.com, e-mail: reservas@lacasonadelaciudad.com).

The newly-remodeled **Hotel Don Javier** is perfectly located on a pedestrian street just off Plaza España around the corner from the TI (Sb-€57, Db-€95, extra bed-€15, includes breakfast buffet but not tax, 15–20 percent less in June–July & Nov–Feb, 10 percent discount if you show this book, CC, José Aparicio 3, tel. 952-871-052, fax 952-878-001, www.ronda.net/usuar/laespanola/, e-mail: laespanola@ronda.net, SE).

MODERATELY PRICED
Hotel La Española, across from Hotel Don Javier, is run by the same family. Each of its 18 rooms is newly remodeled and comfy, with air-conditioning and modern bathrooms (Sb-€41, Db-€80, big Db suite-€98, Tb-€105, includes breakfast buffet but not tax, 15–20 percent less in June–July & Nov–Feb, 10 percent discount if you show this book, CC, José Aparicio 3, tel. 952-871-052, fax 952-878-001, www.ronda.net/usuar/laespanola/, e-mail: laespanola@ronda.net, SE).

Family-run **Hotel San Gabriel** has 16 pleasant rooms, a friendly staff, and a fine garden terrace (Sb-€60, Db-€72, Db suite-€78, CC, air-con, Calle Jose M. Holgado 19, just off Plaza Poeta Abul-Beca, tel. 952-190-392, fax 952-190-117, www.hotelsangabriel.com, e-mail: info@hotelsangabriel.com, friendly Ana SE). If you are a cinema-lover, settle into one of the seats from the old Ronda theater that now grace the charming TV room. Ask to see the Don Quixote movie that was partially filmed in the hotel.

Alavera de Los Baños, located next to ancient Moorish baths at the bottom of the hill, has 10 clean and colorful rooms (Db-€66, 15 percent more Aug–Sept, includes tax and breakfast, CC, Calle San Miguel, tel. & fax 952-879-143, www.andalucia.com/alavera, e-mail: alavera@ctv.es, Christian & Imma SE). This hotel offers a rural setting within the city, a swimming pool, a peaceful garden, and a wonderful restaurant (see "Eating," below).

The gorge-facing **Don Miguel** is just left of the bridge. Many of its 30 comfortable rooms have balconies and gorgeous views at no extra cost, but street rooms come with a little noise (Sb-€45, Db-€66, breakfast-€3.15, CC, air-con, elevator, parking garage a block away-€8/day, Plaza de España 4, tel. 952-877-722, fax 952-878-377, www.dmiguel.com, e-mail: reservas@dmiguel.com, SE).

Relaxed and friendly **Hotel Enfrentearte Ronda** has 11 spacious rooms and a peaceful garden (Sb-€45, Db-€78–90, extra bed-€36, 10 percent discount for more than 3 nights, air-con, Real 40, tel. 952-879-088, fax 952-877-217).

LOWER PRICED
Hotel Royal has 29 clean and spacious rooms—although they are boring and many are on a busy street. Ask for a *tranquilo* room in the back (Sb-€26, Db-€42, Tb-€52, CC, air-con, Virgen de la Paz 42, 3 blocks off Plaza España, tel. 952-871-141, fax 952-878-132,

www.ronda.net/usuar/hotelroyal/, e-mail: hroyal@ronda.net, some English spoken).

Hostal Ronda Sol has a homey atmosphere with 15 cheap but monkish rooms (S-€10.50, D-€17, no CC, Almendra 11, tel. 952-874-497, friendly Maria NSE). Next door, and run by the same owner, **Hostal Biarritz** offers 21 similar rooms, some with private baths (S-€10.50, D-€17, Db-€21, T-€25, Tb-€32, includes tax, no CC, Almendra 7, tel. 952-872-910, NSE).

The 65-room **Hotel El Tajo,** remodeled in 2002, has pleasant, quiet rooms once you get past the tacky Moorish decoration in the foyer (Sb-€27, Db-€48, parking-€6/day, CC, air-con, Calle Cruz Verde 7, a half-block off the pedestrian street, tel. 952-874-040, fax 952-875-099, SE).

Hotel San Francisco offers 25 small, nicely decorated rooms a block off the main pedestrian street in the town center (Db-€40–45, Tb-€42, includes tax, CC, air-con, Maria Cabrera 18, tel. 952-873-299, fax 952-874-688).

Hostal Andalucía, a plain but clean place with 11 comfortable rooms, is immediately across the street from the train station (Sb-€22, Db-€34, includes tax, CC, air-con, easy street parking, Martinez Astein 19, tel. & fax 952-875-450, NSE).

Eating in Ronda

Dodge the tourist traps. They say the best meal in Ronda is at the **parador** (*muy* elegant, figure €21). **Plaza del Socorro,** a block in front of the bullring, is a wonderful local scene, where families enjoy the square and its restaurants. Take a *paseo* with the locals down pedestrian-only Carrera Espinel and choose a place with tables spilling out into the action. The best drinks and views in town are enojyed on the terraces of the **Hotel Don Miguel** or the parador.

Restaurante Pedro Romero, assuming a shrine to bull-fighting draped in *el toro* memorabilia doesn't ruin your appetite, gets good reviews but is touristy (€11 menus, daily 12:30–17:00 & 19:30–23:30, air-con, across the street from bullring at Calle Virgen de la Paz 18, tel. 952-871-110). Rub elbows with the local bullfighters or dine with the likes (well, photographic likenesses) of Orson Welles, Hemingway, and Franco.

Restaurante Santa Pola offers traditional food with friendly service and gorge views (3-course dinners-€11, good foie gras on apples and tempura eggplant, lunch from 12:30, dinner 19:30–23:30, flamenco shows, crossing New Bridge, take the first left downhill and you'll see the sign, Calle Santo Domingo, tel. 952-879-208).

Alavera de los Baños, located in the hotel of the same

name, serves tasty Moorish specialties such as lamb and chicken *tajine*, along with vegetarian dishes, and offers great outdoor dining (dinner only for non-guests, Calle San Miguel, tel. 952-879-143.) **Restaurante del Escudero** serves tasty Spanish cuisine on a terrace over the gorge (€30–35 à la carte, Mon–Sat 12:00–16:00 & 19:00–23:00, Sun 12:00–16:00, Paseo Blas Infante 1, tel. 952-871-367).

Trendy, spendy **Restaurante Tragabuches** serves "nouvelle cuisine Andalouse" (multicourse menu–€50, à la carte around €45, Tue–Sat 13:30–15:30 & 20:30–22:30, Sun 13:30–15:30, closed Mon, José Aparicio 1, tel. 952-190-291, www.tragabuches.com).

The no-frills **Café & Bar Faustino** offers the cheapest tapas in town (€0.90–1) to a lively crowd of students, blue-collar workers, and tourists (Tue–Sun 12:00–24:00, closed Mon, just off Plaza Carmen Abela, Santa Cecilia 4, tel. 952-190-327).

Casa Manolo, a 10-minute walk from the town center, is a new, affordable option popular with locals, especially at lunchtime (3-course lunch–€6, daily 12:00–16:00 & 20:30–23:00, Lauria 54; go up Espinel, left on Montejeras, then third right; tel. 952-878-050.)

Transportation Connections—Ronda
By bus to: Algeciras (1/day, Mon–Fri only), **Arcos** (4/day, 2 hrs), **Benaoján** (2/day, 30 min), **Jerez** (4/day, 3 hrs), **Grazalema** (2/day, 1 hr), **Zahara** (2/day, Mon–Fri only, 1 hr), **Sevilla** (5/day, 3 hrs; also see trains below), **Málaga** (5/day, 1.75 hrs; access other Costa del Sol points from Málaga), **Marbella** (5/day, 75 min), **Fuengirola** (5/day, 2 hrs), **Nerja** (4 hrs, transfer in Málaga; can take train or bus from Ronda to Málaga). There's no efficient way to call "the bus company" because there are four sharing the same station; it's best to just drop by and compare schedules (on Plaza Concepción García Redondo, several blocks from train station).

By train to: Algeciras (4/day, 2 hrs), **Bobadilla** (4/day, 1 hr), **Málaga** (3/day, 2.5 hrs, transfer in Bobadilla), **Sevilla** (3/day, 3.5 hrs, transfer in Bobadilla), **Granada** (3/day, 2.5 hrs, transfer in Bobadilla), **Córdoba** (2/day, 2 hrs direct, 3.5 hrs with transfer in Bobadilla), **Madrid** (5/day, 5 hrs, 1 direct night train—23:20–8:40). It's a sleepy station serving only 11 trains a day. Transfers are a snap and time-coordinated in Bobadilla; with four trains arriving and departing simultaneously, double-check that you've jumped on the right one. Train info: tel. 902-240-202.

MORE ANDALUSIAN HILL TOWNS: THE ROUTE OF THE PUEBLOS BLANCOS
There are plenty of undiscovered and interesting hill towns to explore. About half the towns I visited were memorable. Unfortunately, public transportation is frustrating; I'd do these towns

Route of the White Hill Towns

only by car. Good information on the area is rare. Fortunately, a good map, the tourist brochure (pick it up in Sevilla or Ronda), and a spirit of adventure work fine. Along with Arcos, Zahara and Grazalema are my favorite white villages.

ZAHARA

This tiny town in a tingly setting under a Moorish castle (worth the climb) has a spectacular view. While the big church facing the town square is considered one of the richest in the area, the smaller church has the most-loved statue. The Virgin of Dolores is Zahara's answer to Sevilla's Virgin of Macarena (and is similarly paraded through town during Holy Week). Zahara is a fine overnight stop for those who want to hear only the sounds of wind, birds, and elderly footsteps on ancient cobbles. (**TI** open Mon–Sat 9:00–14:00 & 16:00–19:00, Sun 10:00–14:00, tel. 956-123-114.)

▲**Zahara Castle**—During Moorish times Zahara lay within the fortified castle walls above today's town. It was considered the gateway to Granada and a strategic stronghold for the Moors by the Christian forces of the Reconquista. Locals tell of the Spanish conquest of the Moors' castle as if it happened yesterday: After the Spanish failed several times to seize the castle, a clever Spanish soldier noticed that the Moorish sentinel would check to see if any attackers were hiding behind a particular section of the wall by tossing a rock to set the pigeons in flight. If they flew, the sentinel figured there was no danger. One night a Spaniard hid there with a bag of pigeons and let them fly when the sentinel tossed his rock. Seeing the birds fly, the guard assumed he was clear to enjoy a snooze. The clever Spaniard then scaled the wall and opened the door to let his troops in, and the castle was conquered. That was in 1482. Ten years later Granada fell, the Muslims were back in Africa, and the Reconquista was complete. Today the castle is little more than an evocative ruin (free, always open) offering a commanding view. The lake is actually a reservoir. Before 1991 the valley had only a tiny stream.

El Vínculo—This family-run olive mill welcomes visitors for a look at its traditional factory and a taste of some homemade sherry and the olive oil that the Urruti family has been producing on this site for centuries (€4, daily 9:30–20:00, on CA531 just outside Zahara, tel. 956-123-002).

Sleeping and Eating in Zahara
(€1 = about $1, country code: 34, zip code: 11688)
Hostal Marqués de Zahara is the best central hotel and a good value, with 10 comfortable rooms gathered around a cool, quiet courtyard. The wife cooks traditional specialties in the restaurant (Sb-€28, Db-€40, less Nov–March, breakfast-€3, CC, air-con, San Juan 3, 11688 Zahara, tel. & fax 956-123-061, www.zaharadelasierra.info, e-mail: hostal@vialutil.com, Santiago SE).
Pensión Los Tadeos is a simple, blocky place just outside of town by the municipal swimming pool (*piscina*) offering 10 remodeled rooms with great views (D-€37–50, basic breakfast-€1.50, Paseo de la Fuente, tel. 956-123-086, family Ruiz NSE).
Hotel Arco de la Villa—long on comfort, short on character—has 17 rooms with views just five minutes from the main square (Sb-€30, Db-€49, extra bed-€11, Camino Nazari, tel. 956-123-230, fax 956-123-244, www.tugasa.com/zahara.html, e-mail: info@tugasa.com).

Eating: Sr. Manolo Tardio runs **Meson Los Estribos,** a fine little restaurant with great views across from the church (Tue–Sun 13:00–16:00 & 20:00–23:00, closed Mon), and rents affordable apartments (CC, tel. 956-123-145).

GRAZALEMA
Another postcard-pretty hill town, Grazalema offers a royal balcony for a memorable picnic, a square where you can watch old-timers playing cards, and plenty of quiet, whitewashed streets to explore. Plaza de Andalucía, a block off the view terrace, has several decent little bars and restaurants and a popular candy store. Situated on a west-facing slope of the mountains, the town catches clouds and is famous as the rainiest place in Spain—but I've had only blue skies on every visit (**TI** open March–Sept Tue–Sun 10:00–14:00 & 18:00–20:00, Oct–Feb Tue–Sun 10:00–14:00 & 17:00–19:00, closed Mon, tel. 956-132-225). For horseback riding, consider Al-Hazan

(€15/1–3 hr, €70/full-day with lunch, tel. 956-132-296, www
.al-hazan.com, e-mail: al-hazan@airtel.com, run by Hanna, SE).
Sleeping in Grazalema: The **Casa de las Piedras** has 30 comfortable rooms just a block up from the town center—ask for a room
in their new wing (Sb-€26, D-€18, Db-€42, Tb-€56, includes
tax, buffet breakfast-€6, CC, Calle Las Piedras 32, 11610 Grazalema, tel. & fax 956-132-014, SE). **Villa Turistica Grazalema** is
a big, popular, happy place for locals enjoying their national park.
It has 38 apartments and 24 regular hotel rooms, with balconies
on the first floor or opening onto the swimming-pool garden on
the ground floor (Sb-€31, Db-€49, plus tax, extra person-€9.60,
apartments-€62–103, includes breakfast, 15 percent more in Aug,
CC, restaurant, 1 km outside town, tel. 956-132-136, fax 956-132-
213, www.tugasa.com/g-hotel.html).

JEREZ

Jerez, with nearly 200,000 people, is your typical big-city mix
of industry, garbage, car bandits, and dusty concrete suburbs,
but it has two claims to touristic fame: horses and sherry.

Jerez is ideal for a noontime (or midday) visit on a weekday.
See the famous horses, sip some sherry, wander through the old
quarter, and swagger out.

Orientation

Tourist Information: The helpful TIs give out free maps and
info on the sights. You'll find one at Plaza Alameda Cristina
(tel. 956-331-150) and another at Plaza Arenal (tel. 956-359-654).
Both have the same hours: June–Sept 9:30–14:30 & 17:00–19:00,
Sat–Sun 9:30–15:30; Oct–May Mon–Fri 9:30–14:30 & 16:30–
18:30, Sat–Sun 9:30–15:30.

Arrival in Jerez: The bus station (at Calle Cartuja and
Madre de Dios) has a simple baggage checkroom open weekdays
(€0.40/piece, if it looks closed, knock on the window; it's open
until 22:00). *Consigna* is the Spanish word for "baggage check."
The train station, a block away, has 30 lockers; buy a €2.40
locker token *(ficha)* at the ticket window.

Exit the bus station farthest from the WCs and turn left.
The center of town and the Plaza Alameda Cristina TI are a
20-minute walk away. At the five-way intersection angle right
on Honda until you reach Plaza Alameda Cristina—the TI is
tucked away on your right.

If you're arriving by train, angle right as you leave the station.
Cross the intersection. The bus station is on your left. Continue
straight, following directions from the bus station, above. Taxis
from the station to the horses cost about €4.

If you're headed to Alcázar, the Plaza Arenal TI is more convenient. Exit the bus station at the exit closest to the WCs and turn right, head to Plaza de las Augustias, then on to Plaza Arenal.

Sights—Jerez

▲▲**Royal Andalusian School of Equestrian Art**—If you're into horses, this is a must. Even if you're not, this is horse art like you've never seen. The school does its Horse Symphony show at noon every Thursday, as well as every Tuesday from March through October, and every Friday from July through October (€12–18, CC, reservations tel. 956-319-635 or 956-318-008, fax 956-318-014, call for current schedule, www.realescuela.org).

This is an equestrian ballet with choreography, purely Spanish music, and costumes from the 19th century. The stern horsemen and their talented and obedient steeds prance, jump, and do-si-do in time to the music, to the delight of an arena filled with mostly local horse aficionados.

Training sessions, open to the public on Monday, Wednesday, and Friday (plus Tuesday Nov–Feb) from 11:00 to 13:00 and from March through October 10:00 to 13:00, offer a €6 sneak preview. Practice sessions can be exciting or dull, depending on what the trainers are working on.

Amble along (Mon and Wed only) during a one-hour guided tour of the stables, horses, tack room, and horse health center. Sip sherry in the arena's bar to complete this Jerez experience.

If you're driving, follow signs from the center of Jerez to Real Escuela Andaluza de Arte Ecuestre (street parking). Otherwise it's a 30-minute walk from the train station, a 10-minute walk from the TI on Plaza Alameda Cristina, or a short €4 taxi ride.

▲▲**Sherry Bodega Tours**—Spain produces more than 10 million gallons per year of this fortified wine, ranging in taste from *fino* (dry) to *amontillado* (medium) to *oloroso* (sweet). The name "sherry" comes from English attempts to pronounce Jerez. While traditionally the drink of England's aristocracy, today it's more popular with Germans. Your tourist map of Jerez is speckled with wine barrels. Each of these barrels is a sherry bodega that offers tours and tasting.

Sandeman Sherry Tour: Just over a fence from the horse school is the venerable Sandeman Bodega (which has been producing sherry since 1790 and is the longtime choice of English royalty). This tour is the aficionado's choice for its knowledgeable guides and their quality explanations of the process (€4, tours Mon, Wed, and Fri 10:30–14:30 on the hour, Tue and Thu 10:00–15:00 every hour, Sat 11:30 and 13:30, bottling finishes at 14:00, closed Sun, finale is a chance to taste 3 varieties, tel. 956-151-700 for English tour times and to reserve a place, fax 956-302-626).

Jerez

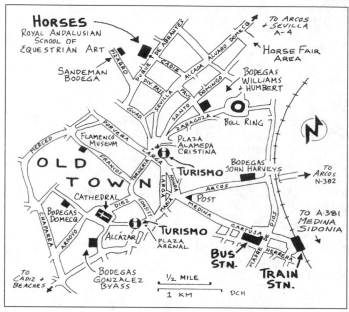

Harvey's Bristol Creme: Their 90-minute English tours (Mon–Fri at 10:00 and noon (or by arrangement) aren't substantial but include a 10-minute video and all the sherry you like in the tasting room (€3, Calle Pintor Munoz Cebrian, reservations recommended, tel. 956-3460-00, fax 956-349-427).

Gonzalez Byas: The makers of the famous Tío Pepe offer a tourist-friendly tour with more pretense and less actual sherry-making on display (it's done in a new, enormous plant outside of town), but it's the only bodega that offers daily tours (€7, March–Nov 11:30–17:30 every hour except 14:30, closed Dec–Feb, Manuel Maria Gonzalez 12, tel. 956-357-000, fax 956-357-046). Gonzales Byas is Disneyfying its tours, and schedules change frequently—call for the latest.

Alcázar—This gutted castle looks tempting, but don't bother. The €1.20 entry fee doesn't even include the camera obscura. Its underground parking is convenient for those touring Gonzalez Byas Bodega (€0.90/hr).

Transportation Connections—Jerez

Jerez's bus station is shared by six bus companies, each with its own schedules, some specializing in certain destinations, others sharing popular destinations such as Sevilla and Algeciras. Shop around for the best departure time. By car it's a zippy 30 minutes from Jerez to Arcos.

By bus to: Tarifa (3/day, 2 hrs), **Algeciras** (8/day, 2.5 hrs), **Arcos** (hrly, 30 min), **Ronda** (4/day, 2.5 hrs), **Sevilla** (12/day, 90 min), **Málaga** (1/day, 5 hrs), **Córdoba** (1/day, 3 hrs), **Madrid** (7/day, 7 hrs). Bus info: tel. 956-345-202.

By train to: Sevilla (12/day, 1 hr), **Madrid** (2/day, 4 hrs), **Barcelona** (2/day, 12 hrs). Train info: tel. 902-240-202.

Drivers note: In Jerez, blue-line zones require prepaid parking tickets on your dashboard on weekdays 9:00–13:30 and 17:00–20:00 and on Saturday 9:00–14:00; Sundays and July and August afternoons are free. Otherwise there's the handy underground parking lot near the Alcázar and at Plaza Alameda Cristina.

Easy Stops for Drivers

If you're driving between Arcos and Tarifa, here are several sights to explore.

Yeguada de la Cartuja—This breeding farm, which raises Hispanic Arab horses according to traditions dating back to the 15th century, offers shows on Saturday at 11:00 (€9, Finca Fuente del Sucro, Ctra. Medina–El Portal, km 6.5, Jerez de la Frontera, tel. 956-162-809, www.yeguadacartuja.com). From Jerez take the road to Medina Sidonia, then take a right in direction of El Portal—you'll see a cement factory on your right. Drive for five minutes until you see the Yeguada de la Cartuja. A taxi from Jerez will charge around €12 one-way.

Medina Sidonia—The town is whitewashed as can be surrounding its church and castle ruins–topped hill. Give it a quick look. Signs to Vejer and then *Centro Urbano* route you through the middle to Plaza de España—great for a coffee stop. Or, if it's lunchtime, consider buying a picnic, as all the necessary shops are nearby and the plaza benches afford a fine workaday view of a perfectly untouristy Andalusian town at play. You can drive from here up to Plaza Iglesia Mayor to find the church and TI (Tue–Sun 10:00–14:00 & 18:00–20:00 in summer, 10:00–14:00 & 16:00–18:00 in winter, closed Mon, tel. 956-412-404). At the church, a man will show you around for a tip. Even without a tip you can climb yet another belfry for yet another vast Andalusian view. The castle ruins just aren't worth the trouble.

Vejer de la Frontera—Vejer, south of Jerez and just 35 kilometers north of Tarifa, will lure all but the very jaded off the highway. Vejer's strong Moorish roots give it a distinct Moroccan (or Greek island) flavor—you know: Black-clad women whitewashing their homes and lanes that can't decide if they're roads or stairways. Only a few years ago women wore veils. The town has no real sights (other than its women's faces) and very little tourism, but it makes for a pleasant stop. (TI open Mon–Sat 10:00–14:00 & 17:00–20:00, closed Sun, Marques de Tamaron 10, tel. 956-450-736.)

The coast near Vejer is lonely, with fine but windswept beaches. It's popular with windsurfers and sand flies. The Battle of Trafalgar was fought just off Cabo de Trafalgar (a nondescript lighthouse today). I drove the circle so that you need not.

Sleeping in Vejer: A newcomer on Andalucía's tourist map, the old town of Vejer has only two hotels. **Convento de San Francisco** is a poor-man's parador in a classy refurbished convent (Sb-€41, Db-€59, breakfast-€3.50, prices soft off-season, CC, La Plazuela, 11150 Vejer, tel. 956-451-001, fax 956-451-004, e-mail: convento-san-francisco@tugasa.com, Ines SE). They have the rare but unnecessary Vejer town map. A much better value is the clean and charming **Hostal La Posada** (S-€15, Db-€30, cheaper off-season, Los Remedios 21, tel. & fax 956-450-258, NSE). Both are at the entrance to the old town, at the top of the switchbacks past the town's lone traffic cop.

Route Tips for Drivers—Andalucía

Arcos to Tarifa (130 km): Drive from Arcos to Jerez in 30 minutes. If you're going to Tarifa, take the tiny C343 road at the Jerez edge of Arcos toward Paterna and Vejer. Later you'll pick up signs to Medina Sidonia and then to Vejer and Tarifa.

Sevilla to Arcos: The remote hill towns of Andalucía are a joy to tour by car with Michelin map #446 or any other good map. Drivers can zip south on N-IV from Sevilla along the river, following signs to Cádiz. Take the fast toll freeway (blue signs, E5, A4). The toll-free N-IV is curvy and dangerous. About halfway to Jerez, at Las Cabezas, take CA403 to Villamartin. From there, circle scenically (and clockwise) through the thick of the Pueblos Blancos—Zahara and Grazalema—to Arcos.

It's about two hours from Sevilla to Zahara. You'll find decent but winding roads and sparse traffic. It gets worse if you take the tortuous series of switchbacks over the 1,385-meter (4,500-foot) summit of Puerto de Las Palomas on the direct but difficult road from Zahara to Grazalema. Remember to refer to your "Ruta de Pueblos Blancos" pamphlet.

Traffic flows through old Arcos only from west to east (coming from the east, circle south under town). The TI, my recommended hotels, and parking (Paseo Andalucía) are all in the west. Driving in Arcos is like threading needles. But if your car is small and the town seems quiet enough, follow signs to the parador, where you'll find the only parking lot in the old town.

COSTA DEL SOL:
SPAIN'S SOUTH COAST

It's so bad, it's interesting. To northern Europeans the sun is a drug, and this is their needle. Anything resembling a quaint fishing village has been bikini-strangled and Nivea-creamed. Oblivious to the concrete, pollution, ridiculous prices, and traffic jams, tourists lie on the beach like game hens on skewers — cooking, rolling, and sweating under the sun.

Where Europe's most popular beach isn't crowded by high-rise hotels, most of it's in a freeway choke hold. Wonderfully undeveloped beaches between Tarifa and Cádiz and east of Almería are ignored, while lemmings make the scene where the coastal waters are so polluted that hotels are required to provide swimming pools. It's a fascinating study in human nature.

Laugh with Ronald McDonald at the car-jammed resorts. But if you want a place to stay and play in the sun, unroll your beach towel at Nerja.

You're surprisingly close to jolly olde England. The land of tea and scones, fish and chips, pubs and bobbies awaits you—in Gibraltar. And beyond "The Rock" is the whitewashed port of Tarifa, the least developed piece of Spain's generally over-developed south coast and a good place to rest up for a visit to Morocco (see next chapter).

Planning Your Time
My opinions on the "Costa del Turismo" are valid for peak season. If you're there during a quieter time and you like the ambience of a beach resort, it can be a pleasant stop. Off-season it can be neutron-bomb quiet.

The whole 240 kilometers (150 miles) of coastline takes six hours by bus and four hours to drive (probably less when the

Costa del Sol

new freeway opens between Algeciras and Marbella). You can resort-hop by bus across the entire Costa del Sol and reach Nerja for dinner. If you want to party on the beach, it can take as much time as Mazatlán.

To day-trip to Tangier, Morocco, you can take a tour from Gibraltar, Algeciras, and—possibly in 2003—from Tarifa.

NERJA

Somehow Nerja, while cashing in on the fun-in-the-sun culture, has actually kept much of its quiet, Old World charm. It has good beaches, a fun evening *paseo* (strolling scene) that culminates in the proud Balcony of Europe terrace, enough pastry shops and nightlife, and locals who get more excited about their many festivals than the tourists do. For a taste of the British expatriate scene, pick up the monthly *Street Wise* magazine or tune in to Coastline Radio at 97.7 FM.

Orientation

Tourist Information: The helpful, English-speaking TI has bus schedules, tips on beaches and side trips, and brochures for nearby destinations such as Málaga and Gibraltar (Mon–Fri 10:00–14:00 & 17:30–20:30, Sat 10:00–13:00, closed Sun, Puerta del March 2, just off Balcony of Europe, tel. 952-521-531, www.nerja.org, e-mail: turismo@nerja.org). Ask for a free city map (or buy the more detailed version for €0.60). Pick up the free "Villa de Nerja Cultural Center" flier with the latest theater and musical events, and the "Leisure Guide" with a comprehensive listing of activities.

Their booklet on hiking is suitable only for drivers; you need a car to reach the trailheads. Another TI is located at the Caves of Nerja (Mon–Fri 10:00–14:00 & 16:00–18:30, Sat 10:00–13:00, closed Sun, tel. 952-529-024).

Internet Access: The most scenically situated of Nerja's few Internet cafés are Med Web C@fé, at the end of Calle Castilla Pérez, on a square overlooking the beach (daily 10:00–24:00, 10 computers, tel. 952-527-202), and next door, Europa@web (same hours, tel. 952-526-147).

Market: The lively open-air market is colorful and fun (Tue 9:30–14:00 and Sun 9:30–14:00, along Calle Almirante Ferrándiz, in the west end of town).

Getting Around Nerja

You can easily walk anywhere you need to go. A goofy little **tourist train** does a 30-minute loop through town every 45 minutes (€3, daily 10:30–22:00, until 24:00 July–Aug, departs from Plaza Cavana, you can get off and catch a later bus using same ticket, route posted on door of train). Nerja's **taxis** charge set fees (e.g., €6 to Burriana beach, taxi tel. 952-524-519). To clip-clop in a **horse-and-buggy** through town, it's €20 for about 20 minutes (hop on at Balcony of Europe).

Sights—Nerja

▲▲**Balcony of Europe (Balcón de Europa)**—This bluff over the beach is the center of the town's *paseo* and a magnet for street performers. The mimes, music, and puppets can draw bigger crowds than the balcony, which overlooks the Mediterranean, kilometers of coastline, and little coves and caves below.

Promenades—Pleasant seaview promenades lead in opposite directions from the Balcony of Europe, going east to Burriana Beach (promenade may be closed for renovation most of 2003) and west to Torrecilla Beach (10-min walk). Even if you're not a beach person, you're likely to enjoy the views. At Torrecilla Beach, the promenade ends at the delightful Plaza Los Congrejos, with cascading terraces of cafés (with Internet access) and greenery spilling into an overlook of the beach (at the end of Avenida Castilla Pérez).

Beaches—Nerja has several good beaches. The sandiest—and most crowded—is Playa del Salon, down the walkway to the right of the Restaurante Marissal, just off the Balcony of Europe. The pebblier beach, Playa Calahonda, is full of fun pathways, crags, and crannies (head down through the arch to the right of the TI office) with a fine promenade (mentioned above, may be closed in 2003) leading east to a bigger beach, Playa de Burriana. This is Nerja's leading beach, with paddleboats and entertainment options.

Nerja

* NOT TO SCALE -
BUS INFO KIOSK TO
BALCON DE EUROPA
IS A 10 MIN WALK

← N-340 AV. DE PESCIA
TO MALAGA

BUS INFO KIOSK

TO CAVES & GRANADA ↗

N-340

❶ Plaza Cavana	❺ Hostal Lorca	❾ Don Peque
❷ Hotel Puerta del Mar	❻ Pension El Patio	❿ Bar El Pulguilla
❸ Balcon de Europa	❼ Mena	⓫ Bar El Chispa
❹ Hostal Marissal	❽ Atembeni	⓬ Los Cunaos Bar

Another beach, Playa de la Torrecilla, is a 10-minute walk west of the Balcony of Europe. All of the beaches have showers, bars, restaurants, and—in season—beach chairs (about €4/day). Beware of red flags on the beach, which indicate that seas are too rough for safe swimming.

▲**Caves of Nerja (Cuevas de Nerja)**—These caves, four kilometers east of Nerja, have the most impressive array of stalactites and stalagmites I've seen anywhere in Europe, their huge caverns filled with expertly backlit formations and appropriate music. The visit is a 30-minute unguided ramble deep into the mountain, up and down lots of dark stairs congested with Spanish families. At the end you reach the Hall of the Cataclysm, where you'll circle what, according to Guinness, is the world's largest stalactite-made column. Someone figured that it took one trillion drops to make the column. Then you hike out (€5, daily 10:00–14:00 & 16:00–18:30, until 20:00 July–Aug, tel. 952-529-520).

A new exhibit in the Centro de Interpretacion (next to bus parking) explains the cave's history and geology—the exhibit's in Spanish, but it includes a 10-minute video in English.

To get to the caves, catch a bus from the Nerja bus stop on Avenida de Pescia (€0.75, 14/day, 15 min). During the festival held here the last week of July, the caves provide a cool venue for hot flamenco and classical concerts.

Frigiliana—This picture-perfect whitewashed village, only six kilometers from Nerja, is easy by car or bus (7/day, 15 min, €0.75). It's a worthwhile detour from the beach, particularly if you don't have time for the Pueblos Blancos hill towns (see www.frigiliana.com for more information).

Sleeping in Nerja
(€1 = about $1, country code: 34, zip code: 29780)

Sleep Code: **S** = Single, **D** = Double/Twin, **T** = Triple, **Q** = Quad, **b** = bathroom, **s** = shower only, **CC** = Credit Cards accepted, **no CC** = Credit Cards not accepted, **SE** = Speaks English, **NSE** = No English spoken.

To help you easily sort through these listings, I've divided the rooms into three categories, based on the price for a standard double room with bath during high season:

Higher Priced—Most rooms more than €100.
Moderately Priced—Most rooms €100 or less.
Lower Priced—Most rooms €50 or less.

The entire Costa del Sol is crowded during August and Holy Week, when prices are at their highest. Reserve in advance for peak season, basically mid-July through mid-September, prime time for Spanish workers to hit the beaches. Any other time of year you'll find Nerja has plenty of comfy, low-rise, easygoing, resort-type hotels and rooms. Room rates are three-tiered, from low season (Nov–March) to high season (July–Sept). Compared to the pricier hotels, the better hostels (Marissal and Lorca) are an excellent value.

HIGHER PRICED
Hotel Plaza Cavana overlooks a plaza lily-padded with cafés. If you like a central location, marble floors, modern furnishings,

an elevator, and a small rooftop swimming pool, dive in (35 rooms, Sb-€54, €64, or €74; Db-€74, €88, or €103; Tb-€94, €108, or €124; some view rooms, includes breakfast, tax extra, CC, air-con, a second small pool in basement, your car can ride an elevator down into the garage for €6/day, 2 blocks from Balcony of Europe at Plaza Cavana 10, tel. 952-524-000, fax 952-524-008, www.hotelplazacavana.com, e-mail: hotelplazacavana @infonegocio.com, SE).

Hotel Puerta del Mar, just around the corner and run by the same owners, offers 24 modern rooms at a better value (Sb-€42, €52, €62, €72, or €82; Db-€79, €91, or €113; Qb-€103, €113, or €123; apartments €60–150, breakfast next door-€3, CC, air-con, use of Cavana pool, Calle Gómez, tel. 952-527-304).

The most central place in town is **Balcón de Europa,** right on the water and on the square, with the prestigious address Balcón de Europa 1. It has 110 rooms with all the modern comforts, including a pool and an elevator down to the beach. All the suites have a seaview balcony and most regular rooms come with a sea view (Sb-€60, €70 or €90; standard Db-€80, €98, or €117; add about €20 extra for sea view and balcony; Db suite with Jacuzzi-€152, €177, or €201; breakfast-€8, CC, air-con, elevator, drivers should follow signs to parking garage, parking-€7.25/day, tel. 952-520-800, fax 952-524-490, www.hotel -balconeuropa.com, e-mail: balconeuropa@spa.es, SE).

Nerja's **parador,** housed in a new office-type building rather than a castle, lacks character but has 98 spacious, suite-like rooms and overlooks Burriana Beach (Sb-€75, €90, or €110; Db-€119, €120, or €130; less Nov–Feb, CC, air-con, free parking, large-for-Nerja swimming pool, 10-min walk from town center, Almuñecar 8, tel. 952-520-050, fax 952-521-997, e-mail: nerja@parador.es, SE).

MODERATELY PRICED

Hotel Paraiso del Mar, next to the parador, is a destination place, with 16 attractive rooms, a great setting on the bluff, and a pool and two terraces en route to a private stairway to Burriana Beach. You might not feel the need to make the 10-minute walk to the town center (Sb-€50, €65, or €75; Db-€55, €77, or €87; about €?20 extra for sea view and Jacuzzi, suites available for 50 percent more, includes buffet breakfast, tax extra, CC, quiet, air-con, friendly dog Ringo, underground parking, Calle Prolongación de Carabeo 22, tel. 952-521-621, fax 952-522-309, www.hotelparaisodelmar.com, e-mail: info@hispanica-colint.es, Alicia SE).

Hostal Marissal, just next door to the fancy Balcón de Europa hotel, has an unbeatable location and 21 modern, spacious rooms, six with small view balconies overlooking the action on the Balcony of Europe (Db-€39, €48, or €57, CC, air-con, Balcón de Europa 3, reception at Marissal café, tel. & fax 952-520-199, e-mail: marissal@terra.es, Maria SE).

LOWER PRICED
A quiet residential section five minutes from the center (and 3 blocks from the bus stop) offers two good options (near a small, handy grocery store):

Hostal Lorca—run by a friendly young Dutch couple, Femma and Rick—has nine modern, comfortable rooms and an inviting, compact backyard that contains a terrace, palm tree, singing bird, and small pool. You can use the microwave and take drinks—on the honor system—from the well-stocked fridge. This quiet, homey place is a winner (Sb-€28–34, Db-€35–40, extra bed-€9, includes tax, breakfast-€3.30, no CC, Mendez Nunez 20, look for yellow house, near bus stop, tel. 952-523-426, www.hostallorca.com, e-mail: hostallorca@teleline.es, SE).

Pensión El Patio has five clean, simple rooms. If you want to go local, this is worth the communication struggles (Sb-€18–36, Db-€25–37, Tb-€36–48, no CC, Mendez Nuñez 12, near bus stop, tel. 952-522-930, Angeles NSE). If no one answers, ask at the nearby grocery shop.

The following three places are central—within three blocks of the Balcony of Europe—but none will stun you with warmth. **Hostal Residencia Mena** is erratically run but has 11 fine rooms, four with terraces and sea views, and a quiet breezy garden (Sb-€18–24, Db-€27–39, includes tax, street noise, CC, El Barrio 15, tel. 952-520-541, fax 952-528-345, e-mail: hostalmena@hotmail .com, Maria speaks some English). The family-run **Hostal Atembeni** has 19 basic rooms (Sb-€20, €26, or €30; Db-€25, €33, or €38; includes tax, no breakfast, CC, ceiling fans, Diputación 12, tel. 952-521-341, some English spoken). **Hostal Residencia Don Peque**, across from Hostal Atembeni, has 10 simple rooms (with older bathrooms), eight with balconies, and an indifferent manager. Front rooms over the noisy street have air-conditioning (Db-€25–39, includes tax, breakfast-€3, CC, Diputación 13, tel. & fax 952-521-318, some English spoken).

Your cheapest and often most interesting bet may be a room in a private home (*casa particular*). Walk around with your backpack on the residential streets within about a six-block radius of Calle La Parra or Calle Nueva. Ask around.

Eating in Nerja
There are three Nerjas: the private domain of the giant beachside hotels; the central zone packed with fun-loving expatriates and

tourists enjoying great food with trilingual menus; and the back streets, where local life goes on as if there were no tomorrow (or tourists). The whole old town around the Balcony of Europe sizzles with decent restaurants. It makes no sense for me to recommend one over the others. Wander around and see who's eating best.

Farther inland, prices go down and locals fill the bars and tables. A 10-minute hike uphill takes you into the residential thick of things, where the sea views come thumbtacked to the walls. These three great places cluster within two blocks of each other around Herrera Oria (see map). Each specializes in seafood and is fine for a sit-down meal or a stop on a tapas crawl. Remember that tapas are snack-size portions. To turn tapas into more of a meal, ask for a *ración, media* (half) *ración*—or a menu.

El Pulguilla specializes in seafood, with clams so fresh they squirt (Tue–Sun 13:00–16:00 & 19:30–24:00, closed Mon, Bolivia 1, tel. 952-521-384). **El Chispa** is similarly big on seafood, with an informal restaurant terrace on the side (Tue–Sun 11:00–16:00 & 19:30–24:00, closed Mon, San Pedro 12, tel. 952-523-697). **Los Cuñaos** is most fun late in the evening, when families munch tapas, men watch soccer on TV, women chat, and stray kids wander around like it's home (daily 12:00–16:00 & 19:00–23:00, good seafood and prices, Herrera Oria 19, tel. 952-521-107). These places are generally open all day for tapas and drinks; I've included just their serving hours in case you're hungry for a meal.

If you're out late, consider **Bar El Molino** for folk singing after 23:00; it's touristy but fun (Calle San Jose 4).

Transportation Connections—Nerja
The Nerja bus station is actually just a bus stop on Avenida de Pescia with an info booth (daily 8:00–20:00, helpful schedules posted on booth, tel. 952-521-504).

By bus to: Nerja Caves (14/day, 15 min), **Frigiliana** (7/day, 15 min), **Málaga** (17/day, 70–90 min), **Granada** (3/day, more frequent with Motril transfer, 2.5 hrs), **Córdoba** (1–2/day, 4 hrs), **Sevilla** (3/day, 4 hrs).

Transportation Connections—Málaga
The train station nearest Nerja is an hourly 90-minute bus ride away in Málaga. Málaga's train and bus stations—a block apart from each other—each have pickpockets and lockers (train station lockers are better). You can rent a car at the train station.

From Málaga by train to: Ronda (3/day, 2 hrs, transfer in Bobadilla), **Madrid** (5/day, 4.25 hrs on Talgo train), **Córdoba** (10/day, 2–2.75 hrs, fastest on Talgo), **Granada** (2/day, 2.5–3.25 hrs, transfer in Bobadilla), **Sevilla** (5/day, 2.5 hrs), **Barcelona** (2/day, 13.5 hrs). Train info: tel. 902-240-202.

   Buses: Málaga's bus station, a block from the train station, has a helpful information office with bus schedules (daily 7:00–22:00, on Paseo de los Tilos, tel. 952-350-061).

   By bus to: Algeciras (8/day, 1.45 hrs), **Nerja** (17/day, 70–90 min), **Ronda** (4/day, 2 hrs), **La Línea/Gibraltar** (4/day, 3 hrs), **Sevilla** (10/day, 3 hrs), **Jerez** (1/day, 5 hrs), **Granada** (16/day, 2 hrs), **Córdoba** (5/day, 3 hrs), **Madrid** (12/day, 6 hrs).

Sights—From Nerja to Gibraltar

Buses take five hours to make the Nerja-to-Gibraltar trip. They leave nearly hourly and stop at each town mentioned.

Fuengirola/Torremolinos—The most built-up part of the region, where those most determined to be envied settle down, is a bizarre world of Scandinavian package tours, flashing lights, pink flamenco, multilingual menus, and all-night happiness. Fuengirola is like a Spanish Mazatlán with a few less-pretentious, older, budget hotels between the main drag and the beach. The water here is clean and the nightlife fun and easy. James Michener's idyllic Torremolinos has been strip-mauled and parking-metered.

Marbella—This is the most polished and posh town on the Costa del Sol. High-priced boutiques, immaculate streets, and beautifully landscaped squares are testimony to Marbella's arrival on the world-class-resort scene. Have a *café con leche* on the beautiful Plaza de Naranjas in the old city's pedestrian section. Wander down to new Marbella and the high-rise beachfront apartment buildings to check out the beach scene. Marbella is an easy stop on the Algeciras–Málaga bus route (as you exit the bus station, take a left to reach the center of town).

San Pedro de Alcantara—This town's relatively undeveloped sandy beach is popular with young travelers. San Pedro's neighbor, Puerto Banus, is "where the world casts anchor." This luxurious jet-set port, complete with casino, is a strange mix of Rolls-Royces, yuppies, boutiques, rich Arabs, and budget browsers.

GIBRALTAR

One of the last bits of the empire upon which the sun never set, Gibraltar is a fun mix of Anglican propriety, "God Save the Queen" tattoos, English bookstores, military memories, and tourist shops. The few British soldiers you'll see are enjoying this cushy assignment in the Mediterranean sun as a reward for enduring and surviving an assignment in another remnant of the British Empire: Northern Ireland. While things are cheaper in pounds, your euros work as well as your English words here.

The 30,000 Gibraltarians have a mixed and interesting heritage. The Llanitos (pron. yah-nee-tohs), as the Spanish call them, speak a Creole-like Spanglish. They are a fun-loving and tolerant mix of British, Spanish, and Moroccan.

You'll need your passport to cross the border (and you may still be able to charm an official into stamping it—ask or you'll get just a wave-through). Make Gibraltar a day trip (or just an overnight); rooms are expensive compared to Spain.

Planning Your Time

For the best day trip to Gibraltar, consider this plan: Walk across the border, catch bus #3 and ride it to the end, following the self-guided tour (see below). Ride bus #3 back to the cable-car station, then catch the cable-car to the top, and walk down via St. Michael's Cave and the Apes' Den. From there, either walk or take the cable car back into town. Spend your remaining free time in town before returning to Spain.

Tourists who stay overnight find Gibraltar a peaceful place in the evening, when the town can just be itself. No one is in a hurry. Families stroll, kids play, seniors window-shop, and everyone chats.

If you won't make it to Tarifa or Algeciras, but want to carve out a day for Morocco, see "Day Trip to Tangier, Morocco," below.

Orientation

(tel. code: 9567 from Spain, 350 from other countries)

Tourist Information: Gibraltar's main TI is at Casemates Square, the grand square at the entrance of town (Mon–Fri 9:00–17:30, Sat–Sun 10:00–15:00, tel. 74982, www.gibraltar.gi). Another TI is in the Duke of Kent House on Cathedral Square, nearer the town center (Mon–Fri 8:45–17:30, closed Sat–Sun, bus #3 stops here, just after NatWest House, tel. 74950). More TIs are at Customs where you cross the border and at the Coach Park (bus terminal). The TIs give out free maps and can arrange tours of caves and the WWII tunnels that crisscross the island (€8.25/£5 per tour, 3 hrs).

Helpful Hints

Telephone: To telephone Gibraltar from Spain, dial 9567 followed by the five-digit local number. To call the Rock from European countries other than Spain, dial 00-350-local number. To call from America or Canada, dial 011-350-local number. If you plan to make calls from Gibraltar, note that phone booths take English coins or Gibraltar phone cards (available at kiosks).

Electricity: If you have electrical gadgets, note that Gibraltar, like Britain, uses three-prong plugs. Your hotel may have an adapter (which plugs onto a European plug) to loan you.

Gibraltar

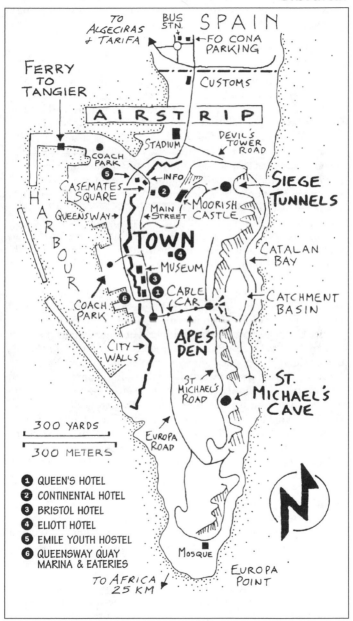

TO
ALGECIRAS
& TARIFA

BUS
STN.

SPAIN

FO CONA
PARKING

FERRY
TO
TANGIER

CUSTOMS

A I R S T R I P

DEVIL'S
TOWER
ROAD

STADIUM

COACH
PARK

❺

CASEMATES
SQUARE

INFO

❷

MOORISH
CASTLE

SIEGE
TUNNELS

H A R B O U R

QUEENSWAY

MAIN
STREET

TOWN

❹

MUSEUM

CATALAN
BAY

❸

CABLE
CAR

CATCHMENT
BASIN

❻

COACH
PARK

CITY
WALLS

APE'S
DEN

ST
MICHAEL'S
ROAD

ST.
MICHAEL'S
CAVE

300 YARDS

300 METERS

EUROPA
ROAD

❶ QUEEN'S HOTEL
❷ CONTINENTAL HOTEL
❸ BRISTOL HOTEL
❹ ELIOTT HOTEL
❺ EMILE YOUTH HOSTEL
❻ QUEENSWAY QUAY
   MARINA & EATERIES

TO AFRICA
25 KM

MOSQUE

EUROPA
POINT

N

Internet Access: Café Cyberworld has pricey Internet access (daily 12:00–24:00, Queensway 14, in Ocean Heights Gallery, near Casemates end of town, tel. 51416).

Arrival in Gibraltar

By Bus: Spain's La Línea bus station is a five-minute walk from the Gibraltar border. If you're day-tripping to Gibraltar, you can store luggage at the La Línea station (15 lockers, €2.40/£1.50 each) or at Gibraltar's airport, an eight- to ten-minute walk away from the border (£1–3/€1.60–4.70 per day depending on size; ask at airport information desk).

From the La Línea bus station walk to the border (flash your passport) and then take a quick bus ride into town: Catch either the #3 minibus to the TI at Cathedral Square (can stay on to continue self-guided tour, below) or the double-decker bus #9 to Casemates Square—which also has a TI (€0.70/40 pence, every 15 min). Otherwise it's a 30-minute walk between the border and the center: From the "frontier" (as it's called), walk straight across the runway (look left, right, and up), then head down Winston Churchill Avenue, angling right at the Shell station on Smith Dorrien Avenue.

Avoid taking an expensive taxi ride into town. Compare the cost of a taxi from the border to the cable-car lift (€7.25/£5) with the cost of bus #3 (€0.70/40 pence).

By Car: After taking the La Línea–Gibraltar exit off the main Costa del Sol road, continue as the road curves left with the Rock to your right. The traffic light with the *Aduana* (customs) sign is just at the border; a right turn will take you into Gibraltar, or a left turn will take you immediately to La Línea (the Gibraltarians call this street Winston Churchill Avenue, the Spanish call it the 20th of April). Avoid long lines of cars going into Gibraltar by turning left and parking in La Línea. From here you make the five-minute walk across the border on foot. The handiest place to park is at the Fo Cona underground parking lot (€0.90/hr, €6/day, left on 20th of April, 100 meters on your left). You'll also find blue-lined parking spots in this area (€1/hr from meter, bring coins, leave ticket on dashboard, Sun free).

If you insist on driving into Gibraltar, there are plenty of parking lots (like the huge one near the cable car), but be prepared for up to a 90-minute wait both ways at the border.

Tours of Gibraltar

It's easy to visit the Rock's uppermost sights on your own at your own pace (e.g., walk or take bus #3 to the cable-car lift, take the lift up and hike down to the sights). Those with more money than

Spain vs. Gibraltar

Spain has been annoyed about Gibraltar ever since Great Britain snagged this prime 6.5-square-kilometer territory through the 18th-century Treaty of Utrecht at the end of the War of Spanish Succession. Although Spain long ago abandoned efforts to reassert its sovereignty by force, it still tries to make Gibraltarians see the error of their British ways by messing up things like border crossings and the phone system. Still, given the choice—and they got it from the U.N. in 1967—Gibraltar's residents steadfastly remain Queen Elizabeth's loyal subjects, voting overwhelmingly to continue as a self-governing British dependency.

Gibraltar, a key British military base in World Wars I and II, and a banking, shipping, and tourist magnet, is connected to Spain by a sandy isthmus. Over the years, Spain has limited air and sea connections and choked traffic at the 1.2-kilometer border in efforts to convince Gibraltar to give back the Rock. And then there's the phone issue. Spain refuses to recognize (or dial) a separate country code for Gibraltar, which essentially ends up making Gibraltar's phone system part of Spain's. This means that Spain can decide how many numbers Gibraltar residents get—and it's a lot less than they want. That's why when you call Gibraltar from Spain, you first dial 9567, the area code for the Spanish province of Cádiz, and when you call Gibraltar from anywhere else, you dial the country code, 350. There are similar problems at work with mobile phones; at this point, they only work near the border. Gibraltar, a European Union member, has made its case all the way up to the European Commission, which told Spain and Britain to sort it out. Please hold....

time take a tour (covers admission to the Upper Rock Nature Reserve sights included on tour). There are two types of tours: by minibus and by taxi. For the minibus tours, book at a travel agency. You can catch a taxi tour at the border (or cheaper at taxi stands at squares in the center).

By Minibus: Travel agencies offer approximately 90-minute tours for a set fee (around €18–21.25/£11–13). Stops include St. Michael's Cave, the Apes' Den, and Siege Tunnels. Consider Thomas Cook Exchange Travel (tours on Mon, Wed, and Fri, 241 Main Street, near Marks & Spencers, tel. 76151), Bland

Travel (tours also on Mon, Wed, and Fri, 220 Main Street, tel. 79068), or Parodytur (priciest but offers tours daily, Cathedral Square, tel. 76070). If you call ahead to reserve a seat, you pay when you arrive in Gibraltar. Or just drop by any agency when you're in town (usually open Mon–Fri 9:30–18:00, closed Sat–Sun). Nearly every travel agency in town offers the tour, with only minor variations.

By Taxi: Lots of aggressive cabbies at the border would love to take you for a ride—about €25/£16 per person if the taxi is packed. More people in a taxi means a lower cost per person; try to buddy up with other travelers. Cabbies at taxi stands in the center of Gibraltar are more low-key and charge a bit less (though it's harder to gather a group). The basic tour consists of four stops: an overlook over the Strait, St. Michael's Cave (for a 15–20-minute visit), near the top of the Rock, and the Siege Tunnels (for 15–20 minutes). A fifth stop—the ATM at NatWest House—is added for people who mistakenly thought they could pay for this tour with a credit card.

The Quick, Cheap, Bus #3 Self-Guided Orientation Tour

At the border, pick up a map at the customs TI. Then walk straight ahead for 200 meters to the bus stop on the right. Catch minibus #3 (4/hr, pay driver €0.70/40 pence) and enjoy the ride.

You enter Gibraltar by crossing an **airstrip.** Forty times a week, the entry road into Gibraltar is closed to allow airplanes to land or take off. (You can fly to London for as little as $180.) The airstrip, originally a horse racing stadium, was filled in with stones excavated from the 50 kilometers of military tunnels in the Rock. This airstrip was a vital lifeline in the days when Spain and Britain were quarreling over Gibraltar and the border was closed.

Just after the airstrip, the bus passes a road leading left (which heads clockwise around the Rock to the town of Catalan Bay, peaceful beaches, and the huge mountainside rainwater catchment wall). As you pass apartments on the left, find the **Moorish castle** above (now a prison; only the tower is open to the public).

Over the bridge and on the right after the next stop you'll see **World War memorials.** The first is the American War Memorial (a building-like structure with a gold plaque and arch), built in 1932 to commemorate American sailors based here in World War I. Farther along you'll see 18th-century cannons and a memorial to Gibraltarians who died in World War II.

The following sights occur in rapid succession: Passing the NatWest House office tower on the left, you'll immediately see a **synagogue** (only the top peeks out above a wall; the wooden doors in the wall bear the Star of David). In the 19th century half of Gibraltar was Jewish. The Jewish community now numbers 600.

Just after the synagogue is little **Cathedral Square,** with a playground, TI, and the Moorish-looking Anglican church (behind the playground).

Now you'll pass a loooong wall; most of it is the back of the Governor's Residence (also called the Convent). At the front of the Residence (not visible from the bus), a miniature Changing of the Guard occurs at midday.

The bus stops before the old **Charles V wall,** built in response to a 1552 raid in which the pirate Barbarossa captured 70 Gibraltarians into slavery.

Immediately after you pass under the wall, you'll see—on your left—a green park that contains the **Trafalgar cemetery** (free, daily 9:00–19:00). Buried here are the British sailors who died defeating the French off the coast of Portugal's Cape Trafalgar in 1805.

The next stop is at the big parking lot for the **cable car** to the top of the Rock, as well as for the **botanical gardens** (free, daily 8:00–sunset) at the base of the lift. You can get off now or later, on the ride back into town.

Heading uphill out of town you pass the big ugly casino and the path leading up the Rock (a 2.5-hour hike). Reaching the end of the Rock you pass modern apartments and the mosque. The lighthouse marks the windy Europa Point—end of the line. Buses retrace the route you just traveled, departing about every 15 minutes (check schedule before exploring farther).

The **Europa Point,** up the mound from the bus stop and tourist shop (on right), is an observation post. A plaque here identifies the mountains of Morocco 25 kilometers across the strait. The light of the lighthouse (from 1841, closed to visitors) can be seen from Morocco.

The **King Fahad Mosque,** a gift from the Saudi sultan, was completed in 1997. Gibraltar's 300 Muslims worship here each Friday. Here—as across the strait in Morocco—five times a day the imam sings the call to prayer. Visitors (without shoes) are welcome outside of prayer time.

Sights—Gibraltar's Upper Rock Nature Reserve

▲▲▲**The Rock**—The real highlight of Gibraltar is the spectacular Rock itself. From the south end of Main Street, catch the cable car to the top (€6.50/£4 one-way, €9/£6 round-trip, or €12/£7 to include admission to all of the Upper Rock Nature Reserve sights, Mon–Sat 9:30–17:15, last cable car down at 17:45, 6/hr, closed Sun and when it's windy, brochure with necessary map included with ticket). The lift, usually closed on Sunday, may open on Sunday during peak season, June through September.

The cable car drops you at a slick **restaurant/view terrace** at the very top of the Rock, from which you can explore old ramparts and drool at the 360-degree view of Morocco, the Strait of Gibraltar, the bay stretching west toward Algeciras, and the twinkling Costa del Sol arcing eastward. Below you stretches the giant catchment system that the British built to catch rainwater in the not-so-distant past, when Spain allowed neither water nor tourists to cross its disputed border. The views are especially crisp on brisk off-season days.

Buying a one-way ticket up saves a little money and gives you a chance to hike down to all of the sites. Allow 90 minutes to hike down—or as much as 2.5 hours if you stop at the following listed sights in the Upper Rock Nature Reserve, which you'll see in order as you descend from the top of the Rock.

If you get a round-trip ticket, your best strategy is to take the cable car up, hike downhill to St. Michael's Cave and the Apes' Den, and then take the cable car down into town from the Apes' Den, skipping the other sights. Why hike at all, you ask? Because you'd miss St. Michael's Cave if you relied solely on the cable car.

The entire Upper Rock Nature Reserve is open daily from 9:30 to 19:00. Only the Apes' Den is free with your cable-car ticket. A pass for admission to the other sites is €12/£7 (better value if purchased with cable-car ticket—the same price includes the lift).

Approximate hiking times: From the top of cable-car lift to St. Michael's Cave, 15 min; from the Cave to Apes' Den, 10 min, from the Apes' to Siege Tunnels, 35 min; from the Tunnels to *City Under Siege* exhibit, 5 min; from exhibit to Moorish Castle, 5 min; and down to town, 10 min.

▲▲**O'Hara's Battery**—If the Battery is still closed for renovation in 2003, it's not worth the 20-minute hike from the top of the cable-car lift (confirm status at cable-car lift or local TI). At 430 meters (1,400 feet), this is the highest point on the Rock. A 28-ton, 9-inch gun sits on the summit where a Moorish lookout post once stood. It was built after World War I, and the last test was fired in 1974. Locals are glad it's been mothballed. During test firings, if locals didn't open their windows to allow air to move freely after the concussion, their windows would shatter. Fifty kilometers of tunnels, like the tiny bit you see here, honeycomb this strategic rock. During World War II an entire garrison could have survived six months with the provisions stored in this underground base (Mon–Sat 10:00–17:30, closed Sun; from top of cable-car lift, walk 10 min down and then 10 min up). The iron rings you might see are anchored pulleys used to haul up guns such as the huge one at O'Hara's Battery.

▲**St. Michael's Cave**—Studded with stalagmites and stalactites, eerily lit and echoing with classical music, this cave is dramatic, corny, and slippery when wet. Considered a one-star sight since Neolithic times, these caves were alluded to in ancient Greek legends—when the Rock was one of the Pillars of Hercules, marking the end of the world, and the caves were believed to be the Gates of Hades. In the last century they were prepared (but never used) as a World War II hospital and are now just another tourist site with an auditorium for musical events. Notice the polished cross-section of a stalagmite showing weirdly beautiful rings similar to a tree's. Spelunkers who'd enjoy a three-hour subterranean hike through the lower cave can make arrangements in advance at the TI (€8.25/£5 per person). To continue to the Apes' Den, refer to your map (free with lift ticket) and take the left fork.

Apes' Den—This small zoo without bars gives you a chance for a close encounter with some of the famous (and very jaded) apes of Gibraltar. Keep your distance from the apes and beware of their kleptomaniac tendencies. The man at the little booth posts a record of the names of all the apes. If there's no ape action, wait for a banana-toting taxi tour to stop by and stir some up. (The cable car stops here; you can catch the car down to town from here or continue on foot to see the following sights.)

▲**Siege Tunnels**—Also called the Upper Galleries, these chilly tunnels were blasted out of the rock by the Brits during the Spanish and French siege of 1779 to 1783. Hokey but fun dioramas help recapture a time when Brits were known more for conquests than for crumpets. The tunnels are at the northern end of the Rock, about 1.5 kilometers from the Apes' Den.

Gibraltar, A City Under Siege **Exhibition**—A spin-off of the Siege Tunnels, this excuse for a museum gives you a look at life during the siege. It's worth a stop only if you already have a combo-ticket (just downhill from Siege Tunnels).

Moorish Castle—Actually more tower than castle, this building offers a tiny museum of Moorish remnants and carpets. The original castle was built by the Moor Tarik-ibn-Zeyad in 711, but his name lasted longer than the castle: "Gibel-Tarik" (or Tarik's Hill) became "Gibraltar." The tower marks the end of the Upper Rock Nature Reserve. Head downhill to reach the lower town and Main Street.

Sights—Lower Gibraltar

Gibraltar Museum—Built atop a Moorish bath, this museum in Gibraltar's lower town tells the story of a rock that has been fought over for centuries. Highlights are the history film and the prehistoric remains discovered here.

On the ground floor, you can see the 15-minute film, a

"teaser" prehistoric skull display, and the empty rooms of the 14th-century Moorish baths. The first floor contains military memorabilia, a model of the Rock, paintings by local artists, and, in a cave-like room off the art gallery, a collection of prehistoric remains and artifacts. The famous skull of a Neanderthal woman found in Forbes' Quarry is a copy (original in British Museum in London). This first Neanderthal skull was found in Gibraltar in 1848, though no one realized its significance until a similar skull found years later in Germany's Neanderthal Valley was correctly identified—stealing the name, claim, and fame from Gibraltar (€3.40/£2, Mon–Fri 10:00–18:00, Sat 10:00–14:00, closed Sun, no photos, on Bomb House Lane off Main Street).

▲**Catalan Bay**—Gibraltar's tiny second town originated as a settlement of Italian shipwrights whose responsibility was keeping the royal ships in good shape. Today it's just a huddle of apartments around a cute little Catholic church and the best beach on the Rock (fully equipped). Catch bus #4 from opposite the Governor's Residence or the roundabout near the airport.

Dolphin-Watching Cruises—Numerous companies take you on two-hour cruises of the bay to look for dolphins (€24.50–33/£15–20). Nautilus runs boats with glass fronts and sides (€33/£20, 4/day, Admirals Walk 4, tel. 73400) and Dolphin World refunds your money if dolphins aren't sighted (€25/£16, 3/day, Admirals Walk, Marina Bay Pier, cellular 5448-1000).

Day Trip to Tangier, Morocco

Virtually any travel agency in Gibraltar offers day trips to Tangier (ask at the TI for their "Tangier Day Trips" list, stop by any travel agency in Gibraltar, or check with Thomas Cook Exchange Travel and Parodytur—both listed in "Tours of Gibraltar," above). Depending on the company, you'll pay about €57–74/£35–45 for the tour, which covers the ferry crossing, a tour of Tangier, lunch, a shopping stop at the market, and the return by ferry. Some tours leave from Gibraltar, others from Algeciras. But because Gibraltar is pricey compared to Spain, it makes sense to use your time here just to see the Rock, and day-trip to Morocco from a cheaper homebase such as Tarifa (a 30-min bus ride from the port of Algeciras).

Sleeping in Gibraltar

(€1 = about $1.50, tel. code: 9567 from Spain or 350 international, zip code: 29780)

Sleep Code: **S** = Single, **D** = Double/Twin, **T** = Triple, **Q** = Quad, **b** = bathroom, **s** = shower only, **CC** = Credit Cards accepted, **no CC** = Credit Cards not accepted. Exterior rooms (with views and traffic noise) often cost more than interior rooms (quiet, without a view).

To help you easily sort through these listings, I've divided the rooms into three categories, based on the price for a standard double room with bath during high season:

Higher Priced—Most rooms more than €100/£60.
Moderately Priced—Most rooms €100/£60 or less.
Lower Priced—Most rooms €50/£30 or less.

To call Gibraltar from Spain, dial 9567 plus the five-digit local number. To call from Europe, dial 00-350-local number. To call from America or Canada, dial 011-350-local number.

HIGHER PRICED

Eliott Hotel is four stars and then some—it has a roof-top pool with a view, bar, and terrace; fine sit-a-bit public spaces; and 114 modern, settle-in rooms (Db-€156–270/£95–165, breakfast-€13–20/£8–12, CC, air con, laundry service, elevator, nonsmoking floor, free parking, centrally located at Governor's Parade, tel. 70500, fax 70243, www.gib.gi/eliotthotel, e-mail: eliott@gibnet.gi).

Bristol Hotel offers drab, overpriced rooms in the heart of Gibraltar (Sb-€80–87/£49–53, Db-€105–113/£64–69, Tb-€121–133/£74–81, more for interior rooms, breakfast-€8.25/£5, CC, air con, elevator, swimming pool oddly located off breakfast room in the annex, free parking, Cathedral Square 10, tel. 76800, fax 77613, www.gib.gi/bristolhotel, e-mail: bristhtl@gibnet.gi).

MODERATELY PRICED

Queen's Hotel, near the cable-car lift, has 62 comfortable rooms in a noisy location (S-€40/£26, Sb-€66/£40, D-€56/£36, Db-€71–90/£46–55, Db with sea view-€108/£66, Tb-€98/£60, Qb-€119/£77, includes breakfast, 20 percent discount for students with ISIC—15 percent if paying with CC, free parking, elevator, at #3 bus stop, Boyd Street 1, tel. 74000, fax 40030, www.queenshotel.gi, e-mail: queenshotel@gibnynex.gi).

Continental Hotel isn't fancy but has a friendly feel. Its 18 high-ceilinged, air-conditioned rooms border an unusual ellipical atrium (Sb-€69/£42, Db-€90/£55, Tb-€115/£70, Qb-€139/£85, includes small breakfast, CC, elevator, in pedestrian area just off Main Street, a couple of blocks from Casemates TI, Engineer Lane, tel. 76900, fax 41702, e-mail: contiho@gibnet.gi). The hotel runs an inexpensive café downstairs.

LOWER PRICED

The cheapest place in town is **Emile Youth Hostel Gibraltar** (37 beds, D-€43/£27, dorm bed-€19.75/£12, includes breakfast, lockout 10:00–17:00, just outside Casemates Square entry on Montagu Bastion, tel. & fax 51106).

Eating in Gibraltar

Casemates Square, newly refurbished, makes a grand entrance to Gibraltar. This big square contains a variety of restaurants, ranging from fast food (fish-'n'-chips joint, Burger King, and Pizza Hut) to pubs spilling out into the square. Consider the **All's Well** pub, near the TI, with €8.25/£5 meals and pleasant, umbrellaed tables under leafy trees (daily 9:30–24:00, CC).

Queensway Quay Marina is the place to be when a misty sun sets over the colorful marina and rugged mountains of Spain. The string of restaurants that line the promenade have indoor and outdoor seating, offer seafood and other dishes, and are usually open daily for lunch and dinner. Next door to each other are two popular choices: **Raffles Restaurant** (daily, tel. 40362) and **Claus on the Rock Bistro** (Mon–Sat, closed Sun, colorful menu from around the world, good cigar and wine selection, tel. 48686). **Waterfront,** farther on, is less expensive, and the **Jolly Parrot** (just tapas and drinks) offers the cheapest seat on the promenade. Queensway Quay is at the cable-car end of town (walk through Ragged Staff Gate toward the water).

Main Street is dotted with sidewalk cafés perfect for people-watching. Tourists hang out at **Roy's** fish 'n' chips outside the Governor's House (a.k.a. the Convent) to watch the miniature Changing of the Guard ceremony around midday (exact time not announced for security reasons, shorter version every 30 min).

For good-value meals, consider **The Little Chef,** an adventure when the one English-speaking guy is off-duty. They have tasty, cheap €5.80/£3.50 meals but no menu. You just ask—in Spanish if necessary—what's cooking (daily 8:00–15:00, no dinner, Cornwalls Parade 7, a few blocks from Casemates Square). **The Clipper** has filling €8.25/£5 pub meals (on Irish Town, at intersection with tiny Irish Place). The **Carpenter's Arms** at the Methodist church does a cheap €5/£3 lunch special, open to anyone. Their tea and apple pie for €1.60/£1 is a local favorite, particularly at "elevens," as the British say, when hunger pangs strike before lunch (Mon–Fri 9:30–14:00, closed Sat–Sun, no smoking, Main Street 297).

Grocery: A Checkout supermarket is on Main Street, off Cathedral Square, next to Marks & Spencer (Mon–Sat 8:30–20:00, Sun 10:00–15:00, has a take-away window with roast chicken to go). Fruit stands bustle at the Market Place (Mon–Sat 9:00–15:00, closed Sun, outside entry to Casemates Square).

Transportation Connections—Gibraltar

If you're leaving Gibraltar without a car, you must walk five minutes from Gibraltar's border into Spain to reach La Línea, the nearest bus station. The region's main transportation hub is Algeciras, with lots of train and bus connections, and ferries to Tangier and Ceuta. (For Algeciras connections, see "Tarifa," below.) If you're traveling between La Línea and Algeciras, buy tickets on the bus. Otherwise buy tickets inside the station.

La Línea by bus to: Algeciras (2/hr, 45 min), **Tarifa** (8/day, 1 hr), **Málaga** (4/day, 3 hrs), **Granada** (2/day, 5 hrs), **Sevilla** (3/day, 4 hrs), **Jerez** (2/day, 3.15 hrs), **Huelva** (1/day, 6.15 hrs), **Madrid** (2/day, 8 hrs). Tel. 956-170-093 or 956-172-396.

TARIFA

Europe's most southerly town is a pleasant alternative to gritty, noisy Algeciras. It's an Arab-looking town with a lovely beach, an old castle, restaurants swimming in fresh seafood, inexpensive places to sleep, and enough windsurfers to sink a ship. If you're going to Morocco, Tarifa is a far quieter and more liveable homebase than Algeciras.

As I stood on Tarifa's town promenade under the castle, looking out at almost-touchable Morocco across the Strait of Gibraltar, I regretted only that I didn't have this book to steer me clear of Algeciras on earlier trips. Tarifa has no blockbuster sights (and is pretty dead off-season), but it's a town where you just feel good to be on vacation.

Orientation

Tourist Information: The TI is on Paseo Alameda (June–Sept daily 10:00–14:00 & 16:00–20:00, Oct–May Mon–Sat 11:00–13:00 & 17:00–19:00, tel. 956-680-993).

Arrival in Tarifa: The bus station (really just a ticket office) is at Batalla de Salado 19 (Mon–Sat 7:30–11:00 & 14:30–19:00, Sun 15:00–20:00, tel. 956-684-038). When you get off the bus, orient yourself by facing the old-town gate. The recommended hotels in the old town are through the gate; the hotels in the newer part of town are a couple of blocks behind you.

Internet Access: Try Pandora, in the heart of the old town, across from Café Central and near the church (15 computers, cheap prices, long hours).

Ferry to Morocco

Boats to Tangier, Morocco, sail from both Algeciras and Tarifa. Anyone can sail from Algeciras to Tangier, whether solo or with a tour. The boats leaving Tarifa for Tangier have been open only to people from countries that are members of the European Union, but this is expected to change to include Americans in 2003. Even if it doesn't, I'd still homebase in Tarifa for a trip to Tangier (taking the 30-min bus ride to Algeciras, then the boat to Tangier and back, returning by bus in the evening to Tarifa). Certainly it'd be more convenient to sail directly from Tarifa to Tangier. For the latest on whether non-Europeans can make this crossing, call the Tarifa TI (tel. 956-684-038) or the Marruecotur travel agency in Tarifa (tel. 956-681-821 or 956-681-242). Note that the Spanish refer to Tangier as Tanger, with a guttural "g" (said at the back of the throat, sounding like tahn-hair).

Tours: Marruecotur in Tarifa offers a day trip that takes you by bus from Tarifa to Algeciras, by fast ferry from Algeciras to Ceuta (a Spanish possession in Morocco), with three-hour (basically shopping) stops in both Tetuan and Tangier (€51, daily year-round, leave Tarifa at 8:00, return by 19:45, guide joins you in Algeciras, includes lunch at Tetuan; 2-day tour option available with overnight in Tangier for €110 for 1 person, €87 apiece for 2 people). Marruecotur's office is across the street from the Tarifa TI (daily 7:40–21:00, also books flights, trains, and some long-distance buses to destinations in Spain and Portugal, Avenida Constitución 5, tel. 956-681-821 or 956-681-242, fax 956-680-256, e-mail: mcotur1@e-savia.net). **Speedlines Tours,** across from the bus station, also books tours to Tangier (and books flights, trains, car and bike rentals, and so on, Batalla del Salado 10, tel. 956-627-048, www.speedlines-tours.com).

If and when non-Europeans are allowed to sail directly from Tarifa to Tangier, tours offered from Tarifa will concentrate on Tangier (without Tetuan), and **FRS Maroc** will be another travel agency for you to consider, either for tours or ferry tickets (tel. 956-681-830, at the Tarifa dock; currently they work only with people from the European Union).

Sights—Tarifa

Castle of Guzman El Bueno—This castle was named after a 13th-century Christian general who gained fame in a sad show of courage while fighting the Moors. Holding Guzman's son hostage, the Moors demanded he surrender the castle or they'd kill the boy. Guzman refused, even throwing his own knife down from the ramparts. It was used on his son's throat. Ultimately, the Moors withdrew to Africa, and Guzman was a hero. *Bueno.* The castle itself is a concrete hulk in a vacant lot, interesting only for the harbor views from the ramparts (€1.20, mid-June–Sept Tue–Sun 11:00–14:00 & 18:00–20:00, Oct–mid-June Tue–Sun 11:00–14:00 & 16:00–18:00, closed Mon).

Church of St. Matthew—Tarifa's main church faces its main drag. Most nights it seems life squirts from the church out the front door and into the fun-loving Calle El Bravo. Wander inside

Tarifa

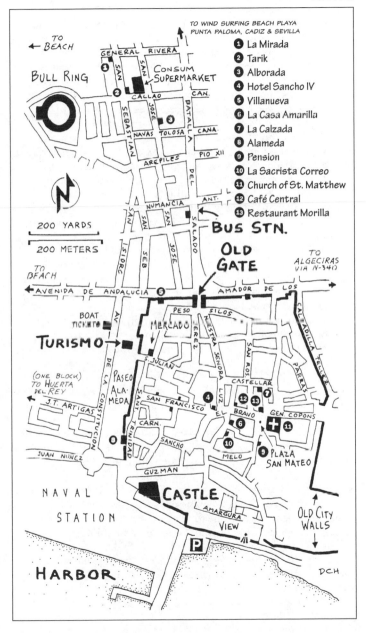

TO WIND SURFING BEACH PLAYA
PUNTA PALOMA, CADIZ & SEVILLA

1 La Mirada
2 Tarik
3 Alborada
4 Hotel Sancho IV
5 Villanueva
6 La Casa Amarilla
7 La Calzada
8 Alameda
9 Pension
10 La Sacrista Correo
11 Church of St. Matthew
12 Café Central
13 Restaurant Morilla

TO ← BEACH

BULL RING

CONSUM SUPERMARKET

GENERAL RIVERA
SAN
SAN
CALLAO
CAN.
SEBASTIAN
JOSE
BATALLA
NAVAS TOLOSA
CANA.
CANA
AREPILES
PIO XII
DEL
NUMANCIA
ANT.
SAN
SAN
SAN
SALADO

200 YARDS

200 METERS

TO BEACH

BUS STN.

OLD GATE

TO ALGECIRAS VIA N-340

AVENIDA DE ANDALUCIA 5 AMADOR DE LOS

BOAT TICKETS

TURISMO →

(ONE BLOCK) TO HUERTA DEL REY

J.T. ARTIGAS

PESO SILOS
MERCADO
NUESTRA SEÑORA
JEREZ
SAN ROS
CADILLA
PARRAS
FELIX

AV
DE LA CONSTITUCION

PASEO ALAMEDA

S. JULIAN

SAN FRANCISCO

CASTELLAR

LUZ

4 12 13 7

MANT TRINIDAD

CARN.

SANCHO

EL BRAVO
6

GEN COPONS

+ 11

8

10

MELO

9 PLAZA SAN MATEO

JUAN NUÑEZ

GUZMAN

NAVAL

STATION

CASTLE

AMARGURA

VIEW

P

OLD CITY WALLS

HARBOR

DCH

(daily 9:00–13:00 & 17:30–1:00, English leaflets—unless they're out—are inside on the right).

1. Find the tiny square (about the size of a piece of copier paper) of **ancient tombstone** in the wall just before the transept on the right side. Probably the most important historic item in town, it proves there was a functioning church here during Visigothic times, before the Moorish conquest. The tombstone reads, in a kind of Latin Spanish, "Flaviano lived as a Christian for 50 years, a little more or less. In death he received forgiveness as a servant of God on March 30, 674. May he rest in peace." If that gets you in the mood to light a candle, switch on an electric "candle" for a coin.

2. Step into the transept beyond the candles. The centerpiece of the **altar** is a boy Jesus. By Andalusian tradition he used to be naked, but these days he's clothed with outfits that vary with the Church calendar. On the left is a fine 17th-century statue of the "Virgin [protector] of the Fishermen."

3. A statue of **St. James the Moorslayer** (missing his sword) is on the right wall of the main central altar. Since the days of the Reconquista, James has been Spain's patron saint.

4. The chapel to the left of the main altar harbors several **statues** that go on parade through town during Holy Week. The **Captive Christ** (with hands bound) goes back to the days when Christians were held captive by Moors.

5. Circling around to the left side you'll find a side door, the **"door of pardons."** For a long time, Tarifa was a dangerous place—on the edge of the Reconquista. To encourage people to live here, the Church offered a huge amount of forgiveness to anyone who lived in Tarifa for a year. One year and one day after moving to Tarifa, they would have the privilege of passing through this special "door of pardons," and a Mass of thanksgiving would be held in that person's honor.

Bullfighting—Tarifa has a third-rate bullring where novices botch fights on occasional Saturdays through the summer. Professional bullfights takes place the first week of September. The ring is a short walk from the town. You'll see posters everywhere.

▲**Whale-Watching**—Daily whale- and dolphin-watching excursions are offered by several companies in Tarifa. For any of the tours, it's wise to reserve one to three days in advance, though same-day bookings are possible. You'll get a multilingual tour and a two-hour trip (usually no WC on board). Sightings occur over 90 percent of the time. Dophins and pilot whales frolic here any time of year, while sperm whales visit May through June and orcas stay July through August. Depending on the wind and weather, boats may leave from Algeciras instead (drivers follow in a convoy, people without cars usually get rides from staff).

The best company is the Swiss nonprofit **FIRMM** (Foundation for Information and Research on Marine Mammals), which gives a 15-minute educational talk prior to departure—and if you don't see any dolphins or whales, you can go on another trip for free (€27 per person, no CC, runs 1–5 trips/day April–Oct, Pedro Cortés 4, around the corner from Café Central—one door inland, also offers courses, details on their Web site, tel. 956-627-008, fax 956-681-424, cellular 619-459-441, www.firmm.org, e-mail: firmm98@aol.com, SE). Another company is **Whale Watch España,** across from the TI (€27 per person, CC, runs 1–4/day Jan–Oct, Avenida de la Constitución, tel. 956-682-247, cellular 639-476-544, www.whalewatchtarifa.com, e-mail: wwe27013 @teleline.es, SE). Yet another option is **Mar de Ballenas** (tel. 956-682-253).

▲**Windsurfing**—The vast, sandy beach **Playa Punta Paloma** lies about eight kilometers northwest of town. On windy summer days the sea is littered with sprinting windsurfers while the beach holds a couple hundred vans and fun-mobiles from northern Europe. Under mountain ridges lined with modern energy-generating windmills, it's a fascinating scene. Drive down the sandy road and stroll along the beach. You'll find a cabana-type hamlet with rental gear, beachwear shops, a bar, and a hip, healthy restaurant with great lunch salads.

For drivers, it's a cinch to reach. Without a car, you're in luck July through September, when Speedlines Tours runs a cheap bus that does a circuit of nearby campgrounds, all on the waterfront (€1.50, Mon–Fri every 90 min 8:00–24:00, Sat–Sun 8:00–3:00, the stop Punta Paloma is best; Speedlines Tours, across from the bus station, is at Batalla del Salado 10, tel. 956-627-048).

Sleeping in Tarifa
(€1 = about $1, country code: 34, zip code: 11380)
Sleep Code: **S** = Single, **D** = Double/Twin, **T** = Triple, **Q** = Quad, **b** = bathroom, **s** = shower only, **CC** = Credit Cards accepted, **no CC** = Credit Cards not accepted, **SE** = Speaks English, **NSE** = No English spoken.

To help you easily sort through these listings, I've divided the rooms into three categories, based on the price for a standard double room with bath during high season:

Higher Priced—Most rooms more than €100.
Moderately Priced—Most rooms €100 or less.
Lower Priced—Most rooms €50 or less.

Room rates vary with the season (3 seasonal tiers vary but are, roughly: high—mid-June–Sept; medium—spring and fall; and low—winter). Breakfast is usually extra.

Sleeping outside the City Wall

These hotels are right off the main drag—Batalla del Salado—with easy parking, in the modern, plain part of town. To get oriented if arriving by bus, face the old-town gate. These hotels are several blocks behind you.

MODERATELY PRICED

Hotel La Mirada has 25 modern rooms, some of which come with sea views at no extra cost (Sb-€30, €36, or €42; Db-€54, €60, or €66; extra bed-€9, breakfast-€3.60, extra for American-type breakfast, includes tax, CC, elevator, great views from large terrace, attached restaurant, Calle San Sebastián 41, tel. 956-684-427, fax 956-681-162, www.hotel-lamirada.com, Antonio and Salvador speak some English). It's two blocks off the main drag and about five blocks away from the old town.

The 22-room motel-style **Hostal Tarik** is a lesser value. Clean but noisy, it's a bit tattered, and short on windows on the ground floor; ask for a room upstairs (Db-€30, €42, or €54; Tb-€42, €60, or €78; tax extra, CC, Calle San Sebastián 34, tel. 956-680-648, Mario speaks some English). Surrounded by warehouses, it's one block toward the town center from Hotel La Mirada.

LOWER PRICED

Hostal Alborada is a squeaky-clean 25-room place with an attractive courtyard. It's a couple of blocks closer to the old town on a plain street (Sb-€23, €29, or €36; Db-€31, €38, or €49; Tb-€40, €53, or €65; get your price and then show this book for a 10 percent discount any time of year *except* high season—mid-June–Sept, tax extra, CC, laundry and Internet services, Calle San José 52, tel. 956-681-140, fax 956-681-935, www.hotelalborada.com, fun-loving Rafael Mesa Rodriguez and his wife Juaquina speak only a little English).

Sleeping on or inside the City Wall

HIGHER PRICED

La Sacristia, formerly a Moorish stable, offers 10 high-quality rooms, each decorated differently (Sb-€80–90, Db-€90–108, extra bed-€30, CC, nonsmoking rooms, fans, sauna, roof terrace with views, San Donato 8, tel. 956-681-759, www.lasacristia.net).

MODERATELY PRICED

Hostal La Calzada has eight airy, well-appointed rooms right in the noisy-at-night, old-town thick of things (Db-€42, €48, or €54; Tb-€48, €54, and €60; includes tax, closed Oct–March,

CC, Calle Justino Pertinez 3, veer left and down from the old-town gate, tel. 956-680-366 or 956-681-492, NSE).

Hostal Alameda glistens with pristine marble floors and pastels. It overlooks a square where the local children play. Its 11 bright rooms, five with a view, are above its restaurant, which serves great gazpacho (Db-€39, €45, or €60; Tb-€43, €57, or €75; breakfast-€2.70, includes tax, CC, Paseo Alameda 4, tel. & fax 956-684-029, some English spoken).

La Casa Amarilla (the Yellow House) offers 11 posh apartments with modern decor and miniature kitchens (Db-€40–55, Tb-€52–73, Qb-€64–91, tax extra, 20 percent deposit requested, CC, across street from Café Central, Calle Sancho IV El Bravo 9, entrance on alley, tel. 956-684-029, fax 956-680-590, www.lacasaamarilla.net, e-mail: lacasaamarilla@lacasaamarilla.net).

Hotel Sancho IV has 12 comfortable, newly remodeled, spacious rooms. The top-floor suite is grand, with private elevator access, a Jacuzzi, great views, and a big terrace—worth the splurge. Friendly and casual management (Sb-€34, €42, or €67, Db-€52, €70, or €88, top-floor Db suite-€99, €133, or €175, tax extra, breakfast after 9:00, CC, double-paned windows, elevator, restaurant on ground floor, a block from Café Central, Sancho IV Bravo 18, tel. 956-627-083, fax 956-62-7-055, e-mail: hotelsancho4@terra.com).

LOWER PRICED

Hostal Villanueva is your best budget bet. It's simple, clean, and friendly, newly remodeled with double-paned windows, and includes a great terrace overlooking the old town. It's on a busy street, and the quiet rooms in the back come with the best views (12 rooms, Sb-€15–18, Db-€33–51, includes tax, breakfast-€1.80, CC for 2-night min, attached restaurant, Avenida de Andalucía 11, just west of the old-town gate, with access outside the wall, tel. & fax 956-684-149, Pepe SE).

Pension Correo rents eight simple rooms at a good value (Db-€30–40, extra bed-€15-17, no CC, reservations accepted only within 24 hours of arrival, roof garden, Coronel Moscardo 8, tel. 956-680-206, Maria José and Lucca SE).

Eating in Tarifa

You'll find good tapas throughout the old town. **Café Central** is the happening place nearly any time of day. The tapas are priced at €1.20; go to the bar and point. They also offer great, ingenious €5 salads (study the menu) and impressively therapeutic, healthy fruit drinks (late hours daily, off Plaza San Mateo, near church, tel. 956-680-560). Across the street, the popular **El Barrilito** makes interesting sandwiches (€1.80–2.40) with a tapas option and indoor/outdoor seating. Next door, the tiny **La Calzada Panaderia** makes sandwiches-to-go and also has a few outdoor tables. A few doors down, in front of the church, **Restaurant Morilla** serves good local-style food and paella on the town's prime piece of people-watching real estate (long hours, every day, Calle Sancho IV El Bravo, tel. 956-681-757).

From Café Central follow the cars 100 meters to the first corner on the left to reach the simple, untouristy **Bar El Frances** for its fine tapas (generally €0.80), especially snails (*caracoles,* June–mid-July only), pork on tomato sauce *(carne con tomate)*, and pork with spice *(chicharrones).* Show this book and be treated to a glass of local white wine *(vino de chiclana)* with your tapa (bar has no sign, it's at #21A).

The nearby **Café Bar los Melli** is family-friendly and serves a good chorizo sandwich and *patatas bravas*—potatoes with a hot tomato sauce served on a wooden board (from Bar El Frances, cross parking lot and take Calle del Legionario Rios Moya up 1 block). **Bar El Pasillo,** next to Melli, has tapas.

From Melli you can circle around toward the church past some very gritty and colorful tapas bars. Just to the seaside of the church you'll see the mysterious **Casino Tarifeño.** This is an old-boys' social club "for members only," but it offers a big, musty Andalusian welcome to visiting tourists, including women. Wander through. There's a low-key bar with tapas, a TV room, a card room, and a lounge.

From the town center, walk the narrow Calle San Francisco to survey a number of good restaurants, such as the classy, quiet **Guzman El Bueno** (indoor seating and outdoor seating in a court-yard, CC), the cheap and popular **Pizzeria La Capricciosa** (indoor seating only, also does take-out), and the only place offering out-door seating on the street, **El Rincon de Juan** (sample the local fish—*hurta* and *voraz*, CC).

The street Huerta del Rey is a family scene at night. Stop by the produce shop for fruit and veggies, the *heladeria* for ice cream, or **El Tuti** for a drink (outside the old city walls, 2 blocks west; a clothing market is held here Tue 9:00–14:00).

Confiteria la Tarifeña serves super pastries and flan (at the top of Calle Nuestra Señora de la Luz, near the main old-town gate).

With a car, head to the bars on Camping de La Pena to check out Tarifa's popular windsurfing scene—give **Chozo** or **Spin Out** a try.

Picnics: Stop by the *mercado municipal* (Mon–Sat 8:00–14:00, closed Sun, in old town, inside gate nearest TI), any grocery, or the **Consum supermarket** (Mon–Sat 9:00–21:00, closed Sun, simple cafeteria, at Callao and San José, near the hotels in the new town).

Transportation Connections—Tarifa

By bus to: La Línea/Gibraltar (7/day, 1 hr, first departure at 9:40, last return at 20:00), **Algeciras** (12/day, 30 min, first departure from Tarifa weekdays at 6:30, on Sat 8:00, on Sun 10:00; return from Algeciras as late as 21:00), **Jerez** (3/day, 2 hrs), **Sevilla** (4/day, 3 hrs), **Huelva** (1/day, 5 hrs), and **Málaga** (2/day, 3.5 hrs). Bus info: tel. 956-684-038.

Transportation Connections—Algeciras

Algeciras is only worth leaving. It's useful to the traveler mainly as a transportation hub, offering ferries to Tangier (see that chapter) and trains and buses to destinations in southern and central Spain. The **TI** is on Juan de la Cierva, a block inland from the port, and on the same street as the train station and the Comes bus station which runs buses to Tarifa (Mon–Fri 9:00–14:00, tel. 956-572-636).

Trains: The train station is four blocks inland on the far side of Hotel Octavio (up Juan de la Cierva, lockers on platform for €3—buy token at ticket window, tel. 956-630-202). If arriving by train, head down Juan de la Cierva toward the sea for the TI and port.

By train to: Madrid (2/day, 6 hrs during day, 11 hrs overnight), **Ronda** (4/day, 2 hrs), **Granada** (3/day, 4.5 hrs), **Sevilla** (3/day, 5 hrs, transfer in Bobadilla), **Córdoba** (4/day, 4.5–5 hrs; 2 direct, 2 with transfers in Bobadilla), **Málaga** (3/day, 4 hrs, transfer in Bobadilla). With the exception of the route to Madrid, these are particularly scenic trips; the best is the mountainous journey to Málaga via Bobadilla.

Buses: Algeciras has three bus stations.

The **Comes bus station** (half block away from train station, next to Hotel Octavio, tel. 956-653-456) runs buses to **La Línea** (2/hr, 45 min, from 7:00–21:30), **Tarifa** (11/day, 7/day on Sun), **Sevilla** (5/day, 3.5 hrs), **Jerez** (3/day, 2.5 hrs), **Huelva** (1/day, 6 hrs), and **Madrid** (4/day, 8 hrs).

The **Portillo bus station** (on waterfront, kitty-corner from the port, Calle Virgen Carmen 15, next door to Restaurant Portillo, tel. 956-654-304) offers frequent, direct buses to **Málaga** (7/day, 2 hrs) and **Granada** (4/day, 4 hrs).

The **Linesur bus station** (also on waterfront, 1 long block past Portillo station, Calle Virgen Carmen 31, tel. 956-667-649) offers the most frequent direct buses to **Sevilla** (8/day, 3.25 hrs) and **Jerez** (8/day, 1.25 hrs).

Route Tips for Drivers

Tarifa to Gibraltar (45 min): It's a short drive, passing a silvery-white forest of windmills, from peaceful Tarifa past Algeciras to La Línea (the Spanish town bordering Gibraltar). Passing Algeciras, continue in the direction of Estepona. At San Roque take the La Línea–Gibraltar exit.

Gibraltar to Nerja (210 km): Barring traffic problems, the trip along the Costa del Sol is smooth and easy by car—much of it on new highways. Just follow the coastal highway east. After Málaga follow signs to Almería and Motril.

Nerja to Granada (130 km, 90 min, 100 views): Drive along the coast to Salobrena, catching N323 north for about 65 kilometers to Granada. While scenic side trips may beckon, don't arrive late in Granada without a firm reservation.

MOROCCO

- About 447,000 square kilometers, or 172,000 square miles (a little bigger than the state of California)
- 31 million people (70 people per square kilometer)
- 10.5 dirhams = about $1

Morocco is culture shock—both bad and good. It makes Spain and Portugal look meek and mild. You'll encounter oppressive friendliness, brutal heat, the Arabic language, the Islamic faith, ancient cities, and aggressive beggars.

Most of the English-speaking Moroccans that the tourist meets are hustlers. Most visitors have some intestinal problems. Most women are harassed on the streets by horny but generally harmless men. Things don't work smoothly. In fact, compared to Morocco, Spain resembles Sweden for efficiency.

While Morocco is clearly a place apart from Mediterranean Europe, it doesn't really seem like Africa either. It's a mix, reflecting its strategic position between the two continents. Situated on the Strait of Gibraltar, Morocco has been flooded by waves of invasions over the centuries. The Berbers, the native population,

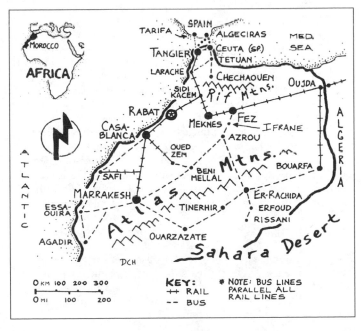

have had to contend with the Phoenicians, Carthaginians, Romans, Vandals, and more.

The Arabs brought Islam to Morocco in the seventh century A.D. and stuck around, battling the Berbers in various civil wars. A series of Berber and Arab dynasties rose and fell; the Berbers won out and still run the country today.

From the 15th century on, European countries carved up much of Africa. By the early 20th century, most of Morocco was under French control. In 1956, France granted Morocco independence

Morocco—a young country with an old history—is a photographer's delight and a budget traveler's dream. It's cheap, exotic, and comes with plenty of hotels and decent transportation. Along with a rich culture, Morocco offers plenty of contrast—from beach resorts to bustling desert markets, from jagged mountains to sleepy mud-brick oasis towns.

When you cruise south across the Strait of Gibraltar, leave your busy itineraries and split-second timing behind. Morocco must be taken on its own terms. In Morocco things go smoothly only *"Inshallah"*—if God so wills.

Helpful Hints

Friday: Friday is the Muslim day of rest, when most of the country (except Tangier) closes down.

Money: Change money only at banks, or even easier, at ATMs (available at most major banks), all of which have uniform rates. The black market is dangerous. Change only what you need and keep the bank receipt to reconvert if necessary. Don't leave the country with Moroccan money. (If you do, the Bank of Morocco branch in Algeciras may buy it back from you.)

Health: Morocco is much more hazardous to your health than Spain or Portugal. Eat in clean—not cheap—places. Peel fruit, eat only cooked vegetables, and drink reliably bottled water (Sidi Harazem or Sidi Ali). When you do get diarrhea—and you should plan on it—adjust your diet (small and bland meals, no milk or grease) or fast for a day but make sure you replenish lost fluids. Relax; most diarrhea is not serious, just an adjustment that will run its course.

Information: For an extended trip, bring travel information from home or Spain. The guides published by Lonely Planet, Rough Guide, and Let's Go (*Let's Go: Spain and Portugal* includes Morocco) are good. The green *Michelin Morocco* guidebook is worthwhile (if you read French). Buy the best map you can find locally—names are always changing, and it's helpful to have towns, roads, and place-names written in Arabic.

Language: The Arabic squiggle-script, its many difficult sounds, and the fact that French is Morocco's second language make communication tricky for English-speaking travelers. A little French goes a long way, but learn a few words in Arabic. Have your first local friend help you pronounce *min fadlik* ("please"; pron. meen FAD-leek), *shókran*

Arabic Numerals

0	•	Sifr
1	١	Waahid
2	٢	Itneen
3	٣	Talaata
4	٤	Arba'a
5	٥	Khamsa
6	٦	Sitta
7	٧	Sab'a
8	٨	Tamanya
9	٩	Tis'a
10	١٠	'Ashra

("thank you"; SHOW-kron), *ismahli* ("excuse me"; ees-MAY-lee), *yeh* ("yes"; EE-yuh), *lah* ("no"; lah), and *maa salama* ("good-bye"; mah sah-LEM-ah). In markets, I sing "la la la la la" to my opponents. *Lah shókran* means, "No, thank you." Listen carefully and write new words phonetically. Bring an Arabic phrase book. Make a point of learning the local number symbols; they are not like ours (which we call "Arabic").

Keeping your bearings: Navigate the labyrinthine medinas (old towns) by altitude, gates, and famous mosques or buildings. Write down what gate you came in so you can enjoy being lost—temporarily. *Souk* is Arabic for a particular market (such as leather, yarn, or metalwork).

Hustlers: While Moroccans are some of Africa's wealthiest people, you are still incredibly rich to them. This imbalance causes predictable problems. Wear your money belt. Assume con artists are more clever than you. Haggle when appropriate (prices skyrocket for tourists). You'll attract hustlers like flies at every famous tourist sight. They'll lie to you, get you lost, blackmail you, and pester the heck out of you. Never leave your car or baggage where you can't get back to it without your "guide." Anything you buy in their company gets them a 20 percent commission. Normally locals, shopkeepers, and police will come to your rescue when the hustlers' heat becomes unbearable. I usually hire a guide, since it's helpful to have a translator, and once you're "taken," the rest seem to leave you alone.

Marijuana: In Morocco marijuana *(kif)* is as illegal as it is popular, as many Westerners in local jails would love to remind you. Some dealers who sell it cheap make their profit after you get arrested. Cars and buses are stopped and checked by police routinely throughout Morocco—especially in the north and in the Chefchaouen region, which is Morocco's *kif* capital.

   Getting around Morocco: Moroccan trains are quite good. Second class is cheap and comfortable. Buses connect all smaller towns quite well. By car, Morocco is easy, but drive defensively and never rely on the oncoming driver's skill. Night driving is dangerous. Pay a guard to watch your car overnight.

TANGIER

Go to Africa. As you step off the boat you realize that the cross-ing (1–2.5 hrs, depending on the port you choose) has taken you farther culturally than did the trip from the United States to Iberia. Morocco needs no museums; its sights are living in the streets. Offered daily and year-round, the one-day excursions from Algeciras and Gibraltar (and Tarifa, once this port is opened to non-Europeans) are well-organized and reliable. Given that tours from Spain (rather than pricier Gibraltar) are virtually the cost of the boat passage alone, the tour package is a good value for those who can spare only a day for Morocco. For an extended tour of Morocco, see below.

Morocco in a Day?

There are many ways to experience Morocco, and a day in Tangier is probably the worst. But all you need is a passport (no visa or shots required), and if all you have is a day, this is a real and worthwhile adventure. Tangier is the Tijuana of Morocco, and everyone there seems to be expecting you.

You can use ATMs in Tangier to get Moroccan dirhams, but for a short one-day trip, there's no need to change money. Everyone you meet will be happy to take your euros, dollars, or pounds.

Whether on a tour or on your own, carefully confirm the time your return boat departs from Tangier. The time difference between the countries can be up to two hours. (I'd keep my watch on Spanish time and get my departure time clear in Spanish time.) Plan on spending one hour of your day in lines (passport control and so forth).

On Your Own: Just buy a ferry ticket at the port or from a local travel agency. Both Algeciras and Gibraltar have fine ferry terminals (for a look at Gibraltar's, see www.gibraltar.gi). When the Tarifa port opens up to non-Europeans—expected in 2003— crossing there will be the best option for most (more pleasant than Algeciras, cheaper than Gibraltar).

If you plan to sail from Algeciras, buy your ticket at the port instead of one of the many divey-looking travel agencies littering the town. To find the right office at the Algeciras port, go to the very farthest building, which is labeled in large letters: Estación Maritima Terminal de Pasajeros (lockers available here and at train station; easy parking at port). Inside this main port building, directly behind the helpful little info kiosk (daily 6:45–21:45, tel. 956-585-463, SE), are the official offices of the seven boat companies. Buy your ticket here. There are 8–18 crossings daily to Tangier.

By Tour: You rarely need to book a tour more than a day in advance, even during peak season. Tours generally cost about €50 from Spain or €60–75 from Gibraltar. This includes a round-trip crossing and a guide who meets you at a prearranged point and hustles you through the hustlers and onto your bus. Excursions vary, but usually offer a city tour, possibly a trip to the desolate Atlantic Coast for some rugged African scenery and the famous ride-a-camel stop, a walk through the medina (old town) with a too-thorough look at a sales-starved carpet shop, and lunch in a palatial Moroccan setting with live music.

Sound cheesy? It is. But no amount of packaging can gloss over how exotic and different this culture really is. This kind of cultural voyeurism is almost embarrassing, but it's nonstop action and more memorable than another day in Spain. The shopping is—Moroccan. Bargain hard!

The day trip is so tightly organized you'll have hardly any time alone in Tangier. For many people, that's just fine. Some, however, spend a night there and return the next day. If you're interested, ask travel agencies about the two-day tour (sample cost: one-day tour—€52, two-day tour including single room at hotel—€110, double room—€88 apiece). The first day of a two-day tour is the same as the one-day tour; you just go to a fancy hotel (with dinner) rather than to the afternoon boat and catch the same boat 24 unstructured hours later.

Tour tips: If you get a voucher when you pay for your tour at a travel agency, exchange it at the boat office to get your ticket prior to boarding. Confirm where you will meet the guide. You may need to relinquish your passport for the day; you will get it back. Note that there are variations on the tour; for instance, Marruecotur in Tarifa offers a tour that includes a crossing from Ceuta and a stop in Tetuan (for details, see "Tarifa" in Costa del Sol chapter).

Travel Agencies Offering Tours

There are dozens, particularly in Algeciras. Here are several.

In Algeciras: Marruecotur is at the port (€48 for one-day tour, Estación Maritima C-6, tel. 956-656-185, fax 956-653-132, e-mail: mcotur@e-savia.net).

In Tarifa: Marruecotur is across from the TI (€48, daily in summer 7:40–21:00, Avenida Constitución 5, tel. 956-681-821 or 956-681-242, fax 956-680-256, e-mail: mcotur1@e-savia.net). Another is **Speedlines Tours,** across from Tarifa's bus station (Batalla del Salado 10, tel. 956-627-048, www.speedlines-tours.com).

In Gibraltar: Consider Thomas Cook Exchange Travel (€57/£36 for one-day tour, 241 Main Street, tel. 76151) and Parodytur (€74/£47, Cathedral Square, tel. 76070). Agencies are open Monday through Friday from 9:30 to 18:00 (closed Sat–Sun).

Ferries to Morocco

Ferries have mediocre cafeteria bars, plenty of WCs, stuffy indoor chairs, and grand views. Boats are most crowded in August, when the Costa del Sol groups come en masse. Only a few crossings a year are canceled because of storms, mostly in winter.

The following information is for people going to Tangier on their own. If you're taking a tour, skip this.

From Algeciras to: Tangier (12/day in summer, 8/day in winter, 2.5 hrs by slow boat—no faster option at this time, €22.50 one-way, €46 round-trip; to bring a car: €70 one-way, €140 round-trip), **Ceuta** (hrly in summer, 7 ferries/day in winter, 35 min by Fast Ferry, €20.50 one-way, €37 round-trip; to bring a car: €60 one-way, €108 round-trip). Ceuta, an uninteresting Spanish possession in North Africa, is the best car-entry point (for info on the crossing, see "Extended Tour of Morocco," below) but is not for those relying on public transport.

From Tarifa to Tangier: 1/day, 1 hr (currently this crossing is open only to residents of the European Union, but may open to others in 2003).

From Gibraltar to Tangier: 2/day, 1 hr (€30 one-way, €50 round-trip, the morning boat returns from Tangier later the same day; the afternoon sailing forces an overnight in Tangier, returning the next day).

TANGIER

Tangier is split into two. The new town has the TI and fancy hotels. The medina (old town) has the markets, the Kasbah (with its palace), cheap hotels, decrepit homes, and 2,000 wanna-be guides. The twisty, hilly streets of the old town are caged within a wall accessible by keyhole gates. The big square, Grand Socco, is the link between the old and new parts of town.

Orientation (area code: 39)

Many assume they'll be lost in Tangier—because it's in Africa. This makes no sense. The town is laid out very simply. From the boat dock you'll see the old town—circled by its medieval wall—on the right (behind Hotel Continental). The new town sprawls past the industrial port zone to the left. Nothing listed under "Sights" (below) is more than a 15-minute walk from the port. Petit Taxis are a godsend for the hot and tired tourist. Use them generously and go ahead and just pay double the meter for any ride.

Tourist Information: Get a free map and advice at the TI (Mon–Sat 8:30–12:00 & 14:30–18:30, Boulevard Pasteur 29, in newer section of town, tel. 94-80-50, fax 94-86-61).

Exchange rate: 10.5 dirhams = about $1.

Telephone: To call Tangier from Spain, dial 00 (international access code), 212 (Morocco's country code), 39 (Tangier's city code), then the local six-digit number.

Arrival in Tangier

If you're taking a tour, follow the leader.

Independent travelers will take a five-minute walk from the boat, through customs, and out of the port. Consider hiring a guide (see "Guides," below). Taxis at the port are more expensive. Ask the cost before taking one. The big yellow Port de Tanger gateway defines the end of the port area and the start of the city. Leave mental bread crumbs so you can find your way back to your boat. It will just stay put all day. Just outside the port gate on the busy traffic circle you'll find plenty of fair, metered Petit Taxis along with a line of decent fish restaurants, the boulevard arcing along the beach into the new town, and stairs leading up into the old town and the market (on the right).

Planning Your Time

Catch a Petit Taxi to the TI. From there you can walk to the Grand Socco and market. Or, to minimize uphill walking, catch a taxi to the Place de la Kasbah at the top of the old town and work your way downhill to the port.

In the old town, start at the Museum of the Kasbah, then wander through the fortress (Dar el-Makhzem) and the Old American Legation Museum. Then shop through the Petit Socco. Walk out of the old town into the noisy Grand Socco. From there, catch a taxi to the beach (Place el Cano) and sightsee along the beach and then along Avenue d'Espagne back to the port.

Guides

If you're on your own, you'll be fighting off "guides" all day. In order to have your own translator and a shield from less scrupulous touts that hit up tourists constantly throughout the old town, I recommend hiring a guide. Stress your interest in the people and culture rather than shopping. Guides, hoping to get a huge commission from your purchases, can cleverly turn your Tangier day into a Marco Polo equivalent of the Shopping Channel.

I've had good luck with the private guides who meet the boat. These hardworking, English-speaking, and licensed guides offer their services for the day for €18. Aziz Begdouri is great ($12 or €18 for 5 hrs, easier to reach him from Spain on his Spanish cellular, tel. 607-897-967, than his Moroccan cellular, tel. 00-212-6163-9332, e-mail: aziztour@hotmail.com). The TI also has official guides (half-day for $12, or 120 dirhams, tel. 94-80-50, or call guides' association directly at tel. 93-13-72).

If you don't want a guide, ask directions of people who can't leave what they're doing (such as the only clerk in a shop) or of women who aren't near men. Ask "Kasbah?" or wherever you want to go, and you'll get pointed in the right direction. Fewer hustlers are in the new (but less interesting) part of town.

Sights—Tangier

Kasbah—This is the fortress atop old Tangier. You'll find a history museum in a former palace on Place de la Kasbah (10 dirhams, Wed–Mon 9:00–12:30 & 15:00–17:00, closed Tue, tel. 93-20-97) and a colorful gauntlet of Kodak moments waiting to ambush tour groups as they wander through: snake charmers, squawky dance troupes, and colorful water vendors. Before descending out of the Kasbah, don't miss the ocean viewpoint, the Mosque de la Kasbah, and Dar el-Makhzen, the fortress of the pasha of Tangier.

The Medina and Petit Socco—From the Kasbah, a maze of winding lanes and tiny alleys weave through the old-town market area. Petit Socco, a little square in the old town, is lined with tea shops. A casual first-time visitor cannot stay oriented. I just wander, knowing that if I keep going downhill, I'll eventually pop out at the port; if I veer to the right while going downhill, I'll come to a gate leading into the modern town probably via the Grand Socco, the big and noisy market square. The market is filthy and reportedly dangerous after dark. Plain-clothed tourist police are stationed throughout, making sure you're safe as you wander.

Tangier American Legation Museum—Morocco was the first country to recognize the United States as an independent country. This building, given to the United States by the sultan of Morocco, became the American government's first foreign possession.

Tangier

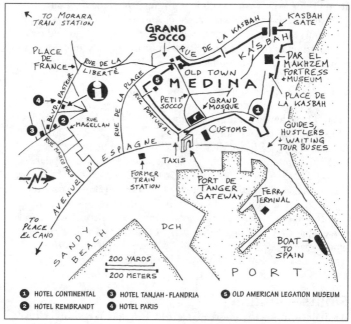

● HOTEL CONTINENTAL   ● HOTEL TANJAH-FLANDRIA   ● OLD AMERICAN LEGATION MUSEUM
● HOTEL REMBRANDT   ● HOTEL PARIS

It served as our embassy or consulate from 1821 to 1956, is still owned by the United States, and is the only U.S. national historic landmark overseas. Today this 19th-century mansion is a strangely peaceful oasis within Tangier's intense old town. It offers a warm welcome, lots of interesting paintings, and a reminder of how long the United States and Morocco have had good relations (free, donations appreciated, Mon–Fri 10:00–13:00 & 15:00–17:00, during Ramadan 10:00–15:00, closed Sat–Sun, Rue America 8, tel. 93-53-17).

Grand Socco—This big square is a transportation hub. From here, a gate leads into the old-town market; Rue de la Kasbah leads uphill along the old wall to Port de la Kasbah (a gate leading into the Kasbah); Rue de la Liberté leads to Place de France and Boulevard Pasteur (TI and recommended hotels); and Rue de la Plage leads to the train station, the port, and the beach.

Tangier Beach—This fine, white-sand crescent beach stretching eastward from the port, is lined by fun eateries and packed with locals doing what people around the world do at the beach—with a few variations. You'll see lazy camels and people, young and old, covered in hot sand to combat rheumatism.

Sleeping in Tangier
**(10.5 dirhams = about $1,
country code: 212, area code: 39)**
Sleep Code: **S** = Single, **D** = Double/Twin, **T** = Triple, **Q** = Quad,
b = bathroom, **s** = shower only, **CC** = Credit Cards accepted,
no CC = Credit Cards not accepted, **SE** = Speaks English,
NSE = No English.

To help you easily sort through these listings, I've divided
the rooms into three categories, based on the price for a standard
double room with bath (during high season):

Higher Priced—Most rooms more than 400 dirhams.
Moderately Priced—Most rooms 400 dirhams or less.
Lower Priced—Most rooms 300 dirhams or less.

These hotels are centrally located, near the TI and
American Express (Boulevard Pasteur 54), and within walking
distance of the market. The first two are four-star hotels.
To reserve from Europe, dial 00 (Europe's international
access code), 212 (Morocco's country code), 39 (Tangier's
city code), then the local number. July through mid-September
is high season, when rooms may be a bit more expensive
and a reservation is wise.

HIGHER PRICED
Hotel Rembrandt, with a restaurant, bar, and swimming
pool surrounded by a great grassy garden, has 75 clean, comfortable rooms, some with views (Sb-387 dirhams, Db-474
dirhams, breakfast-52 dirhams, CC, air-con, elevator, Boulevard Pasteur, tel. 93-78-70 or 33-33-14, fax 93-04-43, SE).

Hotel Tanjah-Flandria, across the street, is more formal,
stuffy, and comfortable but a lesser value (151 rooms, Sb-425
dirhams, Db-530 dirhams, breakfast-65 dirhams, CC, air-con,
elevator, restaurant, rooftop terrace, small pool, Boulevard
Pasteur, tel. 93-32-79, fax 93-43-47, SE).

MODERATELY PRICED
Hotel Continental, the Humphrey Bogart option, is a
grand old place sprawling along the old town. It overlooks
the port, with lavish, evocative public spaces, a chandeliered
breakfast room, and 70 spacious bedrooms with rough hardwood floors. Jimmy, who runs the place with a Moroccan
flair, says he offers everything but Viagra. When I said,
"I'm from Seattle," he said, "206." Test him. He knows
your area code (Db-360 dirhams, includes tax and breakfast, Dar Baroud 36, tel. 93-10-24, fax 93-11-43, e-mail:
hcontinental@iam.net.ma, SE).

LOWER PRICED
Hotel Paris, across from the TI, is noisy, dingy, and friendly. Ask for a room in the back—and a mop. (28 rooms, Sb-210 dirhams, Db-250–310 dirhams, price varies according to size, no CC, Boulevard Pasteur 42, tel. 93-18-77; the helpful and informative manager, Abdullatif, SE.)

Extended Tour of Morocco

Morocco gets much better as you go deeper into the interior. The country is incredibly rich in cultural thrills—but you'll pay a price in hassles and headaches. It's a package deal, and if adventure's your business, it's a great option.

To get a fair look at Morocco, you must get past the hustlers and con artists of the north coast (Tangier, Tétouan). It takes a minimum of four or five days to make a worthwhile visit—ideally seven or eight. Plan at least two nights in either Fès or Marrakech. A trip over the Atlas Mountains gives you an exciting look at Saharan Morocco. If you need a vacation from your vacation, check into one of the idyllic Atlantic beach resorts on the south coast. Above all, get past the northern day-trip-from-Spain, take-a-snapshot-on-a-camel fringe. Oops, that's us. Oh, well.

If you're relying on public transportation for your extended tour, sail to Tangier, blast your way through customs, listen to no hustler who tells you there's no way out until tomorrow, and hop into a Petit Taxi for the Morora train station four kilometers away (24 dirhams, or $2.30). From there, set your sights on Rabat, a dignified, European-type town with fewer hustlers, and make it your get-acquainted stop in Morocco. Trains go farther south from Rabat.

If you're driving a car, sail from Algeciras to Ceuta, a Spanish possession. Crossing the border is a bit unnerving, since you'll be jumped through several bureaucratic hoops. You'll go through customs at both borders, buy Moroccan insurance for your car (cheap and easy), and feel at the mercy of a bristly bunch of shady-looking people you'd rather not be at the mercy of. Don't pay anyone on the Spanish side. Consider tipping a guy on the Morrocan side if you feel he'll shepherd you through. Relax and let him grease those customs wheels. He's worth it. As soon as possible, hit the road and drive to Chefchaouen, the best first stop for those with their own wheels.

Sights—Moroccan Towns

▲▲**Chefchaouen**—Just two hours by bus or car from Tétouan, this is the first pleasant town beyond the Tijuana-type north coast. Monday and Thursday are colorful market days. Stay in the classy old Hotel Chaouen on Plaza el-Makhzen. This former

Spanish parador faces the old town and offers fine meals and a refuge from hustlers. Wander deep into the whitewashed old town from here.

▲▲**Rabat**—Morocco's capital and most European city, Rabat is the most comfortable and least stressful place to start your North African trip. You'll find a colorful market (in the old neighboring town of Salé), bits of Islamic architecture (Mausoleum of Mohammed V), the king's palace, mellow hustlers, and fine hotels.

▲▲▲**Fès**—More than just a funny hat that tipsy Shriners wear, Fès is Morocco's religious and artistic center, bustling with crafts-men, pilgrims, shoppers, and shops. Like most large Moroccan cities, it has a distinct new town from the French colonial period and an exotic—and stressful—old Arabic town, where you'll find the market. The Fès marketplace is Morocco's best.

▲▲▲**Marrakech**—Morocco's gateway to the south, this market city is a constant folk festival bustling with djellaba-clad Berber tribespeople and a colorful center where the desert, mountain, and coastal regions merge. The new city has the train station, and the main boulevard (Mohammed V) is lined with banks, airline offices, a post office, a tourist office, and comfortable hotels. The old city features the mazelike market and the huge Djemaa el-Fna, a square seething with people—a 43-ring Moroccan circus.

▲▲▲**Over the Atlas Mountains**—Extend your Moroccan trip several days by heading south over the Atlas Mountains. Take a bus from Marrakech to Ouarzazate (short stop) and then to Tinerhir (great oasis town, comfy hotel, overnight stop). The next day go to Er Rachidia and take the overnight bus to Fès.

By car, drive from Fès south, staying in the small mountain town of Ifrane, and then continue deep into the desert country past Er Rachidia and on to Rissani (market days: Sun, Tue, and Thu). Explore nearby mud-brick towns still living in the Middle Ages. Hire a guide to drive you past where the road stops and head cross-country to an oasis village (Merzouga) where you can climb a sand dune and watch the sun rise over the vastness of Africa. Only a sea of sand separates you from Timbuktu.

Transportation Connections—Morocco

In Tangier, all train traffic comes and goes from the suburban Morora train station, four kilometers from the city center and a short Petit Taxi ride away (24 dirhams, $2.30). Upon your return, take a taxi or catch the bus, which meets every train arrival and takes passengers all the way to the port for 3 dirhams. The bus also goes from downtown one hour before each departure but is not worth the trouble.

From Tangier by train to: Rabat (4/day, 6 hrs), **Casablanca** (5/day, 6 hrs), **Marrakech** (5/day, 10 hrs), **Fès** (2/day, 6 hrs), **Ceuta** and **Tétouan** (hrly buses, 1 hr).

From Fès to: Casablanca (8/day, 5 hrs), **Marrakech** (4/day, 9 hrs), **Rabat** (7/day, 4 hrs), **Meknes** (10/day, 1 hr), **Tangier** (5/day, 5 hrs).

From Rabat to: Casablanca (12/day, 90 min), **Fès** (6 buses/day, 5.5 hrs), **Tétouan** (2 buses/day, 4 hrs).

From Casablanca to: Marrakech (6/day, 5 hrs).

From Marrakech to: Meknes (4/day, 10 hrs), **Ouarzazate** (4 buses/day, 4 hrs).

By Plane: Flights within Morocco are convenient and cheap (around $80 to Casablanca).

PORTUGAL

- About 92,000 square kilometers, or 36,000 square miles (the size of Indiana), 15 percent of the Iberian Peninsula
- 10 million people (110 people per square kilometer)
- 1 euro (€1) = about $1
- Time zone difference: Portuguese time is generally one hour earlier than Spanish time.

Portugal is underrated. The country seems somewhere just beyond Europe. The pace of life is noticeably slower than in Spain. Roads are rutted. Prices are cheaper. While the unification of Europe is bringing sweeping changes, the traditional economy is based on fishing, cork, wine, and textiles. Be sure to balance your look at Iberia with enough Portugal.

Portugal isn't touristy—even its coastal towns lack glitzy attractions. The beach and the sea are enough, as they have been for centuries, the source of Portugal's seafaring wealth long ago and the draw for tourists today.

The locals, not jaded by tourists, will meet you with warmth—especially if you learn at least a few words of Portuguese instead of launching into Spanish.

Over the centuries, Portugal and Spain have had a love-hate, on-again, off-again relationship, but they have almost always remained separate, each with their own distinct language and culture.

Portugal bucked the Moors before Spain did, establishing its present-day borders 800 years ago.

A couple of centuries later, the Age of Discovery (1500–1700) made Portugal one of the world's richest nations.

Prince Henry the Navigator, Bartolomeu Dias, and Vasco da Gama traveled to Africa seeking—and finding—a trade route to India. Portuguese-born Ferdinand Magellan, sailing for Spain, was the first to circumnavigate the globe.

Portugal, a naval superpower for a century, established colonies throughout Africa and Brazil. The gold that flowed into the country led to an explosion of the arts back home. (Now known as the Manueline period, after King Manuel, its finest architecture is in Lisbon, represented by Belém's tower and monastery.) But no country can corner the market on trade for long, and as with Spain, Portugal underwent a long decline.

Portugal endured the repressive regime of António de Oliveira Salazar from 1932 to 1974—the longest dictatorship in Western European history. Salazar (and his successor Caetano) pumped money into fighting wars to hang on to the last of the country's African colonies. When Portuguese military officers staged a coup in 1974, the locals were on their side. Portugal lost its colonies, but the Portuguese—and their former colonies—won their freedom.

Portugal, the poorest European Union country, has worked hard to meet EU standards... and has enjoyed heavy EU investment. Today Portugal is a success story, with huge improvements in its infrastructure and a relatively strong economy. But prices have remained low, making Portugal prime territory for budget travelers.

LISBON
(LISBOA)

Lisbon is a ramshackle but charming mix of now and then. Old wooden trolleys shiver up and down its hills, bird-stained statues mark grand squares, taxis rattle and screech through cobbled lanes, and well-worn people sip coffee in Art Nouveau cafés.

While Lisbon's history goes back to the Romans and Moors, its glory days were the 15th and 16th centuries, when explorers such as Vasco da Gama opened new trade routes around Africa to India, making Lisbon one of Europe's richest cities. Portugal's "Age of Discovery" fueled an economic boom, which fueled the flamboyant art boom called the Manueline period—named after King Manuel I (ruled 1495–1521). In the early 18th century, the gold and diamonds of Brazil, one of Portugal's colonies, made Lisbon even wealthier.

Then, on All Saints' Day in 1755, while most of the population was in church, the city was hit by a tremendous earthquake. Candles quivered as far away as Ireland. Two-thirds of Lisbon was leveled. Fires started by the many church candles raged through the city, and a huge tidal wave blasted the waterfront. Of Lisbon's 270,000 people, 30,000 were killed.

Under the energetic and eventually dictatorial leadership of Prime Minister Marques de Pombal—who had the new city planned within a month of the quake—Lisbon was rebuilt on a progressive grid plan, with broad boulevards and square squares. Remnants of pre-earthquake Lisbon charm survive in Belém, the Alfama, and the Baírro Alto district. The bulk of your sightseeing will likely be in these neighborhoods.

The heritage of Portugal's Age of Discovery was a vast colonial empire. Except for Macao and the few islands off the Atlantic coast, the last bits of the empire disappeared with the

Lisbon

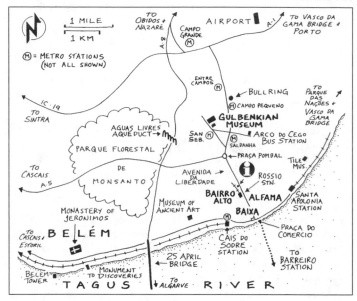

1974 revolution, which delivered Portugal from the right-wing Salazar dictatorship. Imigrants from former colonies such as Mozambique and Angola have added diversity and flavor to the city, making it more likely that you'll hear African music than Portuguese fados these days.

But Lisbon's heritage survives. The city—with newly restored downtown squares and a financial boost from the European Union—seems better organized, cleaner, and more prosperous and people-friendly than ever. With its elegant outdoor cafés, exciting art, entertaining museums, a hill-capping castle, a salty sailors' quarter, and the boost given the city after hosting the 1998 World's Fair, Lisbon is a world-class city. And with some of Europe's lowest prices, enjoying Lisbon is easy on the budget.

Planning Your Time

With three weeks in Iberia, Lisbon is worth two days. Remember, many top sights are closed on Monday, particularly in Belém.

Day 1: Start by touring Castle São Jorge at the top of the Alfama, and surveying the city from its viewpoint. Hike down to another fine viewpoint, Miradouro de Santa Luzia, and descend into the Alfama. Explore. Back in the Baixa (pron. bai-shah; "lower city"), have lunch on or near Rua Augusta and walk to the funicular near Praça dos Restauradores. Kick off the described walk through the Baírro Alto with a ride up the funicular. Take a joyride on trolley #28. Art-lovers can then taxi to the Gulbenkian Museum. Consider dinner at a fado show in the Baírro Alto.

Day 2: Trolley to Belém and tour the tower, monastery, and Coach Museum. Have lunch in Belém. Tour the Museum of Ancient Art and spend the rest of your afternoon browsing through the Rossio, Bairro Alto, and Alfama neighborhoods.

A third day is best spent in Sintra touring the Pena Palace and exploring the ruined Moorish castle. (If you only have two days, this is possible but rushed if you see Sintra instead of the ancient art museum on the second afternoon.)

Orientation

Greater Lisbon has around two million people and some frightening sprawl, but for the visitor, the city can be a delightful small-town series of parks, boulevards, and squares bunny-hopping between two hills down to the waterfront. The main boulevard, Avenida da Liberdade, goes from the high-rent district downhill, ending at the grand square called Praça dos Restauradores. From here the Baixa—the post-earthquake, grid-planned lower town, with three fine squares—leads to the riverfront. Rua Augusta is the grand pedestrian promenade running through the Baixa to the river.

Most travelers focus on the three characteristic neighborhoods that line the downtown harborfront: Baixa (flat, in the middle), the Baírro Alto (literally "high town," Lisbon's "Latin Quarter" on a hill to the west), and the tangled, medieval Alfama (topped by the castle on the hill to the east).

From ye olde Lisbon, Avenida da Liberdade storms into the no-nonsense real world, where you find the airport, bullring, Edward VII Park, and breezy botanical gardens.

Tourist Information

Lisbon has several hardworking tourist offices, and additional info kiosks sprout around town late each spring. Main TIs are at the Palacio Foz (at the bottom of Praça dos Restauradores, daily 9:00–20:00, tel. 213-463-314; TI for Portugal in same office, tel. 218-494-323 or 213-463-658), "Ask Me Lisbon" center (Praça do Comércio, 9:00–20:00, tel. 210-312-810), airport (daily 6:00–24:00), Castle São Jorge (kiosk open April–Sept daily 10:00–13:00 & 14:00–18:00), and Belém (kiosk open daily 10:00–13:00 & 14:00–18:00, in front of monastery, tel. 213-658-435). Two good Web sites are www.atl-turismolisboa.pt and www.portugalinsite.pt.

Lisbon's free city map has a helpful inset of the town center

Central Lisbon

(but the TI's Gray Line and Cityrama tour brochures have a better city map). Pick up the free monthly *Follow Me Lisboa.*

LisboaCard: This card covers all public transportation (including the Metro) and free entrance to most museums (including Sintra sights) and discounts on others, plus discounts on city tours and the Aero-Bus airport bus. You can buy this only at Lisbon's TIs (including the airport TI), not at participating sites. If you plan to museum-hop, the card is a good value, particularly for a day in Belém (covers your transportation and sightseeing), but don't get the card for Sunday, when many sights are free until 14:00, or for Monday, when most sights are closed (24-hr card/€12, 48-hr card/€19, 72-hr card/€24; includes excellent explanatory guidebook). You choose the start date and time. While Lisbon's Shopping and Restaurant Cards unnecessarily complicate your time, the LisboaCard saves a frugal and busy sightseer about 30 percent (well over €30 if you did all the sights recommended).

Arrival in Lisbon

By Train: Lisbon has four train stations—Santa Apolónia (to Spain and most points north), Rossio (for Sintra, Óbidos, and Nazaré), Barreiro (for the Algarve), and Cais do Sodre (for Cascais and Estoril). If leaving Lisbon by train, see if your train requires a reservation (boxed R in timetable).

Santa Apolónia Station covers international trains and nearly all of Portugal (except the south). It's just past the Alfama. It has ATMs and good bus connections to the town center (buses #9 and #39 go to Praça dos Restauradores; #46 and #90 continue up Avenida da Liberdade—as you exit the station, these bus stops are to your left and run alongside the station). A taxi from Santa Apolónia to any recommended hotel costs around €4.

Rossio Station is in the town center (an easy walk from most recommended hotels, ATM near track 5) and handles trains to Sintra (direct, 4/hr) and to Óbidos and Nazaré (both require a transfer at Cacém). Its all-Portugal ticket office on the ground floor is handy (Mon–Fri 7:00–20:00, closed Sat–Sun, sells long-distance and international tickets to virtually everywhere except nearby destinations such as Sintra, no CC). You can buy tickets to Sintra upstairs in the lobby in front of the tracks, either at the ticket office or from the simple-to-use machines (select English, pop in coins—about €1.10, TV monitor in lobby lists departure times, usually :08, :23, :38, and :53 in both directions).

Barreiro Station, a 30-minute ferry ride across the Tagus River (Rio Tejo) from the dock at Lisbon's Praça do Comércio, covers trains to the Algarve and points south (the €1 ferry ticket is generally sold to you with a train ticket). Note that the same Lisbon dock handles boats to Cacilhas and cruises on the Tejo. To catch a ferry to the Barreiro train station, go to the two-story white building on the dock that actually looks like a train station.

Caís do Sodre Station, on the waterfront (just west of Praça do Comércio) handles the 40-minute rides to Cascais and Estoril.

By Bus: Lisbon's modern bus station has ATMs, a leaflet rack of schedules (near entrance/exit) next to a nifty computer that can display your route, and two info offices—one for buses in Portugal, the other for international routes (both closed Sun). If you plan to leave Lisbon by bus, you can virtually always buy a ticket just a few minutes before departure, but you can also buy it up to seven days in advance if you prefer the peace of mind. The station is at Arco do Cego. To get downtown from the station, it's a €3.50 taxi ride or a short Metro trip (3-block walk to Metro stop Saldanha; exiting the bus station, turn left on Avenida João Crisostomo, then left on busy Avenida da República, look for red M for Metro, near McDonald's, bus info: tel. 213-545-439).

By Plane: Lisbon's easy-to-manage airport is eight kilometers northeast of downtown, with a 24-hour bank, ATMs, two TIs (daily 6:00–24:00), reasonable taxi service (€10, 15 min to center), good bus connections into town (#44, #45, €1), and an airport bus, Aero-Bus #91. The Aero-Bus runs from the airport to Avenida da Liberdade, Praça dos Restauradores, Rossio, and Praça do Comércio (€2.30, 3/hr, 30 min, daily 7:45–20:45, buy ticket on bus). Your ticket is actually a one-day Lisbon transit pass that covers bus, trolley, and funicular rides, but not the Metro (3-day transit pass for €5.50 also sold on bus). If you fly in on TAP airline, show your boarding pass to get a free lift into town on the airport bus (TAP tel. 218-416-644). Airport info: tel. 218-413-700.

While you're at the airport, take advantage of the all-Portugal tourist office across from the Lisbon TI (daily 6:00–24:00, tel. 218-493-689).

Getting around Lisbon

A day pass that covers the Metro, lifts, trolleys, and buses costs €2.50 (sold at Metro stations and Carris booths—on Praça da Figueira and behind the Santa Justa elevator). Note that the LisboaCard covers it all.

By Metro: Lisbon's simple, fast subway is handy for trips to the Gulbenkian Museum, Chiado, bullfights, Colombo Mall, Parque das Nacoes, and long-distance bus station. Bring change for the machines, as many stations are not staffed (€0.60 per ride, 10-pack for €4.50, or €1.50 all-day pass, covered by LisboaCard). Remember to stamp your ticket in the machine. Metro stops are marked with a red M. *Saida* means exit. If you can't find a Metro map, look in the TI's free *Follow Me Lisboa.*

By Trolleys, Funicular, and Buses: For fun and practical public transport, use the trolleys and the funicular. If you buy your ticket from the driver, one ride costs €0.90 (no transfers). You get two rides for €1 if you buy your ticket from a Carris kiosk (on Praça da Figueira; at the bullfight ticket kiosk at Praça dos Restauradores; or behind the Santa Justa elevator—open daily 8:00–19:30; can mix forms of transportation).

Transit passes cover all public transportation—including the extensive city bus system—except for the Metro (1-day/€2.50, 3-day/€5.50). Like San Francisco, Lisbon sees its trolleys as part of its heritage and is keeping a few. Trolleys #12 (circling the Alfama), #28 (scenically across the old town), and #15 (to Belém) are here to stay.

By Taxi: Lisbon cabbies are good-humored, abundant, and use their meters. Rides start at about €2, and you can go anywhere in the center for around €3. Decals on the window clearly spell out all charges in English. The most typical scam is the cabbie setting his meter at the high price tarif. The meter should read Tarif 1 (6:00–22:00) or Tarif 2 (nights and weekends); if it's Tarif 3, 4, or 5, simply tell him to change it.

Especially if you're traveling with a companion, Lisbon's cabs are a cheap time-saver. For an average trip, couples save less than a dollar by taking public transport and spend an extra 15 minutes to get there—bad economics. If time is limited, taxi everywhere. If you're having a hard time flagging one down, ask for a *praça de taxi* (pron. PRAH-sah dee taxi; taxi stand).

Helpful Hints

Calendar Concerns: Bullfights take place most summer Thursdays in Lisbon (though closed through 2003) and most Sundays nearby. Tuesdays and Saturdays are flea-market days in the Alfama. The national museums are free on Sunday (all day or until 14:00) and closed all day Monday.

Pedestrian Warning: Sidewalks are narrow, and drivers are daring; cross streets with care. Lisbon has piles of people doing illegal business on the street. While it's generally safe, if you're looking for trouble, you may find it. For late-night strolling, choose your neighborhood wisely. Pickpockets target tourists on the trams (especially #12 and #28) and old-time cable-cars.

Language: Remember to try to start conversations in Portuguese (see "Survival Phrases," near the back of this book). Fortunately, many people in the tourist trade speak English. Otherwise, try Portuguese, French, or Spanish, in that order. Locals call their city Lisboa (pron. LEEZH-bo-ah) and their river the Tejo (pron. TAY-zhoo). Squares are major navigation points and are called *praça* (pron. PRA-sah).

Time Change: Portuguese time is one hour earlier than Spanish time during daylight savings months.

Banking: ATMs are the way to go, giving more euros per dollar all over Lisbon (and Portugal). Banks offer fine rates but high fees to change checks or cash (bank hours are generally Mon–Fri 8:30–15:00, closed Sat–Sun). American Express cashes any kind of traveler's check at mediocre rates without a commission. Their office is not central (Mon–Fri 9:30–13:00 & 14:30–18:30, closed Sat–Sun, in Top Tours office at Avenida Duque de Loule 108, Metro: Rotunda, tel. 213-194-190).

Internet Access: The TI has a list of the latest. The Ask Me Lisbon office on Praça do Comércio has computers upstairs (€2.50/30 min).

Post Office and Telephones: The post offices *(correios)* on Praça do Comércio (Mon–Fri only) and at Praça dos

Restauradores 58 have easy-to-use metered phones and Internet points (Mon–Fri 8:00–22:00, Sat–Sun 9:00–18:00). The telephone center on the northwest corner of Rossio Square sells phone cards and also has metered phones (daily 8:00–23:00, accepts CC).

Travel Agency: Agencies line the Avenida da Liberdade. For flights (but not train tickets), Star Turismo is handy and helpful (Mon–Fri 9:30–18:30, closed Sat–Sun, Praça dos Restauradores 14, southwest corner of square, tel. 213-460-336).

Guides: The city has no regular walking tours and the sights come with no audioguides. A local guide can be a big help. For a private guide contact the Guides' Union (€76/4 hrs, €126/full day, tel. 213-467-170). Christina Quental has been sharing the wonders of her hometown with visitors for 20 years and can tailor a visit to whatever you like (cellular 919-922-480 or tel. 219-625-191, e-mail: duartecancella@dcanews.com). Claudia da Costa is another good local guide (cellular 965-560-216, e-mail: claudiadacosta@hotmail.com).

Tours—Lisbon

▲▲**Ride a Trolley**—Lisbon's vintage trolleys, most from the 1920s, shake and shiver through the old parts of town, somehow safely weaving within inches of parked cars, climbing steep hills, and offering sightseers breezy views of the city for less than a euro (rubberneck out the window and you easily die). Trolley #28 is a Rice-A-Roni Lisbon joyride. Stops from west to east include Estrela (the 18th-century late-Baroque Estrela Basilica and Estrela Park—cozy neighborhood scene with pond-side café and a "garden library kiosk"); the top of the Bica funicular (which drops steeply through a rough-and-tumble neighborhood to the riverfront); Chiado square (the café and "Latin Quarter"); Baixa (on Rua da Conceição between Augusta and Prata); the cathedral (Sè); Largo Santa Luzia (the Alfama viewpoint); Largo das Portas do Sol; Santa Clara Church (flea market on Tue and Sat morning); and the pleasant and untouristy Graca district. Just pay the conductor as you board, sit down, and catch the pensioners as they lurch by at each stop. For a quicker circular Alfama trolley ride, catch #12 on Praça da Figueira (departs every few minutes, 20-min circle, driver can tell you when to get out for the Largo Santa Luzia viewpoint near the castle—about three-quarters through the ride).

Carris City Bus and Tram Tours—Carris Tours offer a confusing array of bus and tram tours giving tired tourists a lazy overview of the city. While uninspiring and not cheap, they're handy and offered daily year-round. They all start and end at Praça do Comércio—trams on one side, buses (with info booth) on the other.

The **Tejo Tour** (which loops around west Lisbon) and the **Orient Express** (which loops east) are double-decker hop-on hop-off bus tours: You can get off, tour a sight, and catch a later bus. Major stops on the Tejo Tour are the Gulbenkian Museum and Belém sights (runs twice hourly from 9:00–17:00 March–Oct, later in summer, less in winter). The major stops of the Orient Express are Parque das Nações and the Tile Museum (runs hourly 10:15–17:15 March–Oct, less in winter). Both tours use audioguides. And in each case, your ticket functions as a transit pass the rest of the day, covering trams, buses, and lifts (but not the Metro, which is owned by a different company). You can't hop on and hop off between the two tours. They cost €13 apiece.

Carris' **Discovery Tour** goes to Belém (90 min, live guide, €16). Their **Sintra Tour** makes a swing around the scenic and historic peninsula (an hour free in Sintra but no Pena castle visit) all the way out to Cabo da Roca—which is frustrating to reach on your own even if you have a car (daily at 14:00, 4.5 hours, with a live 3-language guide, €40 cost includes one of their €16 tram tours as a bonus).

Carris offers four tram tours, including the **Hills Tramcar** tour, which takes you on a 1900s tramcar through the Alfama and Baírro Alto. Scenic ride...sparse information (€16, 90-min tour with no stops and a live bilingual guide, about 11/day March–Oct). A two-day ticket for €30 allows you to take all four 90-minute tours. For more information, stop by their yellow info bus (with an awning, west side of Praça do Comércio, no CC, discount with LisboaCard, tel. 213-613-010).

Tejo River Cruise—Cruzeiros no Tejo runs two-hour trips from the Terreiro do Paço dock off Praça do Comércio, cruising to the Vasca da Gama bridge and Parque das Nações, east to Belém and back (€15, discount with LisboaCard, April–Sept 2/day, at 11:00 and 15:00—confirm time at TI or the kiosk at dock entrance, 4-language narration includes English, hop-on hop-off option at Parque das Nações and Belém sometimes possible on weekends, drinks included, WC on board, tel. 218-820-348).

Do-It-Yourself Walking Tours

The Baírro Alto and Chiado Stroll

Elevator da Gloria—For a ▲▲ walk, rise above the lower town on the funicular called "Elevator da Gloria," near the obelisk at Praça dos Restauradores. Leaving the funicular on top, turn right to enjoy the city view from Miradouro de São Pedro Alcantara (San Pedro Park belvedere). Wander over to the tile map, which helps guide you through the view, stretching from the castle

Pombal's Lisbon

After the earthquake of 1755, Prime Minister Marques de Pombal rebuilt much of Lisbon. He had served as a diplomat in London, where he picked up some city-planning ideas—considered pretty wild by 18th-century Lisbon. (A forceful figure, Pombal not only rebuilt Lisbon, but also ended the Inquisition and expelled the Jesuits, who were the intellectual power behind the Inquisition.)

Avenida da Liberdade is the tree-lined grand boulevard of Lisbon, connecting the old town near the river (where most of the sightseeing action is) with the newer upper town. Before the great earthquake this was a royal promenade. After 1755 it was the grand boulevard of Pombal's new Lisbon—originally limited to the aristocracy. The present street, built in the 1880s and inspired by Paris' Champs-Élysées, is lined with banks, airline offices, nondescript office buildings ... and eight noisy lanes of traffic. The grand "rotunda"—as the roundabout formally known as Praça Marques de Pombal is called—tops off the Avenida da Liberdade with a commanding statue of Mr. Pombal, decorated with allegorical symbols of his impressive accomplishments. (A single-minded dictator can do a lot in 27 years.) Beyond that stretches the fine Edward VII Park. The 20-minute downhill walk from the Rotunda (Metro: Rotunda) along the 1.5-kilometer-long avenue to the old town is enjoyable. The black-and-white cobbled sidewalks are a Lisbon tradition.

Praça dos Restauradores is the monumental square at the lower end of Avenida da Liberdade. Its centerpiece, an obelisk, celebrates the restoration of Portuguese independence from Spain in 1640. (In 1580 the Portuguese king died without a direct heir. The closest heir was Philip II of Spain—yuck. He became Philip I of Portugal, ushering in an unhappy 60 years during which three Spanish Philips ruled Portugal.) Within a few meters of the obelisk is the neo-Manueline-style Rossio train station, Lisbon's oldest hotel (Hotel Avenida Palace, built to greet those arriving by train), the Art Deco facade of the Eden Theater from the 1920s, the TI, bullfight ticket kiosk, a funicular that climbs to the high town, a Metro station, and Lisbon's restaurant row "eating lane."

Baixa, between Avenida da Liberdade and the harbor, is the flat, lower city. The grid plan (with many streets named for the crafts and shops historically found there) and most of the five-story facades are Pombal's from just after 1755. Baixa's pedestrian streets, inviting cafés, bustling shops, and elegant old storefronts give the district a certain magnetism. I find myself doing laps in a people-watching stupor. The mosaic-decorated Rua Augusta (with the grand arch near the river framing the equestrian statue of King José I) has a delightful strolling ambience—reminding many of Barcelona's Ramblas. Notice the uniform and utilitarian Pombalan architecture with its decoration limited to wrought iron and tiles. In the years after the earthquake Lisbon did a lot of building without a lot of money.

Midway down the Baixa you'll see the 45-meter-tall **Santa Justa Elevator.** It was built in 1892 (a few years after, and inspired by, the Eiffel Tower) to connect the lower town with the high town. While you can no longer enter the Baírro Alto from the skyway at the top, you can still ride the lift for a fine city view and a cup of coffee (€1.80, daily 7:00–23:45).

The Baixa has three great squares, each ornamented with a statue of a Portuguese king. **Rossio** and **Figueira** squares—congested with buses, subways, taxis, and pigeons leaving in all directions—stand side-by-side at the top. Rossio has been the center of Lisbon since medieval times. The small Largo San Domingos (between Restauradores and Figueira) has a fascinating ambiance. Immigrants from Portugal's former colonies in Africa hang out here. This is the neighborhood grapevine, where they share news from home, share strategies on gaining legal residency, and trade various food products from their homelands. Lisbon's most classic *ginjinha* bar faces this square.

Praça do Comércio, or Trade Square—where the ships used to stop and sell their goods—borders the Baixa at the riverfront. Nicknamed "Palace Square" by locals, for 200 pre-earthquake years it was the site of Portugal's royal palace. It's ringed by government ministries and is the departure point for city tours and the boat across the Tejo. The area bordering this opposite the harbor was conceived as a residential neighborhood for the upper class but they chose the suburbs and it's been pretty dead for the last century. The statue is of King José I, the man who put Pombal to work rebuilding the city.

birthplace of Lisbon on the right to the towers of the new city
in the distance on the left. The centerpiece of the park is a bust
honoring a 19th-century local journalist. This district is famous
for its writers, poets, and bohemians.

Port Wine Institute—If you're into port (the fortified wine that
takes its name from Oporto, a city just north of here), you'll find
the world's greatest selection directly across the street from the
lift at **Solar do Vinho do Porto** (run by the Port Wine Institute,
Mon–Sat 14:00–24:00, closed Sun, WCs, Rua São Pedro de Alcantara 45, tel. 213-475-707). In a plush, air-conditioned living room
you can, for €1 to €22 per glass (poured by an English-speaking
bartender), taste any of 300 different ports—though you may want
to try only 150 or so and save the rest for the next night. Fans
of port describe it as "a liquid symphony playing on the palate."
Browse through the easy menu; the colheita is particularly good.
Munchies are in the back.

Follow the main street (Rua São Pedro de Alcantara,
which turns into Rua Misericordia) downhill a couple of blocks.
Throughout this walk, look up and notice the fine old tile work
on the buildings.

When you reach the small square, Largo Trindade Coelho,
the São Roque Church will be on your left.

São Roque Church—Step inside and sit on a pew in the middle
(8:30–17:00). Built in the 16th century, the church of St. Roque is
one of Portugal's first Jesuit churches. The painted wood ceiling
is perfectly flat. The acoustics here are top-notch, important in a
Jesuit church where the emphasis is on the sermon. Notice all the
numbered doors on the floor. These are tombs—nameless because
they were for lots of people. They're empty now—the practice
was stopped in the 19th century when parishioners didn't want
dead plague victims rotting under their feet. Survey the rich side
chapels. The highlight is the Chapel of St. John the Baptist (left of
altar, gold and blue). It looks like it came right out of the Vatican
because it did. Made in Rome out of the most precious materials,
it was the site of one papal Mass; then it was shipped to Lisbon—
probably the most costly chapel per square inch ever constructed.
Notice the mosaic floor (with the spherical symbol of Portugal)
and the three paintings that are actually intricate, beautiful mosaics—
a Vatican specialty (designed to avoid damage from candle smoke
that would darken paintings). The São Roque Museum, with
some old paintings and church riches, is not as interesting as the
church itself (€1, discount with LisboaCard, Tue–Sun 10:00–
17:00, closed Mon).

After a visit with the poor pigeon-drenched man in the
church square (WC), continue downhill along Rua Nova da

Trindade. At #20 you can pop into Cervejaria da Trindade, the famous "oldest beer hall in Lisbon" (see "Eating," below), for a look at the 19th-century tiles. Once the refectory of a monastery, it became a brewery after the monks were expelled in 1834. If you're tired of all this history, continue downhill to #16—Lisbon's biggest used bookstore—where you can sell this book. Otherwise continue down the hill anyway, where, at the next intersection, signs point left to the ruined Convento do Carmo. Follow the inside trolley tracks downhill to the next square...

Largo do Carmo—On this square, the police guard the head-quarters of the National Guard—famous among locals as the last refuge of the fascist prime minister before the people won their democracy in the Revolution of 1974. It was a peaceful revolution, called the Carnation Revolution, because of the flowers they put in the guns of the soldiers as people power made it clear it was time for democracy in Portugal.

On Largo do Carmo, check out the ruins of the **Convento do Carmo** (Tue–Sun 10:00–18:00, closed Mon). At first glance the church seems intact, but look closer, through the windows. After the church was destroyed by the 1755 earthquake, Marques de Pombal directed that its delicate Gothic arches be left standing as a permanent reminder of that disastrous event.

If you're hungry, consider Leitaria Academica, a venerable lit-tle working-class eatery with tables spilling onto the breezy square.

Next, leave Largo do Carmo walking a block uphill on Travessa do Carmo. At the square take a left (on Rua Serpa Pinto) downhill to Rua Garrett where—in the little pedestrian zone on the right—you'll find a new Metro stop across from an old café.

Rua Garrett and Chiado—On the pedestrian street, Rua Garrett, coffeehouse junkies enjoy the grand old **A Brasileira** café, reeking of smoke and the 1930s. Drop in for a *bica* (Lisbon slang for an espresso) and a *pastel de Belém* (€1 cream cake—a local specialty). The statue outside is of the poet Fernando Pessoa—who was a regular at Brasileira. This café was the literary and creative soul of Lisbon in the 1920s and 1930s when the country's avant-garde—poets, painters and writers—would hang out here.

At the new Chiado Metro stop, a slick series of escalators whisks people effortlessly between the Chiado square and the lower town. It's a free and fun way to survey a long, long line of Portuguese—but for now, we'll stay in the Chiado neighborhood. (If you'll be coming up here for fado in the evening, consider zipping up the escalator to get here; the recommended fado restaurant, Canto do Camões, is roughly three blocks away; see "Nightlife," below.)

This district, the **Chiado** (pron. SHEE-ah-doo), is popular for its shopping and theaters. Browse downhill on Rua Garrett, lined with fine shops, peeking into the classy stores such as the venerable Bertrand bookstore (at #73, English books and a good guidebook selection in room 5). Notice that the street lamps are decorated with the symbol of Lisbon: a ship—carrying the remains of St. Vincent—guarded by two ravens. Rua Garrett ends abruptly downhill at the entrance of the six-story vertical mall, Armazens do Chiado.

To end this walk, you have several options: Catch the subway (Chiado) to your next destination, walk down Rua do Carmo to Rossio (facing the mall entrance, it's the road to your left), or enter the Armazens mall (eateries on top floor, see "Eating," below). To get from the mall to Baixa—the lower city—take the elevator down (press 0) or the escalators (you'll pass through the Intersports shop on the lower floors—exit through ground level of store).

The São Jorge Castle-Alfama Stroll

For another ▲▲ walk, explore the colorful sailors' quarter—the Alfama, dating back to Visigothic days. It was a busy district during the Moorish period, and finally the home of Lisbon's fisherfolk (and of the poet Luis de Camões, who wrote, "our lips meet easily, high across the narrow street"). The tangled street plan here is one of the few aspects of Lisbon to survive the 1755 earthquake, helping make the Alfama a cobbled playground of Old World color. A visit is best during the busy midmorning market time or in the cooler hours in the late afternoon or early evening, when the streets teem with locals. Market days are Tuesday and Saturday on Campo de Santa Clara (8:00–15:00, best in morning).

Start your walk at São Jorge Castle—the highest point in town. Get to the castle gate by taxi (€3) or bus #37 from Praça da Figueira. (Trams #28 and #12 go to the Largo Santa Luzia farther below.)

São Jorge Castle Gate—Just inside the castle gate (on left) is a statue of St. George, England's patron saint—because in the 14th century, Portugal had a homesick English queen. A sensitive guy, the king dedicated the castle to St. George (São Jorge; pron. saaaoow zhor-zhuh). Follow the cobbles uphill past the first lanes of old Lisbon to the . . .

View Terrace (Miradouro São Jorge)—Enjoy the grand view. The Tejo River (pron. TAY-zhoo) is one of five main rivers in Portugal, all of which come from Spain. While Portugal and Spain generally have very good relations, the major sore point is the control of all this water. From here you have a good view of the 25th of April Bridge which leads to the Cristo Rei statue (both described below).

Stroll along the **ramparts** inland for a more extensive city view of Pombal's Lisbon (the square and grid streets leading up to the big Edward VII Park on the far right). Before the restaurant (after walking under the second arch), take a right (past a WC) and a left to enter the actual inner castle (free and empty offering only a chance to climb up for more views, sometimes exhibitions are housed here, daily 9:00–21:00).

The **castle** was first built by the Moors in the eighth century. After Portugal's King Alfonse Henriques (his statue stands here) beat the Moors in the 12th century, the castle began its four-century-long stint as a royal residence. In the 16th century the king moved and the castle fell into ruins. What you see today was mostly rebuilt by the dictator Salazar in the 1960s.

Heading back out, you'll pass...

Olisiponia (Roman name for Lisbon)—This high-tech syrupy multimedia presentation offers a sweeping video overview of the city's history in English (€3, discount with LisboaCard, Thu–Tue 10:00–18:00, closed Wed and often for lunch). Near the castle-wall entrance is a little **TI** kiosk (daily 9:00–13:00 & 14:00–18:00).

Leave the castle. Across the ramp from the castle entrance/exit is the recommended restaurant Arco do Castello (see "Eating," below). Facing the restaurant, go left, take your first right, and follow the striped lane downhill through the small square Largo do Contador Mor—which contains the recommended restaurants A Tasquinha and Comidas de Santiago, past another restaurant, Farol de Santa Luzia—to a great Alfama viewpoint at...

Largo Santa Luzia—From this square (a stop for trolleys #12 and #28), admire the panoramic view from the small terrace, Miradouro de Santa Luzia, where old-timers play cards in the shade of the bougainvillea amid lots of tiles. Find the wall of 18th-century tiles that shows the Praça do Comércio before the earthquake. The 16th-century Royal Palace (on the left of tile work) was completely destroyed in the quake. For another view, hike left around the church to the catwalk. This is the place for the most scenic cup of coffee in town—at the Cerca Moura's café terrace (kiosk opens at 11:00, Largo das Portas do Sol 4). Next door to Cerca Moura's main café on the square, you'll find the...

Museum of Decorative Arts—This offers a unique (but nearly meaningless, with its lack of decent English descriptions) stroll through aristocratic households richly decorated in 16th- to 19th-century styles (€4, discount with LisboaCard, Tue–Sun 10:00–17:00, closed Mon, Largo das Portas do Sol 2, tel. 218-862-183). Descend into...

The Alfama—From Largo das Portas do Sol (Cerca Moura bar), go down the stairs (Rua Norberto de Araujo, between the church and the catwalk) into the Alfama. The old wall used to mark the end of Moorish Lisbon. As soon as the stairs end, turn left… down more stairs.

Explore downhill from here until you end up on Rua de São Pedro, a main drag a few blocks below. The Alfama's urban-jungle roads are squeezed into tangled, confusing alleys; bent houses comfort each other in their romantic shabbiness; the air drips with laundry and the smell of clams and raw fish. Get lost. Poke aimlessly, peek through windows, buy a fish. Locals hang plastic water bags from windows to try to keep away the flies. Favorite saints decorate doors protecting families. St. Peter—protector of fishermen—is big in the Alfama. Churches are generally closed since they share a roving priest. The street plan is labyrinthine— to frustrate invaders trying to get up to the castle. The neighborhood here is historically tightly knit—families routinely sit down to communal dinners in the streets. Feuds, friendships, and gossip are all intense. When a woman loses her husband (even today), she typically wears black for the rest of her life. If a black widow goes back to colors, neighbors question her respect and love for her dead husband.

If you see carpets hanging out to dry, a laundry is nearby. Every neighborhood has a public laundry and bathroom. Few accommodations have bathrooms, one of the reasons young people are choosing to live elsewhere.

Rua de São Pedro, the fish market and liveliest street around, leads left downhill to the square called Largo do Chafariz de Dentro and the fado museum.

House of Fado and Portuguese Guitar—This museum tells the story of fado in English. Push the buttons throughout for music, don't miss the male student voices of Coimbra's fado, and finish with a rest in a simulated fado bar to watch old Alfama videos and hear the Billie Holidays of fado. As you leave, notice— on the wall by the door—the fado lyrics censored by the dictator Salazar (€2.50, discount with LisboaCard, daily 10:00–13:00 & 14:00–18:00, Largo do Chafariz de Dentro, tel. 218-823-470). A few steps off this square is the recommended Parreirinha de Alfama fado bar (see "Nightlife," below).

To get back downtown: From the fado museum, you can walk a block to the main waterfront drag (facing museum, go to the left around it) where Avenida Infante dom Henrique leads back to Praça do Comércio downtown (a 10-min walk, plenty of taxis, buses #9 and #39 go to Praça dos Restauradores, #46 and #90 continue up Avenida de Liberdade). The recommended Jardim do Marisco fish restaurant is on the waterfront just across the boulevard.

Sights—Lisbon

▲▲▲**Gulbenkian Museum**—This is the best of Lisbon's 40 museums. Calouste Gulbenkian, an Armenian oil tycoon, gave his art collection (or "harem," as he called it) to Portugal in gratitude for the hospitable asylum granted him during World War II. (He lived in Lisbon from 1942 until he died in 1955.) This great collection, spanning 2,000 years and housed in a classy modern building, offers the most purely enjoyable museum experience in Iberia. It's cool, uncrowded, gorgeously lit, and easy to grasp, displaying only a few select and exquisite works from each epoch.

Savor details as you stroll chronologically through the ages past the delicate Egyptian, vivid Greek (fascinating coins), and exotic Oriental sections, and the well-furnished Louis land (much of the furniture was actually once owned by French royalty). There are masterpieces by Rembrandt, Rubens, Renoir, Rodin, and artists whose names start with other letters. Just wandering through the paintings, you gain an appreciation for Gulbenkian's taste. The nubile finale is a room filled with Art Nouveau jewelry by the French designer Rene Lalique—just another buddy in Gulbenkian's impressive circle of friends (€3, free Sun, discount with LisboaCard, Tue–Sun 10:00–18:00, closed Mon, pleasant gardens, good air-con cafeteria, take Metro from Rossio to São Sebastião and walk 200 meters, or €4 taxi from downtown, Berna 45, tel. 217-823-000, www.gulbenkian.pt).

The Portuguese consider Gulbenkian—whose estate is still a growing and vital foundation promoting culture in Portugal—an inspirational model for how to be thoughtfully wealthy.

▲▲**Museum of Ancient Art (Museu Nacional de Arte Antiga)**— This is the country's best for Portuguese paintings from her glory days, the 15th and 16th centuries. (Most of these works were gathered from Lisbon abbeys and convents after their dissolution in 1834.) You'll also find the great European masters—such as Bosch, Jan van Eyck, and Raphael—and rich furniture, all in a grand palace. Here are some highlights:

Third floor—Portuguese paintings: The *Adoration of St. Vincent* is a many-paneled altarpiece by the late-15th-century master Nuno Goncalves. A gang of 60 real people—everyone from royalty to sailors and beggars—surrounds Lisbon's patron saint.

Second floor—Japanese screen and jewels: Find the fascinating and enchanting Namban screen painting (Namban means "barbarians from the south"). It shows the Portuguese from a 16th-century Japanese perspective—with long noses and great skill at climbing rigging (like acrobats). The Portuguese, the first Europeans to make contact with Japan, gave the Japanese guns, Catholicism (Nagasaki was founded by Portuguese Jesuits), and the word for "thank you" (ever notice how similar *arigato* is to *obrigado*?).

On the same floor (in a free-standing glass case) is the Monstrance of Belém, made for Manuel I from the first gold brought back by Vasco da Gama. Squint at the fine enamel creatures on the base, the 12 apostles gathered around the glass case for the Communion wafer (the fancy top pops off), and the white dove hanging like a mobile under the all-powerful God bidding us all peace on earth. There is another impressive monstrance nearby, as well as more jewels and fine porcelain on the rest of this floor.

First floor—European paintings: Look for Bosch's *Temptations of St. Anthony* (a 3-paneled altarpiece fantasy, c. 1500) and Dürer's *St. Jerome*.

Cost, Hours, and Location: €3, free until 14:00 on Sun, free with LisboaCard, Tue 14:00–18:00, Wed–Sun 10:00–18:00, closed Mon, may close for lunch in 2003 (from Praça da Figueira take trolley #15 or bus #49, #27, or #60, Rua das Janeles Verdes 9, tel. 213-912-800). The museum has a good cafeteria with seating in a shaded garden overlooking the river.

▲**National Tile Museum (Museu Nacional do Azulejo)**—This museum, filling the Convento da Madre de Deus, features piles of tiles, which, as you've probably noticed, are an art form in Portugal. The presentation is low-tech, but the church is sumptuous, and the tile panorama of pre-earthquake Lisbon (upstairs) is fascinating (€3, free until 14:00 on Sun, free with LisboaCard, Tue 14:00–18:00, Wed–Sun 10:00–18:00, closed Mon, 10 min on bus #105 from Praça da Figueira, Rua da Madre de Deus 4, tel. 218-147-747).

Lisbon's City Museum—This sounds good but it's way out from the center, comes without a word in English, and is a disappointment.

Cathedral (Sè)—The cathedral, just a few blocks east of Praça do Comércio, is not much on the inside, but its fortress-like exterior is a textbook example of a stark and powerful Romanesque fortress of God. Started in 1150, after the Christians retook Lisbon from the Islamic Moors, its crenellated towers made a powerful statement: The Reconquista was here to stay.

The church is built upon the supposed birthplace of St. Anthony—another favorite saint of Portugal (locals appeal to him for help in finding a parking spot, a true love, and for lost causes generally). Also, St. Vincent is buried here—legend has it that in the 12th century his remains were brought to Lisbon on a ship guarded by two sacred black ravens, the symbol of the city. The **cloisters** are peaceful and an archaeological work in progress, uncovering Roman ruins (€0.50). The humble **treasury** is worthwhile only if you want to support the church and climb some stairs (€2, free with LisboaCard, 10:00–17:00, on Largo da Sè, several blocks east of Baixa, take Rua da Conceição east, turns into Rua de Santo António da Sè).

Liquid Sightseeing—*Ginjinha* (pron. zheen-zheen-yah) is the diminutive name for a favorite Lisbon drink. *Ginjinha* is a sweet liquor made from the sour cherry–like *ginja* berry, sugar, and schnapps. It's sold for €0.80 a shot in funky old hole-in-the-wall shops throughout town. The only choices are with or without berries (*com* or *sem fruta*) and *gelada* (if you want it poured from a chilled bottle—very nice). In Portugal, when people are impressed by the taste of something, they say, "*Sabe melhor que nem ginjas*" ("It tastes even better than *ginja*"). The oldest *ginjinha* joint in town is a colorful hole-in-the-wall at Largo de São Domingos #8 (just off northeast corner of Rossio Square, across from entrance of "eating lane" —Rua das Portas de Santo Antão). Another *ginjinha* bar is nearby, on Rua das Portas de Santo Antão, next to #59 (nearly across the street from recommended Casa do Alentejo).

Sights—Away from the Center

Parque das Nações—Lisbon celebrated the 500th anniversary of Vasco da Gama's voyage to India by hosting Expo '98. The theme was "The Ocean and the Seas," emphasizing the importance of healthy, clean waters in our environment. The riverside fairgrounds are east of the Santa Apolónia train station in an area suddenly revitalized with luxury condos and crowd-pleasing terraces and restaurants. Ride the Metro to the last stop (Oriente— meaning east end of town), walk to the water, turn right, and join the riverside promenade. You can rent a bike by the hour, go up the Vasco da Gama tower (€2.50, discount with LisboaCard, daily 10:00–20:00, tel. 218-969-869), or visit Europe's biggest aquarium, the Oceanario, which simulates four different oceanic underwater and shoreline environments (€8.50, discount with LisboaCard, daily 10:00–20:00). Popular café/bars—such as Bar de Palha—line the waterfront just south of the tower. This area is fully open on Monday (when many Lisbon museums are not) and most vibrant on Sunday afternoons.

Vasco da Gama Bridge—Europe's second-longest bridge (17 km) was opened in 1998 to connect the Expo grounds with the south side of the Tejo and to alleviate the traffic jams on Lisbon's only other bridge over the river.

▲**25th of April Bridge**—At 3 kilometers long (1 km between the towers), this is one of the longest suspension bridges in the world. It was built in 1966 by the same company that did its San Francisco cousin (but notice the lower deck for train tracks). Originally named for the dictator Salazar, the bridge was renamed for the date of Portugal's 1974 revolution and liberation. For a generation locals showed their political colors by choosing what name to use. While conservatives called it the Salazar bridge, liberals called it the 25th of April bridge. Now most people simply call it "the bridge over the river," perhaps choosing to keep their politics private.

Cristo Rei—A huge statue of Christ (à la Rio de Janeiro), with outstretched arms symbolically blessing the city, overlooks Lisbon from across the Tejo River. It was built as a thanks to God, funded by Lisboetas grateful that Portugal stayed out of World War II. While it's designed to be seen from a distance, a lift takes visitors to the top for a great view (€3, daily 9:30–18:00). Catch the ferry from downtown Lisbon (6/hr, from Praça do Comércio) to Cacilhas, then take a bus marked "Cristo Rei" (4/hr, from ferry dock). Because of bridge tolls, taxis to or from the site are expensive. For drivers, the most efficient visit is a quick stop on your way south to the Algarve.

Sights—Lisbon's Belém District

Five kilometers from downtown Lisbon, the Belém District is a stately pincushion of important sights from Portugal's Golden Age, when Vasco da Gama and company turned the country into Europe's richest power. Belém was the send-off point for voyages in the Age of Discovery. Sailors would stay and pray here before embarking. The tower would welcome them home. For some reason, the grand buildings of Belém survived the great 1755 earthquake. Consequently, this is the only place to experience the grandeur of pre-earthquake Lisbon. After the earthquake, safety-conscious and rattled royalty chose to live here—in wooden rather than stone buildings. And the modern-day president of Portugal calls Belém home. To celebrate the 300th anniversary of independence from Spain, a grand exhibition was held here in 1940, resulting in the fine parks, fountains, and monument. Remember, sights are closed on Monday.

Getting to Belém: You'll get here quickest by taxi (€5 from downtown), or slower (30 min) and cheaper by trolley #15 (catch at Praça da Figueira or Praça do Comércio) or bus #28 (Praça do Comércio). In Belém, the first stop is the Coach Museum; the second is the monastery. If you miss the first subtle stop (named Belém), you can't miss the second stop, the massive monastery.

Consider doing Belém in this order: the Coach Museum, pastry and coffee break, Monastery of Jerónimos, Maritime Museum (if interested) and/or lunch at its cafeteria (public access, museum admission not required), Monument to the Discoveries,

Belém

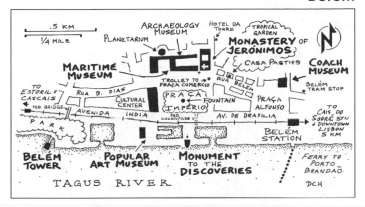

and Belém Tower. By taxi, start at Belém Tower, the farthest
point. Belém also has a cultural center, children's museum, and
a planetarium—non-priorities for a quick visit.

Tourist Information: The little TI kiosk (daily 10:00–13:00
& 14:00–18:00, tel. 213-658-455) is directly across the street from
the entrance of the monastery. A little red-and-white **Mini Train**
does a handy 25-minute hop-on hop-off circuit of the sights—
which feel far-flung if you're tired—departing nearly every hour
from the entrance of the monastery (€2.50, discount with Lisboa-
Card, daily except Mon year-round at 10:00, 11:00, 12:00, 14:00,
15:00, 16:00, and 17:00, plus 18:00 and 19:00 June–Sept; can get
off to explore a sight and catch the next bus; live guide does tour
in Portuguese, English, and French).

Eating in Belém: You'll find snack bars at Belém Tower, a
cafeteria at the Maritime Musuem, and fun little restaurants along
Rua de Belém, between the Coach Museum and the monastery;
I like **Restaurante Jerónimos** at Rua de Belém 74 (closed Sat,
next to the pastry place, see below).

The **Casa Pasteis de Belém** café is the birthplace of the
wonderful cream tart called *pastel del Nata* throughout Portugal.
Here they're called *pastel del Belém.* Since 1837 locals have come
here to get them warm out of the oven (daily 8:00–24:00, Rua de
Belém 88). Sit down. Enjoy one with a *café com leite.* Sprinkle on
the cinnamon and powdered sugar.

For a wonderfully untouristy little adventure, consider having
lunch across the river. Immediately in front of the Coach Museum
is the dock for boats to Porto Brandão (8-min cruise, 2/hr until
23:00, €0.60 each way), a relaxed port town whose harborfront
square has several good fish restaurants such as **O Parafuso.**

Lunch or dinner here is a good opportunity to try *cataplanas*, a traditional fish and veggie stew.

▲▲**Coach Museum (Museu dos Coches)**—In 1905 the Queen of Portugal—seeing that cars would soon obliterate horse-drawn carriages as a means of getting around—decided to use the palace's riding-school building to preserve her fine collection of royal coaches. Claiming to be the most-visited sight in Portugal, it is impressive, with more than 70 dazzling carriages (described in English) in the elegant old riding room. The oldest is the crude and simple coach used by King (of Spain and Portugal) Philip II to shuttle between Madrid and Lisbon around 1600. Notice that this coach has no driver's seat; its drivers would actually ride the horses. You'll have to trust me on this, but, if you lift up the cushions, you'll find two potty holes—also handy for road sickness. Imagine how slow and rough the ride would be with bad roads and no suspension. Study the evolution of suspension from the first coach, or "Kotze," made in a Hungarian town of that name in the 15th century. Look for the highly symbolic ornamentation of the later coaches. The newly restored "Ocean Coach" stands shining in the center, with gold fingers at the stern symbolizing the Atlantic and Indian Oceans holding hands, a reminder to all of Portugal's mastery of the sea. The second room shows sedan chairs and the evolution of carriages as a common means of transport—lighter and faster, including 18th-century "sport cars" and an early Lisbon horse-drawn taxi (€3, free Sun until 14:00, free with LisboaCard, Tue–Sun 10:00–17:30, closed Mon, tel. 213-610-850, taxi stand across the street).

Rua de Belém leads from the Coach Museum and the monastery past the guarded entry to Portugal's presidential palace, some fine pre-earthquake buildings, and a famous pastry shop (obligatory stop, see "Eating in Belém," above).

▲▲▲**Monastery of Jerónimos**—King Manuel (who ruled from 1495) had this giant church and its cloisters built (starting in 1505) with "pepper money"—a 5 percent tax on spices brought back from India—as a thanks for the discoveries. Sailors would spend their last night here in prayer before embarking on their frightening voyages. Here's a tour, starting outside the monastery:

1. South portal: The ornate south portal, facing the street, is textbook Manueline style. Manueline—like Spain's Plateresque but with sea motifs—bridged Gothic and Renaissance. Henry the Navigator stands between the doors with the king's patron saint, St. Jerome (above on the left, with the lion). This door is only used when Mass lets out.

As you pass through the entrance, the church (free) is on your right and the cloisters (€3, free Sun until 14:00, free with

LisboaCard) are straight ahead (hours for both: May–Sept
Tue–Sun 10:00–18:30, Oct–April 10:00–17:00, closed Mon,
last entry 30 min before closing).

2. Church interior: View the interior from near the high
altar looking back toward the entrance. See how Manueline is a
transition between Gothic and Renaissance. While in Gothic
architecture massive columns break the interior into a nave with
low-ceilinged ambulatories on either side, here the slender palm
tree–like columns don't break the interior space, and the ceiling is
all one height. Find some of the Manueline motifs from the sea:
rope-like arches, ships, and coral. Exotic new animals—another
aspect of the Age of Discovery—hide in the capitals. It is, after all,
the sea that brought Portugal 16th-century wealth and power and
made this art possible.

3. Front of church: Now, close your eyes, and turn 180
degrees toward the front. You can see that the rest of the church
is Renaissance. Nearly everything but the stained glass (replacement glass is from 1940) survived the 1755 earthquake. In the
main chapel in the apse (at the far front), elephants—who
dethroned lions as the most powerful and kingly beasts—support
two kings and two queens (King Manuel I is front-left). Walk
back on the side with the seven wooden confessional doors (on
your right). Notice the ornamental carving around the second
one: A festival of faces from newly discovered corners of the world.
Ahead of you (near the entry) is the tomb of Vasco da Gama.

4. Tombs: Vasco da Gama's tomb is decorated with richly
symbolic carvings: The proud sailboat (in the middle of the side of
the tomb) is a Portuguese caravel. This was a technological marvel
in its day, with a triangular sail that could pivot quickly to catch
the wind efficiently. The sphere is a common Manueline symbol.
Some say the diagonal slash is symbolic of the unwritten pact and
ambition of Spain and Portugal to split the world evenly. Even the
ceiling—a *Boy Scout's Handbook* of rope and knots—carries a whiff
of the sea. The second tomb—with literary rather than maritime
motifs—is a memorial (he's buried elsewhere) to Portugal's much-
loved poet, Luis de Camões.

5. Cloisters: Leave the church (turn right, buy a ticket) and
enter the cloisters. These cloisters are the architectural highlight
of Belém. The lacy lower arcade is textbook Manueline; the simpler top floor is Renaissance. Study the carvings. Upstairs you'll
find a bookshop and better views of the church and the cloisters
(women's WC upstairs, men's downstairs).

Maritime Museum (Museu de Marinha)—If you're interested
in the ships and navigational tools of Portugal's Age of Discovery,
this museum, which fills the east wing of the monastery, has good

332 Rick Steves' Spain & Portugal

English descriptions and is worth a look. Sailors love it (€3, free with LisboaCard, June–Sept Tue–Sun 10:00–18:00, Oct–May 10:00–17:00, closed Mon; decent cafeteria with separate entrance; as you face planetarium, museum entrance is to your right; Praça do Império).

▲Monument to the Discoveries—This giant riverside monument was built in 1960 to honor Prince Henry the Navigator on the 500th anniversary of his death. Huge statues of Henry, Magellan, Vasco da Gama, and other heroes of Portugal's Age of Discovery—with a grace typical of fascist Salazar's rule—line the giant concrete prow of a caravel. The inside offers only an elevator ride to a tingly view (€2, free with Lisboa-Card, Tue–Sun 9:00–17:00, closed Mon, tel. 213-620-034). Notice the marble map chronicling Portugal's empire-building (on the ground leading to the monument). Follow the years as Portuguese explorers gradually worked their way around Africa. Today, all that remains of Portugal's once-huge empire are the Azores and Madeira (whose original inhabitants were Portuguese).

▲Belém Tower—Perhaps the purest Manueline building in Portugal (built 1515–1520), this white tower protected Lisbon's harbor and today symbolizes the voyages that made Lisbon powerful. This was the last sight sailors saw as they left and the first when they returned, loaded with gold, spices, and social diseases. When the tower was built, the river went nearly to the walls of the monastery and the tower was mid-river. Its interior is pretty bare, but the views of the bridge, river, and Cristo Rei are worth the 120 steps (€3, free Sun until 14:00, free with Lisboa-Card, May–Sept Tue–Sun 10:00–18:30, Oct–April 10:00–17:00, closed Mon, exhibitions sometimes held here, tel. 213-620-034). The float-plane on the grassy lawn is a monument to the first flight across the South Atlantic (Portugal to Brazil) in 1922. The original plane is in Belém's Maritime Museum.

If you're choosing between towers, Monument to the Discoveries is probably the better choice because of its elevator and better view of the monastery. Both towers are interesting to see from the outside whether or not you go up.

Folk Art Museum (Museu de Arte Popular)—This museum—likely closed for restoration—takes you through Portugal's folk art one province at a time, providing a sneak preview of what you'll see throughout the country (€1.75, free Sun until 14:00, free with LisboaCard, Tue–Sun 10:00–12:30 & 14:00–17:00, closed Mon, between the Monument and the Tower on Avenida Brasilia—but it's not the white restaurant in the middle of the pond).

Shopping in Lisbon

Flea Market—On Tuesday and Saturday, the Feira da Ladra flea market hops in the Alfama on Campo de Santa Clara (best in the morning). A Sunday market—with coins, books, antiques, and more—is at Parque das Nações (10:00–18:00, in garden Garcia da Horta, Metro: Oriente).

Colombo Shopping Mall—While downtown Lisbon offers decaying but still-elegant department stores, a shopping center (described below), classy specialty shops, and a teeming flea market, nothing is as impressive as the enormous Centro Colombo, the largest shopping center in Spain and Portugal. More than 400 shops—including the biggest FNAC department store, 10 cinemas, 60 restaurants, and a health club—sit atop Europe's biggest underground car park and under a vast and entertaining play center. There's plenty to amuse children here and the place offers a fine look at workaday Lisbon (daily 10:00–24:00, pick up a map at info desk, Metro: Colegio Militar takes you right there, tel. 217-113-636).

Armazens do Chiado—This grand six-floor shopping center connects Lisbon's lower and upper towns with a world of ways to spend money (lively food circus on 6th floor—see "Eating," below). Amid other buildings the same height, it doesn't stand out. So here's how to find it: If you approach from Chiado, Rua Garrett dead-ends at the main entrance. From the Baixa (lower town), head up Rua Assuncão toward the mall, where you'll find three subtle entrances on Rua do Crucifixio—through the Intersports store (take their escalators up into the mall), or at #113 or #89 (where small, simple doorways lead to elevators).

El Corte Inglés—The Spanish mega–department store has arrived in Lisbon with a huge store at the top of Edward VII park (daily 10:00–22:00, Metro: S. Sebastiao, tel. 213-711-700).

Nightlife

Nightlife in the Baixa seems to be little more than loitering prostitutes and litter stirred by the wind. But head up into the Baírro Alto and you'll find lots of action. The Jardím do São Pedro is normally festive and the Rua Diario de Noticias is lined with busy bars.

The trendy hot spot lately for young locals is the dock district under the 25th of April Bridge. The Docas (pron. dock-ash) is a 400-meter-long strip of warehouses turned into restaurants and discos. Popular places include Hawaii, Salsa Latina, Havana, and Friday's (catch a taxi or trolley #15 from Praça da Figueira to the stop Avenida Infante Santo, take overpass, then a 10-min walk toward bridge).

▲▲**Fado**—Fado, which means "fate," is the folk music of Lisbon's back streets. Since the mid-1800s it's been the Lisbon blues— mournfully beautiful, haunting ballads about lost sailors, broken hearts, and sad romance. To the lilting accompaniment of the Portuguese *guitarra* (like a 12-string mandolin), the singer longs for what's been lost. While generally sad, fado can also be jaunty ... but in a nostalgic way.

Fado has become one of Lisbon's favorite late-night tourist traps, but it can still be a great experience. The Alfama has a few famous touristy fado bars, but the Baírro Alto is better (and safer late at night). Wander around Rua Diario de Noticias and neigh- boring streets either for a late dinner (after 22:00) or later for just drinks and music. Homemade "fado tonight" *(fado esta noite)* signs in Portuguese are good news, but even a restaurant filled with tourists can come with good food and fine fado. Prices for a fado performance vary greatly. Many have a steep cover charge, while others just want you to buy a meal. Any place recommended by a hotel has a bloated price for the kickback.

Fado in Baírro Alto: **Canto do Camões,** run by friendly English-speaking Gabriel, is my favorite. It's a great value, with good food, music, and an honest style of business (open at 20:00, music from 21:00 until around 01:00, €22-or-more meal required, after 22:00 €11 minimum if seats are available, CC, Travessa da Espera 38, from Rua Misericordia, go 2.5 blocks west on Tra- vessa da Espera, call ahead to reserve, tel. 213-465-464, e-mail: canto.do.camoes@clix.pt). The meal is punctuated with sets of three fado songs from different singers. For a snack, a good vintage port goes nicely with a plate of *queijo da serra* (sheep cheese) and *pancetta* (salt-cured ham). Relax, spend some time, and close your eyes or make eye contact with the singer. Let the music and wine collaborate.

Restaurante Adega do Ribatejo is a dark, homey place crowded with locals who enjoy open-mike fado nightly (except Sunday) from around 8:30. This is just around the corner from Gabriel's Canto do Camões—less touristy but less of a "show." This place really is an adventure—a fado dinner with the lights off (€15 meals, Mon–Sat from 19:00, Rua Diario de Noticias 23, tel. 213-468-343).

Fado in the Alfama: **Parreirinha de Alfama** is a cozy, 15- table place known for its owner, singer Argentina Santos, who also does the cooking. People usually eat around 20:30 or 21:00, and Tina starts singing about 21:30 and ends around 1:00. For just music and a drink you're welcome—with a €10 minimum—after 23:00 (open nightly, no cover charge for fado, just have dinner—around €15, and drinks, CC, Beco do Espirito Santo 1, with back to fado museum on Largo do Chafariz de Dentro, Parreirinha is at 2 o'clock, 20 meters up a little alley, take right fork, tel. 218-868-209).

Club de Fado is a big, bustling, touristy place with good food and good fado nightly around the corner from the cathedral (€30 dinners, 20:30 serving meals, 21:30 music starts, reservations smart, CC, Rua São João da Praça 94, tel. 218-882-604).

▲▲▲**Portuguese Bullfight**—The bullring, which was closed for renovation in 2002, will likely reopen in 2004. If you always felt sorry for the bull, this is Toro's Revenge—in a Portuguese bullfight, the matador is brutalized along with the bull. After an exciting equestrian prelude in which the horseman (*cavaleiro*) skillfully plants barbs in the bull's back while trying to avoid the padded horns, a colorfully clad eight-man suicide squad (called a *forcado*) enters the ring and lines up single file facing the bull. With testosterone sloshing everywhere, the leader prompts the bull to charge—slapping his knees and yelling *toro!*—and then braces himself for a collision that can be heard all the way up in the cheap seats. As he hangs onto the bull's head, his buddies then pile on, trying to wrestle the bull to a standstill. Finally, one guy hangs on to el toro's tail and "water-skis" behind him. Unlike at the Spanish *corrida*, the bull is not killed in front of the crowd at the Portuguese *tourada* (but it is killed later).

Given that Lisbon's bullring is closed for renovation, you'll most likely see a bullfight in nearby Cascais or on the Algarve (Easter–Oct, flyers at TI and in hotels). When Lisbon's bullring reopens, fights will again be held on Thursday at 22:00 mid-June through September (tickets €10–50). The ring is small; there are no bad seats. To sit nearly at ringside, try the cheapest *bancada* seats, on the generally half-empty and unmonitored main floor (Metro: Campo Pequeno).

Important note: Half the fights are simply Spanish-type *corridas* without the killing. For the real slam-bam Portuguese-style fight, confirm that there will be *grupo de forcados*. Tickets are nearly always available at the door (no surcharge, tel. 217-932-143 to confirm). For a 10 percent surcharge you can buy them at the green ABEP kiosk (also sells concert and movie tickets) at the southern end of Praça dos Restauradores.

Movies—In Lisbon, unlike in Spain, most films are in the original language with subtitles. (That's one reason the Portuguese speak better English than the Spanish.) Many of Lisbon's theaters are classy, complete with assigned seats and ushers. Check the newspaper for what's playing. Or drop by the ABEP kiosk (see "Portuguese Bullfight," above), where a list of all the movies playing in town is taped to a side window (on the left).

Sleeping in Lisbon
(€1 = about $1, country code: 351)
Sleep Code: **S** = Single, **D** = Double/Twin, **T** = Triple, **Q** = Quad,
b = bathroom, **s** = shower only, **CC** = Credit Cards accepted,
no CC = Credit Cards not accepted, **SE** = Speaks English,
NSE = No English. Breakfast is included unless otherwise noted.

To help you easily sort through these listings, I've divided
the rooms into three categories, based on the price for a standard
double room with bath during high season:

Higher Priced—Most rooms more than €115.
Moderately Priced—Most €115 or less.
Lower Priced—Most rooms €60 or less.

With a few exceptions, cheaper hotels downtown feel like
Lisbon does downtown: tired and well-worn. Singles cost nearly
the same as doubles. Addresses such as 26-3 stand for building #26,
third floor (which is fourth floor in American terms). If the minibar
is noisy, unplug it. For hotel locations, see map on page 338.

Be sure to book in advance if you'll be in Lisbon during its
festival—Festas de Lisboa—the last three weeks of June, when
parades, street parties, concerts, and fireworks draw crowds to
the city. Conventions can clog Lisbon at any time.

Sleeping in the Center
Central as can be, the Baixa district bustles with lots of shops, traffic, people, street musicians, pedestrian areas, and urban intensity.

HIGHER PRICED
On Rossio Square: The central **Hotel Metropole,** which keeps
its 1920s style throughout its 36 rooms, is elegant. While a bit overpriced, you're paying for its prime location. The smaller back rooms
are quieter (Sb-€130–140, Db-€150–170, includes breakfast buffet,
CC, air-con, elevator, Rossio 30, tel. 213-219-030, fax 213-469-166,
www.almeidahotels.com, e-mail: metropole@almeidahotels.com).

On Praça dos Restauradores: Hotel Avenida Palace—the
most characteristic five-star splurge in town—was built with the
Rossio Station in 1892 to greet big-shot travelers back when trains
were new and this was the only station in town. The lounges are
sumptuous, dripping with chandeliers, and the 82 rooms mix
old-time elegance with modern comforts (Sb-€185, Db-€205,
superior Db-€230, more expensive suites, includes breakfast,
CC, air-con, elevator, laundry service, free parking but few spaces,
hotel's sign is on square, but entrance is at Rua 1 de Dezembro
123, tel. 213-218-100, fax 213-422-884, www.hotel-avenida-palace
.pt, e-mail: hotel.av.palace@mail.telepac.pt). Same-day drop-ins
can save 25 percent in slow times.

Orion Eden Apartment Hotel rents 134 slick and modern compact apartments (with small kitchens) and has a rooftop swimming pool and terrace with city and river views. The building used to be a 1930s cinema, hence the Art Deco architecture and the slightly pie-shaped rooms. Perfectly located at the Rossio end of Avenida da Liberdade, this is a clean, quiet pool of modernity amid the ramshackle charm of Lisbon and an intriguing—though not cheap—option for groups or families of four (Db-studio-€125, 2-bedroom apartment with bed-and–sofa bed combo that can sleep 4 people-€180, breakfast-€8.50, CC, air-con, elevator, Praça dos Restauradores 24, tel. 213-216-600, fax 213-216-666, e-mail: aparthoteledcn@viphotels.com).

MODERATELY PRICED

Near Praça da Figueira: The **Hotel Lisboa Tejo** (pron. LEEZH-boah TAY-zhoo) is an oasis, with 58 comfortable rooms and an attentive and welcoming staff (Sb-€70–80, Db-€80–90, prices vary according to room size, 10 percent discount with this book, includes buffet breakfast, CC, air-con, laundry service, elevator, Poço do Borratém 4, from southeast corner of Praça da Figueira, walk 1 block down Rua Dos Condes de Monsanto and turn left, tel. 218-866-182, fax 218-865-163, e-mail: hotellisboatejo@evidenciagrupo.com).

Hotel Mundial is a massive four-star hotel overlooking a park-like square. It has 255 plush business-class rooms, doormen, revolving doors, lots of tour groups, and a recommended top-floor Varanda restaurant—with superb city views, especially at night (small Db-€93, big Db-€115, includes breakfast, CC, air-con, free parking, 1 block northeast of Praça da Figueira, Rua D. Duarte 4, tel. 218-842-000, fax 218-842-110, e-mail: mundial.hot@mail.telepac.pt).

LOWER PRICED

On or Near the "Eating Lane" and Rossio Square: Pensão Residencial Gerês, a good budget bet downtown, has 20 bright, basic, cozy rooms with older plumbing. The pension lacks the dingy smokiness that pervades Lisbon's cheaper hotels (S-€40, Sb-€50, D-€45, Db-€50–60, Tb-€75–90, high-end prices June–Oct, no breakfast, CC, Calçada do Garcia 6, uphill a block off the northeast corner of Rossio, tel. 218-810-497, fax 218-882-006, Nogueira family speaks some English).

Residencial Florescente rents 72 rooms on the "eating lane," a thriving pedestrian street a block off Praça dos Restauradores. It's an Old World slumber mill with narrow halls but comfortable and clean rooms (Sb-€40, Db-€45, Db/twin-€50, Tb-€60, includes

Lisbon Hotels

1 Hotel Metropole
2 Hotel Avenida Palace
  & Orion Eden Apt. Hotel
3 Hotel Lisboa Tejo
4 Hotel Mundial
5 Pensão Gerês
6 Residencial Florescente
7 Albergaria Insulana
8 Pensao Aljubarrota
9 To Hotel Lisboa Plaza & Pensão
  Residencial 13 da Sorte
10 To Hotel Britania & Ibis Hotels
11 Residencia Roma
12 To Hotel da Torre

breakfast, CC, air-con, Rua Portas S. Antão 99, tel. 213-463-517, fax 213-427-733, SE).

On Rua da Assuncão: The **Albergaria Residencial Insulana,** on a pedestrian street, is professional—dark, masculine, and a bit smoky—with 32 quiet and comfortable rooms (Sb-€50, Db-€55, extra bed-€10, includes breakfast, CC, elevator, air-con, Rua da Assuncão 52, tel. 213-423-131, fax 213-428-924, www.insulana.cjb.net, e-mail: insulana@netc.pt, SE).

Pensão Aljubarrota is a fine value if you can handle the long climb up four floors (nearly 80 steps), narrow hallways, and bubbly black-vinyl flooring. Once you're on top, you'll find small, rustically furnished, ramshackle rooms with cute balconies from which to survey the Rua Augusta scene (2-night minimum stay, S-€24, D-€38, Ds-€45, big Ds-€50, T-€58, 10 percent discount with cash and this book, further discount for 3-night stays, all but singles have balconies, CC, Rua da Assuncão 53-4, tel. & fax 213-460-112, Malik, Soraia, and lovely Rita SE).

Sleeping along Avenida da Liberdade

HIGHER PRICED

These listings are a 10-minute walk or short Metro ride from the center. The following two places, jointly owned, offer a deal in July and August: Free entrance to Lisbon's museums for guests who stay at least three nights.

Hotel Lisboa Plaza, a four-star gem, is a spacious and plush mix of traditional style with bright-pastel modern elegance. It offers all the comforts, snappy polite service, and a free glass of port with this book (Sb-€130–154, Db-€146–170, Tb-€180–210, the higher prices apply March–June and Sept–Oct, larger "superior" rooms cost 20 percent more, buffet breakfast-€12.50, CC, air-con, laundry service, nonsmoking floor, parking-€9/day, well located on a quiet street off busy Avenida da Liberdade, a block from Metro: Avenida at Travessa do Salitre 7, from Metro, walk downhill and turn right at Salitre, tel. 213-218-218, fax 213-471-630, www.heritage.pt, e-mail: plaza.hotels@heritage.pt).

Hotel Britania maintains its 1940s-Art-Deco feel throughout its 30 spacious rooms, offering a clean and professional haven on a quiet street one block off Avenida da Liberdade. Run by the Lisboa Plaza folks (above), it offers the same four-star standards for the same prices—and also a free glass of port upon check-in with this book (air-con, elevator, laundry service, nonsmoking floor, free street parking or €9/day in next-door garage, Rua Rodrigues Sampaio 17, Metro: Avenida, from Metro stop, walk uphill on boulevard, turn right on Rua Manuel de Jesus Coelho and take first left, tel. 213-155-016, fax 213-155021, www.heritage.pt, e-mail: britania.hotel@heritage.pt).

LOWER PRICED

Residencia Roma, a sweet little place a block off busy Avenida da Liberdade and two blocks up the street from the Rossio Station, has 24 comfortable rooms and a secure feeling (Sb-€42, Db-€55, extra bed-€13, prices 10 percent higher July–Oct, includes breakfast, CC, air-con, back rooms quieter, Travessa da Gloria 22-A, tel. 213-460-558, call to reserve then send fax with CC number and expiration date, tel. & fax 213-460-557, e-mail: res.roma@mail.telepac.pt). Some rooms have a kitchen (at no extra cost); breakfast is not included if you use the kitchen.

Pensão Residencial 13 da Sorte is simple but cheery, with 22 doll-house rooms and bright tiles throughout (Sb-€40, Db-€54, Tb-€60, no breakfast, CC, 10 percent discount for 5 nights, elevator, just off Avenida da Liberdade near the Spanish Embassy at Rua do Salitre 13, 10-min walk from center, 50 meters from Metro: Avenida, tel. 213-539-746, fax 213-531-851, friendly Alexandra SE).

Sleeping away from the Center

MODERATELY PRICED
In Belém: For modern comfort on the edge of town, consider **Hotel da Torre,** which offers 59 rooms next to the monastery (Sb-€73, Db-€85, request the newly renovated rooms—a better value, includes breakfast, CC, air-con, elevator, double-paned windows; facing monastery, it's on the street to the right, Rua dos Jerónimos 8, tel. 213-616-940, fax 213-616-946, e-mail: hoteldatorre.belem@mail.telepac.pt).

LOWER PRICED
Hotel Ibis—Two Ibis hotels offer plain, modern comforts with no character and no stress for a good price in soulless areas away from the center but handy to Metro stations. Each has cookie-cutter rooms, nonsmoking floors, air-conditioning, and €4 breakfasts: **Ibis Saldanha** (Sb/Db-€58, CC, Avenida Casal Ribeiro 23, 2-min walk from Metro: Saldanha, tel. 213-191-690, fax 213-191-699, www.ibishotel.com) and **Ibis Lisboa-Centro** (Sb/Db-€54, CC, next to Metro: Praça de Espanha, Avenida Jose Malhoa, tel. 217-235-700, fax 217-235-701, www.ibishotel.com).

Eating in Lisbon
One dinner of your stay in Lisbon should be accompanied by a fado performance. Several good options for this musical dinner are listed under "Nightlife," above.

Eating between the Castle and the Alfama Viewpoint
(These are listed in order from the castle to the viewpoint.)
Arco Do Castello, an eight-table Indo-Portuguese restaurant, dishes up delicious fish and shrimp curries (how spicy is up to you) from Goa, a former Portuguese colony in India. Top your €10 meal off with a shot of the Goan firewater, *feni*, made from cashews (Mon–Sat 12:30–24:00, closed Sun, CC, just across from ramp leading into castle, Rua Chão da Feira 25, tel. 218-876-598).
Largo do Contador Mor is a wispy cobbled square a block

above the Miradouro de Santa Luzia and a block below the castle with two eateries: **A Tasquinha Restaurante,** with great outdoor seating at the top of the square, is touristy with marginal service but beautifully located and serves fine plates of grilled sardines (*sardinhas assadas*-€7.50, Mon–Sat 12:00–15:00 & 19:00–24:00, closed Sun, setting better than the food, Largo do Contador Mor 5, tel. 218-876-899). Eat fast, cheap, and healthy at **Comidas de Santiago,** a little salad bar with great summer gazpacho (choose 2 salads on small plate for €2.60 or 4 on big plate for €4.30, understand your bill, daily 11:00–18:00, Largo do Contador Mor 21, tel. 218-875-805).

For a quality seafood feast, consider dining high in the Alfama at the **Farol de Santa Luzia** restaurant (€14 fixed-price *menu turistico,* Mon–Sat 12:00–15:00 & 19:00–24:00, closed Sun, CC, Largo Santa Luzia 5, across from Santa Luzia viewpoint terrace, no sign but a window full of decals, tel. 218-863-884).

To mix some adventure in with your sardines, walk past Portas do Sol and follow the trolley tracks along Rua da São Tome to a square called Largo Rodrigues Freitas where you'll find **Nossa Churrasqueira**—busy feeding chicken, sardines, and cod on rickety tables to finger-lickin' locals with meager budgets (Tue–Sun 12:00–22:00, closed Mon). This neighborhood, a gritty chunk of pre-earthquake Lisbon, is full of interesting eateries. Brighten a few dark bars. Have an aperitif, taste the *branco seco* (local dry white wine). Make a friend, pet a chicken, ponder the graffiti, and pick at the humanity ground between the cobbles.

Seafood on the Harborfront
Jardim do Marisco is a big, bright, and thriving place on the waterfront immediately below the Alfama in a small modern dock mall, Doca Jardim do Tobaco. Survey the seafood as you enter. The menu is a verbal aquarium of shellfish—easy in English. Cockles and barnacles (*percebes*) are sold by the 100-gram unit (try 100 grams of barnacles, but get eating instructions from your waiter). Be sure to specify how much you want (a quarter-pound is about 200 grams). You can eat dressy on one side or casual and cheaper on the other (open daily until late when it's most lively, Doca Jardim do Tabaco, Ave Infante Dom Henrique, tel. 218-824-242). The same mall also has an Italian place, and if you're looking for red meat, a Brazilian place upstairs.

Eating in Bairro Alto
Lisbon's "high town" is full of small, fun, and cheap places. Just off São Roque's Square you'll find the inexpensive, basic **Casa Trans-Montana** (Mon–Sat 12:00–15:00& 19:00–22:00, Sun

Lisbon Restaurants

1 Arco do Castello
2 A Tasquinha Rest. & Comidas de Santiago
3 Largo Santa Luzia
4 Nossa Churrasqueira
5 Jardin do Marisco
6 Casa Trans-Montana
7 Cervejaria da Trindade
8 Travessa de Santo Antão
9 Casa Do Alentejo
10 Casa Suica
11 Café Pic-Nic

12 Armazens do Chiado shopping center
13 Rest. Beira-Gare
14 Terreiro do Paco
15 Rua dos Correeiros
16 Pingo Doce
17 Varanda de Lisboa
18 To Cerevejaria Ribadouro
19 Canto Camões Fado
20 Rest. Adega do Ribatejo
21 Parreirinha de Alfama
22 Club de Fado

19:00–22:00, down the steps of Calcada do Duque at #43). The bright and touristy **Cervejaria da Trindade,** a Portuguese-style beer hall, is full of historic tiles, seafood, and tourists. It's over-priced and in all the guidebooks, but people enjoy the bright and boisterous old-time atmosphere (€15 meals, confirm prices, daily 12:00–24:00, liveliest 20:00–22:00, closed holidays, CC, air-con, courtyard, a block down from São Roque at Rua Nova da Trindade 20C, tel. 213-423-506). They have five Portuguese beers on tap—Sagres is the standard lager. Preta Sagres is a good dark beer. Bohemia is sweet and with more alcohol. Light meals and snacks are served at the bar and in the front. You'll find many less-touristed restaurants deeper into the Baírro Alto on the other (west) side of Rua Misericordia. See "Fado," under "Nightlife," above, for the best option.

Eating in and near Rossio

Rua das Portas de Santo Antão is Lisbon's "eating lane"—a galaxy of eateries with good seafood (off the northeast corner of Rossio Square). The place has pushy waiters and is very touristy but lively with happy eaters and fun to browse. For cheap, tasty chicken and fries, find the small side street, Travessa de Santo Antão, where three restaurants—**Rei da Brasa, Rei dos Frangos,** and **Restaurante Machaco**—all crank out simple, decent meals inside or streetside. **Casa do Alentejo,** specializing in Alentejo cuisine, fills an old ballroom on the second floor of a building that's a cultural and social center for people from the traditionalist southern province of Portugal (see jokes in Évora chapter, page 378) living in Lisbon (2-course special of the day-€11, daily 12:00–15:00 & 19:00–22:00, slip into closed-looking building at Rua das Portas de Santo Antão 58 and climb the stairs, tel. 213-469-231). While the food is mediocre, the ambience is fabulous. For a full-bodied Alentejo red wine, go with the Borba.

 Casa Suíça (pron. swee-sah) is a bright, modern, air-conditioned place popular with locals because it's classy but affordable and free of riff-raff. They serve more than pastry—try the light meals, salads, and fruit cups (daily 7:00–21:00, inexpensive at the bar, reasonable at tables, inside or outside overlooking your choice of both Rossio and Praça da Figueria squares). Across the Rossio, **Café Pic-Nic** is a lively diner—a little more lowbrow—for breakfast or a light meal, people-watching on the sidewalk.

 Armazens do Chiado Shopping Center has a sixth-floor food circus with few tourists in sight, offering a huge selection of fun eateries from traditional Portuguese to Chinese (daily about 10:00–23:30, between the low and high towns, between Rua Garrett and Rua Assuncão, from the low town find the inconspicuous elevator at Rua do Crucifixo 89 next to the Chiado Metro entrance). Some of the mall's eateries are actual restaurants (that get quiet from about 15:00–18:00); others are smaller fast-food counters that share a common eating area and serve all day. **Chimarrão,** a Brazilian place, offers an impressive self-serve pay-by-the-weight salad-and-meat buffet with tropical fruits and desserts and juices. This is where healthy eaters assemble the plate of their dreams—by far the best vegetarian and fruity place I found. Study the exotic fruit sheet on the table. On the same floor you'll find **Loja das Sopas,** offering hearty soups with six €4 menus (find a table in the food circus nearby), and **Café de Roma** for a great variety of fancy coffee drinks.

For cod and vegetables prepared faster than a Big Mac and served with more energy than a soccer team, stand or sit at **Restaurant Beira-Gare** (a greasy-spoon diner in front of Rossio train station at the end of Rua 1 de Dezembro, Mon–Sat 6:30–24:00, closed Sun). Their house-special pork sandwich is *bifane no pão.*

Terreiro do Paco is a dressy new place right on Praça do Comércio serving traditional Portuguese cuisine in an elegant modern setting and getting rave reviews from locals (€20–40 meals, Mon–Sat 13:00–15:00 & 20:00–24:00, closed Sun, air-con, CC, reservations smart, next to Lisboa TI on Praça do Comércio, tel. 210-312-850).

The Rossio's Rua dos Correeiros is lined with competitive restaurants, lively and fun for lunch but dead at dinner. Walk the street and determine the prevailing menu of the day. If it's the same fish, that's what was fresh at the market today and it should be good. The chain of little **Ca das Sandes** sandwich shops, found here on Correeiros and scattered about town, offer healthy sandwiches that you design Subway-style, salads, and usually outdoor seating (daily 9:00–20:00). **Pingo Doce** is a fine supermarket one block southwest of Rossio (daily 8:30–21:00, kitty-corner from a Ca das Sandes shop, on Rua 1 de Dezembro and Calçada do Carmo).

For a splurge with a view, consider **Varanda de Lisboa,** the restaurant on the top floor of the recommended Hotel Mundial. Dressy locals enjoy the beautifully presented food, live piano music, and a commanding view of floodlit Lisbon (allow about €25 per person with wine, daily 12:30–15:00 & 19:30–22:00, CC, reserve in advance for dinner, particularly Fri–Sat nights, tel. 218-842-000).

Up Avenida da Liberdade: Cervejaria Ribadouro is a popular splurge with locals, for quality meat and shellfish (€15 meals, daily 12:00–24:00, Avenida da Liberdade 155, at intersection with Rua do Salitre, Metro: Avenida, tel. 213-549-411). Note that seafood prices are listed by the kilogram; the waiter will help you determine the cost of a portion. To limit the cost, actually write down the number of grams you want. For a fun, quick meal or snack anytime, order 100 grams of *percebes* (barnacles) at the bar with toasted bread and a little beer.

Transportation Connections—Lisbon

By train to: Madrid (1/day, overnight 22:05–8:25, first class-€65, second class-€51, ticket and bed: €70 in quad, €90 in double, €128 in single; discount with railpass—for example, about €35 for a bed in quad; Rossio station can sell these, no CC; train departs from Santa Apolónia, station takes CC), **Paris** (1/day, 18:05–16:25, 21.5 hrs, departs Santa Apolónia), **Évora** (5/day, 2.5–3.5 hrs, departs Barreiro, 3 are direct, 2 require transfer in Casa Branca; bus is faster), **Lagos** (4/day, 3.5 hrs, departs Barreiro, likely transfer in Tunes), **Faro** (2 fast trains/day, 3.5 hrs, departs Barreiro), **Coimbra** (hrly, 2–2.5 hrs, departs Santa Apolónia), **Nazaré Valado** (4/day, 2.5–3.5 hrs, departs Rossio, transfer in Cacém), **Sintra** (4/hr, 45 min, departs Rossio). Train info: tel. 218-884-025.

To Salema: Both the bus and train take about five hours from Lisbon to Lagos (details in Algarve chapter). Trains from Lisbon to the south coast leave from the Barreiro station across the Tejo from downtown. Boats shuttle train travelers from Praça do Comércio to the Barreiro train station, with several departures hourly (€1, 30-min ride; note that schedule times listed are often when the boat sails, not when train departs). The 23:10–6:28 overnight train, while no fun, allows you to enjoy the entire day on the Algarve.

By bus to: Coimbra (12/day, 2.5 hrs, €8), **Nazaré** (6/day, 2 hrs), **Fatima** (10/day, 2 hrs), **Alcobaça** (5/day, 2 hrs), **Évora** (12/day, 2 hrs), **Lagos** (8/day, 5 hrs, €12, easier than train, must book ahead, get details at TI), **Madrid** (2/day, 8 hrs, 9:30–19:00 or 20:30–06:30, €38, Intercentro Lines), **Sevilla** (5–6 buses/week, departs Tue–Sun at 7:00, off-season not on Wed, 7 hrs, €32 one-way, buy ticket at station, reservations not necessary, Eurolines, www.eurolines.es). All buses leave from Lisbon's Arco do Cego bus station (Metro: Saldanha, tel. 213-159-277).

Flying: You can generally buy a plane ticket to Madrid on short notice for about €150. Flying one-way on a round-trip is a little cheaper.

Driving in Lisbon

Driving in Lisbon is big-city crazy. If you enter from the north, a series of boulevards takes you into the center. Navigate by following signs to *Centro*, Avenida da República, Praça dos Marques de Pombal, Avenida da Liberdade, Praça dos Restauradores, Rossio, and Praça do Comércio. Consider hiring a taxi (cheap) to lead you to your hotel. If you are turning in your car upon arrival in Lisbon, consider driving to the airport (rent-a-car turn-in clearly signposted, no extra expense to drop it here, very helpful TI open late) and ride a taxi for €8 sweat-free to your hotel. If starting your trip in Lisbon, don't rent a car until you're on your way out.

There are many safe underground pay parking lots (follow the blue P signs), but they get more expensive by the hour and can cost €33 per day (at the most central Praça dos Restauradores).

NEAR LISBON: SINTRA, CABO DA ROCA, CASCAIS, AND ESTORIL

For centuries, Portugal's aristocracy considered Sintra the natural escape from Lisbon. Now tourists do, too. Climb through the Versailles of Portugal, the Pena Palace; romp along the ruined ramparts of a deserted Moorish castle on a neighboring hilltop; and explore the rugged and picturesque westernmost tip of Portugal at Cabo da Roca. You can also mix and mingle with the jet set (or at least press your nose against their windows) at the resort towns of Cascais or Estoril.

Planning Your Time

These sights make fine day trips from Lisbon—and there are two bullrings out here (at Cascais and Estoril). Without a car, I'd skip Cabo da Roca and do Sintra as a side trip from Lisbon. For a slam-bam swing around the peninsula, consider a Carris bus tour (€40, 4.5 hrs).

By car, the 110-kilometer circular excursion (Lisbon–Belém– Sintra–Cabo da Roca–Cascais–Lisbon) makes for a fine day, but traffic congestion around Sintra can mess up your schedule. Follow the coast from Praça do Comércio west, under the bridge to Belém. Continue west to just before Cascais, where Sintra (11 km) is signposted. Sintra itself is far easier by train than by car from Lisbon. Consider not picking up your rental car until after Sintra.

Drivers eager for beach time can leave Lisbon, do the Sintra circle, and drive directly to the Algarve that evening (4 hrs from Lisbon). From Sintra/Cascais, get on the freeway heading for Lisbon and exit at the Sul Ponte A2 sign, which takes you over the 25th of April Bridge and south on A2.

SINTRA

For centuries, Sintra—just 18 kilometers northwest of Lisbon— was the summer escape of Portugal's kings. Those with money and a desire to be close to royalty built their palaces in lush gardens in the same neighborhood. Byron called this bundle of royal fancies and aristocratic dreams a "glorious Eden," and today it's mobbed with tourists. You can easily spend a day in this lush playground of castles, palaces, sweeping coastal views, and exotic gardens.

Sights near Lisbon

Tourist Information: Sintra has two TIs, a small one in the train station, and a larger TI a block off the main square (both open daily June–Sept 9:00–20:00, Oct–May 9:00–19:00, tel. 219-231-157 or 219-241-623, www.cm-sintra.pt). Pick up a free map, the helpful Sintra guide, and a schedule for the #434 shuttle bus to the sights. The TI can arrange *quartos* (rooms in private homes, Db-€30–50) for overnighters.

Arrival in Sintra: Arriving by train, stop by the station TI for a map. To reach the center by bus, exit station right, and cross the street to get to bus stop #434 (see "Getting Around," below). By car, park it. The main lot is at Volta do Duche, near the center. A small lot is next to the train station. The most central free parking is in the valley below town—Rio do Porto.

Planning Your Time

Day Trip from Lisbon by Train: Catch an early Lisbon-to-Sintra train (4/hr from Rossio station, 45 min—it's the last stop in both directions so relax or pass the time stretching, using the train car as a gym). If you like modern art, visit Sintra's new Museum of Modern Art (near train station). From the station, catch shuttle bus #434 (€3.30, valid all day) to the main square, and visit the National Palace. Catch bus #434 up to Pena Palace. Have a picnic lunch in Pena Gardens (see below for details). Tour the palace. Walk down to the Moorish castle and explore. Hike from the

Moorish castle into town (30-min steep, wooded path; fork in path leads down from within the castle grounds—get instructions and map at entry). Catch train back to Lisbon for dinner. Note that the Pena Palace and Museum of Modern Art are closed Monday, and the National Palace is closed Wednesday.

Getting around Sintra

Cars are the curse of Sintra. Traffic and parking can be terrible. But public transportation puts the "glorious" back into Byron's Eden. Bus #434 loops together all the important stops: the train station (stop is across street from station); old town/TI/National Palace (stop is at TI); Moorish ruins; Pena Palace; and back to the station (3/hr, 2/hr in winter, €3.30 ticket good for 24 hours, buy from driver; first bus starts at 10:20 from station, last one leaves station at 17:15, entire circuit takes 30 min). It's an enjoyable level 10-minute walk from the station to the old town and National Palace. Taxis don't use a meter but have set fares (e.g., from town center or train station to Pena Palace-€8). If you decide (probably regrettably) to drive to the sights, you'll take a one-way winding loop and be encouraged to park "as soon as you can" or risk having to drive the huge loop again.

Sights—Sintra

▲▲**National Palace (Palacio Nacional)**—While going back to Moorish times, most of what you'll see is from the 15th-century reign of João I and later Manueline work. This oldest surviving royal palace in Portugal is still used for official receptions. Housing royalty for 500 years until 1910, it's fragrant with history (€3, free with LisboaCard, Thu–Tue 10:00–17:30, last entry 17:00, closed Wed, no photos; it's the white, Madonna-bra building in the town center, a 10-min walk from train station).

The palace is a one-way romp with little information provided. As you tour the place, notice the following:

Swan Room: This first room is the palace's banquet room. A king's daughter—who loved swans—was married into a royal house in Belgium. He missed the princess so much that he decorated the ceiling with her favorite animal.

Courtyard: This was a fortified medieval palace, so rather than fancy gardens outside, it has a stay-awhile courtyard within its protective walls. Notice the unique chimneys. Hans Christian Andersen said they look like two grand bottles of champagne. I disagree. Whatever they look like, they give the kitchen a marvelous open-domed feeling as you'll see at the end of your tour.

Magpie Room: King João I was caught kissing a lady-in-waiting by his queen. Frustrated by his court—abuzz with gossip—

Sintra

João had this ceiling painted with magpies. The 15th-century tiles are Moorish from Spain, brought in before the development of the famous, ubiquitous Portuguese tiles.

King's Bedroom: The king portrayed on the wall was a gung-ho medieval-type monarch who went to battle in Africa chasing the Moors even after they were chased out of Europe. He disappeared at age 18, leaving Portugal in unstable times with a distant heir who soon died. The throne passed to cousin King Philip II of Spain, leading to 60 years of Spanish rule (1580–1640). Note the ebony, silver, and painted copper headboard of the Italian Renaissance bed. The tiles in this room are considered the first Portuguese tiles—from the time of Manuel I. The corn-on-the-cob motif is a reminder of American discoveries. Wander through more rooms, upstairs, and through more rooms to the blue and gold . . .

Stag Room: This most-striking room in the palace honors Portugal's loyal nobility. Study the richly-decorated ceiling. The king's coat of arms at the top is surrounded by the coats of arms of his children, and below that, the coats of arms of all but one of Portugal's noble families. That family schemed a revolt and got only a blank niche. The Latin circling the room reads, "Honoring all the noble families who've been loyal to the king." The 18th-century tiles feature scenes that hang from the walls like tapestries. Enjoy the view—a lush garden-like land dotted with mansions of noble families who located here to be close to their king, the hill-capping castle, and the wide-open Atlantic. Believe it or not, you're in the westernmost room of the westernmost palace on the European continent.

Kitchen: With all the latest in cooking technology, the chef could roast an entire cow on the spit, keep his plates warm in the iron dish warmer (with drawers below for the charcoal), and get really dizzy by looking up and spinning around three times. OK, you can go now.

▲▲**Pena Palace (Palacio de Pena)**—This magical hilltop palace sits high above Sintra, a steep 15-minute hike above the ruined Moorish castle. In the 19th century, Portugal had a very romantic prince. German-born Prince Ferdinand was a contemporary and cousin of Bavaria's "Mad" King Ludwig (of Disney-esque Neuschwanstein Castle fame). Ferdinand was also a cousin of England's Prince Albert (Queen Victoria's husband). Flamboyant Ferdinand hired a German architect to build him a fantasy castle, mixing elements of German and Portuguese style. He ended up with a crazy neo-fortified casserole of Gothic, Arabic, Moorish, Disney, Renaissance, and Manueline architectural bits and decorative pieces (€5 for required park/palace combo-ticket, free with LisboaCard, Tue–Sun 10:00–18:30, closed Mon, last entry 45 min before closing, closes an hour early off-season, tel. 219-237-300). To avoid the very long uphill climb (and enjoy a free lift back down) catch the shuttle bus just inside the gate at the *Paragem* sign (€1.50 round-trip, departures every few minutes in fake vintage Lisbon trolley).

The palace, built in the mid-1800s, is so well preserved that it feels as if it's the day after the royal family fled Portugal in 1910 (during a popular revolt making way for today's modern republic). This gives the place a charming intimacy rarely seen in palaces. English descriptions throughout give meaning to the rooms. Here are the highlights.

Entry: Buy your ticket, cross the drawbridge that doesn't draw, and join an onion-domed world of tourists frozen in deep kneebends with their cameras cocked. Bags and cameras need to be checked. Stow your camera in a pocket or give it up. At the base of the stairs you'll see King Ferdinand, who built this castle from 1840 until 1885 when he died. While German, he was a romantic proponent of his adopted culture, doing much to preserve the architectural and artistic heritage of Portugal.

Courtyard: Note how the palace was built upon the arcaded remains of a ruined 16th-century monastery. In spite of its plushness, it retains the coziness of a bunch of small rooms gathered in two levels around this cloister.

King's Bedroom: The king enjoyed cutting-edge comforts, including the shower/tub imported from England—and even a telephone (you'll see the switchboard later). The palace is decorated in classic Romantic style—dark, heavy, and busy with collectables.

Queen's Bedroom and Dressing Room: Study the melancholy photos of Queen Emilia, King Charles, and their family in this room. The turn of the 20th century was a rocky time for Portugal's royal family. In 1908, after the queen's husband and eldest son were killed, Emilia fled to France. The palm frond on the headboard of her bed was from her last Palm Sunday Mass in Portugal. Poke around. If you lean you can see Emilia's toilet. And in the next room, what about that padded velvet bidet?

View Balcony: On the upper floor, enjoy a sweeping view from Lisbon to the mouth of the Tejo. Find Cristo Rei and the 25th of April bridge. The statue on the distant ridge honors the palace's architect. After the abundant kitchen, a view café welcomes peasants.

▲**Moorish Castle (Castelo dos Mouros)**—Sintra's thousand-year-old Moorish castle ruins, lost in an enchanted forest and alive with winds of the past, are a castle-lover's dream come true and a great place for a picnic with a panoramic Atlantic view. Though built by the Moors, the castle was taken by Christian forces in 1147. What you'll climb on today, while dramatic, was much restored in the 19th century. To get from Sintra to the ruins, hike three kilometers, taxi, or ride bus #434—see "Getting around Sintra," above (€3, or free if you enter by hiking up from the town, free flier includes English info and a rough map, daily 9:00–20:00, last entry at 19:00, closes an hour early in off-season).

▲**Sintra Museum of Modern Art: The Berardo Collection**—Modern art–lovers rave about this private collection, one of Iberia's best. The collection rotates, with 120 of its 800 pieces shown at any given time. The art is presented with thoughtful English descriptions for each section in hopes of giving the novice a better grip on post-1945 art (€3, Tue–Sun 10:00–18:00, closed Mon, 500 meters from train station, in Sintra's former casino on Avenida Heliodoro Salgado, exit right from station and go straight—for about 8 min, tel. 219-248-170, www.berardocollection.com).

Quinta da Regaleira—This neo-Manueline 1912 mansion and garden, with mystical and Masonic twists, was designed by an Italian opera-set designer for a wealthy but disgruntled monarchist two years after the royal family was deposed. The included and required two-hour English tour is mostly in the garden (as the palace is quite small) and can be longish unless you're into quirky Masonic esoteria (€10, by reservation only, 12 tours/day in summer, 4/day in winter, max 30 persons, book by calling 219-106-650 during these hours: Mon–Fri 9:30–13:00 & 14:30–19:00—if this is important to you, call several days in advance as the mansion is likely to be booked up; a 10-min walk from downtown Sintra, café, www.regaleira.pt). Ask a local to pronounce "Regaleira" for you.

Toy Museum—Just for fun, you can wander through a collection of several thousand old-time toys, from small soldiers, planes, cars, trucks, and old trikes to a dolls' attic upstairs. The 20th-century owner João Arbués Moreira started collecting toys when he was 14, and just never quit (€3, free with LisboaCard, Tue–Sun 10:00–18:00, closed Mon, Rua Visconde de Monserrate, 1 block in front of National Palace, tel. 219-242-171, www.museu-do-brinquedo.pt).

Monserrate—Just outside of Sintra is the wonderful garden of Monserrate. If you like tropical plants and exotic landscaping, a visit is time well spent (€3, daily 10:00–17:15, less in winter). Some say that the Pena Gardens (below the palace) are just as good as the more famous Monserrate.

Sleeping and Eating in Sintra
(€1 = about $1, country code: 351, zip code: 2710)
Casa Miradouro is a beautifully restored mansion from 1890. With six spacious, stylish rooms, an elegant lounge, castle and sea views, and a wonderful garden, it's a worthy splurge. The place is graciously run by Frederic, who speaks English with a Swiss accent (Sb-€80–108, Db-€90–120, priciest May–Sept, CC, nonsmoking rooms, closed Jan–Feb, street parking, Rua Sotto Major 55, from National Palace go past Hotel Tivoli Sintra and 400 meters downhill, note that it's a stiff uphill hike to return to center, tel. 219-235-900, fax 219-241-836, www.casa-miradouro.com, e-mail: mail@casa-miradouro.com).

Vila Marques, another elegant old mansion, is funkier but filled with pride. It has an eccentric-grandmotherly flair, hardwood floors, fine rooms, and a great garden with birds. It's 100 meters behind Hotel Tivoli and 200 meters from the National Palace (S-€30, D-€40, D/twin-€45, €5 more JuneSept, no sinks in rooms, the €75 Db rooms on the garden lack the character of the cheaper rooms actually in the mansion, no CC, Rua Sotto

Mayor 1, tel. 219-230-027, fax 219-241-155, Sra. Marques and her hard-working maid Maria NSE).

Dining in Sintra: The hardworking, tourist-friendly **Restaurant Regional de Sintra** feeds locals and tourists well (€13 meals, Thu–Tue 12:00–22:30, closed Wed, 200 meters from train station at Travessa do Municipio 2, exit station left, go downhill to the first square—far right corner, tel. 219-234-444).

A Quick Lunch: The touristy little cobbled lane Rua das Padarias is lined with charming shops and eateries. For a light lunch, try **Pastelaria Vila Velha** (Rua das Padarias 8, tel. 219-230-154). The venerable **Piriquita Tea House** calls itself an *"antiga fabrica de Queijadas"*—historic maker of tiny tasty cheese cakes (at the base of Rua das Padarias); it's a fine place for a sweet and coffee. For a bakery sandwich-to-go, stop by **Padarias Reunidas de Sintra,** across the square from the National Palace. Bus drivers and tour guides grab a quiet and cheap lunch in the homey, if a little bleak, **O Pelourinho Cafe** (homemade-style soups and salad, around corner from palace and main square, behind horse-drawn carriages at Calcada do Pelourinho 2, tel. 219-231-979). At the train station, Pizza Hut's salad bar is an easy place to get a cheap, healthy salad-to-go for a picnic in Sintra or the ride back to Lisbon,

Transportation Connections—Sintra
To: Lisbon's Rossio Station (4 trains/hr, 45 min, see "Transportation Connections—Lisbon," above, for details), **Cascais** (hourly buses also stop at Cabo da Roca, 45–60 min, bus stop at the Sintra train station, buy €2.80 ticket from driver).

CABO DA ROCA
Wind-beaten, tourist-infested Cabo da Roca is the westernmost point in Europe. It has a little shop, a café, and a tiny TI that sells a "proof of being here" diploma (daily 9:00–20:00). Nearby, on the road to Cascais, you'll pass a good beach for wind, waves, sand, and the chance to be the last person in Europe to see the sun set. For a desolate beach, drive to Praia Adraga (north of Cabo da Roca).

CASCAIS AND ESTORIL
Before the rise of the Algarve, these towns were the haunt of Portugal's rich and beautiful. Today they are quietly elegant, with noble old buildings, beachfront promenades, a bullring, a casino, and more fame than they deserve. Cascais is the more enjoyable of the two; it's not as rich and stuffy and has a cozy touch of fishing village, great seafood, and a younger, less-pretentious atmosphere (TI tel. 214-663-813). Both are an easy day trip from Lisbon (4 trains/hr, 40 min from Lisbon's Caís do Sodre station).

THE ALGARVE

The Algarve was once known as Europe's last undiscovered tourist frontier. But it's well discovered now, and if you go to the places featured in tour brochures, you'll find it much like Spain's Costa del Sol—paved, packed, and pretty stressful. But there are a few great beach towns left, mostly on the western tip, and this part of the Algarve is the south coast of any sun worshiper's dreams.

For some rigorous rest and intensive relaxation in a village where the tourists and the fishermen sport the same stubble, make sunny Salema your Algarve hideaway. It's just you, a beach full of garishly painted boats, your wrinkled landlady, and a few other globetrotting experts in lethargy. Nearby sights include Cape Sagres (Europe's "Land's End" and home of Henry the Navigator's famous navigation school) and the beach-party-jet-ski resort of Lagos. Or you could just work on a tan and see how slow you can get your pulse in sleepy Salema. If not now, when? If not you, who?

Planning Your Time

The Algarve is your vacation from your vacation. How much time it deserves depends upon how much time you have and how much time you need to recharge your solar batteries. On a three-week Iberian blitz, I'd give it three nights and two days. After a full day of sightseeing in Lisbon or Sevilla, I'd push it by driving four hours around dinnertime to gain an entirely free beach day. With two days, I'd spend one enjoying side trips to Cape Sagres and Lagos and another just lingering in Salema. The only other Algarve stop to consider is Tavira. (If you're visiting in winter, Tavira—which is lively year-round—makes a better stop than tiny Salema, which closes down.)

The Algarve

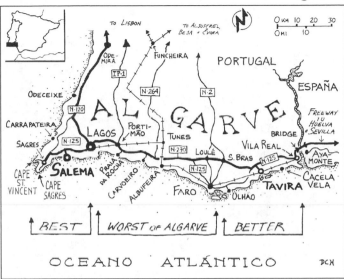

BEST | WORST of ALGARVE | BETTER

OCEANO · ATLÁNTICO

Getting around the Algarve

Trains and buses connect the main towns along the south coast (skimpy service on weekends). Buses take you west from Lagos, where trains don't go. The freeway—which covers the east half of the Algarve and will cover the west within a couple of years—makes driving quick and easy. (See "Route Tips for Drivers in the Algarve," at the end of this chapter.)

SALEMA

One bit of old Algarve magic still glitters quietly in the sun—Salema. It's at the end of a small road just off the main drag between the big city of Lagos and the rugged southwest tip of Europe, Cape Sagres. This simple fishing village, quietly discovered by British and German tourists, has a few hotels, time-share condos up the road, some hippies' bars with rock music, English and German menus, a classic beach—with a new, paved promenade, and endless sun.

Helpful Hints

Tourist Information: There's no TI in Salema, but the Horizonte Travel Agency and people in the bars, restaurants, and pensions have heard all the questions and are helpful. Online, see www.salema.info.

Salema

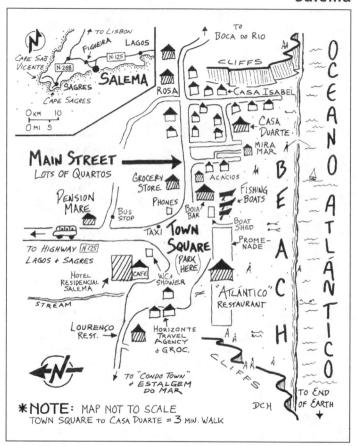

✳NOTE: MAP NOT TO SCALE
TOWN SQUARE TO CASA DUARTE = 3 MIN. WALK

Coastal Boat Tours: Local English-speaking guide Sebastian offers a two-hour scenic cruise along the coast. He gives a light commentary on the geology and the plant and bird life as he motors halfway to Cape Sagres and back. Trips include nipping into some cool blue natural caves. Morning trips are best for bird-watching. Kicking back and watching the cliffs glide by, I felt like I was scanning a super-relaxing gallery of natural art. Consider being dropped at (nude) Figueira Beach just before returning to Salema (it's a 20-min walk home to Salema—bring shoes, a picnic, and extra water). Easygoing and gentle Sebastian charges little more than what it costs to run his small boat (€15 per person, daily 10:30 and 13:30 June–Aug, 2–5 passengers, tel. 282-695-458, ask for Sebastian at beachside fishermen's hut or book his tour through Pensión Mare or Horizonte Travel Agency).

Travel Agency: Horizonte Travel Agency changes money at fair rates; posts bus and train schedules; sells long-distance bus tickets to Lisbon (same price as bus station); rents cars, mopeds, and mountain bikes; books hotels and flights (such as cheap stand-bys to Germany and Britain); offers weekly condo rentals in Salema; and runs all-day €36 jeep tours to the nature park on the southwest coast (open normally Mon–Sat 9:30–19:00, Sun 9:30–13:00; Oct–May closed at lunch and on Sun, CC, across stream from Hotel Residencial Salema, tel. 282-695-855, tel. 282-695-920; e-mail: horizonte.passeios.turis@mail.telepac.pt, Andrea and Barbel SE).

Changing Money: Salema may get its first ATM in 2003. Many places don't take credit cards. Bring lots of euros.

Taxi: Your hotel can arrange a taxi. Or call Jose direct at cellular 919-385-139. Jose and his wife Isabel have two cars and, for a price, are at your service: €15 to Lagos bus station, or €20 for a 75-minute quick, scenic tour of Cape Sagres/Cape St. Vincent with short stops and a commentary (this can be a great value when 2 couples team up to share the excursion); they may wait in Sagres for €7 an hour. For €225, you could taxi to Lisbon or Évora. You'll see Jose at the taxi stall in the center parking lot.

Salema Beach Bum's Quickie Tour

Salema has a split personality: The whitewashed old town is for locals, the other half was built for tourists. Locals and tourists pursue a policy of peaceful coexistence. Tourists laze in the sun while locals grab the shade.

Market action: Salema's flatbed truck market rolls in most mornings—one truck each for fish, fruit, and vegetables, and a five-and-dime truck for clothing and other odds and ends. The tooting horn of the fish truck wakes you at 8:00. The bakery trailer sells delightful fresh bread and "store-bought" sweet rolls each morning (about 8:00–11:00). And weekday afternoons around 14:30 the red mobile post office stops by.

Fishing scene: Salema is still a fishing village. While the fishermen's hut no longer hosts a fish auction, you'll still see the old-timers enjoying its shade, oblivious to the tourists, mending their nets and reminiscing about the old days when life was only fish and hunger. In the calm of summer, boats are left out on buoys. In the winter, the community-subsidized tractor earns its keep by hauling the boats ashore. (In pre-tractor days, such boat-hauling was a 10-man chore.) The pottery jars stacked every-where are octopus traps. Unwritten tradition allocates different

chunks of undersea territory to each Salema family. The traps
are tied about a meter apart in long lines and dropped offshore.
Octopi, thinking these would make a cozy place to set an ambush,
climb in and get ambushed. When the fishermen hoist them in,
they hang on—unaware they've made their final mistake.

Beach scene: Locals, knowing their tourist-based economy
sits on a foundation of sand, hope and pray that sand returns after
being washed away each winter. Some winters turn the beach into
a pile of rocks. Beach towns must provide public showers and
toilets, such as Salema's Balneario Municipal (daily 14:00–19:00
in summer, showers €1). The fountain in front of it is a reminder
of the old days. When water to the village was cut off, this was
always open. Locals claim the beach is safe for swimming. But
the water is rarely really warm.

On the west end of the beach, you can climb over the rocks
past tiny tide pools to the secluded Figuera Beach. While the old
days of black widows chasing topless Nordic women off the beach
are gone, nudism is still risqué today. If you go topless, do so
with discretion. Over the rocks and beyond the view of prying
eyes, Germans grin and bare it.

Community development: The whole peninsula (west of
Lagos) has been declared a natural park, and further development
close to the beach is forbidden. Salema will live with past mistakes,
such as the huge hotel in the town center that pulled some mysterious strings to go two stories over the height limit. Up the street is
a huge community of Club Med–type vacationers who rarely leave
their air-conditioned bars and swimming pools. Across the highway
a kilometer or two inland is an even bigger golfing resort with a
spa, pool, and tennis (worth exploring by car). The ramshackle
old village of Salema is less and less ramshackle—gradually being
bought by northern Europeans for vacation or retirement homes.

Salema after dark: Salema has several late-night bars, each
worth a visit. Consider a Salema pub crawl. Local drinks you might
want to try: *Armarguinha* is a sweet, likeable almond liqueur. *Licor
beirão* is Portuguese ameretto, a "double distillation of diverse
plants and aromatic seeds in accordance with a secret old formula."
Caipirinha (pron. kai-peer-een-ya), tasty and powerful, is made
of fermented Brazilian sugarcane. And *moscatel* is the local sweet
dessert wine.

The **Boia Bar** offers beachfront drinks and music. Guillerme
Duarte's **Atabua Bar** is the liveliest (across the street, famous
sangria). **A Aventura Bar** offers a pleasant atmosphere for sipping
drinks and sending e-mail (€4.50/hr, just past the Salema Market).
And, up the hill (next to Lourenço's restaurant), the on-again-off-
again **Carioca Bar** is a more bohemian-style hangout.

Sleeping in Salema
(€1 = about $1, country code: 351, zip code; 8650)

Sleep Code: **S** = Single, **D** = Double/Twin, **T** = Triple, **Q** = Quad,
b = bathroom, **s** = shower only, **CC** = Credit Cards accepted,
no CC = Credit Cards not accepted, **SE** = Speaks English,
NSE = No English. When a price range is given, the lowest is
the winter rate and the highest is the peak-season summer rate.

Salema is crowded July through mid-September. August is hor-
ribly crowded. The water is swimmable May, June, late September,
and October. I got a sunburn late last April. And the place is closed
down and dead in the winter. The town has three streets, five restaurants, several bars, a lane full of fisherfolk who happily rent out
rooms to foreign guests, and a circle of modern condo-type hotels,
apartments, and villas up the hillside. Parking is free and easy on
the street (beware of the No Parking signs near the bus stop).

For maximum comfort there's no need to look beyond John's
Pensión Mare. For economy and experience, go for the *quartos*
(rooms—usually with separate private entrances rented out of
homes; see www.salema.info).

MODERATELY PRICED: PENSIÓNES AND HOTELS

Pensión Mare, a blue-and-white building looking over the village
above the main road into town, is the best good, normal hotel
value in Salema (Sb-€33–38, Db-€45–60, Tb-€65–75, includes
good breakfast, 10 percent discount with this book and cash if
arranged discretely and in advance, CC, guests-only laundry
service €4 per kilo, Praia de Salema, Budens 8650-194, Algarve,
tel. 282-695-165, fax 282-695-846; the excellent Web site www
.algarve.co.uk has a virtual tour of every room and some good
Salema information). An easygoing Brit, John, runs this place,
offering seven comfortable rooms (see prices above), three fully
equipped apartments (Db-€50–75, breakfast not available), and
a tidy paradise. John will hold a room with a phone call and a
credit card. He also rents a gem of a fisherman's two-bedroom
cottage on the "*quartos* street" (Db-€75, Qb-€100) and Casa
Alegria, a colorful apartment with a splash of Santa Fe and a
fantastic view (about €80/night, sleeps up to 6, 7-night min).

Hotel Residencial Salema, the oversized hotel towering
crudely above everything else in town, is a good value if you
want a modern, comfortable room handy to the beach. Its 32
red-tiled rooms all have air-conditioning, balconies, and partial
views (Sb-€45–65, Db-€50–75, 10 percent discount with this
book, extra bed-30 percent more, includes breakfast, CC,
elevator, rents cars and mopeds, closed Nov–March, tel. 282-
695-328, fax 282-695-329, e-mail: hotel.salema@clix.pt, SE).

Estalagem Infante do Mar is a peaceful three-star resort hotel on a bluff high above the village. Its 30 rooms are plain but all have balconies and spectacular views (Sb-€40–60, Db-€45–80, the manager Carla offers a 10 percent discount with this book, extra bed-30 percent more, includes small breakfast, CC, pool, Internet access, laundry service, bar, restaurant, free parking, closed Nov–Feb, tel. 282-690-100, fax 282-690-109, www.infantedomar.com, mail@infantedomar.com, SE). It's a stiff 10-minute walk uphill from town. From the Hotel Residencial Salema, cross the bridge and then head up. Or ask for their free shuttlebus pick-up or drop-off.

LOWER PRICED: QUARTOS AND CAMPING

Quartos abound along the residential street (running left from the village center as you face the beach). Ask one of the locals at the waterfront or ask at the Boia Bar or Salema Market. Prices vary with the season, plumbing, and view, but if you're only staying one night, you're bad news (doubles-€25–45, forget breakfast and credit cards). Many places offer beachfront views. It's worth paying extra for *com vista* (view) rooms. Some apartments are bright and sprawling while some rooms are dark and musty. Few *quartos'* landladies speak English, but they're used to dealing with visitors. Many will clean your laundry for about €3 or so. If you're settling in for a while or are on a tight budget, park your bags and partner at a beachside bar and survey several places. Except for August weekends, there are always rooms available for those dropping in. Especially outside of July and August, prices can be soft.

Maria Helena and Jorge Ribeiro, a helpful young couple, rent two small, simple doubles (D-€30 all year, one has a tiny view) and a charming tree house–type apartment with a kitchen, fine view terrace, and view toilet for €40 (Rua dos Pescadores 83, tel. 282-695-289, SE).

Casa Duarte has five pleasant rooms (4 with views), a communal kitchenette, and two terraces (D-€25–35, €5 penalty for 1-night stays, tel. 282-695-206 or their English-speaking daughter Cristina at tel. 282-695-307; son Romeu, who owns the Salema Market, also SE). From "*quartos* street," turn right at the Clube Recreativo and then left on the paved path. Duarte's is #7, the first building on the right.

Isabel Bernardo rents two tidy rooms which share a WC/shower and terrace. One rooms sleeps four with a bunk (D-€25–35, at top of lane past Casa Duarte at Rua da Alegria 22, tel. 282-695-190, cellular 966-843-392, NSE).

Friendly **Rosa** rents a small double with a big terrace (Db-€35–40) and a comfortable apartment with balcony that can sleep two couples and a child. This is a super value at €50, worth the hike (near top of hill, 5-min walk from center, Rua dos Pescadores 18, tel. 282-695-255, NSE).

The **Acacio family** rents a humble ground-floor double (D-€25–30) and a fine upstairs apartment with kitchenette, balcony, and a great ocean view for up to four people (Db-€45, Tb-€50, Qb-€70, on "*quartos* street" at #91, tel. 282-695-473, Silvina NSE). She pouts if you're staying only one night.

Campers (who don't underestimate the high tides) sleep free and easy on the **beach** (public showers available in the town center) or at a well-run **campground** with bungalows a kilometer inland, back toward the main road.

Eating in Salema

Fresh seafood, eternally. Look for grilled golden bream *(dorada)* and giant prawns *(camarão)*. Salema has six or eight places all serving fine meals for €8 or less. Happily, those that face the beach (the first 3 listed below) are the most fun and have the best service, food, and atmosphere. For a memorable last course at any of these places, consider taking your dessert wine *(moscatel)*, Brazilian sugar-cane liquor *(caipirinha)*, or coffee to the beach for some stardust.

The **Boia Bar and Restaurant,** at the base of the residential street, has a classy beachfront setting, noteworthy service by friendly Paolo and his gang, and a knack for doing whitefish just right—always with free seconds on good orange and green vegetables. Their vegetarian lasagna and salads are popular, as is their €6 bacon and eggs breakfast (daily 9:30–1:00, serving until 22:00; try to arrive for dinner by 19:00, CC, tel. 282-695-382).

The **Atlantico**—noisier, big, busy, and right on the beach—originated as a temporary beach restaurant. It's moving into a permanent building in 2003. It has long dominated the Salema beach scene and is known for good fish and friendly service (daily 12:00–24:00, serving until 22:00, CC, tel. 282-695-142).

The intimate **Mira Mar,** farther up the residential street, is run by Florentine and Dieter, who offer a more creative menu for those venturing away from seafood. Their tapas plate—a hearty array of cold meats, veggies, and munchies—is good for a meal and their Portuguese stew is a meat and vegetables delight (daily 12:00–24:00, serving until 23:00, no CC, tel. 282-269-250).

Restaurante Lourenço, off the beach and a block up the hill, offers good-value meals, has a local clientele, and is the place for *cataplanas* (fish, tomatoes, potatoes, onions, and whatever else is available, cooked long in a traditional copper pot—between a pressure cooker and a steamer, €13 for 2 people). They make the best coffee in town (€8 menu, daily 8:00–24:00, no CC, from Hotel

Residencial Salema cross bridge, restaurant is a half-block uphill on your left, tel. 282-698-622).

Need a break from fish? At **Carapau Frances,** in the town square, a Greek/French couple serves good Greek and Italian food, including cheap pizzas (Fri–Wed breakfast from 9:00, lunch from 12:00, dinner from 18:00, closed Thu, no CC).

Romeu's **Salema Market** has all the fixings for a great picnic (fresh fruits, veggies, bread, sheep's cheese, sausage, and *vinho verde*—new wine, a Portuguese specialty with a refreshing taste) to take with you to a secluded beach or Cape Sagres. Helpful Romeu also changes money and gives travel advice (daily 8:00–13:00 & 15:00–20:00, on the "*quartos* street"). Another good grocery store, **Alisuper,** is just up from the beach on a tiny strip mall across from Hotel Residencial Salema.

Drivers who want a classy meal outside of town should consider the elegant **Restaurant Vila Velha** in Sagres (tel. 282-624-788) or the romantic **Castelejo Restaurante** at Praia do Castelejo (see "Cape Sagres," below).

CAPE SAGRES

This rugged southwestern tip of Portugal was the spot closest to the edge of our flat Earth in the days before Columbus. Prince Henry the Navigator, determined to broaden Europe's horizons and spread Catholicism, sent sailors ever farther into the unknown. His navigators' school was here, where shipwrecked and frustrated explorers were carefully debriefed as they washed ashore. (TI open Tue–Sat 9:30–13:00 & 14:00–17:30, closed Sun–Mon, on main street Rua Comandante Matoso, tel. 282-624-873.)

Portugal's "end of the road" is two distinct capes. Windy **Cabo St. Vincent** is actually the most southwestern tip. It has a desolate lighthouse that marks what was referred to even in pre-historic times as "the end of the world" (open to the public daily 10:00–17:00, snoop around, peek over the far edge, ask the attendant to spin the light for you). Outside the lighthouse, salt-of-the-earth merchants sell figs, fritters, and seaworthy sweaters (€20 average). **Cape Sagres,** with its old fort and Henry the Navigator lore, is the more historic cape (2 or 3 maritime history exhibits per year, old church, dramatic views). At either cape, look for dare-devil windsurfers and fishermen casting off the cliffs (and actually occasionally falling to their deaths).

Lashed tightly to the windswept landscape is the salty town of Sagres, above a harbor of fishing boats and near the lavish **Pousada do Infante** (Db-€145, tel. 282-624-222, fax 282-624-225). For a touch of local elegance, pop by the *pousada* for breakfast. For €9 you can sip coffee and nibble on a warm croissant while gazing out to sea. The classy *pousada*, a reasonable splurge with a magnificent setting, offers a warm welcome to anyone ready to pay so much for a continental breakfast.

Sagres is a popular gathering place for the backpacking crowd, with plenty of private rooms in the center and a great beach and bar scene. From Salema, Sagres is a 20-minute drive or hitch, a half-hour bus trip (nearly hourly trips from Salema, check return times), or a taxi ride (€20 for a 75-min round-trip, plus €7/hr for waiting time in Sagres).

Many beaches are tucked away on the drive between Salema and Cape Sagres. Most of them require a short walk after you stop along N-125. In some cases you leave your car on access roads or cross private property to reach the beaches—be considerate. In Salema, ask at Pensión Mare or the Horizonte Travel Agency for directions to beaches before you head to Sagres. Furnas beach is fully accessible by car. Ingrina and Zavial beaches are accessed by turning south in the village of Raposeira. Many beaches have bars.

The best secluded beach in the region is **Praia do Castelejo,** just north of Cape Sagres (from the town of Vila do Bispo, drive inland and follow the signs for 15 min). If you have a car and didn't grow up in Fiji, this really is worth the drive. Overlooking the deserted beach is **Castelejo Restaurante**, which specializes in *cataplanas,* hearty seafood stew (daily 12:00–22:00, 12 km from Salema at Praia do Castelejo, tel. 282-639-777).

LAGOS

Lagos, with a beach-party old town and a jet-ski marina, is as enjoyable as a big-city resort can be. The major town on the west end of the Algarve was the capital of the Algarve in the 13th and 14th centuries. The first great Portuguese maritime expeditions embarked from here, and the first African slave market in Europe was held here. (Though not advertised by the local TI, the slave market does appear on the town map.)

The old town, defined by its medieval walls, stretches between Praça Gil Eannes and the fort. It's a whitewashed jumble of pedestrian streets, bars, funky craft shops, outdoor restaurants, and sunburned tourists. The church of San Antonio and the adjoining regional museum (€2, Tue–Sun 9:30–12:30 & 14:00–17:00, closed Mon) are worth a look, but the morning fish market at the Mercado Municipal is more interesting (produce upstairs, closed Sun, on main square, facing marina). The beaches with the exotic rock formations—of post-card fame—begin just past the fort.

Tourist Information: The TI, a bleak six-minute walk from the bus station, is oddly located on a traffic roundabout on the entrance into town (Mon–Fri 9:30–13:00 & 14:00–17:30, closed

Sat–Sun, behind bus station, take Rua Vasco da Gama to the
right, and continue straight, on roundabout en route to Portimão,
tel. 282-763-031).

Arrival in Lagos: The train and bus stations are a five-
minute walk apart, separated by the marina and pedestrian bridge
over a river. Neither the bus station nor the train station has
luggage storage.

Sights—Lagos

Coastal Boat Tours—Along the harborfront, you'll be hustled
to take a sightseeing cruise. Old fishermen ("who know the nick-
name of each rock along the coast") sit at anchor under umbrellas
while their salespeople on the promenade hawk 45-minute exotic
rock and cave tours for €10. More serious maritime adventures are
sold (April–Oct) by a string of established companies with offices
just over the marina bridge. Bom Dia offers three different tours
by sailboat: a two-hour €15 grotto tour (with a chance to swim), a
half-day €35 BBQ cruise (basically a grotto tour with a meal), and
a full-day €50 round-trip to Sagres (no CC, in marina at Lagos 10,
WC on board, smart to reserve a day ahead in Aug, tel. 282-764-
670 or 917-810-761, www.bomdia.info). Dolphin Seafari offers
90-minute dolphin-watching cruises (about 80 percent of trips see
a dolphin) and 45-minute speedboat tours just for fun (1/day in
late afternoon, no CC, big sturdy inflatable lifeboat used for both
trips, tel. 282-792-586 or 919-359-359).
Bullfight—Lagos has a small, just-for-tourists bullfight in its dinky
ring from June through September on most Saturdays at 18:30.
Seats are a steep €20, but the show is a thriller. Signs all along
this touristy coastline advertise this *stierkampf.*

Sleeping in Lagos
(€1 = about $1, country code: 351, zip code: 8600)
When a price range is given, the lowest is the winter rate, the
highest is the August rate. Lagos is enjoyable for a resort its size,
but I must remind you that Salema is a village paradise and is only
a 20-minute taxi ride (€15, no meter, settle price first) or half-hour
bus ride away. If you missed the last bus to Salema (leaves Lagos
around 20:30), Albergeria Marina Rio and Pensão Residencial
Solar are both within 100 meters of the bus station.

MODERATELY PRICED
Caza de São Goncalo de Lagos, a beautifully decorated 18th-
century home with a garden, lovely tile work, parquet floors, and
elegant furnishings, is a fine value. While the downstairs rooms are
relatively plain, upstairs you'll find a plush Old World lounge, a

dreamy garden, and 13 classy old rooms with all the comforts (Sb-€30–60, Db-€45–70, Qb-€70–100 depending on room and season, includes breakfast, closed Nov–March, CC—AmEx only, Rua Candido dos Reis 73, on a pedestrian street 2 blocks off Praça Luis do Camões, a square that's a block behind the main square, tel. 282-762-171, fax 282-763-927, SE).

Hotel Riomar, next door, is a new, blocky, and tour-friendly place providing more comfort than character for a decent price (42 rooms, Db-€45–60, includes breakfast, CC—AmEx only, air-con, elevator, rooms on back lack street noise, Rua Candido dos Reis 83, tel. 282-770-130, fax 282-763-927).

The big, slick **Albergeria Marina Rio** faces the marina and the busy main street immediately in front of the bus station. Its modern, air-conditioned rooms come with all the amenities. Marina views come with noise. Quieter rooms are in the back (Db-€48–90, extra bed-€13.50–27, CC, small rooftop pool and terrace, elevator, Internet access, laundry service, Avenida dos Descobrimentos-Apartado 388, tel. 282-769-859, fax 282-769-960, www.marinario.com, e-mail: marinario@ip.pt, SE).

LOWER PRICED
Pensão Residencial Solar rents 29 very basic rooms (Sb-€28–45, Db-€40–70, includes breakfast and a fan, extra bed-€5, cheaper D-€20–40 rooms in annex up the hill, CC, elevator, Rua Antonio Crisogono dos Santos 60, tel. 282-762-477, fax 282-761-784, SE).

The Club Med–like **youth hostel** is a lively, social, and cushy, hammocks-in-the-courtyard experience (dorm bed in quad-€10–15, five Db-€28–42, includes breakfast, kitchen facilities, Internet access, priority given to hostel members, non-members of any age are welcome, Rua Lancarote de Freitas 50, tel. 282-761-970, fax 282-769-684, e-mail: reservas@movijovem.pt).

Transportation Connections—Lagos
Lagos to: Lisbon (5 trains/day, 5 hrs, usually transfer in Tunes; 5 direct buses/day, 5 hrs, €14 for bus or train; bus is more convenient since it arrives in Lisbon whereas the train arrives across the river, a ferry ride away from Lisbon), **Évora** (2 buses, at 7:00 and 15:00, 6 hrs, €12; 2 trains, at 8:20 and 17:15, 6–7 hrs, with one transfer, €10), **Vila Real St. Antonio** (4 trains/day, 4.5 hrs), **Tavira** (7 trains/day, 3.5 hrs, 2 daily express trains do it in 2 hrs). Train info: tel. 282-762-987, bus info: tel. 282-762-944.

Lagos to Salema: Lagos is your Algarve transportation hub and the closest train station to Salema (15 km). Buses go nearly hourly between Lagos and Sagres (30-min ride, last bus departs Lagos around 20:30, fewer buses on weekends); about half the buses go right into the village of Salema—the others (marked *cruzt* in the schedule) drop you at the top of the road (that must be *cruzt*) into Salema (bus continues to Figueira). From here it's a 20-minute walk downhill into the village.

In Lagos, to get to the bus station from the train station (ignore the "*quartos* women" who tell you Salema is 60 km away), walk straight out of the train station, go left around the big building, walk past the marina, cross the pedestrian bridge and then the main boulevard, and walk straight into the white-and-yellow EVA bus station (tel. 282-762-944). If you venture into Lagos, buses to Salema (marked with the final destination, Sagres) also stop on the waterfront. Allow €15 for a taxi from Lagos to Salema (settle price first). Before heading to Salema, pick up return bus schedules and train schedules for your next destination, particularly if you're going to Sevilla (though as a fallback, Horizonte Travel Agency in Salema has posted schedules).

Lagos to Sevilla: The €15 direct bus from Lagos to Sevilla runs twice daily from May through September (sometimes starts in April and continues into Oct, doesn't run off-season). The bus departs the Lagos bus station at 7:30 and at 14:00, arriving at Sevilla's Plaza de Armas bus station respectively at 12:45 and 19:15 (schedule from Sevilla to Lagos: 7:30–11:00, 16:30–20:00). Note that Spanish time is one hour later than Portuguese time during daylight saving months. To get from Salema to Lagos, take the bus or taxi (€15).

Off-season options: If you're traveling off-season, when the direct Lagos-Sevilla bus doesn't run, getting to Sevilla is a very long day (roughly 8–10 hrs). There are two options from Lagos: 1) take buses—with transfers in Faro, Portugal and Huelva, Spain— all the way to Sevilla, or 2) take a train/ferry/bus combination.

The all-bus option is simpler and usually faster, but isn't as good a choice on weekends when bus frequency drops dramatically. You take the bus from Lagos to Faro (7/day, 2 hrs), then catch the bus to Sevilla (2/day, 4 hours with transfer in Huelva). Note that only two buses from Faro run to Sevilla. Get an early start in order to catch a bus from Faro; ideally call (or have a local person call) the Faro bus station (tel. 289-899-760 or 289-899-761) to find out the times of the two departures for Sevilla (or see www.eva-bus.com for Lagos–Faro–Huelva bus schedules; from Huelva buses run hourly to Sevilla, 1-hr trip).

Taking a train/ferry/bus combination between Lagos and Sevilla is the most time-consuming of all (about 10 hours) but it's predictable and runs daily year-round (frequency drops on weekends but it's still doable). Take the train from Lagos to the last stop in Vila Real de San Antonio (4/day includes 2 morning departures, allow 4.5 hours with transfer in Tunes or Faro). The Vila Real train station is about a kilometer from the dock (exit straight from station—on Rua Eça de Queiroz, walk about 5 min, turn left on Rua Ayamonte, leads to dock; or take a €3 taxi ride). Ferries run frequently between Vila Real and Ayamonte, Spain (€1, 17/day, 26/day July–Sept, 15 min, last ferry runs about 22:00).

Ayamonte is a pleasant border town. The bus station is a 15-minute walk from the dock; pick up a map and bus schedules from the TI at the Ayamonte dock (Mon–Sat 10:00–13:30 & 17:00–20:00, closed Sun, open later and on Sun afternoon in summer, tel. 959-502-121). To reach the bus station from the dock, angle right though the pedestrian area to Avenida Andalucía, then follow this road past the lake straight to the station (tel. 959-321-171).

From Ayamonte to Sevilla, catch a direct bus to Sevilla (6/day, fewer on weekends, 2.5 hrs) or transfer at Huelva (10/day, 1 hr, easy transfer). From Huelva, buses run hourly to Sevilla (1 hr, tel. 959-256-900). From Huelva, you could take one of four daily trains to Sevilla (2 hrs), but it's simpler to take the bus. Huelva's bus and train stations are connected by a 15-minute walk along Avenida Italia. Sunday schedules are limited and more frustrating. (See "Transportation Connections" near the end of the Sevilla chapter for more specifics.)

TAVIRA

Straddling a river, with a lively park, chatty locals, and boats sharing its waterfront center, Tavira is a low-rise, easygoing alternative to the other, more aggressive Algarve resorts. It's your best east Algarve stop. Because Tavira has good connections by bus and train (it's on the trans-Algarve train line, with nearly hourly departures both east and west), many travelers find the town more accessible than Salema. And it's the perfect midway stop on the four-hour drive from Sevilla to Salema (just 3 kilometers off the freeway).

The many churches and fine bits of Renaissance architecture sprinkled throughout Tavira remind the wanderer that 500 years ago the town was the largest on the Algarve (with 1,500 dwellings according to a 1530 census) and an important base for Portuguese adventurers in Africa. The silting up of its harbor, a plague, the 1755 earthquake, and the shifting away of its once-upon-a-time lucrative tuna industry left Tavira in a long decline. Today the town has a wistful charm and lives off its tourists.

Orientation

Tavira straddles the Rio Gilão three kilometers from the Atlantic. Everything of sightseeing and transportation importance is on the south bank. A clump of historic sights—the ruined castle and main

Tavira

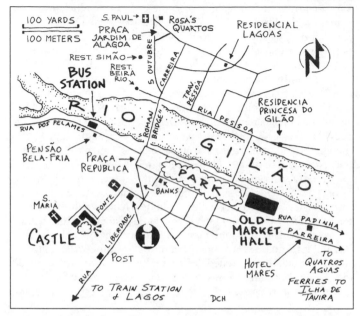

church—fills its tiny fortified hill and tangled Moorish lanes. But today the action is outside the old fortifications along the riverside Praça da República and the adjacent shady, fountain- and bench-filled park. The old market hall is beyond the park. And beyond that is the boat to the beach island. The old pedestrian-only "Roman Bridge" leads from Praça da República to the north bank (2 recommended hotels and most of the evening and restaurant action).

Tourist Information: The TI is up the cobbled steps from the inland end of the Praça da República (normally daily 9:30– 18:00, closed during lunch and on Sun off-season, Rua Galeria 9, tel. 281-322-511). Guided town walks leave from the TI daily most of the year and twice daily in summer (€2.50, call TI or 281-321-946 for information, reserve 2 days in advance, particularly July–Aug).

Arrival in Tavira: The train station is a 10-minute walk from the town center. To get to the center, leave the station following the yellow Turismo sign and follow this road downhill to the river and Praça da República. The riverside bus station is three blocks from the town center; simply follow the river into town. Drivers drive to the riverside main square where pay parking *(zona pago)* meters will take €0.50 per hour. If you're arriving in Portugal, stock up on €0.50 coins as this is the largest coin parking meters will take.

Sights—Tavira

The TI's free map describes a dozen churches with enthusiasm. But for most tourists, the town's sights can be seen in a few minutes. Uphill from the TI you'll find the ruined **castle,** offering only plush gardens and a city view (free, 9:00 or 10:00–17:00). Just beyond the castle ruins is the town's most visit-worthy church, the **Church of Santa Maria.** From there I'd enjoy the riverside park at **Praça da República** and the fun architecture of the low-key 18th-century buildings facing the river. After dinner take a stroll along the fish-filled river, with a pause on the pedestrian bridge or in the park if there's any action in the bandstand.

Beaches—The big hit for travelers is Tavira's great beach island, **Ilha da Tavira.** The island is a long, almost treeless sandbar with a campground, several restaurants, and a sprawling beach. A summer-only boat takes bathers painlessly from downtown Tavira to the island (July–mid-Sept about hourly from 8:00–20:00, timetable at TI, €1 round-trip, departs 200 meters downriver from former market hall). It's an enjoyable ride even if you just go round-trip without getting out. Or you can bus, taxi, ride a rental bike, or bake during a shadeless two-kilometer trip out of town to Quatro Aguas, where the five-minute ferry shuttles sunbathers to Ilha da Tavira (€1, ferry runs constantly with demand all year, last trip near midnight in high season to accommodate diners).

Another fine beach, the **Barril Beach resort,** is four kilometers from Tavira. Walk, rent a bike, or take a city bus to Pedras del Rei and then catch the little train (usually runs year-round) or walk 10 minutes through Ria Formosa National Park to the resort. Get details at the TI.

Sleeping in Tavira
(€1 = about $1, country code: 351, zip code: 8800)
Prices usually shoot up in August.

Residencial Lagoas is spotless, homey, and a block off the river. Friendly English-speaking Maria offers a communal refrigerator, a rooftop patio with a view made for wine and candles, and laundry washboard privileges (S-€18, D-€28, Db-€38, Tb-€43, no gouging in July and Aug, cheaper off-season, no breakfast, no CC, Rua Almirante Candido dos Reis 24, tel. 281-322-252, easy phone reservations). Cross the Roman footbridge from Praça da República, follow the middle fork on the other side, and turn right where it ends.

The modern, hotelesque **Residencia Princesa do Gilão** offers 22 bright, modern rooms. Choose riverfront or quiet on the back with terrace (Db-€40–50, includes breakfast, no CC, Rua Borda de Agua de Aguiar 10, cross Roman bridge and turn right along river, tel. & fax 281-325-171, SE).

Pensão-Residencial Bela Fria is a shiny eight-room place with a rooftop sun terrace overlooking the river. Its simple air-conditioned rooms are quiet, modern, and comfortable (Sb-€25–35, €60 July–Aug; Db-€40–50, €90 July–Aug; includes breakfast, no CC, Rua dos Pelames 1, directly across from bus station, tel. & fax 281-325-375, e-mail: residencial@belafria.com, SE). Guests get a free half-hour at the adjacent cybercafé.

For quiet, spacious, comfort, **Rosa's Quartos** are worth the communication struggles. Rosa rents 14 big, gleaming, marble-paved rooms on a quiet alley. Request her best rooms, which are in a separate building across the alley in back (Db-€25–35, no CC, over bridge and through Jardim da Alagoa square to Rua da Porta Nova 4, immediately across from St. Paul's church, unmarked door, tel. 281-321-547, friendly Rosa NSE).

Residencial Mares, on the busy side of the river amid all the strolling and café ambiance, has good rooms, a restaurant, and a rooftop terrace. Some rooms on the second floor have balconies overlooking the river (Sb-€30–50, no singles in Aug; Db-€40, €65 in July and Sept, €80 in Aug; includes breakfast, CC, air-con, Rua Jose Pires Padinha, on the TI side of the river just beyond old market hall, tel. 281-325-815, fax 281-325-819, e-mail: maresresidencial@mail.telepac.pt, SE).

Eating in Tavira

Tavira is filled with reasonable restaurants. A couple of lively places face the riverbank just beyond the old market hall. A few blocks inland, hole-in-the-wall places offer more fish per dollar.

Crossing the pedestrian bridge, turn left, go upstream through the tunnel and find the rickety riverside tables of two good choices: **Restaurante Beira Rio** has great fish and an extensive menu (€14 meals, nightly 18:00–22:30, tel. 281-323-165). **Restaurante Casa Simão** is simpler with grilled fish—cheap and tasty.

The following places are all within two blocks of the pedestrian Roman bridge, just over the river from the town center. For seafood, I enjoyed the inexpensive and relaxed **Restaurant Bica,** below Residencial Lagoas (see first hotel listing, above). The **Patio,** on a classy rooftop, is worth the extra euros (Mon–Sat 18:00–23:00, closed Sun). For Italian cuisine, consider English-friendly **Patrick's** (good lasagna and curry dishes).

Anazu Pasteleria is the place to grab an inexpensive

breakfast or nurse a late riverside drink (on Rua Pessoa, 1 block east of Roman bridge, cheap Internet access).

Transportation Connections—Tavira
To: Lisbon (train or bus works fine: 4 trains/day, 5 hrs; 5 buses/day, 5 hrs), **Lagos** (train is better: 12 trains/day, change in Faro or Tunes, 2–3 hrs), **Sevilla** (bus is better: 2 buses/day, 3.5 hrs, transfer in Huelva; can also hook up with morning Lagos–Sevilla bus in Ayamonte—ask TI or local travel agency for current schedule). Train info: tel. 281-322-354, bus info: tel. 281-322-546.

CACELA VELHA
Just a few kilometers east of Tavira (1 km off the main road), this tiny village sits happily ignored on a hill with its fort, church, one restaurant, a few *quartos*, and a beach with the open sea just over the sandbar, a short row across its lagoon. The restaurant serves a sausage-and-cheese specialty fried at your table. If you're driving, swing by, if only to enjoy the coastal view and imagine how nice the Algarve would be if people like you and me had never discovered it.

Route Tips for Drivers in the Algarve
Lisbon to Salema (240 km, 4 hrs): Following the blue *Sul Ponte* signs, drive south over Lisbon's 25th of April Bridge. A short detour just over the bridge takes you to the giant concrete statue of Cristo Rei (Christ in Majesty). Continue south past Setúbal to the south coast (following signs to Algarve, Vila do Bispo, Sagres, Lagos, and Salema). Just east of Vila do Bispo, you'll hit the tiny road to the beach village of Salema. Decent roads, less traffic, and the glory of waking up on the Algarve make doing this drive at night a reasonable option.

Algarve to Sevilla (240 km): Drive east along the Algarve. In Lagos, park along the waterfront by the fort and the Mobil gas station. From Lagos follow the signs to Faro and then, near Loule, hit the freeway (direction: España) to Tavira. It's a two-hour drive from Salema to Tavira. Leaving Tavira, follow the signs to España. You'll cross over the bridge into Spain (where it's 1 hour later during daylight savings months) and glide effortlessly (90 min by freeway) into Sevilla. At Sevilla follow the signs to *Centro Ciudad* (city center) and drive along the river until you see the cathedral and tower.

ÉVORA

Deep in the heart of Portugal, in the barren, arid plains of the southern province of Alentejo, historic Évora (pron. EH-voh-rah) has been a cultural oasis for 2,000 years. With an untouched provincial atmosphere, fascinating whitewashed old town, museums, a cathedral, a chapel of bones, and even a Roman temple, Évora stands proudly amid groves of cork and olive trees.

The major sights—the Roman Temple of Diana and early Gothic cathedral—crowd close together at the town's highest point. A subtle but still-powerful charm is contained within the town's medieval wall. Find it by losing yourself in the quiet lanes of Évora's far corners.

Planning Your Time

With frequent bus connections (12/day, 2 hrs) to Lisbon, Évora makes a decent day trip from Portugal's capital city. You can stop by for an overnight en route to or from the Algarve, five hours away (2 buses and 2 trains a day, about €12). Drivers can sandwich Évora between Lisbon and the Algarve, exploring dusty droves of olive groves and scruffy seas of peeled cork trees along the way. The highway from the Algarve is great (3 hours via Beja—don't take the freeway).

With a day in Évora, take the Introductory Walk outlined below, have a quick lunch, see the remaining sights, and enjoy a leisurely, top-notch dinner. After dinner, stroll the back streets and ponder life with the retired men on the squares.

Tourist Information: The TI is on the main square, at Praça do Giraldo 73 (April–Oct Mon–Fri 9:00–19:00, Sat–Sun 9:00–12:30 & 14:00–17:30, Nov–March daily 9:00–12:30 & 14:00–17:30, tel. 266-702-671).

Évora

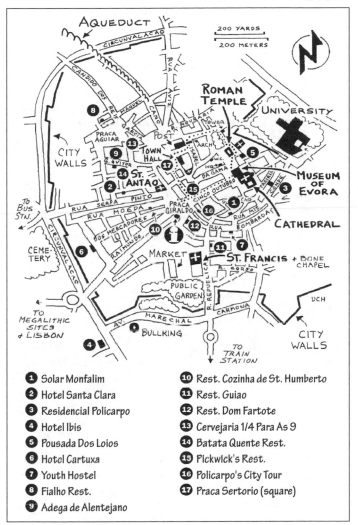

- ❶ Solar Monfalim
- ❷ Hotel Santa Clara
- ❸ Residencial Policarpo
- ❹ Hotel Ibis
- ❺ Pousada Dos Loios
- ❻ Hotel Cartuxa
- ❼ Youth Hostel
- ❽ Fialho Rest.
- ❾ Adega de Alentejano
- ❿ Rest. Cozinha de St. Humberto
- ⓫ Rest. Guiao
- ⓬ Rest. Dom Fartote
- ⓭ Cervejaria 1/4 Para As 9
- ⓮ Batata Quente Rest.
- ⓯ Pickwick's Rest.
- ⓰ Policarpo's City Tour
- ⓱ Praca Sertorio (square)

Arrival in Évora: The bus station is on Avenida S. Sebastião. To reach the center from the station, it's either a short taxi ride (€3.50) or a 10-minute walk (exit station right, and continue straight all the way into town, passing through the city walls at the halfway point). The train station is on Avenida Dr. Barahona. From the train station to the center, it's a taxi ride (€3.50) or

25-minute walk straight up Avenida Dr. Barahona, continuing straight—on Rua da República—after you enter the city walls.

Helpful Hints

Walking Tour: Policarpo's City Tour offers a walking tour of Évora's historic center for €18 (minimum 2 people, reserve ahead, 2.5 hrs, Alcárcova de Baixo 43, a block from TI, from main square take shopping street—Cinco de Outubro—then first right, tel. 266-746-970; see "Sights near Évora," below, for their daily excursions).

Local Guide: Maria Pires is a good local guide (€35 for private 2-hour tour for up to 5 people, tel. 917-232-147).

Taxis: Cabs are helpful in this small but confusing town. They're parked on the main square (€3.50 minimum).

Introductory Old Town Walk

Évora's walled city is small. These sights are all within a five-minute walk of the main square, Praça do Giraldo (pron: PRA-suh doo zhee-RAHL-doo). The walk will take about an hour or so, plus time visiting sights. If it's a hot day, take this walk early in the morning or late in the afternoon (before sights close, cathedral at 17:00).

Évora was once a Roman town (2nd century B.C. to 4th century A.D.), important because of its wealth of wheat and silver, its proximity to a river (easy to ship goods), and its location on a trade route to Rome. We'll see Roman sights, though most of Évora's Roman past is buried under the houses and hotels of today (often uncovered by accident when plumbing work needs to be done in basements). The town fell under Moorish rule from the eighth century to the 12th century. And during its glory years (15th–16th centuries), Évora was favored by Portuguese kings, even serving as the home of King John III. From Romans to Moors to Portuguese kings, this little town has a big history.

The Main Square: Start at Praça do Giraldo, Évora's main square. It was named after Giraldo the Fearless, the Christian knight who led a surprise attack and retook Évora from the Moors in 1165. As thanks, Giraldo was made governor of the town—and the symbol of the city (Évora's coat of arms is a knight on a horse—see it crowning the lampposts). On this square, all that's left of several centuries of Moorish rule is their artistry, evidenced by the wrought-iron balconies of the buildings that ring the square (and an occasional distinctive Mudejar "keyhole" window throughout the town).

Until the 16th century, the area behind the TI was the Jewish Quarter. Because Christians figured the Bible forbade the charging of interest, Jews did the money-lending, hence the

Évora Old Town Walk

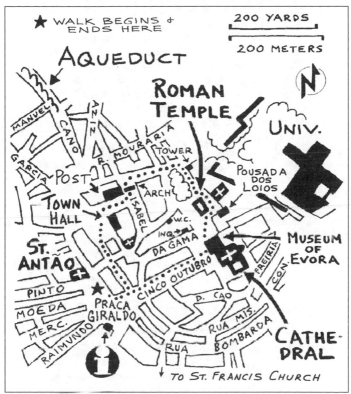

★ WALK BEGINS &
ENDS HERE

200 YARDS

200 METERS

AQUEDUCT

ROMAN TEMPLE

UNIV.

N

MANUEL CANO

GARCIA

POST

TOWN HALL

R. MOURARIA

TOWER

ARCH

ISABEL

W.C.

ING. DA GAMA

POUSADA DOS LOIOS

ST. ANTÃO

PINTO

MOEDA

MERC.

RAIMUNDO

PRACA GIRALDO

CINCO OUTUBRO

D. CAO

RUA

RUA MIS.

BOMBARDA

MUSEUM OF EVORA

FREIRIA

CON.

CATHE-DRAL

↓ TO ST. FRANCIS CHURCH

names of the streets such as Rua Moeda (road of money) and Rua de Mercadores (road of merchants).

The Roman triumphal arch that used to stand on this square was demolished in the 16th century to make way for the Church of St. Antão (at the end of the square). In front of the church is a 16th-century fountain—once an important water source for the town (it marks the end of the aqueduct) and now a popular hang-out for young and old.

The Portuguese King John III lived in Évora for 30 years in the 16th century. The TI is inside the palace where the king's guests used to stay. Others weren't treated as royally. A fervent proponent of the Inquisition, King John sanctioned the deaths of hundreds of people who were burned as heretics on this square. On Tuesday mornings, the square is a traditional cattle and produce market with ranchers and farmers gathering (without their goods) to make deals—a medieval stock exchange based on trust. Notice the C.M.E. board (opposite the TI, near the start of Rua Cinco de Outubro) where people gather to see who's died lately.

From the Main Square to the Roman Sights and Cathedral: Leave the square on Rua Cinco de Outubro (opposite the TI office). The name of the road celebrates the date, October 5, 1910, when Portugal shook off royal rule and became a republic. This little street has been a main shopping street since Roman times (we'll return to it later). Take the first left (at Restaurante Mr. Pickwick's) on Alcárcova de Cima, which in Arabic means "the place with water." A few steps farther on, you'll see a portion of Roman wall built into the buildings on your right. After this, a series of modern windows show more of this wall, which used to surround what is now the inner core of the town. Below the last window you can actually see the red paint of a Roman villa built over by the wall. (The wall that presently encircles Évora is 14th-century, fortified in the 17th century during Portugal's fight for independence from Spain.)

Ahead of you, across the intersection, is the blunt, granite, columned end of a 16th-century **aqueduct.** You can see the arches of the aqueduct embedded in shops to your left. Continue straight (on Travessa de Sertorio). The abnormally high sidewalk to your left is another part of the aqueduct.

Keep going straight. Within a block you'll reach a square, Praça Sertorio. The tallest white building on the square is the **town hall.** Go inside (Mon–Fri 9:00–17:00, closed Sat–Sun, computers offering free Internet access). In the dark corner (on the right) is a view of a Roman bath uncovered during some building repair. To the right of this overlook is more of the excavation, with a map showing the layout of the Roman site. The map also indicates other Roman sights in Évora (we'll see all but the last one on this walk).

Exit the town hall to the right and take an immediate right around the town hall building. Across Rua de Olivença is a church built into a Roman tower (once part of the Roman wall you saw earlier) and farther on, the arcaded post office (*correios*).

Walk alongside the post office and take the first left, on Rua de Dona Isabel. You'll immediately see the **Roman arch**— Porta de Dona Isabel—once a main gate in the Roman wall.

When you pass under the Roman wall, you're entering a neighborhood called Mouraria (for the Moors). After Giraldo the Fearless retook Évora, the Moors were still allowed to live in the area, but on the other side of this gate, beyond the city walls. They were safe here for centuries . . . until the Inquisition expelled them in the 16th century.

Turn right, passing a modern café and a patch of grass show-ing Évora's coat of arms—Giraldo on horseback. Turn right at the tower—called the Five Corners (Cinco Quinas) for its five sides—and walk a block uphill to Évora's sight-packed square. Here you'll see the Roman temple, fancy Pousada dos Loios, a public garden, and the dressy Jardim do Paço restaurant, known for its beautiful garden setting and pricey food.

The **Pousada dos Loios,** once a 15th-century monastery, is now a luxurious hotel with small rooms (blame the monks). To the left of the *pousada,* stairs lead down to a church—Igreja dos Loios dos Duques de Cadaval—with an impressive gold altarpiece. This is the lavish mausoleum chapel of the noble Cadaval family (still a big-time family—owners of the *pousada*). Look for the two small trapdoors in the floor flanking the aisle midway up the church. One opens up to a well (imagine the thoughts going through a bad boy's mind while sitting on this pew during a long service), the other reveals an ossuary stacked with Cadaval bones. The tile work around the altar is 17th century—mere decoration with tradi-tional yellow patterns. Along the nave, the tiles are 18th century—with scenes to tell Bible stories. This coincided with the popularity of tapestries in France and Belgium that had the same teaching purpose. The room to the right of the altar contains tile work, ancient weaponry, and religious art, including a cleverly painted Crucifixion (Cadaval church-€2.50, Tue–Sun 10:00–14:30 & 16:00–18:00, closed Mon, no photos).

The **Roman temple** was once part of the Roman forum and the main square in the first century A.D. Today the town's open-air concerts and events are staged here, against an evocative temple backdrop. It's beautifully floodlit at night. While known as the Temple of Diana, it was more likely dedicated to the emperor.

The Roman forum sprawled where the **Museum of Évora** stands today. In fact, an excavated section of the forum is in the courtyard of the museum, surrounded by a delightful mix of Roman finds, medieval statuary, and 16th-century Portuguese and Flemish paintings, along with exhibitions on the top floor and in the basement (€1.50, Tue–Sun 9:00–12:30 & 14:00–18:00, closed Mon).

Across the square from the museum is a white building, now used by the university, but notorious as being the **tribunal of the Inquisition.** Here thousands of innocent people (many Moors and Jews) were tried and found guilty. After being condemned, the prisoners were taken in procession through the streets to be burned on the main square. In front of this building is a granite sculpture of a coffin with a body inside—a memorial to those who were killed.

Alentejo: Corks and Jokes

Driving from Lisbon to the Algarve, you'll pass through the Alentejo region, known for producing cork. Portugal, the world's leading producer of that wonderful, tasteless, odorless seal for wine bottles, produces 30 million corks a day. In Alentejo, you'll drive through vast fields of cork oaks. Twenty years after planting, they're ready to be stripped. Every seven to nine years the bark is stripped again, leaving a sore red underskin. Even with the rise of plastic "corks," the cork business remains strong with insulation and acoustic uses.

The Alentejo region is also known for being extraordinarily traditional. Throughout Europe, what a tourist might see as quaint is seen by city folk as backward. The people of Alentejo are the butt of local jokes. It's said you'll see them riding motorcycles in pajamas . . . so they can better lay into the corners. Many Portuguese call porno flicks "Alentejo karate." I met a sad old guy from Alentejo. When I asked him what was wrong, he explained that he was on the verge of teaching his burro how to live without food . . . but it died. The big event of the millennium in Lisbon was the arrival of the Alentejanos for Expo '98.

The little street to the left of the Inquisition headquarters is **Rua de Vasco da Gama.** Globetrotting da Gama lived on this street after he discovered the water route to India in 1498 (his house, not open to the public, is 30 meters down the street at the smudged number #15 on your right). Backtrack and turn right for the cathedral.

The **cathedral,** behind the museum, was built after Giraldo's conquest—on the site of the mosque. (For more on the cathedral, see "Sights," below.) The first cardinal of this church was Dom Henrique, who founded the town's university in 1559 (see "Sights," below). Later Dom Henrique became King Henrique after his great-nephew, the young King Sebastian, died in North Africa in a disastrous attempt (get this) to chase the Moors out of Africa. Henrique, who ruled only two years before he died, left no direct descendants (he was a cardinal and therefore supposedly chaste). The throne of Portugal passed to his cousin, King Philip II of Spain, starting a bleak 60-year period of Spanish rule (1580–1640) and the beginning of Évora's decline.

From the Cathedral back to Main Square: Take the little street opposite the cathedral's entrance, downhill. It's the shopping street, Rua Cinco de Outubro, which connects Évora's main sights with its main square. The street is lined with products of the Alentejo region: cork (even postcards), tile, leather, iron-work, and Arraiolos rugs (made with a distinctive weave in the nearby town of Arraiolos).

On the shopping street, after you pass the intersection with Rua de Burgos, look left to see a blue **shrine** protruding from the wall of a building. The town built it as thanks to God for sparing it from the 1755 earthquake that devastated much of Lisbon. Ahead of you is the main square. The Chapel of Bones and town market are just a few blocks away on your left.

Sights—Évora

▲▲**Cathedral**—Portugal has two archbishops, and one resides here in Évora. This important cathedral (of Santa Maria de Évora), built in the late 12th century, is a transitional mix of Romanesque and Gothic. The tower to the right is Romanesque (more stocky and fortress-like), and the tower to the left is Gothic (lighter, more windows). As usual, this was built upon a mosque (after the Reconquista succeeded here) and that mosque was built upon a Christian Visigothic chapel (religious and military tit-for-tat is nothing new).

Inside the cathedral, midway down the nave on the left, is a 15th-century statue of a pregnant Mary. It's thought that the first priests, hoping to make converts out of Celtic pagans who worshiped mother goddesses, thought they'd have more success if they kept the focus on fertility. Throughout Alentejo, there's a deeply felt affinity for this ready-to-produce-a-savior Mary. Across the aisle, a more realistic Renaissance Gabriel, added a century later, comes to tell Mary her baby's not just any baby. The 18th-century high altar is neoclassical, with a muscular Jesus—though carved in wood—matches the Portuguese marble all around.

Admission to the museum, choir, and cloisters costs €3 (church open daily July–Aug 9:00–17:00, Sept–June 9:00–12:30 & 14:00–17:00, museum/choir/cloisters close at 16:30 and on Monday, no photos, WC under cloister entry). Each corner of the **cloister** bears a carving of one of the four evangelists. In the corner closest to the entry, a spiral stairway leads to the "roof," providing a close-up view of the cathedral's fine lantern tower and the fortress-like crenellations. This fortress of God design was typical of Portuguese Romanesque. Back on ground level, a simple chapel niche (on opposite corner from cloister entry) has a child-sized statue of another pregnant Virgin Mary (midway up wall) and the sarcophagai of four recent archbishops.

The **museum** is interesting for the art in its first and last rooms. Center-stage in the first room is an intricate 14th-century, French-made, puzzle-like ivory statue of Mary (Virgem do Paraiso). Her "insides" open up to reveal the major events in her life. A photo below shows Mary folded up and ready to travel. Next, a long room lined with crude 15th-century Alentejo paintings has an extremely dramatic Rococo crucifix and the sacred treasures of this richest church in Alentejo. In the last room, a glass case displays a sparkling reliquary, containing pieces of the supposed True Cross (in a cross-shape), heavily laden with more than a thousand true gems, rotating to show off every facet.

The sunlit **choir** (late 15th to early 16th century) overlooks the cathedral. Its oak stalls are carved with scenes of daily life (hunting boars, harvesting, rounding up farm animals). The huge contraption in the middle is a music stand. Notice the wide edge on the ends of the seats. Even the older clerics were expected to stand up for much of the service. But when the seat is flipped up, the edge becomes a ledge, making it possible for clerics to sit while they respectfully "stood."

▲▲▲**Church of St. Francis and the Chapel of Bones**—To get to the church from the main square, take the road to the left of the imposing Bank of Portugal. At the end of the arcade, turn right on Rua da República. You'll see the church just ahead.

Imagine the church in its original pure style—simple as St. Francis would want it. It's wide—just a nave lined by chapels. In the 18th century it became popular for wealthy families to buy fancy chapels, resulting in today's gold-leaf hodgepodge. The huge Baroque chapel to the left of the altar is over the top—with St. Francis and his partner in Christ-like simplicity surrounded by anything but poverty.

The entrance to the **bone chapel** is outside, to the right of the church entrance. The intentionally thought-provoking message above the chapel reads: "We bones in here wait for yours to join us" (€1, pay the €0.25 to take photos, daily 9:00–13:00 & 14:30–17:30). Inside the macabre chapel, bones line the walls and 5,000 skulls stare blankly at you from walls and arches. They were unearthed from various Évora churchyards. This was the work of three monks who, concerned about the way society was going, thought this would provide Évora with a helpful place to meditate on the transitoriness of material things in the undeniable presence of death. The bones of the monks responsible for the interior decorating are in the small white coffin by the altar.

After reflecting on mortality, pop into the **market** (immediately in front of the church entrance), busiest in the morning and on Saturday (closed Mon). Wander around. It's a great slice-of-life look at this community. People are proud of their produce. *Provar?* (pron. proo-vahr) means "Can I try a little?" *Provar* some cheese.

Now take a refreshing break in the **public gardens** (Jardim Publico, to the left as you exit church, at the bottom of Praça 1 de Maio). The little kiosk café next to the goldfish pond sells freshly baked goods and drinks. For a fine little lunch, try an *empada de galinha* (tiny chicken pastry) and a local specialty—*queijada* (pron. kay-ZHAH-duh, sweet cheesecake). The gardens, bigger than they look, contain an overly restored hunk of the 16th-century Royal Palace. Behind the palace, look over the stone balustrade to see a kids' playground and playfields. Life goes on—make no bones about it.

▲**University**—Originally known as the College of the Holy Spirit, this was established as a Jesuit university in 1559 by Dom Henrique, the cathedral's first archbishop (who later became a cardinal and then king). Two hundred years later, Marques de Pombal, the powerful minister of King Jose, decided that the Jesuits had become too rich, too political, and—as the sole teachers of society—too closed to modern thinking. He abolished the Jesuit society in 1759—and confiscated their wealth. The university was closed until 1973 when it reopened as a secular school. Injecting 8,000 students into this town of 50,000 people (with 14,000 inside the walls), brought Évora a new vitality... and discos. Rather than the American-style campus, the colleges are scattered throughout the town.

The main entrance of the university is the old courtyard on the ground level (downhill from the original Jesuit chapel). Enter the courtyard (free weekdays and Sat morn, pay €1.50 on Sat 15:00–18:00, Sun 10:00–14:00 &15:00–18:00). Attractive blue-and-white *azulejo* tiles ring the walls and the classrooms, with the theme of the class portrayed in the tiles. Poke into a classroom to see the now-ignored pulpit. Originally, Jesuit priests were the teachers and information coming from a pulpit was not to be questioned.

Enter the room directly across the courtyard from the entrance. Here major university events are held, under the watchful eyes of Cardinal Henrique (the painting to the left) and young King Sebastian (to the right).

The university shop to the right of this room gives you a great look at the tiles. In the 16th century this was a classroom for students of astronomy—note the spheres and navigational instruments mingled with cupids and pastoral scenes. Imagine the class back then. Having few books, if any, the students (males only) took notes as the professor taught in Latin from the lectern in the back.

Behind this courtyard is a smaller courtyard, with a café off its far right corner (Mon–Fri 8:30–19:00, Sat 9:00–12:00, closed Sun).

In front of the café is a huge marble fountain where students used to wash their hands. The food is the cheapest in town and the public is welcome. Strike up a conversation with a student.

Sights near Évora

Megalithic Sights—Near Évora, you'll find menhirs (standing stones, near Guadalupe and elsewhere); dolmens (rock tombs at Anta do Zambujeiro and Capela-anta de São Brissos); cromlechs (rocks in formation *à la* Stonehenge, at Cromlech dos Almendres); and a cave with prehistoric paintings (Gruta do Escoural). Depending on how much you want to see, you can do a 25- to 70-kilometer loop from Évora by tour (see below), by **car** (list of rental-car agencies available at Évora's TI), or by rental bike (details at TI).

    Policarpo's City Tour offers bus tours of the megaliths (€25, 2-person minimum, 3 hrs, offered daily depending on demand, no CC, Alcárcova de Baixo 43; to reach their office from main square, head up shopping street—Cinco de Outubro—and take first right; in summer book 2 days in advance, tel. 266-746-970, SE). Policarpo also offers other tours, including an €18 walking tour of Évora and a €75 full-day trip (2-person minimum) to nearby castles, a marble quarry, and a ceramic workshop.

Bullfighting—Bullfights are rare in Évora, but nearby towns advertise fights on Saturday and Sunday through the season (roughly June–Sept). Notice women are on the docket now (perhaps to give a tired sport a little kick).

Sleeping in Évora

(€1 = about $1, country code: 351, zip code: 7000)

Sleep Code: **S** = Single, **D** = Double/Twin, **T** = Triple, **Q** = Quad, **b** = bathroom, **s** = shower only, **CC** = Credit Cards accepted, **no CC** = Credit Cards not accepted, **SE** = Speaks English, **NSE** = No English.

    To help you easily sort through these listings, I've divided the rooms into three categories, based on the price for a standard double room with bath:

    Higher Priced—Most rooms more than €100.
    Moderately Priced—Most rooms €100 or less.
    Lower Priced—Most rooms less than €50.

HIGHER PRICED

The classy **Pousada dos Loios**, once a 15th-century monastery, is now a luxury hotel renting 30 well-appointed cells. While the rooms are small, the place sprawls with many fine public spaces, courtyards, and a small swimming pool (Db-€185, more on Fri,

Sat, and Sun, less Nov–March, includes breakfast, CC, air-con, free parking, Convento dos Loios, across from Roman temple, reserve with Central Booking Office at tel. 218-442-001, fax 218-442-085, www.pousadas.pt, e-mail: guest@pousadas.pt).

Hotel Cartuxa is a big tour-group place, with greedy shops lining its long corridors. Though not as central as the *pousada*, is has 85 far-more-spacious rooms, lower prices, a swimming pool big enough to swim in, and a big garden bordered by the city wall (Sb-€125, Db-€145, includes breakfast, 20 percent less Nov–March, CC, air-con, elevator, parking-€4, attached restaurant/bar, Travessa da Palmeira 4/6, 5-min walk from center, tel. 266-739-300, fax 266-739-305, www.hoteldacartuxa.com, e-mail: comercial@hoteldacartuxa.com, SE).

MODERATELY PRICED

Solar Monfalim, a 16th-century noble house, seems unchanged from when it received its first hotel guests in 1892. This elegant hacienda-type place, with homey lounges and a Valium ambience, rents 26 rooms in a central and quiet location (Sb-€65, Db-€80, Tb-€105, includes breakfast, CC, air-con, pleasant breakfast room with balcony, parking-€3, Largo da Misericordia 1, tel. 266-750-000, fax 266-742-367, www.monfalimtur.pt, e-mail: reservas@monfalimtur.pt, SE).

Residencial Policarpo, filling another 16th-century nobleman's mansion, also has a homey feel, with 22 simple rooms tucked around a courtyard. Joquim and Michele Policarpo carry on the family tradition of good hospitality (prices in July–Aug: S-€25, Ss-€38, Sb-€45, D-€30, Ds-€43, Db-€50, Tb-€63, 15 percent less in April–June and Sept, even less off-season, includes breakfast, no CC, double-paned windows, air-con, terrace, fireplace, easy parking, 2 entrances: Rua da Freiria de Baixo 16 and Rua Conde da Serra, near university, tel. & fax 266-702-424, http://localnet.pt/residencial -policarpo/, e-mail: incoming.alentejo@policarpo.net, SE).

Hotel Santa Clara, renting 40 rooms on a quiet side street, is a solid, professional, tour-friendly place with no character but a good location and price and lots of comfort (Sb-€45, Db-€56, includes breakfast, CC, air-con, Travessa do Milheira 19, from Praça do Giraldo, take Rua Pinta Serpa downhill, then right on Milheira; coming from the bus station, turn left on Milheira after you enter city wall, tel. 266-704-141, fax 266-706-544, e-mail: hotelsantaclara@mail.telepac.pt).

Hotel Ibis, a cheap chain hotel, has 87 identical, Motel 6–type rooms a 15-minute walk from the center, just outside the city walls. Easy to find and offering easy parking, it's a cinch for drivers—but staying here is like eating at McDonald's in Paris (Sb/Db-€50,

€55 in July–Sept, breakfast-€4, one child sleeps free, CC, air-con, elevator, parking, Quinta da Tapada, tel. 266-744-620, fax 266-744-632, www.ibishotel.com, e-mail: h1708accorhotels.com).

LOWER PRICED

Évora's **hostel** is glorious as hostels go, with a central location, rooftop terrace, 16 doubles, and 16 multibed rooms, all with a WC and shower (84 beds total, Db-€28–35 per person, dorm bed-€10–12.50, top prices for mid-June through mid-Sept, non-members of any age pay €2 extra per night, includes breakfast, air-con, elevator, lockout 11:00–14:00 for cleaning, 2 blocks off town square, Rua Miguel Bombarda 40, tel. 266-744-848, fax 266-744-843). It's wise to book in advance through the Central Booking Office (tel. 213-596-000, fax at 213-596-001, www.pousadasjuventude.pt, e-mail: reservas@movijovem.pt).

Eating in Évora

Dining

Restaurante Cervejaria ¹/₄ Para As 9 ("quarter to nine") is steamy with local families chowing down on traditional favorites such as *arroz de tamboril* (a rice and seafood stew) and *açorda de marisco* (a spicy soup with clams, mixed seafood, and bread spiced with Alentejano herbs). The place gets packed, so arrive before 8:45 (€15 dinners, nightly from 19:00, Rua Pedro Simões 9, tel. 266-706-774).

Batata Quente Restaurante ("hot potato") has a more flamboyant menu than most, with traditional and creative dishes, strong on vegetables (€10 meals, Tue–Sun 19:00–22:30, closed Mon, air-con, near the center at Largo Santa Catarina 25, tel. 266-741-161).

Restaurante Cervejaria Fialho is a famous place where white-coated waiters feed traditional Alentejo cuisine to Bogart-like locals. With €25 meals, it's expensive, but this is arguably the best food in town (Tue–Sun 12:00–24:00, closed Mon, arrive before 20:00 or make a reservation, CC, air-con, Travessa Mascarenhas 14, from main square go right alongside church—Rua João de Deus—for a 5-min walk, take first left after garden square, tel. 266-703-079).

Adega do Alentejano is like an above-ground wine cellar. A huge clay wine cask crowds the entry. Inside, locals choose from cheap (€7 per plate), traditional dishes scrawled on placemats thumbtacked to the wall (Mon–Sat 12:00–15:00 & 19:00–22:00, closed Sun, no CC, Rua Gabriel Victor do Monte Pereira 21,

from main square go right alongside church—on Rua João de
Deus, then take third left, tel. 266-744-447).

Eating near Praça do Giraldo

These are within a block of Praça do Giraldo, the main square.
The first three are popular with tourists, but known for quality
traditional cuisine: **Restaurante Cozinha de St. Humberto**
(closed Thu, pricey, Rua da Moeda 39, tel. 266-704-251), **Restaurante Guião** (closed Mon, Rua da República 81, between
main square and Church of St. Francis, tel. 266-703-071), and
Mr. Pickwick's Restaurante, more peaceful, with a few fun outdoor tables and a sedate interior just a block up Rua 5 de Outubro
from the main square (serving traditional—in spite of the name—
€8 plates with veggies and salad, lunch from noon, dinner from
19:00, closed Sun, Alcarcova de Cima 3, tel. 266-706-999).

To crank up the local atmosphere, eat at **Dom Fartote**
(cheap and basic fare, daily 12:00–15:00 & 19:00–24:00, Rua Romao
Ramalho 11, a few steps off the main square, tel. 266-700-081).

Transportation Connections—Évora

To: Lisbon (by bus: 12/day, 2 hrs; by train: 4/day, 2.5–3.5 hrs
including ferry from Barreiro Station to Lisbon), **Lagos** (by bus:
2/day, 5 hrs, transfer in Albufeira; by train: 3/day, 5.5 hrs with
transfers at Casa Branca and Funcheira), **Coimbra** (12/day,
4 hrs), **Madrid** (2 buses/day, 7.5–10 hrs, buy 1 day in advance
to insure a seat; the 7.5-hr bus is overnight), **Sevilla** (1 bus/day
on Wed, Fri, Sat, and Sun, 7.5 hrs). Bus info (no English spoken):
tel. 266-769-410.

CENTRAL PORTUGAL:
COIMBRA AND NAZARÉ

While the far north of Portugal has considerable charm, those with limited time enjoy maximum travel thrills on or near the coast of central Portugal. This is an ideal stop if you're coming in from Salamanca or Madrid or are interested in a small-town side trip north from Lisbon.

The college town of Coimbra (3 hrs north of Lisbon by train, bus, or car) is Portugal's Oxford and its easiest-to-enjoy city. Browse through the historic university, fortress-like cathedral, and lively Old Quarter of what was once Portugal's leading city.

Nazaré, an Atlantic-coast fishing-town-turned-resort, is black-shawl traditional and beach friendly. You'll be greeted by the energetic applause of the surf, widows with rooms to rent, and big plates of steamed shrimp. Have fun in the Portuguese sun in a land of cork groves, eucalyptus trees, ladies in seven petticoats, and men who stow cigarettes and fishhooks in their stocking caps.

Several other worthy sights are within easy day-trip distance of Nazaré. You can drop by the Batalha Monastery, the patriotic pride and architectural joy of Portugal. If the spirit moves you, the pilgrimage site at Fatima is nearby. Alcobaça has Portugal's largest church (and saddest romance). And Portugal's incredibly cute walled town of Óbidos is just down the road.

Planning Your Time
Few Americans give Portugal much time, visiting only Lisbon and the south coast. But on a three-week trip through Spain and Portugal, Coimbra and Nazaré each merit a day. There's another day's worth of sightseeing in Batalha, Alcobaça, and Fatima. If you're connecting Salamanca with Lisbon, I'd do it this way (for specifics see Salamanca's and Coimbra's "Transportation Connections").

By Car

Day 1: Leave Salamanca early, breakfast in Ciudad Rodrigo, early afternoon arrival in Coimbra, tour university and old cathedral.
Day 2: Shop and browse the Old Quarter, lunch at Batalha, tour church, visit Fatima, evening in Nazaré.
Day 3: Make the 16-kilometer side trip from Nazaré to Alcobaça (town, monastery, wine museum). Spend afternoon back in Nazaré with a look at Sitio and beach time. Seafood dinner.
Day 4: Visit Óbidos on your way to Lisbon. Arrive in Lisbon by noon.

By Public Transportaton

Day 1: You have only one train option and it's miserable: the 4:38–8:40 Salamanca–Coimbra train connection (5-hr trip, 1 hr gained in Portugal); upon arrival, spend the day sightseeing in Coimbra. The Salamanca–Coimbra bus offers a more liveable departure time but doesn't run daily, leaving Salamanca on Monday, Friday, Saturday, and Sunday at 15:00 (4-hr trip).
Day 2: If you arrived in Coimbra by train and did your Coimbra sightseeing yesterday, catch the morning bus to Nazaré today. If you arrived in Coimbra by bus yesterday evening, sightsee Coimbra this morning, and catch an afternoon bus to Nazaré. Set up and relax in Nazaré, Sitio, and on the beach. Seafood dinner.
Day 3: Do the triangular loop (Nazaré Batalha–Alcobaça–Nazaré) by bus, or enjoy beach time.
Day 4: Train into Lisbon.

COIMBRA

Don't be fooled by Coimbra's drab suburbs. Portugal's most important city for 200 years, Coimbra (pron. KWEEM-bra) remains second only to Lisbon culturally and historically. It served as Portugal's leading city while the Moors controlled Lisbon. Only as Portugal's maritime fortunes rose was landlocked Coimbra surpassed by the ports of Lisbon and Porto. Today Coimbra is Portugal's third-largest city (pop. 100,000) and home to its oldest and most prestigious university (founded 1290). When school is in session, Coimbra bustles. During school holidays, it's sleepy. It's got a great Arab-flavored Old Quarter—a maze of people, narrow streets, and tiny *tascas* (restaurants with just a few tables).

Orientation

Coimbra is a mini-Lisbon—everything good about urban Portugal without the intensity of a big city. I couldn't design a more enjoyable city for a visit. There's a small-town feeling in the winding streets set on the side of the hill. The high point is the

Coimbra

TO BUS STN.
(BORING 15 MIN WALK)
PORTO +
ECOVIA P & R

PRAÇA
8 MAIO

Post   MARKET

S. BANDEIRA

TO PRAÇA
REPUBLICA

FERMIXO

LARGO
OLARIAS

MARTINS DE CAVALHO

RUA
QUEBRA
COSTAS

DOS APOSTOLOS

PADEIRAS

PAPRE ANT VEIRA

VISCONDE DA LUZ

LARGO
DA SÉ VELHA

MAGALHAES

VEIGA

COUTINHOS

LOUREIRO

TRAIN
STN
'A'

AZEITEIRAS

SÉ

LARGO
FEIRA

NAVARRO

WC

WC

SIOTA

PRACA
DINIS

BORGES

LARGO
PORTAGEM

OLD
UNIV

PORTA FERREA

FALCÃO

LISBOA

PONTE S. CLARA

NAVARRO

BRASIL

JARDIM   BOTANICO

TO
SANTA CLARA
CONVENT
+
LITTLE
PORTUGAL

RIO
MONDEGO

0 M   100   200

0 YDS   200

REGRAS

CASTRO

TO E.3
NAZARÉ +
LISBOA

|||| UNIVERSITY

DCH

- ❶ Praca do Comercio
- ❷ Iron gate entry to
  University courtyard
- ❸ Machado de Castro Museum
- ❹ Hotel Astoria
- ❺ Hotels Oslo & Braganca
- ❻ Residencia Moderna
- ❼ Ibis Hotel
- ❽ Pensao Santa Cruz &
  free internet
- ❾ Hospedaria Simoes
- ❿ Residencial Larbelo
- ⓫ Rest. Trovador
- ⓬ Adega Paco do Conde Rest.
- ⓭ Rest. Jardim da Manga
- ⓮ Elevator
- ⓯ Fado Diligencia
- ⓰ Casa Bizarro

old university. From there, little lanes meander down like a
Moroccan medina to the main pedestrian street. This street
(named Visconde da Luz at the top, turning into Rua de Ferreira
Borges halfway down) runs from the Praça 8 de Maio to the
Mondego River, dividing the old town into upper (Alta) and
lower (Baixa) parts.

From the Largo da Portagem (main square by the river)
everything is within an easy walk. The Old Quarter spreads out
like an amphitheater—timeworn houses, shops, and stairways all
lead up to the university. The best views are looking up from the

far end of Santa Clara Bridge and looking down from the observation deck of the university. The TI and plenty of good budget rooms are within several blocks of the train station.

Tourist Information

Pick up a map and the monthly cultural calendar at the helpful English-speaking TI at Largo da Portagem (July–Sept Mon–Fri 9:00–19:00, Sat–Sun 10:00–13:00 & 14:30–17:30; Oct–June Mon–Fri 9:00–18:00, Sat–Sun 10:00–13:00 & 14:30–17:30, entrance on Navarro, tel. 239-855-930, www.turismo-centro.pt, e-mail: rtc-coimbra@turismo-centro.pt). Here you can get bus schedules (printed out for you) and information on sights in central Portugal. Other TIs are on Largo Dinis (Mon–Fri 9:00–18:00, Sat–Sun 9:00–12:30 & 14:00–17:30, tel. 239-832-591) and Praça da República (Mon–Fri 10:00–18:30, closed Sat–Sun, tel. 239-833-202; both near the university).

While the city doesn't offer walking tours, the TI has a list of private guides (such as Cristina Bessa at tel. 239-835-428, €75/half-day).

Helpful Hints

Bus Tickets: The Abreu travel agency sells bus tickets to Salamanca and beyond (Mon–Fri 9:00–12:30 & 14:30–18:30 plus March 15–mid-Oct Sat 9:00–12:30, closed Sun, CC, Rua da Sota 2, near train station A, tel. 239-855-520); if you're heading to Salamanca, the bus is a far better option than the train (for more info, see "Transportation Connections—Coimbra," below). ATMs and banks (Mon–Fri 8:30–15:00, closed Sat–Sun) are plentiful. Avis has an office in the train station A (Mon–Fri 8:30–12:30 & 15:00–19:00, closed Sat–Sun, tel. & fax 239-834-786, www.avis.com) and Hertz is at Rua Padre Estevão Cabral (tel. 239-834-750).

Internet Access: Internet Coimbra Camara Municipal has five computers and offers free access for a half-hour. Bring paper for print-outs (Mon–Fri 10:00–20:00, Sat–Sun 10:00–22:00, from the pedestrian street, past Praça 8 Maio on your left). Internet Centralmodem Cyberlounge has 14 computers (Mon–Fri 11:00–04:00, Sat–Sun 16:000–4:00, Rua Quebra Costas 42–44).

Arrival in Coimbra

By Train: There are two Coimbra train stations, A and B. Major trains (e.g., from Lisbon and Salamanca) stop only at B (big). From there, you can take a free three-minute shuttle train to the very central A station (free, included with ticket that got you to B station). To find out exactly which train to take to get to the A station, go to the *informações* office and ask at the ticket window:

"Comboio [pron. kom-boy-oo] *para Coimbra?"* Local trains (e.g.,
to Nazaré) stop at both stations. Station B has an ATM in an outside wall of the station, opposite the *informações* office. Taxis wait
across the tracks (about €4 to Station A or your hotel). Station A
has a helpful English-speaking *informações* office, tucked away in
a waiting room, where you can get schedules (daily 9:00–14:00 &
15:00–19:00, tel. 239-834-998). Across the street from Station A
are two Multibanco ATMs.

By Bus: The bus station, on Avenida Fernão de Magalhaes
(tel. 239-855-270) has a luggage check across from the *informações*
office to the right (€1 per bag, daily 8:00–18:30). The station
is a boring but easy 10-minute walk from the center. Exit the
bus station to the right and follow the busy street into town or
take a taxi (€2). Local buses are expensive (€1.20), and by the
time bus #29 or #35 comes along, you could already have walked
downtown. If you're heading for the bus station to leave Coimbra
by bus, take Avenida Fernão de Magalhaes past its intersection
with Cabral and look on the left—the Neptuno café marks the
station's subtle entrance. If you're planning to walk to the bus
station simply to get bus schedules, go to the TI instead, which
will print timetables for you.

Do-It-Yourself Orientation Tour
of Coimbra's Old Quarter

Coimbra is a delight on foot. You'll find yourself doing laps along
the straight (formerly Roman) pedestrian-only main drag. Do it
once following this quickie tour, which includes an elevator ride
that transports you to the top of the hill:

Start at **Santa Clara Bridge.** This has been a key bridge
over the Mondego River since Roman times. For centuries it
had a tollgate *(portagem).* Cross the bridge for a fine Coimbra
view, a lowbrow popular fairground, and free parking.

The square, **Largo da Portagem** (at the end of the bridge
on the Coimbra side), is a great place for a coffee or a pastry.
Pastelaria Briosa's pastries are best.

Stroll down the **pedestrian street.** After a gauntlet of clothing stores, take the stairs (to your left) leading to a terrace overlooking the square below (pay public WC, *sanitarios,* in the
stairwell). The square is the pleasant **Praça do Comércio** (shaped
like a Roman chariot racecourse—and likely to have been one
2,000 years ago) and the heart of the old town. Look at your map.
The circular street pattern outlines the wall used by Romans,
Visigoths, Moors, and Christians to protect Coimbra. Historically
the rich could afford to live within the protective city walls (the
"Alta" or high town). Even today, the Baixa, or low town, remains

a poorer section, with haggard women rolling their wheeled shopping bags, children running barefoot, and men lounging on the square like it's their life's calling. But it's a fun area to walk around during the day. Return to the pedestrian street.

Across the street from the overlook, steps lead up through an ancient arched gateway—Arco de Almedina—into the old city and to the old cathedral and university. Later, we'll finish this walk by going through this arch, when we come downhill after visiting the university.

Farther along the pedestrian drag, stop at the picturesque corner just beyond the cafés (where the building comes to a triangular corner). The steep road climbs into Coimbra's historic ghetto (no Jewish community remains).

You'll know it's graduation time if graduation photos are displayed in photographers' windows. Check out the students decked out in their traditional university capes (displaying rips on the hem for girlfriends) and color-coded sashes (yellow for medicine, red for law, and so on).

The pedestrian street ends at Praça 8 de Maio with the **Church of Santa Cruz** and its ornate facade. The shiny "necklace" on the angel behind the trumpeter is actually electrified to keep pigeons from dumping their corrosive load on the tender limestone. The church holds the tomb of Alfonso Henriquez, the king who reconquered most of Portugal from the Moors and Sancho I.

People (and pigeons) watch from the terrace of the recommended **Café Santa Cruz** (to the right of church). Built as a church but abandoned with the dissolution of the monasteries in 1834 (the women's room is in a confessional), this was the 19th-century haunt of local intellectuals.

Go around the church to your right to find the great **Self-Service Restaurant Jardim da Manga** directly behind the church (in park with fountain, see "Eating," below). Beyond the restaurant is the **covered market** (Mon–Sat 8:00–14:00, closed Sun, could buy a picnic here) and beyond the market (exit by the fish section, then go right) is the sleek new city elevator.

Take this **Elevador do Mercado,** (inaugurated in 2002) to the top of the hill (well worth €0.90 for 2 trips, Mon–Fri 7:30–23:30, Sat–Sun 9:00–23:30). The lift whisks you up the long, steep hill (stop midway to transfer), offering commanding views of Coimbra en route. Exit to the right and follow signs up to *Universidade*. After you pass a church and the **Machado de Castro Museum** (described in "Sights," below, may be closed for restoration in 2003), the Iron Gate entry of the university will be on your right.

Explore the university (details below), then head down the

extremely steep Rua Quebra Costas, the "Street of Broken Ribs." At one time this lane had no steps and literally was the street of broken ribs. During a strong rain this becomes a river. Going downhill, you'll pass the old **cathedral** (Sè Velha, described below), the recommended **Restaurante Trovador** (offering fado performances nearly nightly, facing cathedral), and lots of shops, showing off the fine local blue-and-white ceramic work called *faianca*. If you can't make it to Morocco, this dense jungle of shops and markets may be your next-best bet.

Rua Quebra Costas ends at the **Arco de Almedina** (literally "gate to the medina"; this is the arch we saw earlier from the pedestrian street). Part of the old town wall, this is a double gate with a 90-degree kink in the middle for easier defense. The two square holes in the ceiling, through which boiling oil would be poured, turned attacking Moors into fritters. Passing through the arch, you'll end up unscathed on the pedestrian street.

Sights—Coimbra's Old University

Coimbra's 700-year-old university was modeled after Bologna's university (Europe's first, A.D. 1139). It's a stately, three-winged former royal palace (from when Coimbra was the capital), beautifully situated overlooking the city. At first, law, medicine, grammar, and logic were taught. Then, with Portugal's seafaring orientation, astronomy and geometry were added. While Lisboa's university is much larger, Coimbra's university is still the country's most respected.

Cost and Hours: A combo-ticket for the two university sites that cost money to see—the Grand Hall and King John's Library—is €4 (otherwise €2.50 per site, daily May–Sept 9:00–19:00, Oct–April 9:30–12:00 & 14:00–17:00). To get to the university, consider taking the elevator from the covered market to the top of the hill (see "Do-It-Yourself Orientation Tour," above) or take a taxi to the Iron Gate, then sightsee Coimbra downhill.

Iron Gate—Find the gate to the old university (on Praça da Porta Ferrea). Before entering, stand with your back to the gate (and the old university) and look across the stark modern square at the fascist architecture of the new university. In what's considered one of the worst cultural crimes in Portuguese history, the dictator Salazar tore down half the old town of Coimbra to build these university halls. Salazar, proud that Portugal was the last European power to hang onto its global empire, wanted a fittingly monumental university here. After all, Salazar—along with virtually all people of political importance in Portugal—was educated in Coimbra. If these bold buildings are reminiscent of Mussolini's EUR in Rome, perhaps it's because they were built in part by Italian architects for Portugal's little Mussolini.

Coimbra's Old University

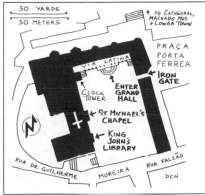

OK, now turn and walk through the Iron Gate. Traditionally, freshmen, proudly wearing their black capes for the first time, pass through the Iron Gate to enroll. But to get out they find an Iron Gate gauntlet of butt kicks from upperclassmen. Walk into the . . .

Old University Courtyard—The statue in the square is of King John III. While the university was established in 1290, it went back and forth between Lisbon and Coimbra (back then, university students were adults, privileged, and a pain to have in your town). In 1537 John III finally established the school permanently in Coimbra (away from Lisbon). Standing like a good humanist (posing much like England's Renaissance King Henry VIII), John modernized Portugal's education system Renaissance-style. But he also made the university the center of Portugal's Inquisition.

Survey the square with your back to the gate. The dreaded sound of the clock tower's bell—named the "baby goat" for its nagging—called the students to class. On several occasions the clapper has been stolen. No bell . . . no class. No class . . . big party. A larger bell (the "big goat") rings only on grand and formal occasions.

The university's most important stops all face this square: the Grand Hall (up the grand stairway on the right between you and the clock tower), St. Michael's Chapel (straight ahead, through the door, then to the left), and King John's Library (across the square, farthest door on left, flanked by columns).

The arcaded passageway (upstairs) between the Iron Gate and the clock tower is called Via Latina, from the days when only Latin was allowed in this part of the university. Purchase your ticket at the end of Via Latina immediately under the tower. See the following sights in any order you like.

The Grand Hall (Sala dos Capelos)—Enter from the middle of Via Latina and show your ticket (ask the ticket-taker about the *varanda* view; see next paragraph). The Grand Hall is the site of the university's major academic ceremonies, such as exams and graduations. This was originally the throne room of the royal palace. Today the rector's light-green chair sits thronelike in front. While students in their formal outfits filled the benches, teachers sat along the perimeter, and gloomy portraits of Portuguese kings looked down. Since there is no clapping during these formal rituals, a brass band (on the platform in the back) would punctuate the ceremonies with solemn music. Tourists look down from balconies above the room.

View Catwalk: Continue around the Grand Hall and out onto the narrow observation deck for the best possible views of Coimbra. The viewpoint will likely be open, but may be closed if there aren't sufficient staff to monitor the "only 10 people on the balcony at a time" rule. Ask the ticket-taker, *"A varanda esta aberta?"*—Is the veranda open? Request the key by making a hand sign for "key" or saying *"chave"* (pron. SHAH-veh).

From the viewpoint, scan the old town. Remember, before Salazar's extension of the university, this old town surrounded the university. The Baroque facade breaking the horizon is the "New" Cathedral—from the 16th century. Below that, with the fine arcade, is the Machado de Castro Museum, housed in the former bishop's palace and sitting on a Roman site (see below). And below that, like an armadillo, sits the old cathedral. If you see any noisily painted yellow and blue windows, it marks a *república*. Traditionally, Coimbra students from the same distant town would live together in groups of about a dozen in communal houses called *repúblicas*. Today these function as tiny fraternities—some are highly cultured, others are mini–Animal Houses. Look beyond the houses to the Mondego River, the longest entirely Portuguese river. Over the bridge and above the popular fairgrounds is the 17th-century Santa Clara Convent—at 180 meters (590 feet), the longest building in Coimbra.

St. Michael's Chapel—This chapel is behind the 16th-century Manueline facade (enter through the door to the right of the facade—once inside, push the door on the left marked *capela*, free admission). The architecture of the church interior is Manueline; notice the golden "rope" trimming the arch before the altar. The decor is from a later time. The altar is 17th-century Mannerist, with steps unique to Portugal (and her South American colonies), symbolizing the steps the faithful take on their journey to heaven. The 2,100-pipe 18th-century German-built organ is notable for its horizontal "trumpet" pipes. Found only in Iberia, these help the organist perform the allegorical fight between good and evil—with the horizontal pipes trumpeting the arrival of the good guys. Finally, above the loft in the rear are the box seats for the royal family.

The **Museum of Sacred Art,** farther down the corridor, may still be closed for renovation in 2003. When it reopens, a painting of John the Baptist will again point the way to art that nuns and priests find fascinating. The museum was created in 1910 to keep the art in Coimbra when the new republic wanted to move it all to Lisbon. (Also in the corridor, you'll find a café with WCs and a lovely view of the river from the terrace.)

King John's Library—This grand library displays 30,000 books in 18th-century splendor. The zealous doorkeeper locks the door at every opportunity to keep out humidity. Buzz to get into this temple of thinking. You might have to wait outside (until other tourists who are inside are ready to leave). Inside, at the "high altar," stands its founder, the Divine Monarch John V. The reading tables inlaid with exotic South American woods (and ornamented with silver ink wells) and the precious wood shelves (with clever hide-away staircases) are reminders that Portugal's wealth was great—and imported. Built Baroque, the interior is all wood. Even the marble is just painted wood. Look for the trompe l'ocil Baroque tricks on the painted ceiling. Gold leaf (from Brazil) is everywhere, and the Chinese themes are pleasantly reminiscent of Portugal's once-vast empire. The books, all from before 1755, are in Latin, Greek, or Hebrew. Imagine being a student in Coimbra 500 years ago. As you leave, watch how the doorman uses the giant key as a hefty doorknob.

More Sights—Coimbra

Machado de Castro Museum—The museum may be closed for restoration in 2003, but check to be sure. Housed in the old bishop's palace, it contains ceramics, 14th- to 16th-century religious sculpture (mostly taken from the dissolved monasteries), and a Roman excavation site. Upstairs, look for the impressive 14th-century *Cristo Negro* carved in wood. Until a decade ago when this statue was cleaned (and the black—from candle soot—came off), it was considered to be a portrait of a black Christ. Just before you return downstairs, enjoy the views from the top-floor arcade.

The Roman building, crisscrossed with empty tunnels, in the basement provided a level foundation for an ancient Roman forum that stood where the museum does today. At the entrance read the Latin-inscribed Roman stone: bottom line—"Aeminiens," referring to the people who lived in Roman Coimbra, then called Aeminium; fifth line—the fourth-century emperor of the day, Constantio; and the second line—a reference perhaps to an early alliance of barbarian tribes from the North Atlantic. Notice the few economical "plug-on" Roman busts—from the days when they'd keep the bodies but change the heads according to whoever the latest emperor was. The museum sometimes houses art exhibitions here in the Roman tunnels or on the ground floor (€3, includes any exhibitions, free Sun morning, Tue–Sun 9:30–12:30 & 14:00–17:30, closed Mon). Visit this before or after the old university, since both are roughly at the same altitude.

Old Cathedral (Sè Velha)—Same old story: Christians push out Moors (1064), tear down their mosque, and build a church. The Arabic script on a few of the stones indicates that rubble from the mosque was used in the construction. The facade of the main entrance even feels Arabic. Notice the crenellations along the roof of this fortresslike Romanesque church; the Moors, though booted out, were still considered a risk.

The three front altars are each worth a look. The main altar is a fine example of Gothic. The 16th-century chapel to the right is one of the best Renaissance altars in the country. The apostles all look to Jesus as he talks, while musical angels flank the holy host. To the left of the High Altar, the Chapel of St. Peter shows Peter being crucified upside down. The fine points of the carving were destroyed by Napoleon's soldiers.

The giant holy-water font shells are a 19th-century gift from Ceylon, and the walls are lined with 16th-century tiles from Sevilla.

On the right just before the transept is a murky painting of a queen with a skirt full of roses. She's a local favorite with a sweet legend. Against the wishes of the king, she always gave bread to the poor. One day, when he came home early from a trip, she was busy doling out bread from her skirt. She pulled the material up to hide the bread. When the king asked her what was inside (suspecting bread for the poor), the queen—unable to lie— lowered the material and, miraculously, the bread had turned to roses.

The peaceful cloister (entrance near back of church) is the oldest Gothic cloister in Portugal. Its decaying walls, neglected courtyard, and overgrown roses offer a fine framed view of the cathedral's grassy dome (church is free, cloisters cost €1; church hours: Mon–Thu 10:00–18:00, Fri 10:00–13:00, Sat 10:00–18:00, cloister closes from 13:00–14:00 Sept–June; closed Sun, the public is welcome to come to Mass, ask TI for schedule, WCs on your right).

Little Portugal (Portugal dos Pequenitos)—This is a children's (or tourist's) look at the great buildings and monuments of Portugal in miniature, scattered through a park a couple of blocks south of town, across the Santa Clara Bridge (€4 for gardens and monuments, €5 for gardens plus maritime and clothing museums, daily March–June 10:00–19:00, July–mid-Sept 9:00–20:00, mid-Sept–Feb 10:00–17:00).

Kayaks, Cruises, and Adventure Sports—O Pioneiro do Mondego takes you from Coimbra to Penacova (25 km away) by minibus and leaves you with a **kayak** and instructions on getting back. It's a three-hour paddle downstream on the Rio Mondego to Coimbra (€15, 10 percent discount with this book, daily April–mid-Oct, 1- and 2-person kayaks available, book by phone, meet at park near TI, tel. 239-478-385 to reserve, best time to phone is 20:00–22:00, SE). Most people stop to swim or picnic on the way back, so it often turns into an all-day journey. For the first 20 kilometers you'll go with the flow, but you'll get your exercise paddling the last five flat kilometers.

If you'd rather let someone else do the work, Basofias boats **cruise** up and down the river daily except Monday (€8, 3/day in summer, fewer off-season, 75 min, depart in afternoon from dock across from TI, get schedule at TI, tel. 239-491-900).

Capitao Dureza in Foz da Figueira specializes in **adventure sports**—at your own risk: rappelling, rafting, and canyoning (book by tel. & fax 233-427-772).

Sights—Near Coimbra

▲**Conimbriga Roman Ruins**—Portugal's best Roman site is impressive... unless you've been to Rome. Little remains of the city, in part because its inhabitants tore down buildings to throw up a quick defensive wall against an expected barbarian attack. Today this wall cuts crudely through the site. Highlights are the fine mosaics of the Casa dos Fonts (under the protective modern roofing) and a delightful little museum (€3, site open daily mid-March–mid-Sept 9:00–20:00, mid-Sept–mid-March 9:00–18:00; museum open 10:00–16:30, closed Mon). The ruins are 15 kilometers south of Coimbra on the Lisbon road. On weekdays two buses leave for the ruins each morning from Coimbra's A station (AVIC bus stop is on the riverside just in front of the station) and return late afternoon (€1.50, 30-min trip). Buses run twice per hour to Condeixa but leave you 1.5 kilometers from the site. Check bus schedules at the Coimbra TI.

Sleeping in Coimbra
(€1 = about $1, country code: 351, zip code: 3000)

Sleep Code: **S** = Single, **D** = Double/Twin, **T** = Triple, **Q** = Quad, **b** = bathroom, **s** = shower only, **CC** = Credit Cards accepted, **no CC** = Credit Cards not accepted, **SE** = Speaks English, **NSE** = No English. Breakfast isn't included unless noted.

To help you easily sort through these listings, I've divided the rooms into three categories, based on the price for a standard double room with bath during high season:

Higher Priced—Most rooms €80 or more.
Moderately Priced—Most less than €80.
Lower Priced—Most rooms less than €50.

The listings are an easy walk from the central A station and Santa Clara Bridge. For the cheapest rooms, simply walk from the A station a block into the old town and choose one of countless *dormidas* (cheap pensions). River views come with traffic noise.

HIGHER PRICED

Hotel Astoria gives you the thrill of staying in the city's finest old hotel (Sb-€85–100, Db-€100–115, price varies depending on season, extra bed-€25–30, includes breakfast, 10 percent discount by showing this book at check-in, CC, air-con, elevator, fine Art Deco lounges, public parking opposite hotel-€5/day, closed parking €7.50/day, central as can be at Avenida Navarro 21, tel. 239-853-020, fax 239-822-057, www.almeidahotels.com, e-mail: astoria@almeidahotels.com, SE). Rooms with river views cost nothing extra.

MODERATELY PRICED

Hotel Oslo rents 36 good business-class rooms a block from the A station. Rooms are small but hint of Oslo (Sb-€40–45, Db-€50–65, third person-€15 extra, includes breakfast buffet with view of old Coimbra, also a top-floor view bar that sometimes has free fado show for guests on Sat nights at 21:00, CC, air-con, elevator, free parking, Avenida Fernão de Magalhaes 25, tel. 239-829-071, fax 239-820-614, e-mail: hoteloslo@sapo.pt, SE).

Ibis Hotel is a modern high-rise. Its orderly little rooms come with all the comforts and American Motel 6 charm. Well-located on a riverside park, it's three blocks past the Santa Clara Bridge and the Old Quarter (110 rooms, Sb/Db-€40–59, breakfast-€4, CC, easy €3/day parking in basement, elevator, some smoke-free rooms, Avenida Emidio Navarro 70, tel. 239-852-130, fax 239-852-140, e-mail: h1672@accor-hotels.com, SE).

Hotel Braganca's ugly lobby disguises 83 clean, comfortable, but sometimes smoky rooms (ask to sniff several) with modern bathrooms (Sb/shower-€33, Sb/tub-€50, Db/shower-€56, Db/tub-€63, Tb/tub-€75, 10 percent discount with this book, save money by requesting a room with a shower—*chuveiro*, includes breakfast, CC, air-con, elevator, free parking in small lot if space available, Largo das Ameias 10, next to A station, tel. 239-822-171, fax 239-836-135, e-mail: hbraganza@mail.telepac.pt, SE). To minimize street noise, ask for a quieter room in the back.

LOWER PRICED

Residencial Moderna hides 16 delightful little rooms overlooking a pedestrian street. The six top-floor rooms come with parquet floors and a balcony—request *"com varanda"* (Db-€35–45, 10 percent discount with this book, breakfast-€3, no CC, air-con, free parking nearby daily 20:00–8:00, Rua Adelino Veiga 49, 2nd floor, a block from A station, tel. 239-825-413, fax 239-829-508, Fernandes family NSE).

Residencia Aeminium, run by the recommended Hotel Oslo and right next door, has 10 clean, comfortable rooms (Sb-€25–30, Db-€35–45, Tb-€45–55, includes breakfast at Hotel Oslo, no CC, air-con, double-paned windows, Avenida Fernão Magalhaes 17, tel. 239-829-071, fax 239-820-614, e-mail: hoteloslo@sapo.pt, SE).

Pensão Santa Cruz overlooks the charming and traffic-free square called Praça 8 de Maio at the end of the pedestrian mall. It's a bright, homey place, with 15 simple rooms that van Gogh would have enjoyed painting. You'll find lots of stairs, dim lights, and some balconies worth requesting (D-€12.50–20, Db-€20–€30, most expensive June–Aug, prices are soft so ask for relief if you need it, no CC, Praça 8 de Maio 21, 3rd floor, tel. & fax 239-826-197, www.pensaosantacruz.com, e-mail: mail @pensaosantacruz.com, Walter, Anna, and Oswald SE).

Residencial Larbelo—on Largo da Portagem, in front of the bridge—is rundown but has character, mixing frumpiness and former elegance. The old-fashioned staircase, elegant breakfast room, and friendly management take you to another age (Sb-€20, Db-€25–35, Tb-€35–45, depending on season and plumbing, includes breakfast, CC—Visa only, Largo da Portagem 33, tel. 239-829-092, fax 239-829-094, NSE).

Hospedaria Simões is a last resort. It's buried in the heart of the old town, just below the old cathedral. Run by the Simões family, it offers 18 clean, well-worn rooms, but only eight have real windows; to get a window, ask for a *quarto com janela* (Sb-€15–18, Db-€20–23, Tb-€25, Qb-€30, no breakfast, no CC, fans, piles of stairs, from Rua Ferreira Borges, go uphill through old gate toward cathedral, take first right, Rua Fernandes Thomas 69, tel. 239-834-638).

The youth hostel, **Pousada de Juventude,** on the other side of town in the student area past the Praça da República, is friendly, clean, and well-run, but is no cheaper than a simple *pensão* (€10.50 for members, €8.50 off-season, 4- to 6-bed rooms, closed 12:00–18:00, Rua Antonio Henriques Seco 14, tel. 239-822-955, SE).

Eating in Coimbra

Eating with Fado
Restaurante Trovador, while a bit touristy, serves wonderful food in a classic and comfortable ambience, with entertaining dinner fado performances nearly nightly after 21:00. It's the place

for an old-town splurge (daily menu-€27.50, Mon–Sat 12:00–15:00 & 19:30–22:30, closed Sun, CC, facing the old cathedral, Largo de se Velha 15, reservations recommended to eat with the music—ask for a seat with a music view, tel. 239-825-475).

Fado Diligencia is a good spot for a fado sing-along in a warm, relaxed atmosphere. Food and drinks are reasonable (shows daily 22:30–2:00, Rua Nova 30, from Praça 8 Maio take Rua Sofia to your second left, Diligencia is 2 blocks up on your right, tel. 239-827-667).

Eating without Fado
Adega Paço do Conde knows how to grill. Choose your seafood or meat selection from the display case, and it's popped on the grill. Students, solo travelers, and families like this homey place (€5 meals, Mon–Sat 11:00–22:00, closed Sun, Rua Paço do Conde 1, CC, from Praça do Comércio, take the last left—Adelino Veiga, opposite the church, and walk 2 blocks to small square—Largo do Paço do Condo, tel. 239-825-605, Alfredo SE).

For a quick, easy, and cheap meal with locals next to a cool and peaceful fountain, slide a tray down the counter at **Self-Service Restaurant Jardim da Manga** (€6 meals, Sun–Fri 8:00–23:00, closed Sat, in Jardim/Garden da Manga, behind Church of Santa Cruz, tel. 239-829-156).

The **Santa Cruz Café**, next to the Church of Santa Cruz, is Old World elegant, with outdoor tables offering great people-watching over Praça 8 Maio.

For an acceptable meal on an atmospheric square—Praça do Comércio—eat at **Restaurant Praça Velha,** but don't let the waiters con you (daily 8:00–01:00, Praça do Comércio 72).

Tiny **Casa Bizarro** serves up tasty Portuguese food at a good price (Sun–Fri 12:00–15:00 & 18:00–22:00, Sat 12:00–15:00, Rua Sargento Mor 44).

Boemia Bar, a happy student place, serves €5 grilled-pork meals near the old cathedral, behind the recommended Restaurant Trovador (Mon–Sat 19:00–24:00, closed Sun).

Picnics: Shop at the inviting covered *mercado* behind the Church of Santa Cruz, newly renovated in 2002 (Mon–Fri 7:00–19:00, Sat 7:00–14:00, closed Sun), or at hole-in-the-wall groceries in the side streets. The central "supermarket" **Minipreço**—behind the A station—is disappointing, selling fruit only in large quantities and lacking real juice. But in case they have something you want, they're open long hours (Mon–Sat 8:30–20:00, Sun 9:00–13:00 & 15:00–19:00). The well-maintained gardens along the river across from the TI are picnic-pleasant.

Transportation Connections—Coimbra

By bus to: Alcobaça (2/day, 90 min), **Batalha** (3/day, 75 min), **Fatima** (9/day, 1 hr), **Nazaré** (5/day, 1.75 hrs, €8.50), **Lisboa** (17/day, 2.5 hrs), **Évora** (12/day, 4 hrs), **Lagos** (5/day, 10 hrs with 1 change). Bus info: tel. 239-855-270. Frequency drops on weekends, especially Sunday.

By train to: Nazaré/Valado (6/day, 3.5 hours, transfer in Bifurcação de Lares, bus is better). The Nazaré/Valado train station is five kilometers away from Nazaré. Train info: tel. 808-208-208 (www.cp.pt).

To Salamanca: One **train** per day departs at 19:56 and drops you in Salamanca at 2:25 in the morning (5.5 hrs, 1-hr time difference). The far better option is the direct **bus,** but it runs only four times a week (€20, departs Mon, Fri, and Sat at 10:15, arrives 15:45, departs Sun at 18:15, arrives 23:45, 4.5 hrs, 1-hr time difference during daylight saving months); to guarantee a place, book two days in advance. You can confirm schedules and buy your bus ticket by phone or in person at the Abreu travel agency in Coimbra (see "Helpful Hints," above) more easily than at Coimbra's bus station (Intercentro, tel. 239-827-588, NSE).

NAZARÉ

I got hooked on Nazaré when colorful fishing boats littered its long, sandy beach. Now the boats motor comfortably into a new harbor a 30-minute walk south of town, the beach is littered with frolicking families, and it seems most of Nazaré's 10,000 inhabitants are in the tourist trade. But I still like the place.

Even with its summer crowds, Nazaré is a fun stop offering a surprisingly good look at old Portugal. Somehow the traditions survive, and the locals are able to go about their black-shawl ways. Wander the back streets for a fine look at Portuguese family-in-the-street life. Laundry flaps in the wind, kids play soccer, and fish sizzle over tiny curbside hibachis. Squadrons of sun-dried and salted fish are crucified on nets pulled tightly around wooden frames and left under the midday sun. Locals claim they are delightful—but I don't know. Off-season Nazaré is almost empty of tourists—inexpensive, colorful, and relaxed, with enough salty fishing-village atmosphere to make you pucker.

Nazaré doesn't have any blockbuster sights. The beach, tasty seafood, and funicular ride up to Sitio for a great coastal view are the bright lights of my lazy Nazaré memories.

Plan some beach time here. Sharing a bottle of *vinho verde* (new wine, a specialty of Portugal) on the beach at sundown is a good way to wrap up the day.

Nazaré Fashions:
Seven Petticoats and Black Widows

Nazaré is famous for its women who wear skirts with seven petticoats. While this is mostly just a creation for the tourists, there is some basis of truth to the tradition. In the old days, women would sit on the beach waiting for their fishermen to sail home. To keep warm during a cold sea wind and stay modestly covered, they'd wear several petticoats in order to fold layers over their heads, backs, and legs. Even today, older and more traditional women wear short skirts made bulky by several—but not seven—petticoats.

You'll see some women wearing black, a sign of mourning. Traditionally, if your spouse died you wore black for the rest of your life. This tradition is still observed, although in the last generation, widows began remarrying—considered quite racy at first.

Orientation

Nazaré faces its long beach, stretching north from the new harbor to the hill-capping old town of Sitio. Leaving the bus station, turn right and walk a block to the waterfront and survey the town. Scan the cliffs. The funicular climbs to Sitio (the hilltop part of town). Also to your right, look at the road kinking toward the sea. The building (on the kink) with the yellow balconies is the Ribamar Hotel, next to the TI. Just beyond the Ribamar you'll find the main square (Praça Sousa Oliveira, with banks and ATMs) and most of my hotel listings.

Sitio, which feels like a totally separate village sitting quietly atop its cliff, is reached by a frequent funicular (€0.60). Go up at least for the spectacular view.

Tourist Information: The TI faces the beach a block south of the main square (May–June daily 10:00–13:00 & 15:00–19:00, July–Aug daily 10:00–22:00, Oct–April daily 9:30–13:00 & 14:30–18:00, tel. 262-561-194). Ask about summer activities, bullfights in Sitio, and music on the beach (Sat–Sun 22:00).

Internet Access: Try the Cultural Center Library (free, Mon–Fri 9:30–13:00 & 14:00–19:00, Sat 15:00–19:00, closed Sun, on main road along beach en route to harbor) or the post office (Mon–Fri 9:00–12:30 & 14:30–18:00, closed Sat–Sun, on Rua Mouzinho Albuquerque, about 5 blocks inland, also has metered phones).

Laundry: At Lavanderia Nazaré, close to the bus station, Lucia will wash, dry, and fold your laundry in less than 24 hours

Nazaré

TO VALADO TRAIN STN. & ALCOBAÇA

TO N-242 OBIDOS & LISBON

RUA DOS BARRANCOS

POST

100 YARDS
100 METERS

SUB-VILA

REDOL

BUS STATION

R. OCIDENTAL

SITIO FUNICULAR STATION

REPUBLICA

TO PORT & SÃO MARTINHO

RUA LEIRIA

BEACH

TO SITIO

AVENIDA

PRAÇA ARRIAGA

ATLANTIC OCEAN

WC & SHOWERS

DCH

PRAÇA SOUSA OLIVEIKA (MAIN SQUARE)

❶ Ribamar Hotel Rest.
❷ Albergaria Mar Bravo
❸ Residencial A Cubata
❹ Hotel Mare
❺ Casa dos Frango Rest.
❻ Restaurante A Tasquinha
❼ Oficina Restaurante
❽ Laundry

(€3/kg, Mon–Sat 9:30–13:00 & 15:00–19:00, closed Sun, Rua Branco Martins 17, tel. 262-552-761).

Sights—Nazaré

The Beach—Since the harbor was built in 1986, boats are no longer allowed on the beach. Before that they filled the squares in the winter and the beaches in the summer. Today it's the domain of the beach tents—a tradition in Portugal. In Nazaré, the tents are run as a cooperative by the old women you'll see sitting in the shade ready to collect €6 or more a day. The beaches are groomed and guarded. Flags indicate danger level: red (no one in the water), yellow (wading is safe), green (no problem). If you see a mass of children parading through town down to the beach, they're likely from a huge dorm in town that provides poorer kids from this part of the country with a summer break.

Funicular to Sitio—Nazaré's funicular was built in 1889—the same year as the Eiffel Tower—by the same disciple of Eiffel who built the much-loved elevator in Lisbon. Ride up the lift (called *ascensor*); it goes every five minutes (€0.60 each way, runs 7:00–1:00, every 5 min 7:00–21:30, otherwise every half-hour, WCs at base). Notice how the locals get off while it's still moving. Walk to the staggering Nazaré viewpoint behind the station at the top, then the main viewpoint past the many vendors at the promontory (wave to America). Sitio feels different. Its people are farmers, not fishing folk.

Activities—Sitio stages Portuguese-style **bullfights** on Saturday nights from July through early September (tickets from €10 at kiosk in Praça Sousa Oliveira). Sitio's **NorParque** is a family-friendly **water park** with a pool, slides, and Jacuzzi (adults-€9, kids ages 6–11-€7.50, less after 14:30, June–mid-Sept 10:30–19:00, closed mid-Sept–May, opening may be delayed until July depending on weather, confirm hours at TI, watch for free shuttle bus). A **flea market** pops up near Nazaré's town hall every Friday (9:00–13:00, at the inland end of the street the bus station is on) and the colorful **produce market** bustles in the morning (daily 8:00–12:00, Oct–May closed Mon, kitty-corner from bus station).

Sleeping in Nazaré
(€1 = about $1, country code: 351, zip code: 2450)
Sleep Code: **S** = Single, **D** = Double/Twin, **T** = Triple, **Q** = Quad, **b** = bathroom, **s** = shower only, **CC** = Credit Cards accepted, **no CC** = Credit Cards not accepted, **SE** = Speaks English, **NSE** = No English.

You should have no problem finding a room, except in August, when the crowds, temperatures, and prices are all at their highest. You'll find plenty of hustlers meeting each bus and Valado train and waiting along the promenade. Even the normal hotels get into the act during the off-season. I've never arrived in town without a welcoming committee inviting me to sleep in their *quartos* (rooms in private homes).

I list a price range for each hotel: The lowest is for winter (roughly Jan–March), the sky-highest for mid-July through August. The rest of the year (approximately April–mid-July and Sept–Dec) expect to pay about midrange. You will save serious money if you arrive with no reservations and bargain, even at hotels.

HIGHER PRICED
Hotel Mare, just off the Praça Sousa Oliveira, is a big, modern, American-style hotel with 36 rooms, some tour groups, and a rooftop terrace (Sb-€49–75, Db-€50–95, Tb-€54–108, includes breakfast, CC, all with air-con and balconies, double-paned

windows, elevator, free parking lot, Rua Mouzinho de Albuquerque 8, tel. 262-561-122, fax 262-561-750, e-mail: hotel
.mare@mail.telepac.pt, SE).

Albergaria Mar Bravo is on the main square and the
waterfront. Its 16 comfy rooms are great—modern, bright, and
fresh, with balconies, eight with views—but the staff is not gen-
uinely friendly (Sb-€50–90, Db-€60–102, depending on view
and month, view breakfast room, CC, air-con, elevator, Praça
Sousa Oliveira 71-A, tel. 262-569-160, fax 262-569-169, e-mail:
mar_bravo@clix.pt, SE).

MODERATELY PRICED
Ribamar Hotel Restaurant has a prime location on the waterfront, with an Old World, hotelesque atmosphere, including
24 rooms with dark wood and four-poster beds (Sb-€25–45,
Db-€30–80, prices flexible, includes breakfast, CC, 5 rooms with
balconies, good attached restaurant downstairs, parking-€5/€10
in Aug, Rua Gomes Freire 9, tel. 262-551-158, fax 262-562-224,
some English spoken). Look for the yellow awnings and balconies.

Residencial A Cubata, a friendly place on the waterfront on
the north end, has 22 small, comfortable rooms and older bathrooms (Sb-€25–50, Db-€33–75, depends on view and season,
includes breakfast, 10 percent discount with this book if you pay
cash, CC, noisy bar below—though they've added soundproofing,
Avenida da República 6, tel. 262-561-706, fax 262-561-700, some
English spoken). For a peaceful night, forgo the private balcony,
take a back room (saving some money), and enjoy the communal
beachfront balcony.

LOWER PRICED QUARTOS
I list no dumpy hotels or cheap pensions because the best budget
option is *quartos.* Like nowhere else in Iberia, locals renting spare
rooms clamor for your business in Nazaré. Except perhaps for weekends in August, you can stumble into town any day and find countless
women hanging out on the street (especially around the bus station)
with fine modern rooms to rent. I promise. The TI's partial list of
quartos totals 200. If you've got a backpack, they've got a room.
Their rooms are generally better than hotel rooms—for half the cost.
Your room is likely to be large and homey, with old-time-elegant
furnishings (with no plumbing but plenty of facilities down the hall)
and in a quiet neighborhood, six short blocks off the beachfront
action. I'd come into town and have fun looking at several places.
Hem and haw and the price goes down. **Nazaré Amada** rents seven
fine rooms (average price for Db-€20, €30 July–Sept, Rua Adriao
Batalha, garage, tel. 262-552-206, cellular 962-579-371, SE).

Eating in Nazaré

Nazaré is a fishing town, so don't order *hamburguesas*. Fresh seafood is great all over town, more expensive (but affordable) along the waterfront, and cheaper farther inland. Waiters will sometimes bring you food (such as olives or bread) that you didn't order. Just wave it away or else you'll pay for it.

In this fishing village even the snacks come from the sea. *Percebes* are local boiled barnacles, sold as munchies in bars and on the street. Merchants are happy to demonstrate how to eat them and let you sample one for free. They're great with beer in the bars.

Vinho verde, a Portuguese specialty, is a very young wine— picked, made, and drunk within a year. It's refreshing and a bit like champagne without the bubbles. Generally white, cheap, and on every menu, it goes great with shellfish. *Amendoa amarga* is the local amaretto.

The family-run **Oficina** serves home-style seafood dishes, not fancy but filling, in a friendly setting that makes you feel like you're eating at someone's kitchen table (daily 12:00–15:00 & 19:00–22:00, if it's quiet it may be closed at night, Rua das Flores 33, off Praça Dr. Manual Arriaga; facing the restaurant Casa dos Frango, take street immediately left, tel. 262-083-703).

Chicken addicts can get roasted chickens to go at **Casa dos Frango** (daily 9:30–13:00 & 15:30–20:30, Praça Dr. Manual Arriaga 20), while picnic gatherers can head for the covered *mercado* across from the bus station (daily 8:00–12:00, closed Mon Oct–May).

Family-run **Restaurante A Tasquinha** serves home-style Portuguese cooking in a cozy picnic-bench setting, popular among locals and some tourists (Tue–Sun 12:00–15:00 & 19:00–22:30, closed Mon, Rua Adriao Batalha 54, tel. 262-551-945).

Restaurante O Luis in Sitio serves excellent seafood and local cuisine to an enthusiastic crowd in a cheery atmosphere. While few tourists go here, friendly waiters make you feel welcome. This place is worth the trouble if you want to eat well in Nazaré: Ride the lift up to Sitio and walk five minutes to Praça de Toros (€10 dinners, Fri–Wed 12:00–24:00, closed Thu, air-con, CC, from funicular take steps down to main drag, turn right on main drag and walk to bullring, take street downhill left of bullring, Rua Dos Tanques 7, tel. 262-551-826).

Transportation Connections—Nazaré

Nazaré's bus station is in the center, on Avenida Vieria Gumaraes, a block inland from the waterfront. The nearest train station is at Valado (5 km toward Alcobaça, connected by semiregular €1.25 buses and reasonable, easy-to-share €6 taxis). To avoid this headache, consider using intercity buses instead of trains.

If you're heading to Lisbon, trains and buses work equally well. While the train station is five kilometers from Nazaré and a trip to Lisbon requires a transfer in Cacém, you'll arrive at Lisbon's very central Rossio station (near recommended hotels). Lisbon's bus station is a Metro (or taxi) ride away from the center.

Nazaré/Valado by train to: Coimbra (6/day, 3.5 hrs, change at Bifurcação de Lares; see bus info below), **Lisbon** (7/day, 2-3 hrs). Train info: tel. 808-208-208.

Nazaré by bus to: Alcobaça (stopping at Valado, 12/day, 20 min), **Batalha** (7/day, 1 hr, some change at São Jorge), **Óbidos** (5/day, 1 hr; bus is better than train), **Fatima** (3/day, 60 min), **Coimbra** (5/day, 1.75 hrs; bus is better than train), **Lisbon** (8/day, 1.5 hrs). Buses are scarce on Sunday. Bus info: tel. 262-551-172.

Day-Tripping from Nazaré to Alcobaça, Batalha, Fatima, or Óbidos: Traveling by bus you can see both Alcobaça and Batalha in one day (but not on Sun, when bus service is sparse). Alcobaça is easy to visit on the way to or from Batalha (and both are connected by bus with Óbidos). Ask at the bus station or TI for schedule information and be flexible. Fatima has the fewest connections and is farthest away. Without a car, for most, Fatima is not worth the trouble. A taxi from Nazaré to Alcobaça costs about €10.

BATALHA

The only reason to stop in the town of Batalha is to see its great monastery. Considered Portugal's greatest architectural achievement and a symbol of its national pride, the Batalha (which means "battle") Monastery was begun in 1388 to thank God for a Portuguese victory that kept it free from Spanish rule. Why the battle? The Portuguese king died leaving only a daughter who was married to the king of Spain as an heir. This left the King of Spain ruling Portugal. The Portuguese went to war to keep their independence. Vastly outnumbered but with English aid, the Portuguese won. A hero of the Portuguese victory was a bastard named John (João). The Portuguese people choose him to be their king. Furthering ties with England, John married an Englishwoman who became Portugal's Queen Philippa.

Tourist Information: The TI, behind the monastery, has free maps and information on buses (daily April–Sept 10:00–13:00 & 15:00–19:00, Oct–March 10:00–13:00 & 14:00–18:00, Praça Mouzinho de Albuquerque, tel. 244-765-180). Batalha's market day is Monday morning (market is 200 meters behind monastery).

Arrival in Batalha: If you take the bus to Batalha, you'll be dropped off within a block of the monastery and TI. There's no official luggage storage, but you can leave luggage at the TI or monastery's ticket desk while you tour the cloisters.

Nazaré Area

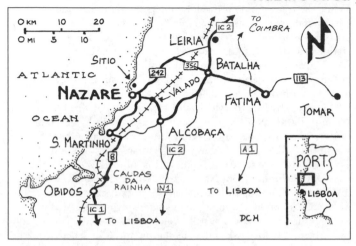

Monastery of Santa María

Here's a self-guided tour of the town's most important sight (€3, daily April–Sept 9:00–18:00, Oct–March 9:00–17:00, tel. 244-765-180).

Monastery Exterior: The equestrian statue outside the church is of Nuno Alvares Pereira, who commanded the Portuguese in the battle and masterminded the victory over Spain. Before entering the church, study the carving on the west portal. Noticing the two ranks of figures: first rank—angels with their modesty wings; second rank—the angel band with different instruments including a hillbilly washboard. Also, flanking the door are two coats of arms: Portugal's on the right and the House of Lancaster on the left (a reminder of Portugal's indebtedness to England for its victory). Stepping inside you'll be struck by the tall, pure Gothic lines of this appropriately uncluttered Dominican abbey church. The first chapel on the right is the...

Founder's Chapel: Center-stage is the double sarcophagus (that's English style) of King John and his English Queen Philippa. Their son, Henry the Navigator, is entombed opposite the entry—wearing the church like a crown on his head. Speaking of crowns, notice that this square room is ingeniously capped by an octagonal dome.

Cloisters: Pay €3 before entering. The greatness of Portugal's Age of Discovery shines brightly in the royal cloisters, which combine the simplicity of Gothic with the elaborate decoration of the Manueline style.

Chapter Room: This is famous for its fine and frighteningly broad vaults. The ceiling was considered so dangerous to build (it collapsed twice) that only prisoners condemned to death were allowed to work on it. Today unknowing tourists are allowed to wander under it. Portugal's Tomb of the Unknown Soldier sits under a mutilated cricifix called *Christ of the Trenches*—which accompanied Portuguese soldiers into battle on the WW I western front. The three small soldiers under the flame—which burns Portuguese olive oil—are dressed to represent the three most valiant chapters in Portuguese military history: fighting Moors in the 12th century, Spaniards in the 14th century, and Germans in the 20th century.

The adjacent monks' dining hall, or refectory, holds a museum of World War I memorabilia. Notice the photo of the *Christ of the Trenches* in battle (just inside the door on right).

Keep your ticket, exit the first cloister to a square behind the church where signs to the right (WC is to the left) direct you to the...

Unfinished Chapels: The unfinished chapels *(capelas imperfeitas)* were started for King Duarte around 1435 to house the tombs of his family and successors. Never finished, the building with the best Manueline details you'll see here—is open to the sky. Study the elaborate carvings of the entry gate. This is classic Manueline—tangled with symbols of the age: artichokes (used to fend off scurvy), corn (from American discoveries), and Indian-inspired motifs (from the land of pepper). Across from the elaborate doorway are the tombs of King Duarte and his wife, their recumbent statues hand-in-hand, blissfully unaware of the work left undone.

Transportation Connections—Batalha

By bus to: Nazaré (5/day, 1 hr), **Alcobaça** (10/day, 30 min), **Fatima** (3/day, 30 min), and **Lisbon** (6/day, 2 hrs). Expect fewer buses on weekends. By car, Batalha is an easy 16-kilometer drive from Fatima. You'll see signs from each site to the other.

FATIMA

On May 13, 1917, the Virgin Mary, "a lady brighter than the sun," visited three young shepherds and told them peace was needed. World War I raged on, so on the 13th day of each of the next five months, Mary dropped in again to call for peace. On the 13th of October, 70,000 people witnessed the parting of dark storm clouds as the sun wrote "God's fiery signature" across the sky. Now, on the 13th of May, June, July, September, and October, and on the 19th of August, thousands of pilgrims gather at the huge neoclassical **Basilica of Fatima** (evening torchlit processions for 2 nights, starting the night before, usually the 12th and 13th). In 1930 the Vatican recognized the Virgin of Fatima as legit, and in 1967, on the 50th anniversary, 1.5 million pilgrims—including the Pope—gathered here. Fatima welcomes guests. Near the basilica is the TI (daily April–Sept 10:00–13:00 & 15:00–19:00, Oct–March 10:00–13:00 & 14:00–18:00, Avenida Jose Alves Correia da Silva, tel. 249-531-139).

The impressive **basilica** stands in front of a mammoth square lined with parks. (Dress modestly to enter the church.) Surrounding the square are a variety of hotels, restaurants, and tacky souvenir stands.

Visitors may want to check out two museums (both open daily 9:30–18:30 and cost about €6). The **Museo de Cera de Fatima** is a series of rooms telling the story of Fatima's visitation one scene at a time with wax figures (English leaflet describes each vignette). The **Museu-Vivo Aparicões,** a low-tech sound and light show, tells the same story (worthless without English soundtrack playing—ask). While the wax museum is better, both exhibits are pretty cheesy for those who are inclined not to take Fatima seriously.

Apart from the 12th and 13th of most months, cheap hotel rooms abound.

Buses go from Fatima to **Batalha** (3/day, 30 min), **Leiria** (15/day 30 min), and **Lisbon** (12/day, 1.5–2.5 hrs, depending on route); service drops on Sunday.

ALCOBAÇA

This pleasant little town is famous for its church, one of the most interesting in Portugal. I find Alcobaça a better stop than Batalha.

Tourist Information: The English-speaking TI is across the square from the church (daily May–Oct 10:00–13:00 & 15:00–19:00, Nov–April closes at 18:00, Praça 25 de Abril, tel. 262-582-377).

Arrival in Alcobaça: If you arrive by bus, it's a five-minute walk to the town center and monastery: Exit right from the station (on Avenida Manuel da Silva Carolino), take the first right, and continue straight (on Avenida dos Combatentes).

Sights—Alcobaça

▲▲**Cistercian Monastery of Santa María**—This abbey church— the best Gothic building and the largest church in Portugal—is a clean and bright break from the heavier Iberian norm. It was started in 1178 after this area was reconquered from the Moors. It became one of the most powerful abbeys of the Cistercian Order and a cultural center of 13th-century Portugal. The abbey, clean and simple, is designed to be filled with hard work, prayer, and total silence. The abbey and cloisters cost €3 (worthwhile €1 English leaflet, daily April–Sept 9:00–19:00, Oct–March 9:00–17:00, tel. 262-505-120).

Nave and Tombs of Dom Pedro and Inês: A long and narrow nave leads to a pair of finely carved Gothic tombs (from 1360). These are of Portugal's most tragic romantic couple, Dom Pedro (King Peter I, on the right) and Dona Inês de Castro (on the left). They rest feet-to-feet in each transept so that on Judgment Day they'll rise and immediately see each other again. Pedro, heir to the Portuguese throne, was in love with the Spanish aristocrat Inês. Concerned about Spanish influence, Pedro's father, Alfonso IV, forbade their marriage. You guessed it—they were married secretly. The angry father-in-law, in the interest of Portuguese independence, had Inês murdered. When Pedro became king (1357), he ripped out and ate the hearts of the murderers. And even more interesting, he had Inês' rotten corpse exhumed, crowned it, and made the entire royal court kiss what was left of her hand. Now that's *amore*.

The carvings on the tomb are just as special. Like religious alarm clocks, the attending angels are poised to wake the couple on Judgment Day. The "Wheel of Life" below the finely-combed head of Pedro shows scenes from his life with Inês. Elsewhere on the coffin you can see scenes from the life of St. Bartholomew—being skinned alive. Pedro's tomb is supported by lions, a symbol of royalty. Inês' tomb is supported by the lowly scum who murdered her . . . one holding money, a symbol of evil. Study the relief at the feet of Inês: Heaven, the dragon mouth of Hell, and jack-in-the-box coffins on Judgment Day. Napoleon's troops vandalized the tombs.

More Tombs and Relics in the Sacristy: Near the king's tomb, step into the neo-Gothic Hall of Tombs for more deceased royalty. Behind the High Altar is the sacristy. In the round room decorated with painted wooden sculptures, the little glassed-in hollows in the statues and beams hold relics (tiny bits of bones or clothing) of the monks who died in the monastery. In the rear of the nave, find the . . .

Hall of Kings: This hall—where you pay to enter—features statues of most of Portugal's kings and 18th-century tiled walls telling the story of the 12th-century conquest of the Moors and the building of the monastery.

Cloisters: Cistercian monks built the abbey in 40 years, starting in 1178. They inhabited it until 1834 (when the Portuguese king disbanded all monasteries). Cistercian monks spent most of their lives in silence and were allowed to speak only when given permission by the abbot. To enjoy this cloister like the monks did, meditate, pray, exercise, and connect with nature. As you multitask, circle counterclockwise until you reach the fountain—where the monks washed up before eating. In the cloisters, the fountain marks the entry to the...

Refectory or Dining Hall: Imagine the hall filled with monks eating in silence as one reads from the Bible atop the "Readers' Pulpit." Food was prepared next door.

Kitchen: The 18th-century kitchen's giant three-part oven could roast seven oxen simultaneously. The industrious monks rerouted part of the River Alcoa to bring in running water. And how about those hard surfaces?

▲**Mercado Municipal**—An Old World Safeway is housed happily here under huge steel-and-fiberglass domes. Inside the covered market, black-clad, dried-apple-faced women choose fish, chicks, birds, and rabbits from their respective death rows. Wander among figs, melons, bushels of grain, and nuts (Mon–Sat 9:00–13:00, closed Sun, best on Mon). It's a five-minute walk from the TI or bus station; ask a local, *"Mercado municipal?"*

▲▲**National Museum of Wine (Museu Nacional do Vinho)**— This museum, a kilometer outside Alcobaça (on the road to Batalha and Leiria, right-hand side), offers a fascinating look at the wine of Portugal (€1.50, May–Sept Tue–Fri 9:00–12:30 & 14:00–17:30, Sat–Sun 10:00–12:30 & 14:00–18:00, closed Mon; Oct–April Mon–Fri 9:00–12:30 & 14:00–17:30, closed Sat–Sun, tel. 262-582-222; your car is safer parked inside the gate). Run by a local cooperative winery, the museum teaches you everything you never wanted to know about Portuguese wine in a series of rooms that used to be fermenting vats. With some luck you can get a tour—much more hands-on than French winery tours—through the actual winery.

Transportation Connections—Alcobaça

By bus to: Lisbon (5/day, 2 hrs), **Nazaré** (12/day, 30 min), **Batalha** (4/day, 30 min), **Fatima** (3/day, 75 min, more frequent with transfer in Batalha). Bus frequency drops on Sunday. A taxi to the Nazaré/Valado train station costs about €6; to Nazaré, up to €10. Bus info: tel. 262-582-221.

ÓBIDOS

Postcard perfect, Óbidos sits atop a hill, its 14th-century wall (13 meters/43 feet tall) corralling a bouquet of narrow lanes and flower-bedecked whitewashed houses. Óbidos is ideal for photographers who want to make Portugal look prettier than it is.

Founded by Celts (c. 300 B.C.), then ruled by Romans,

Visagoths, and Moors, Óbidos was unique as Portugal's "wedding city"—the perfect gift for a king to give to a queen who has everything. (Beats a toaster.) Today this medieval walled town is popular for lowly commoners' weddings. Preserved in its entirety as a national monument, it survives on tourism. Every summer morning at 9:30, the tour groups flush into town. Óbidos is especially crowded in August. It's worth a quick visit. Ideally, arrive late in the day and leave early the next and enjoy the town as you would a beautiful painted tile. Or arrive mid-day and play Rowdy Yates with the *Rawhide* crush of tour groups.

Tourist Information: TI is at Óbidos' main gate (daily Mon–Fri 9:30–18:00, shorter on weekends and off-season, tel. 262-959-231).

Arrival in Óbidos: Ideally, take a bus to Óbidos and leave by either bus or train. If you arrive at the train station, you're faced with a 20-minute uphill hike into town. The bus drops you off much closer (go up the steps and through the archway on the right). There's no official place to store luggage.

Introductory Walk through Óbidos

Main Gate: Enter through the main gate in Óbidos' 14th-century wall. Like Dorothy entering a medieval Oz, you're confronted by two wonderful cobbled lanes. The top lane is the town's main drag, littered with tourists shopping and leading straight through Óbidos to its castle (ahead you can see its square tower, where this walk finishes). Above on the left is the end of the wall walk, which makes a scenic if treacherous half-circle return from the castle. But for now, follow the...

Lower Brick Road: Wander along this lane less traveled, noticing the whitewash that keeps things cool; the bright blue-and-yellow trims, traditionally designed to define property lines; and the potted geraniums, which bloom most of the year, survive the summer sun well, and keep mosquitos away. At the Church of St. Peter (which has a fine, newly restored, Baroque altar, covered with Brazilian gold leaf), turn left to climb uphill to the main tourist drag. Then turn right on the...

Main Shopping Drag: Walking toward the castle, you'll pass typical shops and a public WC before reaching the...

Town Square: The lone column at the side of the road is the 16th-century pillory. Locals were tied to this to endure whatever punishment was deemed appropriate. The huge pots you see once held olive oil. The small Municipal Museum, across the square, is not worth the €1.50 unless you enjoy stairs, religious art, and Portuguese inscriptions. But do enter the...

Church of St. Mary of Óbidos: Grab a seat on a front pew, surrounded by classic 17th-century tiles. Notice the fine painted-wood ceiling. To the left of the altar is a niche with a delicate Portuguese Renaissance tomb, featuring a pietà carved out of local limestone. On the right are three paintings by a well-respected female artist of the 17th century—Josefa d' Óbidos. Return to the main shopping drag, and turn left for the...

Final Stretch to the Castle: On the right, pop into the **Don Ramiro Wine House.** This welcoming showcase for regional products—wine, cheese, and meat—serves your choice of wine by the glass, and if you'd like a light meal, a sampler plate of meats and cheese. Its atmospheric setting is dominated by a big old grape press (open daily, on the main drag). Across the street, **Bar Ibn Errik Rex** is the most characteristic of several Óbidos *ginjinha* bars. Óbidos is famous for this much-loved Portuguese liqueur (see description of the cherry schnapps—€2.50 a glass—in Lisbon chapter). The main drag dead-ends at the top of the town and the castle, which is now a fancy hotel, or *pousada* (9 rooms, Db-€185, CC, tel. 262-959-105, fax 262-959-148). A lane to the right leads to the stairs accessing the town wall. But go uphill to the left, following the *pousada* signs to the terrace with the telescope for a city view. You can return to your starting point three ways: hiking along the upper town wall, exporing photogenic side lanes, or shopping and drinking your way back down the main drag.

Sights near Óbidos

Caldas da Rainha—A 10-minute drive or taxi ride from Óbidos, Caldas da Rainha is famous for its therapeutic springs, which have attracted royalty for rheumatism cures and aristocrats who wanted to make the scene. A venerable hospital now sits upon the source of those curative waters. The town's charming old center is more work-aday than Óbidos, providing a good glimpse of everyday Portugal with the charm punched up just a notch. Ideally, drop by this town any morning (except Monday) when its farmers' market fills Praça da República with fruits, veggies, nuts, flowers, and lots of busy locals.

Sleeping in Óbidos
(€1 = about $1, country code: 351, zip code: 2510)
To enjoy the town without tourists, spend the night. Here are four reasonable values in this overpriced toy of a town.

MODERATELY PRICED
Albergaria Rainha Santa Isabel is a hotelesque place marked by flags on the main drag in the center of the old town. If bold and driving, call first to let them know you're approaching, stop long enough to drop your bags and get a parking permit, and drive

on to the the town square to park (Sb-€58, Db-€75, higher in
Aug, third person-€18 extra, includes breakfast, CC, air-con,
elevator, on the main one-lane drag, Rua Direita, tel. 262-959-323,
fax 262-959-115, e-mail: arsio@oeste.online.pt, SE).

Casa de S. Thiago de Castelo, a fancy and characteristic
little guesthouse at the base of the *pousada*/castle, rents 10
elegantly-appointed rooms around a chirpy *Better Homes and
Tiles* patio (Db-€85 April–Oct, includes breakfast, CC, parking,
Largo de S. Thiago, tel. & fax 262-959-587, Helena SE).

LOWER PRICED
Casa do Poço, with four dim, basic rooms around a bright folksy
courtyard, is just one of many homes renting rooms in the old
center (Db-€45–58, includes breakfast, Travessa da Mouraria,
follow main street past square and see sign on right, tel. 262-
959-358, fax 262-959-282).

Casa do Relogio is a rustic eight-room place at the downhill end of town, just outside the wall. It's friendly, easy-going,
and provides no-stress parking and great comfort for the price
(Db-€45, €58 in peak of summer, includes breakfast, Rua da
Graca Apartado 12, tel. 262-959-282 or 262-959-772, fax 262-
959-282, Sarah SE).

Eating in Óbidos

At **Restaurant Ó Barco,** professionals Mariana and Walter fill
a chalkboard with daily international and Portuguese specials—
served with a Dutch accent by a sunbeam named Alice. The
dining room is small, so it can be smoky. Breezy terrace seating is
available in summer (€15, Tue–Sun 12:30–14:30 & 19:30–22:00,
closed Mon, walk down from St. Mary's Church, Largo Dr. João
Lourenço, tel. 262-950-925).

Restaurante A Ilustre Casa de Ramiro is a bigger place
50 meters downhill (outside the wall) from O Barco. It's dressy
and characteristic but more touristy, with a four-language menu
(€20 dinners, Fri–Wed 12:30–15:00 & 19:30–22:30, closed Thu,
Rua Porta do Vale, tel. 262-959-194).

Picnics: Óbidos is tough on the average tourist's budget. Pick
up your picnic at the small grocery store just inside the main gate
(on the lower brick road), the larger grocery in the center on Rua
Direita, or the tiny market just outside the town wall.

Transportation Connections—Óbidos

To: Nazaré (4 buses/day, 1 hr), **Lisboa** (5 buses/day, 75 min;
7 trains/day, 2 hrs, transfer in Cacem), **Alcobaça** (6 buses/day,
1 hr), **Batalha** (4 buses/day, 2 hrs). Far fewer buses run on Sunday.

Route Tips for Drivers in Central Portugal

Lisbon to Coimbra: This is an easy 2-hour straight shot on the slick Auto-Estrada A1 (toll: €11). You'll pass convenient exits for Fatima and the Roman ruins of Conimbriga along the way. Leave the freeway on the easy-to-miss first Coimbra exit and then follow the *centro* signs. Four kilometers after leaving the freeway you'll cross the Mondego River. Take Avenida Fernão de Magalhaes directly into town; you'll find free parking near the Ponte de Santa Clara (bridge), on the side opposite the city center. Most hotels are near the train station and this bridge.

Óbidos to Lisbon: Don't drive into tiny, cobbled Óbidos. Ample tourist parking is provided outside of town. From Óbidos, the tollway zips you directly into Lisbon (€7). For arriving and parking in Lisbon, see that chapter. If going to Sintra, follow signs to Cascais as you approach Lisbon.

APPENDIX

Iberian History

The cultural landscape of modern Spain and Portugal was shaped by the various civilizations that settled on the peninsula. Iberia's sunny weather and fertile soil made it a popular place to call home.

The Greeks came to Cadiz around 1100 B.C., followed by the Romans, who occupied the country for almost 1,000 years, until A.D. 400. Long after the empire crumbled, the Roman influence remained and could be found in things like cultural values, building materials and techniques, and even Roman-style farming equipment, which was used well into the 19th century. And, of course, there was wine.

Moors (711–1492)

The Moors—North Africans of the Muslim faith who occupied Spain—had the greatest cultural influence on Spanish and Portuguese history. They arrived on the Rock of Gibraltar in A.D. 711 and moved north. In the incredibly short time of seven years, the Moors completely conquered the peninsula.

The Moors established their power and Muslim culture in a subtle way. Non-Muslims were tolerated and often rose to positions of wealth and power; Jewish culture flourished. Rather than brutal subjugation, the Moorish style of conquest was to employ their sophisticated culture to develop whatever they found. For example, they encouraged wine-making, although for religious reasons they themselves weren't allowed to drink alcohol.

The Moors ruled for more than 700 years. Throughout that time, pockets of Christianity remained. Local Christian kings fought against the Moors whenever they could, whittling away at the Muslim empire, gaining more and more land. The last Moorish stronghold, Granada, fell to the Christians in 1492.

The slow, piecemeal process of the Reconquista split the peninsula into the independent states of Portugal and Spain. In 1139 Alfonso Henriques conquered the Moors near present-day Beja in southern Portugal and proclaimed himself king of the area. By 1200 the Christian state of Portugal had the borders it does today, making it the oldest unchanged state in Europe. The rest of the peninsula was a loosely-knit collection of smaller kingdoms. Spain's major step toward unity was in 1469, when Fernando II of Aragon married Isabel of Castile. Known as the "Catholic Monarchs," they united the other kingdoms under their rule.

The Golden Age (1500–1700)

The expulsion of the Moors set the stage for the rise of Portugal and Spain as naval powers and colonial superpowers. The Spaniards, fueled by the religious fervor of the Reconquista, were interested in spreading Christianity to the newly discovered New World. Wherever they landed, they tried to Christianize the natives—with the sword, if necessary.

The Portuguese expansion was motivated more by economic concerns. Their excursions overseas were planned, cool, and rational. They colonized the nearby coasts of Africa first, progressing slowly around Africa to Asia and South America.

Through exploration (and exploitation) of the colonies, tremendous quantities of gold came into each country. The aristocracy and the clergy were swimming in money. It was only natural that art and courtly life flourished during this Golden Age.

Slow Decline

The fast money from the colonies kept Spain and Portugal from seeing the dangers at home. Great Britain and the Netherlands also were becoming naval powers, and defeated Spain's "Invincible Armada" in 1588. Portugal's imperial economy imported everything. They stopped growing their own wheat and neglected their fields.

During the centuries when science and technology in other European countries developed as never before, Spain and Portugal were preoccupied by their failed colonial politics. In the 18th century Spain under the rule of the French Bourbon family. (This explains the French Baroque architecture that you'll see, such as La Granja near Segovia and the Royal Palace in Madrid.) Endless battles, wars of succession, revolutions, and counterrevolutions weakened the countries. In this chaos there was no chance to develop democratic forms of government. Dictators in both countries made the rich richer and kept the masses underprivileged.

During World War I Portugal fought on the Allied side and Spain stayed neutral. In World War II both countries were neutral, uninterested in foreign policy as long as they were at peace. In the 1930s Spain suffered a bloody and bitter civil war between fascist and democratic forces. The fascist dictator Francisco Franco prevailed, ruling the country until his death in 1975.

Democracy in Spain and Portugal is still young. After a bloodless revolution, Portugal held democratic elections in 1975. After 41 years of a fascist dictatorship, Spain finally had elections in 1977.

Today socialists are in power in both countries. They've adopted moderate policies to minimize the stress on their young democracies, fighting problems such as unemployment and foreign debts with reasonable success. Today Spain and Portugal are members of the European Union. Though not considered wealthy or powerful, both countries are prospering, thanks in part to you and tourism.

Art

The "Big Three" in Spanish painting are El Greco, Velázquez, and Goya.

El Greco (1541–1614) exemplifies the spiritual fervor of much Spanish art. The drama, the surreal colors, and the intentionally unnatural distortion have the intensity of a religious vision.

Diego Velázquez (1599–1660) went to the opposite extreme. His masterful court portraits are studies in realism and cool detachment from his subjects.

Goya (1746–1828) matched Velázquez's technique but not his detachment. He let his liberal tendencies shine through in unflattering portraits of royalty and in emotional scenes of abuse of power. He unleashed his inner passions in the eerie, nightmarish canvases of his last, "dark" stage.

Not quite in the league of the Big Three, Murillo (1617–1682) painted a dreamy world of religious visions. His pastel, soft-focus works of cute baby Jesuses and radiant Virgin Marys helped make Catholic doctrine palatable to the common folk at a time when many were defecting to Protestantism.

You'll also find plenty of foreign art in Spain's museums. During its Golden Age, Spain's wealthy aristocrats bought wagonloads of the most popular art of the time—Italian Renaissance and Baroque works by Titian, Tintoretto, and others. They also loaded up on paintings by Rubens, Bosch, and Brueghel from the Low Countries, which were under Spanish rule.

In the 20th century Pablo Picasso (see his inspirational antiwar *Guernica* mural in Madrid), Joan Miró, and surrealist Salvador Dalí made their marks. Great museums featuring all three are in or near Barcelona.

Architecture

The two most fertile periods of architectural innovation in Spain and Portugal were during the Moorish occupation and in the Golden Age. Otherwise, Spanish architects have marched obediently behind the rest of Europe.

The Moors brought Middle Eastern styles with them, such as the horseshoe arch, minarets, and floor plans designed for mosques. Islam forbids the sculpting or painting of human or animal figures ("graven images"), so artists expressed their creativity with elaborate geometric patterns. The ornate stucco of Granada's Alhambra, the elaborate arches of Sevilla's Alcázar, and decorative colored tiles are evidence of the Moorish sense of beauty. Islamic and Christian elements were blended in the work of Mozarabic (Christians living under Moorish rule) and Mudejar (Moors living in Spain after the Christian reconquest) artists.

As the Christians slowly reconquered the country, they turned their fervor into stone, building churches both in the heavy, fortress-of-God Romanesque style (Lisbon's cathedral) and in the lighter, heaven-reaching, stained-glass Gothic style (Barcelona, Toledo, and Sevilla). Gothic was an import from France, trickling into conservative Spain long after it swept through Europe.

The money reaped and raped from Spain's colonies in the Golden Age spurred new construction. Churches and palaces were built using the solid, geometric style of the Italian Renaissance (El Escorial) and the more ornamented Baroque. Ornamentation reached unprecedented heights in Spain, culminating in the Plateresque style of stonework, so called because it resembles intricate silver filigree work. Portugal's highly ornamented answer to Plateresque is called "Manueline." Both Plateresque and Manueline were transitional stages—the final over-the-top flowering of the Gothic age at the dawn of the Renaissance.

In the 18th and 19th centuries, innovation in both countries died out. Spain's major contribution to modern architecture is the Art Nouveau work of Antonio Gaudí early in the 20th century. Most of his "cake-left-out-in-the-rain" buildings, with asymmetrical designs and sinuous lines, can be found in Barcelona.

Bullfighting—Legitimate Slice of Spain or Cruel Spectacle?

The Spanish bullfight is as much a ritual as it is a sport. Not to acknowledge the importance of the bullfight is to censor a venerable part of Spanish culture. But it also makes a spectacle out of the cruel killing of an animal. Should tourists boycott bullfights? I don't know.

Today bullfighting is less popular among locals. If this trend continues, bullfighting may survive more and more as a tourist event. When the day comes that bullfighting is kept alive by our tourist dollars rather than the local culture, then I'll agree with those who say bullfighting is immoral and that tourists shouldn't encourage it by buying tickets. Consider the morality of supporting this gruesome aspect of Spanish culture before buying a ticket. If you do decide to attend a bullfight, here is what you'll see.

While no two bullfights are the same, they unfold along a strict pattern. The ceremony begins punctually with a parade of participants across the ring. Then the trumpet sounds, the "Gate of Fear" opens, and the leading player—*el toro*—thunders in. A ton of angry animal is an awesome sight, even from the cheap seats (with the sun in your eyes).

The fight is divided into three acts. Act 1 is designed to size up the bull and wear him down. The matador (literally "killer"), with help from his assistants, attracts the bull with the shake of the cape, then directs the animal past his body, as close as his bravery allows. The bull sees only things in motion and (some think) red. After a few passes the *picadors* enter, mounted on horseback, to spear the swollen lump of muscle at the back of the bull's neck. This tests the bull as the matador watches studiously. It also lowers the bull's head and weakens the thrust of his horns. (Until 1927 horses had no protective pads and were often killed.)

In Act 2, the matador's assistants *(banderilleros)* continue to enrage and weaken the bull. The *banderillero* charges the charging bull and, leaping acrobatically across its path, plunges brightly-colored barbed sticks into the bull's vital neck muscle.

After a short intermission, during which the matador may, according to tradition, ask permission to kill the bull and dedicate the kill to someone in the crowd, the final, lethal Act 3 begins. The matador tries to dominate and tire the bull with hypnotic cape work. A good pass is when the matador stands completely still while the bull charges past. Then the matador thrusts a sword between the animal's shoulder blades for the kill. A quick kill is not always easy, and the matador may have to make several bloody thrusts before the sword stays in and the bull finally dies. Mules drag the dead bull out, and his meat is in the market mañana (barring "mad cow" concerns—and if ever there were a mad cow...). *Rabo del toro* (bull-tail stew) is a delicacy.

Throughout the fight, the crowd shows its approval or impatience. Shouts of "*¡Olé!*" or "*¡Torero!*" mean they like what they see. Whistling or rhythmic hand-clapping greets cowardice and incompetence.

You're not likely to see much human blood spilled. In 200 years of bullfighting in Sevilla, only 30 fighters have died (and only three were actually matadors). If a bull does kill a fighter, the next matador comes in to kill him. Historically, even the bull's mother is killed, since the evil qualities are assumed to have come from the mother.

After an exceptional fight, the crowd may wave white handkerchiefs to ask that the matador be awarded the bull's ear or tail. A brave bull, though dead, gets a victory lap from the mule team on his way to the slaughterhouse. Then the trumpet sounds, and a new bull charges in to face a fresh matador.

Fights are held on most Sundays, Easter through October (at 18:30 or 19:30). Serious fights with adult matadors are called *corrida de toros*. These are often sold out in advance. Summer fights are often *novillada*, with teenage novices doing the killing. *Corrida de toros* seats range from €20 for high seats facing the sun to €100 for the first three rows in the shade under the royal box. *Novillada* seats are half that, and generally easy to get at the arena a few minutes before showtime. Many Spanish women consider bullfighting sexy. They swoon at the dashing matadors who are sure to wear tight pants (with their *partas nobles*—noble parts—in view, generally organized to one side, farthest from the bull).

A typical bullfight lasts about two hours and consists of six separate fights—three matadors (each with his own team of *picadors* and *banderilleros*) fighting two bulls each. For a closer look at bullfighting by an American aficionado, read Ernest Hemingway's classic, *Death in the Afternoon*.

The Portuguese bullfight is different from the Spanish bullfight. For a description, see the Lisbon chapter. In Portugal, the bull is not killed in front of the crowd, though it is killed later.

Festivals and Public Holidays

Spain and Portugal erupt with fiestas and celebrations throughout the year. Semana Santa (Holy Week) fills the week before Easter with processions and festivities all over Iberia, but especially in Sevilla. To run with the bulls, be in Pamplona—with medical insurance—the second week in July.

This is a partial list of holidays and festivals. For more information, contact the Spanish or Portuguese National Tourist Offices (listed in this book's introduction) and check these Web sites: www.whatsonwhen.com, www.holidayfestival.com, www.whatsgoingon.com, and www.festivals.com.

Jan 1	New Year's Day, Spain & Portugal
Jan 6	Epiphany, Spain
Early Feb	La Candelaria (religious festival), Madrid (Spain)
Late Feb	Carnival (Mardi Gras), Portugal
Feb 28	Day of Andalucía (some closures), Andalucía (Spain)
Easter	Holy Week leading to Easter (April 20), Spain & Portugal
early May	April Fair, Sevilla (Spain)
April 25	Liberty Day (parades, fireworks), Portugal
May–June	Algarve Music Festival, Algarve (Portugal)
May 1	Labor Day (closures), Spain & Portugal

2003

JANUARY						
S	M	T	W	T	F	S
			1	2	3	4
5	6	7	8	9	10	11
12	13	14	15	16	17	18
19	20	21	22	23	24	25
26	27	28	29	30	31	

FEBRUARY						
S	M	T	W	T	F	S
						1
2	3	4	5	6	7	8
9	10	11	12	13	14	15
16	17	18	19	20	21	22
23	24	25	26	27	28	

MARCH						
S	M	T	W	T	F	S
						1
2	3	4	5	6	7	8
9	10	11	12	13	14	15
16	17	18	19	20	21	22
23/30	24/31	25	26	27	28	29

APRIL						
S	M	T	W	T	F	S
		1	2	3	4	5
6	7	8	9	10	11	12
13	14	15	16	17	18	19
20	21	22	23	24	25	26
27	28	29	30			

MAY						
S	M	T	W	T	F	S
				1	2	3
4	5	6	7	8	9	10
11	12	13	14	15	16	17
18	19	20	21	22	23	24
25	26	27	28	29	30	31

JUNE						
S	M	T	W	T	F	S
1	2	3	4	5	6	7
8	9	10	11	12	13	14
15	16	17	18	19	20	21
22	23	24	25	26	27	28
29	30					

JULY						
S	M	T	W	T	F	S
		1	2	3	4	5
6	7	8	9	10	11	12
13	14	15	16	17	18	19
20	21	22	23	24	25	26
27	28	29	30	31		

AUGUST						
S	M	T	W	T	F	S
					1	2
3	4	5	6	7	8	9
10	11	12	13	14	15	16
17	18	19	20	21	22	23
24/31	25	26	27	28	29	30

SEPTEMBER						
S	M	T	W	T	F	S
	1	2	3	4	5	6
7	8	9	10	11	12	13
14	15	16	17	18	19	20
21	22	23	24	25	26	27
28	29	30				

OCTOBER						
S	M	T	W	T	F	S
			1	2	3	4
5	6	7	8	9	10	11
12	13	14	15	16	17	18
19	20	21	22	23	24	25
26	27	28	29	30	31	

NOVEMBER						
S	M	T	W	T	F	S
						1
2	3	4	5	6	7	8
9	10	11	12	13	14	15
16	17	18	19	20	21	22
23/30	24	25	26	27	28	29

DECEMBER						
S	M	T	W	T	F	S
	1	2	3	4	5	6
7	8	9	10	11	12	13
14	15	16	17	18	19	20
21	22	23	24	25	26	27
28	29	30	31			

May 2	Day of Autonomous Community, Madrid
May 13	Pilgrimage to Fatima, Fatima (Portugal)
Mid-May	Feria del Caballo (horse pageantry), Jerez (Spain)
May 15–25	San Isidro (religious festival), Madrid (Spain)
June 10	Portuguese National Day, Portugal
June 13	St. Anthony's Day, Lisbon (Portugal)
June 13	Pilgrimage to Fatima, Fatima (Portugal)
June	Lisbon's Festival, Lisbon (Portugal)
Mid-June	Corpus Christi, Spain
Late June	La Patum (Moorish battles), Barcelona (Spain)
June 24	St. John the Baptist's Day, Spain
June 29	St. Peter's Day, Lisbon (Portugal)
Late June– Early July	International Festival of Music and Dance, Granada (Spain)
Mid-July	Running of the Bulls, Pamplona (Spain)
July 13	Pilgrimage to Fatima, Fatima (Portugal)
Aug	Gràcia Festival, Barcelona (Spain)

Aug 6–15	Verbena de la Paloma (folk festival), Madrid (Spain)
Aug 15	Assumption (religious festival), Spain & Portugal
Aug 19	Pilgrimage to Fatima, Fatima (Portugal)
Sept 13	Pilgrimage to Fatima, Fatima (Portugal)
Mid-Sept	Our Lady of Nazaré Festival, Nazaré (Portugal)
Mid-Sept– mid-Oct	Autumn Festival (flamenco, bullfights), Jerez (Spain)
Late Sept	La Mercé (parade), Barcelona (Spain)
Oct 5	Republic Day (businesses closed), Portugal
Oct 12	Spanish National Day, Spain
Oct 13	Pilgrimage to Fatima, Fatima (Portugal)
Nov 1	All Saints' Day, Spain & Portugal
Nov 9	Virgen de la Almudena, Madrid (Spain)
Mid-Nov	International Jazz Festival, Madrid (Spain)
Dec 1	Independence Restoration Day, Portugal
Dec 6	Constitution Day, Spain
Dec 8	Feast of the Immaculate Conception, Spain & Portugal
Dec 13	Feast of Santa Lucia, Spain
Dec 25	Christmas, Spain & Portugal
Dec 31	New Year's Eve, Spain & Portugal

Let's Talk Telephones

This is a primer on telephoning in Europe. For specifics on Spain and Portugal, see "Telephones" in the introduction.

Dialing Direct

Making Calls within a European Country: What you dial depends on the phone system of the country you're in. About half of all European countries use area codes; the other half uses a direct-dial system without area codes.

If you're calling within a country that uses a direct-dial system (Spain, Portugal, Belgium, the Czech Republic, France, Italy, Switzerland, Norway, and Denmark), you dial the same number whether you're calling within the city or across the country.

In countries that use area codes (such as Austria, Britain, Finland, Germany, Ireland, the Netherlands, and Sweden), you dial the local number when calling within a city, and you add the area code if calling long-distance within the country. Example: The phone number of a hotel in Munich is 089-264-349. To call it in Munich, dial 264-349; to call it from Frankfurt, dial 089-264-349.

Making International Calls: You always start with the international access code (011 if you're calling from the United States or Canada, 00 from virtually anywhere in Europe), then dial the country code of the country you're calling (see list below).

What you dial next depends on the particular phone system of the country you're calling. If the country uses area codes, you drop the initial zero of the area code, then dial the rest of the area code and the local number. Example: To call the Munich hotel from Spain, dial 00, 49 (Germany's country code), then 89-264-349.

Countries that use direct-dial systems (no area codes) differ in how they're accessed internationally by phone. For instance, if you're making an international call to Spain, Portugal, Italy, the Czech Republic, Norway, or Denmark, you simply dial the international access code, country code, and phone number. Example: The phone number of a hotel in Madrid is 915-212-900. To call it from Portugal, dial 00, 34 (Spain's country code), then 915-212-900. But if you're calling Belgium, France, or Switzerland, you drop the initial zero of the phone number. Example: The phone number of a Paris hotel is 01 47 05 49 15. To call it from Madrid, dial 00, 33 (France's country code), then 1 47 05 49 15 (the phone number without the initial zero).

Country Codes
After you dial the international access code (00 if you're calling from Europe, 011 if you're calling from America or Canada), dial the code of the country you're calling.

Austria—43	Greece—30
Belgium—32	Ireland—353
Britain—44	Italy—39
Canada—1	Morocco—212
Czech Rep.—420	Netherlands—31
Denmark—45	Norway—47
Estonia—372	Portugal—351
Finland—358	Russia—7
France—33	Spain—34
Germany—49	Sweden—46
Gibraltar—350	Switzerland—41
(9567 from Spain)	United States—1

Directory Assistance
In Spain, dial 1003 for local numbers and 025 for international numbers (expensive). In Portugal, dial 118 for local numbers and 177 for international numbers. (Note: In Spain a 608 or 609 area code indicates a mobile phone.)

European Calling Chart

Just smile and dial, using this key:
AC = Area Code, LN = Local Number.

European Country	Calling long distance within...	Calling from the U.S.A./ Canada to...	Calling from another European country to...
Austria	AC (Area Code) + LN (Local Number)	011 + 43 + AC (without the initial zero) + LN	00 + 43 + AC (without the initial zero) + LN
Belgium	LN	011 + 32 + LN (without initial zero)	00 + 32 + LN (without initial zero)
Britain	AC + LN	011 + 44 + AC (without initial zero) + LN	00 + 44 + AC . (without initial zero) + LN
Czech Republic	LN	011 + 420 + LN	00 + 420 + LN
Denmark	LN	011 + 45 + LN	00 + 45 + LN
Estonia	LN	011 + 372 + LN	00 + 372 + LN
Finland	AC + LN	011 + 358 + AC (without initial zero) + LN	00 + 358 + AC (without initial zero) + LN
France	LN	011 + 33 + LN (without initial zero)	00 + 33 + LN (without initial zero)
Germany	AC + LN	011 + 49 + AC (without initial zero) + LN	00 + 49 + AC (without initial zero) + LN
Gibraltar	LN	011 + 350 + LN	00 + 350 + LN From Spain: 9567 + LN
Greece	LN	011 + 30 + LN	00 + 30 + LN

European Country	Calling long distance within...	Calling from the U.S.A./ Canada to...	Calling from another European country to...
Ireland	AC + LN	011 + 353 + AC (without initial zero) + LN	00 + 353 + AC (without initial zero) + LN
Italy	LN	011 + 39 + LN	00 + 39 + LN
Morocco	LN	011 + 212 + LN (without initial zero)	00 + 212 + LN (without initial zero)
Netherlands	AC + LN	011 + 31 + AC (without initial zero) + LN	00 + 31 + AC (without initial zero) + LN
Norway	LN	011 + 47 + LN	00 + 47 + LN
Portugal	LN	011 + 351 + LN	00 + 351 + LN
Spain	LN	011 + 34 + LN	00 + 34 + LN
Sweden	AC + LN	011 + 46 + AC (without initial zero) + LN	00 + 46 + AC (without initial zero) + LN
Switzerland	LN	011 + 41 + LN (without initial zero)	00 + 41 + LN (without initial zero)
Turkey	AC (if no initial zero is included, add one) + LN	011 + 90 + AC (without initial zero) + LN	00 + 90 + AC (without initial zero) + LN

- The instructions above apply whether you're calling a fixed phone or cell phone.
- The international access codes (the first numbers you dial when making an international call) are 011 if you're calling from the U.S.A./Canada, or 00 if you're calling from virtually anywhere in Europe. Finland and Lithuania are the only exceptions. If calling from either of these countries, replace the 00 with 990 in Finland and 810 in Lithuania.
- To call the U.S.A. or Canada from Europe, dial 00 (unless you're calling from Finland or Lithuania), then 1 (the country code for the U.S.A. and Canada), then the area code and number. In short, 00 + 1 + AC + LN = Hi, mom!

U.S. Embassies

Madrid, Spain: Serrano 75, tel. 915-872-240 or 915-872-200,
www.embusa.es/cons/services.html
Lisboa, Portugal: Avenida das Forças Armadas,
tel. 217-273-300, www.american-embassy.pt
Gibraltar: Call embassy in Madrid (above).
Casablanca, Morocco: 8 Boulevard Moulay Youssef,
tel. 22/26-45-50, www.usembassy-morocco.org

Numbers and Stumblers

- Europeans write a few of their numbers differently than we do.
  1 = 1 , 4 = 4 , 7 = 7 . Learn the difference or miss your train.
- In Europe, dates appear as day/month/year, so Christmas is
  25/12/03.
- Commas are decimal points and decimals commas. A dollar
  and a half is 1,50, and there are 5.280 feet in a mile.
- When pointing, use your whole hand, palm down.
- When counting with fingers, start with your thumb. If you hold
  up your first finger to request one item, you'll probably get two.
- What Americans call the second floor of a building is the first
  floor in Europe.
- Europeans keep the left "lane" open for passing on escalators
  and moving sidewalks. Keep to the right.

Metric Conversion (approximate)

1 inch = 25 millimeters	32 degrees F = 0 degrees C
1 foot = 0.3 meter	82 degrees F = about 28 degrees C
1 yard = 0.9 meter	1 ounce = 28 grams
1 mile = 1.6 kilometers	1 kilogram = 2.2 pounds
1 centimeter = 0.4 inch	1 quart = 0.95 liter
1 meter = 39.4 inches	1 square yard = 0.8 square meter
1 kilometer = .62 mile	1 acre = 0.4 hectare

Climate Chart

First line, average daily low; second line, average daily high; third line, days of no rain.

	J	F	M	A	M	J	J	A	S	O	N	D
SPAIN												
Madrid												
	35°	36°	41°	45°	50°	58°	63°	63°	57°	49°	42°	36°
	47°	52°	59°	65°	70°	80°	87°	85°	77°	65°	55°	48°
	23	21	21	21	21	25	29	28	24	23	21	21
Barcelona												
	43°	45°	48°	52°	57°	65°	69°	69°	66°	58°	51°	46°
	55°	57°	60°	65°	71°	78°	82°	82°	77°	69°	62°	56°
	26	23	23	21	23	24	27	25	23	22	24	25
Almeria (Costa del Sol)												
	46°	47°	51°	55°	59°	65°	70°	71°	68°	60°	54°	49°
	60°	61°	64°	68°	72°	78°	83°	84°	81°	73°	67°	62°
	25	24	26	25	28	29	31	30	27	26	26	26
PORTUGAL												
Lisbon												
	46°	47°	50°	53°	55°	60°	63°	63°	62°	58°	52°	47°
	57°	59°	63°	67°	71°	77°	81°	82°	79°	72°	63°	58°
	16	16	17	20	21	25	29	29	24	22	17	16
Faro (Algarve)												
	48°	49°	52°	55°	58°	64°	67°	68°	65°	60°	55°	50°
	60°	61°	64°	67°	71°	77°	83°	83°	78°	72°	66°	61°
	22	21	21	24	27	29	31	31	29	25	22	22
MOROCCO												
Marrakesh												
	40°	43°	48°	52°	57°	62°	67°	68°	63°	57°	49°	42°
	65°	68°	74°	79°	84°	92°	101°	100°	92°	83°	73°	66°
	24	23	25	24	29	29	30	30	27	27	27	24

Basic Spanish Survival Phrases

Good day.	**Buenos días.**	**bway**-nohs **dee**-ahs
Do you speak English?	**¿Habla usted inglés?**	**ah**-blah oo-**stehd** een-**glays**
Yes. / No.	**Sí. / No.**	see / noh
I (don't) understand.	**(No) comprendo.**	(noh) kohm-**prehn**-doh
Please.	**Por favor.**	por fah-**bor**
Thank you.	**Gracias.**	**grah**-thee-ahs
I'm sorry.	**Lo siento.**	loh see-**ehn**-toh
Excuse me.	**Perdóneme.**	pehr-**doh**-nay-may
(No) problem.	**(No) problema.**	(noh) proh-**blay**-mah
Good.	**Bueno.**	bway-noh
Goodbye.	**Adiós.**	ah-dee-**ohs**
one / two	**uno / dos**	**oo**-noh / dohs
three / four	**tres / cuatro**	trays / **kwah**-troh
five / six	**cinco / seis**	**theen**-koh / says
seven / eight	**siete / ocho**	see-**eh**-tay / **oh**-choh
nine / ten	**nueve / diez**	**nway**-bay / dee-**ayth**
How much is it?	**¿Cuánto cuesta?**	**kwahn**-toh **kway**-stah
Write it?	**¿Me lo escribe?**	may loh ay-**skree**-bay
Is it free?	**¿Es gratis?**	ays grah-**tees**
Is it included?	**¿Está incluido?**	ay-**stah** een-kloo-**ee**-doh
Where can I buy / find...?	**¿Dónde puedo comprar / encontrar...?**	**dohn**-day **pway**-doh kohm-**prar** / ayn-kohn-**trar**
I'd like / We'd like...	**Quiero... / Queremos...**	kee-**ehr**-oh / kehr-**ay**-mohs
...a room.	**...una habitación.**	**oo**-nah ah-bee-tah-thee-**ohn**
...the bill.	**...la cuenta.**	lah **kwayn**-tah
...a ticket to ___.	**...un billete para ___.**	oon bee-**yeh**-tay **pah**-rah
Is it possible?	**¿Es posible?**	ays poh-**see**-blay
Where is...?	**¿Dónde está...?**	**dohn**-day ay-**stah**
...the train station	**...la estación de trenes**	lah ay-stah-thee-**ohn** day **tray**-nays
...the bus station	**...la estación de autobuses**	lah ay-stah-thee-**ohn** day ow-toh-**boo**-says
...the tourist information office	**...la Oficina de Turismo**	lah oh-fee-**thee**-nah day too-**rees**-moh
Where are the toilets?	**¿Dónde están los servicios?**	**dohn**-day ay-**stahn** lohs sehr-**bee**-thee-ohs
men	**hombres, caballeros**	**ohm**-brays, kah-bah-**yay**-rohs
women	**mujeres, damas**	moo-**heh**-rays, **dah**-mahs
left	**izquierda**	eeth-kee-**ehr**-dah
right	**derecha**	day-**ray**-chah
straight	**derecho**	day-**ray**-choh
When does this open / close?	**¿A qué hora abren / cierran?**	ah kay **oh**-rah **ah**-brehn / thee-**ay**-rahn
At what time?	**¿A qué hora?**	ah kay **oh**-rah
Just a moment.	**Un momento.**	oon moh-**mehn**-toh
now / soon / later	**ahora / pronto / más tarde**	ah-**oh**-rah / **prohn**-toh / mahs **tar**-day
today / tomorrow	**hoy / mañana**	oy / mahn-**yah**-nah

Basic Portugese Survival Phrases

When using the phonetics, try to nasalize the n and w.

Good day.	**Bom dia.**	bohn **dee**-ah
Do you speak English?	**Fala inglês?**	**fah**-lah een-**glaysh**
Yes. / No.	**Sim. / Não.**	seeng / now
I (don't) understand.	**(Não) compreendo.**	(now) kohn-pree-**ayn**-doo
Please.	**Por favor.**	poor fah-**vor**
Thank you. (said by male)	**Obrigado.**	oh-bree-**gah**-doo
Thank you. (said by female)	**Obrigada.**	oh-bree-**gah**-dah
I'm sorry.	**Desculpe.**	dish-**kool**-peh
Excuse me (to pass).	**Com licença.**	kohn li-**sehn**-sah
(No) problem.	**(Não) á problema.**	(now) ah proo-**blay**-mah
Good.	**Bom.**	bohn
Goodbye.	**Adeus.**	ah-**deh**-oosh
one / two	**um / dois**	oon / **doysh**
three / four	**três / quarto**	**traysh** / kwah-**troo**
five / six	**cinco / seis**	seeng-**koo** / **saysh**
seven / eight	**sete / oito**	seh-**teh** / oy-**too**
nine / ten	**nove / dez**	naw-**veh** / **dehsh**
How much is it?	**Quanto custa?**	**kwahn**-too **koosh**-tah
Write it?	**Escreva?**	ish-**kray**-vah
Is it free?	**É gratis?**	eh **grah**-teesh
Is it included?	**Está incluido?**	ish-**tah** een-kloo-**ee**-doo
Where can I find / buy...?	**Onde posso encontrar / comprar...?**	ah **ohn**-deh **paw**-soo ayn-kohn-**trar** / kohn-**prar**
I'd like / We'd like...	**Gostaria / Gostaríamos...**	goosh-tah-**ree**-ah / goosh-tah-**ree**-ah-moosh
...a room.	**...um quarto.**	oon **kwar**-too
...the bill.	**...a conta.**	ah **kohn**-tah
...a ticket to ___.	**...um bilhete para ___.**	oon beel-**yeh**-teh **pah**-rah
Is it possible?	**É possível?**	eh poo-**see**-vehl
Where is...?	**Onde é que é...?**	**ohn**-deh eh keh eh
...the train station	**...a estação de comboio**	ah ish-tah-**sow** deh kohn-**boy**-yoo
...the bus station	**...a terminal das camionetas**	ah tehr-mee-**nahl** dahsh kahm-yoo-**neh**-tahsh
...the tourist information office	**...a informação turistica**	ah een-for-mah-**sow** too-**reesh**-tee-kah
...the toilet	**...a casa de banho**	ah **kah**-zah deh **bahn**-yoo
men	**homens**	**aw**-maynsh
women	**mulheres**	mool-**yeh**-rish
left / right	**esquerda / direita**	ish-**kehr**-dah / dee-**ray**-tah
straight	**em frente**	ayn **frayn**-teh
What time does this open / close?	**A que horas é que abre / fecha?**	ah keh **aw**-rahsh eh keh **ah**-breh / **feh**-shah
At what time?	**A que horas?**	ah keh **aw**-rahsh
Just a moment.	**Um momento.**	oon moo-**mayn**-too
now / soon / later	**agora / em breve / mais tarde**	ah-**goh**-rah / ayn **bray**-veh / m?sh **tar**-deh
today / tomorrow	**hoje / amanhã**	**oh**-zheh / ah-ming-**yah**

For 336 more pages of survival phrases for your next trip to Iberia, check out *Rick Steves' Spanish and Portuguese Phrase Books*.

Faxing Your Hotel Reservation

Use this handy form for your fax or find it online at
www.ricksteves.com/reservation. Photocopy and fax away.

One-Page Fax

To: _____ @ _____
           hotel   *fax*

From: _____ @ _____
            name   *fax*

Today's date: ____ / ____ / ____
              day *month* *year*

Dear Hotel _____,

Please make this reservation for me:

Name: _____

Total # of people: _____   # of rooms: _____   # of nights: _____

Arriving: ____ / ____ / ____   My time of arrival (24-hr clock): _____
          day *month* *year*

(I will telephone if I will be late)

Departing: ____ / ____ / ____
           day *month* *year*

Room(s): Single___ Double___ Twin___ Triple___ Quad___

With: Toilet___ Shower___ Bath___ Sink only___

Special needs: View___ Quiet___ Cheapest___ Ground Floor___

Credit card: Visa___ MasterCard___ American Express___

Card #: _____

Expiration date:_____

Name on card: _____

You may charge me for the first night as a deposit. Please fax, e-mail, or
mail me confirmation of my reservation, along with the type of room
reserved, the price, and whether the price includes breakfast. Please also
inform me of your cancellation policy. Thank you.

_____
Signature

_____
Name

_____
Address

_____
City   *State*   *Zip Code*   *Country*

_____
E-mail Address

Road Scholar Feedback for SPAIN & PORTUGAL 2003

We're all in the same travelers' school of hard knocks. Your feedback helps us improve this guidebook for future travelers. Please fill this out (or use the online version at www.ricksteves.com/feedback), attach more info or any tips/favorite discoveries if you like, and send it to us. As thanks for your help, we'll send you our quarterly travel newsletter free for one year. Thanks! Rick

Of the recommended accommodations/restaurants used, which was:

Best _____

Why? _____

Worst _____

Why? _____

Of the sights/experiences/destinations recommended by this book, which was:

Most overrated _____

Why? _____

Most underrated _____

Why? _____

Best ways to improve this book:

_____

_____

I'd like a free newsletter subscription:

____ Yes   ____ No   ____ Already on list

_____
Name

_____
Address

_____
City, State, Zip

_____
E-mail Address

Please send to: ETBD, Box 2009, Edmonds, WA 98020

INDEX

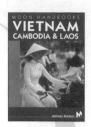

FREE TRAVEL GOODIES FROM

Rick Steves

EUROPEAN TRAVEL NEWSLETTER

My *Europe Through the Back Door* travel company will help you travel better *because* you're on a budget—not in spite of it. To see how, ask for my 64-page *travel newsletter* packed full of savvy travel tips, readers' discoveries, and your best bets for railpasses, guidebooks, videos, travel accessories and free-spirited tours.

2003 GUIDE TO EUROPEAN RAILPASSES

With hundreds of railpasses to choose from in 2003, finding the right pass for your trip has never been more confusing. To cut through the complexity, visit www.ricksteves.com for my online *2003 Guide to European Railpasses.* Once you've narrowed down your choices, we give you unbeatable prices, including important extras with every Eurailpass, **free:** my 90-minute *Travel Skills Special* video or DVD and your choice of one of my 24 guidebooks.

RICK STEVES' 2003 TOURS

We offer 20 different one, two, and three-week tours (200 departures in 2003) for those who want to experience Europe in Rick Steves' Back Door style, but without the transportation and hotel hassles. If a tour with a small group, modest family-run hotels, lots of exercise, great guides, and no tips or hidden charges sounds like your idea of fun, ask for my 48-page 2003 Tours booklet.

YEAR-ROUND GUIDEBOOK UPDATES

Even though the information in my guidebooks is the freshest around, things do change in Europe between book printings. I've set aside a special section at my website (www.ricksteves.com/update) listing *up-to-the-minute changes* for every Rick Steves guidebook.

*Visit **www.ricksteves.com** to get your...*

☑ **FREE EUROPEAN TRAVEL NEWSLETTER**
☑ **FREE 2003 GUIDE TO EUROPEAN RAILPASSES**
☑ **FREE RICK STEVES' 2003 TOURS BOOKLET**

Rick Steves' Europe Through the Back Door
130 Fourth Avenue North, PO Box 2009, Edmonds, WA 98020 USA
Phone: (425) 771-8303 ■ Fax: (425) 771-0833 ■ www.ricksteves.com

Free, fresh travel tips, all year long.

Visit **www.ricksteves.com** to get Rick's free 64-page newsletter... and more!